AF477944

Adis Merdzanovic

Democracy by Decree

Prospects and Limits
of Imposed Consociational Democracy
in Bosnia and Herzegovina

Adis Merdzanovic

DEMOCRACY BY DECREE

Prospects and Limits
of Imposed Consociational Democracy
in Bosnia and Herzegovina

ibidem-Verlag
Stuttgart

Bibliographic information published by the Deutsche Nationalbibliothek

Die Deutsche Nationalbibliothek lists this publication in the Deutsche Nationalbibliografie; detailed bibliographic data are available in the Internet at http://dnb.d-nb.de.

Bibliografische Information der Deutschen Nationalbibliothek

Die Deutsche Nationalbibliothek verzeichnet diese Publikation in der Deutschen Nationalbibliografie; detaillierte bibliografische Daten sind im Internet über http://dnb.d-nb.de abrufbar.

This work was accepted as a PhD thesis by the Faculty of Arts and Social Sciences, University of Zurich in the autumn term 2014 on the recommendation of the Doctoral Committee: Prof Dr Josette Baer Hill (main supervisor) and Prof Dr Francis Cheneval.

ISBN-13 Paperback edition: 978-3-8382-0792-6

ISBN-13 Hardback edition: 978-3-8382-0812-1

© *ibidem*-Verlag / *ibidem* Press

Stuttgart, Germany 2015

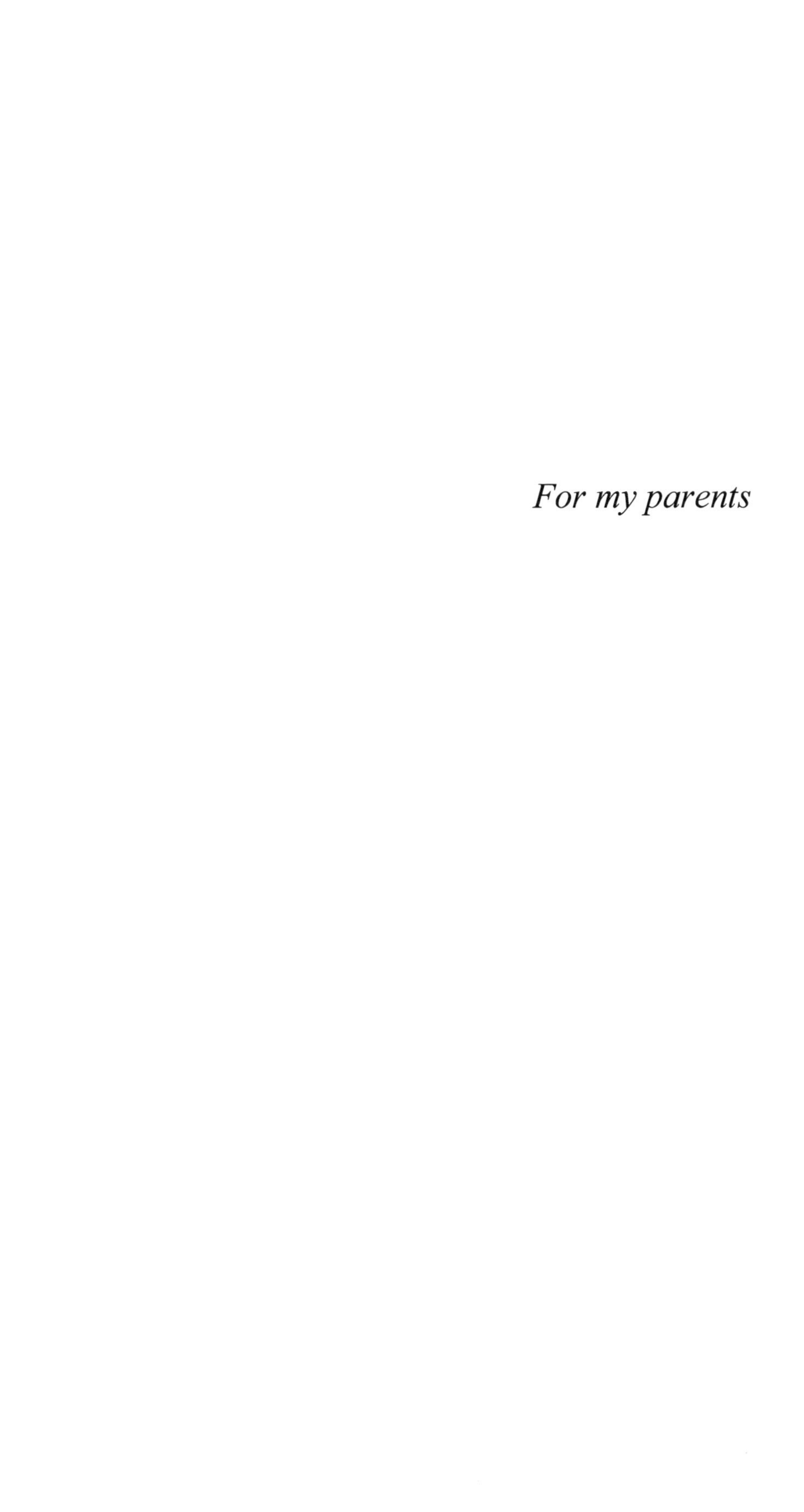

For my parents

TABLE OF CONTENTS

ACKNOWLEDGEMENTS

This book, which is based on my PhD thesis at the Departments of Political Science and Philosophy of the University of Zurich, would never have been possible without the support of many people and institutions. My deepest gratitude belongs to my primary doctoral supervisor Josette Baer Hill and my secondary supervisor Francis Cheneval for their support and encouragement. The study furthermore received substantial funding from the University of Zurich. My thanks go to the commissions of the *Forschungskredit* that not only approved my initial grant proposal, but, when the project ran longer than expected, also extended the funding (Grant-Nr. FK-13-072). The *Forschungskredit* allowed me to finish my study without financial worries, while being part of a stimulating academic community and enjoying the benefits of institutional support.

As far as the content of the study is concerned, I would like to express my gratitude to the interview partners who readily accepted to meet me and patiently answered my questions. These include former High Representatives in Bosnia and Herzegovina—Carlos Westendorp, Wolfgang Petritsch, Paddy Ashdown, Christian Schwarz-Schilling, and Miroslav Lajčák—who have given part of their time to me, and a much bigger part of it to Bosnia and Herzegovina. I cannot be anything but impressed by their commitment to help a country to which, perhaps a decade before the war, many of them had presumably no connection. Whatever one may think of their performances during their mandates, it is beyond doubt that coming to Bosnia and Herzegovina and dealing with Bosnian politics is no easy job; it is not something just anyone would happily agree to do. Rather, it takes a special kind of commitment and a particular kind of person to accept the task of rebuilding a state and unifying a society that has just come from a bloody war. Having met and talked to them, I honestly believe that all former High Representatives included in this study implemented policies that they thought best for the country at the time. All of them had the best intentions and acted accordingly. Naturally, not all of their policies fulfilled the expectations and some had rather serious unintended consequences. Even though it is the aim of this study to scientifically examine such consequences by putting them into a larger theoretical context, my intent is by no means to discredit the records of those fine individuals for whom I have the utmost respect. Furthermore, I am greatly thankful to my Bosnian interview partners, to whom I will refer as Bosnia's 'political elite' throughout the book. I wish to thank Haris Silajdžić, Mladen Bosić, Mladen Ivanić, Dragan Čović, Božo Ljubić, Nebojša Radmanović, and Željko Komšić for their time and readiness to participate in the interviews. Their contribution helped me understand the problems of the contemporary Bosnian political system, whereas their political stances made me realise how difficult it would be to achieve a real, post-conflict 'solution'.

To be clear: In this study, my loyalties are not with a particular case and not with Bosnia and Herzegovina as such; rather, my goal is to present an academic contribution to existing literature on consociationalism and post-conflict state building. I am thus sincerely confined by respective standards when reviewing the collected material and, especially, when analysing the interviews with international and local decision makers. Almost by definition, my analysis will disagree with some of the views presented during these interviews and point to inconsistencies and false assumptions contained in some statements. I hope such critique is perceived as substantiated, i.e. founded on facts and trustworthy sources and presented in a comprehensible manner. I would like to thank my interview partners for their understanding in this regard.

On a more personal level, I wish to thank colleagues, with whom I had numerous occasions to discuss my theoretical ideas and empirical thoughts. This list includes Anja Heidelberger, Sylvie Ramel, Sevan Pearson, Julianne Funk, as well as Nenad Stojanović and Daniel Bochsler. Special thanks are also in order for Donald L. Horowitz, who was kind enough to comment on my theoretical model during a seminar in Zurich, and Stefan Troebst, who did the same during a conference in New Orleans. Needless to say, all errors in the manuscript are my own. Finally, I owe the greatest amount of gratitude to my parents, Ibrahim and Senada, to whom this book is dedicated for their unbelievable and unconditional support.

A.M.

Oxford/Zurich, April 2015

LIST OF ACRONYMS

ABiH	Army of Bosnia and Herzegovina
BiH / BH	Bosnia and Herzegovina
BOSS	*Bosanska Stranka*, Bosnian Party
BPS	*Bosanska Patriotska Stranka*, Bosnian Patriotic Party
CD BiH	*Koalicija za cjelovitu i demokratsku BiH*, Coalition for a United and Democratic BiH
DF	*Demokratski Front*, Democratic Front
DPA	Dayton Peace Agreement, General Framework Agreement for Peace in Bosnia and Herzegovina
EU	European Union
EUFOR	European Union Force
EUSR	European Union Special Representative to Bosnia and Herzegovina
FBiH	Federation of Bosnia and Herzegovina
GDS	*Gradjanska demokratska stranka*, Citizen's Democratic Party
HDZ	*Hrvatska Demokratska Zajednica Bosne i Hercegovine*, Croat Democratic Union of Bosnia and Herzegovina
HDZ1990	*Hrvatska Demokratska Zajednica 1990*, Croat Democratic Union 1990
HSS	*Hrvatska Seljačka Stranka*, Croat Peasants' Party
HVO	*Hrvatsko vijeće obrane*, Croat Defence Council (Croatian military forces in Bosnia)
HZ HB	*Hrvatska Zajednica Herceg Bosna,* Croatian Community of Herceg Bosna (a Croat parastate during the Bosnian war)
IFOR	NATO Implementation Force
LDS	*Liberalno Demokratska Stranka*, Liberal Democratic Party
NARS	*Narodna skupština Republike Srpske*, National Assembly of the Republic of Srpska
NHI	*Nova Hrvatska Inicijativa*, New Croat Initiative

OHR	Office of the High Representative of the International Community in Bosnia and Herzegovina
PDP	*Partija Demokratskog Progresa*, Party of Democratic Progress
PIC	Peace Implementation Council
RBiH	Republic of Bosnia and Herzegovina (1992-1995)
RS	*Republika Srpska*, Republic of Srpska
SAA	Stabilisation and Association Agreement
SB	Steering Board
SBB	*Stranka za Bolju Budućnost*, Party for a Better Future
SBiH	*Stranka za Bosnu i Hercegovinu*, Party for Bosnia and Herzegovina
SDA	*Stranka Demokratske Akcije*, Party for Democratic Action
SDP	*Socijaldemokratska Stranka Bosne i Hercegovine*, Social Democratic Party of Bosnia and Herzegovina
SDS	*Srpska Demokratska Stranka*, Serb Democratic Party
SFOR	NATO Stabilisation Force
SNS	*Srpski Narodni Savez*, Serb National Alliance
SNSD	*Savez Nezavisnih Socijaldemokrata*, Alliance of Independent Social Democrats
SPRS	*Socijalistička Partija Republike Srpske,* Socialist Party of the Republic of Srpska
SR BiH	*Socijalistička Republika Bosna i Hercegovina,* Socialist Republic of Bosnia and Herzegovina (used in this book for the entire Yugoslav period until 1992)
SRS	*Srpska Radikalna Stranka*, Serbian Radical Party
UDSB	*Unija Bosanskih Socijaldemokrata*, Union of Bosnian Social Democrats
UN SC	United Nations Security Council

1 Introduction

As we approach the twentieth anniversary of the Dayton Peace Accords—this fundamental set of treaties that ended the 1992–1995 war in Bosnia-Herzegovina[1] as well as the battles between Croatia and the significantly shrunk Yugoslavia (i.e. Serbia)—we find ourselves wishing for a larger conclusion, some sort of a thorough assessment of their merits two decades after the fact. While the Accords are generally credited for the conclusion of military hostilities and thus for putting an end to the human suffering in the narrower region, especially the General Framework Agreement for Peace in Bosnia and Herzegovina (usually referred to as the Dayton Peace Agreement, DPA) is often criticised for establishing a suboptimal post-war state structure; the latter, it is said, institutionalises the ethno-national segregation of the society, discriminates against national minorities, makes the political system inefficient as well as prone to patronage politics, and is generally not apt for the challenges of the century in which we live. Since the Bosnian political system reflects the philosophy of the so-called consociational power-sharing model that tries to integrate different groups into a common state through a particular set of political institutions, the failure to establish a self-sustaining democracy in this particular country has become one of the major arguments for discrediting the model itself. Critics of consociationalism tend to point to Bosnia in order to emphasise the general inadequateness of this institutional solution for establishing stable democratic rule in divided post-war societies.

What such critics often fail to see, however, is that the Bosnian consociation did not develop autonomously or in a power vacuum, but as part of a larger international context. International actors heavily affected not only the negotiations of the peace treaty but also the post-war development of the political system. While I have no intention to present a final judgement on the Bosnian case—that would be presumptuous–, I nevertheless want to emphasise that any serious attempt to reflect on the benefits and failures of the DPA has to account for external influence. In this respect, I wish to shine a light on a particular aspect of Bosnia's post-war development that necessarily needs to form an integral part of any larger narrative. The internationals had a significant effect on how the consociational system worked in practice and they therefore also share part of the responsibility for the contemporary situation.

---

[1] For linguistic reasons, I shall use the shortened term 'Bosnia' or the abbreviations 'BiH' or 'BH' throughout the text.

In a nutshell, this book explores the relationship between international actors and consociational democracy in post-war Bosnia and Herzegovina. But like Arend Lijphart's first treatise on consociational politics in the Netherlands, it is not conceptualised 'as a country study in the conventional sense' but as 'an extended theoretical argument based on a single case of particular interest'[2] for consociational theory. So even though the major part of the text deals with the case study, the research aim goes well beyond the understanding of this particular country. It is directed at what we may call a fundamental misconception of consociational theory. Especially in its contemporary form, consociationalism tends to argue that stable democratic rule is the necessary result of a post-war political system that includes the four consociational institutions of a grand coalition, proportional representation, veto powers, and group autonomy.

Against this background, I shall argue that power sharing works in a different manner in post-war societies than in other kinds of divided societies, since the former cannot be regarded and analysed independently of the international contexts in which they are situated. Unfortunately, this has indeed been done with some regularity in the past. In such studies, the performance of institutions as well as prevailing group dynamics and incentive structures are examined from an intra-state perspective while little attention is given to the importance of external actors. The underlying separation is also visible in the larger context of political science research. While international relations experts primarily focus on questions surrounding humanitarian intervention and the feasibility of maintaining a common state after the intervention, comparative political scientists tend to analyse the inner workings of political systems by focusing on specific institutions like the parliamentary or electoral systems. There is thus a visible research gap between these two kinds of studies, especially in the field of political theory. Despite some notable exceptions in recent years—for example, Michael Kerr's wonderful study analysing external inference in four power-sharing arrangements in Northern Ireland and Lebanon,[3] or recent articles and books by Florian Bieber and Soeren Keil focusing on the influence of internationals in the Balkans[4]—a theoretically based approach towards internationally enforced consociational the-

---

[2] Arend Lijphart, *The Politics of Accommodation: Pluralism and Democracy in the Netherlands*, Second Revised Edition (London: University of California Press, 1975), 15, Fn. 42.

[3] Michael Kerr, *Imposing Power-Sharing: Conflict and Coexistence in Northern Ireland and Lebanon* (Dublin: Irish Academic Press, 2005).

[4] Florian Bieber and Soeren Keil, "Power-Sharing Revisited: Lessons Learned in the Balkans?," *Review of Central and East European Law* 34, no. 4 (2009): 337–60; Florian Bieber, "The Balkans: The Promotion of Power Sharing by Outsiders," in *Power Sharing in Deeply Divided Places*, ed. Joanne McEvoy and Brendan O'Leary (Philadelphia: University of Pennsylvania Press, 2013), 312–26; Soeren Keil, *Multinational Federalism in Bosnia and Herzegovina* (Farnham: Ashgate, 2013).

ory is still lacking. With the model developed in this study, I seek to contribute to the closure of this gap.

Furthermore, I wish to advocate for the benefits of a multidisciplinary approach towards the analysis of post-conflict societies. In what follows, I firstly try to bridge the gap between international relations and comparative politics in the field of consociational theory; secondly, I attempt to enrich the field of normative consociational theory by presenting a model that incorporates a theoretical foundation for external influences; thirdly, by choosing the option of an in-depth case study and including a thorough historical discussion of the case as necessary background information, I seek to bridge the divide between political science and historical studies.

The research subject of this study is the political system. In my understanding, this term refers not only to the set of legal and formal institutions foreseen in a constitution, but also to the actual as well prescribed forms of political behaviour and to the true, functioning logics of the state.[5] My interest is thus not primarily dedicated to specific aspects or subsystems of political action, but to its framework. Therefore, I shall analyse adjacent systems like the economy or the electoral system only insofar as they influence the performance and incentive structures of the political system from which they emerged. My main focus is the behaviour of the political elite that is subject to the incentive structures that the political institutions provide.

The primary research questions of this study are: (1) How can the influence of external actors equipped with far-reaching powers be introduced into the normative theory of consociational democracy? (2) How does the existence of external actors with far-reaching powers change the prevailing incentive structure and influence the achievability of consociationalism's main goals, i.e. group cooperation and stable democratic rule? I shall try to answer these questions in both a theoretical and an empirical way. Through a meta-theoretical analysis of the evolution of consociational theory, this research intends to clarify the normative characteristics of the approach and to contemplate the consequences if one were to alter the prevailing assumptions. As a result, it proposes a new theoretical model called 'imposed consociation' that is applicable to a specific kind of consociational post-conflict polities. In an in-depth study of post-war Bosnia and Herzegovina, this theoretical model shall be compared to a real-world example and further substantiated. Finally, these analyses should tell us something about the general applicability of a consociational system in other post-conflict polities as well as lead to some interesting practical recommendations.

---

[5] "Political System," *Encyclopedia Britannica*, accessed December 25, 2013, http://www.britannica.com/EBchecked/topic/467746/political-system.

1.1　Case Selection

This study follows a particular understanding of the aims of political theory. In my belief, normative political theory has to be concerned with the empirical feasibility of the proposed concepts in order to be justifiably employed. As an empirically grounded normative theory, consociationalism adheres to this principle. Consequently, in order to advance normative consociational theory, we need to contrast the theoretical expectations with empirical evidence in order to construct valid normative models. In itself, this is a huge task; one that I am not attempting in this study. Instead, my aims are much more humble and limited in scope, for I try to fine-tune my theoretically developed expectations in order to detect flaws in the theoretical argument and to increase the depth of the 'imposed consociational' model. Hopefully, this process will result in a theoretical construct that one day can be tested in a larger context on other cases. For now, my endeavour remains to develop such a model in a coherent and theoretically as well as empirically sound manner. In this sense, the theoretical aspiration of the present study remains closely connected to the case on which it is based.

The case selected for these purposes must fulfil all the theoretical preconditions the model of an 'imposed consociation' envisions.[6] Concretely, the selected case has to be (a) a divided post-conflict society, (b) whose political system incorporates the four consociational institutions to such a degree that the polity itself can accurately be termed a consociation. With respect to the composition of the society, the case has to (c) be clearly divisible with respect to the different groups, meaning that the main dividing lines must be politicised in a way that allows us to call them cleavages. These groups have to display internal political struggles so that (d) internal group coherence is absent. Furthermore, the decision-making power regarding political issues must lie not only in the hands of the local political leaders, but—completely or partially—in the ones of an (e) 'International Regulating Body', which is not hesitant to use its 'intervention prerogative'. In short, we need a case that is a consociation with a well-structured international influence but without group coherence.

Post-war Bosnia and Herzegovina is such a case. First, it closely follows the principle of consociational democracy. Proportionality—and, in fact, equality—between the three constituent peoples (Bosniaks, Croats, and Serbs) determines the composition of the most important state institutions as well as the administrative positions. Territorial autonomy is respected in the form of two lower federal units called entities, the Bosniak-Croat Federation of Bosnia and Herzegovina (FBiH) and the Serb-dominated Republika Srpska (RS). The Federation is further divided into cantons, most of which have either a Bosniak or Croat majority. Finally, the adaptation of laws in the two chambers of parliament requires qualified

---

[6]　See chapter 6 for the context and theoretical substantiation of these assumptions.

majorities, which, together with the so-called vital interest clause, constitutes the veto powers within the Bosnian consociation.[7] We are thus confronted with an almost ideal-typical situation, in which we have a fully-fledged consociational system where we can analyse the prevailing dynamics.

Second, Bosnia and Herzegovina is a divided, post-conflict state.[8] That the Bosnian territory witnessed some of the cruellest atrocities, human rights abuses, and genocide during the war is owed to the despicable philosophy of ethnic homogenisation and ethnic cleansing, which tended to hit the ethnically heterogeneous places most brutally. Due to its historical trajectory since the Middle Ages, Bosnia was such a heterogeneous place, encompassing at least three different religious communities. Beginning with the nationalist movements in neighbouring countries in the nineteenth century, those communities gradually turned into national groups. And even though we can doubt the importance of societal division in Yugoslav pre-war Bosnia, there can be no doubt that its contemporary society is highly divided along the cleavage of ethno-national belonging, not least due to the experiences of the war.

Third and perhaps most importantly, in order to ensure the implementation of the civilian aspects of the Dayton Peace Agreement, the international community created the Office of the High Representative (OHR). In 1997, the OHR was given the authority to impose laws if the local legislatures fail to do so and to remove public officials from their posts if they violate the DPA in any form. Since the introduction of these so-called Bonn powers, Bosnia has been regarded as a quasi-protectorate. The OHR has used its intervention prerogative on a regular basis—not only to set up the respective state structures foreseen by Dayton but also to expedite the work of those structures.[9] As I shall argue throughout the text, this created a completely new kind of consociational system: one in which the general advantages of consociationalism are turned upside down, and one that does not end in stable democratic rule but in a challenging dependency on the international community. From a practical point of view, we are in the lucky position of being able to retrace this entire process, for all Bonn-power decisions are documented and publicly available.[10]

---

[7]   A detailed discussion of Bosnia's political system and its consociational qualities is provided in chapter 7.

[8]   The term 'post-conflict' is not unproblematic. While I use it to describe the state after the armed conflict, i.e. the 1992-1995 war, I do not wish to imply that the societal conflict between the three national groups has ended. In this sense, a negative rather than a positive reading of the peace achieved through the Dayton Peace Agreement in 1995 determines my terminology.

[9]   Chapter 9 provides a detailed account of OHR policies in Bosnia since the end of the war to date.

[10]   Through the website of the OHR: www.ohr.int.

Bosnia and Herzegovina has been the subject of many studies, some of which have also focused on the consociational character of the post-war society or the interactions between the international community and the local political system.[11] The present study, however, differs from those predecessors in two respects. First, it concentrates on the political system as such, not specific aspects of it. Its goal is thus at the same time larger and smaller than what previous research has attempted. It tries not to explain any specific outcome, but the framework that makes certain outcomes probable in the first place. Second, this study deals with the dynamics and incentive structures within the political elite. To my knowledge, there exists no other analysis to date that focuses on the behaviour of the Bosnian political elites (their views, motives, and actions), the behaviour of the High Representatives (their philosophies, actions, and practical constraints), nor such a detailed analysis of the interactions between these two actors. Given that I work with first-hand information collected through in-depth interviews with the respective decision-making leaders (see below), I believe the current study may not only contribute to our analytical and theoretical understanding of the case within the framework of consociational theory but also provide some novel data regarding the post-war development of Bosnia and Herzegovina in general.

1.2   Methodology

Like consociationalism, 'imposed consociationalism' is deemed a flexible theoretical model. One cannot observe the envisioned mechanisms on day one after the establishment of consociational institutions, for the model incorporates certain learning effects that result from political gains and losses. However, the significant groundwork in the form of consociational principles has to be laid out in the beginning for the specific kind of political behaviour to develop later on. As far as methodology goes, this absolutely prescribes a temporal approach, which allows not only for the model to be fine-tuned but can answer additional questions as well: How do such mechanisms develop? How does a post-conflict consociational settlement turn into an 'imposed consociation'? With respect to the present

---

[11]   See, for example: Sumantra Bose, *Bosnia after Dayton: Nationalist Partition and International Intervention* (London: C. Hurst, 2002); David Chandler, *Bosnia: Faking Democracy after Dayton* (London; Sterling, VA.: Pluto Press, 2000); Florian Bieber, *Post-War Bosnia. Ethnicity, Inequality and Public Sector Governance* (Hampshire: Palgrave Macmillen, 2006); Roberto Belloni, *State Building and International Intervention in Bosnia* (London: Routledge, 2007). Historical analyses of the Bosnian case include: Noel Malcolm, *Bosnia: A Short History*, New Updated Edition. (New York: New York University Press, 1996); Marie-Janine Calic, *Krieg und Frieden in Bosnien-Hercegovina*, Erweiterte Neuausgabe (Frankfurt: Suhrkamp Verlag, 1996); Marko Attila Hoare, *How Bosnia Armed* (London: Saqi Books, 2004); Marko Attila Hoare, *History of Bosnia: From the Middle Ages to the Present Day* (London: Saqi Books, 2007).

study, therefore, the timeframe analysed is from 1996 to 2012/3; the starting date corresponds to the beginning of DPA implementation, while the end date relates to the beginning of this project. Later developments will be included in the analysis where needed.

Such a longitudinal analysis allows us to trace back the developments within the state and to map out the consequences of international intervention with regard to the system's mechanisms and the political leaders' behaviour. In order to describe the dynamics between the international and the national levels as accurately as possible, I shall use international reports and documents, perform an original analysis of local newspapers, and supplement my analysis with secondary literature about Bosnia's post-war development. As far as the newspapers are concerned, I shall analyse articles published in the three biggest local newspapers *Dnevni Avaz* (Daily Newspaper), *Oslobođenje* (Liberation), and *Nezavisne Novine* (Independent Newspaper). For the first part of the analysis (1996-2000), the newspapers have been consulted in the National Library in Bosnia's capital Sarajevo. For their more recent articles, the analysis was performed in the *Mediacentar* Sarajevo, a privately owned company possessing and currently digitalising many newspapers in the region.[12] From 1996 to somewhere between 2004 and 2005, the analysis was done manually, by consulting the printed editions of the newspapers directly. After this date, however, the contents of all the three newspapers are digitalised and accessible online.[13]

In order to analyse the data in an efficient manner, articles were included in the analysis only if they relate to general topics dominating the political scene at a particular time and if they furthermore testify to the involvement of external actors, namely the Office of the High Representative or the Peace Implementation Council (PIC). Moreover, in addition to secondary literature I consulted the decisions of the OHR and the communiqués and declarations of the PIC that are accessible through the OHR website.[14] The combination of these documents allowed me to determine what political issues dominated a particular period of time, the positions of the different groups, and the strategies employed by the international actors as well as the local political group leaders. The importance of an issue is thereby reinforced through its repetition in the different documents and newspaper articles. Since we are concerned with the political system, the issues analysed are well known and hard to miss. Therefore, rather than concentrating on every single decision by the High Representative—something which is hardly feasible—I concentrated on larger patterns and developments.

---

[12]   See www.media.ba.

[13]   See http://www.idoconline.info/digitalarchive/public/index.cfm.

[14]   See www.ohr.int, especially the decisions archive (http://www.ohr.int/decisions/archive.asp) and the archive of declarations and communiqués by the Peace Implementation Council (http://www.ohr.int/pic/archive.asp?sa=on).

In addition to the document analysis described above, I performed open and in-depth interviews[15] with the main political decision makers, i.e. former High Representatives and local party leaders. In an open interview only the general topics are pre-determined, whereas their importance and relevance varies from one interviewee to another. An in-depth-interview, on the other hand, is more structured because a general topic guide is used; the conversation generally follows this topic guide but the researcher has the ability to ask clarifying and follow-up questions regarding specific topics that were either mentioned or concern aspects of particular interest. Open interviews thus allow for particular events to be analysed, while in-depth interviews secure more comparability between the different interviewees.

The interviews with former High Representatives were conducted in an open form. While the questions were individual and based on specific events during their time in office, all interviews had a similar structure. They included (a) a description of the situation they found upon assuming their office (i.e. their determination of the main challenges), (b) their impressions of the local Bosnian politicians, (c) their view regarding the Bonn powers, including their usage, and (d) their vision for a future of Bosnia. In addition, I discussed specific events during their mandates that previous analysis suggested as significant. For the local politicians, an in-depth interview guide was used, which can be found in the annex. Rather than establishing a historic perspective, the goal here was to understand the relations and dynamics between the international community and the local politicians. Therefore, the interview partner was invited to explain this dynamic using a political issue he deemed important, which in itself yielded some interesting information. Selected for interviews were the leaders or high-ranking officials of the main parties within the three groups. The respective list is also provided in the annex. Due to persistence, amicable networks, and some luck, I was in the position to interview true decision makers within the political scene of Bosnia and Herzegovina. In total, I conducted twelve interviews, seven with local politicians and five with former High Representatives. The interviews with locals were conducted in Bosnian/Serbian/Croatian, whereas the internationals were interviewed in English (Westendorp, Ashdown, Lajčák) or in German (Schwarz-Schilling, Petritsch). As with all non-English material, I translated all statements into English before including them in the present thesis.

This approach raises methodological concerns. The people I interviewed express a particular point of view that does not necessarily reflect the 'true' nature

---

[15]   Regarding the methodology for open and in-depth interviews, see Jane Ritchie and Jane Lewis, *Qualitative Research Practice: A Guide for Social Science Students and Researchers* (London: Sage, 2003); Paul Thompson, *The Voice of the Past. Oral History*, Third Edition. (Oxford: Oxford University Press, 2000). In general, the corset of semi-structured interviews was deemed too strict for the present project.

of Bosnian politics. The same holds true for the media outlets that tend to show a particular bias. Addressing such methodological challenges means, first of all, acknowledging that personal interviews are as biased as other available sources and should therefore be assessed on equal terms. In the words of Paul Thompson:

> The basic tests of reliability …—searching for internal consistency, cross-checking details from other sources, weighing evidence against a wider context—are just the same as for other sources. All are fallible and subject to bias, and each has varying strengths in different situations. In some contexts, oral evidence is best; in others it is supplementary, or complementary, to that of other sources.[16]

Personal interviews with local and international decision makers give us a unique opportunity to examine a person's argumentative strategy, which is a key ingredient of the 'imposed consociation' model. In this sense, we are as interested in determining a particular bias as we are in understanding the functional logic of the system itself. Furthermore, interviews may provide information that is otherwise unobtainable. For example, interviews with former High Representatives give us a rare insight into the black box of OHR decision making, i.e. into the reasons and processes of particular decisions. Lacking other sources that may provide such information, there seems to be no alternative than to rely on personal interviews.

This does by no means eradicate the basic challenge in distinguishing between truth and bias, and may even make it more acute. The only way to deal with reliability issues is to supplement the interviews (or the newspaper articles) with other material. It is for this reason that I include sources such as secondary literature, official documents, available statistical data, etc. into the present analysis. The interviews do thus not stand alone, but are integrated into a wider context, which means that they are not only examined in light of internal consistency but also cross-checked with other sources and weighted against the wider context.

1.3   Structure

This book is divided into four parts. Given that we are dealing with a case study, I shall begin with an in-depth introduction into the Bosnian situation through the prism of nationalism theory. Contemporary political science, especially in its quantitative form, tends to neglect the importance of the historical context. Even though there is no need to include historical arguments in every analysis, inclusion is surely of paramount importance within the context of a case study. Only through the prism of history do we really understand the deeper reasons for certain political demands. This is even more important in the Balkans where, as has been argued,[17] time does not elapse chronologically but overlaps. Especially in

---

[16]   Thompson, *The Voice of the Past. Oral History*, 153.

[17]   Gordon N. Bardos, "Balkan Ethnoconfessional Nationalism: Analysis and Management," *Südosteuropa* 59, no. 2 (2011): 192–213.

the field of national recollections, historical memories are kept alive through storytelling over generations so that they can be recalled at the appropriate moment. In other words, generations living centuries apart know the same stories and can relate to the respective historical figures and their demands. A deeper analysis of this area is therefore key in order to understand the Bosnian case.

Additionally, the Bosnian case presents an interesting challenge for existing theories of nationalism. Perhaps most tellingly, the Czech historian Miroslav Hroch neither mentions the Bosnians nor the Bosnian Muslims in his typology of national movements in smaller European states.[18] While it is undoubtedly difficult to place a traditionally multi-national country into a typology of national states, the question nevertheless remains whether Bosnia and its three national groups would fit such a model. In order to answer this question, we need to analyse the historical developments in the country following a specific framework—which in our case will be Miroslav Hroch's three-phase model—and with respect to each of the three groups. This naturally includes a study of neighbouring nationalisms that provided the ideological blueprints as well as substantial practical support for the local groups during the process of nationalisation. While I cannot claim that such an analysis will yield new findings in terms of historical inquiry, I believe that it will prove illuminating from a political science point of view.

Part I consists of three chapters. Chapter 2 is dedicated to a short introduction into theories of nationalism and the important differences between the development of national movements in horizontal relations in Western Europe and such movements within larger empires in Eastern Europe. The third chapter takes a comparative look at the national movements in Bosnia-Herzegovina, Serbia, Croatia, and the 'two Yugoslavias' (1918-1941, 1945-1991/2). Furthermore, through an analysis of commonalities, this chapter also elaborates on the ideological structures of group nationalism; it tries to show the non-cohesiveness of the nationalist argument as such. Finally, the fourth chapter is dedicated to nationalist developments in Bosnia-Herzegovina. In its totality, these three chapters serve as necessary background information before a study of Bosnian politics can be attempted.

Part II of the thesis is dedicated to the development of the theoretical model called 'imposed consociation'. In chapter 5, I briefly introduce consociational theory and present a meta-theoretical analysis of its evolution. My main goal is to show how the theory has changed and how an originally empirical explanation for a deviant case became a normative model directed to stabilise democracy in any kind of divided society. It seems obvious, even though I have never seen it admitted anywhere that such an evolution could not have happened without serious

---

[18]   Miroslav Hroch, *Das Europa der Nationen. Die moderne Nationsbildung im europäischen Vergleich*, 1st ed. (Göttingen: Vandenhoeck & Ruprecht, 2005).

trade-offs from which consociational theory suffers to this day. The subsequent chapter 6 tries to illustrate some of the trade-off involved by combining the approaches to international intervention in post-conflict societies with the general claims of consociational theory. Through the model of the 'imposed consociation', I shall try to exemplify the consequences of a continuous influence from an outside body on the consociational system and the prevailing incentive structures that determine the behaviour of the elites.

Part III deals with the real-world example of an 'imposed consociation' in Bosnia and Herzegovina. Chapter 7 introduces the contemporary political system and reflects on some of its major challenges. Chapter 8 is dedicated to the behaviour of political elites, their views and guiding principles. As such, it investigates the prevailing incentive structure within the political system. Together with chapter 9, which presents an in-depth analysis of OHR policies since 1996, this chapter is surely the empirical heart of the present study. In chapter 10, I combine the findings of the three previous chapters in order to show that the model of an 'imposed consociation' is best suited to explain the current dynamics of the Bosnian system and that this system is the result of specific interactions between the international and the national levels of politics since the end of the war.

Part IV, which consists of chapter 11, is designed to conclude the present discussion and to contemplate the lessons learned form the Bosnian case. It furthermore includes practical recommendations for consociational state building in divided post-conflict societies.

Finally, I have included a short epilogue that seeks to modestly look beyond the confines of the current case study to the cases of Macedonia and Kosovo. Its goal is to illustrate the merits of the analytical framework of an 'imposed consociation' and to show where further research in this area may start.

Part I:
Nationalism

2 Theories of Nationalism—A Brief Survey

The moment of Yugoslavia's dissolution in the early 1990s was not surprising. With the fall of the Iron Curtain and the disappearance of the Soviet Union, the makeup of the world order became fluid. Owing its decade-long privilege to the special status as a non-aligned communist country inhabited by various ethno-national groups, Yugoslavia was bound to be part of the greater turmoil in its immediate geographic proximity. But such interpretations explain only the moment of the dissolution. As far as its actual origins are concerned, several other arguments have been advocated.[1] In this first part of the study, I shall deal with the most-well known 'nationalist hypothesis', which holds ethnically or religiously rooted 'nationalism' to be the main perpetrator of the Yugoslav catastrophe. Within this explanatory pattern, 'nationalism' is neither merely a political ideology that best suits the needs of a political elite at a specific time, nor a contextual phenomenon of a particular historical moment. Instead, it is seen as a perpetually valid independent variable that can explain virtually all conflicts involving the former Yugoslav spaces. Being independent of the larger context, 'nationalism' thus becomes a factuality to which one must adapt. The international community is especially guilty of advocating this 'ancient hatreds' thesis as an excuse for neither preventing the outbreak of war on the European continent nor making serious attempts to consciously disentangle the region's history of ethnic diversity from the economy and power-based conflicts of interests. By the end of the 1980s, the latter collided in a changing geopolitical environment and an aggravated economic situation. Since these conflicts were articulated along ethno-national lines and interpreted in terms of national conflicts by insiders and outsiders alike,[2] the examination of the 'nationalist hypothesis' remains important. For in this form, 'nationalism' is indeed the prime culprit.

Although 'nationalism' has been called 'the most important ideology of the modern era',[3] general statements about the establishment of a 'nation', the emergence of 'nationalism', or its goals are almost impossible to make. We usually

---

[1] See overview in Dejan Jovic, *Yugoslavia: A State That Withered Away* (West Lafayette, Indiana: Purdue University Press, 2008).

[2] Richard Holbrooke, *To End a War* (New York: Random House, 1999), 22. See also Calic, *Krieg und Frieden in Bosnien-Hercegovina*, 160–2, 219–20.

[3] John Breuilly, "Reflections on Nationalism," *Philosophy of the Social Science / Philosophie Des Sciences Sociales* 15, no. 1 (1985): 65.

find ourselves confronted with a huge amount of related literature.[4] Different authors use different concepts, definitions, and/or patterns in order to describe or explain similar phenomena. The study of 'nationalism' is thereby confronted by a general ambiguity. Retracing the emergence of 'nationalism' in Europe through the examination of philosophical currents and historical events leading to the establishment of particular nation states provides better knowledge about such cases. However, such particular explanatory patterns decrease the ability to generalise, thus preventing the emergence of generally valid 'theories of nationalism'. On the other hand, theories aimed at explaining general trends and causal mechanisms of 'nationalism' tend to fail when applied to concrete cases, especially in ethnically diverse regions. This ambiguity is not be regretted but regarded as an extremely interesting intellectual challenge that can succeed only if the limitations of such an endeavour are *a priori* admitted. First, the goal of Part I cannot be to develop a new approach to the phenomenon of 'nationalism'. The results of one particular case study can hardly ever be generalised. Instead, this section will use already established theories in order to test their accuracy with regard to the present research subject. Second, the use of specific terms like 'nationalism', 'nation', or even 'ethnicity' cannot be regarded as commonly established. The concepts behind these terms cannot be defined in a way that would enjoy widespread scientific agreement. Therefore, when referring to the broadly undefined, general ideas, I shall use quotation marks; these will be omitted when referring to the definitions I use. It is important to note that the definitions used refer only to the present study. While their use in other contexts may be adequate, they were designed for this purpose only. And third, the goal of chapters 2, 3, and 4 is not to develop a well-founded history of 'nationalism' in the Western Balkans, or even in Bosnia. It is also not to show where such region-specific analysis could or should begin. Instead, this section is to set the background needed in order to understand the differences between the three main groups in current Bosnia and their historic origins and legacies. As such, it is more an introduction to the case study than an intellectual contribution of its own.

---

[4]   See for example: Ernest Gellner, *Nations and Nationalism* (Ithaca: Cornell University Press, 2009); Eric J. Hobsbawm, *Nations and Nationalism since 1780: Programme, Myth, Reality*, 2nd ed. (Cambridge: Cambridge University Press, 1990); Anthony D. Smith, *Ethnic Origins of Nations* (London: Blackwell, 1986); Anthony D. Smith, *National Identity* (Reno: University of Nevada Press, 1991); Benedict Anderson, *Imagined Communities* (London: Verso, 2006); Rogers Brubaker, *Nationalism Reframed. Nationhood and the National Question in Europe* (Cambridge: Cambridge University Press, 1997); Adrian Hastings, *The Construction of Nationhood. Ethnicity, Religion and Nationalism* (Cambridge: Cambridge University Press, 1997); Hroch, *Das Europa der Nationen*; John Hutchinson and Anthony D. Smith, *Nationalism* (Oxford: Oxford University Press, 2001).

2.1   Nation and Nationalism

2.1.1 Modernists and Primordialists

We can distinguish two main approaches within the theories of nationalism. One side of the debate belongs to the modernist faction, the 'dominant orthodoxy of scholarship in nationalism'.[5] It includes authors like Ernest Gellner, Benedict Anderson, or Eric Hobsbawm.[6] They all understand 'nationalism' as a phenomenon connected to the modernising processes of the industrial society of the late eighteenth and the nineteenth centuries. Only the technical and industrial progress of that time, they argue, made the establishment of a sufficiently large *communauté de destin* possible. Accordingly, 'nationalism' as well as 'nations, national states, national identities and the whole "inter-national" community' are products of the modern era.[7] On the other side, we find the primordialist faction, represented by authors like Clifford Geertz or Edward Shils. In their understanding, 'nations', in one sense or another date much further back than the modernists imagine. In fact, they 'exist in the first order of time and lie at the root of subsequent processes and developments'.[8] Modern 'nations' thus represent only the contemporary versions of ancient social and cultural communities, which makes the element of ethnic ancestry key.

Both approaches face apparent challenges. The modernist perspective fails to sufficiently explain why it was particularly the 'nationalist' ideology that found so much support among the people. After all, industrialisation and modernity affected all contemporary and future ideologies in similar ways (even though not to similar degrees). So what made 'nationalism' so particular that it could overpower other concepts of belonging? Similarly, primordialists have to explain why the historical social and cultural community exercised so much political influence at that particular moment in time and with respect to that particular group. This paradigm simply cannot explain 'why people become attached to certain historic collectivities and not others (for example, Germany rather than Prussia), and why such attachments vary in scope, intensity and timing'.[9]

However, it seems possible to successfully reconcile those two approaches. In fact, the most convincing approach to the study of 'nationalism' is to argue for an eclectic and mixed position between modernist and primordialist claims, as

---

[5]   Anthony D. Smith, *Nationalism* (Cambridge: Polity Press, 2001), 49.

[6]   Marko Attila Hoare, *History of Bosnia: From the Middle Ages to the Present Day* (London: Saqi Books, 2007), 21–25; Smith, *Nationalism*, chap 3.

[7]   Smith, *Nationalism*, 47.

[8]   Ibid., 51.

[9]   Ibid., 54.

advocated by scholars like Anthony D. Smith[10] and Adrian Hastings.[11] Their basic claim is very simple: although the pre-modern communities are not to be fully equated with modern 'nations', they nevertheless possess, in Hastings' terminology, 'proto-national' qualities. As one historian writes, '[t]hat these [historically previous] forms of national or proto-national identity were not simply equivalent to their modern (…) counterparts is readily believable; that they were wholly dissimilar is much less so'.[12] 'Nations' need to be seen as *modern* phenomena which have their roots in *primordial* communities. Intellectually and practically, they are dependent on specific proto-national bonds. As has been convincingly shown with regards to the nation-building process in Europe, feelings, symbols, and myths used for the construction of modern 'nations' were not randomly selected; instead, they were closely connected to the cultural heritage of the people involved.[13] The so-called ethno-symbolist faction within nationalism theory, which developed as a critique to modernism, precisely emphasises the importance of such 'myths, symbols, memories, values and traditions' for the 'formation, persistence and change of ethnicity and nationalism'.[14] In other words, the primordial attributes of community were the 'raw material' for the modern 'nation'-building of the nineteenth century, which relied on the technological accomplishments of the time to succeed.[15] I believe that only this reconciled position, which takes into account the primordial bonds as well as the effects of modernisation, is capable to explain both the timing and the content of 'nationalism'.

2.1.2   The 'Nation'

We can understand the inner components of a 'nation' by looking at three classical definitions proposed by Ernest Renan, Stalin, and Max Weber. I chose those definitions because they exemplify in a proto-typical manner the different approaches one may take towards a definition. Renan famously defined the 'nation' as a 'large-scale solidarity, constituted by the feeling of the sacrifices that one has

---

[10]   Smith, *Ethnic Origins of Nations*.

[11]   Hastings, *The Construction of Nationhood.*

[12]   Hoare, *History of Bosnia*, 22. Hoare also heavily criticises Gellner, stating that to 'accept Gellner's thesis—indeed, even to accept the intellectual significance of Gellner's thesis—is an act of faith rather than of reason' (Ibid.).

[13]   Hanspeter Kriesi, *Vergleichende Politikwissenschaft 1: Grundlagen. Eine Einführung* (Baden-Baden: Nomos, 2007).

[14]   Anthony D. Smith, "Ethno-Symbolism", in *Encyclopedia of Nationalism*. Ed. A.S. Leoussi, 84 (London: Transaction Publishers, 2001); quoted in Umut Özkirimli, *Theories of Nationalism. A Critical Introduction,* 2nd ed. (Houndsmill: Palgrave Macmillan, 2010), 143.

[15]   Kriesi, *Vergleichende Politikwissenschaft 1*, 94–95.

made in the past and of those that one is prepared to make in the future'.[16] Accordingly, the 'nation' is no fixed category, but a 'daily plebiscite'. It depends on the will of the people and is subject to changing attitudes within society. Due to this aspect of voluntariness, a 'nation' can succeed only if it enjoys the support of the masses that are actively willing to sacrifice themselves for its survival. If, as a result of external or internal quarrels, the 'national' idea were to lose its unifying character, the 'nation' would cease to exist.

In contrast to Renan, Stalin[17] promotes an intellectually more exigent definition when he defines a 'nation' as 'a historically constituted, stable community of people formed on the bases of a common language, territory, economic life and psychological make-up manifested in a common culture'.[18] The voluntariness to which Renan alluded is thus based on specific elements of commonality that constitute the substrate of the 'nation'. Typically, those include a common language, a commonly inhabited territory, a common culture and history in the form of shared experiences and memories, or a common ethnic ancestry. These elements reinforce the bonds within society and provide the sociological foundation for the readiness to sacrifice oneself so that the 'nation' can live. They also help explain the supremacy of certain solidarity bonds over others in that 'national' bonds are seen as more deeply rooted in the human character than, say, other kinds of relationships.

However, following Weber, the elements of commonality—or peculiarity, in his terminology—are not the foundation of the 'nation' *per se* but the expressions of an underlying and unique 'feeling of solidarity' against outsiders, which forms the subjective base for a 'nation' to exist.[19] A Weberian 'nation' is thus a 'prestige community' that is unified through cultural values 'that are to be preserved and developed only through the cultivation of the peculiarity of the group'.[20] Since Weber understands the nation as 'a community of sentiment which would adequately manifest itself in a state of its own' and 'which normally tends to produce a state of its own',[21] he also assumes that political action is inherent to the concept of a 'nation'.

As these three rather distinct definitions exemplify, there are different ways to define a 'nation'. First, one may look at elements of commonality such as language, territory, or culture. That these categories often tend to be 'fuzzy, shifting,

---

[16] Ernest Renan, "Qu'es-ce qu'une nation?", 1882, http://archives.vigile.net/04-01/renan.pdf. Accessed 19 November 2010. Excerpt also available in Hutchinson and Smith, *Nationalism*, 17–18.

[17] Joseph Stalin, 'The Nation', in: Hutchinson and Smith, *Nationalism*, 18–21.

[18] Quoted in Ibid., 20.

[19] Cf. David Beetham, *Max Weber and the Theory of Modern Politics* (Cambridge: Polity Press ; New York: B. Blackwell, 1985), 122.

[20] Max Weber, 'The Nation', in: Hutchinson and Smith, *Nationalism*, 21–25.

[21] Quoted in Ibid., 25.

and ambiguous'[22] does not put into question their analytical usefulness but rather the general coherence of the 'nationalist' argument. For all intents and purposes, the elements of commonality remain practically relevant. They express the primordial bonds on which 'nationalist' intellectuals rely. In other words, those elements are the building blocks of modern 'nations'. Moreover, due to being grounded in an—often times highly questionable—examination of historical and societal development, those elements of commonality are directly observable and constitute *objective* criteria for denominating a group as a 'nation'. Whether a 'nationalist' intellectual chooses language, religion, territory, or all of the above as the foundation for his 'nation' largely depends on the circumstances under which his national ideology is to operate and who the significant 'other' ought to be. This choice is therefore not based on the genuine validity of the elements or historical claims, but on their political and practical usefulness within a particular context.

The elements of commonality are the practical representation of an existing intra-societal system of common values and beliefs. People are thus members of a *communauté de destin* long before they can articulate their feelings in those terms. In this second way of defining it, the 'nation' rests purely on a common solidarity, on the *subjective* element of wanting to be a unified 'nation'. But if such solidarity is—and, by definition, it must be since otherwise the state could not be sustained—inherent to the society and the individual living in it, it is not directly observable. In fact, its existence is only indirectly implied, for example through successful mobilisation on specific aspects of this solidarity.

While the distinction between subjective and objective elements within an analytical definition of the 'nation' characterised the early academic debate of nationalism, it is nowadays widely acknowledged that 'nations' rely on both kinds of bonds in order to underline their distinctive character.[23] An analytically useful definition of the 'nation' thus rests on the successful incorporation of those two kinds of relationships and their interdependence. The Czech historian and political theorist Miroslav Hroch offers such a definition. He argues that the 'nation' is characterised by relations based on different types of bonds among its members. Since these bonds—i.e. linguistic, historic, economic, political, etc. connections—are based on the genuine feeling of a closer link to members of one's own society as a result of communication processes and common experiences, they are mutually inter-exchangeable.[24] Due to these common relationships, the members perceive themselves as part of a 'nation'. Hroch's definition thus successfully combines objective and subjective criteria without neglecting that they influence the subject on different levels. His assertion of 'common bonds' primarily refers

---

22   Hobsbawm, *Nations and Nationalism since 1780*, 6.
23   For a full historical discussion see Hroch, *Das Europa der Nationen*, 13–6.
24   Ibid., 20–21.

to the character and function of these relationships and not to their actual form. Following Benedict Anderson, a 'nation' is 'imagined as a *community,* because, regardless of the actual inequality and exploitation that may prevail in each, the nation is always conceived as a deep, horizontal comradeship'.[25] Such comradeship is based on proto-national bonds as much as it is influenced by elements of commonality as their form of articulation. *A nation, thus, consists of a mutually exchangeable set of bonds and relationships among its members and articulates itself through certain elements of commonality that are influenced by internal and external dynamics.*

This definition, which shall be used in the following analysis, only seemingly excludes the purpose-oriented character of a nation to which Weber has pointed. His assertion that a nation 'would adequately manifest itself in a state of its own' and therefore 'tends to produce a state of its own' does not suppose that every nation will indeed produce a state of its own. More likely, the nation generates the demand that the solidarity, on which the nation is based, 'finds expression in autonomous political institutions'.[26] It thus refers to some kind of political goal or action being inherent to the concept of a nation. Without this aspiration, the nation as such has no further consequences, apart from deeper camaraderie. It is this specific political aspiration that, according to Weber, makes the nation different than other contexts of solidarity. But contrary to Weber's assumption, the inherent purpose of a nation is by no means limited to the aspiration of a nation-state. It may as well lie in the attaining and maintaining of autonomy, unity, and identity for its members.[27] Some purpose or goal of this kind is indeed already inherent to the mere concept of a nation. But its transformation to a level of consciousness cannot only rely on the foundational feeling of solidarity. The awakening of the national feeling is always a conscious action, performed by someone with a specific purpose in mind. Analytically, it therefore constitutes a different part of the argument and as such belongs to the discussion of 'nationalism' rather than the concept of a nation.

2.1.3   Nationalism

'Nationalism' can hardly be debated without provoking an immediate negative connotation. The term is closely associated with hatefulness and intolerance against non-members of one's society or members of an other community as well as with an inherent urge towards expansion and domination.[28] We may refer to 'nationalism's' contribution to the establishment of modern states and thus try to

---

25   Anderson, *Imagined Communities,* 7.
26   Beetham, *Max Weber and the Theory of Modern Politics,* 122.
27   Smith, *Nationalism,* 9.
28   Hroch, *Das Europa der Nationen,* 28.

present it as a tolerant ideology of inclusion.[29] But we can hardly assume such argument to be convincing, for too devastating are the consequences of real-world 'nationalism'. However, this kind of real-world 'nationalism' is distinctly different from what is of interest to the present discussion. It is the practical application of a deeper ideology and as such subject to the constraints of reality. It is the product of 'nationalism' rather than being 'nationalism' itself. 'Nationalism', as we understand it in the present context, is an ideology based on a particular set of assumptions from which particular political claims are deduced.[30] Whether this ideology succeeds or fails in practical terms, depends less on the ideology itself but on the practicability of the political claims. The same holds true for the diverse forms of appearance that this ideology produces.

As an ideology, 'nationalism' rests on a vague and simple claim. It 'places the nation at the centre of its concerns and seeks to promote its well-being'.[31] It is a political theory primarily concerned with the question what is best for the nation. But because of the inherence of a political aspiration in the concept of the nation, the answer is already predetermined; and so are the consequences. Ernest Gellner defines 'nationalism' as a 'theory of political legitimacy, which requires that ethnic boundaries should not cut across political ones'; the congruence of the political and the national unit is what Gellner has termed the 'nationalist principle'.[32] Wherever such congruence is lacking, the political order can be deemed illegitimate and political action against it justified. But instead of treating 'nationalism' as a 'theory of legitimacy'—a compliment it by no means deserves—we should understand it as a call for social and political change. Smith defines 'nationalism' quite accurately when stating that it is 'an ideological movement for attaining and maintaining autonomy, unity, and identity on behalf of a population deemed by some of its members to constitute an actual or potential "nation"'.[33] 'Nationalism' as an ideology thus produces a predetermined outcome, namely the fight for autonomy, unity, or identity. This fight, of course, is always subject to the laws of practicability and feasibility. On this level, 'nationalism' obviously becomes a political programme.

However, not every nation makes it thus far and not every political programme is necessarily successful. National ideology may, and in fact most often does, fall victim to practical constraints. Adrian Hastings argues that every ethnic group has 'a nation-state potentially within it but in the majority of cases that potentiality will never be activated because its resources are too small, the allurement of incorporation within an alternative culture and political system too pow-

---

[29]   Ibid.
[30]   For other meanings of 'nationalism', cf. Smith, *Nationalism*, 5–9.
[31]   Ibid., 9.
[32]   Gellner, *Nations and Nationalism*, 1.
[33]   Smith, *National Identity*, 73. Original emphasis.

erful'.[34] Hastings presents an argument similar to the 'threshold principle' that Hobsbawm has advocated.[35] According to this principle, nationality, expressed *inter alia* through the right of self-determination, only applies to nationalities of a certain size, for only they can form an economically sustainable unit.[36]

Implicit in the claim of sustainability is the pragmatic realisation that such states can never be truly homogenous. Convincing people that they nevertheless are, however, is no small part of the nationalist task. The group of individuals aspiring to become the founding fathers of a nation state have to penetrate the feeling of solidarity within the people thus allowing them to feel as a nation based on some elements of commonality. Only after having defined the people in whose name they want to question existing authority, can they really fulfil the prophecy of national ideology. They need to lobby upper and lower classes for their idea to become a meaningful political force. This is the moment when all the elements we have analysed separately so far come together: the nation, nationalism as an ideology, the political programme, and, last but by no means least, the constraints of feasibility of real-world nationalism. In order to fully understand the phenomenon of nationalism, a 'fruitful combination of historical analysis and theory' is thus needed.[37]

In sum, when dealing with 'nationalism', we have to distinguish between two phenomena. First, the attitude the members of a nation possess when they care about their identity as members of that particular nation; and second, the actions the members of a nation take in seeking to achieve (or sustain) some form of political sovereignty.[38] Leaving moral aspects of 'nationalism' aside, we thus need to distinguish between the foundation of the nation (*'the national ideology'*) and the actions performed in order to ensure or sustain that nation (*'the nationalist movement'*). While those two aspects usually appear in concert, they are analytically distinct in content and consequence. The former thereby structurally predates the latter. In order for the nationalist movement to become a political—and historical—force,[39] the ideological foundation has previously to be established, at least in a minimal form. A structural cluster composed of unifying factors and stances had to exist in order for either the people or the elites to be mobilised by nationalist rhetoric. By its mere nature, such rhetoric is based on unifying feelings, common threats, goals, or disappointments. The creation of the national ideology is the task of intellectuals, while its implementation is the one of national leaders. Especially in Eastern Europe, intellectuals were crucial in discovering,

---

34   Hastings, *The Construction of Nationhood*, 13.
35   Even though on all other counts, Hastings is a sharp critic of Hobsbawm.
36   Hobsbawm, *Nations and Nationalism since 1780*, chap. 1.
37   Breuilly, "Reflections on Nationalism", 66.
38   Beetham, *Max Weber and the Theory of Modern Politics*, 122.
39   Hroch, *Das Europa der Nationen*, 46.

re-discovering, or sometimes even inventing the foundations for the national ideology and, thusly, the nation itself; without their efforts, the nationalist movements of the nineteenth century would hardly have been successful.[40]

2.2   Analysing Nationalism in Contextual Terms

In order to fully understand the nationalist argument in a particular case, we have to investigate events, institutions, and views expressed before the formation of a nation state; examine the elements of commonality that articulate the national feeling of solidarity; look at the effects of modernisation and industrialisation; think about the conflicts of interest within the society; and, finally, analyse the role a mobilisation of feelings plays in the formation of the nation state.[41] With this general task in mind, specific research questions permit a pragmatic combination of those research interests and make the endeavour more manageable in the present context. In light of our research subject, Bosnia-Herzegovina, we shall concentrate on certain contextual factors under which the ideology of nationalism has developed, both in the nineteenth as well as in the twentieth centuries. Our analytical framework will focus on three particular contexts: the geographical, the historical, and the procedural context. These contexts are of course interconnected, which makes clear analytical separation impossible. This holds especially true for the separation between geography and history. For what passes as a geographical explanation of the phenomenon of nationalism has, in the present context, very little to do with geography as such. While the importance of certain geographical features cannot be denied—for example the significance of the Drina river in terms of separating the Bosnian and the Serbian lands or, even before that, the eastern or western parts of the Roman empire –, they only contribute indirectly to the phenomenon of nationalism. Instead, they can be seen as a reason for certain 'natural barriers' of political action and as such influence nationalism only via the element of history.

Nevertheless, the combination of these three contexts possesses a strong explanatory power; in one way or another, these contexts figure prominently in most of the theories of nationalism. Moreover, these contexts allow the introduc-

---

[40]   For the general context, see Hroch, *Das Europa der Nationen*. Specific works dealing, for example, with Slavic and Slovak intellectual history, respectively, are: Josette Baer, *Slavic Thinkers or the Creation of Polities: Intellectual History and Political Thought in Central Europe and the Balkans in the 19th Century* (Washington, DC: New Academia Publishing, 2007); Josette Baer, *Revolution, Modus Vivendi or Sovereignty?: The Political Thought of the Slovak National Movement from 1861 to 1914* (Stuttgart: Ibidem, 2010). The philosophy of the Bosnian Muslim intellectual Adil Zulfikarpašić is the focus of Šaćir Filandra and Enes Karić's, *Bošnjačka ideja* (Zagreb: Narodni zavod Globus, 2002).

[41]   As presented in Hroch, *Das Europa der Nationen*, 38.

tion of case-specific elements into the discussion; a feature that grand theories of nationalism often times fail to provide. Nationalism as an ideology and political programme depends on these kinds of elements not only with regard to its form and content, but also regarding its success or failure.

2.2.1   The geographical and historical contexts

Following Anderson, nationalism is by no means a European invention. It started with the 'creole pioneers' in the new South American republics that had already been administrative and territorial units from the sixteenth to the eighteenth century.[42] Consequently, all European cases were able to work from visible 'blueprints' provided by their distant and, after the French revolution, close predecessors. The extent to which these models were known to European nationalists is of course open to debate. But the similarity of crucial elements suggests that there was indeed some form of 'ideological transfer' involved in the process of establishing nationalism in Europe. However, as Anderson rightly points out, the European nationalists did not strictly follow these models but adapted them to their specific needs and political environments.[43] This spirit of, in Anderson's terms, 'selective pirating' was especially embraced in the 'Eastern' parts of the continent. In her study of Slavic political thinkers, Josette Baer argues that eclecticism can be seen as a 'basic principle of political thought' in Eastern Europe. The 'Eastern' intellectuals 'absorbed Western political ideas of the Enlightenment, liberalism, and nationalism adjusting them to fit the political circumstances they were trying to change'.[44]

Since these political circumstances were rather different in Eastern and Western Europe, two distinct kinds of nationalism developed that differed not only regarding the events leading to their emergence but also in their ideological foundation and political claims. On one part of the continent, we find the so-called Western model—also termed 'unificatory nationalism' (Gellner), the 'civic-territorial' model (Smith), or 'liberal nationalism' (Hobsbawm)—while on the other, the so-called Eastern model prevails—also called 'the classical Habsburg-and-east-and-south type of nationalism' (Gellner), the 'ethnic-genealogical' model (Smith), or 'transformed nationalism' (Hobsbawm). The cited thinkers of nationalism acknowledge the two models as well as their correspondence to the areas of Eastern and Western Europe. But even though they are argued in geographic terms, they do not presuppose the importance of geography as such. In fact, they neglect geography almost entirely and make an argument based on history and political circumstances. The Western parts of Europe experienced a multitude of

---

42   Anderson, *Imagined Communities*, chap. 4.
43   Ibid., 81–82.
44   Baer, *Slavic Thinkers or the Creation of Polities*, 16.

different rulers with territorially small and limited jurisdictions. The Eastern parts, and especially the Balkans, were integrated into larger empires and as such were collectively subject to foreign reign. These different circumstances that happen to correspond to the different parts of the continent were the actual origin of the two distinct types of nationalism that developed subsequently. In this sense, geography is not a context of nationalism *per se*, but one of the manifestations of historical trajectories.

The two types of nationalism differed in terms of ideology, i.e. their different cultural foundations. According to Smith,[45] the Western model is predominately a spatial or territorial concept. Nations must possess compact, well-defined territories that are connected to a historical homeland. The concept of the nation is based on 'a measure of common culture and a civic ideology',[46] which puts legal and political rights of the individual at the centre. Its counterpart, Smith's 'non-Western' model that is found in Eastern Europe or Asia, is based on a strictly 'tribal' concept of a nation. By merit of birth and ethnic descent the individual is for all times and circumstances identified as a member of a particular nation. Consequently, a nation is 'first and foremost a community of common descent', a fictitious 'super-family'[47] of sorts.

While these general distinctions are indeed empirically defensible, any subliminal connotations need to be rejected. Ernest Gellner, for example, concurs with John Plamnatz'[48] general characterisation of the Eastern (Balkan) type being 'nasty' and the Western type (Italy and Germany) being 'benign and nice'. The inappropriateness of such terms for analytical analysis is striking, let alone their uselessness from the point of view of scientific neutrality. Gellner sees the lack of a 'well developed high culture', meaning a 'literate, training-sustained'[49] culture as the deeper cause for the different character of Eastern nationalism:

> This kind of Eastern nationalism did not operate on behalf of an already existing, well defined and codified high culture, which had as it were marked out and linguistically pre-converted its own territory by sustained literary activities ever since the early Renaissance or since the Reformation, as the case might be. Not at all. This nationalism was active on behalf of a high culture not as yet properly crystallized, a merely aspirant or in-the-making high culture. It presided, or strove to preside, in ferocious rivalry with similar competitors, over a chaotic ethnographic map of many dialects, with ambiguous historical or linguo-genetic allegiances, and containing

---

[45]   Smith, *National Identity*, chap. 1.

[46]   Ibid., 11.

[47]   Ibid., 11–2.

[48]   John Plamnatz, 'Two Types of Nationalism", in *Nationalism*, E. Kamenka, Ed. (London: Edward Arnold, 1976 [1973]), quoted in Gellner, *Nations and Nationalism*, 96–7.

[49]   Ibid., 37.

populations which had only just begun identify with these emergent national high cultures.[50]

There is truth in Gellner's argument that the cultural and linguistic unity resulting from earlier centuries made Western nationalism more manageable. What Gellner fails to see, however, is that it was not the lacking high culture *per se* that made Eastern nationalism complicated. Take the example of the Serbian and Croatian national movements to which we shall come in the next chapter. Here, it is questionable whether a high culture was indeed lacking in the cases. Serbs could rely on the church as the bearer of national identity even during the times of Ottoman suzerainty, and the Croat nobility enjoyed some form of self-determination in the Habsburg Empire. This surely made the position of contradicting allegiances within the general public difficult. But even if one accepts the notion that a high culture was lacking, Gellner's argument neglects that this lack was by no means the reason for a different development in Western and Eastern Europe. Instead, it was merely a reflection of the completely different political, and thus historical circumstances under which these two nationalisms developed. Western nationalism was 'horizontal' in character; it was a negotiation of belonging and territory between different areas of jurisdiction and identification that all belonged to the same level. In contrast, Eastern nationalism developed under the conditions of existing empires and as such involved elements of 'verticality'. The nationalists had not only to convince their co-nationals of their nation-character, but also to strip the existing rulers of authority as a matter of principle, not space. It is highly doubtful that Western nationalism would have been 'benign' if it had to operate under the same circumstances as in the East. Western nationalism is in no way morally superior to Eastern nationalism; it is just different.

Miroslav Hroch has magnificently explained the consequences of the different contexts of emergence for the forms and ideologies of nineteenth century nationalisms.[51] Accordingly, the Western type of a state-nation (*Staatsnation*) is characterized through an efficient administration and an effective tax collecting system, which helps finance the needs of the ruling class and especially the wars of conquest. In order to be effective, an educational elite had developed and a police apparatus had been formed. The latter's task was, in Hroch's view, not only to guarantee the observance of the laws but also, in cooperation with the church, to supervise the attitude of the subordinates. The legitimacy of this social order was thus religious. Political rights were reserved for a few who used the term nation in order to define themselves. According to Hroch, the formation of modern nations as a community of politically equal citizens was in this respect a reaction to a crisis of legitimacy of the old political and religious order. The sovereignty

---

[50]   Ibid., 97.
[51]   Hroch, *Das Europa der Nationen*, 41–47. The argument in this paragraph follows Hroch.

had to pass over from the rulers to the nation, i.e. to the community of free citizens. Since the administrative framework for the state was already established before the modern nationalising process started, mobilisation of the masses was not needed. This is the main difference to the Eastern kind of nationalism that Hroch observes. For national movements within multi-ethnic empires, nationalism was the project of a non-ruling ethnic group. It aimed at obtaining full national existence, but independence in the form of a nation state was not necessarily a goal. As Hroch explains, on the cusp of the nineteenth century there were over twenty non-ruling ethnic groups within the territories of the three big empires, i.e. the Austro-Hungarian, the Ottoman, and the Russian. Some of those groups already formed their own ethnic communities, but unlike nations, they did not possess a complete social structure and a common culture. Under these circumstances, they could not rely on a sentiment of solidarity that included the complete social structure, from the workers to the employers and the educated classes. The nation, according to Hroch, was something that had to be constructed.

But the distinction between Eastern and Western types of nationalism is incomplete insofar as it neglects important variations within those types. These variations primarily concern the form of nationalism and only to a lesser degree its causes. Rogers Brubaker famously claimed that the relationships between the nation and nationalism 'are governed by the properties of political fields, not by properties of collectiveness'.[52] Depending on their emergence and position, Brubaker distinguishes between three different kinds of nationalism: (i) 'nationalising nationalisms' of newly independent or newly reconfigured states, where the state is understood as belonging to one core nation; (ii) 'homeland nationalisms', where states intervene in order to protect the interests and rights of 'their' ethno-national kin in other states; and finally (iii) the nationalism of national minorities that hold citizenship to one country but have ethnic ties to another, which is why they fight for recognition of certain collective and cultural rights.[53] Large, multi-ethnic empires seemingly present the natural birthplace for all three kinds of nationalism. But the relationship between them is by no means fixed; instead it needs to be regarded as an area of competing stances. As Brubaker writes, 'the triadic relation between these three "elements" is, therefore, a *relation between relational fields*; and relations between the three fields are closely intertwined with relations *internal to*, and *constitutive of*, the fields'.[54] Internal changes of power equilibria within as well as in relation to the three different nationalisms thus alter the political demands each kind of nationalism is likely to produce. While Brubaker's taxonomy tells us little about the emerging process of nationalisms, it provides a helpful framework in order to approach the subject at hand. In

---

[52] Brubaker, *Nationalism Reframed*, 17.
[53] Ibid., chap. 3.
[54] Ibid., 67, original emphasis.

a specific manner, it helps distinguish and explain political claims of equal or similar groups depending on their position within the triadic nexus.

2.2.2   The procedural context

While the historical and geographical context explains the emergence of different forms of nationalisms, it tells us little about the actual process of their emergence. Miroslav Hroch provides a useful analytical framework in order to explain nationalism within smaller European states located at the southeastern edges of the continent.[55] Analytically as well as procedurally, Hroch distinguishes three different phases of national uprising. A precondition for the emergence of nationalism was the adaptation of certain elements of commonality. In combination with an already existing, but rather vague feeling of common solidarity, these elements would create the true and indistinguishable nation. The respective process included the concretisation of the national territory; the production of knowledge regarding important events in the nation's past; the elaboration of cultural traditions unique to the nation; as well as the description of the nation's membership criteria and its member's way of life. In Western state-nations, this process was often done by state-paid intellectuals, while in multi-ethnic empires this task had to be performed by private citizens. Either way, this *'phase A'* was an intellectually dominated phase that defined the framework of the nation.

In *'phase B'*, according to Hroch's model, these intellectuals decided to spread their concept of national belonging among certain members of the said nation. This decision led to the establishment of a particular portion within the national movement as the founding fathers of the nation; in other words, it created the national elite. They established the political and conceptual framework of the nation and provided, based on the political and structural circumstances, the foundation of a later political programme. In Western Europe, where this national elite usually controlled large portions of public administration, they were able to take over national institutions by themselves. They were not dependent on the mobilisation of the masses, i.e. *'phase C'* in Hroch's model.

Minority nationalisms within large empires, on the other hand, relied on mass mobilisation in order to be successful. Only when the masses had taken over and accepted the idea of being a nation, could the national movement become a 'material force'.[56] It is only in relation to this phase that national movements could also elaborate a differentiated national political programme, for the validity of such programmes always depends on the means available in order to put them into action. Only when the Eastern national leaders could rely on some sort of public support were they really able to fight for their political programme. How-

---

[55]   Hroch, *Das Europa der Nationen,* 45–47.

[56]   Ibid., 46.

ever, the seeds of the programme itself were already laid in *'phase B'* or even in *'phase A'*, for a nation never develops without intrinsic political motives. The establishment of a nation state presents the ultimate success of nationalism in its narrower understanding.

Hroch's framework provides clear tools based on which nationalism can be analysed. However, it is important to remember that the model is of an ideal-typical character. Almost none of the small-nation nationalisms followed exactly this path, which makes Hroch's model analytical and not historical. Furthermore, we should avoid the assumption that the 'self-evident success of nationalism means that nationalism is very strongly rooted in the thought and behaviour of [common] people'.[57] To put it bluntly, this is simply not true. Peasants participating in the beginnings of a Serbian national movement, for example, did not sign on to the idea of a Serb nation, which at that time was still lacking clear contours. They rather opposed certain aspects of Ottoman rule that did in fact not primarily concern the foundation of Serb identity, i.e. Orthodox Christianity, but their everyday lives. In general, mobilising factors not primarily connected to national identity deserve much credit for the success of national movements. As Eric Hobsbawm has put it, '[t]he combination of social and national demands, on the whole, proved very much more effective as a mobilizer of independence than the pure appeal of nationalism'.[58]

Nevertheless, nationalism remains an important channel to funnel all sorts of emotions. Therefore, we should have a closer look at the different phases that Hroch has introduced in relation to our region of concern, the Western Balkans. As we have seen, a nationalist ideology relies on the individual only within the context of group identification. Personal freedoms are thus only obtained through the identification with a nation, understood as a community of peoples of equal descent and character. Within 'phase A', nationalist intellectuals had to choose elements of communality that would support such a claim. In Eastern Europe, they put special emphasis on 'the study and purification of language, since [they] regarded this manifestation of national character as perhaps the most important'.[59] Language was indeed an obvious choice; not only did it include all members of the potential nation regardless of social class, but it was also omnipresent in their everyday life and thus allowed simple and quick identification. But at the same time, there hardly existed any standardised language to date (which, in Gellner's terms, would indeed testify to a lack of high culture). As Eric Hobsbawm has written, languages 'are usually attempts to devise a standardized idiom out of a multiplicity of actually spoken idioms, which are thereafter downgraded to dia-

---

[57]   Breuilly, "Reflections on Nationalism", 73.
[58]   Hobsbawm, *Nations and Nationalism since 1780*, 125.
[59]   Barbara Jelavich, *History of the Balkans: Volume 1* (Cambridge: Cambridge University Press, 1999), 172.

lects, the main problem in their construction being usually, which dialect to chose as the base of the standardized and homogenized language.'[60] And Adrian Hastings, in many respects a critic of Hobsbawm and the modernist tradition, argues that the point in time when 'ethnicities', defined as groups of people with a shared cultural identity and spoken language, turn into nations is exactly when 'their specific vernacular moves from an oral to written usage to the extent that is being regularly employed for the production of a literature, and particularly for the translation of the Bible'.[61] If language is such an important parameter of nationality, the choice of a national idiom and its codification are highly political acts to begin with. The same holds true for the later use of such language in order to create a national sentiment strong enough to battle authority. Combined with the technical means of spreading the national idea around to fellow co-nationals, it was language that made an imagined community possible in the first place.[62] This can be observed in the northern Balkans, where between 1800 and 1850 three distinct literary languages were formed: Slovene, Serbo-Croat, and Bulgarian.

But closely connected to the issue of language were the issues of history, ethnicity, and territory. According to Smith, the first wave of Eastern nationalism in the early to late nineteenth century was characterised by the ethnic self-determination of the peoples subject to 'foreign' rule.[63] Through the mobilisation of the middle and lower strata into a vernacular politicised culture, the nationalists of this time sought to achieve the independence of their own 'historic territory' from a larger political unit, such as the Habsburg, Romanov, and Ottoman Empires. Unsurprisingly, this provoked a response by these empires that started their own nationalising efforts.[64] Following Smith, the goals of the national movements included (1) the creation of a literary 'high' culture for the community where it was lacking; (2) the formation of a culturally homogenous 'organic' nation; (3) securing a recognized 'homeland' and preferably an independent state for the community; and (4) turning a hitherto passive ethnic group into an active ethno-national community.[65] While not all of this was the task of the intellectuals, they played an important role in designing the parameters that would make nationalism possible. But usually they did not form the nations themselves nor did they *a priori* think that one nation is superior to the other and thus has to rule or be ruled, respectively. For the most part, they only argued that the best place for

---

[60]   Hobsbawm, *Nations and Nationalism since 1780*, 54.

[61]   Hastings, *The Construction of Nationhood*, 12.

[62]   Anderson, *Imagined Communities*, chap. 5.

[63]   Smith, *National Identity*, chap. 6.

[64]   The controversy over the official language in the Habsburg Empire (German v. Hungarian, Hungarian v. Croatian) can be seen as a proof for this claim.

[65]   Smith, *National Identity*, 126.

an individual is within his nation, which is defined by a specific set of elements of commonality. 'It was only later, when these vague conceptions were transformed into practice and into political programs, that national leaders came to emphasize the unique and marvellous qualities of their own people and to use this argument to justify their control over others'.[66] The intellectuals spread the word around and the elites, sometimes together with the intellectuals, reacted with a political programme.

In Eastern Europe, the implementation of such programmes was bound to happen only if the participation of the peoples could be secured. This task was made easier by the position of subject peoples within the empire. The masses, mostly peasants, were not repressed primarily by local nobles alone, but by foreign powers and local nobles cooperating with them. Since the acquisition of national consciousness cannot be separated from other forms of social and political consciousness in the period of nationalism,[67] it was a mixture of political demands and national self-determination claims that mobilised the masses.

---

[66]   Jelavich, *History of the Balkans Volume 1*, 173.
[67]   Hobsbawm, *Nations and Nationalism since 1780*, 130.

3 A Comparative Look at Western Balkan Nationalisms

Nationalism, as it appeared in the late 1980s in Yugoslavia, was a combination of two different kinds of nationalist thought. It melded together the eighteenth and nineteenth centuries ideas of national identity and respective memories in order to create not only an explanation for the contemporary political developments but also a mobilising feeling of a historical continuation of national struggle. This endeavour succeeded because past events were kept alive through their continuous recollection in various forms of storytelling. The result was a 'chronological overlap' that 'creates links between individuals and generations living in different eras and compresses the elapsed time between generations or historical events'.[1] Discontent for authority and perceived domination could thus easily be awakened once a suitable situation presented itself. Calling Muslims *Turci* ('Turks') was as small a step as calling members of the Serb and Croat communities *Ustaše* and *Četnici*, respectively. Everybody knew what the context was and what such terms signified; everybody remembered the stories, poems, and songs dedicated to the respective struggles in previous times. A comprehensive analysis of contemporary ethno-nationalisms has thus to take into account historical forms of the nationalist struggle in the region. This is especially true for the case of Bosnia-Herzegovina where the medley of different ethno-national groups created unique circumstances for nationalism to spread.

The first section of this chapter analyses the elements of commonality on which Croatian, Serbian, and Bosnian nationalisms are based. While this task is relatively unchallenging for the first two, it is quite complex for the third. Nevertheless, the first section of this chapter will treat Bosnian nationalism as a given in order to elaborate on its differences from the other two. Conceptually, I understand the term 'Bosnian' more as a geographical than a national concept for the moment. This approach is justified since different groups put forward distinctively Bosnian elements of commonality in order to underline their political arguments. In historical terms, for example, the connection between medieval Bosnian territory and national identity is not an element solely attributed to the nationalism of Bosnian Muslims. Nor is the term Bosniak solely used to depict members of the Muslim faith with a Bosnian background. Since many groups originating on Bosnian soil have used the common elements of a distinctly Bosnian identity in order to justify their projects and political claims, these elements have to be

---

1   Bardos, "Balkan Ethnoconfessional Nationalism: Analysis and Management," 201.

analysed largely detached from the group nationalisms with which they are associated today.

The second and third sections of this chapter deal with national awakenings in the neighbouring states of Serbia and Croatia. These will lay ground for analysing the cross-border influences with respect to the incorporation of their co-nationals living on Bosnian territory. The forth section is dedicated to the particular form of Yugoslav multi-nationalism. In their totality, these four sections provide the necessary background for the analysis of nationalism in Bosnia-Herzegovina, which is the subject of the next chapter.

3.1   Elements of Commonality within Bosnian, Croat, and Serb Nationalisms

The main dividing line between the three national communities in Bosnia is religion. Bosnian Muslims, Bosnian Croats, and Bosnian Serbs, I believe, do not really differ in terms of their ethnic ancestry, language, or even culture due to centuries of close contact and amalgamation. Even though such differences are often introduced in treatises about national identities, they tend to be structurally unfounded in historical terms, as we shall see shortly. Be that as it may, the objective validation of such claims is secondary to their *de facto* appeal, as subjective traits do not necessarily have to correspond to objective ones for the creation of national identity.[2] Furthermore, even though religious distinctions form the foundation of the respective nationalisms, the nationalists have made sure to broaden this foundation as much as possible. They tried to justify their claim to nationhood not only based on their religious differences, but also with regards to territory, ethnic ancestry, or history. What element they chose depended largely on the audience they were addressing. Croats, for example, underlined the claim of historical statehood in their autonomy struggle against the Habsburg Empire in the nineteenth century. In the 1990s, when they needed to differentiate themselves from the Serbs and Bosnian Muslims, they claimed an origin rooted in European (and Catholic) civilisation; they opposed their counter-nationalists on rather cultural arguments. The accumulation of such fragmented audiences and purposes of communication, combined with the intellectual need to possess all the elements of nationhood that respected nations possess, led to the creation of holistic concepts of national identity. All groups claiming nationhood could thus present distinct ethnic, religious, linguistic, and historical-cultural arguments to support their claims.

---

2   Calic, *Krieg und Frieden in Bosnien-Hercegovina*, 23–23.

3.1.1 Ethnicity

In the present context, I understand ethnicity as historical ancestry.[3] The Slavs, an Indo-European people, arrived in the Balkans in the sixth and seventh centuries when, unlike most previous invaders, they settled the land as peasants.[4] The internal structure of the Slavic community is subject to debate. Some historians claim that the sixth century Slavs included different tribes, two of them being the Croats and the Serbs.[5] Noel Malcolm, for example, argues that these two tribes were, 'from the earliest times, distinct but closely connected, living and migrating in tandem'.[6] Edgar Hösch, on the other hand, maintains that the Slavic tribes were not distinct but simply 'summarized' as 'Croats' and 'Serbs'.[7] Probably most prominently, Ivo Banac rejects the premise of different tribes altogether by stating that the first settlers 'were undifferentiated Slavs, who identified themselves only with the common Slavic name and according to the local–pre-Slavic–toponyms'.[8] According to Banac, it was only after the first South Slavic states were constructed that, as a result of new waves of Slavic immigrants, three distinct South Slavic 'matrix-nationalities' emerged: the Croats, the Serbs, and the Bulgars. Through new tribal alliances and the imposition of control over the tribes in their immediate area of settlement, the 'Croat and Serb states, emerging respectively as sovereign principalities in the late ninth and twelfth centuries, created traditions of nationhood where previously there had been only tribal agriculturists'.[9]

What may seem an academic debate about minor categorisation and timing issues is of crucial importance for the study of nationalism in the region. Differentiated Slavic tribes are a necessary condition for the claim of different ethnic ancestries of the South Slavic peoples. In other words, they are the breeds for a distinct national history. In order to secure this item of national identity, some Croatian nationalists have even gone as far as to claim that Goths, not the South Slavs, were their (and, by implication, Bosnians') original ancestors.[10] They were able to make such a claim because different tribes passed through the Balkan Pen-

---

[3] For all the different concepts of ethnicity, see the Oxford Reader by Hutchinson and Smith, especially the introduction: John Hutchinson and Anthony D. Smith, *Ethnicity* (Oxford: Oxford University Press, 2009), 3–14.

[4] Jelavich, *History of the Balkans Volume 1*, 15.

[5] Alex J. Bellamy, *The Formation of Croatian National Identity: A Centuries-Old Dream?* (Manchester: Manchester University Press, 2004), 33.

[6] Malcolm, *Bosnia*, 9.

[7] Edgar Hösch, *Geschichte der Balkanländer: Von der Frühzeit bis zur Gegenwart*, 5., aktualisierte und erweiterte Auflage. (Munich: Beck, 2008), 38.

[8] Ivo Banac, *The National Question in Yugoslavia. Origins, History, Politics* (London: Cornell University Press, 1988), 33.

[9] Ibid., 34.

[10] Malcolm, *Bosnia*, 5.

insula prior to the Slavs—but without leaving much of a cultural heritage.[11] In a similar manner, the Bosniak historian Mustafa Imamović correctly defines Bosnian Muslims as ethnic Slavs who settled the area of the later medieval Bosnian kingdom. But he maintains that throughout their ethno-genesis, the Bosnian Slavs, unlike the Slavs on the peripheries, hardly mingled with other people because they inhabited a territory in the centre of the geographical South Slavic ethnic space. He goes on to claim that even after converting to Islam, they did not mingle with Muslims of non-Slavic origin 'despite the strong spiritual ties'. In his view, this makes the Bosnian Muslims 'the oldest and the purest Slavs in Bosnia'.[12] There is no need to address the validity of such questionable and morally reprehensible claims in the context of the present study, since its use in nationalist rhetoric is instrumental, not factual. It is only in the modern era that the ethnic substrate of the ancient South Slavic tribes would become important as the basis for the formation of the Yugoslav tribes.[13]

3.1.2 Historical association

More important than ethnic ancestry for the national awakening in the Balkans was historical association. 'National revival' in the Balkans 'was a process of remembering the cultural, linguistic, and historic facets of identity, based on the nations' glorious kingdoms in the Middle Ages'.[14] The fact that a specific group inhabited certain areas in the past, i.e. that they constitute their *historic homeland*, is often presented as a legitimisation of current territorial aspirations. Usually, and quite understandably, these nations aspire to owning and governing the territory their group inhabited at the apex of their territorial power. For Serb nationalists, the historic reference is the reign of Stephen Dušan of the Nemanić dynasty.[15] Shortly after succeeding to the crown in 1331, he undertook a series of expeditions between 1334 and 1348 so that his dominions ultimately 'stretched from

---

[11] Before the Slav invasion, different tribes occupied the territory of modern Bosnia. According to Malcolm, the earliest historically traceable inhabitants were the Illyrians, who spoke an Indo-European language related to Albanian. In the third century, Gothic tribes started their conquest of the Balkans but, after some victories, they withdrew to Italy and Dalmatia. Apart from the Goths, Asiatic Huns and Iranian Alans visited the region in the forth and fifth centuries, and the Avars in the sixth century. All these tribes left some ancestors in the region that were soon absorbed by the common population. Ibid., 2–6.

[12] Mustafa Imamović, *Historija Bošnjaka* (Sarajevo: Preporod, Bošnjačka Zajednica Kulture, 1996), 23. Without referencing specific sources, Imamović states that he concurs with other researchers, namely Milenko S. Filipović, Špiro Kulišić, and Muhamed Hadžijahić, whose analyses have supported the claim of purity and the oldest historical ancestry of the Bosnian Muslims.

[13] Calic, *Krieg und Frieden in Bosnien-Hercegovina*, 21.

[14] Baer, *Slavic Thinkers or the Creation of Polities*, 123.

[15] Hösch, *Geschichte der Balkanländer*, 41.

the Danube to the Gulf of Corinth, from the Adriatic to the Aegean'; Dušan was the 'strongest ruler in the Balkans' aiming at creating a powerful Serbian-Hellenic state.[16] He styled himself the 'king of Serbia and Romania', 'lord of almost all the empire of Romania', and in 1346, 'emperor of the Serbs and the Greeks'. Later on, he would add the Bulgarians and Albanians to the title as well.[17] Dušan ruled over a vast empire, intent 'on becoming the master of the Balkan peninsula'.[18] But even though his land incorporated the territory of Hum (modern Herzegovina), it did not include Bosnia proper. (In fact, the presence of Serbs within the territory of Bosnia proper primarily dates from the periods after the arrival of the Ottoman Empire.[19] The subsequent claim of Serb nationalists regarding the territory of modern Bosnia and Herzegovina can therefore not be legitimised through territorial expansions of the medieval kingdoms.) After Dušan's death, his kingdom 'broke up into a plethora of dynastic principalities, making itself vulnerable to the imposition of Ottoman supremacy'.[20]

The Croat equivalent to the reign of Dušan was the medieval kingdom of Tomislav (910-928),[21] even though it was in place for only a comparably short period of time. Tomislav, the first ruler to take the title of a king, had his centre in Biograd on the Dalmatian coast.[22] At its apex, the realm included Northern and Southern Dalmatia, several islands in the Adriatic Sea, Istria, as well as Bosnia.[23] The importance of Tomislav's reign lies less in the geographical extent of his dominion but rather in the unification of Northern Croatia with coastal Dalmatia, which were ruled as one single polity. This union 'formed a major part of the so-called national dream of the Croats'.[24] Tomislav's realm thus enabled Croatian nationalists to substantiate their claim to Croatia's *continued* historical statehood with regards to all three parts of its territory, i.e. Dalmatia, Croatia, and Slavonia. For this reason, early Croat nationalism is primarily based on the historical statehood narrative. It states that Croatia, despite being incorporated into the 'Hungarian Empire' since the beginning of the twelfth century, always stayed independent to such a degree that can legitimise its claim to national independence and sover-

---

[16]   Stevan K. Pavlowitch, *Serbia: The History Behind the Name* (London: C Hurst & Co Publishers, 2002), 4.

[17]   Jelavich, *History of the Balkans Volume 1*, 19; Pavlowitch, *Serbia*, 4; Hösch, *Geschichte der Balkanländer*, 70.

[18]   Banac, *The National Question in Yugoslavia*, 37.

[19]   Tim Judah, *The Serbs: History, Myth and the Destruction of Yugoslavia* (New Haven: Yale University Press, 2009), 80.

[20]   Banac, *The National Question in Yugoslavia,* 37.

[21]   Hösch, *Geschichte der Balkanländer*, 41.

[22]   Jelavich, *History of the Balkans Volume 1*, 21.

[23]   Hösch, *Geschichte der Balkanländer*, 56.

[24]   Bellamy, *The Formation of Croatian National Identity*, 36.

eignty.[25] The crucial importance of the historical argument is underlined by the fact that many of Croatia's contemporary national symbols, like the currency (the *Kuna*) or the chequerboard coat of arms (called *Šahovnica*), date back to the medieval kingdom.[26] However, the invasion by the Hungarians in 1102, the subsequent establishment of authority over Croat lands in 1526, as well as the incorporation of Croatia within the Yugoslav states of 1918 and 1945 profoundly challenges the claim of Croatia's continued statehood—understood in the sense of sovereign self-rule by Croat nobility. In administrative terms, however, there is some merit to the argument.

Similar to their Serb and Croat counterparts, Bosnians as well looked to medieval times to find their territorial reference and located it in the reign of Ban Stephen Tvrtko (1353-91).[27] Already under his predecessor, Ban Stephen Kotromanić (1322-1353), Bosnia had expanded to include the territories of Hum (in 1326)—which made Bosnia and Herzegovina a single political entity for the first time in history—and several formerly Croatian areas west of the Banat.[28] Under Tvrtko, Bosnian expansion continued and its realm comprised large parts of the Dalmatian coast as well as Zeta (modern Montenegro).[29] According to one historian, 'during the second half of Tvrtko's reign Bosnia was the most powerful state within the western Balkans'.[30] The geographic circumference of his realm made it possible for Tvrtko to be crowned king of 'the Serbs, Bosnia, and the Croats' in 1377; later, he would add Dalmatia to this title.[31]

The notion of a historic homeland is crucial to the nationalist argument not only as a legitimisation of current territorial aspirations but as the foundation of a distinct *cultural* connection between the 'core' lands and the nation itself. Naturally, those 'core' lands are smaller than the territories of the medieval empires, for they solely comprise the first settlements of the alleged ethnic ancestors. For the Serbs, this is the historical heartland of Raška (Rascia), a town near modern Novi Pazar.[32] The Croats originally settled areas in 'the coastal territory from the mouth of Raša in Istria to the Cetina River' and their territory went 'as far east as the Vrbas River in present-day Bosnia'.[33] The 'core' lands of the Bosnians were situated at the source of the Bosna River just outside modern Sarajevo. Due to

---

25   The entire argument regarding the historical statehood narrative can be found in Ibid., chap. 3.
26   Ibid., 36.
27   Hösch, *Geschichte der Balkanländer*, 41.
28   Malcolm, *Bosnia*, 17.
29   Hösch, *Geschichte der Balkanländer*, 75.
30   Malcolm, *Bosnia*, 13.
31   Jelavich, *History of the Balkans Volume 1*, 25; Malcolm, *Bosnia*, 18–20.
32   Banac, *The National Question in Yugoslavia*, 37.
33   Ibid., 35.

such 'core lands', ethnicity and historical association become so closely inter-linked that they form an almost indistinguishable part of the nationalist argument.

The different territorial claims of the three groups inhabiting modern Bosnia are thus all (more or less) valid, yet mutually exclusive. During different times in history, different parts of modern Bosnia-Herzegovina were under Bosnian, Serb, or Croat control. This would allow its territory to be presented as originally Serbian, Croatian, or Bosnian. Strictly speaking, the historical argument therefore cannot hold true for any of the three groups with regards to Bosnia. Instead, the specific territorial circumstances of Bosnia-Herzegovina strengthened a unique regional character within its population. In the words of Ivo Banac:

> Indeed, although the Serbs and Croats participated in Bosnia's earliest national integrations and continued to do so into the modern period, the growth of Bosnia's pronounced regional character may derive from strong presence of the undifferentiated Slavs from the first migration. An alternative interpretation is to view Bosnia as a nationally polarised Croat-Serb state, which, like many other peripheral medieval states with mixed population (Savoy, Burgundy), fostered a state-preserving regional consciousness.[34]

Regardless of their ethnic ancestry, people inhabiting medieval Bosnia developed a common regional consciousness, which would exert influence over the next centuries. This uniquely Bosnian identity was a product of (a) the administrative structures of the Bosnian state, which would be preserved even under Ottoman and Habsburg rule; (b) the specific Bosnian script *Bosančica* as the expression of cultural distinctiveness; and (c) the medieval Bosnian church, that differed to some extent from the Catholic and Orthodox churches of that time. Bosnians, regardless of the national identity they later developed, are not simply co-nationals of Croats and Serbs, as the nationalist propaganda of the nineteenth and twentieth centuries would claim. They possessed a multi-layered regional identity that would at first make the nationalist project quite difficult (see next chapter).

3.1.3 Religion

In 1459 and 1463, respectively, Orthodox Serbia and still (more or less) Catholic Bosnia fell under the control of the Porte. Since the Ottomans were not able to conquer Croatia, it remained under Hungarian and thus Catholic influence. With the establishment of these rival empires in the Balkans Peninsula, religion was to become a key issue for governing those territories. What is more, this situation helped build distinct religious identities.

The history of Serbian Orthodoxy starts with St Sava, the founder and first head of the Serbian Orthodox Church. In 1219, this third son of Stephan Nemanja secured religious autonomy for the Serbs from the Byzantine emperor. Since reli-

---

[34] Ibid., 39.

gious autonomy was administered communally, St Sava *de facto* established the foundations of 'Serbian statehood and national identity'.[35] Shortly after its creation, the church's centre was moved to Peć in Kosovo, which made the region the spiritual and administrative centre of the Serbian Church. However, Kosovo's importance as an attribute of Serbian national identity was mainly due to the battle at *Kosovo Polje*, the Field of Blackbirds, between the Serbs and the Ottomans in 1389. When the Ottoman Sultan Murad defeated the Serbian army under the leadership of Prince Lazar,[36] he effectively gave rise to a myth of Serbian martyrdom that would echo for centuries.[37] In Serbian ecclesiastical mythology, Prince Lazar's death was interpreted as 'a martyr's sacrifice for the Christian faith' and 'physical defeat was turned into spiritual victory'.[38] In accordance with this understanding, Lazar's alleged last words to his men on the eve of the battle were that 'it is better to die in battle than to live in shame'.[39] The creation of the Serbian Church and the spiritual re-interpretation (or integration) of the defeat at *Kosovo Polje* unified Serbian Orthodoxy with Serbian national identity.

In the Ottoman Empire, the *millet* system allowed non-Muslim organisations to maintain their legal, economic, and administrative structures. This possibility transformed the churches from cultural and administrative bodies into the preservers of a religion-specific cultural identity. In the words of one prominent historian, 'as the bearer of the whole cultural, religious, and political life, the Orthodox and Catholic churches played a central role in the development of a national self-consciousness of the Serbs and the Croats, respectively'.[40] Against this background, the independence from the Porte that Serbia ultimately achieved at the Congress of Berlin has a peculiar significance: it presented not only the liberation of the 'Turkish yoke' but some sort of compensation for the centuries-old injustice that the Serbs suffered at *Kosovo Polje*.

In its Catholic form, Christianity is also essential to Croat national identity, albeit not in purely religious terms. The Croats were Christianized somewhere between the seventh and the ninth centuries,[41] mostly due to Aquileian missionary activity.[42] Presumably, Catholicism was fully established in Croatia only after the arrival of the Hungarians in 1102. Since the latter were of the same faith as the Croats, the religious component played a secondary role to the statehood argu-

---

[35]   Judah, *The Serbs*, 20.
[36]   Lazar was supported *inter alia* by the army of the Bosnian king Tvrtko.
[37]   'The battle was not as catastrophic as later legend would suggest. Closer to a draw, it was nevertheless a great massacre in which both Lazar and Murad died, and which impressed contemporaries as a portentous event.' See Pavlowitch, *Serbia*, 10.
[38]   Ibid.
[39]   Judah, *The Serbs*, 29. The words were passed down by the Serbian patriarch Danilo.
[40]   Calic, *Krieg und Frieden in Bosnien-Hercegovina*, 27.
[41]   Malcolm, *Bosnia*, 8–9.
[42]   Banac, *The National Question in Yugoslavia*, 61.

ment in the formation of Croat national ideology in the nineteenth century. It is only in the last decades of the twentieth century that religion and culture were re-integrated into the Croat national mythology. While the Serbs had to preserve their religion throughout Ottoman times, the Croats faced no such challenge. This is why, within the Croatian context, the religious component is always intermingled with a much more fundamental claim of a 'clash of civilisations', to borrow Samuel Huntington's famous phrase. Croat nationalists like the later President of independent Croatia, Franjo Tuđman, referred to the consequences of the division of the old Roman Empire in 395 in order to distinguish the Serbs form the Croats. In a 1992 interview, he said:

> Croats belong to a different culture—a different civilization from the Serbs. Croats are part of Western Europe, part of the Mediterranean tradition. Long before Shakespeare and Moliere, our writers were translated into European languages. The Serbs belong to the East. They are peoples like the Turks and Albanians. They belong to the Byzantine culture… despite similarities in language we cannot be together.[43]

This ancient division served both as an integrative argument towards Europe and a distinguishing element with respect to the others, in this case the Serbs. It was the foundation of a self-identification as part of a European civilisation as well as the neglect of the other's right to the same. Tuđman insisted on the relevance of this division well into the 1990s. According to his ideology, the Croats served as an *'antemurale christianitis'* defending Christian Europe from Islam during the Ottoman conquests.[44] However, since they did so as part of the 'Western civilisation' this component of their national identity could not serve in the struggle for national recognition against the Habsburg Empire. The nineteenth century Croatian national narrative thus centred more on the territorial and autonomy components of national self-determination than on religion. As far as Croats inhabiting the areas of Croatia, Slavonia, and Dalmatia were concerned, sovereignty and territorial autonomy were the main challenges for the establishment of a truly Croat nation. Croats living under Ottoman rule, on the other hand, formed part of the non-Muslim population known as *raya* and as such did not enjoy the same rights as those individuals who adhered to Islam. Apart from general discrimination and taxation issues, the consequences of this policy were especially striking in the area of land ownership, which was a prerogative of Muslims.

Religion is also the key determinant for the Bosnian Muslim national ideology. But it is not the Islamisation of Bosnian territory *per se* that makes religion relevant. In fact, many Bosniaks have Catholic and Orthodox ancestors. In their national narrative, the gradual conversion of Bosnians to the Muslim faith is seen as some sort of a culmination of distinct religious traditions that would establish a genuinely Bosnian Muslim identity. According to this view, (Catholic) Bosnians

---

[43]   Quoted in Bellamy, *The Formation of Croatian National Identity*, 68.

[44]   Ibid., 69.

were some sort of community distinct from Serbs and Croats even before they became Muslims. They shared certain elements of commonality, most importantly their links to the territory of Bosnia, which makes a clear distinction between Bosniaks and Bosnians almost impossible. The modern term *Bošnjak* (Bosniak) accurately connotes 'Bosnian Muslims' and is the result of an intellectual and political process during the Bosnian war in the 1990s. The newly created *Bošnjački Sabor* (Bosniak Assembly) decided in 1993 that Bosnian 'Muslims' should henceforth be called 'Bosniaks' justifying this choice through a series of arguments linked to history, territory, the relationship to the other communities (Serbs and Croats), and religion.[45] Since this change coincided with an attempt by the pan-Islamist elite within the main Muslim party, the SDA, to re-Islamise the society, the Assembly chose an exclusive terminology.[46] Bosniak would henceforth only equal Bosnian Muslim.

Bosniak nationhood rests on three pillars that are well known within nationalist theory: religion, history, and territory. But contrary to intuition, Bosnian Muslims, or Bosniaks, do not see their religious ancestry solely in the period of the Ottoman Empire. Their claim to religious individuality dates back to the time before the Ottoman conquest: as a 'unique Bosnian phenomenon', the medieval Bosnian Church 'lies at the heart of Bosniak nationhood'.[47] This church encompassed the medieval Bosnian realm and followed practices different than those of the Catholic and Orthodox churches.[48] But its exact character is highly disputed among historians—and has been for the last 120 years when the first books on the subject were published by Franjo Rački (1867) and Božidar Petranović (1967).[49] Rački claimed that the Bosnian Church is of Bogumil descent, a dualist Bulgar heretical movement of the tenth century. Petranović, on the other hand, saw the church as part of the Eastern Orthodox tradition, even though it incorporated some heretical beliefs. Other authors, like Luka Petrović, completely rejected the dualist character of the church and tried to prove its monastic origins; if successful, this would basically make it a Catholic Church.[50]

It is difficult to determine the validity of such claims in general; within the context of the present study it is impossible. What seems clear though, is that the

---

[45]   Sevan Pearson, "Bošnjaci instead of Muslimani: A Symbolic Change in Wartime Bosnia-Herzegovina in 1993", Francis Cheneval and Sylvie Ramel, ed., *Special Issue of Transitions: From Peace to Shared Political Identities. Exploring Pathways in Contemporary Bosnia-Herzegovina* 51, no. 1–2 (2011): 201–220.

[46]   They thus neglected other concepts, put forward by Adil Zulfikarpašić and Muhamed Filipović, see Ibid., 212–213.

[47]   Imamović, *Historija Bošnjaka*, 84.

[48]   Malcolm, *Bosnia*, chap. 3.

[49]   Ibid.; Imamović, *Historija Bošnjaka*, 84–92; Banac, *The National Question in Yugoslavia*, 39–40.

[50]   Imamović, *Historija Bošnjaka*, 88.

claim of Bogumil ancestry has to be rejected. There is no proof that the Bogumils ever penetrated Bosnian soil. But even if the Bosnian Church was Bogumil in character, it was already collapsing well before the Ottoman conquest.[51] It could thus hardly be the bearer of a distinct Bosniak nationhood, at least not in terms of accurate history telling. Moreover, it is difficult to reflect on the degree of difference between the Bosnian Church and the other two churches. There simply are no sources from *inside* Bosnia regarding the organisation, the ceremonies, and the theology of the Bosnian Church.[52] According to Malcolm, the most convincing theory contains elements of both the Eastern Orthodox and Catholic theory.

More important from a nationalist point of view is that 'the *ecclesia Bosniensis* represented a religious assertion of Bosnian individuality'.[53] As it was later on monopolised by the Bosnian Muslims, it allowed them to claim that 'their direct ancestors were originally separate from either the Orthodox or the Catholic inhabitants and would obviate equally vehement Croat and Serb claims on Bosnian land based on the supposition that Bosnia was an integral part of their respective cultural legacies'.[54] Bosniak identity is thus crucially linked to the Bogumil tradition within the Bosnian Church narrative. This also explains the territorial aspect of Bosniak identity, for the Bosnian Church is closely connected to the medieval kingdom. It not only presented a religious phenomenon but also the manifestation of a socio-political situation in a feudal medieval realm.[55] According to Imamović, the church weakened the ruling class and strengthened particularism; by simultaneously fighting the supremacy of the Pope, the Catholic-Croat, and the Orthodox-Serb authorities, it strengthened the independence of the medieval state and defended it against external dangers.[56]

3.1.4 Language

The study of language was the 'most important attribute' of nationality for nineteenth century nationalists.[57] With historical association as the legitimisation of territorial claims, language, along with ethnicity and religion, was the foundation of a distinct cultural heritage. But a distinction based on language between the different South Slavs proved to be very difficult. It is commonly assumed that since the middle of the nineteenth century, Croats, Serbs, Montenegrins, and Bosnian Muslims in the South Slavic lands used the same literary language. This

---

[51] Pearson, "Bošnjaci instead of Muslimani", 214.

[52] Malcolm, *Bosnia*, 31.

[53] Banac, *The National Question in Yugoslavia*, 40, original italics.

[54] Francine Friedman, *The Bosnian Muslims. Denial of A Nation* (Colorado: Westview Press, 1996), 12–3.

[55] Imamović, *Historija Bošnjaka*, 92.

[56] Ibid.

[57] Jelavich, *History of the Balkans Volume 1*, 177.

language could be differentiated into Eastern and Western types and included three different dialects: *štokavian*, *kajkavian*, and *čakavian*—based on the usage of the word 'what' ('*što*', '*kaj*', or '*ča*').[58] In light of the geopolitical situation (the multinational empires), the choice of one of these dialects as the foundation of a common South Slavic literary language was inherently political. The example of the Croat Ljudevit Gaj, who, 'though a native speaker and writer of *kajkavian* Croat switched his own writings from this dialect to *štokavian* in 1839, in order to underline the basic unity of southern Slavs'[59] illustrates this quite well. In most parts of Croatia as well as in Serbia, Montenegro, and Bosnia, *štokavian* was the dominant dialect,[60] which means that language facilitated the unification of the South Slavs.

Developments in Serbia influenced Gaj's choice. The Serbian intellectual Vuk Karadžić (1787–1864), who continued the studies of Dositej Obradović (1739–1811), chose the same dialect for the Serbian literary language, for he was impressed by the purity of this vernacular spoken in Herzegovina.[61] In 1850, Croatian and Serbian intellectuals, along with politicians codified *štokavian* as the foundation of Serbian and Croatian literary language(s).[62] Unity in language, however, is not to be confused with unity of national ideologies. While Gaj was aiming to transcend the national differences between Serbs, Croats, and Slovenes by arguing that they shared common ancestry,[63] Karadžić opposed this idea. Instead, his 'linguistic vision was that all speakers of his pure and ennobled vernacular were really Serbs, whatever their religious affiliation or self-definition'.[64] Although common, language was to remain an important element of *division* for the South Slavs. Linguistic separation was thereby facilitated by the division of *štokavian* into three regional types: *ekavian*, *ikavian*, and *ijekavian* (e.g. '*dete*', '*dite*', '*dijete*' for 'child'); *ijekavian* was spoken in Croatia, Bosnia-Herzegovina,

---

[58]   Calic, *Krieg und Frieden in Bosnien-Hercegovina*, 25.
[59]   Hobsbawm, *Nations and Nationalism since 1780*, 54–55.
[60]   Calic, *Krieg und Frieden in Bosnien-Hercegovina*, 25.
[61]   Jelavich, *History of the Balkans Volume 1*, 177; Pavlowitch, *Serbia*, 35; Malcolm, *Bosnia*, 102. Some controversy is attached to the fact that in Ottoman Bosnia local writers called their language 'Bosnian' which could lead to the conclusion of a distinct Bosnian language independent of Serbo-Croat. However, as Malcolm explains, these sources simply meant 'the language spoken in Bosnia: they were not suggesting that it was quite separate from the language spoken anywhere else' (Ibid., 102.). Additionally, some linguists argue that in Bosnia-Herzegovina, where the Eastern and Western versions of the Serbo-Croat language intermingled, a discrete Bosnian language could be found (Calic, *Krieg und Frieden in Bosnien-Hercegovina*, 26.).
[62]   In the *1850 Vienna Literary Agreement* (Calic, *Krieg und Frieden in Bosnien-Hercegovina*, 26.)
[63]   Bellamy, *The Formation of Croatian National Identity*, 44.
[64]   Pavlowitch, *Serbia*, 47.

Montenegro and parts of Serbia, while most people in Serbia spoke *ekavian*.[65] In order to foster unity, Yugoslav linguists established in the *Novi Sad Agreement* of 1954 that the dialects spoken in Zagreb and Belgrade were indeed two types of the same language, the exact name of which was not specified. But starting in the 1960s, especially Croats would question this agreement and ask for Croatian to be accepted as a language of its own.[66] These efforts culminated in the 1990s with the creation of a 'pure' Croatian standard language[67] and the introduction of new grammar and dictionaries in Serbian, Croatian, and Bosnian.[68]

3.2 Nationalism in Serbia—Martyrdom and Uprising

Even though the revolutions of 1804 and 1815 set the Serbs on their path towards national independence, they did not start as actual projects of nationalism. They were popular uprisings against an unsecure environment within the Ottoman Empire which threatened the survival of the people subjected to the Porte's rule. As an 'insurgency movement',[69] the popular awakening had only a minimal theoretical foundation at its beginning. The intellectual 'phase A' of the nation building process, which establishes the parameters of national identity and the foundation of its basic ideas, was therefore almost completely missing before the revolution. The formation of the nation and the determination of its elements through the standard nationalist tools—researching the past, codification of language, determining the importance of religion, and distinction from others—were key tasks once a state of sufficient autonomy was achieved. In other words, the popular uprisings preceded the establishment of an intellectual foundation of the Serb nation and were not its consequences.

This argument, put forward by Hroch, is convincing insofar as it refers to the actual revolutions of 1804 and 1815 and their immediate origins. The autonomy movement gradually gained power from the second uprising until the Congress of Berlin in 1878 when Serbian independence was internationally codified. The main part of the usual content of 'phase A' was indeed done in the years after Serbia gained a substantial amount of autonomy as a principality within the Ot-

---

[65] Calic, *Krieg und Frieden in Bosnien-Hercegovina*, 26.

[66] Bellamy, *The Formation of Croatian National Identity*, 55; Pavlowitch, *Serbia*, 174. In the 1967 'Declaration concerning the name and position of the Croatian literary language', Croatian intellectuals argued that Croatian had been downgraded to a local dialect. They demanded that Croatian becomes the official language in Croatia and as such to be taught in school. After the abolition of the Croatian spring in 1971, the 1974 Yugoslav Constitution guaranteed all nations the right to use their own languages (Bellamy, *The Formation of Croatian National Identity*, 55, 139.)

[67] See the study by Bellamy, *The Formation of Croatian National Identity*, chap. 6.

[68] Calic, *Krieg und Frieden in Bosnien-Hercegovina*, 27.

[69] Hroch, *Das Europa der Nationen,* 105, 107.

toman Empire, i.e. after 1830. Nevertheless, stating that the creation of the Serb *national idea* happened only after the establishment of the national state—or in the time immediately preceding it—is inaccurate. The basic idea of unifying all Serbs into one state is in no small part a consequence of the Serbian Church being split between empires. While church dogma depicted all Serbs as part of one ethnic and religious community, one part of the population was subject to Ottoman rule and the other to Habsburg control. The prevalence of such dogma was even more important because the Serbian national movement was not unified in its leadership. This opened up the field for potentially contrasting concepts of national unity. The difficult relationship between the Karađorđević and Obrenović families can be understood not only as a manifestation of two competing, legitimising principles but as a separation within the Serbian nobles once the fight against the Ottomans began to yield its first results.

3.2.1   Before the uprisings: The ideological foundation of the Serbian uprising

The first Serbian uprising in 1804, led by Đorđe Petrović (or, as he would later be known, Karađorđević), was not a national uprising in the sense of a fight for independence or autonomy. The territorial unification of Serb lands and Serb people, to paraphrase Gellner's definition of nationalism, was by no means the intention of the revolutionaries. Quite the contrary: the uprising was not aimed against the sovereignty of the Sultan at all, but against the 'unruly and brigand elements' within the empire that the Porte was unable to control.[70] The janissary corps especially terrified the population and committed grave massacres. As a reaction to the brutal killing of some seventy native elders, '[f]rightened rural notables organized the resistance of the terrified peasantry with outlaws and former Austrian servicemen and auxiliaries'.[71] Thus, even though the people rose against an important element of the Ottoman administration, they did not seriously challenge the general rule of the Porte.

While the first uprising was rather a contextual effect without far-reaching political planning or intellectual background, Pavlowitch insists that 'it did give new impetus both to the memory of medieval Serbia and to the tradition of defiance and defeat'.[72] In order to legitimise his actions and motivate the troops, Karađorđević specifically referred to the need of removing the Turkish yoke 'that Serbia had borne since the battle of Kosovo'; he furthermore tried to legitimise his authority through the usage of king Dušan's symbols. All this does indeed support Pavlowitch's interpretation of events. However, he insists that there was

---

[70]   Jelavich, *History of the Balkans Volume 1*, 192.
[71]   Pavlowitch, *Serbia*, 28.
[72]   Ibid., 31.

no 'great idea' to restore Dušan's empire,[73] no desire for a greater Serbia. This fight was thus not nationalistic in character. Moreover, it seems questionable that Karađorđević referred to the Porte when talking about 'the Turks'; more likely, he might have meant the janissary corps and he may have reminded his soldiers of their people's greatness as a means of boosting troop moral.

But the crucial question is why Karađorđević chose exactly those elements in order to gain public support or legitimacy. The ideas of the 'Turkish yoke' and 'Lazar's martyrdom' at *Kosovo Polje* had been passed from one generation to the next through the institution of the Serbian Church, operating under the *millet* system within the Ottoman Empire. The treaty of Belgrade in 1739 put Serbia under Ottoman sovereignty and led to migrations of the Serb Patriarch Arsenje IV and the Christian elite. The new archbishopric was set up in Karlovci. In the Habsburg Empire, Orthodox Serbs enjoyed some equivalent of the *millet* system, meaning that they could practice their religion and form assemblies.[74] This archbishopric, which was also to harbour the remains of Prince Lazar, had an important role in defining Serb identity. In response to the question why someone called himself a Serb, one catechism of 1772 read: 'I call myself a Serb because of my birth and of my language, which is that of the people from whom I originate and who called themselves Serbs.'[75] The catechism introduces ideas of birth and ancestry thus underlining the element of common ethnicity and origin. It also mentions a common language as an important element of Serb identity, presumably in opposition to the language(s) spoken in the Habsburg Empire. Being a parochial source, the element of religion is present as well. It is worth mentioning that such ideas of Serbdom were not confined to the Habsburg dominion. Members of the Serb merchant class frequently travelled across the Habsburg-Ottoman border, which also made it possible to transport books. Two books were of particular importance in shaping Serb national ideology: Jovan Rajić's history of the Slavs published in 1768 and Hristopher Žefarović's *Stemmatografija* printed in 1741.[76] As a collection of portraits and coats of arms of Slavic saints, monarchs, and bishops, the *Stemmatografija* turned out to be especially influential. It not only suggested a direct line between Patriarch Arsenje IV and the Nemanić family, but also contained several coats of arms used by Karađorđević and his troops.

---

[73] Ibid.

[74] Ibid., 22.

[75] Ibid., 23.

[76] Judah, *The Serbs*, 54–55. In fact, the *Stemmatografija* was an adapted version of the same book by Croat national ideologist Vitezović, which was updated under the direction of Arsenje IV. See Banac, *The National Question in Yugoslavia*, 74.

Among those was also the modern Serbian coat of arms, which consists of a square cross and four Cyrillic letter Cs (Ss in Latin script).[77]

All these circumstantial effects support the argument that the nationalists of the nineteenth century heavily relied on relicts, ideas, and philosophies that the Orthodox Church had preserved or composed in order to keep the elements of Serb identity alive throughout the centuries of Ottoman and Habsburg control. Even though certain aspects of national identity, like the language issue, were only properly introduced into the nationalist debate later on, the church prepared the ground for such moves. This suggests that the Serbian 'uprising nationalism' had in fact an intellectual foundation of some sort, even if it was not the leading force behind Karađorđević's revolution. In fact, while the revolution itself was apolitical and unintellectual, it led to the widespread introduction of the Serb national identity idea based on the elements described. But it also prompted a political programme that reached beyond the demand of getting rid of the janissary corps. This programme was a logical consequence—first of the revolution's military component, i.e. the idea that military success and sacrifice should be rewarded and, second, of the features unique to the concept of nationalism that relies on full self-determination and territorial integrity. What we can observe is a perfect example for methodologically combining modernist and primordialist approaches towards nationalism as outlined in the previous chapter. While the national revolution and what would follow were indeed an element unique to the nationalist logic of the nineteenth century (not strictly of modernisation, though), these events depended on primordialist concepts guarded and perfected over centuries by the Orthodox Church. However, we need to be aware of the dichotomy of those two approaches. It would be anachronistic to characterise the idea of Serbdom before the Karađorđević/Obrenović uprisings as an idea of national identity. We may assume that this identity was 'a combination of different bonds and relationships'. But those were not yet combined with a political and social concept of a nation and lacked the integral parts of a national political programme. This became one of the main focuses of the nation-building policies of the first autonomous governments.

3.2.2   From the revolution to the national state and beyond

After the first uprising had begun, the Serbian leadership tried to round up foreign support as 'some sort of great-power guarantee of their autonomy'. They established links with Russia, Austria-Hungary, and other Balkan Christians, 'in par-

---

[77]   As Judah writes, most Serbs now believe the four Ss stand for '*Samo sloga Srbina spašava*' (Only unity saves the Serbs), even though they were not originally meant to be letters but representations of fire-lighting flints. See Judah, *The Serbs*, 55.

ticular their brother Serbs living in Bosnia, Montenegro, and Hercegovina'.[78] The first real battle with Sultan Selim's army in 1805 ended with a Serbian victory. This victory 'marks the commencement of the Serbian revolution in the real sense of the word' since, for the first time, 'the Serbs fought not against a Muslim rebel force, but against the Sultan's troops'.[79] Several other victories followed and in December 1806, the Serb troops captured Belgrade and expelled the Ottoman army. In light of this event and the war between the Ottoman Empire and Russia that had started the same summer, the Porte was ready to compromise. It basically agreed to the entire Serb programme, which consisted of removing the janissaries, limiting Ottoman presence in the *pashalik* (i.e. the district) of Belgrade in general, using local troops to garrison Serbian fortresses, and transferring some administrative autonomy to Serbian officials (tax collection).[80] In effect, the Porte was ready to give some form of autonomy to the Serbs. But some Russian officials presented a better offer. In exchange for military support in the war against the Ottomans, 'Russia' was ready to give the Serbs full independence. Unaware that such offers had not been approved by St Petersburg, the Serb leadership chose the two birds in the bush instead of the one in the hand. Their position was substantially weakened when Russia and the Porte signed the armistice of Slobozia in August 1807. In August 1809 an Ottoman army marched on Belgrade and, in October 1813, occupied it. Karađorđević, whose leadership was already subject to internal critique, fled to Austria and the first uprising came to an end.

Since this also meant that local conditions remained largely unchanged, there was hardly any chance for peace. The second Serbian uprising in April 1815, therefore, was only surprising in its proximity to the first's failure. It happened under the leadership of Miloš Obrenović who was involved in the first uprising as well but did not flee in 1813.[81] As the Serbian leadership and the Porte were generally ready to compromise, by November a '*de facto* agreement had been reached, with village elders once again collecting taxes and Miloš Obrenović accepted as "paramount elder" and sole Serbian representative'.[82] The subsequent events proved that Obrenović's approach would have a more lasting effect than Karađorđević's.[83] After 1830, Serbia was legally an autonomous tributary

---

[78]   Jelavich, *History of the Balkans Volume 1*, 197.

[79]   Ibid., 198.

[80]   Ibid., 198–9.

[81]   Pavlowitch, *Serbia*, 32.

[82]   Ibid.

[83]   In 1817, Obrenović had Karađorđević killed after the latter returned secretly to Serbia as part of a larger Greek-inspired plan for a general Christian uprising against the Ottomans. This marked the beginning of the fight between the Karađorđević and Obrenović dynasties. This fight would determine large parts of Serbian history from this point on. See Jelavich, *History of the Balkans Volume 1*, 240; Pavlowitch, *Serbia*, 33.

principality whose frontiers were fixed in 1843; '[e]xcept for thc sultan's ultimate sovereignty, the military presence of garrisons, and limited economic advantages, what remained of the Ottoman régime was largely formal'.[84] After the establishment of formal authority over its dominion, Prince Miloš, as Obrenović now called himself, had to establish domestic institutions and consolidate his power. He 'wished to strengthen his personal position and win further autonomous rights for the state'.[85] Since Miloš ruled with the 'unlimited authority of the supreme leader who had obtained the rights that Serbia now enjoyed… he had acquired the farming of the sultan's revenues in Serbia, appropriated reclaimed lands, traded, collected most of the pig export business, and amassed a fortune, which he invested in Wallachian estates and in Viennese banks'.[86] Despite his general distrust of bureaucrats[87] and notables' resentment for efficient central authority,[88] Miloš established a strong domestic administration.

With the establishment of governing capabilities, the young Serbian state had to formulate a national policy. This included (a) the definition of relations towards neighbours and the positioning of one's government in relation to the great powers of the century; and (b) the consolidation of a national ideology within the people.[89] This second task is of special interest in the present context. Following Hroch's model, the Serbian nationalist leaders had to create the idea of a Serb nation, spread it around among the elites, and convey it to the masses. They benefitted from efforts of the Serbian Church in preserving the idea of Serbdom as well as from Karađorđević's insistence on those elements in motivating his troops. But since the revolution was successful before a national identity was fully established, the intellectual formation of the Serb nation was a key task of the new state. In other words, Hroch's 'phase A' was split in two, before and after the uprisings. Perhaps more accurately, we may assume that the uprising gave rise to the full elaboration of the national idea. The new government thus faced the need to approach all phases of nationalism almost simultaneously—and perhaps in a more coordinated manner. In Brubaker's terms, it had to pursue a 'nationalising nationalism'. This meant that intellectuals had to establish the nation and teach its meaning to the general public as part of one all-encompassing project. Referring to Balkan nationalisms in general, one distinguished historian writes:

> It is impossible to judge the extent to which the people in any Balkan area held deeply nationalistic convictions—that is, in the sense of believing that the nation-state was the natural moral and political division for mankind and that it should command

---

84   Pavlowitch, *Serbia,* 33.

85   Jelavich, *History of the Balkans Volume 1,* 238.

86   Pavlowitch, *Serbia,* 34.

87   Ibid., 35.

88   Jelavich, *History of the Balkans Volume 1,* 239.

89   Ibid., 236.

the first allegiance of the citizen. The majority of peasants were probably emotionally most closely attached to their families and regions and perhaps their local churches. Certainly the new governments did take seriously the task of *teaching patriotism* to the population. National propaganda, both for internal and foreign consumption, became a major *state industry* and was perhaps the strongest component of the education given in the new school systems.[90]

Given the close link between the public and the church, governments assumed ideas and responsibilities previously held by clerics. Apart from education and social welfare, this also included the moral guidance of the people. The new 'state' conceptualised itself around church ideology by adopting an 'idealized form of "nation state"', in which 'ethnicity and culture were one'.[91] Since this transformation had to be explained and internalised by the people, nationally oriented educational systems became crucial. Dositej Obradović, Karađorđević's minister of education (between 1808-1811), was responsible for the establishment of the first institution of higher education in Belgrade, the so-called Great School.[92] His main goal was to 'disseminate the ideas of the Enlightenment through didactic writings in the spoken language'.[93] This also meant codifying this spoken language. Vuk Karadžić carried on Obradović's programme. He not only significantly contributed to the development of the Serbian language and a Cyrillic script suitable for it, but he also published a collection of Serbian epic poems, 'which rendered them accessible to the emerging classes and enabled them to play an important role in the growth of the new nationalism'.[94] Karadžić was convinced that all the Slavs in the region 'were not different peoples but rather one people divided by religion—that is, Orthodoxy, Catholicism and Islam'.[95] Therefore, his concept of a Serb nation had to encompass all those people, which meant that it could not be exclusively based on religion. In fact, by choosing *štokavian* as the national language for the Serbs, he implicitly stated that the Serb nation was by no means exclusively Orthodox; as long as they spoke *štokavian*, Catholics and Muslims had to be Serbs as well.[96]

It was in this regard that Karadžić laid the foundation of the Greater Serbia ideology. When understood in terms of *realpolitik*, his definition meant that the people living in Croatia or Bosnia were in fact Serbs, as long as they were of Slavic origin. But Karadžić's ideology was not as much aimed at unifying the South Slavs as it was designed to subject them to Serbian rule. Contrary to the philosophy of the Illyrian movement (that sought to unite the Slavs behind a

---

[90]   Ibid., 237. My emphasis.

[91]   Pavlowitch, *Serbia*, 43.

[92]   Judah, *The Serbs*, 55.

[93]   Pavlowitch, *Serbia*, 35.

[94]   Judah, *The Serbs*, 55.

[95]   Ibid.

[96]   Banac, *The National Question in Yugoslavia*, 80.

common ancestry that is neither Serb nor Croat nor any other of the current nations, see next section), Karadžić wanted to subsume the Slavs under Serb ethnicity in order to justify Serb sovereignty. Almost as important as Karadžić in
terms of creating the intellectual foundation of a Serbian nation was prince-
bishop Petar II Petrović-Njegoš of Montenegro.[97] In 1847, he published the poem
The Mountain Wreath glorifying Miloš Oblić, the legendary Kosovo hero said to
have killed the Sultan. Many years later, this poem inspired the young Bosnian
Serb Gavrilo Princip to assassinate the Austro-Hungarian Archduke Franz Ferdinand in Sarajevo, initiating World War I.

Unifying Serb culture and ethnicity also incorporated territorial aspects. Internally, it meant that the territory of Serbia had to be depopulated of people loyal
to the Porte, for the emerging nationalism had, like all uprising nationalisms, a
clearly anti-empire orientation.[98] Externally, and as a consequence of Karadžić's
ideas of national unity, it meant that Serbia's territorial aspirations were by no
standard fulfilled within the current extent of Serbian dominion. There were still
many Serbs living outside those parameters. Karadžić was thus also the intellectual father of a greater Serbian ideology that would find its expression in the 1844
document known as *Načertanje* (Outline), written by Ilija Garašanin. By then, the
political landscape in Serbia had changed. Prince Miloš' authoritarianism had
faced serious opposition by the so-called Constitutionalists—primarily merchants,
local elders, and wealthier peasants—who demanded that the Prince's powers be
limited by a constitution.[99] When he abdicated in 1839, Miloš was succeeded by
his son Milan who died of tuberculosis before even officially assuming the
throne. His brother Michael was installed in 1840 but faced serious opposition by
the Constitutionalists and by people still loyal to his father, Prince Miloš. In 1842,
an assembly dominated by the Constitutionalists dismissed Michael and installed
Aleksander Karađorđević as prince, the son of the first uprising's leader.[100] With
this change in leadership, the Constitutionalists effectively secured their power
over Serbia. In terms of policy, they, *inter alia,* intensified their educational efforts and began financing higher education abroad, mostly in Paris. As a consequence, young people educated in Europe brought back not only knowledge, but
also 'a broader outlook on culture and politics'.[101] Garašanin, who was a leading
figure in the Constitutionalist movement, became minister of the interior under
Aleksander Karađorđević.

---

[97]   Judah, *The Serbs*, 63–4.

[98]   Pavlowitch, *Serbia*, 43. Pavlowitch notes that the Ottomans, regardless of their
origin and language, left 'as a result of the arrangements stipulated with the Porte',
'under economic pressure', or 'voluntarily'.

[99]   Ibid., 37.

[100]   Jelavich, *History of the Balkans Volume 1*, 243.

[101]   Pavlowitch, *Serbia*, 42.

The *Načertanje* was an outline of Serbia's long-term foreign policy. It centred on the idea of unifying Serbia with Montenegro, Bosnia, Herzegovina, and parts of northern Albania.[102] Its central premise and basic principle was that 'Serbs, wherever they lived, should enjoy self-determination and self-government, which [Garašanin] equalled to the conservative rule of a Serbian dynasty, by no means a democracy or a union of South Slavs'.[103] But Garašanin's *Great Serbia* 'had nothing to do with the Serb ethno-nationalism and mass expulsion of [the] 20th century, but followed the 19th century rationale of the poor agrarian states in the Balkans: territorial expansion for reasons of economic sustainability'.[104] Despite this rationale behind his policy, Garašanin relied on a nationalistic argument when justifying his claims. As Baer explains, his text included a definition of Serb nationhood evolving around the components of language, culture, to some extent Orthodoxy, and self-liberation as a consequence of what she termed the 'theorem of historical continuity': the idea that Serbian statehood was to be understood as a process toward an empire that began in the thirteenth and fourteenth centuries (and included, *inter alia,* Dušan's empire) and was interrupted by the Ottomans.[105] The autonomy achieved by Prince Miloš was therefore only a first step in a gradual effort to establish a larger Serbian state—the second step being the enlargement of the province under Aleksander Karađorđević. Serbia was to become the Balkan Piedmont.[106] In Garašanin's view, '[t]he restoration of the Serb Empire should not only demonstrate that the Serbs were a considerable political factor in the Balkans, but that they had a historical duty, a moral task' to restore their legacy.[107]

Of particular importance was the territorial claim on Bosnia, whose population had to be persuaded—not forced—to join the project. Otherwise, as Garašanin wrote, 'it would follow that the Serbs would be split into small provincial principalities under separate dynasts, who would without fail surrender themselves to foreign influence, because they would rival and envy each other'.[108] This restoration project, however, was not the immediate goal of Serbian foreign policy but rather a long-term aspiration. It was used in order to justify other, lesser aims, for Serbia clearly lacked the capabilities necessary to put Garašanin's outline into action. The outline therefore expressed the state of mind that prevailed in Serbia's educated class.[109]

---

[102]   Ibid., 45.

[103]   Baer, *Slavic Thinkers or the Creation of Polities,* 147.

[104]   Ibid., 146.

[105]   Ibid., 150–1.

[106]   Marie-Janine Calic, *Geschichte Jugoslawiens im 20. Jahrhundert* (Munich: Beck, 2010), 48–53.

[107]   Baer, *Slavic Thinkers or the Creation of Polities,* 151.

[108]   Quoted in Banac, *The National Question in Yugoslavia,* 84.

[109]   Pavlowitch, *Serbia,* 45.

By the middle of the nineteenth century, the idea of a Serbian national identity was fully developed including all the components it still enjoys today. The Orthodox religion—closely interwoven with the memory of the Kosovo battle and the Nemanić dynasty—had served as the central component of the new nation in the beginning of the uprisings. It remained important throughout the entire nation-building process as well as in the attempted implementation of the corresponding project of a Greater Serbia. But especially in the first decades, Orthodoxy was not the linchpin of Serbian nationhood. In fact, the first national governments were generally of secular orientation. However, by taking over significant responsibilities of the church, the state incorporated the structure of the church itself and, more importantly, established a clear hierarchy: 'What happened at this point was not a separation of church and state, as happened in liberal Western Europe, but the subordination of the religious to the secular authorities'.[110] Religion in general, and the ecclesiastical structures in particular, became dependent on the state they helped to create. The extent to which religious dogma and structures mattered in every-day politics varied according to the interests of the dominant political elites. This understanding was a clear consequence of Garašanin's thinking. His plan clearly foresaw the revival of the Serbian empire based on an ethnic, not a religious concept. He wrote: 'If we consider the revival of the Serb Empire from this standpoint, then other South Slavs will easily understand this idea and accept it with joy.'[111]

With Orthodoxy and ethnicity as two separate, but nevertheless crucial components of Serb national identity, the Serb nation can be defined in more strict or more liberal terms depending on which of those two components one wishes to emphasise. This makes it a perfect tool of political management, for either of the two components can be introduced depending on the political goal and the prevailing circumstances. The same is true for language, which, as noted earlier, can be understood as either an element of unity or an element of separation between the South Slavs. A liberal Serb identity is basically compatible with the later concepts of Yugoslav identity, which were based on some form of brotherhood and unity. But it is also compatible with the exclusive ethno-nationalist understanding later advocated by Dobrica Ćosić and put into action by Slobodan Milošević. This is not to say that there are no frictions between these different types of national identities, indeed there are many. But those identities could be brought together or separated one way or another, provided the political will to do so. Such 'liberalism' was possible because the South Slavic peoples did not until recently finalise their national formation process. Different concepts of the nation still prevailed at the turn of the century: the cultural nation (based on Johann

---

[110]   Jelavich, *History of the Balkans Volume 1*, 237.
[111]   Quoted in Baer, *Slavic Thinkers or the Creation of Polities*, 151.

Gottlieb Herder) that would favour a unified South Slavic state; and the religious nation (as a legacy of the Ottoman period) that would acknowledge the linguistic similarities but concentrate on the religious differences.[112] Calic furthermore notes that distinct historical and political traditions created dividing lines that were too deep to overcome through anything other than instrumentation from above, which would happen with the kingdom of the Serbs, Croats, and Slovenes (the SHS state) in 1918.

3.3   Nationalism in Croatia—Historic Statehood Rights

As part of the Habsburg Empire, the territories of modern Croatia played an important role in the general division of power between the Austrians and the Hungarians. Vienna controlled Dalmatia and the Military Frontier region, while Croatia proper and Slavonia were under the supervision of Hungary.[113] The majority of Croats (and Habsburg Serbs) thus lived in 'Hungarian' lands, meaning that their fate was closely associated to that of the Hungarians.[114] But despite formally being under the regime of a *Ban* (governor) appointed by the crown, the Croats acted partly autonomously through the Croat assembly, the *Sabor.* This parliament included the great landowners, representatives of the lesser nobility, the Catholic prelates, delegates from free towns and some others.[115] Unified in their desire to maintain an existence apart from Austrian or Hungarian direct control, the Croat nobility generally chose not to pick sides in the quarrels between the Hungarian and Austrian nobility.[116]

3.3.1   The Illyrian movement

The ideological foundation of the Croat national movement was the tradition of Illyrianism, which centred on the question of language and gained traction in the early to mid-nineteenth century. With the growth of Hungarian nationalism, in reaction to similar attempts from Vienna with regards to use of the German, Hungarian nationalists demanded a change of the official language in the areas they controlled. Hungarian should replace Latin in government and education.[117] Since it was a part under Hungarian dominion, this change would affect the official language in Croatia as well. The reaction of Croatian nobility to such tendencies remains subject to debate. According to Barbara Jelavich, the nobility was in its majority not nationally minded and thus showed little resistance to the Hungarian

---

112   Calic, *Geschichte Jugoslawiens,* 27.
113   Jelavich, *History of the Balkans Volume 1,* 304.
114   Ibid., 139.
115   Ibid., 141.
116   Ibid.
117   Ibid., 305.

decision. The *Sabor* approved the learning of Hungarian as a compulsory subject in Croatian schools—a move for which it was highly criticised by the Croatian national opposition.[118] In contrast, Ivo Banac claims that the Croat nobility generally opposed the introduction of Hungarian in Croatian schools as it deemed it an expression of Magyarization. Following Banac, the nobility only refrained from a big battle because the Croats knew that only an alternate Croat national programme was able to counter the Hungarian national idea.[119]

At that time, the national opposition enunciating and defending Croat national interests was a group 'drawn from the educated sections of the population, including men from the lower nobility, the clergy, the professions, and the army' as well as the 'educated youth', which had studied in Graz or Vienna.[120] It was, in other words, an intellectual cast in pursuit of a common national ideology. Philosophically influenced by the ideas of Herder and the actuality of the Croats' unfortunate position between Hungarian, Italian, and German hegemonic aspirations, those intellectuals advocated an ethnic, cultural, and linguistic kinship between the Slavs.[121] To foster unity between the different South Slavic peoples, they claimed that all were decedents of the Illyrians, an ancient people inhabiting the Balkan Peninsula before the arrival of the undifferentiated Slavs.

Among the most important supporters of this idea was Ljudevit Gaj, who, apart from crafting a unique South Slavic history, was crucial in determining the national language. In order to strengthen his claim of a unified South Slavic culture, 'he wished the differences in language to be minimised as much as possible'.[122] This is the reason why he chose the *štokavian* dialect for the codified language. This choice, by no means obvious,[123] would allow all South Slavs to join the Illyrian project. That many Croats abandoned their native *kajkavian* was, in the words of Ivo Banac, 'a unique gesture in the history of the nineteenth century national movements and was possible only in the context of tolerant Illyrianist ideology, which was so preoccupied with the conciliatory give and take'.[124]

Illyrianism was thus an intellectually dominated project, which represented 'phase A' of the Croat national movement. The intellectuals involved, however, did not yet see themselves as the bearers of a Croat national identity. In fact, they refrained from using the word 'Croat' at all, for it 'tended to be identified with the opposition and those who supported cooperation with Hungarians against the

---

[118]   Ibid.

[119]   Banac, *The National Question in Yugoslavia. Origins, History, Politics*, 76.

[120]   Jelavich, *History of the Balkans Volume 1*, 305.

[121]   Calic, *Geschichte Jugoslawiens*, 44.

[122]   Jelavich, *History of the Balkans Volume 1*, 306.

[123]   The choice of *kajkavian* would also have been possible from a purely ideological standpoint. See, Banac, *The National Question in Yugoslavia. Origins, History, Politics*, 76–79.

[124]   Ibid., 78.

Habsburg government on the old basis'.[125] Nevertheless, '[d]ue to their historic importance, the Croats held a special position within the Illyrian movement, which was never clearly defined, leaving the understanding of *Illyrianism* open to various interpretations that were oscillating between elitist demands for Croatian leadership in the movement and the egalitarian view of the integration of all South Slavs.'[126] Such heavy dependence on Croat national and cultural traditions was responsible for the failure of Illyrianism to attract support from the other South Slavs.[127] Illyrianism did, however, manage to unify the Croats from different regions—Croatia, Slavonia, Dalmatia, Bosnia-Herzegovina, etc.—behind 'the Illyrian nomenclature and Gaj's linguistic and orthographic standards'.[128] Furthermore, the desire of political South Slavic unity, although simply implied in the intellectual framework, was inherent to the Illyrian concept. In this regard, the Illyrian movement was not so much a predecessor of Croat nationalism but of Yugoslavism. Its inclusiveness would later allow the different people to unite behind a concept of commonality based on 'über-ethnic' cooperation.[129]

3.3.2   The Croat national movement

By questioning Habsburg authority, Illyrianism also established an ideological framework for the Croat national movement. The leaders of this 'anti-Illyrian', or rather 'pro-Croat' nationalist current were Eugen Kvaternik and Ante Starčević. An early adherent of the Illyrian ideology, Starčević became frustrated after the revolution of 1848 had failed and resulted in a renewal of absolutism and German/Hungarian cultural assimilation within the empire.[130] With the establishment of a closely centralised system, it became difficult for adherents of Illyrianism to believe in a 'federated Monarchy, in which the South Slavs, under Croat leadership, would enjoy extended autonomy'.[131] Consequently, Starčević abandoned the Illyrian ideology in order to adopt a Croat nationalist one.

He based his philosophy on the *historic state rights* argument. Accordingly, the Croat nobility actively and freely elected the authority of the Hungarian crown in 1102 and did *not* effectively surrender Croatia's sovereignty.[132] Its historical right to statehood was deemed a direct consequence of the Slavic conquest

---

[125]   Jelavich, *History of the Balkans Volume 1*, 308.

[126]   Baer, *Slavic Thinkers or the Creation of Polities*, 171.

[127]   Banac, *The National Question in Yugoslavia* , 78.

[128]   Ibid., 79.

[129]   Calic, *Geschichte Jugoslawiens*, 45.

[130]   Baer, *Slavic Thinkers or the Creation of Polities*, 167; Banac, *The National Question in Yugoslavia,* 85.

[131]   Banac, *The National Question in Yugoslavia*, 85.

[132]   Calic, *Geschichte Jugoslawiens*, 45; Baer, *Slavic Thinkers or the Creation of Polities*, 168.

of the homeland in the sixth and seventh centuries.[133] Starčević and Kvaternik neglected the distinctiveness of the different South Slavic peoples and claimed that
Serbs and Slovenes were essentially Croats.[134] They furthermore introduced the
concept of a Croat 'political people'. In medieval times the *populus* of Croatia
was its nobility. However, at the beginning of the eighteenth century the responsibility to defend the people was transferred to popularly based standing armies
such that the nobility, according to Starčević and Kvaternik, lost its rights of exclusive representation.[135] Consequently, the realm of Croat territorial aspirations
was not limited to the lands possessed by the nobility, but far exceeded them.
Starčević thus 'claimed... lands that were never Croatian and justified these
claims with his radical view of Croatian cultural superiority, which has been lost,
[and] thus should be revived.'[136] His idea of a Greater Croatia was born by con-
verging the arguments of a common Croat ancestry for all the South Slavs and the
attribution of political rights to this people, for 'there could be only one political
people in a given state'.[137] Kvaternik saw the border of the Croat homeland running from the Alps to the Drina, from Albania to the Danube, while Starčević
pushed this line as far as to the Serbian-Bulgarian border.[138]

It is no coincidence but a manifestation of path dependency that Croat nationalists chose the *historic* state rights narrative in order to justify their claims
for territory and autonomy. Referring to Pavao Ritter Vitezović (1652–1713),
who first used the Croat name to include all Slavs, Ivo Banac explains this remarkable historic process:

> The legitimist way of arguing was, in a sense, imposed upon the Croats. The Habs-
> burg court, the Venetians of Vitezović's times, and later the Hungarian legal theo-
> rists, all advanced historical arguments in favour of diminishing Croatia's territorial
> integrity or its ancient municipal autonomy (*jura municipalia*). As a result, begin-
> ning with Vitezović's generation, Croat national apologetics were lopsidedly histori-
> cist. The Croats never felt safe enough with strict national–linguistic and cultural–
> arguments in favour of their autonomy and statehood. They clearly believed that the
> rusty weapon of historical and state right were most effective in the struggle against
> Habsburg and Hungarian centralism.[139]

---

[133]   Banac, *The National Question in Yugoslavia*, 86.
[134]   Calic, *Geschichte Jugoslawiens*, 45.
[135]   Banac, *The National Question in Yugoslavia*, 86.
[136]   Baer, *Slavic Thinkers or the Creation of Polities*, 169.
[137]   Banac, *The National Question in Yugoslavia*, 86.
[138]   Ibid., 86–7.
[139]   Ibid., 74. The historic state rights argument, in a downscaled model, is also important
         with respect to what Franjo Tuđman would later term the 'centuries-old dream' of
         the Croat national movement: the unification of Slavonia, Croatia proper, and Dal-
         matia in one state (see Bellamy, *The Formation of Croatian National Identity*, 5.)
         This, of course, refers back to the medieval kingdoms of Tomislav, who is said to
         have united Croatia and Dalmatia, and Krešimir Petar, who consolidated the Croat
         lands into a single Triune Kingdom (Croatia-Slavonia-Dalmatia) (see Ibid., 36.)

Starčević's and Kvaternik's ideas present the first intellectual approach to establish a unified Croat nationhood. Their efforts served as blueprints for similar attempts in later history. In their ideological foundation, they relied on the Illyrian movement, whose central elements they rearranged into a new Croat identity. In this sense, the Illyrian movement and the Croat national movement shared a partly common 'phase A'. However, unlike the Illyrian movement that found its political expression only once Yugoslavism became reality (see below), the Croat nationalist movement always had a clear political component. It was more than an intellectual exercise and Starčević and Kvaternik were more than the intellectual backbone of the movement. In 1861, when they founded the Party of Rights (*Stranka prava,* meaning the Party of [Croat State] Rights), they set out a political programme that made the continuation of Habsburg sovereignty borderline impossible. The Party 'wished a permanent partnership neither with Vienna nor with Buda' and, at best, 'would accept union only through a common monarch'.[140] By the end of the century, it had become the main Croat opposition to the 1867 *Ausgleich*—which divided the Empire in two halves; Croatia-Slavonia belonged to Hungary while Dalmatia and Istria came under Austrian control—and the subsequent Croat-Hungarian *Nagodba* of 1868, an agreement formalising Croatia's subjection to Hungarian control. Furthermore, Starčević's ideology influenced many young students and intellectuals as well as the first generations of Croat political leaders in Dalmatia, Istria, and Bosnia-Herzegovina.[141]

3.4 Yugoslavism—Two Forms of a Failed Idea

3.4.1 Yugoslavism—*Jugoslovenstvo*

The Yugoslav national movement was ideologically based on Illyrianism. In a somehow different form and despite harsh attacks by Serb and Croat nationalists, Catholic Bishop Josip Strossmayer and Franjo Rački revived this ideology in the 1860s. Strossmayer was the leader of the Illyrian National Party founded in 1841, and Rački a leading historian and first head of the Yugoslav Academy established in 1866 by Strossmayer.[142] Central to their philosophy, which was to become the most important current among the Croat intelligentsia,[143] was the idea of *Jugoslovenstvo* (Yugoslavism). Like Illyrianism, Yugoslavism sought 'the spiritual unification of the South Slavs, founded upon a common culture and literary lan-

---

140   Jelavich, *History of the Balkans Volume 1*, 318–9.
141   Banac, *The National Question in Yugoslavia*, 86.
142   Ibid., 89; Jelavich, *History of the Balkans Volume 1*, 319; Calic, *Geschichte Jugoslawiens*, 45.
143   Calic, *Geschichte Jugoslawiens*, 45.

guage'.[144] But contrary to Illyrianism, Yugoslavism understood Croats and Serbs as two tribes of essentially the same people, which perhaps may have included the Slovenes as well.[145] Adherents of the ideology deliberately chose to ignore the separating elements, like religion, tradition, and historical myths, as they deemed the unification of all South Slavs the only strategy potentially capable of securing the survival of the Croats within the Habsburg Empire.[146] In other words, Illyrianism partly fulfilled the requirements of 'phase A' for the Yugoslav movement. It established the general ideas, which many political and ideological leaders would fine-tune in the decades to come. The ideas of Gaj and others served as the backbone of Strossmayer's Yugoslavism.

However, Strossmayer broadened the concept as far as possible in order to make it inclusive of all the South Slavic peoples, without neglecting their distinctiveness. For example, this is why he argued for a separation of the Catholic Church and the Croat national sentiment; 'His great dream was to reconcile Rome and the Eastern Churches and bring an end to the religious schism that was so harmful to the Slavic peoples.'[147] If we were to label this early Yugoslavism in simplified terms, the label would surely be 'unity in diversity'. Nevertheless, Strossmayer and Rački also shared the 'political peoples' argument of the Croat national movement. Unlike Kvaternik and Starčević they did not deny that Serbs and Slovenes were indeed a people of their own with particular cultural and emotional peculiarities, but 'inasmuch as they formed one political nation with the Croats, their task was to sustain Croat political nationhood as the "form of national development" best suited "in the struggle against Magyar supremacy and German centralization"'.[148] Despite this subordination under Croat political dogma, the Yugoslav state they envisioned would respect the equality between the different peoples.

In order to make his concept more popular and comprehensive, Strossmayer 'encouraged and financed various cultural institutions, which were designed to bring the Croats out of their provincial isolation and expose them to the modern European cultural trends, and, in addition, to encourage the building of a genuinely South Slavic national culture'.[149] He furthermore encouraged publications and the establishment of philosophical circles. In terms of Hroch's model, this would correspond to 'phase B' of spreading the idea of nationality from the intellectual to other layers of the population. On a political level, Strossmayer's programme,

---

[144]   Banac, *The National Question in Yugoslavia*, 89.

[145]   Calic, *Geschichte Jugoslawiens*, 45.

[146]   Ibid.

[147]   Banac, *The National Question in Yugoslavia. Origins, History, Politics*, 90.

[148]   Ibid. Banac quotes a polemical article published in 1863 in the populist *Pozor* (Notice).

[149]   Ibid., 89.

echoed by the National Party, included the demand of territorially uniting Slavonia, Dalmatia, and Croatia proper (thus re-establishing the Triune Kingdom) and the introduction of autonomy rights for the Croats, first within and later outside the Habsburg Empire.[150] The Yugoslav political programme was a gradual one. Rački and Strossmayer fought for the establishment of a South Slavic region within a federalised Habsburg Empire. Yet their ultimate goal was a 'federal South Slavic state, built on the ruins of Habsburg Monarchy and embracing Serbia and Montenegro'.[151] Nevertheless, a majority within the National Party accepted the terms of the 1868 *Nagodba* thereby weakening Croat opposition to Magyar control.[152]

Even though the ideology of Yugoslavism would eventually yield first results in political terms, it faced serious competition at the end of the nineteenth century. Especially the period between Serbia's independence at the Congress of Berlin (1878) and the end of the First World War in 1918 saw a real boost of mass mobilisation behind different national ideologies. According to Calic, this 'radicalisation' had two origins:[153] first, a vertical and horizontal mobilisation of the society through the emergence of new middle classes, combined with better means of education and communication (print), which led to the development of a new, nationally oriented political community. In this sense, the mobilisation of the masses followed the process envisioned by Benedict Anderson and created a nationally oriented imagined community. Second, developments connected to industrialisation and urbanisation led to a tendency to perceive clashes of interests as national rather than social or political conflicts. This led to the establishment of nationally distinct clusters and to a differentiation along ethnic lines among the public. Not surprisingly, this development coincides with the emergence of national and religious parties.[154] In Bosnia, for example, Muslim, Serb, and Croat parties were founded between 1906 and 1908. However, during the same time, ideas of South Slavic (Serb-Croat) unity, based on the concept of Yugoslavism, began spreading. Despite their different intentions, South Slavic Socialists as well as the revolutionary youth movements of the 1890s articulated this very same concept. Since young people dominated this pre-Yugoslav movement, a new generation—including, *inter alia,* the later Nobel laureate Ivo Andrić—evolved, not only ideologically believing, but also practically living out Yugoslavism.[155]

---

[150]   Calic, *Geschichte Jugoslawiens*, 45.

[151]   Banac, *The National Question in Yugoslavia. Origins, History, Politics*, 90.

[152]   Ibid., 90–1.

[153]   Calic, *Geschichte Jugoslawiens*, 56.

[154]   Ibid., 58–61.

[155]   Ibid., 60. While Andrić identified himself as a Yugoslav, contemporary Serb national ideologues claim that he was really a Serb.

With distinct national ideologies (Serb, Croat, perhaps even Muslim) as well as a common ideology for the South Slavs (Illyrianism/Yugoslavism), the end of the nineteenth century witnessed an ideological competition in the South Slavic lands that would repeat itself one hundred years later. However, Yugoslavism in the form advocated by Strossmayer and Rački included the ideas of the particular nationalisms of the three groups, with the exception of the Bosnian Muslims' that had not yet developed its own national traits. Within the concept of Yugoslavism, Serbs, Croats, and Slovenes were accepted as distinct peoples or nations. Certain elements of their national identity were thus deemed legitimate and, consequently, the ideology of Yugoslavism was open, inclusive, and allowed for different interpretations.[156] In other words, the new Yugoslav identity incorporated elements of peculiarity for the different peoples as well as elements of commonality.

If Yugoslavism was to be successful, it had to integrate the already existing particular identities within a larger context. However, this also meant that particular nationalisms based on those identities would remain virulent and could not be eradicated by the concept of Yugoslavism. In fact, as long as Yugoslavism was perceived as something more than the national identity of a particular people it had the potential to unite the South Slavic peoples. This presupposed the absence of highly politicised cleavages based on elements of particularity. When, however, Yugoslavism is perceived as an empty shell because issues based on elements of particularity determine the political discourse, those virulent national ideologies can become more powerful than the all-encompassing concept of Yugoslavism. In this respect, it is no coincidence that the ideology of Yugoslavism suffered more during the time of the first Yugoslavia (when the federalist-centralist debate between the Serbs and Croats overshadowed everything) than during the high time of Titoist socialism, for socialism offered an inclusive ideology in addition to the Yugoslav foundation. Nevertheless, finding the right balance between Yugoslavism and particular nationalisms by its people remained a constant struggle for the entire period of Yugoslavia's existence.

At the turn of the century, international developments as well as political necessities determined which of the different ideologies would survive the subsequent upheavals. In the course of deep troubles within the Habsburg Empire and the assassination of King Aleksandar Obrenović in Serbia in 1903, Serbs and Croats in the Empire found their common 'New Course' in 1905. It opposed Austro-Hungarian dualism, advocated the unification of Croatia-Slavonia with Dalmatia, and implicitly incorporated the idea of mutual recognition for Serb and Croat equality.[157] Influenced by the writings of the Czech philosopher Tomáš G. Masaryk, their lifetime goal was the 'liberation and unification of our people (...)

---

[156]   Ibid., 66.
[157]   Banac, *The National Question in Yugoslavia*, 97–8.

from Tyrol to Macedonia'.[158] When dealing with the Habsburg officials, Croats and Serbs formed a Croato-Serb coalition under the general motto of *narodno jedinstvo* (National Oneness or National Unity).[159] According to this vague concept, Croats and Serbs formed one people with two names, perhaps even three if one adds the Slovenes. While this idea may seem to be the predecessor of a concrete Yugoslav national programme, Ivo Banac insists that Serb and Croat leaders within the coalition generally maintained their aspirations of South Slavic unity under Serb or Croat control, respectively; nevertheless, the idea of *narodno jedinstvo* contained the seed of an 'integralist and unitarist Yugoslavism'.[160]

However, the still heterogeneous idea of Yugoslavia was in need of a deeper theoretical foundation. In a series of articles published in 1913, one offspring of the Yugoslav youth movements, Milan Marjanović, in addition to promoting Serb superiority, claimed that 'the Turks entirely destroyed all South Slavic "tribal-state" formations and created a single "Yugoslav national mass." At the beginning of the nineteenth century there were no Serbs or Croats, only a "mass of peoples that *no longer* had states or political life, a mass which was *not yet* anything akin to a people either in whole or in parts."'[161] The Yugoslav people were thus a people in development. Like many nationalist ideologies before, the unitarist Yugoslav tradition was 'a genuine ahistorical faction'.[162] It denied the historical developments unique to the nationalist awakening of the nineteenth century and focused on other elements of commonality, like language. Intellectuals and people engaged in the cultural sector formed the backbone of the new Yugoslav idea. The synthesis of cultural, linguistic, and political factors was perceived as the common ground for a Yugoslav identity, in which every people was to bring own elements.[163] Since Serb national literature and poems were rich in heroisms, they constituted the core of a Yugoslav national ethos after being updated to fit their modern connotation.[164] These efforts, in fact, present a renewal of 'phase A' of Yugoslavism, which is distinctly different than 'phase A' of the Illyrian and early Yugoslav movements. This time, the political programme of unifying all South Slavs within one state was the focal point of all ideological foundations.

The culmination of the different ideologies and national programmes was the formal annexation of Bosnia and Herzegovina by the Habsburg Empire in May 1908. It radicalised the existing national movements and broadened the base for revolutionary ideas. Part of this development was the organisation of '*Mlada*

---

[158]   Calic, *Geschichte Jugoslawiens*, 55.
[159]   Banac, *The National Question in Yugoslavia*, 98.
[160]   Ibid., 99.
[161]   Quoted in Ibid., 101.
[162]   Ibid., 102.
[163]   Calic, *Geschichte Jugoslawiens*, 62–3.
[164]   Ibid., 63.

Bosna', a revolutionary group of young students united in their wish to end Habsburg rule over Bosnia. Its member Gavrilo Princip assassinated Archduke Franz Ferdinand and his wife in Sarajevo in 1914 thus initiating the First World War. The war presented the best opportunity to unite the South Slavs in one state and make Yugoslavia a political reality. The proposal of the Yugoslav Committee in London under the leadership of Ante Trumbić understood Serbs, Croats, and Slovenes as one people with different names. This idea was codified in the declaration of Corfu, signed on 20 July 1917. And even though Bosnian Muslims as well as Macedonian and Montenegrin representatives formulated some reservations, the idea of a common state under these circumstances gradually gained support as the war came to an end.[165]

There is neither need nor space to elaborate the political situation in the Kingdom of the Serbs, Croats, and Slovenes (SHS, 1918-1929) or the subsequent Kingdom of Yugoslavia (1929-1941) in this chapter. Suffice it to say that the SHS kingdom was not a state based on the common rights of the peoples but, in line with the Western-European ideal of a state-nation, based on the freedoms of the individual.[166] Its major political challenge was constitutional design. The debate between Serbian centralism and Croatian/Slovene federalism echoed the former nationalist conflicts between supremacy and subordination of different peoples. The presumption that Yugoslav unification would end national conflicts turned out to be false and the national question 'became the most important problem of Yugoslavia's internal relations.'[167] This issue anticipated the central struggle that was to determine Yugoslavia's fate:

> Whereas proponents of unitarism sought to obliterate all historically derived differences between the Serbs, Croats, and Slovenes by means of a strictly centralised state, the majority of Serbian political parties used centralism to further Serbian predominance. This meant that the partisans of a unitarist and a Great Serbian version of Yugoslavia were counterposed to the representatives of the non-Serb national movements, who either demanded a federated (or confederated) state structure or sought guarantees for their national aspirations outside the framework of Yugoslavia.[168]

As a countermeasure to its dividing tendencies, the government tried to advocate the idea of collective Yugoslavism. The unification of Yugoslavia was promoted as a process similar to the Western European unifications of Italy or Germany.[169] This project of 'nationalisation from above' faced serious obstacles. The network of social communications within the respective groups was already too thick for

---

[165]   Ibid., 79–80.
[166]   Ibid., 85.
[167]   Banac, *The National Question in Yugoslavia*, 214.
[168]   Ibid., 214–5.
[169]   Calic, *Geschichte Jugoslawiens*, 87.

an all-encompassing national ideology to be successfully introduced.[170] Yugoslavism, based on three equal but different tribes, left much room for the coexistence of national and 'supranational' identities. Due to social networks and everyday political interests, national collective identities had always prevailed in the hearts and minds of the peoples. The political discussion between centralisation and federation was thus necessarily interpreted in national terms, which undermined the idea of Yugoslavism even further.

When in 1929 King Aleksander Karađorđević abolished the SHS kingdom and proclaimed the 'Kingdom of Yugoslavia', he changed the territorial borders of the provinces in order to weaken regionalist and nationalist tendencies and to create a common feeling of belonging. But the establishment of an absolutist monarchy and the rearrangement of internal political boundaries were hardly suited to foster a sense of community. Karađorđević's actions did not yield the results for which he hoped. In fact, they may have had the contrary effect. The constant political and economic crises disappointed many intellectuals and led many politically interested people to question this kind of ideology in general.[171] The *Sporazum* (Agreement) between the Serbs and the Croats in 1939, which granted the Croats significant territorial autonomy within Yugoslavia in form of its own Croat entity (Banovina of Croatia), was not able to calm the situation. Quite to the contrary, it led to similar claims by other nationalities and resistance against such political deliberations in general.[172] Even without the Second World War, it is doubtful that this solution would have prevailed.

3.4.2   Yugoslav 'brotherhood and unity'

Constant political struggles opened up the space for ideological debates outside the familiar national continuum. The fascists under the leadership of Josip Frank opposed Yugoslavism and argued for an ethnically homogenous Croatia. This movement, after being officially prohibited in 1929, survived as an underground organisation by the name of *Ustaše* under the leadership of Ante Pavelić. Pavelić's ideology was 'anti-Yugoslav, anti-Serb, anti-liberal, and anti-communist' and his declared goal was the forceful creation of a 'Great Croatia' that would include Bosnia-Herzegovina, the *Sandžak*, Montenegro and parts of Vojvodina.[173] This movement became especially important when fascist Italy and Nazi Germany occupied Yugoslavia during the Second World War and established the puppet state *Nezavisna Država Hrvatska* (the Independent State of Croatia, NDH). Previously, however, the *Ustaše* movement had only marginal

---

[170]   Ibid., 88.
[171]   Ibid., 123.
[172]   Ibid., 134.
[173]   Ibid., 125.

support. As the leading ideology and political force in the NDH, this movement naturally faced serious challenges. As the military counterpart to the *Ustaše* movement, the Serb resistance to the German and Italian forces formed around the nationally oriented guerrilla troops called *Četnici* and led by Dragoljub (Draža) Mihailović. In times of renewed Serb patriotism, the *Četnici* revived the emblems and habits of the First World War liberation fighters. And even though the *Četnici* lacked a coherent ideological programme,[174] they nevertheless adhered to concepts of a Greater Serbia without minorities.[175]

While fascism never attracted large parts of the population in the region, the same cannot be said for communism. In 1920, the Communist Party won 12.5 per cent of the votes in the first post-war Yugoslav elections; especially impressive were 33% in Macedonia and 36% in Montenegro, which the party achieved through a pragmatist approach to the national question, i.e. by acknowledging the nationhood of these two peoples.[176] However, just as Yugoslavism as a national ideology is inherently contradictory with regard to the coexistence of different national groups within one supra-nationality, Communism seems structurally unable to coexist with any national ideology.[177] Consequently, the Communist Party of Yugoslavia (KPJ)[178] initially regarded the national question as secondary to class affiliation. In its view, 'national tensions were a curse of the old regimes, especially of the Austro-Hungarian Monarchy, and they would be eradicated with the creation of the new "national" state of the South Slavs'.[179] Even though the Communist party subscribed to the doctrine of *narodno jedinstvo*—and, as a result thereof, centrism or unitarism—and generally adopted this terminology for pragmatic purposes, there was no common concept of what that understanding

---

[174]   Ibid., 146.

[175]   See Sabrina P. Ramet, *The Three Yugoslavias: State-Building and Legitimation. 1918-2005.* (Bloomington, Indiana: Indiana University Press, 2006).

[176]   Calic, *Geschichte Jugoslawiens*, 127–8. In 1921, the Communist Party was banned from the public sphere as a reaction to an assassination attempt committed by a few Communist gunmen (and other incidents). It was thus forced underground and heavily decimated in its membership. See Banac, *The National Question in Yugoslavia. Origins, History, Politics*, 329, 332.

[177]   Ivo Banac talks about a never quite resolved paradox implicit in Yugoslav Communist philosophy: '*Narodno jedinstvo* was, after all, a variant of nationalism: specifically, the prototype of South Slav supranationalism. Yet, in Communist perception, it somehow managed to coexist with a different, but no less powerful strain of decisively Marxist derivation, that is, the concept of internationalist humanity, which, as the liberated entity of the postrevolutionary, genuinely historic epoch, would shed all the elements of the alienation characteristic of class societies, including nationality.' (Banac, *The National Question in Yugoslavia*, 337–8.)

[178]   Until June 1920, the *Komunistička partija Jugoslavije* (KPJ, Communist Party of Yugoslavia) was called the *Socijalistička radnička partija Jugoslavije (komunista)* (Socialist Workers' Party of Yugoslavia (communist)).

[179]   Banac, *The National Question in Yugoslavia*, 333.

entailed. While Communists from formerly Austro-Hungarian areas *de facto* denied the individuality of the different South Slavic peoples[180] and argued for a common nationhood, their Serbian counterparts were less ideological: 'their unitarism was more a matter of temporary expediency than of a total commitment to *narodno jedinstvo*.'[181]

Despite the vagueness of the concept and the fact that the KPJ never truly abandoned the view that national differences were secondary to class differences, the party sharply criticised the ruling class, i.e. the bourgeoisie, for failing to achieve national oneness. Conversely, it claimed to represent 'one of the strongest pillars of national unification'[182] of the South Slavs. But in fact, the KPJ advocated many different positions with regards to the internal structure of Yugoslavia as it relates to the national question. In the late twenties, when the debate between centralism and federalism was at its peak, the KPJ supported a breakup of Yugoslavia and the independence of Croatia and Slovenia; in the thirties, after the establishment of the dictatorship, it cooperated with Croat and Macedonian nationalists.[183] And it was only after Josip Broz (Tito) took the lead that the KPJ 'adopted a federalist solution to Yugoslavia's national question, a stand that it has pursued, with significant swervings, from the time of its victory in the Second World War'.[184] In fact, Tito transformed the party following a Leninist model and equipped it with a strong 'elite leadership', which included many of the later designers of the Second Yugoslavia such as Milovan Djilas, Aleksandar Ranković, and Edvard Kardelj.[185] Furthermore, the Communist Party abandoned its ultra-leftist position and opened up its structures for Liberals, Social Democrats, and all the other anti-fascist groups of the Popular Front in the 1930s.[186] In an article published in 1942, Tito explained that the fight for national liberation 'would only be a phrase, even deception, if it were not (…) to have an own national meaning for every people too, if it did not mean, apart from the liberation of Yugoslavia, the liberation of the Croats, Slovenes, Serbs, Macedonians, Albanians, Muslims, etc.'[187]

---

[180] They understood the differences among the South Slavic peoples as 'mere "tribal" idiosyncrasies, which would disappear in a unified nation in which they no longer had a historical foundation'. (Ibid., 335.)

[181] Ibid.

[182] This was the view expressed by Sima Marković, one of the leading KPJ theoreticians. Quoted in Ibid., 337.

[183] Ibid., 339.

[184] Ibid.

[185] Calic, *Geschichte Jugoslawiens*, 129.

[186] Banac, *The National Question in Yugoslavia*, 339; Calic, *Geschichte Jugoslawiens*, 129.

[187] Quoted in Calic, *Geschichte Jugoslawiens*, 151.

The political left gained much support among the population and the intelligentsia. Ideologically, Yugoslav Communism became a strange alternative and a counter-argument to tendencies of growing nationalism. It was especially attractive for young people, who like the youth movements preceding them, understood Yugoslavism not as a mere vision, but as a daily practice.[188] Tito tried to avoid mistakes that, in his view, proponents of the first Yugoslavia had made. They had advocated Yugoslavism as some kind of overall national ideology that would supersede or replace the national peculiarities of the different peoples. He did not want to unite the people by neglecting their differences, but by acknowledging them. His ideology of 'brotherhood and unity' (*bratstvo i jedinstvo*) meant that the people inhabiting Yugoslavia were indeed distinct but of common descent. Despite their peculiarities, they were all brothers that should work together in order for socialism to succeed. In terms of solving the national question, Tito's Communist party opted for a pragmatist solution. Each nation was given a state on their own, with the exception of Bosnia-Herzegovina that, lacking a clear national majority, was to become 'neither Serb, nor Muslim, nor Croat, but simultaneously Serb, and Muslim, and Croat', following a decision by the Communist leadership in 1943.[189] While the specific consequences of this ideology for Bosnia-Herzegovina will be examined in the next chapter, it is worth noting that Tito *de facto* planted the seeds of Bosnia-Herzegovina's later statehood through his decision to award it the status of a republic.[190] However, given the history of failure of the first Yugoslavia, the Communists knew that their ideology had to be defended and, in fact, disseminated once the situation of acute conflict was over. The establishment of a common language (Serbo-Croat or Croato-Serb) served as a propaganda tool in this regard.

In ideological terms, the Yugoslav paradigm of 'brotherhood and unity' tried to incorporate existing traditions of the different people and interpret them in a way that was compatible with socialism.[191] Combined with the Soviet threat, the personality cult around Tito, and the first results of incipient industrialisation in the 1960s, this approach actually yielded promising results. In fact, a study in 1969 found that Yugoslavs indeed exhibited split identities and loyalties: as citizens towards the Yugoslav state and as members of their people towards their respective national groups.[192] However, the dangers of 'brotherhood and unity' appear obvious, be it only in retrospect. With the death of Tito the central building block of Yugoslav unity was removed. With the worsening economic situation of the 1980s, the financial burden on the central state became gradually unbearable.

---

[188]   Ibid., 129.
[189]   Quoted in Ibid., 181.
[190]   For the general argument, see Hoare, *History of Bosnia*.
[191]   Calic, *Geschichte Jugoslawiens*, 203.
[192]   Ibid., 217.

The admittedly high standards of the social systems became less and less sustainable, which also affected the cooperation between the republics. That some of them insisted on constitutionally granted autonomy competencies, put the entire state in peril while a coalescent political elite was lacking. Finally, the collapse of the Soviet Union (and the removal of the Soviet threat) made the Non Aligned Movement practically irrelevant. What is more, it deprived Yugoslavia of its privileged partnership with the West and subsequently made its financial burden much more virulent.

All of these developments caused instability in the Yugoslav system.[193] But it was the Communist ideology of 'brotherhood and unity' and the federal structure of Yugoslavia that would finally decide which way the giant was to fall. Since the Republics were *de facto* based on nationality for pragmatic reasons, each political issue could be perceived in national terms. Structural inequalities between the Republics thus easily became inequalities between nations, which were perceived and interpreted as being unfair or unjust. Furthermore, since the 'brotherhood and unity' ideology in fact philosophically acknowledges the distinct national traditions of the peoples, it could not effectively serve as a counter-argument to nationalism. If anything, the Republic structure made the argument of the historical association of people, land, and self-government much easier. For this reason the dissolution of Yugoslavia inevitably started on a national foundation and with a national connotation.

3.4.3 Renewed nationalism and the collapse of Yugoslavia

Since the 'brotherhood and unity' ideology was structurally incapable to counter nationalist tendencies, nationalism was by no means eradicated in the times of Tito's rule. Especially after the 1960s, historians detect an uprising in nationalist rhetoric and actions. Key intellectuals, such as the later president of Croatia Franjo Tuđman or the later 'father' of Serbian nationalism Dobrica Ćosić began questioning the policy of 'brotherhood and unity'. Tuđman, at that time a professor of history, understood historical developments necessarily in national terms. His main academic mission was to prove that Croats were the key victims of Serbia's hegemonic aspirations.[194] He was among the ones arrested following the 'Croatian spring' of 1971, a visible rupture in Yugoslavia's multi-national ceiling that questioned the existing political and social system and demanded more rights for the Croats. The Croatian Communist party voiced opposition against central-

---

¹⁹³ While I summarise the aforementioned currents in this paragraph, the respective arguments can be found in numerous publications, e.g. Sabrina P. Ramet's *Balkan Babel. The Disintegration Of Yugoslavia From The Death Of Tito To The Fall Of Milosevic*. 4th ed. (London: Westview Press, 2002).

¹⁹⁴ Calic, *Geschichte Jugoslawiens*, 237–254.

ism from Belgrade and took to the streets. During the days of the MASPOK (*masovni pokret,* mass mobilisation), the leadership of the local party, the national and cultural organisation *Matica Hrvatska,* as well as student representatives and the local media even called for Croatian independence.[195] It would be too easy to present the 'Croatian spring' solely as a nationalist uprising, for it was indeed connected to efforts by linguists to codify a Croatian standard language. But the motivation of the different factions participating in the events was rather diverse,[196] and so were their opinions. Nevertheless, the 'Croatian spring' showed the perils of national agitation. After the failure of the protest, members of the Croat Communist party were either expelled, or, as in the case of Tuđman, thrown in jail. In 1981, another process against Franjo Tuđman took place. He had publicly claimed that Croats were discriminated in Yugoslavia and questioned the number of casualties in the concentration camp Jasenovac.

Unlike Tuđman, who advocated autonomy for the Republics, Dobrica Ćosić asserted a stronger role for the federal government. Until the mid-1960s, Ćosić had been an adherent of Titoist communism. But his faith in communism declined, mostly due to a 'trivial' event: 'the failure of the League of Writers of Yugoslavia (*Savez kniževnika Jugoslavije*) to reorganize along aesthetic [i.e. non-national/non-Republic] lines in the early 1960s'.[197] He interpreted the failure of his literary initiative as a failure of the Communist elite to establish an integral version of Yugoslavism. Consequently, 'Ćosić's trust in Yugoslav supranationalism dwindled; he soon became convinced that the failure of his attempts to keep integration on track implied the continued division and perhaps eventual destruction of the *Serbian* nation'.[198] While Ćosić was ready to curtail his Serbian identity for communist Yugoslavism, he surely would not settle for anything less. Quite to the contrary, he started actively claiming his Serbian nationhood and 'focused even more on defending Serbia's culture under communism, as opposed to Yugoslavia's'.[199] He put special emphasis on Kosovo as the 'heartland of Serbia'.[200] Since Tito was in fact giving more governmental competencies to the Kosovo Albanians at that time, this emphasis inevitably produced friction. Ćosić consciously centred his ideology on Serbian nationhood and thus laid the foundation for later Serbian nationalism.

---

[195]   Ibid., 252.

[196]   For example, it also included economic demands.

[197]   Nicholas J. Miller, "The Nonconformists: Dobrica Ćosić and Mića Popović Envision Serbia," *Slavic Review* 58, no. 3 (1999), 518.

[198]   Ibid., 520.

[199]   Ibid., 520–1.

[200]   In a speech before the Fourteenth Plenum of the Central Committee of the League of Communists of Serbia in May 1968, quoted in Ibid., 522.

The process of 're-nationalisation'[201] started to have political implications for the Bosnian Muslims as well. In the 1960s, the communist administration recognised them gradually as a nationality. As a result, the Muslims became more self-conscious and gained power within the administration, which was, *inter alia,* based on ethnic quotas. This led to a strengthening of Muslim national feelings and the intellectualisation of Islam within the Balkan context through Alija Izetbegović, a member of the secret anti-Communist youth organization 'the Young Muslims' (*Mladi Muslimani*) that also existed during the Second World War. The Communists understandably did not appreciate the renewed waves of nationalism and chose a familiar course of action. In Kosovo, members of the 'Revolutionary Movement for the Unification of Albania' were brought to court. In Sarajevo in 1983, Izetbegović and twelve others had to face charges for promoting Islamism and discrediting the principle of 'brotherhood and unity'. Others who suggested changes within the existing structure of Yugoslavia following rather diverse ideologies, like Milovan Djilas or Vojislav Šešelj, were also tried before the courts.[202]

In this climate of repression against dissidents and nationalists as well as the obvious shortcomings of 'brotherhood and unity', nationalism found fertile ground. At first it was masked behind appeals for more democratic rights and free speech but its true character became clear rather soon. This process culminated in Kosovo. After Tito's death, the ethnic Albanians wanted Kosovo to become a Republic instead of remaining an autonomous province. Naturally, this displeased the Serbian leadership and especially the Serbian intellectuals who had always put special emphasis on Kosovo for Serbian national identity. A secret memorandum of the Serbian Academy of Science and Arts, which was published in 1986 in parts, claimed that Serbia was in a perpetual crisis and that there was a 'genocide' on-going against the Serbs in Kosovo.[203] This document provided some kind of intellectual foundation for renewed Serbian nationalism, which it presented as a reaction to the injustices the Serbs had to endure in Communist Yugosla-

---

[201] Apart from the intellectual's disappointment with Yugoslavia or the restatement of national individuality, the re-emergence of nationalism had also a structural foundation. According to Calic, the speedy modernisation proved a catalyst of national identity for the different people. As a result of higher education, mobility, and mass communication, competition between the different nationalities emerged. This led to the need for community and provoked a revival of national cultures. Media, associations, and educational institutions provided the ideological space for such communications. The society differentiated internally even within the groups and those new strata adopted national ideas, which until then were reserved to the rather limited layers of intellectuals and the bourgeoisie. Finally, demographical shifts occurred that changed the national composition of the state. Especially in Bosnia and Kosovo, the Muslim population was steadily growing. See Calic, *Geschichte Jugoslawiens*, 237–254.

[202] These examples are taken from Ibid., 268–9.

[203] Ibid., 275.

via. Slobodan Milošević, a high-ranking official within the Serbian Communist Party, captured this sentiment among his people when, during a visit to Kosovo in 1987, he articulated his almost magic words to the Kosovo Serbs: 'Nobody has the right to beat you!' Even though in the course of history Milošević proved himself rather a pragmatist than a pure nationalist, he clearly saw the appeal of nationalism for politics. Its full potential, however, would only be released under the circumstances of the war.

4   Nationalism in Bosnia-Herzegovina

But we belong to no one, we're always on some frontier, always someone's dowry. Is it then surprising that we are poor? For centuries we've been trying to find, trying to recognise ourselves. Soon we won't even know who we are, we're already forgetting that we've ever been striving for anything. Others do us the honour of letting us march under their banners, since we have none of our own. They entice us when they need us, and reject us when we're no longer any use to them. The saddest land in the word, the most unhappy people in the world. We're losing our identity, but we cannot assume another, foreign one. We've been severed from our roots, but haven't become part of anything else; foreign to everyone, both to those who are our kin and those who won't take us in and adopt us as their own. We live at the crossroads of worlds, at the border between peoples, in everyone's way. And someone always thinks we're to blame for something. The waves of history crash against us, as against a reef. We're fed up with those in power and we've made a virtue out of distress: we've become noble-minded out of spite.

Death and the Dervish, Meša Selimović[1]

For the analysis of nationalism, Bosnia-Herzegovina presents a rather curious case: as the common homeland of Bosnian Muslims, Bosnian Croats, and Bosnian Serbs; as a traditional border country between the so-called East and West; and as the only entity that in its entirety belonged to both the Ottoman and the Habsburg empires. Originating in its medieval structure, Bosnia developed a particular sense of regional identity that would shape the various forms of national ideology within its territory. At the same time, nationalism in Bosnia would be highly influenced from the outside, namely by Serbian and Croatian ideologists who, after the establishment of their national ideologies, tried to incorporate it and its population into their own national projects. But only after their re-emergence in the second Yugoslavia were such group nationalisms powerful enough to make a distinctively Bosnian Croat or Bosnian Serb identity, respectively, a conceptual and practical impossibility for large parts of the population. A Bosnian Croat, for example, could henceforth only belong to the Croat nation and was, by definition, associated with the Croatian homeland, whatever concrete geographical extent it had at that time. On a political level, representatives in Serbia and Croatia saw themselves not only as representatives of their concrete electorates but also as spokespeople for the entire Croat and Serb nations,[2] which, again by definition,

---

[1]   Meša Selimović, *Death and the Dervish*. Bogdan Rakić and Stephen M. Dickey, transl. (Evanston: Northwestern University Press, 1996 [1966]), 330.

[2]   Igor Štiks, "Being Citizen the Bosnian Way. Transformations of Citizenship and Political Identities in Bosnia-Herzegovina," Francis Cheneval and Sylvie Ramel, ed., *Special Issue of Transitions: From Peace to Shared Political Identities. Exploring Pathways in Contemporary Bosnia-Herzegovina* 51, no. 1–2 (2011): 253.

included Bosnian Croats and Bosnian Serbs. The situation was furthermore com-plicated by the fact that Bosnian Muslims, who by then had acquired a specific type of national identity of their own, had no (other) corresponding kin-state to turn to, which made them even more eager to preserve Bosnian statehood, first in a multi-national, later in a largely mono-national structure based on the Islamic religion.

This chapter explores the central ambiguity in the Bosnian national charac-ter and its consequences for the political movements that were to dominate the early 1990s. In terms of historical events and their incorporation into the larger picture of nineteenth and twentieth century development I rely on research done by a group of distinguished historians. Those especially include Marko Attila Hoare, Noel Malcolm, Barbara Jelavich, Marie-Janine Calic, and Xavier Bougarel.[3] My contribution is not to evaluate their epistemological claims from a historical point of view, but rather to present an interpretation of their findings in the context of the methodological approach and the general aim of the present study.

In this respect, there are two predominant and seemingly irreconcilable per-spectives from which to choose. One may hold that the events in the 1990s were the result of a centuries-old communitarian structure and thus the genuine out-come of longstanding ethnic division (an argument somewhat along the lines of the 'ancient hatreds'-thesis mentioned in the previous chapter, though far more sophisticated); or one may believe that these events presented in fact a betrayal of Bosnia's tradition of coexistence and symbiosis among the thee major national communities on its soil. Those views are not as contradictory as may appear at first sight. One can illustrate the major difference between the two perspectives by looking at the historical analyses put forward by Xavier Bougarel and Marko Attila Hoare. The former insists that, historically speaking, there never existed a genuinely Bosnian citizenship in the form of a common national identity among the people; as he says, 'the principle which has given structure to the Bosnian po-litical order has not been citizenship, but rather communitarian identity. All elec-tions held in Bosnia since 1910 have been dominated by national parties.'[4] While the latter is certainly true, Hoare offers a slightly different take on the former claim: 'The Bosnians have never comprised a single nation, nor have they ever comprised three wholly separate nations, a paradox that helps to explain the many

---

[3]   Hoare, *History of Bosnia*; Malcolm, *Bosnia*; Jelavich, *History of the Balkans Volume 1*; Barbara Jelavich, *History of the Balkans: Volume 2* (Cambridge: Cambridge University Press, 1999); Calic, *Krieg und Frieden in Bosnien-Hercegovina*; Cf. Calic, *Geschichte Jugoslawiens;* Xavier Bougarel, "Bosnia and Herzegovina - State and Communitarianism", David A. Dyker and Ivan Vejvoda, Ed., *Yugoslavia and After. A Study in Fragmentation, Despair and Rebirth* (London: Longman, 1996): 87-115.

[4]   Ibid., 87.

other paradoxes of Bosnian history.'[5] Hoare insists that even after the Catholics and Orthodox of Bosnia started articulating a sense of, respectively, Croat and Serb nationhood in the nineteenth century, 'this did not mean that they negated Bosnia-Herzegovina as the focus of their patriotic loyalty; rather, they articulated their Bosnian patriotism in Serb and Croat terms respectively.'[6]

Tasked with reconciling those two positions, one is forced to conclude that there are many similarities between the two views. Both historians agree that the societal distinction in Bosnia is the product of the Ottoman times. The *millet* system led to a differentiation among religious lines and 'created' the three religious communities; furthermore, the Ottoman administration, due to the way in which land ownership was organised, had also an economic dimension that strengthened communal distinction. Bougarel and Hoare also agree that by the time of the Habsburg Empire the proto-national communities had become sufficiently differentiated for a common Bosnian (or Bosniak, as it was called at that time) identity to be imposed upon the population. The nationalist sentiments among the Bosnian Serbs and Bosnian Croats grew rapidly during the Dual Monarchy. Both historians furthermore agree, I believe, that it was during the first Yugoslavia (1918-41), i.e. when the political debate between federalism and centralism began, that the Bosnian Serb and Bosnian Croat communities started gradually identifying with their kin in Serbia and Croatia, respectively. It is true that even before 1918, Bosnians were internally segregated into the three different communities, which also expressed itself in the electoral results mentioned by Bougarel. But it is probable that they also had some distinctively Bosnian traits to their identity, which made them different than Serbs from Serbia or Croats from Croatia, respectively. Whether we can call these traits 'patriotism', as Hoare does, depends on whether or not we believe that those traits were sufficiently strong. Put differently, we may conclude that the major division between the two historical perspectives is one of degree rather than essence. If, for whatever reason, one holds the Bosnian traits to have been weak, one is likely to follow Bougarel; if one deems them strong enough, one is probably convinced by Hoare's argument.

Since this is still an unresolved and much debated question—not least among national and nationalist historians and theoreticians—there exists no widely accepted and unanimously supported historical analysis for the Bosnian case. In this chapter, I will therefore base my argument on a combination of these two perspectives. Since I am particularly interested in the Bosnian traits within the national identities of the three local communities and seek to contrast the genealogies of their national movements with the theoretical claims in Miroslav Hroch's model of national agitation and the national movements in Serbia and Croatia, re-

---

[5]   Hoare, *History of Bosnia,* 413-4.

[6]   Hoare, *History of Bosnia,* 413.

spectively, my main line of argument will follow Hoare's narrative. However, taking this approach does not mean that I negate or, which would be worse, am unaware of the internal segregation within Bosnia. In fact, whenever referring to some distinctively Bosnian element, I will try to substantiate the underlying claim through the usage of additional historical accounts by the other distinguished scholars cited above. Furthermore, I will in no ways neglect the communitarian perspective and regularly refer to Bougarel in order to outline major differences, provided that I think that such differences may affect my interpretation of the historical argument. To remind the reader, my main goal in this chapter is not to deliver a new approach for the understanding of nationalism in Bosnia but to apply Miroslav Hroch's argument to the Bosnian case.

4.1   Historical Roots of Bosnian Identity: Medieval Bosnia

Bosniaks as well as liberals in contemporary Bosnia-Herzegovina usually invoke the historical argument when debating Bosnian statehood and identity.[7] Its core can be traced back to medieval times. During the reign of *Ban* Tvrtko (1353-91), the independent Bosnian state not only enjoyed its largest territorial extent[8] but also possessed a clear-cut feudal structure. Feudalism was a by-product of sorts of the economic prosperity that Bosnia experienced already under Tvrtko's predecessor, *Ban* Stephan Kotromanić (1322-1353). Bosnia benefitted from the mining of precious metals and the subsequent trade with Dubrovnik and other places, which led to the establishment of medieval cities all over its territory. In order to consolidate his power, Kotromanić had awarded lands to the nobility, who had redistributed their shares to personal vassals or serfs.[9] This system of land ownership was the core of the nobility's 'economic and political power'.[10] Under Tvrtko, the Bosnian kingdom got its own state structure, which included a parliament and, according to Hoare, 'may have entrenched a sense of Bosnian unity among Bosnian elites, for which the crown was the symbol irrespective of its holder'.[11]

Bosnia's distinct statehood expressed itself through the king as the representative of a political order. Despite being formally a vassal to the Hungarian crown, Tvrtko 'removed the Hungarian double cross from his coat-of-arms, replacing it with the Angevin fleur-de-lys symbol'.[12] This act, which originally underlined Tvrtko's Catholicism, provided the Bosnian state with a symbol that

---

[7]   See also the discussions of the statehood argument in chapter 8 of the present book.

[8]   Malcolm, *Bosnia*, 13–20. Hoare, *History of Bosnia*, 35.

[9]   Imamović, *Historija Bošnjaka*, 54.

[10]   Ibid., 55.

[11]   Hoare, *History of Bosnia*, 37.

[12]   Ibid., 35.

Bosniaks would later perceive as genuinely Bosnian. Similarly, Bosnia's language and script (*Bosančica,* as the latter was called), both of which were later employed as expressions of the land's cultural sovereignty, fuelled the perception of distinctiveness. In conjunction with institutions and cultural and political artefacts of statehood, the specific system of land ownership finally may have produced a distinct kind of Bosnian identity within the nobility. Since later emperors of Bosnia, i.e. Ottoman and Habsburg, 'established forms of administration in the country that respected the Bosnian identity of the Bosnian nobles',[13] this regional identity was preserved throughout the coming centuries. In the words of Calic, Bosnia's regional identity was not artificial: rather, 'the multi-ethnic and multi-confessional symbiosis grew historically over the centuries'. Since the Middle Ages, its outstanding characteristic was 'multi-confessionalism, the coexistence of Catholic, Orthodox and Islamic communities of faith', which is why the term 'Bosnian' is, first and foremost, 'a geographical designation of origin that was used by Muslims, Serbs, Croats and other nationalities alike'.[14]

The medieval Bosnian state possessed a third element of particularity, which, as we have seen in chapter 3, is subject to some debate. The distinguished historian John Fine, whose interpretation enjoys widespread agreement, has put forward a distinct explanation for emergence of the Bosnian Church.[15] Despite officially belonging to the Catholic sphere of influence, Bosnia was, in practical terms, not firmly part of either Roman Catholic or Orthodox ecclesiastical institutions due to its position on the borders between those two spheres of influences.[16] Its geographical location and topography made it 'a natural breeding ground for religious practices deemed heretical by enemies on the international plane'.[17] The Bosnian peasant 'did not consider it heretical to synthetize his or her traditional usages with new ones imposed by Christianity',[18] whereas the Pope naturally came to a different conclusion. Justifying their actions as a fight against heresy, the Hungarians thus launched several crusades against Bosnia following the middle of the thirteenth century. When the Pope decided to transfer religious control over Bosnia to the archbishopric of Kalocsa in Hungary, it provoked local resistance, since the Bosnian Catholics and their religious institutions would have come under direct Hungarian control. The rejection of Hungarian crusades and

---

[13]   Ibid., 37.

[14]   Calic, *Krieg und Frieden in Bosnien-Hercegovina,* 46.

[15]   John Fine, *The Bosnian Church: Its Place in State and Society from the Thirteenth to the Fifteenth Century: From the Twelfth to the Fourteenth Century* (London: Saqi Books, 2007).

[16]   Friedman, *The Bosnian Muslims,* 12–13.

[17]   Hoare, *History of Bosnia,* 41.

[18]   Friedman, *The Bosnian Muslims.* 13.

the subordination under Hungarian ecclesiastical leadership led to the emergence of a schismatic Bosnian Church.[19]

In terms of *nationalist* history, the most important feature of the autochthonous Bosnian Church is its incontestably Bosnian character. According to this narrative, the Bosnian Church neither belonged to any larger heretical movement on the continent nor was it considered in line with Orthodox or Catholic traditions.[20] Quite to the contrary, it resisted these influences and was especially directed against political or religious domination by Hungary. As such, it has been an anchor of Bosnian particularism, which has also strengthened the previously mentioned local, regionally based identity of the Bosnian nobility and its subordinates. However, by the end of the medieval conquests, Bosnia had re-acquired a 'religiously more homogenous population', in line with Catholicism: 'From the reign of Kotromanić, Bosnia's rulers were Catholic and its population subject to influences of Catholicism and of the Bosnian Church. The first definitively Orthodox population of Bosnia was acquired in 1326 with the annexation of Hum [i.e. modern Herzegovina].'[21]

In the fourteenth century, at least three different religious practises could be observed in what constitutes contemporary Bosnia-Herzegovina: the Bosnian Church, the Catholic Church (which had a monastic system in place), and the Orthodox Church, with its predominance in Herzegovina/Hum. Especially for nationalist ideologues, it must have been tempting to see these three religious proto-communities as ancestors of the contemporary national groups thus substantiating their claim to the respective land and people. While the connections between Catholic and Orthodox denominations and Croat and Serb national ideologies, respectively, are somewhat easily drawn, they can only be substantiated if one completely neglects the regional, i.e. Bosnian orientation of those religious groups and if one *prima facie* assigns confessional supremacy over other forms of loyalties. As Malcolm explains, Christianity, in whatever form, 'was quite weakly supported by any Church organization in many parts of Bosnia' so that it 'had probably become little more than a set of folk practices and ceremonies, some of them concerned with birth, marriage and death, and others aimed at warding off evil fortune, curing illnesses, securing good harvest, and so on.'[22] In other words, Bosnians wore their religion rather lightly,[23] which is what made the establishment of the Bosnian Church possible in the first place. This prevents serious par-

---

[19]   Hoare, *History of Bosnia*, 41–2.

[20]   Ibid., 42.

[21]   Ibid.

[22]   Malcolm, *Bosnia*, 58. See also below with regards to Islamisation.

[23]   This would also be true for the times under Ottoman sovereignty, as Malcolm (*Bosnia*, 166) states: 'Islamic observance in Bosnia had never been generally "fanatical", though casual observers described it as such; there had indeed been some fiercely orthodox Muslim clergy, but the population at large was more relaxed in its practices.'

ticipants in the discussions from embarking on the line of argument that supports 'historical continuity' since the Middle Ages. Similarly, arguing identity, or at least ideological congruence between adherents of the Bosnian Church and the contemporary Bosniaks is also quite challenging. In fact, it can only succeed if one were to re-interpret the schismatic character of the local church itself—and this is exactly what some Bosnian Muslim historians have proposed. Even though it is hardly backed up by historical evidence, they claim that the local church was Bogumil in orientation and character. If true, and if one accepts the claim of ideological continuity, the Bosniaks would thus be able to substantiate their claim of cultural and religious autonomy by proving the origins of their nation already in pre-Ottoman times. They claim that, when the Ottomans occupied Bosnia, most of the Bosnian Church adherents, i.e. the Bogumils, converted to Islam and thus became the ancestors of the modern Bosniaks. However, as modern historical scholarship has convincingly shown, the conversion of Bosnia's population to Islam was not a phenomenon unique to believers of the Bosnian Church nor was it a singular event (see also below).[24]

Such instrumentalisation of the Bosnian Church notwithstanding, it is hardly possible to underestimate its importance for the later development of the nations in Bosnia. On the one hand, the local church provided a clear reference point for a uniquely Bosnian identity based on a schismatic and quite liberal interpretation of religious traditions and practices. It incorporated several proto-bonds such as territory, religion, and even culture that would become important later on. Through the intellectual proximity of insistence on religious autonomy and resistance to foreign domination both by the Pope and the Hungarians, it furthermore exercised a strong influence in unifying the nobility and giving them a particularly Bosnian denomination. On the other hand, Bosnia's allegedly heretic beliefs provoked a reaction by the Pope not only in military but also in religious terms. From the middle of the fourteenth century on, he sent Franciscan missions to win Bosnia proper back for the Catholic Church.[25] These Franciscans turned out to be rather tolerant of Bosnian particularities; and quite contrary to the hopes of the papacy, they became the bearers of a uniquely Bosnian identity.

4.2 Bosnia under Ottoman Rule

The medieval Bosnian kingdom and its church present the historical substrate for the emergence of proto-national bonds among the population based on attributes of particularity. Even though they contributed significantly to the development of the later nations, they did, for two reasons, not have the strength to unite the three

---

[24]   Malcolm, *Bosnia*, chap. 5.
[25]   Friedman, *The Bosnian Muslims*, 16.

communities into a single national group. Firstly, struggles over power and influence emerged among the nobility after the death of Tvrtko in 1391, leading to the gradual demise of the medieval Bosnian kingdom. The local magnates sought to strengthen their authority at the expense of the central administration,[26] which naturally threatened the existing political rule. Secondly, with the incorporation of Bosnia proper (in 1463) and Herzegovina (in 1482) into the Ottoman Empire, the factual framework for proto-national bonds changed dramatically. Due to the *millet* system and the general way of ruling, religious affiliation became the single most important issue of everyday life. As Hoare writes:

> Although modern Bosnian statehood has its antecedents in the medieval Kingdom of Bosnia, the national identities of its inhabitants originate from the period after the Ottoman conquest of 1463. The division of contemporary Bosnians between three nationalities—Muslim, Serb and Croat—is the product of the religious and social changes brought about by the long Ottoman presence, and in no way corresponds to the ethnic divisions of the pre-Ottoman period. (...) The nationalities of modern Bosnia-Hercegovina grew out of the religious communities of Ottoman Bosnia, not from any alleged primordial ethnicities dating back to the Middle Ages. The peculiar religious mix of Ottoman Bosnia was in turn the product of Bosnia's prior historical path.[27]

Similarly, Bougarel holds that Bosnia's 'contemporary confessional profile' is the result of the early centuries of the Ottoman period.[28] The establishment of Turkish control over Bosnia and Herzegovina had thereby three important consequences for the (non-)formation of a distinctively Bosnian nationhood. First, the Porte preserved the administrative-territorial framework of the Bosnian state.[29] The territorial circumference was respected through the establishment of a separate and historically based *sanjaks* (military districts) of Bosnia and Herzegovina in the first century after the Ottoman conquest, and re-affirmed in 1580 with the consolidation of several *sanjaks* into the '*Eyalet* of Bosnia'. In the lifespan of the *Eyalet* (from 1864, *Vilayet*), Bosnia 'acquired the borders that were to last virtually unchanged until 1929 and that were restored in 1945' with minor changes.[30] Since adherence to Bosnia's historical territoriality also signifies respect of Bosnian peculiarity, it necessarily sustained Bosnian regional identity among the Bosnian nobility. Special privileges to natives were also common in the administrative framework. From 1516 on, for example, only natives to the Bosnian *san-*

---

26   Hoare, *History of Bosnia*, 37.

27   Ibid., 41.

28   Bougarel, "Bosnia and Herzegovina", 88.

29   Hoare, *History of Bosnia,* 37.

30   Ibid., 38. As Hoare writes, in 1875 the *sanjak* of Herzegovina was separated from the *Vilayet* of Bosnia. Despite its re-integration into the *Vilayet* only two years later, Bosnia and Herzegovina were thus two separated entities at the times of the Bosnian uprising in 1875-8, when the country entered public consciousness. This also explains its modern-day name.

jak could own *timars* (military fiefs).[31] As Bougarel notes, 'the local Muslims elites monopolis[ed] power to their personal advantage'.[32]

As part of the incorporation of Bosnia and Herzegovina into the Empire, the Ottomans established a heavily secured military border between themselves and the Austro-Hungarians. Since the border region—the Military Frontier, or *Krajina* as it is nowadays called—was largely depopulated due to the constant military struggles between the two Empires, its establishment meant the conscious resettling of peoples. Encouraged by the Porte, Orthodox *Vlachs* consequently settled the areas of northern and northwestern Bosnia, which 'gave rise to a Serb majority that persists in northwest Bosnia to the present day'.[33] But it was not only the immigration of *Vlachs* that changed the 'ethno-national' map of Bosnia in Ottoman times. Following their expulsion from Spain, Sephardic Jews came to the territory—and so did Muslim immigrants expelled from the Habsburg Empire or, after the Serbian uprisings, from Serbia. The region saw further waves of immigration, for example by Croats from Dubrovnik who settled as craftsmen and builders in Ottoman Sarajevo, or, after the Austro-Hungarian occupation, by other Catholics and Ashkenazi Jews.[34]

The way in which the Porte handled this increased 'ethnic' plurality was the second major consequence of Ottoman rule over Bosnia. According to Ottoman theology, the world was separable into two interconnected domains: the domain of the faithful and the domain of war. Consequently, the ruler's main obligation was not only to defend Islam but to expand the rule of the religion over as wide a territory as possible.[35] Put into practice, this philosophy demanded constant conquests as a religious duty ('holy war'). But what is more, it also justified the fundamental distinction between Muslim and non-Muslim as the central pillar of Ottoman political rule over conquered territories. The latter distinction was much more pestering in light of the fact that the Ottomans, despite their clearly missionary goals, did generally not force conversions in occupied territories. Through the *millet* system, '[c]onquered people of another religion were allowed a definitive place under the direction of their own ecclesiastical authorities'.[36] But even though conversion was not forced *per se*, the structure of government and political rule strongly encouraged it because non-Muslims paid extra taxes[37] and were

---

31 Ibid.

32 Bougarel, "Bosnia and Herzegovina", 88.

33 Hoare, *History of Bosnia*, 43. However, there are areas like Bihać and Cazinska Krajina with a Muslim majority.

34 Ibid., 43–4.

35 Jelavich, *History of the Balkans Volume 1*, 39–40.

36 Ibid., 39.

37 However, as Malcolm (*Bosnia*, 65) writes, we should not forget that even though the non-Muslims paid special taxes, they were for example exempt from other payments such as the alms-tax (*zakat*) and had to perform military duties from which Christians outside of the border regions were usually exempt.

subject to special restrictions and a generally second-class treatment by the authorities. On the other hand, Muslims were obliged to provide military support and serve in the Sultan's army during the numerous conquests.

Among the Balkans population, only two groups converted in large masses to Islam during the time of Ottoman rule: the Albanians and the Bosnians. The latter's conversion is significant insofar as it constitutes the historical core of the modern Bosniak nation. As nationalist histories generally treat historical facts rather freehandedly, fundamental misunderstandings about the process of conversion in Bosnia are hardly surprising. As was already implied, claims that the rulers largely forced conversions in Bosnia or that only the adherents of the Bosnian Church converted belong to the realm of nationalist mythology rather than historical accuracy. Serious inquiry has shown that the process of conversion in Bosnia was gradual and affected all three Christian dominations. It took over 150 years for Bosnia to become a predominantly Muslim region and there were many people registered as Muslims in Ottoman tax records with clear Orthodox or Catholic origins.[38] Apart from socio-economic and legal privileges that Muslims enjoyed, Bosnia's 'Islamisation was assisted by the weak structure of all three Bosnian Christian churches, the absence of a dominant church territorial structure, and the extent of religious syncretism among the population'.[39] Unsurprisingly, '[t]he shift from folk Christianity to folk Islam was not very great; many of the same practices could continue, albeit with slightly different words or names. Without the controlling presence of a Church, warning of danger to one's immortal soul, the shift could be made quite easily'.[40]

While these circumstances help partly explain the psychology behind conversions, there is one important phenomenon to consider: the practice of *devşirisme. Devşirisme,* meaning 'to collect', came into being sometime in the fourteenth century and existed until the mid to late seventeenth century.[41] In irregular intervals, Ottoman officials would forcefully take children from Christian families—Muslims were exempt from this practice—and bring them to Istanbul, where 'they were converted to Islam and trained as janissary troops, or as personal servants to the Sultan, or as officials in the various departments of state'.[42] Even though the cruelty of such action is often rightfully stressed in reports, it must also be acknowledged, as Jelavich writes, that those children 'gained the possibility of acquiring the most advanced education available and the opportunity to rise to the top of the Ottoman system'. In this sense, this practice had more socio-political than religious implications, for it created a specific ruling class composed of subjected peoples in the centre of the empire. This was particularly

---

[38]   Malcolm, *Bosnia*, 52.

[39]   Hoare, *History of Bosnia*, 42–3.

[40]   Malcolm, *Bosnia*, 58.

[41]   Jelavich, *History of the Balkans Volume 1*, 41.

[42]   Ibid. Malcolm, *Bosnia*, 46.

true for Bosnia, where the benefits of this engagement could directly be felt. It is therefore no surprise that Bosnian Muslims asked explicitly to be included into the system of *devşirisme*, [43] which also explains their overrepresentation in the janissary corps. Since Bosnians usually proved useful, they could climb up the hierarchy and assume the highest positions. According to one report from 1530, the Sultan preferred to recruit Bosnian because he believed them to be 'the best, most pious and most loyal people'. [44] In the sixteenth and seventeenth centuries, for example, there were altogether nine grand viziers of Bosnian origins, and from the late fifteenth century on Bosnians were sent back to govern Bosnia. [45] It is estimated that at least 200,000 children from the Balkans passed through the system when the practice was in effect, most of them Slavs. [46]

The Ottoman rule was thus partly responsible for the influx of different groups to the Bosnian territory [47] and entirely responsible for their differentiation along religious lines. But there is also a third consequence of Ottoman rule that would determine the evolution of nationalism in Bosnia, namely the system of land ownership. In what was to become known as the *timar* rule, land was distributed to Muslims in compensation for their military services. As a consequence of the Porte's frequent military engagements, the landholders were usually away from their property for six to nine months a year; during this time, their land was worked by Christian or Muslim peasants, who apart from doing the obligatory work also paid a tithe in kind and other dues. [48] But unlike in the Western European feudal systems, the Muslim landholders had—apart from collecting dues, which they did as representatives of the Porte—no judicial powers over their serfs, who in turn could not only inherit their right to the land but also sell it and move elsewhere. [49] However, it was not the *timar* system *per se* that led to the betterment of Muslim landowners over other groups, especially the Christian peasants. Rather it was exactly its erosion in the late fifteenth century that, due to political and socioeconomic changes, led to 'a new kind of local aristocracy holding large estates in full, hereditary ownership'. [50] These processes, according to Mal-

---

[43]   Jelavich, *History of the Balkans Volume 1*, 41.

[44]   Quoted in Malcolm, *Bosnia*, 65.

[45]   Ibid., 46.

[46]   Jelavich, *History of the Balkans Volume 1*, 41; Malcolm, *Bosnia*, 46.

[47]   Bougarel also mentions 'the installation of substantial orthodox populations and smaller Jewish populations' during Ottoman times as a key element in creating Bosnia's contemporary confessional profile. (Bougarel, "Bosnia and Herzegovina", 88.)

[48]   Malcolm, *Bosnia*, 47.

[49]   Ibid., 48.

[50]   Ibid., 93. According to Malcolm, some of the 'reasons for this change are: the growth of the *devşirisme* class of imperial officials who competed in seventeenth-century Istanbul for grants of non-military private estates; the shift in military importance from *spahis* [i.e. Muslim landlords] to paid infantry; and the general and insatiable need for revenues, which led to large areas of land being handed over to local lords in return for the collection and delivery of taxes in cash.'

colm, resulted in a social and religious polarisation of Ottoman Bosnia. Whereas in the fifteenth century Christians as well as Muslims could be estate-holders and their lands could be worked by either Christian or Muslim peasants, in the nineteenth century the majority of landowners were Muslims and the majority of non-landowning peasants were Christian.[51]

This situation was the result of Bosnia's geographical position. Located on the periphery of the Ottoman Empire and under constant threat by Christian invasion, the Bosnian Muslims lived under peculiar circumstances compared to Muslims somewhere in the midst of the Ottoman womb. Their special status was *de facto* codified when, after the Vienna War in 1699, the Bosnian Muslim peasantry was 'largely freed from feudal obligations to facilitate its mobilisation as a bulwark against Austria and Venice'.[52] The special status of Muslims led not only to the deterioration in the economic status of Christians but also made the communal divisions more rigid, especially since the middle of the eighteenth century. In the early centuries of Ottoman rule, as Bougarel writes, confessional identity was 'very fluid' and there were 'a number of peasant revolts in this period which pitted Muslim peasants against their Muslim feudal lords'. However, the rise to power by the Muslims led to a rather strict division into landowners and peasants. As Bougarel mentions, as late as 1910, 'more than thirty years after the end of the Ottoman presence in Bosnia, 91.1 per cent of the landed proprieters [sic] having *kmetovi* (tenant farmers with feudal obligations) were Muslims, while 95.4 per cent of the *kmetovi* were Orthodox or Catholic.'[53] This situation was only insignificantly mitigated by the existence of a truly prosperous Christian merchant class in all the major towns of Bosnia.[54] However, since this class was usually more tolerant to Muslim rule, the Christian population was *de facto* segregated into four different groups along two dimensions: the urban and rural classes on the one axis and the Catholics and Orthodox on the other. The rupture in leadership would prove to be an important determinant of Bosnian Serb and Bosnian Croat nationalisms, respectively, for it separated the urban intelligentsia from the peasant masses. At the same time, the protection of land-owning privileges became a central pillar of Bosnian Muslim political activity until well into the first Yugoslavia.

4.3   Bosnian Muslims, Bosnian Croats, Bosnian Serbs

When in the nineteenth century the *national* consciousness of the Bosnian communities was activated, Bosnian Catholics and Bosnian Orthodox became Bosni-

---

[51]   Ibid., 94.
[52]   Hoare, *History of Bosnia*, 47.
[53]   Bougarel, "Bosnia and Herzegovina", 88.
[54]   Malcolm, *Bosnia*, 95–6.

an Croats and Bosnian Serbs, respectively. Simultaneously, Bosnian Muslims started claiming more rights of autonomy from the Porte and gradually thought of themselves as a distinct group rather than part of the Ottoman administration. In other words, 'the fluidity of confessional identity and relationships was gradually replaced by a closed communitarianism'. As Bougarel further writes,

> the informal institution of *komšiluk* (good neighbourliness) certainly continued to be the rule in everyday dealings between the communities; but it was based on a constant reaffirmation of community identities and codes, and not their effacement. *Komšiluk* never developed into intimateness. In terms of the relationships it established between the public and private spheres, between communitarian identity and social bonds, it represented the inverse of citizenship, rather than its premise.[55]

Contrary to Bougarel, Hoare claims that even though the political currents among the three communities were different in structure and philosophy, they were all intrinsically bound to the Bosnian homeland, for neither Bosnian Serbs nor Bosnian Croats yet identified with their respective homelands of Serbia and Croatia:

> By the last decades of Ottoman rule, if not earlier, Bosnians were struggling for self-rule for their country in a manner similar to other nineteenth-century European peoples: the Bosnian uprisings of 1830, 1875, 1878 were all Bosnian-autonomist in form, albeit with different degrees of Muslim or Orthodox colouration. Likewise, the Catholic Franciscans were by this time articulating a well-developed sense of Bosniak nationhood.[56]

Again, these two views seem not that far apart. Bougarel actually agrees that the insurrections of 1830 and 1875 'were effectively revolts against the reinforcement of the role of the state. The first certainly represented no kind of nationalist movement; the second only turned into one after the intervention of the youthful neighbouring Serbian state and the internationalisation of this first Bosnian crisis.'[57] Furthermore, both Hoare and Bougarel hold that Austria-Hungary, after initially trying to combat Bosnian sectarianism, later accepted and even favoured it.[58] Following Hoare, I shall now work out the distinctively Bosnian elements within the nationalist movements of the Bosnian Muslims as well as the Bosnian Serbs and Bosnian Croats, all of which developed as a reaction to Ottoman administration and ideological influences from Serbia and Croatia, respectively.

---

[55] Bougarel, "Bosnia and Herzegovina", 88.

[56] Hoare, *History of Bosnia*, 413.

[57] Bougarel, "Bosnia and Herzegovina", 89.

[58] Hoare (*History of Bosnia*, 314) writes: 'The Austro-Hungarian occupation of 1878 ensured the survival of Bosnia-Herzegovina as a multinational country in which no one nation would dominate, and permitted the flowering of modern national politics among the Serbs, Croats and Muslims.' Bougarel ("Bosnia and Herzegovina", 89) states that the Austro-Hungarian Empire, first 'anxious to counteract the influence of Serb and Croat nationalism' by seeking to promote 'a global Bosnian identity', later 'started to accept, and then even to favour, the consolidation of the communitarian structure of social and political life in Bosnia.'

4.3.1 'National' agitation under Ottoman rule

Since Bosnia was of military importance, the Porte entrusted the local leaders with a unique status of autonomy that was especially visible in terms of administrative prerogatives. Consequently, institutions of Ottoman rule became Bosnian institutions of sorts, because the army and the administration relied predominantly on Bosnian Muslim staffers. These institutions made the development of a distinct Bosnian Muslim consciousness possible, even though the Bosnian Muslims 'identified with the Ottoman state and did not yet define themselves in opposition to it'.[59] However, when Ottoman administrative and military structures changed—e.g. with the 1826 creation of a new army corps, which deprived the janissaries of their privileged positions[60]—the Bosnian Muslims realised that their interests might not best be served under the Sultan's rule. A tipping point was reached with the rebellion of 1830, which followed the Sultan's decision to cede six Bosnian municipalities to the Principality of Serbia.[61] Prominent among the rebelling nobles was Husejn-kapetan Gradaščević, the richest landlord in the country. Under his leadership, Bosnians sought independence and autonomy similar to the one the Porte had granted Serbia and, naturally, rejected any territorial changes. Even though Gradaščević managed to secure administrative autonomy for Bosnia and put an end to the constant reforms of Ottoman government, his achievements did not last long.[62] Only two years later, with the help of Herzegovinian kapetans, the Ottomans defeated Gradaščević and effectively dismantled all institutions of Bosnian rule; in 1850-1, Omer-pasha Latas definitively crushed Bosnia's resistance to Ottoman reforms.[63]

The importance of Gradaščević's rebellion lies more in the cause, structure, and ideology of his movement than in the actual result. Bosnian Muslim rule over the territory was closely linked to the systems of Ottoman administration and, more importantly, land distribution. When the reform of the latter began in the nineteenth century,[64] it enraged Bosnian Muslims, and unified and mobilised them against the Porte. Following Bougarel, one has to understand the struggles by the local communities in the nineteenth century within the context of modernisation and Ottoman reforms: 'So while the nationalist movement of Eastern Europe place the state in the centre of the political order, the communitarian mobilisations which took place in Bosnia in the same period sought to keep it at a dis-

---

[59]   Hoare, *History of Bosnia*, 48.
[60]   Malcolm, *Bosnia*, 120.
[61]   Hoare, *History of Bosnia*, 49.
[62]   Malcolm, *Bosnia*, 121.
[63]   Hoare, *History of Bosnia*, 50.
[64]   Cf. Josef Matuz, *Das Osmanische Reich: Grundlinien seiner Geschichte. 6. Auflage.* (Darmstadt: Primus-Verlag, 2010), chap. 9.

tance.' [65] In 1831, an assembly of Bosnian Muslims demanded local self-government. In September of that year, a second assembly meeting was convened, which, apart from military representatives (*kapetans*) now included members from the larger religious elite and representatives from the villages as well. The idea of Bosnian Muslim unification based on common interests was thus already born before any ideological distinctiveness on which modern Bosniakism relies. In this sense, the demands against the Sultan expressed the will of the Bosnian Muslim elite, which performed the function of a party, or lobbying group, rather than the one of a national movement. It is a unique phenomenon in the region that the Bosnian Muslim unification did not start with an ideological foundation that integrated opposition against the ruling structure or, closely associated to it, the establishment of a new and more autonomous structure. Rather, the 1830-2 rebellion was a reactionary elitist movement that sought to protect the existing *status quo* against on-going reforms.

It is thus not surprising that Gradaščević's idea of the Bosnian nation rested on the Muslim faith and that his movement did not actively seek to 'appeal to the Christian population nor move to end the political and economic discrimination against it, nor did their national identity transcend the religious'.[66] But despite this strong link to Islam, the true cause of Bosnian Muslim unity of that time was interest, i.e. the protection of land owning privileges. The distinctively Muslim orientation of the movement it produced reflected political interests, not religious ideology. Nevertheless, the 1830-2 rebellion remains an important element in modern Bosniak political thought. Despite its failure, it still performs an important function in Bosniak folk memory. For example, the street on which the well-known *Holiday Inn* Hotel in modern Sarajevo is located and which became infamous as 'sniper alley' during the last war, bears today Gradaščević's nickname: '*Zmaj od Bosne*', the dragon of Bosnia. Incidentally, Bosnia's national football team, mostly supported by Bosniaks, is also nicknamed 'the Dragons'.

The events leading to the first unification of the Bosnian Muslims cast serious doubt on the adequateness of Miroslav Hroch's model of national agitation for the present case. The rebellion had no real ideological foundation, nor did it advocate national autonomy as a consequence of national distinctiveness. Furthermore, apart from a religious dogma directed against the Ottomans, the movement did not invoke any religious justification of its actions. While it consisted of a unified elite, it lacked ideology and real mass mobilisation. It was thus not a national movement at all, not even one of an uprising character. While the Serbian uprisings had an ideological foundation of sorts with the Serbian Church and could thus easily invoke the respective memories, the Bosnian Muslims owed

---

[65]   Bougarel, "Bosnia and Herzegovina", 89.

[66]   Hoare, *History of Bosnia*, 50.

their very existence as a group to the Ottoman Islamisation of their territory. Furthermore, their unifying trait, land ownership and administrative power, was closely connected to the continuation of Ottoman rule. Their demands could thus not mobilise the Orthodox and Catholic masses, which structurally contained the movement. This would remain true for the rest of Ottoman rule, where the Bosnian Muslims undoubtedly saw themselves as distinct from their rulers, but not necessarily part of the larger South Slavic community. Their loyalty lay primarily at the local level and not with the central government in Constantinople, while their group consciousness relied not on a social, cultural, or conceptual foundation[67] but on geo-political interests. Therefore, it did not amount to anything comparable to the uniformity that Bosnian Serb and Bosnian Croat movements developed, at least partly, in the same time period.

It was in the last century of Ottoman rule that the Bosnian Orthodox and Bosnian Catholics became Bosnian Serbs and Bosnian Croats, respectively. These developments had not so much a genuinely Bosnian cause, but were rather closely connected to the emergence of nationalism in Serbia and Croatia. These neighbouring nationalisms exerted an important influence on their 'co-nationals' on Bosnian territory since the middle of the nineteenth century. However, it took them almost another one and a half centuries to make the Bosnians genuine parts of their respective nations. This is mostly due to the fact that the regional consciousness that we have just observed with the Bosnian Muslim ruling class also applied to Bosnian Serbs and Bosnian Croats, which made the attempts at assimilation and integration of their respective nations more difficult. But consistent with nationalist ideology, the Serbs and Croats saw Bosnians as part of their national substrate. In some readings of this argument, even the Bosnian Muslims were part of those two nations, as they were seen as ethnic brothers whose conversion to Islam did not really change their overall belonging. In this sense, the development of *national* consciousness (as opposed to a purely communitarian one) within the Bosnian peoples was in no small part the result of foreign attempts to include the Bosnians in respective national philosophies and the counter-reactions these attempts produced.

Since the Serbs of Serbia were the first people of the region to embark on their journey towards full independence in form of a nation state, their ideological and political philosophy reached Bosnian soil first. As we have seen, the Orthodox population had been present in Bosnia proper since the arrival of the Ottomans,[68] and in Herzegovina even well before then. It enjoyed the same rights as any other non-Muslim religious community under the *millet* system and was

---

[67]   Friedman, *The Bosnian Muslims*, 43–4.

[68]   Hoare claims that the Orthodox Vlachs that came to Bosnia proper after the fall of the medieval kingdom and had no own traditions or folk memories and therefore absorbed those of the Orthodox Serbs. Cf. Hoare, *History of Bosnia*, 51.

therefore—since the re-establishment of the Serbian Orthodox Patriarchate in 1557 by the Ottoman grand *vizier* Mehmed-pasha Sokolović, who was himself of Bosnian origin[69]—subject to the teachings of the Orthodox Church with all the national implications these teachings included. This created enough of a proto-national substrate to unite the Serbs on both sides of the Drina, at least in principle. But as Hoare convincingly explains, the 'national awakening' of the Bosnian Serbs in the nineteenth century was the result of a particular dichotomy 'between the conditions facing the Bosnian Serb urban population and those facing the Bosnian Serb peasantry'.[70] Accordingly, the urban Serb elites, who enjoyed friendly relationships with their Muslim counterparts and whose 'patriotic' identification was similar to the latter's, were the pioneers of a distinctively Bosnian Serb *national* identity. Given the ethnic heterogeneity of their composition, these distinct elites advocated a national identity that was Bosnian in character and included the Bosnian Muslims and Bosnian Catholics as well. However, this view of early Bosnian Serb nationalists collided with the social conditions and concerns of the Orthodox peasantry, who was subject to Muslim rule as a result of the land distribution system.[71] While it was not hard for them to accept their commonalities with the Serbs from Serbia, the idea of being part of a Bosnian nation on equal footing with their Muslim landlords was much harder to swallow. Since their fiscal and legal obligations rose, their status resembled genuine serfdom, which meant that the subordinate position vis-à-vis the landlords affected their identity. In the end, according to Hoare, it was the view of the peasants that determined the character of the Bosnian Serb national movements thus excluding any commonalities with the Bosnian Muslims or, for that matter, Croats.

Active agitation of Bosnian Serb individuality began in the 1860s due to Serbian activism. A Serb association that, in ethno-cultural terms, tried to unite the different Orthodox groups under the heading of 'Serbianism' was established in Sarajevo. Bogoljub Petranović, an agent of Serbia who 'came to Bosnia with the deliberate aim of stirring Serb nationalist activity there, in order to further Serbia's expansionist plans, and to counter the influence of Austria-Hungary'[72] became its leader. At around the same time, Ilija Garašanin founded a Bosnia-wide organisation mostly targeting the urban Bosnian Serb classes. Its aim was to prepare a Bosnian uprising against the Ottomans. Since Garašanin's programme was national, not social in orientation, it only sought the unification of the Bosnian territory with Serbia and did not advocate a radical agrarian reform to improve

---

[69]   Ibid.

[70]   Ibid., 52-57. The following argument is Hoare's.

[71]   As previously explained, Bougarel as well underlines the economic disparity between the urban and rural communities of the Bosnian Serbs and Croats.

[72]   Hoare, *History of Bosnia*, 54.

the living conditions of the Serb peasantry.[73] However, it was precisely the devastating situation of the peasantry that led to a series of Christian uprisings against the authorities, the most famous of which happened in 1875-8 in Bosnia and in Herzegovina.

This rebellion was essentially Serb in orientation and composition, but at least in Bosnia proper it had an autonomous Bosnian character.[74] While leadership of the movement was provided by the urban Serb elites that not only mobilised the peasants but also sought to unite them under a national heading, the peasantry itself was more concerned with the improvement of their living conditions than with national rhetoric. But this was far more than enough to agitate them. Since the national idea was an import from Serbia and the rebellion in large part the result of Serbian lobbying, it is quite understandable that the Bosnian rebels demanded the unification of Bosnian and Serbian territory in July 1876. Nevertheless, Hoare insists that the rebellion leadership, stemming from the urban Serb classes, possessed a dual identity. The rebels 'identified with both the Serb nation and the Bosnian homeland'.[75] This is why, when in March 1877 Serbia signed a peace treaty with the Ottoman Empire, the rebels altered their stance. The 'Provisional National Bosnian Government' that was elected at a rebel meeting in October 1877 stated in its proclamation to the 'Bosnian nation' that Bosnia sought unification with other Serbian lands; but, given the improbability of achieving this goal at the present moment, 'the Bosnian nation wishes to have its complete freedom and self-government'.[76] This declaration was as much the expression of Bosnian Serb nationalism as it was the rejection of any annexation attempts by Austria-Hungary.

It is of particular importance that the rebels of the 1875 rebellion referred to themselves, and were referred to by others, as 'Bosniaks'. This term, nowadays associated uniquely with the Bosnian Muslims, referred at that time to all the peoples living on the Bosnian territory; as such, it expressed regional rather than national allegiance. The term referred to medieval times and was cultivated and kept alive mostly by the Franciscans sent to the territory by the Pope to catholicise the allegedly heretic Bosnian believers. Just as the Orthodox Church had done for the Serbs, the Franciscans 'used the tradition of this [medieval] kingdom to underpin the legitimacy and integrity of Bosna Srebrena',[77] as the Franciscan province was then called. Especially in the last century of Ottoman rule, the Franciscans experienced a great expansion and erected many new churches and schools for the Catholic community, who referred to their language as 'Bosniak'.

---

[73]   Jelavich, *History of the Balkans Volume 1*, 351.
[74]   Hoare, *History of Bosnia*, 61–66.
[75]   Ibid., 62.
[76]   Cited in ibid., 63.
[77]   Ibid., 58.

According to Hoare, these circumstances made the Franciscans the bearers of the 'Bosniak' nationality as well as the ancestors of the Bosnian Croat movement. In accordance with Illyrian ideology, Bosnians were seen as ethnic Slavs—thus part of the South Slavic movement—but with a distinctively Bosnian trait based on historical developments.

When it originated in the 1860s, the Bosnian Croat national movement was as much the product of outside imposition as it was a counter-reaction to nationalist tendencies of the Bosnian Serbs. The Croat's situation was different from the Serbs insofar as their community was smaller in numbers and their peasants were largely free and thus suffered less under Muslim rule. In terms of the national composition they played a subordinate role in nineteenth century Bosnia, especially since they did not rely on the connection to Croat Catholic ecclesiastical institutions in order to substantiate their feeling of uniqueness. This is the reason why, according to Hoare, they remained mostly politically moderate and with a distinctively Bosnian orientation. In fact, immediately prior to the Austro-Hungarian invasion, the Franciscan order called for an autonomous Bosnia based on the equality of all three beliefs.[78] Even though their conversion from Bosnian Catholics to Bosnian Croats was therefore slower, it was significantly accelerated by activities of Strossmayer and one Sarajevo Franciscan, who respectively founded a Catholic seminar in Đakovo and a Croat gymnasium in Sarajevo.[79] But in fact, it was only after the arrival of the Habsburgs that the Bosnian Croat national movement truly evolved.

4.3.2 Nationalism in Habsburg Bosnia

Fearing that the territory could come under Serbian control, the Habsburgs decided to occupy Bosnia and Herzegovina. They did so partly against their better judgement, for with Bosnia's *de facto* incorporation into the Dual Monarchy following the Congress of Berlin in 1878, 'another national problem [was added] to a state that was unable to handle the [national] controversies it already had'.[80] Either as a result of the structural tendencies in the monarchy or as an expression of distinct local ideologies, the Habsburg rule would lead to the full-fledged development of two nationalisms and one proto-national identity within the three main communities in Bosnia. Given the empire's internal quarrels, Bosnia became a crown land under the joint rule of Austria and Hungary. Administratively, it came under the control of the Common Ministry of Finance. However, the establishment of Habsburg rule had no immediate consequences with regards to the existing administrative structure, since the Ottoman system was considered workable

---

[78]   Ibid., 61.

[79]   Ibid.

[80]   Jelavich, *History of the Balkans Volume 1*, 361.

and essentially kept in place, albeit with some name and personnel changes.[81] Nevertheless, it was during this time that Bosnia saw a colossal economic advancement as a result of huge public investments. The Habsburg authorities built main and local roads, bridges, established a railway system and opened factories.[82]

Closely connected to these economic developments is the emergence of printed, nationally-minded newspapers. Published since the middle of the nineteenth century in Austria-Hungary or by Austro-Hungarian subjects, those publications now reached Bosnian soil in large masses. Moreover, following the occupation, Serbs and Croats from the Habsburg Empire increasingly founded nationally exclusive newspapers in Bosnia itself.[83] Quite understandably, this accelerated the transformation from a communitarian into a national identity. The Habsburgs generally followed a conciliatory course with respect to such group interests. For example, as Malcolm explains, they allowed the three Bosnian communities to keep their segregated schools, even though those were formally subordinate to the state; nevertheless, they made sure to control the appointments of the senior figures of each religious group.[84] Bougarel, however, maintains that the Austro-Hungarians did not only take control over the religious structures of Bosnia, but even forbade 'the use of the terms "Serb" and "Croat" in the titles of cultural associations'.[85]

But more important than the actual practices was the dramatic change of environment that had been stable for many centuries. With its incorporation into the Dual Monarchy, Bosnia came under Catholic influence, which naturally had consequences for all local elites, especially the Bosnian Catholics. As the authorities wanted to make sure not to treat them as a privileged community, Jesuits were brought into the country, whereby the Franciscans lost their monopoly on Catholic dogma.[86] In one accepts Hoare's claim that the Franciscans had been the bearer of a distinct Bosnian—or, at that time, Bosniak—regional identity, the opening up of the religious spectrum signified the decrease of Bosnian individuality not only in religious but, consequently, also in regional and national terms. If the loyalty of the Franciscans to the Bosnian state had for a while retarded the process of nationalisation of Bosnian Catholics as Croats, it was by no means able to avoid this completely; in fact, '[o]nce the Franciscans had been Croatianised, they be-

---

[81]   Malcolm, *Bosnia*, 137. Hoare, *History of Bosnia*, 72.
[82]   Malcolm, *Bosnia*, 141.
[83]   Hoare, *History of Bosnia*, 70–1.
[84]   Malcolm, *Bosnia*, 144.
[85]   Bougarel, "Bosnia and Herzegovina", 89.
[86]   Malcolm, *Bosnia*, 144–5.

came the carriers of Croat identity among the Bosnian Catholics, but in a peculiarly Bosnian form'.[87]

With the arrival of the Habsburgs, Bosnian Muslims lost their centuries-old domination over the territory and saw their lands for the first time under non-Muslim suzerainty. Even though the new rulers chose to govern the country in a centralistic manner from Sarajevo so that the local elite did not entirely lose control, it was clear that the privileges of the landed elite were up for debate. In order to secure them, a minority of Muslims pledged loyalty to the new regime and acquired political influence and power by cooperating with the central government.[88] They also subscribed to the nationalisation efforts by the Hungarian Ban and Minister of Finance (between 1882 and 1903) Benjamin Kállay.[89] In order to counter the emerging group nationalisms, Kállay developed the idea of a common Bosnian nationhood that all three groups could share. Recalling the use of the word in historical terms, his concept of *Bošnjaštvo* (Bosniakism) sought to elevate regional identity beyond religious boundaries.

For his purposes, and as a matter of practical implementation, it was essential that 'the idea of Bosnian nationhood should be taken up first by the Muslims' because they did not have any sponsor-nation on the other side of the border and thus remained committed to the Bosnian homeland.[90] Indeed, the Sarajevo Muslims supported the idea of *Bošnjaštvo* in significant numbers. Mehmed-beg Kapetanović-Ljubušak, the mayor of Sarajevo propagated this formally secular concept when he wrote in 1886: 'The Bosniak, of whatever religion he is, always remains faithful to his nationality; although every Bosnian Muhammedan is a great Muslim—perhaps greater than those who live in Arabia—he has never renounced his nationality, but always guarded it carefully as something holy.'[91] By portraying the Bosnian Muslims 'not as a religious community but as members of a nationality with a strong religious identity', Kapetanović-Ljubušak 'pioneered the concept of a nationality that would be interpreted in different ways by successive Muslim politicians: as religiously Muslim members of a "Yugoslav" nationality by some politicians in the interwar period; as members of a "Muslim" nationality for whom Islam was irrelevant by Communists of the Titoist period; and as members of a "Bosniak" nationality for whom Islam was an important badge

---

[87]   Hoare, *History of Bosnia*, 78.

[88]   Malcolm, *Bosnia*, 146; Hoare, *History of Bosnia*, 74.

[89]   Even though Kállay was Hungarian, Bosnian newspapers drew comparisons between him and the Austrian Wolfgang Petritsch, once the latter assumed the Office of High Representative in 1999 and advocated a policy which sought the revive the ancient congruity between being loyal to the Bosnian state and being a good Croat or Serb, respectively. Cf. Chapter 9 of the present study.

[90]   Malcolm, *Bosnia*, 148.

[91]   Quoted in Hoare, *History of Bosnia*, 75.

of identity by nationalist politicians since 1993.'[92] The formally secular concept had thus clear-cut religious implications and consequences.

With Kapetanović-Ljubušak's attempts to redefine the Bosnian Muslim identity, the major challenge of the Bosnian Muslim national movement was born: the perpetual dilemma between being 'Muslim' in a religious and a national sense. This dichotomy was only resolved some twenty years ago, when the Bosnian Muslims during the most recent war started calling themselves Bosniaks.[93] In Kállay's times, the identity of Bosnian Muslims was still predominantly religious, which is why his concept did not manage to gain significant support outside of the capital. As Bougarel explains, the Austro-Hungarian policy 'found support among the emerging modernisers among the Muslim elites, but met with hostility by the Orthodox elites (Serbs), the Catholic elites (Croats), and by the traditional Muslim elites.'[94] Bosnian Croats and Bosnian Serbs were already too interconnected with the respective nationalisation movements in their kin-states. In fact, as Noel Malcolm argues, Kállay's project might only have stood a chance if he had 'somehow been able to isolate Bosnia's Orthodox and Catholics utterly from the religious, cultural and political developments in neighbouring lands'. Of course, 'such total isolation would have been quite impossible'.[95] Instead of appeasing the existing (proto-)nationalisms and giving them a common philosophy, Kállay's nationalising policies had the contrary effect: they provoked national movements 'directed against the Bosnian centre and aimed at preserving the traditional autonomies of the religious communities'.[96]

The Bosnian Catholics became increasingly involved within the Croat national movements due to the end of Franciscan monopoly. However, when Vienna appointed the Catholic Josip Stadler as the archbishop of Bosnia in a deliberate attempt to weaken the Franciscan organisation, the Franciscans began identifying with the liberal wing of the Croat national movement and advocated crossconfessional political cooperation. Their national movement was born in the 1880s in Mostar and led by the Franciscan Paškal Buconjić.[97] The Bosnian Muslims and Bosnian Serbs organised their counter-movements to Kállay's policies in the form of demands for autonomy of religious and educational institutions. Also in Mostar, a perceived violation of Bosnian Muslim land rights in the 1880s, as well as the authorities' threat of increased presence by Catholic priests in 1899 provoked the development of a genuinely Muslim autonomist movement that was

---

[92]   Ibid., 75.
[93]   Pearson, "Bošnjaci instead of Muslimani."
[94]   Bougarel, "Bosnia and Herzegovina", 89. The fact that Bougarel uses both the religious as well as national terminology suggests that those two identities had not yet become one.
[95]   Malcolm, *Bosnia*, 149.
[96]   Hoare, *History of Bosnia*, 75.
[97]   Ibid., 78.

religious and traditionalist in its ideology but modern in its organisation.[98] Similarly, state interference into the organisation of the Orthodox Church, restrictions on the use of the Cyrillic alphabet, or a ban on the official use of the Serb name 'united the Bosnian Serb population against the government and behind a specifically Serb-national movement for church and school autonomy'.[99]

All of these movements were distinctively Bosnian in character, as Hoare argues; however, they did not constitute a genuinely Bosnian national movement due to the basic historical pattern of religious distinctiveness, which would be in line with the reasoning put forward by Bougarel. As the latter argues:

> With the new Christian commercial and administrative elites in Bosnia making Serbian and Croatian nationalism their own, nationalist sentiment developed rapidly within the Orthodox and Catholic communities in the territory. The Muslim community, for its part, mobilised around its religious and territorial elites, demanding cultural and religious autonomy—a kind of 'millet in reverse' for the Muslim population.[100]

The positions of the three communities became more national in character when the movements organised themselves in the form of parties and national organisations, respectively. In 1906 the 'Muslim National Organisation' was formed, the 'Serb National Organisation' followed a year later. While these organisations could rely on a coherent group structure as their foundation, the Bosnian Croats' were split between the Franciscan liberal model and the hard-line model of Archbishop Stadler. This divide expressed itself in the organisational structure as well. The 'Croat National Union', founded in 1906, saw the Croat's identity in terms of their Bosnian homeland while the 'Croat Catholic Association', whose emergence was the result of a split within the 'Croat National Union' in 1910, put exclusive emphasis on the Catholic faith.[101] Closely connected to the process of institutionalising political demands was the establishment of national educational-cultural societies, which 'became the principal institutional promoters of national identity in Bosnia-Herzegovina in the decades that followed; through financing the education of students from the ranks of their respective nationalities, they acted to create nationally conscious intelligentsias'.[102] The Dual Monarchy 'conceded cultural and religious autonomy to the Serb community in 1906 and to the Muslims in 1909. ... One year later, a provincial constitution instituted a Bosnian parliament, elected on a restricted suffrage and made up of distinct "colleges" (thirty-seven Orthodox deputies, twenty-nine Muslim, twenty-thee Catholic and one Jew).' As

---

[98]   Ibid., 76.
[99]   Ibid., 77.
[100]   Bougarel, "Bosnia and Herzegovina", 89.
[101]   Hoare, *History of Bosnia*, 80.
[102]   Ibid., 81.

Bougarel concludes, the 'introduction of parliamentarism in Bosnia *went hand-in-hand with the institutionalisation of communitarianism.*'[103]

4.3.3   Bosnian national identities in the two Yugoslavias

By the beginning of the twentieth century, the three Bosnian national movements possessed all the elements necessary to spread their national idea. They had the predispositions of distinct elements of commonality and were in the process of establishing large intelligentsias capable of uniting those elements into philosophically coherent and holistic national ideologies. They furthermore had a common enemy in form of the Habsburg state that kept intervening in their religious and cultural institutions thus provoking resistance from all the elites. And, arguably, they possessed a common goal in the form of autonomy for their common homeland. Nevertheless, at this time, the national movements were still largely projects of the elites that lacked clear contours. The Bosnian Croats were split between their religious loyalties that bound them to Croatia and their regional identity, which connected them to the Bosnian homeland. The Bosnian Serbs, even though much less reluctant to accept unification with Serbia than their Croat counterparts did to Croatia, nevertheless insisted on the peculiarity of their Bosnian existence. The Bosnian Muslims still saw themselves as a religious community and were primarily concerned with protecting their property interests. Their movement had thus not yet reached the first stage of national consciousness but remained a community forged around a common political interest. Given this fact, it remains questionable that their path towards national unification could follow Hroch's model. The political interests of a largely aristocratic class transformed, in due time, into a national substrate; the 'nation's' political programme thus preceded the formation of the actual nation.

This general constellation helps understand the future development and political demands of the three national movements. By the time the 1908 annexation of Bosnia changed the geopolitical climate in the region, nationalist movements from Serbia and Croatia had managed to spread their ideology throughout Bosnia and a new generation of more extreme nationalists was born. But other ideologies penetrated the lands as well. Even though it developed out of the Greater Serbia national movement, the organisation Young Bosnia ('*Mlada Bosna*'), for example, rejected Bosnia's traditional religious division. Instead, it advocated for the ideal of Yugoslavism and many of its members subsequently joined the Communists. The assassination of Archduke Franz Ferdinand and his wife in Sarajevo must be seen as the ideological culmination of all the different group ideologies prevailing in the region. The subsequent events presented a window of opportunity for the political reorganisation of the region.

---

[103]   Bougarel, "Bosnia and Herzegovina", 89-90. Original italics.

In particular, the future of Bosnia was at stake when several different options of territorial division were put on the table. As Hoare writes, that 'Bosnia was not formally united with Serbia in 1918, or in the years following, was the direct result of actions taken by the Bosnian elites, particularly the Bosnian Serb elite, in the face of popular pressure from the Bosnian Serb masses'.[104] With the establishment of the SHS kingdom, the Bosnians managed to secure political autonomy for their common homeland. However, while the integration of Bosnia into the kingdom 'made radical changes to the economic and political balance between the communities (agrarian reform and seizure of control over the state apparatus by the Serbs), it did not raise any immediate question marks over the communitarianism inherited from the Austro-Hungarian period'.[105] Quite to the contrary, the Bosnians entered into wider controversies that were to dominate the two Yugoslavias, which especially included the antagonism between Serbian centralism and Croatian/Slovenian federalism. While Bosnian Croats and Bosnian Serbs would gradually identify with the standpoints of their respective political centres in the subsequent years,[106] the Bosnian Muslims' position was determined by their own pragmatism. As their identity was still primarily religious in nature, it is quite understandable that some of their members declared themselves as 'Bosnian Croats' or 'Bosnian Serbs' in those years. Such identification was primarily pragmatical and closely connected to the centralism-federalism debate rather than being a national statement.[107] In fact, this pragmatism helped them acquire political significance in the newly founded state. The adoption of the 1921 Vidovdan Constitution was only possible because the Radicals and Democrats, who favoured a centralist state, bought off the Bosnian Muslims through concessions to Bosnian peculiarity: the Yugoslav Muslim Organisation negotiated special rights with regards to the Islamic community, an indemnity for landlords after land reform, representation of Muslims in the Bosnian government, and, most importantly, the recognition of Bosnia's borders as historical.[108]

Nevertheless, such pragmatism by the Bosnian Muslim community and the volatility of identity should not be interpreted as a lack of common solidarity; as Noel Malcolm claims, 'in practical terms the Muslims were already operating as a community on a par with the others, a community which defended its own identity and actually did so more effectively than any other grouping in Bosnian politics'. While one may challenge the usage of the term 'identity' in this context, the Bosnian Muslims surely knew how to successfully fight for their common interests. This way, the term 'Muslim' acquired 'political significance', as Malcolm

---

[104]   Hoare, *History of Bosnia*, 97.
[105]   Bougarel, "Bosnia and Herzegovina", 90.
[106]   Ibid., 91.
[107]   Malcolm, *Bosnia*, 165.
[108]   Hoare, *History of Bosnia*, 109.

states, while 'the strictly religious basis of the term was being gradually eroded by the secularization influences of the twentieth century.'[109] In fact, as Bougarel explains, the Yugoslav involvement and the decline of the traditional Muslim elites 'produced a profound crisis of identity within the Muslim community. Exposed to the advances and pressures of Serb and Croat nationalism, the Bosnian Muslims were increasingly inclined to take refuge in national indeterminacy and a tactical Yugoslavism'.[110]

Subsequent developments in the first Yugoslavia were, as we have seen, characterised by the centralism-federalism debate, which was gradually understood in national terms. This trend increased in the second Yugoslavia and later led to a general re-emergence of nationalism in the Communist state. However, there is an important difference between the nationalisms in the second half of the twentieth century and those expressed a hundred years earlier on Bosnian soil. The older nationalisms were Bosnian in character insofar as they acknowledged the existence of different groups on Bosnian territory, but deemed them interconnected through the territory itself. These nationalisms were thus based on a common *regional* identity that all the religious groups shared, the degree of which, however, remains contested. But as the nationalist tendencies progressed, the common bond loosened gradually. The ideas of territorial ethnic homogeneity, which would by definition involve 'ethnic cleansing' in ethnically heterogeneous areas such as Bosnia, were already present in the ideas of the *Četnici* and *Ustaše* movements during the Second World War. But it was only in the 1990s that they formed an *integral part of the national ideology* of the newer nationalisms. These more recent group nationalisms were different from the earlier ones insofar as they were based on the belief of incongruity between different national or regional identities. While nineteenth centuries nationalists had tried to argue that members of different groups on the same soil were nevertheless ethnic brothers that could and should be integrated, the 1990s nationalists concluded that their inclusion into a common state was *a priori* impossible. Since the territory was deemed theirs, ethnic expulsion and mass killing were not only the brutal expressions of such an ideology, but its core substrate and logical consequence. Without doubt, this ideology characterised the Serbian and Croatian national movements of the early 1990s.

---

[109]   Malcolm, *Bosnia*, 166.
[110]   Bougarel, "Bosnia and Herzegovina", 91.

Table 4.1: Population Ratios in Bosnia-Herzegovina (% of total population), 1948–1991

	1948	1953	1961	1971	1981	1991
Serbs	44.3	44.4	42.9	37.2	32.0	31.4
Muslims	30.7	31.3	25.7	39.6	39.5	43.7
Croats	23.9	23.0	21.7	20.6	18.4	17.3
Yugoslavs	–	–	8.4	1.2	7.9	5.5
Montenegrins	0.1	0.3	0.4	0.3	0.3	not available
Albanians	0.0	0.1	0.1	0.1	0.1	not available
Slovenes	0.2	0.2	0.2	0.1	0.1	not available
Macedonians	0.0	0.1	0.1	0.1	0.0	0.0
Other	not available	not available	0.9	0.8	1.5	2.1
Bosnia and Herzegovina	100.0	100.0	100.0	100.0	100.0	100.0
Total Population of Bosnia	2,563,764	2,847,459	3,277,948	3,746,111	4,102,783	4,364,574

Source: Friedman, *The Bosnian Muslims,* 156. Friedman's source is: Jure Petričević, *Nacionalnost stanovništva Jugoslavije: Nazadovanje Hrvata, manjine napredovanje Muslimana i Albanaca* (Brugg: Adria, 1983), p. 115. Total population number is taken from the respective censuses and can also be found in Friedman, *The Bosnian Muslims,* 155.

That Bosnia, and consequently the Bosnian Muslims, would suffer most from the re-emergence of this twentieth century nationalism, was the logical result of the historical heterogeneity of Bosnian-Herzegovinian territory. This assertion is closely connected to the changes in ethno-national composition one can observe between 1950 and 1990. As Table 4.1 shows, the relative Muslim majority with which Bosnia is closely associated today is in historical terms a rather recent event. In the 1948 census, only 31 per cent of the population declared themselves to be Muslim (nationally 'undetermined'), while the Serbs held the majority with 44%. In 1971, those two groups are almost equal in size. However, census data in general should be treated with the utmost caution for a number of reasons. The national self-identification as 'Muslim' does not represent the actual number of people adhering to the Muslim faith. As we have seen, for many members of the Muslim community their faith remained a religious rather than ethno-national category. This remained true in the first decades of the second Yugoslavia, when Muslims had to declare themselves in different ways—at times as Serbs or Croats and at times as 'nationally undetermined'. Only after the recognition of the Bosnian Muslims as a *national* group by the Communist government in 1968 did members of the Muslim community gain the opportunity to declare themselves as 'Muslims in the national sense'. This explains both the sudden peak in the Muslim category as well as the decline in the Yugoslav category in the subsequent census. Bosnian Muslim nationalist writers maintain that the national feeling of the Bosnian Muslims was already developed before the 1960s, but that the community as such simply did not yet have a proper way to express its national determination accurately. Alternatively, though far less convincingly, one could argue that the *national* feeling of Bosnian Muslims was not yet sufficiently formed so that many Muslims saw no problem in identifying themselves as Serbs, Croats, or Yugoslavs. While the recognition of the Bosnian Muslims as a national category may be seen as a project by the Communist elites, it undoubtedly increased the number of people identifying this way as some sort of self-fulfilling prophecy.

Such difficulties notwithstanding, the table shows a demographic shift in the national composition of Yugoslav Bosnia as a result of higher birth rates and lower emigration quotas among the Bosnian Muslims. Over time, this shift started to affect the composition of political bodies, which, until then, have been heavily dominated by Bosnian Serbs.[111] At the eve of the 1992 war, Bosnia's initial position was therefore highly complex due to the mixed ethno-national composition. Although there is still no data regarding Bosnia's current post-war composition,[112] in the 1991 Yugoslavian census 43% of the population declared themselves to be Muslims, 31% Serbs, and 17% Croats.[113] The overall picture is furthermore complicated by the fact that the geographical pattern of settlement was mixed as well. As one scholar[114] prominently termed it, the ethnic spread resembled a 'leopard's coat' meaning that although there were certain areas with a majority population, in general a highly entangled picture could be observed. This, of course, made a peaceful separation into larger, ethnically homogeneous areas, i.e. states, impossible.[115]

If we return to our initial discussion of national movements, we still need to address one development in Bosnia, namely the emergence of a Bosnian Muslim national movement in the second Yugoslavia. With the increasing ideological takeover of Bosnia's territory and history by Serbian and Croatian nationalists,[116] the Bosnian Muslim identity strengthened as some sort of counter-argument. Based on the Muslim faith, it faced the general incongruity between Islam and nationalist orientation, for religious dogma saw all Muslims as part of the *umma*, an all-encompassing religious community. This made the establishment of distinct

---

[111] Calic, *Krieg und Frieden in Bosnien-Hercegovina*, 78–9.

[112] The first post-war census was conducted in September 2013; the results are expected in 2015 or 2016.

[113] Friedman, *The Bosnian Muslims*, 155; Calic, *Geschichte Jugoslawiens*, 311.

[114] Adolf Karger, "Das Leopardenfell. Zur regionalen Verteilung der Ethnien in Bosnien-Herzegovina," *Osteurope* 42 (1992): 1102–11. Quoted in Calic, *Geschichte Jugoslawiens*, 45.

[115] Calic, *Geschichte Jugoslawiens*, 45.

[116] For example, in 1969 a Serbian writer published a book claiming that the entire population of Bosnia was really Serb and, in the subsequent decades, Serbian and Croatian nationalists began openly talking about 'carving pieces of [the] "ethnic" territory of Bosnia and incorporating them in Croatia and Serbia respectively'. As Malcolm writes, '[n]o attempts were made to show that the policies of the Bosnian administration were in fact anti-Serb or anti-Croat during this period; purely statistical oppression on the one hand, and bogus ethnic history on the other, were sufficient'. (Malcolm, *Bosnia*, 204.)

national identity based on faith a *contradictio in adjecto*. Owing to the history of its development as well as to the need to resolve such philosophical incongruity, Bosnian Muslim nationalism necessarily emphasised the political consequences of Muslim distinctiveness. Alija Izetbegović's famous *Islamic Declaration* (published in 1970) thus primarily contained the Islamic principles on how to rule a state. And even though it was only applicable to states with a Muslim majority, it was not unreasonably understood as a revolutionary document and a blueprint for the future of the Bosnian state. Not unrelated to the general rise of nationalism in Yugoslavia and the particular rise of Islamic fundamentalist in the world (e.g. with the Iranian Revolution), the Communist authorities in Bosnia imprisoned Izetbegović and twelve other people for 'hostile and counterrevolutionary acts derived from Muslim nationalism' following a trial in 1983;[117] the latter followed the publication of Izetbegović's *Islam between East and West* in 1980.

Even though Izetbegović later became the leader of the Bosnian Muslim national movement, his ideology does not exclusively represent the one of his group. Confronted with the prevailing nationalisms of the Croats and the Serbs, the Bosnian Muslims reacted in two different ways: 'they strengthened their own Muslims nationalism by giving greater emphasis to the most distinctive thing about it, its religious component, and they also emphasised that they stood for the preservation of Bosnia's unique character as a multi-national, multi-religious republic'.[118] In this sense, the Bosnian Muslims remained committed to the tolerance that the three group nationalisms on Bosnian soil had expressed some hundred years earlier. And in fact it was only prior to the war that the Bosnian Muslim leadership abandoned the general idea of a multi-national republic and strengthened its Islamic roots.[119]

4.4 Conclusion

In historical terms, nationalism in Bosnia developed largely as a consequence of nationalising neighbouring states. If one follows Hoare's argument, Bosnians remained faithful to both their common homeland and their different religious traditions up until the establishment of the first Yugoslavia. Despite attempts by

---

[117] Ibid., 208.

[118] Ibid., 218–9.

[119] As Bougarel ("Bosnia and Herzegovina", 96) writes: 'In September 1990, A. Zulfikarpašić and M. Filipović, representatives of the secular Bosnian nationalist trend, denounced the "fact that the party [the SDA] is ruled by eleven people—of conservative and generally religious orientation—and that it is run by a closed and privatised council, held together by family ties". Not long afterwards, these individuals were thrown out of the SDA during an extraordinary assembly of the party.' In an exemplary way, this process is also illustrated with respect to the Army of the Republic of Bosnia-Herzegovina, in Hoare, *How Bosnia Armed*.

neighbouring nationalists to convince Bosnian Catholics and Bosnian Orthodox people to regard themselves as Croats and Serbs, respectively, those groups insisted on their genuinely Bosnian origins. The Bosnian Muslims, as a result of their historical privileges and not lastly due to the general incoherence between Islam and nationalism, remained committed to their religious identity and generally open to other concepts of nationality. As mentioned throughout the chapter, this view seems not substantially at odds with the account put forward by Bougarel, even though the latter puts more emphasis on the communitarian structure than the unifying traits. However, both narratives agree that, upon entering the multi-national federations of the two Yugoslavias, the Bosnians were to gradually lose their commonality and become part of the general inconsistencies within the prevailing identity concepts (Yugoslavism and 'Brotherhood and Unity') and the political discussions (centralism-federalism, the economy etc.). Just as Croatia and Serbia increased their influence on Bosnian Croats and Serbs, the Bosnian Muslims developed a national identity on their own as a counter measure. The reason that a commonly Bosnian nationhood did not develop over the last two centuries was the religious *and* economic distinction that developed during Ottoman times. The *millet* system preserved the traditions of the Orthodox and Catholic Churches, while the system of land distribution allowed for the emergence of a Bosnian Muslim aristocracy. These determinants made a common Bosnian national movement unlikely as the Ottoman bureaucracy in Bosnia was largely staffed with Bosnians. On an organisational level, this prevented the formulation of common interests, for one group was in control and thus reluctant to any change. As a further element, the general split between urban and rural areas, and elites, delayed the development of a common ideology among the Bosnian Serbs. And with the change of rule after Habsburg occupation, the Bosnian Croats were split as well. Finally, the nationalisation attempts by Kállay provoked counter-reactions and effectively ended any hope of a common Bosnian or Bosniak nationhood. These circumstances made the development of a common Bosnian nationhood impossible.

Due to this specific configuration, Bosnia remains a particular conundrum for nationalist theories, and especially Miroslav Hroch's model of national development. Its shortcomings are especially visible in the case of the Bosnian Muslims that, despite entering the latest war with a political programme more or less aimed at preserving the multi-national character of their Bosnian homeland, were still not equipped with a clear-cut and philosophically coherent national ideology. Furthermore, being in effect part of the ruling class up until the establishment of Communism in Bosnia, the developments of Bosnian Muslim nationalism can hardly follow the path of other smaller nations subject to the rule of an empire. It is astonishing how long the Bosnian Muslims held on to a purely religious version of their collective identity *despite* the fact that they acted similar to agents of national movements. For example, when they secured some form of autonomy for Bosnia with the Vidovdan Constitution, they *de facto* fulfilled the task of a national movement. But they still lacked a common national ideology, apart from a close connection to the homeland, whose administrative survival they deemed a precondition to secure the privileges of their class. It seems quite hard to apply Hroch's model to this case, as the Bosnian Muslim national movement was fragmented over several decades and, for a long time, not distinctly national in character. It did not possess clear phases of intellectual formulation of a national idea and the subsequent spread of this idea among the ruling classes, as those classes were already united on the basis of privilege rather than national ideology. Only in light of the changing geopolitical and national climate in the second Yugoslavia did the Bosnian Muslims develop a clear national orientation, which nevertheless respected the multi-nationality of the common homeland and did not *per se* strive towards the unification of political and ethnic space. Similarly, the development of Bosnian Serb and Bosnian Croat nationalism has to be seen as distinct to the one of Serbian and Croatian nationalists rather than as part of it. Even though the genuinely Bosnian aspects of their identity were eradicated over time due to political changes, these two national movements showed different genealogies than their counterparts in their kin states.

Part II:
Consociationalism

5   A brief Introduction to Consociational Theory

In his seminal book *Democracy in Plural Societies,* Arend Lijphart defines his concept of consociational democracy as 'both an empirical and a normative model' for the establishment and maintenance of democracy in plural, i.e. heterogeneous societies.[1] By accentuating the normative character of the model, Lijphart implicitly argues that although the basic mechanisms of consociationalism have been derived from inductive studies of plural yet stable *Western* democracies, its core principles can and should generally be applied to all societies characterised by stark internal divisions. Later writings confirm this interpretation of Lijphart's words, for he would go on stating that 'consociational democracy is not only the *optimal* form of democracy for deeply divided societies but also, for the most deeply divided countries, the *only feasible* solution.'[2] Lijphart's 'categorical affirmation'[3] of consociational democracy has to be understood not just as the expression of firm belief in the empirical foundation of the model, but first and foremost as a mark of confidence in its normative character. From an analytical point of view, it seems highly doubtful that *any* theoretical model, or theory in general, could ever be accurately stated with such determinism—even though the search for this kind of 'universal natural laws' or 'perpetual causal relationships' undoubtedly lies at the heart of political and social research.

Even though not all consociational thinkers are as absolute in their views as Lijphart is, the interesting question is why one of the sharpest thinkers of comparative political science would make such deterministic statements. We may believe that his confidence results, at least partly, from the support consociational institutions enjoy on the practical and theoretical level. Today, consociationalism is widely acknowledged as 'the dominant model of managing ethnically divided societies' and 'few theories have had a more enduring impact on the thinking of analysts and practitioners of democratic governance than the consociational model'.[4] This practical and theoretical success has two reasons. First there is, in the

---

[1]   Arend Lijphart, *Democracy in Plural Societies: A Comparative Exploration,* 4th ed. (New Haven: Yale University Press, 1980), 1.

[2]   Arend Lijphart, "The Wave of Power-Sharing Democracy," in *The Architecture of Democracy. Constitutional Design, Conflict Management, and Democracy* (New York: Oxford University Press, 2002), 38. Italics added.

[3]   Stojanović, "Quotas et Démocracie" (PhD Dissertation, University of Zurich, 2008), chap. 7.

[4]   Rupert Taylor, "Introduction," in *Consociational Theory. McGarry and O'Leary and the Northern Ireland Conflict,* Rupert Taylor, ed. (London: Routledge, 2009), 1–2, references omitted. Taylor quotes in the first part Rob Aitken and in the second René Lemarchand. Cf. Rob Aitken, "Cementing Divisions?," *Policy Studies* 28, no. 3

words of Lijphart, the 'compelling logic' of the model itself. Over the course of history, 'power-sharing [i.e. consociationalism] was developed repeatedly and *independently* as a method of resolving and preventing deep conflicts.'[5] Consociational institutions were introduced in the United Province of Canada (1840–1867), in the Netherlands (1917–67), in Lebanon (1943–75 and from 1989 on), Switzerland (1943), Austria (1945–66), India (1947), Malaysia (1955, with the exception of 1969–71), Colombia (1958–74), Cyprus (1960–63), Belgium (1970), Czechoslovakia (1989–1993), and South Africa (according to the 1994 interim constitution).[6] Other examples include Northern Ireland (1972 and 1998), Macedonia (since the 2001 Ohrid Agreement), and, of course, Bosnia and Herzegovina since the 1995 Dayton Peace Accords.[7] Consociational interpretations have furthermore been suggested for the political functioning of European Union politics.[8] This overwhelming empirical set of evidence, stretching over more than a century and almost the entire globe, proves, in Lijphart's words, that consociationalism is 'the most rational choice to be made in the circumstances of potential or actual civil strife'.[9] In other words, consociationalism is a pragmatic, common sense solution in situations of violent conflict.

This pragmatism constitutes the second reason for its popularity. Consociationalism presents a viable option for integrating different groups into a common state. It does so without establishing a 'tyranny' of the majority over one or more minorities as the latter are given not only a voice in the political process but substantial veto-powers and group rights as well. Inclusion of all groups into parliament and government is an interesting option for the future setup of newly democratic states. This is, firstly, true for instances where the transition from authoritarianism to democracy happens in a non-violent manner, as was the case in Central and Eastern Europe after the fall of Communism. Here, the old elites wish to

---

(2007): 260; René Lemarchand, "Consociationalism and Power Sharing in Africa: Rwanda, Burundi, and the Democratic Republic of the Congo," *African Affairs* 106, no. 422 (2007): 1.

[5]   Lijphart mentions the 'compelling logic' of consociational democracy on two occasions: Arend Lijphart, "Power Sharing, Ethnic Agnosticism, and Political Pragmatism," *Transformation* 21, no. 1993 (1993): 97; Arend Lijphart, *Thinking about Democracy: Power Sharing and Majority Rule in Theory and Practice* (New York: Routledge Chapman & Hall, 2008), 278. The quote is taken from the first publication (original italics).

[6]   Arend Lijphart, "The Puzzle of Indian Democracy: A Consociational Interpretation," *The American Political Science Review* 90, no. 2 (1996): 259.

[7]   Brendan O'Leary, "Debating Consociational Politics: Normative and Explanatory Arguments," in *From Power Sharing to Democracy. Post-Conflict Institutions in Ethnically Divided Societies*, Sid Noel, ed. (Montreal/Kingston: McGill-Queen's University Press, 2005), 18.

[8]   Matthijs Bogaards and Markus M.L. Crepaz, "Consociational Interpretations of the European Union," *European Union Politics* 3 (2002): 357–81.

[9]   Lijphart, *Thinking about Democracy*, 278.

remain key players in the political process and have the comparative advantage of an already existing party organisation, which helps them in the process of democratic campaigning. The new elites, usually suppressed during authoritarian times, embark on their democratic journey without such infrastructure or experience. They naturally have a fear of not being able to accumulate enough votes because of this structural disadvantage. It is in such situations that consociationalism seems to be an optimal compromise for both sides, for their inclusion into government is guaranteed regardless of the actual voting outcome.[10] Secondly, this logic is far more compelling in instances where transition from one political system to another is accompanied by violence. In situations of war between different groups, consociationalism presents a reasonable compromise between diverse interests provided that the warring parties agree upon the continuation of the common state. It allows the termination of atrocities as the later inclusion in government and parliament, combined with substantial autonomy rights, makes such a post-war structure more likely to be adopted during peace negotiations than all other models. However, as we shall see in the next chapter, this logic is far more complicated and less compelling than presented here.

From an analytical point of view, the normative claim of universal applicability of consociational democracy has to be distinguished from the real-world success of consociational democracy and its appeal to political actors. That consociationalism was selected on different occasions as a result of diverse negotiating logics does not *per se* prove that the consociational model is *normatively* valuable, coherent, or superior to other forms of democratic system design. This holds true even if we assume that all of the cases mentioned above are indeed consociational democracies, and if we furthermore disregard the fact that several of them did not stay consociational, or sometimes even democratic, for a very long time. But it is true that consociationalism's real-world success presents a strong incentive to analyse the model in greater detail.

Implicit in the claim of universal applicability is not only (a) the *prescriptive* notion that consociationalism should be applied as a post-armed-conflict political system in cases of turmoil in divided societies regardless of the character of the social cleavage. It also includes (b) the *explanatory* notion that, after the implementation of a consociational set of institutions, the political system will function in a similar manner as in cases where the consociational logic has already been

---

[10] Although presented slightly in a different manner in this paragraph, the basic idea behind this statement was formulated by Stein Rokkan and has been referred to as 'the Rokkan hypothesis' by Arend Lijphart. Rokkan claims that the instrument of proportional representation was partly determined as the expected outcome by the democratisation process itself, for the latter represents a convergence of processes from above (the old elites) and below (the inclusion of the working class). Cf. Arend Lijphart, "Democratization and Constitutional Choices in Czecho-Slovakia, Hungary, and Poland 1989-91," *Journal of Theoretical Politics* 4 (1992): 207–113.

empirically observed. These two elements constitute the core of what I call *normative consociational theory*. This theory is based on the simple assumption that consociational systems are normatively superior to majoritarian systems because they increase the chances of establishing a stable democracy in deeply divided societies. In other words, consociationalism implies that 'under conditions of dissensus and segmentation only elite accommodation institutionalized in consociational devices can produce stability'.[11] The evolution of a normative consociational model based on empirically determined and causally interpreted relationships in consociational democracies constitutes a first shift in consociational thinking. Through generalisation and abstraction, consociational thinkers developed an absolutist framework for divided societies aspiring to become stable democracies. This process, however, resulted in a structurally weak model with only a few concrete theoretical assumptions.[12]

Before moving on to a proper introduction and critical discussion of consociational theory, we need to remember that its core claim is nevertheless a brave and noble one. It runs against the arguments of some of the world's greatest political thinkers. Reflecting on the theory's position within the philosophical realm, Brendan O'Leary notes that consociationalists 'follow Rousseau's declared method in *The Social Contract* that commends taking "men as they are and laws as they might be"' but they simultaneously object to Rousseau's claim that the sovereignty of a people cannot be divided.[13] Instead, they claim that by setting favourable conditions and incentive structures through the 'right' (i.e. consociational) institutional design, shared sovereignty becomes not only theoretically conceivable but also practically possible. In other words, consociationalists presuppose weaknesses in human character and offer solutions on how to overcome them in order to achieve a specific goal. One aspect of such human weakness is what led John Stuart Mill to famously conclude that democracy 'is next to impossible in a country made up of different nationalities' and completely impossible in a society where people 'read and speak different languages'.[14] Consociational theory disagrees with Mill's assessment as much as it does with a purely ethno-national reading of Aristotle's statement that 'a state aims at being, as far as it can

---

11   Brian Barry, "Review Article: Political Accommodation and Consociational Democracy," *British Journal of Political Science* 5, no. 4 (1975): 481.

12   For a detailed discussion of this shift and the relationship between normative and empirical consociational models, see Matthijs Bogaards, "The Uneasy Relationship between Empirical and Normative Types in Consociational Theory," *Journal of Theoretical Politics* 12, no. 4 (2000): 395–423.

13   Brendan O'Leary, "Foreword: The Realism of Power-Sharing," in *Imposing Power-Sharing. Conflict and Coexistence in Northern Ireland and Lebanon*, by Michael Kerr (Dublin: Irish Academic Press, 2005), xxi.

14   Quoted in Lijphart, "The Wave of Power-Sharing Democracy," 38.

be, a society composed of equals and peers'.[15] Consociationalism's core argument is that while the establishment and maintenance of democracy in heterogeneous societies may be *difficult*, it is not at all *impossible*, given the appropriate institutional and societal settlement.[16]

While disagreeing with Rousseau, Mill, and Aristotle, consociationalists can look back at an impressive and long intellectual tradition on their own. It starts with the sixteenth century philosopher Johannes Althusius, who coined the concept of *consociatio*.[17] Consociational ideas can furthermore be traced back to the writings of the two early twentieth-century Austro-Marxists Karl Renner and Otto Bauer.[18] The first modern scholar to develop consociational ideas—even though he did not label them as such—was the economist and Nobel laureate Sir Arthur Lewis who thought about the establishment of democracy in newly independent West African states.[19]

Lijphart himself borrowed the term 'consociational' from David Apter, 'who uses it in the context of African political systems for the type that is "willing to accommodate a variety of groups of divergent ideas in order to achieve a goal of unity"'.[20] While the accommodation component of consociational democracy can be traced back to those writers, its elitist component exhibits some intellectual familiarities to the conservative model of democracy, as was put forward for example by Joseph Schumpeter.[21] Such a connection, however, must be treated with caution. When concerned with a definition of 'democracy', Lijphart specifically refers to Robert A. Dahl's concept of 'polyarchy'[22] while stating that the concept of democracy itself 'virtually defies definition'.[23] Conversely, Lijphart is not the only significant writer for the development of consociational theory. Other early consociationalists were scholars like Lucien Huyse, Gerhard Lembruch, Er-

---

[15]   Aristotle, *Politics,* quoted in Lijphart, *Democracy in Plural Societies*, 1.

[16]   Ibid.

[17]   Arend Lijphart, "Consociational Democracy," *World Politics* 21, no. 2 (1969): 211 fn. 14.

[18]   O'Leary, "Debating Consociational Politics," 3.

[19]   Lijphart writes about Lewis: '[I]n contrast to political scientists like Gerhard Lehmbruch and myself who *discovered* consociationalism a few years later, Lewis *invented* it by trying to think of what would be the logical solution to the problems in West Africa.' (Lijphart, *Thinking about Democracy*, 278.) See also Arthur Lewis, *Politics in West Africa* (London: Allan and Unwin, 1965).

[20]   Arend Lijphart, "Typologies of Democratic Systems," *Comparative Political Studies* 1, no. 3 (1968): 20–21. Lijphart quotes David E. Apter, *The Political Kingdom in Uganda: A Study in Bureaucratic Nationalism* (Princeton: Princeton University Press, 1961).

[21]   Joseph Schumpeter, *Capitalism, Socialism and Democracy* (New York: Harper and Row, 1956). I thank Martin Beckstein for directing my attention to this point.

[22]   Robert A. Dahl, *Polyarchy: Participation and Opposition* (New Haven: Yale University Press, 1971).

[23]   Lijphart, *Democracy in Plural Societies*, 4.

ic A. Nordlinger, G. Bingham Powell Jr., or Jürg Steiner.[24] Even though some of these early authors use the terms 'consociational' or 'consociation', their subject matters vary somewhat. For example, while Lembruch equates 'consociational democracy' to the Swiss term and concept of *'Konkordanzdemokratie'*,[25] Lijphart sees those two models as distinctly different.

We thus need to clarify the usage of the terms in the present context. In this respect, Lijphart seems not to have done scientific researchers a great favour in the way he treated terminological issues of his theory. In his first book on the subject, originally published in 1968, Lijphart coined the term 'the politics of accommodation' in order to describe the functional logics of his model.[26] At around the same time, he introduced the term 'consociational democracy' in his first paper dedicated to the empirical categorisation of different types of democracies.[27] It was later that Lijphart 'abandoned' this analytically useful terminology and started talking about 'power sharing' and 'power-sharing democracies' despite referring to the very same concept. This change, in Lijphart's own words, was due to the fact that he

> started to use consociationalism not only as an analytical concept but also as a practical recommendation for deeply divided societies. While 'consociationalism' worked well enough in scholarly writing, … I found it to be an obstacle in communicating with policy-makers who found it too esoteric, polysyllabic, and difficult to pronounce. Using 'power sharing' instead has greatly facilitated the process of communication beyond the confines of academic political science.[28]

In fact, many scholars have followed Lijphart's example and started using the term 'power sharing' in their *scientific* writings as a synonym for consociational democracy. Admittedly, 'consociationalism' is harder to pronounce and far more elusive a concept than 'power sharing'. Nevertheless, it seems unfortunate, to say the least, to equate these two terms even for the practical purpose of disseminat-

---

24   The respective studies are: Lucien Huyse, *Passiviteit, Pacificatie en Verzuiling in de Belgische Politiek: een sociologische studie* (Antwerp: Standaard Wetenschappelijke Uitgeverij, 1970); Gerhard Lehmbruch, *Proporzdemokratie: Politisches System Und Politische Kultur in Der Schweiz Und in Österreich* (Tübingen: Moor, 1967); Eric A. Nordlinger, *Conflict Regulation in Divided Societies* (Cambridge, MA: Center for International Affairs, Harvard University, 1972); G. Bingham Jr Powell, *Social Fragmentation and Political Hostility: An Austrian Case Study* (Stanford: Stanford University Press, 1970); Jürg Steiner, *Gewaltlose Politik und kulturelle Vielfalt: Hypothesen entwickelt am Beispiel der Schweiz* (Bern/Stuttgart: Haupt, 1970). These studies have been critically reviewed by Hans Daalder, "The Consociational Democracy Theme," *World Politics* 26, no. 4 (1974): 604–21.

25   Gerhard Lehmbruch, "Consociational Democracy in the International System," *European Journal of Political Research* 3, no. 4 (1975): 378.

26   Lijphart, *Politics of Accommodation*.

27   Lijphart, "Typologies of Democratic Systems."

28   Lijphart, *Thinking about Democracy*, 6.

ing consociationalism's central ideas. Firstly, such terminology is questionable because consociationalism presents *only one option* to share political power in a polity.[29] After all, consociationalism's main 'competitor', the 'integrationist' or 'centripetal' model introduced by Donald L. Horowitz[30] and others, is also a power-sharing model. And so are the concepts of multiculturalism and territorial pluralism, according to a recent presentation by Brendan O'Leary and John McGarry.[31] Therefore, reducing the general concept of shared political power to its consociational reading is incredibly pretentious. Secondly, even from the standpoint of consociational theory the proposed terminology is inaccurate, confusing, and reductionist. Even though shared power in the form of executive grand coalitions is the key element of any consociational design, the normative and empirical implications of consociationalism reach far beyond that single institution. Consociationalism is more than executive power sharing; it is a complex system of institutions and systemic incentive structures that seek to achieve accommodation and stable democratic rule in severely divided societies. In the following, I shall therefore refrain from using the admittedly more elegant formulation of 'power sharing' and continue with the usage of the terms 'consociationalism' and 'consociational democracy'. I deem them accurate and useful in an academic context—and in no way esoteric, whatever characteristic of the model (or term) this may refer to.[32]

In the following sections, I shall introduce and define consociationalism properly and contrast the contemporary with the original consociational model. Special focus will be put on the shifts in consociational thinking that are of particular importance for the model of an 'imposed consociation', which shall be the subject of the next chapter.

5.1 Contemporary Consociationalism and its Critics

A rather simple set of assumptions constitutes the core of contemporary consociational theory. Accordingly, interests and demands of different groups in societies deeply divided by nationality, ethnicity, language, or religion can only be ac-

---

29   O'Leary, "Debating Consociational Politics," 37 Fn. 3. .

30   Donald L. Horowitz, *Ethnic Groups in Conflict*, 2nd revised edition (London: University of California Press, 2000).

31   Brendan O'Leary, "Power Sharing in Deeply Divided Places: An Advocate's Introduction," in *Power Sharing in Deeply Divided Places*, Joanne McEvoy and Brendan O'Leary, ed. (Philadelphia: University of Pennsylvania Press, 2013), 1–64.

32   It seems important to note that Lijphart uses the terms 'consociationalism' and 'power sharing' as synonyms; this does not apply to the concept of 'consensus democracy' even though Lijphart himself has sometimes regarded them as interchangeable. See Lijphart, *Thinking about Democracy*, 6–9.

commodated through the establishment of consociational institutions.[33] The alternative in the form of a majoritarian democracy is likely to provoke serious communal conflicts in territories with two or more communities, especially when the political system is based on a single-party government rooted in one group.[34] Consequently, the prospect of establishing and maintaining democracy in such societies is almost entirely determined by the degree to which the state structure follows the contemporary consociational model. This model relies on four institutions whose interaction can be summarised as follows:

> In a consociational democracy, [1] elite cooperation takes the form of executive coalitions in which the main leaders of all social groups are represented; [2] proportional representation in assemblies as well as proportional allocation of offices and resources; [3] autonomy for social groups in the spheres important to them, such as education; and [4] a mutual veto for groups that see their vital interests at stake.[35]

Let us have a closer look at the four institutions, as Lijphart has introduced them:[36]

Grand Coalition: Elite cooperation in the form of grand coalition governments has been termed the 'primary characteristic of consociational democracy'. It presupposes a genuine commitment of political group leaders towards cooperation and, as a result thereof, a 'coalescent' style of leadership.[37] In slight contrast to the general definition presented in the previous paragraph, Lijphart's definition of a 'grand coalition' does not limit elite cooperation to the executive branch. It merely states the principle that all major social groups or, as he calls them, segments[38] should be part of the larger governmental structures. Even though the grand coalition cabinet is seen as the 'prototypical consociational device', the cooperation can as well be institutionalised through formal parliamentarian commissions or *ad hoc* advisory boards with broad powers. As Lijphart explains, the 'essential characteristic of the grand coalition is not so much any particular institutional arrangement as the participation of the leaders of all significant segments in governing a plural society'.[39]

---

[33] Arend Lijphart, "Constitutional Design for Divided Societies," *Journal of Democracy* 15, no. 2 (2004): 96.

[34] O'Leary, "Debating Consociational Politics," 11.

[35] Matthijs Bogaards, "Democracy and Power Sharing in Multinational States: Thematic Introduction," *International Journal on Multicultural Societies* 8, no. 2 (2006): 119.

[36] In the following presentation I rely on Lijphart, *Democracy in Plural Societies*, chap. 2; Lijphart, "The Puzzle of Indian Democracy"; Arend Lijphart, "Consociation and Federation: Conceptual and Empirical Links," *Canadian Journal of Political Science / Revue Canadienne de Sciences Politique* 12, no. 3 (1979): 499–515.

[37] Lijphart, *Democracy in Plural Societies*, 25.

[38] Regarding the relationship between political institutions and societal divisions, see the next section.

[39] Lijphart, *Democracy in Plural Societies*, 31.

Veto Powers: Even though the grand coalition principle ensures representation of all groups within the government, it does not prevent for one group to be outvoted by a majority of other groups. In order to avoid such a situation when a group's vital interests are at stake, each of them is equipped with significant veto powers. It is somehow difficult to assess this provision theoretically, for it has to be understood as a flexible concept. As Lijphart pointed out in one of his later writings, this veto 'usually consists of merely an informal understanding that minorities can effectively protect their autonomy by blocking any attempts to eliminate or reduce it'; the major exception are countries 'in which one or a few minorities face a solid majority (…), and the minority veto is formally entrenched in the constitution'.[40] An informal as well as a formal interpretation of the veto powers is thus in line with the theory, especially since Lijphart qualifies this point by stating that it is *'usually'* applied in informal terms. The distinction between a minority-minority situation with informal veto powers and a majority-minority situation with formal veto powers is indicative in this case. But the decision on whether to chose formal or informal veto rights is not only predetermined by majority-minority relationships but part of a larger process of constitution writing in situations of on-going conflict.[41]

Group Autonomy: While matters important to the common state should be discussed and decided through elite cooperation on that level, in a consociational democracy each group possesses the autonomy to decide all other matters and execute their decisions autonomously. Decision-making authority is thus delegated as much as possible to the different groups, particularly in the areas of education, culture, religion, or language. Therefore, in his later writings, Lijphart calls this institution 'cultural autonomy' rather than simply 'group autonomy'. In practice, he says, the implementation of the autonomy principle has taken one of three main forms: (1) federal arrangements in countries in which state and linguistic areas largely coincide (Switzerland), (2) the right of religious and linguistic minorities to establish and administer their own autonomous schools which are supported financially by the state (Netherlands, Belgium), and (3) separate personal laws concerning e.g. marriage, divorce, or inheritance for religious minorities (Lebanon, Cyprus).[42] In other words, consociational structures rely on either territorial or non-territorial autonomy for the groups.

Proportionality: In a consociational setting, all groups are involved in the decision making of the common state. How much they have to say, however, is dependent on their share within the population, which is reflected proportionally in the composition of government and parliament. This usually prescribes list PR

---

40   Lijphart, "The Puzzle of Indian Democracy," 261.
41   See Donald L. Horowitz, "Constitution-Making: A Process Filled With Constraint," *Review of Constitutional Studies* 12, no. 1 (2006): 1–17.
42   Lijphart, "The Puzzle of Indian Democracy," 260.

as an electoral system and dismisses other propositions like alternative vote.[43] Furthermore, the consociational model includes the provision that the allocation of financial resources and civil service appointments follow the principle of proportionality. (In some presentations of consociational institutions, the proportionality principle is divided into its electoral and its allocation components and therefore counted as two separate consociational institutions.)

Naturally, the implementation of each of these institutions entails certain risks. For the moment, it is sufficient to say that all of them can be interpreted in a rigid or a flexible manner. Depending on what interpretation we choose, we reach completely different conclusions. For example, the dynamic of inter-group cooperation can be expected to vary substantially between a state with formal veto powers and a state with informal ones. While in the first case the inclusion of the other group into the political process is constitutionally required and thus without alternative, in the latter case it entirely depends on the will of the deciding politicians to follow what we could call 'the constitutional spirit' of including the other group's preferences. This leads to two completely different set-ups in terms of political strategy and the incentive structures the political system provides.

But it is not only the functional logic of the consociational system that depends on the degree of its institutions' rigidity. As Brian Barry has claimed, in cases where inclusion in government is constitutionally prescribed, the entire system can become instable 'because it means that any group of people (whether represented in parliament or not) who want to bring down the regime know that all they have to do to achieve their end is to make an "oversized" government unworkable'.[44] Constitutionally required group inclusion—a quota system, in other words—thus may exert counter-productive influences and hinder consolidation and political stability.[45] In theoretical terms, the presented principles therefore lack precision. Additionally, one has to recognise the close connection between the theoretical provisions and the empirical applications. The principles are formulated broadly, presumably in order to be applicable to different societies with little or no adaptation.

On the other hand, this also means that consociationalism is not a 'one size fits all' model but intrinsically adaptable.[46] However, such an interpretation is only accurate in reference to institutions constituting consociationalism such as electoral systems, mechanisms of governmental representation etc. These elements of the theory are indeed conceptually fluid and can be introduced differently depending on the needs of a concrete divided society. But the concept of intrinsic

---

43   Lijphart, "Constitutional Design for Divided Societies."
44   Brian Barry, "The Consociational Model and Its Dangers," *European Journal of Political Research* 3, no. 4 (1975): 410.
45   See also Stojanović, *Dialogue.*
46   Lijphart, "Constitutional Design for Divided Societies," 99.

adaptability of its components contradicts the consociationalists' general claim of universal applicability of the model's core principles. The underlying inconsistency becomes evident if we differentiate between (a) the general characteristics of the society, in which we wish to apply the consociational model; and (b) the way in which the consociational principles are implemented, which also includes the degree of rigidity. It seems obvious that (a) determines (b) to a large extent. But it is far less obvious why, independently of (a) and (b), we should expect a stable democracy as the final outcome (c). In other words, do the 'conditions on the ground', which are responsible for the *form* of consociation, not also apply to the working mechanisms and expectable outcomes of the said consociation? We shall return to this fundamental inconsistency of consociational theory in the next chapter.

Consociational thinkers largely agree on these four institutions as the foundation of contemporary consociational democracy. Nevertheless, these elements have never been equally important. Nowadays, the principles of group autonomy and grand coalition are deemed more important than veto powers and proportionality in terms of achieving democratic stability.[47] As we shall see, in earlier times the principle of elite cooperation enjoyed primacy over all other principles.

In empirical terms, the four consociational principles just introduced allow a categorisation of existing divided democracies. After determining whether or not a country is truly divided—in the sense that it consists of multiple socially based groups and that these societal divisions overshadow all political and social interaction thus preventing the existence of overlapping memberships—one can look whether the political system incorporates institutions like group autonomy, veto possibilities, grand coalition governments, or proportionality.[48] Depending on the degree to which a country incorporates the four consociational institutions, it can be classified as consociational, semi-consociational, or not consociational at all. We shall return to this one-dimensional categorisation of political systems in the next chapter as well.

---

[47]   In one of his latest writings, Lijphart therefore presents the consociational elements in a slightly different manner, when he notes that 'the successful establishment of democratic government in divided societies requires two key elements: power sharing and group autonomy. Power sharing denotes the participation of representatives of all significant communal groups in political decision making, especially at the executive level; group autonomy means that these groups have authority to run their own internal affairs, especially in the areas of education and culture. These two characteristics are the primary attributes of the kind of democratic system that is often referred to as (...) "consociational" democracy.' Cf. Ibid., 97.

[48]   This is the approach Lijphart uses in *Democracy in Plural Societies.* See also Lijphart, "Consociation and Federation," 513.

In the evolution of consociational theory, the empirical categorisation has proved extremely important in terms of determining favourable and unfavourable conditions for the success of consociational democracy. The existence of these favourable conditions 'makes successful consociationalism [i.e. the establishment of stable democratic rule] more probable and its absence makes it less probable'.[49] In a comparative study based on arguments presented by different consociationalists, Ulrich Schneckener has compiled a list of eleven conditions that affect the success of consociational democracy:[50] Consociational democracy is thus more probable to succeed (a) if the state is not dominated by a clear majority but there exists a relative equilibrium with regard to size; (b) if there exist no significant socio-economic differences between the groups; (c) if the groups are territorially segregated so that federalism can be applied; (d) if the groups are bound by an overarching loyalty; (e) if cross-cutting cleavages exist; (f) if there are different parties representing one group (moderate pluralism rather than national fronts); (g) if there are dominant elites; (h) if the parties respect the status quo and desire system maintenance; (i) if traditions of compromise exist; (j) if there is comprehensive participation in the system and at the negotiating table; and finally, (k) if the consociational solution comes from within the system rather than from outside.

It is important to highlight that these conditions only reflect explanatory arguments of success and failure. Although 'successful consociationalism' may be more likely under the above-mentioned circumstances, Lijphart has refrained from including them in his *normative* model, largely because of their non-deterministic character. Even if all the conditions are fulfilled, consociationalism might fail; and even if all of them are lacking, it might succeed.[51] Since a coherent normative model cannot allow such variation, the favourable and unfavourable conditions are largely irrelevant for the normative consociational model. This is especially true if one recalls that these conditions are idiosyncratic to country settings resulting from grand developments like migration, tradition, or history. In this sense, a constitutional engineer's capability to influence them is extremely limited, especially if we take into account arguments of path dependency. The usefulness of these factors thus lies primarily in their capacity for *ex post facto*

---

[49]   Arend Lijphart, *Power-Sharing in South Africa* (Berkeley: Institute of International Studies, University of California, 1985), 115.

[50]   Ulrich Schneckener, "Making Power-Sharing Work: Lessons from Successes and Failures in Ethnic Conflict Regulation," *Journal of Peace Research* 39, no. 2 (1 March 2002): 210–217. See also Lijphart, "The Puzzle of Indian Democracy," 262–3.

[51]   See Adriano Pappalardo, "The Conditions for Consociational Democracy: A Logical and Empirical Critique," *European Journal of Political Research* 9, no. 4 (1981): 366. A critical discussion of these factors can also be found in Matthijs Bogaards, "The Favourable Factors for Consociational Democracy: A Review," *European Journal of Political Research* 33, no. 4 (1 June 1998): 475–496.

explanations of success or failure, while their predictive and normative character is limited, though in some cases not entirely absent, as we shall see.

What I have presented so far is a vague set of institutions and assumptions guiding the theoretical thinking of consociational theory in empirical and normative terms. While all consociationalists usually share these considerations, they nevertheless remain closely associated to the works of Arend Lijphart. In fact, an unfortunately too common mistake of consociational critics is to base their evaluation of consociationalism on a purely early Lijphartian version[52] of consociational thinking. Because of some admittedly existing weaknesses in Lijphart's early understanding of the normative consociational model, those critics are almost inevitably bound to arrive at conclusions that put into question consociationalism's general adequacy as a normative model of post-conflict constitutional design. While I shall deal with some of those weaknesses in the next chapter in greater detail, I would now like to discuss some of the most prominent critiques against this kind of understanding of consociational democracy. It is important to note that these arguments have been addressed, and to varying degrees refuted by contemporary consociational thinkers.[53]

Liberals have put forward one of the most fundamental critiques of consociationalism. Since consociational democracy institutionalises group interests, the definition of group membership is crucial. In early Lijphartian theory, group membership is *a priori* defined for each individual citizen, for it constitutes the basic premise of an individual's interaction with the state. The latter recognizes its citizen only through his or her ascribed group membership because the political structures are set up in a way that reflects the central cleavages of the society. However, with respect to national minorities within consociational systems, this raises questions of democratic equality. An individual not part of the significant groups whose interests are accommodated through the state structure remains structurally discriminated against, for the system has no way to conceive of his or her out-of-structure existence. This practice of pre-determined group membership is furthermore questionable in terms of an individual's right to self-determination, which, in a liberal reading, should also include one's right to approach the state as a citizen equal to all other citizens. This would presuppose that his or her demands are taken as seriously as anybody else's demands within the political system. However, through a structurally prescribed favouritism towards the demands

---

52   What I call 'early Lijphartian' corresponds to what O'Leary and McGarry call the 'corporate' version of consociationalism. The latter's typology will be introduced shortly.

53   Brendan O'Leary has provided one of the best collections of critiques of consociationalism put forward by conservative, liberal, socialist, and feminist traditions. Furthermore, his seminal text includes a modern consociational rebuttal to those critiques. See O'Leary, "Debating Consociational Politics."

of the significant groups, an early Lijphartian consociational system is incapable of fulfilling such requirements. In other words, the consociational model may lead to some illiberal practices.[54] In the case of pre-determined group memberships, such practices become extremely problematic for divided societies. Consociationalists generally 'believe that certain collective identities, especially those based on nationality, ethnicity, language, and religion, are generally fairly durable once formed'; this does not mean that they are either primordial or immutable, as critics often claim, but rather that they can be 'mobilised in a politics of antagonism, perhaps especially during the democratisation of political systems'.[55] As a solution in conflict situations, consociationalism is therefore put forward as a matter of 'moral and political necessity'; one, which is forced upon decision makers by 'a hard confrontation with reality'.[56] In other words, it is only through the accommodation of those identities, whether one likes them or not, that an end to an armed conflict and a stable future democratic rule can be conceived.

There are three immediate consequences of such understanding. First, this assumption does not concern itself with the sincerity of the wartime identities. If they are of a genuinely endogenous origin, as consociationalists maintain through their 'durability' claim, their replication within the state structure might indeed be unavoidable. However, if they are the mere product of recent developments, perhaps even from outside the concerned society (spill-over effects), their replication within the system might strengthen an external and until recently inexistent cleavage. Consociationalism is not concerned with these kinds of distinctions, nor does it pay appropriate attention to the character and origins of societal cleavages. As Matthijs Bogaards explains eloquently, '[u]sing a metaphor from medicine, one could say that consociationalism treats the symptoms without dealing with the cause'.[57] Second, by their replication as the foundation of the post-war political system, all political positions based those wartime identities become *a priori* legitimate arguments. In a system where group membership is the only point of reference for political stances, acting against common sense solutions when they even marginally infringe on a group's rights is a legitimate strategy. The same logic may even legitimise political actions that are directed against other segments of the citizenry (national minorities), provided that they serve to protect the interests of one's group. In its final and almost unthinkable consequence, the primacy of group membership over all other legitimising principles for political ac-

---

[54] For a detailed liberal critique of consociational democracy, see Shane O'Neill, "Recognition, Equality, Difference," in *Consociational Theory. McGarry and O'Leary and the Northern Ireland Conflict*, Rupert Taylor, ed. (London: Routledge, 2009), 87–98.

[55] O'Leary, "Debating Consociational Politics," 8.

[56] Ibid., 9.

[57] Bogaards, "Democracy and Power Sharing," 121.

tions may even defend actions directly threatening the existence of out-groups. Third, the replication of wartime identities through the system has a self-enforcing effect. In this perspective, consociational critics maintain that consociationalism does not resolve conflict but, at best, 'it organises and regulates a stalemate around the relevant collective identities'.[58] It may not only strengthen existing identities, but also create new allegiances based on the identities to which the system responds. For example, in a society where these group memberships are enforced by an electoral system based on proportional representation, the formation of political parties alongside these lines can be expected; this leads to the situation that parties are not elected based on their party programme but based on the group allegiance thus undermining the democratic structure and creating new inequalities and inefficiencies.[59] As a consequence of all three critical points raised, one might end up *not* with stable democratic rule in a divided post-war society, but with a systemic construct similar to what the Bosnian political scientist Asim Mujkić has described as 'ethnopolis'. This term designates 'a community characterised by the primacy of ethnic belonging over the individual'. The primary characteristic of such a system is that this primacy 'is introduced through the democratic process of self-legislation', through which the individual is deprived of any identity other than his or her group membership.[60]

Modern consociationalism has responded to the critiques raised by liberals and undergone some significant changes. Most importantly, contemporary consociational approaches are divided 'between those who favour a "corporate consociation" and those who favour a "liberal consociation", or, differently put, between those who prefer "predetermination" and those who prefer "self-determination"'.[61] While an early Lijphartian reading of consociational democracy would correspond to a 'corporate consociation', John McGarry and Brendan O'Leary have been fierce advocates of the 'liberal consociation' model. They explain the main differences between those two approaches as follows:

> A *corporate or predetermined consociation* accommodates groups according to ascriptive criteria, such as ethnicity or religion, on the assumption that group identities are fixed and that groups are both internally homogeneous and externally bounded. This thinking indeed privileges such identities at the expense of those group identities that are not accommodated, and/or at the expense of intragroup or transgroup identities. Politicians associated with these unprivileged categories find it more difficult to thrive. A *liberal or self-determined consociation*, by contrast, rewards whatever salient political identities emerge in democratic elections, whether these are based on ethnic or religious groups, or on subgroup and transgroup identities. Liberal

---

58   O'Leary, "Debating Consociational Politics," 5.

59   Ibid., 6.

60   Asim Mujkić, *Mi, Građani Etnopolisa* (Sarajevo: Šahinpašić, 2007), 3.

61   John McGarry and Brendan O'Leary, "Iraq's Constitution of 2005: Liberal Consociation as Political Prescription," *International Journal of Constitutional Law* 5, no. 4 (2007): 675.

consociations also take care to ensure that the rights of individuals as well as groups are protected.[62]

In corporate consociations, the political system obliges voters to vote within their own segment and for their own group parties, whereas in liberal consociations all voters are on a common electoral register and may vote for their own group parties, but for other parties as well.[63] In consequence, this means that liberal consociations are better equipped to respond to changes in voter identity, as they potentially allow for parties to form around all issues and non-predetermined identities. If sufficiently successful at the ballot box, these parties may well challenge the consociational regime as such and request a change of system. This is impossible in corporate consociations. Neither do they allow for new identities to be introduced into the general consociational makeup nor are they tolerant enough to discuss political issues outside of the predetermined group-based framework. Here, change is only possible if the group representatives allow it, which, given that such change directly minimises their political power, is hardly ever the case.

In general, a liberal consociation takes the voter more seriously, as it allows for intra-group competition, whereas a corporate consociation simply assumes group cohesion. Consequently, liberal consociationalism is conceivable with a higher degree of voter inclusion. It is, for example, a liberal consociational feature of the 2005 Iraqi Constitution that local constituencies can autonomously decide whether or not they want to amalgamate into the larger federal region of 'Kurdistan'.[64] Conversely, since a liberal consociation does not *a priori* designate the voter to be a member of some group, it can hardly be accused of violating the basic principle of democratic equality or an individual's right to autonomously decide on how to approach the government. Furthermore, a liberal consociation possesses the potential to mitigate the self-enforcing effects of consociational state structures and may, under certain circumstances, prevent the emergence of an 'ethnopolis'. But the concept of liberal consociationalism is only compelling if the 'degree of liberalism' is reduced to a somewhat symbolic and theoretical level. After all, the more liberal a system gets, the less consociational it can be. Consociationalism relies on accommodating group interests; in order to do so, it needs to rely on certain groups and assume the salience of respective identities. Even if the system is open to changes in these group identities, as in the liberal consociational model, consociational institutions like group autonomy and veto powers strictly rely on prevailing group identities. Now, if one assumes that those institutions are constituted in a flexible way, and if one further presupposes that the salience of the original group identities, which the system currently accommodates, is virtually inexistent and that, consequently, the electorate votes are

---

62   Ibid., 675–6. References omitted, my italics.
63   O'Leary, "Debating Consociational Politics," 15–16.
64   McGarry and O'Leary, "Iraq's Constitution of 2005," 687.

based on new and overarching cleavages, one arrives at a basic conundrum: what is the merit of consociationalism under such circumstances? Or to put it differently: will the political system resulting from those configurations be consociational? It hardly will, I believe. It is therefore important to see that liberal consociationalism as a concept is still directed at accommodating wartime identities within the post-war structure, even though it does so in an admittedly cleverer and more liberal way.

To portray liberal consociationalism as something else would contradict basic consociational claims, especially when applied to post-war settlements. According to consociationalists, low levels of trust resulting from wartime atrocities, the predominance of group loyalties based on wartime identities, and the fact that the negotiating politicians dispose of armies, leave no real alternative for negotiators than to start with the wartime identities represented by those leaders. This is true despite the fact that exactly those identities may be responsible for the conflict in the first place. Critics of consociationalism have to accept that the 'compelling logic' is predominant at this point. Whether consociationalism as a state system, i.e. a constitutional order, will lead to a stable democracy and, what logically precedes it, a functioning state structure, is as a completely different question. This implies a distinction between the *general applicability* of the model and its long-term *quality* and *usefulness*. Knowing the shortcomings of implemented approaches and the weaknesses of existing theoretical models might, in the long run, lead to a comprehensive model that would solve both ends of the equation. I understand the concept of an 'imposed consociation' as a small contribution towards this noble and, for now, distant goal.

5.2 The Original Model and Elite Behaviour

The foregoing presentation of contemporary consociational thinking is the result of certain shifts in consociational theory. The accentuation of a more liberal character of the model has been described in the previous section. But there is a somewhat more fundamental change that can be observed by comparing the original and the contemporary model. Contemporary consociationalists put much emphasis on the nature of the four consociational institutions, their design and alleged effects, while remaining rather silent with regard to an element of consociational theory that enjoyed immense importance when the theory was originally formulated. When Lijphart first introduced the concept of consociational democracy in his 1968 article entitled *Typology of Democratic Systems,* he saw the 'nucleus' of consociationalism as follows:

> In fact, the essential characteristic of consociational democracy is not so much any particular institutional arrangement as *overarching cooperation at the elite level* with the deliberate aim of counteracting disintegrative tendencies in the system.[65]

Contrasting this statement with the contemporary understanding of consociationalism gives some insight into the evolution the theory. In fact, the above citation is from Lijphart's *second* treatise on the subject, even though it represents the first time he labelled the observed mechanisms as 'consociational'. In his book *The Politics of Accommodation*,[66] entirely dedicated to the political situation in the Netherlands, Lijphart already includes all of the functioning logics of consociationalism, but presents them in a slightly different manner. This is, of course, not a point of critique, for any theory is further developed as time passes. But the striking feature about this specific development is that the crucial variable of *elite behaviour* seems to have been lost in transition. It is therefore worth analysing Lijphart's case study of the Netherlands in greater detail.

Lijphart starts by observing a puzzle within so-called pluralist theory. This theory's main hypothesis, namely that plural societies tend to be less stable democracies than homogenous ones, is evidently contradicted by the plural, yet stable case of the Netherlands. Lijphart's goal is to analyse this deviant case in some detail, not in order to propose a completely new theory or even a new approach, but simply to introduce a new variable into pluralist theory: elite behaviour. The Netherlands thereby qualifies as a plural society because of its two basic cleavages of class and religion that crosscut each other and lead to a four-fold division of the citizenry into Catholics, Calvinists, Socialists (secular lower and middle strata), and Liberals (secular upper and middle strata). Each of these blocks (that in Dutch are called *zuilen*, i.e. pillars) has a societal base consisting of political parties, interest groups, media for communication, separate schools and education, social organisations etc. Furthermore, as Lijphart shows, even the interpersonal relations are more frequent within a block than between blocks. The only factor binding the Dutch citizenry together is a 'narrow national consensus', based on a weak Dutch nationalism: 'the feeling of belonging to a common nation as well as to one's own block'.[67] But while this narrow consensus is an important prerequisite, the main reason why the pluralist Netherlands are democratic and stable is, according to Lijphart, the elite's deliberate pursuit of a 'politics of accommodation'.

---

65 Lijphart, "Typologies of Democratic Systems," 21. (my emphasis).
66 Lijphart, *Politics of Accommodation*. While the first edition of this book contains no mention of 'consociational democracy', the second edition includes a different last chapter dealing with the breakdown of the politics of accommodation. In this chapter, which is theoretically similar to the article 'Typologies of Democratic Societies', the concept of consociational democracy is introduced.
67 Ibid., 79. National symbols like the monarchy or the airline KLM strengthen this national consensus.

This policy was first introduced in 1917 in order to overcome three divisions that potentially threatened the survival of the Netherlands: (1) the question of the division between church and state, particularly with regards to education, (2) the franchise issue, (3) and the question of collective bargaining and the rights of labour. The elites realised the perils if these questions—virulent since 1878—remained unresolved. Consequently, they came together and found solutions acceptable to all groups. This understanding marks the beginning of the system of accommodative politics, which, ultimately, explains the stability of Dutch democracy. As Lijphart argues:

> [The politics of accommodation] is the secret to [the Netherlands'] success. The term accommodation is here used in the sense of settlement of diverse issues and conflicts where only a minimal consensus exists. Pragmatic solutions are forged for all problems, even those with clear religious-ideological overtones on which the opposing party may appear irreconcilable, and which therefore may seem insoluble and likely to split the country apart. A key element of this conception is the lack of a comprehensive political consensus, but not the complete absence of consensus. (...) The second key requirement is that the *leaders* of the self-contained blocks must be particularly convinced of the desirability of preserving the system. And they must be capable of bridging the gaps between the mutually isolated blocks and resolving serious disputes in a largely non-consensual context.[68]

At this stage, Lijphart does not yet categorically affirm consociationalism as the only solution for stable democracy in divided societies. In fact, his explanatory argument has no normative connotation whatsoever. He is merely a humble analyst trying to explain how a specific set of rules and conditions has played out in a specific case. In light of later consociational developments, it is worth looking closely at his arguments. The Dutch politics of accommodation has some specific features. Because the general public is mutually isolated within the respective blocks, inter-group cooperation takes only place on the level of the elites. In order for it to work, three prerequisites need to be present: (a) the existence of a weak national consensus, (b) the belief that the maintenance of the system is desirable, and (c) the elite's capacity to bridge the gaps between the isolated groups. As far as systemic assumptions are concerned, Lijphart relies on two of them. The first one is coherence within the blocks, making the leaders of each block especially powerful. This coherence, according to Lijphart, is best maintained if the 'transactions between ideologically incompatible groups can be kept to a minimum'. In this sense, the 'self-containment of such groups and their relative isolation from each other can be a positive value'.[69] (Later on, vicious critics would interpret this assumption as an implicit argument for apartheid.) Isolation, combined with distinct lines of cleavages, thus strengthens coherence and leads to a dependent relationship between the leader and the people. The second assumption states that the

---

group leaders 'understand the perils of political fragmentation'; they thus have to commit to the 'maintenance of the system and the improvement of its cohesion and stability'.[70]

While these thoughts clearly show the importance of the elites with respect to the stability of the system, they also tell us something about the implied causality of the relationship between consociational democracy and elite behaviour. In the original version of the theory, the former is based on the latter. In other words, elite cooperation within grand coalitions is not an element or institution of consociational democracy but its prerequisite and foundation. The institutions of the Dutch 'politics of accommodation' were a mere reflection of the group leaders' willingness to solve potentially dangerous divisions within the society. In Lijphart's words, it was in 1913 when the cabinet, aware of the disruptive forces inherent to the three political issues at hand, 'courageously decided to attempt a solution to the dilemma'.[71] It was only later, after this form of cooperation was institutionalised through the Social and Economic Council, that it was properly 'anchored in the country's legal-constitutional framework'.[72]

What is particularly interesting about Lijphart's early argument is the relative unimportance of any institutional settings. Procedurally speaking, elite behaviour, in form of 'the politics of accommodation', leads to the establishment and institutionalisation of consociational institutions, which, in the long run, lead to stable and plural democracy. According to Lijphart, the only prerequisite for this mechanism to work is a *weak national consensus*. However, he does not specify what 'weak' really implies. In fact, he has no reason to do so, for his study has no immediate prescriptive character. But it is important to note that this national consensus has to be present *within the general public*. Apart from such general feelings of solidarity, the public is deferent. It trusts its leaders not to betray them. Consequently, the cohesion of the blocks and the willingness of the elites to cooperate are sufficient conditions to sustain the system. These configurations allow the leaders to pursue a coalescent style of behaviour towards other group interests, even when the public does not approve of a specific action. Lijphart illustrates this with the example of a private radio station that was appreciated by the general public, but later abolished by the government because it destabilised the existing, group-based stations. 'On a major and deeply felt issue, the elite managed not only to defy public opinion, but to do so with the people's approval'.[73]

To conclude this section: In the original consociational argument, patterns of inter-elite accommodation 'form an independent variable that may impede and

---

[70]   Ibid., 216.
[71]   Ibid., 110.
[72]   Ibid., 112.
[73]   Ibid., 161–2.

reverse the centrifugal forces [of cultural fragmentation] at the level of the masses'; elites must govern 'by forming some kind of elite cartel' and purposely depoliticise seemingly controversial matters, so that these can be 'treated in technocratic terms so as to prevent them from catching ideological fire'.[74] This generally includes bargaining behind closed doors. What is of particular importance for the central argument of the present study is that, in the original consociational model, elections play only a secondary role. The processes linked to the rule of the elites

> reduce the importance of elections and even the direct accountability of leaders. Elections are conducted in strong ideological terms. Since political groups cater above all to their own particular ideological clienteles, elections result in little real change. Elite groups therefore remain largely insulated from direct political upsets. And they need this insulation to work out the careful compromises that serve to stabilize highly divided societies. (...) Autonomous elite politics therefore presuppose that the electorate on the whole play a rather passive role—as both a condition and a consequence of stable politics in divided societies.[75]

5.3 The Origins of Cooperation

By comparing the original to the contemporary model, one can observe a third shift in consociational thinking. In fact, this last shift is a direct consequence of a change in the role of the elites, which was already hinted at in the previous section. In a comparatively recent contribution, Lijphart maintains that 'consociational theory places great emphasis on the contribution of prudent and constructive leadership in the development of successful power-sharing systems'.[76] Nevertheless, he admits that the importance of elite behaviour has changed over time. In an article published in 1993, he states:

> I now believe that, especially in my book *Democracies in Plural Societies* ..., I overstated the role of strong leadership and mass deference in consociational democracies. I now think that the two principal types of representative democracy—consociational and competitive and majoritarian (British-style) democracy—barely differ with regard to the political power of the elites and that the major difference between them is the elite's governing style.[77]

What Lijphart claims to have overstated is the strength attributed to the leaders and the deference attributed to the people. In other words, consociational arrangements are still a valid normative option for divided societies if there is no strong leadership and if the public is not generally deferent. What is key is that political elites in majoritarian and consociational systems will *behave* differently, in his words show a different 'governing style'. In a majoritarian democracy, government and opposition attack each other, which makes cooperation rather

---

[74] Daalder, "The Consociational Democracy Theme," 607.
[75] Ibid., 608.
[76] Lijphart, "The Puzzle of Indian Democracy," 262.
[77] Lijphart, "Power Sharing, Ethnic Agnosticism, and Political Pragmatism," 96.

difficult. By contrast, in a consociational system, there is no real opposition as all the groups are included in government and the leaders are generally willing to cooperate. This leads us to an interesting question with regard to the latter political system: From where or what does the willingness to cooperate with the other group originate?

In his case study of Bosnia-Herzegovina, Roberto Belloni has posed this question in a different way. He starts by stating that 'consociationalists never *convincingly* addressed the direction of causation between consociational institutions and cooperation'. He moves on to ask a fairly obvious question: 'does consociationalism encourage cooperation, or is cooperation the result of a previous implicit agreement among the elites that they must reach a mutual accommodation?'[78] The answer to this question necessarily remains contradictory because consociational theory argues for both interpretations. In the original version, elite cooperation was not only the *conditio sine qua non* of stable democracy in plural societies; it was, apart from a not fully defined weak national consensus, the *only* condition. This becomes evident if one looks at Gerhard Lehmbruch's explanation on how consociational systems emerge:

> Consociational systems come into existence when, in culturally segmented societies, the conflicts are repeatedly regulated by bargaining in such a manner that the results are perceived as favourable by each of the rival groups. Cooperative strategies of conflict regulation may then be adopted in a process of 'learning through success' and become internalised as norms which will be transmitted in the institutionalised socialisation process of the political elites (especially in representative parliamentary bodies, but eventually in bureaucratic organisations, too).[79]

It is thus the elite's willingness to cooperate and the good experiences they make that eventually transform into a consociational system based on these rules that, by now, have become norms. In the contemporary version, the relationship between elite behaviour and cooperation is more complex, as Lijphart explains:

> The structure of consociational democracy *strongly encourages* compromise but does not guarantee it. If the segmental representatives absolutely refuse to compromise, the consociation will almost certainly break down. *However*, the realization of this fact may well be a strong incentive for representatives to be more open to compromise.[80]

In this passage, Lijphart only seemingly concedes to his critics in stating that consociational democracy does not *guarantee* cooperation, only to argue that it pro-

---

[78]   Belloni, *State Building and International Intervention in Bosnia*, 49 my italics.

[79]   Lehmbruch, "Consociational Democracy," 379–80.

[80]   Arend Lijphart, *Power-Sharing in South Africa* (Berkeley: University of California Press, 1985), 95 my italics. This statement, of course, rests on the assumptions that the maintenance of a common state is desired and the perils of fragmentation are accepted. As will be explained in the next chapter, especially in post-war societies, these assumptions and their relationships to elite cooperation are problematic.

vides *strong incentives* for compromise in the next sentence. Looking at the normative consociational model consisting of the four consociational principles, one has to repeat Belloni's question regarding the origins of cooperation. The principle of grand coalitions does not contain any reference to the politician's behaviour nor does it prescribe a way of finding compromise. While they guarantee inclusion in decision making and autonomy, the other three principles as well do not explain *how* cooperation should evolve. The precondition of a weak national consensus is not part of the contemporary model (as applicable to post-conflict societies) and can thus not form part of the explanation. Logically, this leads to the conclusion that *cooperation must be the result of the system itself,* i.e. the product of the interaction of the four consociational principles. It is my understanding that this is what Lijphart means when he states that 'the *structure* of consociational democracy' encourages cooperation and compromise. Compromise is the only way to achieve any outcome in this system.

The changes in the role of the elites as well as the roots of cooperation thus raise the general question about the causality of the argument. Lijphart originally presented consociational democracy as an empiric model that developed over years in a specific country. In *Politics of Accommodation,* he does not yet specify consociational institutions but rather defines the 'rules of the game' for inter-elite cooperation.[81] It is in this context, for example, that he introduces proportionality as an important principle of doing business. A consociational setting thus develops over time as a result of elite cooperation. By contrast, in the contemporary model the causal relation is reversed: consociational institutions are the cause of elite cooperation, not its result. This is the reason why the establishment of consociational structures in post-conflict societies, or generally in divided societies, has so forcefully been advocated by consociational theorists: If one manages to bring the leaders of the different groups to agree on a common state, the institutions will do the rest. In this respect, Lijphart argues with regards to Bosnia, patience is the best option:

> In the Netherlands, it took about 50 years of power-sharing and autonomy to give the once hostile and antagonistic religious groups a sufficient feeling of security to moderate their attitudes towards each other and to create a less divided society. South Africa does not seem to have done badly under its power-sharing systems in the last 10 years.[82]

It is unclear to what timeframe Lijphart is referring when comparing Bosnia to the Netherlands. Does he mean the years 1878 to 1917, in which the Netherlands' problems emerged and were finally solved through the establishment of the 'politics of accommodation', or the period between 1917 and 1967 in which the con-

---

81   Lijphart, *Politics of Accommodation*, chap. 7.
82   Email to Roberto Belloni, 2003, quoted in Belloni, *State Building and International Intervention in Bosnia,* 49.

sociational system was slowly developed? Based on the notion of fifty years, the latter interpretation seems more probable. This argument, however, is hardly convincing. First, it is unclear to what segment Lijphart is referring when he says 'the religious groups'. Does he mean the leaders/elite or the general public? As we have seen, different assumptions accompany the roles of these two entities, with the ones being coalescent and powerful and the others being deferent and coherent. Second, he mentions the creation of 'a less divided society', which is a completely different goal than creating a stable democracy, the original aim of the model. Third, he seems to introduce another variable into the argument, the 'sufficient feeling of security' that is to lead to moderate, i.e. cooperative, attitudes. While it can be generally accepted that consociational theory—and any democratic theory, for that matter—is dependent on a secure environment, I fail to see the effect this general security would have on moderating behaviour, especially in the long term. Once security is established, it 'vanishes' from the incentive list and other factors determine the actions of the politicians. Rather than being an intervening variable, security is a key precondition for consociational democracy. Modern consociationalists, such as Brendan O'Leary and John McGarry acknowledge this point when stating that 'in traditional consociational accounts there has been an overly narrow focus on the design of, and need for agreement on, political institutions' while '[l]ess attention has been paid, by contrast, to issues common to violently divided places or those transiting from war to peace'.[83] They maintain that elements like the design of the police organisation, the demobilisation of fighting forces, or issues of transitional justice need to be addressed within a peace framework, for 'security arrangements must underpin peace processes and political settlements'.[84] Finally, and most importantly, Lijphart's analogy fails with respect to states where consociational institutions have been established in order to calm 'tense' situations, like South Africa or Bosnia. This point relates to the processes described above. The initial cooperation agreement in the Netherlands took only four years, 1913–1917, and basically found commonly agreed-upon solutions to three concrete problems. It lay the ground for further elite cooperation, but the institutions to articulate the positions of the different groups and to find common solutions developed over the following decades, largely as a consequence of changed elite behaviour due to the initial agreement. But in a society modelled after consociational theory, the institutions that had to be developed in the Netherlands already exist *in the beginning*. The elites do not have to invent them, but learn to work within then. This process may take its time, too. But it is of a decisively different nature than the one in the Netherlands.

---

[83]   John McGarry and Brendan O'Leary, "Power Shared after the Death of Thousands," in *Consociational Theory. McGarry and O'Leary and the Northern Ireland Conflict*, Rupert Taylor, ed. (London: Routledge, 2009), 45.

[84]   Ibid.

6 'Imposed Consociation'

6.1 Intervention and Imposition

The necessity to impose a post-conflict regime in warring societies can emerge from different reasoning. To name just two possibilities, there may be a wish to end brutal wars and human rights abuses or one to alter existing political, and perhaps even societal structures in order to fit a pre-defined set of norms and expectations. The former is usually referred to as 'humanitarian intervention' while the term 'regime change' describes the latter. Naturally, these different kinds of intervention reasoning revoke different instruments. In the case of humanitarian intervention, the use of heavy military equipment is usually needed, whereas regime change can be done either militarily, or diplomatically, or through activities of intelligence agencies combined with financial sanctions. All these actions, in one form or another, constitute interventions and/or impositions from an external actor into an existing polity. There is therefore a need to clarify the character of imposition with which we are dealing in the present context, namely the goals and instruments of imposing consociational democracy as a post-conflict model in warring polities. Furthermore, it is of utmost importance to distinguish between the act of imposition *of* a post-conflict regime and the act of imposition *within* a post-conflict regime.

The existing literature on humanitarian intervention centres chiefly on the question of whether or not to do it, while the nation-building literature allows for a structurally more satisfying approach to post-conflict societies. However, the latter is not free of conceptual friction either, *inter alia* because the concept of a 'nation' is differently understood on the two sides of the Atlantic. Francis Fukuyama describes the difference between the American and European approaches to nation building as rooted in the central question of the endeavour's goal and result:[1] Should nation building lead to the formation of a 'nation' in the sense of a community based on some elements of commonality? Or should the final goal of nation building be an efficient state structure founded upon common interests of its citizens? The former view is often associated with the European side of the

---

[1] Francis Fukuyama, "Nation-Building and the Failure of Institutional Memory," in *Nation-Building. Beyond Afghanistan and Iraq*, Francis Fukuyama, ed. (Baltimore: The Johns Hopkins University Press, 2006), 3, original italics. While Fukuyama largely agrees with this distinction, he rejects the underlying premiss of the European view that foreigners never succeeded in nation-building by pointing out that some imperial powers have indeed succeded in building nations in their colonies, such as the British in India.

debate, where the concept of the 'nation' is taken somewhat literally. The goal is to create a community of like-minded citizens that, in a teleological manner, expresses itself properly only within a territorial state on its own. In the latter, American understanding, citizens do not have to share a feeling of solidarity for nation building to be deemed successful. They only need to accept the common state institutions as their own; usually, such acceptance is the direct or indirect result of the benefits these institutions provide for a group, or an individual, as contrasted to the alternative of not joining the common political setup. What is meant is rather some form of *state* building, not necessarily *nation* building.

When one looks at the act of externally building either a state or a nation, reconciling these two approaches in normative terms seems impossible. The normative goal of external nation building cannot be defined without taking into account the abilities of the intervening power or institution itself on the one hand, and the characteristics of the society in which one intervenes on the other. In normative as well as practical terms, creating a stable and functioning state—however difficult it may be—is a much easier task than creating a nation, understood as a community based on a common identity. The latter relies directly on subjective factors such as acceptance of each individual and is therefore largely excluded from the realm of public rule; the former can at least be achieved by setting up a legitimate and efficient state structure because it only indirectly targets citizen identities. Nevertheless, both approaches assume, either as precondition or outcome, some identification of the citizens with the state; the main difference is the degree and the form that such identification takes. Fukuyama is thus right in pointing out that

> For all practical purposes, what passes for nation-building is a much more limited exercise in political reconstruction or re-legitimisation, or else a matter of promoting economic development. Outside powers can succeed at negotiating and enforcing ceasefires between, say, rival ethnic groups; it is seldom that they can make these groups understand that they are part of a larger, nonethnic identity.[2]

Within the present context, the use of the term 'state building' is more accurate than 'nation building'. In our discussion, nation building describes the efforts of nationalist intellectuals of the eighteenth and nineteenth centuries that sought to create their own nations based on certain elements of commonality. While the final goal of such efforts was usually the nation state, the legitimacy of this ultimately territorial concept was clearly rooted in the idea of nationhood of its people. In contrast, the concept of state building is much more rational. It can be understood as an exercise in creating a commonly agreed upon as well as politically and economically functional state structures in a polity that, for whatever reason, is lacking both. Common agreement thereby relies on the citizens' acceptance of

---

2   Ibid., 3–4.

the new state structure and its institutions, whereas its territorial circumference is usually a given. It is in this sense—and not by chance—that state building and political theory share the same fundamental goal: the *legitimisation of political rule*.

The normative concept of political legitimacy 'defines which political institutions and which decisions made within them are acceptable, and, in some cases, what kind of obligation people who are governed by these institutions incur'. This legitimacy is either rooted in *consent*, i.e. people implicitly or explicitly agreeing with the establishment and maintenance of political order; in *utility*, with the 'legitimacy of political authority depend[ing] on what morality requires'; or in *public reason and democratic approval* following Rawls' statement that 'political power is legitimate only when it is exercised in accordance with a constitution (written or unwritten) the essentials of which all citizens, as reasonable and rational, can endorse in the light of their common human reason'.[3] Consequently, the main goal of state building in a divided society has to be the establishment of institutions that the citizens deem legitimate; these institutions need to be making acceptable decisions, which the citizens feel obligated to follow.

In analytical terms, we may distinguish between three basic forms of legitimacy as it refers to the political system and its institutions: input, 'throughput', and output legitimacy.[4] Input legitimacy is based on a number of norms connected to 'the values of political equality, active citizenship and popular sovereignty';[5] it is primarily concerned with the processes behind the *formation* (in the sense of constitution) of political institutions. 'Throughput' legitimacy refers to 'certain qualities of the rules and procedures by which binding decisions are made';[6] in other words, it targets the quality of collective decision-making processes *within* the institutions. Ultimately, outcome legitimacy 'concerns the capacity of government to produce certain output and outcomes that actually contribute towards remedying collective problems. It is not the capacity itself which

---

3   Fabienne Peter, "Political Legitimacy," *The Stanford Encyclopedia of Philosophy (Summer 2010 Edition)*, 22 January 2012, http://plato.stanford.edu/archives/sum2010/entries/legitimacy/. Peter quotes John Rawls, *Justice as Fairness: A Restatement* (Cambridge, MA: Harvard University Press, 2001), 41.

4   For an overview, see Victor Bekkers and Arthur Edwards, "Legitimacy and Democracy: A Conceptual Framework for Assessing Governance Practices," in *Governance and the Democratic Deficit Assessing the Democratic Legitimacy of Governance Practices*, Victor Bekkers et al., ed. (Aldershot: Ashgate, 2007), 35–60. While introducing the concepts, Bekkers and Edwards refer to David Easton, *A Systems Analysis of Political Life* (New York: Wiley, 1965); Fritz Scharpf, *Governing in Europe: Effective and Democratic* (Oxford: Oxford University Press, 1998); Ewald Engelen and Monika Sie Dhian Ho, eds., *De Staat Van de Democratie: Democratie Voorbij de Staat* (Amsterdam: Amsterdam University Press, 2004).

5   Bekkers and Edwards, "Legitimacy and Democracy," 43.

6   Ibid., 44.

is judged but the intended and unintended effects which have been realized'.[7] Put differently, outcome legitimacy is concerned with the quality of *the decisions a political institution produces.*

It is debatable whether democracy is necessary in order for legitimacy to exist. If one bases the argument solely on output legitimacy, democratic principles are indeed not a necessary condition. Autocratic regimes, for example, are likely to produce superb outcomes in terms of general public safety (if one excludes the lack of security emerging from the misuse of a monopoly of violence by the political system itself from the considerations). With regards to state building in divided societies, however, one must not base the legitimacy of the political system solely on the quality of the outcomes it generates. By definition, a system's outcomes are subsequent to the *establishment* of said system. A restricted concentration on outcome legitimacy misses that under circumstances of armed conflict, the current political system has lost its legitimacy.[8] Before the legitimacy of any outcomes the new system is able to produce can even properly be conceived, the system itself needs to be deemed appropriate by the people subject to its rule. Under those circumstances, the legitimacy of the system is in large parts, though not exclusively, a consequence of *input legitimacy,* which includes the principles for the mechanisms and procedures of collective decision making. Once the system and its rules have been set up, one may proceed to determine whether the procedures applied and the decisions taken are legitimate with regards to the established principles and standards. This reasoning leaves but one option for legitimate post-conflict regimes: a democratic setup.

Democracy is furthermore inherent to the concept of nation or state building in that it is part of the existing philosophical consensus attached to the institutions and states performing such acts.[9] Admittedly, democracy as a human right is not universally agreed upon, nor is it always declared as a clear goal of intervening powers. But as long as one is talking about *Western international actors* (single states or military alliances such as NATO) and as long as one has a *long-term commitment* of those actors in mind, the practical *long-term goal* of outside interventions has always been the establishment of—however defined—democratic principles connected to economic prosperity. Even though stability-based, geopolitical arguments often prevail in the discussions of external intervention, democratic development almost always follows the stabilising efforts of intervening ac-

---

[7]   Ibid., 45.

[8]   Sabrina P. Ramet has made this argument with regards to the disintegration of the second Yugoslavia. See Sabrina Petra Ramet, *Balkan Babel: The Disintegration Of Yugoslavia From The Death Of Tito To The Fall Of Milosevic,* 4th ed. (London: Westview Press, 2002).

[9]   In this context, see also the remarks by Brandon O'Leary regarding the choice of consociationalism as a post-conflict regime quoted in the next section.

tors. This logic is hardly surprising for adherents of the Kantian inspired democratic peace theory, whose central hypothesis holds that democracies do not wage war against each other. In this sense, there is a security rationale behind this mechanism. Of course, geographic proximity between the intervening power and the state in need of intervention increases these inherent function logics. As history has shown, when intervening on the European continent in such a manner, the concepts of state building, democracy, and legitimacy are closely tied to each other. They can be separated analytically but practically they remain intermingled.

The incremental choice of consociational constitutional design in many cases of international intervention illustrates the inter-dependence between democracy and external intervention rather well. One reason for consociationalism's appeal in situations of international intervention is that such state-building exercises happen increasingly in ethnically or nationally divided places. This is perhaps a reflection of the general increase in intra-state conflicts as opposed to inter-state conflicts in recent decades. When international actors intervene in an on-going ethnic conflict, their *direct* and *indirect* objectives differ. They can have strategic long-term interests in the region and its stability, but they also might just be interested in ending the bloodshed and human suffering in a country. Whatever the reasons for intervention, the *immediate* objective is always to end the hostilities, which is, analytically and practically, clearly distinct from bringing sustainable peace in the form of a legitimate state.[10] On this level, consociational democracy seems the lowest common denominator promising at least the *theoretical* possibility of self-sustainable democratic rule in the future. It is thus a choice of reason and pragmatism, not passion and conviction. This is the reason why no internationally mediated peace settlement follows consociational theory to the letter as local hierarchies and the conditions on the ground have to be taken into account. The inter-entity boundary line in Bosnia-Herzegovina illustrates this point rather well. As Richard Holbrooke, the 'architect' of the Dayton Peace Accords, writes in his memoirs, it was among the hardest issues to negotiate at Dayton; but in the end, it turned out to follow in large part the front line of the war.[11] The situation

---

[10] It is interesting to note that Bosnia is no exception to this rule. Richard Holbrooke tellingly entitled his book 'To End A War' as the primary objective of international intervention, especially following the massacre in Srebrenica in July 1995, was to end the bloodshed in the region. Today, even critics of the DPA agree that this primary goal was successfully completed even though the treaty is a great burden on contemporary Bosnian politics.

[11] Holbrooke, *To End a War*, chap. 17, 18. This is, of course, not to say that the negotiated changes to the line were insignificant, but to merely illustrate that there is a gap between theory and practice. Conversely, the same holds true for the fact that the Bosniaks and Croats in Bosnia share one entity while the Serbs have one on their own.

on the ground determined the composition of the state, not some consociational ideal-type model.

But, as shall be argued in greater detail in a moment, consociationalism is more than an easy political solution determined by practical circumstances and pragmatic considerations. Normative consociational theory is a *theory of democratisation* intending to produce stable democratic rule. The political legitimacy of a consociational system stems in part from the institutions applied (group veto, group autonomy) and in part from the composition of the deciding bodies (proportional representation, grand coalitions). This combination makes consociationalism interesting as a post-conflict solution, especially since such procedural legitimacy can principally be guaranteed at the negotiating table. Whether it is sufficient to sustain the polity as a whole is another issue.

6.2   Consociational Democracy and the International Context

Until recently, the international context was largely neglected in the evolution of consociational theory. Consociational democracies and their structures were deemed more or less independent of the external circumstances in which their polities are situated. Within the theory, international arguments have been put forward solely to explain two specific phenomena. The first one is the apparent correlation between small-sized states and consociational state structures.[12] Arend Lijphart sees 'small size' as a favourable condition for consociational success as it 'directly enhances a spirit of cooperativeness and accommodation, and it indirectly increases the chances of consociational democracy by reducing the burdens of decision-making and thus rendering the country easier to govern'.[13] Especially the latter point is of importance as the smallness of a state renders it, to a certain extent at least, internationally insignificant. A small state is not able to pursue a conflict-oriented foreign policy.[14] But the international context is not only a favourable condition for the maintenance of a consociation. It can also serve as a catalyst for its establishment. In this second phenomenon, the existence of external threats is key. All the classical empirical examples of consociations were either initiated or strengthened during periods of international crises and world wars.[15] Under such conditions, political unity is seen as a better strategy than political quarrel, since an external power might exploit the latter to the disadvantage of the state in question. Of course, this kind of behaviour is not unique to (subse-

---

[12]   Kerr, *Imposing Power-Sharing*, 37–40; O'Leary, "Debating Consociational Politics," 30–36.

[13]   Lijphart, *Democracy in Plural Societies*, 65.

[14]   See also Daalder, "The Consociational Democracy Theme," 611.

[15]   Meaning Switzerland, the Netherlands, and Austria. See Lijphart, "Consociational Democracy," 217. For a critical discussion of the 'size-argument', see Pappalardo, "The Conditions for Consociational Democracy," 375–379.

quently established) consociational democracies. There are many examples of non-consociational states that in times of great crisis form grand coalition governments. Nor is a consociational system the guaranteed outcome of crisis-based grand coalitions. In divided societies, such coalitions lead to the establishment of a consociational system *only* if 'the cooperative strategies are not abandoned after the end of an acute crisis but become internalised as a routine pattern of conflict regulation.'[16]

But even though not formally part of consociational theory, the international context can nevertheless give important insights into the question of how consociations develop—a question rarely addressed in an analytical manner by consociationalists. As we have briefly seen in the previous chapter, consociations in general develop as a consequence of successful learning processes.[17] Following this argument, *imposing* consociational democracy is *a priori* impossible. Its mere coming into existence is based on the repetitiveness of the bargaining process that strengthens inter-group trust and leads to the conviction that consociationalism is the best way to deal with the challenges of political segregation. This argument runs completely against the logic of using consociationalism as an instrument for regulating group-based conflict.

But consociationalists are not as strict in their views. Quite to the contrary, they acknowledge that external actors, one way or the other, *can* impose consociations. As Gerhard Lehmbruch has explained: 'If, as a result of *octroi* or mediation [of external powers], consociational strategies are introduced and turn out to be advantageous for the interested parties, consociational norms of behaviour may be "internalised" in the process of "learning through success"'.[18] Following Lehmbruch's logic, a political system is not consociational simply due to the fact that it encloses consociational elements, but only if the underlying accommodation strategies are repeatedly applied and thus internalised by the ruling elites. *What can be imposed is thus not consociationalism per se, but rather the consociational structure, i.e. its institutions.* It is in the same vein that we have to understand Jürg Steiner's assertion that 'institutions of power sharing are a necessary but not sufficient condition to arrive at some level of democratic stability in deeply divided societies'.[19] In other words, the imposition of proper consociation-

---

[16]   Lehmbruch, "Consociational Democracy in the International System," 382.

[17]   Ibid., 378–380.

[18]   Ibid., 384.

[19]   Jürg Steiner, "In Search of the Consociational 'Spirit of Accommodation,'" in *Consociational Theory. McGarry and O'Leary and the Northern Ireland Conflict*, Rupert Taylor, ed. (London: Routledge, 2009), 201. Note that by combining stability and democracy arguments, consociationalists consciously blur the boundaries between those two concepts. They can thus claim that consociationalism is, and simultaneously is not intrinsically democratic: while attributing their theory to the democratic traditions, consociationalists claim that their approach only aspires towards a democratic system.

alism onto a system is not a singular, but a continuous event. Successful imposition rests as much on the imposed institutions as it does on the group elites' willingness and capacity to internalise consociational strategies of conflict resolution.

Given such complexities surrounding the imposition of consociationalism as a post-conflict instrument, it is astonishing that this approach has become 'the dominant model of managing ethnically divided societies'.[20] Apart from the repeatedly mentioned 'compelling logic' and the security considerations connected to democratisation, consociationalism's popularity can also be explained by the philosophical characteristics of the international system. As Brendan O'Leary suggests, the international community consciously imposed consociationalism in divided societies in order to promote international norms such as proscriptions against genocide or coercive assimilation, the need to reward democratic states and make non-democratic ones pariahs, or an existing bias against partition and secession in the international world order.[21] In O'Leary's view, the combination of these norms 'leaves international organizations and great powers—when they intervene in national, ethnic, and communal conflicts—usually confined to promote one of the three repertoires of conflict regulation: (1) territorial autonomy; (2) integration; or (3) consociation'.[22] In cases where option (1) cannot be applied due to geographically scattered ethnic settlements and option (2) cannot serve due to wartime hostilities and the predominance of different views of future state-models, only option (3) remains.

The largest shortcoming of contemporary consociationalist theory can be found in the assumption that the influence of external actors is limited to imposing this specific kind of political system. Consociationalists tend to conceptualise the consociational system in a country as an inwardly closed entity. They thus fail to see the interactions between the international system and the consociational polity. International actors can, and usually do, affect the implementation of the peace treaties as well as the maintenance of the consociational system, for 'the consociational model is not a self-sufficient model for the regulation of societies divided by ethnic conflict'.[23] The model becomes self-sufficient only when the locals have internalised the consociational norms as the basic principles of doing business.

It is precisely for this reason that Katia Papagianni proposes thinking of the transitional power-sharing phase immediately following the peace agreement as an *extension of peace talks*. According to her, external actors are needed in order to (1) bring groups that did not sign the peace agreement into the political pro-

---

[20]   Aitken, "Cementing Divisions?," 260.

[21]   O'Leary, "Debating Consociational Politics: Normative and Explanatory Arguments," 33.

[22]   Ibid.

[23]   Kerr, *Imposing Power-Sharing*, 32.

cess; (2) provide a secure environment for local politicians to continue negotiating issues not addressed by the peace agreement; and (3) prevent political stagnation in the transitional period by encouraging local politicians to take cooperative decisions despite being under pressure by extremist factions within their groups (outbidding politics).[24] Papagianni also reiterates the argument originally put forward by Lehmbruch that consociational politics needs some time to start working. External actors need therefore to assist the newly established political system because '[r]outine interaction and relationships among the parties are not yet established'.[25]

However, it is important to note that external assistance or pressure does not occur in a vacuum. External actors are themselves bound by their own agendas, timetables, and deadlines. External assistance can, therefore, go both ways, depending on the motives of international action: while positive exogenous pressures increase the likelihood of successful conflict regulation, negative external pressures lead to an actual decrease.[26] Although such statements may sound tautological, they direct the attention towards an important new variable, namely the *degree of external intervention*, or, as Michael Kerr puts it, the degree of sovereignty a country enjoys.[27] Including this kind of influence by foreign actors into the debate of consociationalism is important, for, under certain circumstances, such intervention changes the dynamics of the consociational system. It affects the elite's commitment towards cooperation as well as the political leaders' strategies to achieve their political goals. This is the core of the concept of an 'imposed consociation' that I shall propose.

6.3 The Concept of 'Imposed Consociation'

Consociational democracy is a flexible concept in that 'some [consociations] are more consociational than others'.[28] For example, a political system comprising only two of consociationalism's four main institutions—grand coalition, proportional representation, group autonomy, and veto powers—is less consociational than a system including all four of them. This one-dimensional distinction is as

---

[24] Katia Papagianni, *Power Sharing, Transitional Governments and the Role of Mediation* (Oslo: Centre for Humanitarian Dialogue, 2008), 3–6, http://www.hdcentre.org/uploads/tx_news/60Powersharingfinal.pdf.

[25] Ibid., 4.

[26] Kerr, *Imposing Power-Sharing*, 32–33.

[27] Ibid., 40. While intervening international actors influence the situation in a given consociation in a direct fashion, neighbouring states might also have strategic interests in the country and thus exert some sort of influence as well. While the former one's goals are rather clear as they have to justify the intervention towards the general public, the latter's motives (and especially strategies) are much more complicated to observe and almost impossible to conceptualise in a coherent theoretical model.

[28] Lijphart, "Consociational Democracy," 224.

relevant to a post-conflict society as it is to any other society. But it fails to grasp the concept of an 'imposed consociation' in its entirety, for the latter relies on a second dimension that crosscuts this first and that constitutes a unique feature of post-conflict societies: the degree of external intervention. Figure 6.1 illustrates the continuum with which we are dealing.

Figure 6.1 A two-dimensional representation of democracies

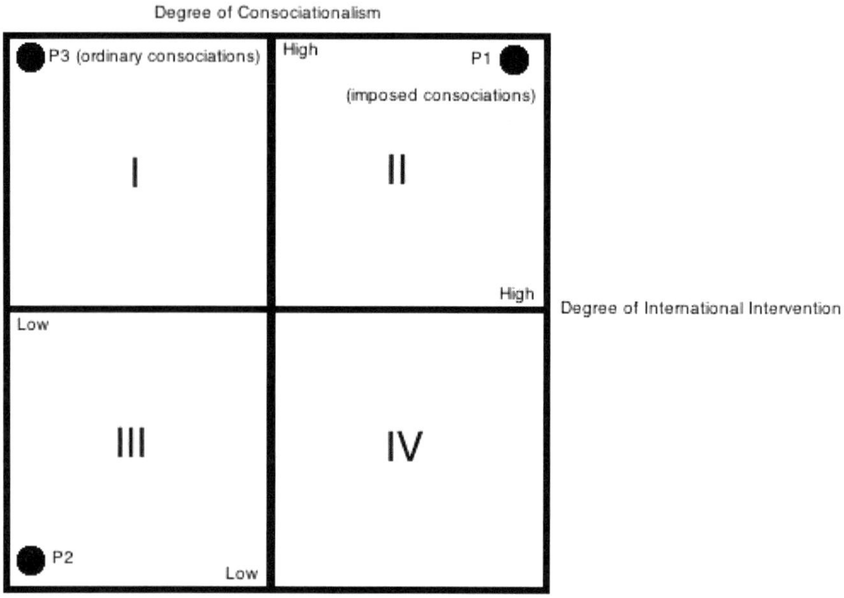

The x-axis represents the degree of foreign intervention into the system while the y-axis reflects the degree of consociationalism a system enjoys. Perfect consociations with a high degree of international intrusion can be found in the upper right corner (P1) while non-consociations with no international intervention are located in the lower left corner (P2). Leaving these two extremes aside for a moment, the graphic concentrates our attention to a much more interesting situation, namely the differences between states at the edges of boxes I and II. Located here are perfect consociations with full (P1) and no international intervention (P3). We shall focus on those two ideal types—termed 'imposed consociation' (P1) and 'ordinary consociation' (P3)—in the following.

But it is important to note that, just as the concept of a consociation itself has to be seen as a continuous categorical spectrum, an 'imposed consociation' has to as well. External actors can exercise different kinds of pressures on the existing system and their intervention strategies may change over time. While unlikely, it is theoretically conceivable that after establishing a consociation in a given polity, external actors refrain from using their influence and let the consociational mechanisms work on their own. On the other hand, it is also possible that external actors establish quasi-protectorates and, while giving the local elites all the consociational devices, they keep the key decisions in their hands. Of course, all variation between those two positions is conceivable as well. This ideal-type depiction is therefore in itself fluid; the degree of external inference may vary from one state to another but also within a state from one point in time to another. The same holds true for the degree of consociationalism, even though this position is probably much more stable over time.

Definition and terminology

Based on our reflections, we can now provide a precise definition of an 'imposed consociation' within the context of the present study. *The term 'imposed consociation' shall be applied when (a) external actors of some sort were crucial in the establishment of the consociational regime in a conflict-torn polity (imposition of), and (b) these external actors (or a fraction of them) continue exerting some kind of influence on the newly created political system (imposition within).* 'External actors' is an open concept, which can include collective international actors—like the United Nations or Peace Implementation Councils –, or be limited to particular states with a strategic interest in the region. The distinguishing feature of those actors is that they do not stem from the *domestic* political system, in which they intervene. They are therefore (largely) not responsible towards its legitimising mechanisms, but towards some higher norms of the *international* system or their own particular regime.

In order to avoid misunderstandings, it seems necessary to point out that the concept of an 'imposed consociation', as it is used in the present context, is only applicable when *both* elements of the definition—establishment of the consociation *and* continued influence by external actors—are present. If the establishment of a consociation is internationally negotiated and the international actors refrain from interfering with the inner workings of the system, we could, as far as semantics go, call this polity an imposed consociation as well. The system was indeed imposed on the local elites. This situation, however, is not captured by my term 'imposed consociation', for in this case international intervention can (probably) be neglected when analysing the inner workings of that system. This is clearly not the case when international engagement becomes pivotal for the continued functioning of the state itself. In this sense, my terminology is much more restricted than its name may suggest. This will become evident within the discussions of the inner workings of imposed consociational regimes.

The term 'imposition' is not without peril since it may lead to debates whether foreigners indeed *imposed* a post-war political system in a particular divided society, meaning that they did so *against the will* of the group elites who might have preferred a different kind of political order. This question, however, is of lesser importance than acknowledging the influence external actors exercise *within* the system *after* it has been set up. In this sense, *the second element of the definition is far more important than the first*; yet I nevertheless believe that the first element is a necessary precondition for the second to exist. If a political system grants an outsider the right to substantially intervene, the system itself has to have its origins in a prior form of intervention or imposition by the outside. This does not necessarily mean that the makeup of the system ran counter to the wishes of the local political elites or that the outside imposition equalled pressuring the locals into accepting a solution that they strongly opposed. It does mean, however, that the locals were not completely independent when they agreed on this kind of external oversight, which is why such kind of provisions are strongly bound to situations of emergency and loss of local political authority with war being but the most obvious one.

Given this qualification, is the term 'imposed' truly adequate? I believe it is, for what distinguishes this kind of consociational regime from the traditional notion—and, in some way, from democratic theory itself—is precisely the fact that an outsider can intervene *by imposing legislative and executive decisions*. As I intend to argue in the remainder of this chapter, the mere act of imposition (first in actuality, later even in potentiality) changes the functioning logics of the consociational system thus transforming it into a new kind of political regime. I believe that 'imposition' carries the terminological gravitas as well as the analytical accuracy and usefulness in order to describe the transformation I have in mind.

It is furthermore important to note that I do not consider imposition *per se* morally wrong or right; within the analytical context, the term should therefore not invoke any kind of negative or positive connotation. What we are dealing with within the concept of an 'imposed consociation' are the *consequences* of such action, which shall be judged based on their effects on consociationalism's main goal of stable democratic rule in divided post-conflict societies. Such a discussion does *not* require a moral assessment of the mere act of external imposition in abstract form. However, it does presuppose some discussion of the motives behind external intervention and behind such acts. These help not only grasp the general philosophical background against which our analysis is set but also influence local political leaders' perceptions of what behaviour can and cannot be tolerated by external actors. Their motivation and philosophy towards imposition within the system become powerful tools for explaining local politicians' behaviour. And it is only in this explanatory fashion that the former's attitude with regards to external imposition becomes relevant.

6.3.1   Assumptions: minimal consensus and group cohesion

Applying consociational conflict-regulation to divided societies has to take into account the effect continued international intervention has on the system. But before we are able to do so, there are additional configurations we have to examine when addressing the matter at hand. These configurations stem from the assumptions consociationalist make regarding the system. As we have seen in the previous chapter, there are not many pre-conditions a polity has to fulfil in order to qualify for a consociational solution. In a strict reading of the theory, only the *existence of a divided society* is required—a feature conflicting societies most certainly possess. Reflecting on the expected working of the theory, however, we distilled two other implicit preconditions: the existence of a *minimal consensus* regarding the common state and the existence of *intra-group cohesion*.

The minimal-consensus precondition is, as already explained, rather vague and therefore hard to conceptualise outside of the examination of particular cases. The basic question remains whether or not the signing of a peace treaty by conflicting parties can be seen as an expression of commitment towards the common state. After all, the agreement to a specific post-conflict regime can be the result of strong military and diplomatic pressures, which may leave the warring parties no real alternatives. In this case, commitment to the common state is the result of coercion rather than conviction. Such coercion, however desirable it may seem, can have negative consequences. The consociational features of the new system make political agreement easier but they do not guarantee some kind of identification with the common state, at least not in the short term. However, the imposing powers' hope is that once the system has started working, the trust in and identification with the political system—legitimacy, in other words—shall follow. The fact that those actors know that coercion is hardly a sustainable tool for democratisation helps for example explain why the creation of common state symbols is of particular importance to intervening powers. These symbols give every citizen the possibility to identify with the state.[29]

Since the establishment of new institutions may very well lead to identification with those institutions, such strategies are not *a priori* doomed to fail. It is therefore conceivable that, over time and under certain conditions, an understanding may emerge that is functionally equivalent to a minimal consensus. In this sense, we may think of the minimal-consensus precondition as some form of a 'conditional precondition'. In terms of achieving the ultimate goal, it is undoubtedly favourable if a minimal consensus is present at the signing of the peace agreement. But it can also emerge during the implementation process itself. This

---

[29]   As we shall see, the introduction of common license plates, a new flag, and a common passport were attempts by the international community to foster the feeling of community within the Bosnian population.

understanding is not to be confused with the position that the signing of the peace treaty *is* the expression of a minimal consensus by the parties. In my view, the peace treaty does not represent the *actuality* of a minimal consensus but only inherits the *potentiality* of the latter's emergence. In theoretical terms, this means that an absolutist reading of the minimal-consensus-precondition has to be rejected when dealing with the mechanics of consociationalism.

This, however, is not true for the second precondition, the assumption of group cohesion. When talking about consociation as a means to resolve, say, an ethnic conflict, can we really assume group cohesion and, as a result thereof, the relative unimportance of elections?[30] In order to answer this question, let us assume that there are multiple warring parties in a state engaged in heavy battles over territory based on different political and philosophical mind-sets. Say that each of these groups is backed by armed forces. The groups are likely to have separate political and military leaderships but a close cooperation between the two branches can be expected, for anything else would weaken the entire intra-group system. This close cooperation between the political and the military representatives, combined with the general spirit of cooperation within the group elites resulting from the necessities of the war situation (comparable to the grand coalition governments in situations of crisis), makes the assumption of general group cohesion plausible. When the international actors intervene in such a situation, they are forced to negotiate with the political establishments of these groups, which, at this particular moment, are indeed the main representatives of the groups. This means that the elite responsible for the implementation of the peace treaty (and the consociational mechanisms) is indeed in the position to rely on a coherent group structure.

But the general plausibility of this assumption does not exclude the possibility for intra-elite rivalry or, to put it in a softer way, the possible existence of different ideas regarding battle strategies or the future state *within* a group. While it may be defendable to assume that such currents are rather weak in situations of conflict, this does not mean that they have to *stay* weak in the post-conflict phase. The mere fact that the elite is willing to compromise can lead to the extreme faction's disapproval of the elite's actions despite their general support of their leaders. This is first of all true for cases where the consociational setting is employed as a transitional device not built on electoral support. As Papagianni writes,

> Following the signing of peace agreements, there are high public expectations for a new kind of inclusive and just politics. The public yearns for meaningful political changes, which, however, rarely come from power-sharing governments that tend to be concerned with maintaining the status quo and their grip on power.[31]

---

[30]   Regarding the connection, see previous chapter.
[31]   Papagianni, *Power Sharing*, 6.

Papagianni uses this situation in order to substantiate the normative claim that international actors should use the political vacuum of the transitional phase (i.e. until the elections) for empowering new political actors. She claims that, once established as a matter of fact, 'power sharing arrangements tend to prevent the emergence of new political leaders'.[32] However, the validity of this claim rests on the existence of a strong and corporately designed consociational system *as well as* the assumption of group cohesion. But assuming the existence of group autonomy in several political fields, what is to guarantee that there will be no different ideas regarding, e.g., the structure and function of the educational system? After all, consociationalism—especially in a liberal, but also in a corporate form—does not prevent a system from having a democratic discourse *within* groups regarding possible political concepts for the future.

It is in this sense that the 'war-leadership', even if it enters the post-conflict phase with a coherent group structure, will be put to the test through continuous elections. Taking the example of the Dutch pillars, group cohesion is enforced through the existence of distinct group-specific organisations like unions, media of communication, etc.; in conflict societies, the only real 'institution' holding the group together is the conflict-situation itself. Once the fighting has ceased—and other identification mechanisms have not yet been established or are not yet working properly—what is to enforce group cohesion at this moment?[33] The general assumption of group cohesion is therefore highly problematic and must be abandoned with regards to post-conflict societies.

6.3.2 Elite behaviour in imposed and ordinary consociations compared

When combining our thoughts about the non-existence of group cohesion and the influence of external actors in divided post-conflict societies, we can start creating a theoretical model on how political elites would probably behave in certain situations. On a *conceptual* level, an 'imposed consociation' is best understood by comparing the inner workings of this kind of consociation with a consociation that does not share its distinct feature: *the intervention prerogative of the so-*

---

[32] Ibid., 8.

[33] This is, of course, not to argue that group cohesion is desirable as a general concept, for the competition of ideas is a basic element of any democratic society. It is just to illustrate that in post-conflict societies we cannot assume group cohesion in the long term, perhaps not even in the short term. Talking about the behaviour of the elites, this means that they have a twofold task. On the one hand, they have to negotiate, compromise, and implement the decisions on which they agree with the elites of the other groups; on the other hand, they have to justify their behaviour to their own group if they do not wish to be voted out of office at the next elections. This significantly changes their incentive structure and influences their behaviour in a way that is not necessarily positive with respect to the establishment of a stable democracy in a post-conflict society.

called International Regulation Body (IRB). This term will be properly explained later in this section. But for the moment, let us start with an ordinary consociation; here, I assume a divided post-conflict society with a complete consociational setting but without group cohesion.

Ordinary consociation

The central argument of contemporary consociational theory is that the institutional setting provides the incentives for elite cooperation. For this to work, however, the decision power must lie entirely within these institutions; otherwise the system works in a completely different way and the advantage of consociational democracy is turned into a disadvantage. In order to understand this claim, let us imagine a consociation in a post-conflict society. All major groups are represented in parliament and government and a qualified majority of sorts is needed in order for major laws to be passed. Let us furthermore assume that the electoral system is designed corporately, meaning that each voter can only vote for parties and candidates of her own group, but that there are different parties she can choose from. To pass laws in this system, elite cooperation is needed, for every group can block decisions (by using their veto powers) and thus stall the political process. At this stage of the argument, no external influence whatsoever is assumed; the system is regarded as a closed microcosm separated from the external environment. How would political group leaders behave in such a consociation (which comes close to P3)?

We need to distinguish between the two roles the elites play in a consociational system. On the one hand, they are the spokespeople of their groups in negotiations with other groups; but as the governing party of their group, they are on the other hand also confronted with some kind of intra-group competition. In other words, an opposition challenges the current elite, as group cohesion is not present in this scenario. Consociational theory now assumes that election campaigns are necessarily dominated by a strong ideological dispute and that every group caters above all to its own segment.[34] In a corporately designed consociation, they have no choice but to do so as their competitors are members of the same group. The central question is who is to best represent this group towards the other groups. It is therefore safe to assume that political group leaders are likely to pursue a strongly ideological, group-targeted election campaign portraying themselves as the only real chance for achieving any progress for their group. On this platform the parties are elected into government and parliament. It is at precisely this moment that they form part of the grand coalition governing the country and thus become the 'group elite' on which consociational theory relies.

---

[34]   Daalder, "The Consociational Democracy Theme," 607–8.

But in order for any important law to pass, these elites—that have dominated the election campaign by using extremely ideological or extremist rhetoric—have to negotiate with the other group elites in order to find solutions for the challenges the state and their group face. The extreme positions they had at the beginning of their mandate need to be transformed into compromised, pragmatic solutions on which all the groups can agree. Put differently, there is simply no alternative to cooperating with others in order to improve the situation for one's own group. As Hans Daalder explained, consociational democracy 'tends to show a curious mixture of ideological intransigence on the one hand and pragmatic political bargaining on the other'.[35]

Inter-group cooperation is thus the only possibility in order to achieve solutions and pass laws. For each of the group-elites, this situation might lead to certain problems with their electorates and enhance intra-group competition. The elites have shown their readiness to change previously held (or at least strongly advocated) positions during the governing process, which makes them vulnerable to attacks by the opposition. It may also lead to voter transitions from the elites to other group parties. The only solution for the elites to justify their behaviour lies in their ability to persuade the electorate that the actions taken were necessary in order to get anything done. In order for this argument to work, however, the situation the electorate is in indeed has to have improved during the mandate or, at least, the electorate has to be convinced that it is about to improve as a result of the policies implemented by the elites. If it has not, the elite party runs the risk of getting voted out of office. Assuming that the group elite parties—or coalitions, for that matter—can persuade their electorate of the two issues just mentioned, their stay in government is likely. This has the additional advantage of showing the voter that compromise is not at all bad. In addition, it makes middle-of-the-road positions generally tolerable as long as they are backed up by results. But even if the elites fail to convince their electoral and the opposition group parties get voted into the government, they, again, will have to compromise and defend their compromises resulting in them adopting middle-of-the-road positions as well.

This is the key consociational argument at work with the difference that internal group-cohesion is not assumed; politicians wishing to become the leaders of their groups have thus to win against other candidates. They make promises based on which they are elected into the government and until the electorate realises the advantages of moderate political behaviour, the leaders are bound to take extreme positions. Furthermore, if their claims are moderate they pre-empt a later compromise and weaken their negotiating strategy. As participation in the government is the only way in order for social, economic, or political change to hap-

---

[35]   Ibid.

pen, parties will pursue the strategy that is deemed the most promising one in order to secure participation, i.e. to ensure their electoral success. This naturally favours extremist rhetoric. Once in government, they have to compromise—independently of their previous positions[36]—in order for any problem to be solved, otherwise the system is completely deadlocked. If a politician is not able to achieve positive outcomes for his[37] group due to his unwillingness to compromise, he is likely to be voted out of office since other parties may claim that a moderate position would be more effective. Over time, so consociational theory tells us, a *general* drift towards the middle can be expected thus guaranteeing political stability. To borrow a term from game theory, in this setting cooperation and compromise in government are a *dominant strategy* of the actors as long as results can be expected.

Some critical remarks on elite behaviour in 'ordinary consociations'
This view of the consociational mechanism under non-group cohesion conditions has an ideal-typical character. It is probably too kind to the consociational model. Overcoming extremist positions and adopting moderate ones is the underlying promise of any consociational argument. But it is also the hardest change in behaviour for the political elites to perform. First, one needs to consider the psychological aspects of the mere act of compromising, which, depending on the society in question can very well be equal to admitting defeat or surrender. The situation is aggravated by the fact that one has to compromise with people formerly fought on the battlefields. Second, there are also strategic considerations that make compromise difficult. Group elites are usually well aware of the fact that compromising makes them vulnerable and can produce intra-group opposition. Even under ideal-type conditions, they fear attacks from their flanks and stick to their extreme positions.[38] It is for precisely this reason that the establishment of a functioning and successful consociational system in which moderate positions dominate takes some time. But this general caveat does by no means put in question the central argument of the 'imposed consociational' model, nor the general mechanism of an 'ordinary consociation' describes so far. If one holds the position that consociational mechanisms are *per se* dysfunctional, one puts into questions the adequateness of this system for post-conflict societies. One may do so by claiming that consociationalism is unlikely to produce moderate positions and, therefore, has a centrifugal effect on the political system. This is an old critique and has

---

[36]   Of course, the compromises are not completely independent of the political positions held before, but the compromised solutions will soften the extreme character of those positions.

[37]   Even tough I shall, from time to time, use the male formulation for reasons of linguistic simplification, female political leaders are of course meant as well. The expected political behaviour is seen as being independent from the gender of the leader.

[38]   Donald L. Horowitz has suggested this aspect to me.

sparked numerous debates between adherents and opponents of the consociational model. But for the purposes of the present study and the model of 'imposed consociationalism', it is not yet necessary to take a position on the general adequateness of the consociational model for post-conflict societies. If one believes the advocates of consociationalism, the political mechanisms and incentive structures presented so far are to be expected. Under conditions of an 'imposed consociation', this generally positive incentive structure is reversed, which makes the system dysfunctional. If one believes consociationalism critics, the consociational system itself is already dysfunctional; in this case, under conditions of an 'imposed consociation', it would be even more dysfunctional than an 'ordinary consociational' system.

My elaborations so far assume the lack of group cohesion, but they do not necessarily assume the presence of different parties within each electoral corpus, at least not at the beginning of the post-conflict period. There can be situations in post-war societies, where there is just one group or party advocating extremely ideological positions and policies. But just as we cannot understand the groups as some kind of monolithic blocks, we cannot assume solely the existence of one philosophical current within them. In such cases, the hypothesised dynamics do not change much from the previous example. The fights are just not fought between an elite party and an opposition party (or parties) but *within* the elite party itself, namely between different wings. It is an easily defensible assumption that these differences in ideas, procedures, or even style of political behaviour will—in due time—take the form of genuine ideological or practical disagreements thus leading to the formation of different parties within the system. To illustrate this point, let us assume that there is, as a result of the conflict, only one party per group adhering to extremist positions present at the first post-conflict elections. Naturally, this party—perhaps made up of the war-leadership—wins the elections and gets into government and parliament. Here, as we have seen, it has to compromise. As compromises by nature produce winners and losers, some politicians, groups, or factions within the party are bound to be frustrated with some compromises, even though these may enjoy majority support. As consociational bargaining benefits from cross-thematic approaches—meaning that wins and losses can be compensated for over different political areas—there is virtually no chance that every party member is always on the winning side. Therefore, intra-group 'opposition' is likely to rise; and when it reaches a critical level, it will probably lead to the creation of new parties. Furthermore, wartime leaderships, even when channelled and articulated through political structures, tend not to be democratic or based on the rule of law. The application of such categories has to be seen as somewhat anachronistic in the context of conflict. But the introduction of such principles is a key post-conflict challenge and raises the possibility of intra-group disagreement. Whatever the argument, it results in the likely assumption that, in the long run, more parties simply have to emerge as a result of the introduced system; after all, if a one-party system prevails, its democratic character needs to be reassessed and so does consociational democracy's place within the field of democratisation theories.

There is a second assumption guiding the above rationale that may lead so some misunderstanding: the role of the masses. Consociational theory gives little respect to the voter and sees him simply as a follower. In fact, while explaining the Dutch 'politics of accommodation', Lijphart notes that it highly benefits from the deference of the public and their belief in their leaders who in return 'do not violate their followers' trust'.[39] In a more abstract form, Lijphart writes that 'widespread approval of the principle of government by elite-cartel' is a 'very obvious factor' favouring consociational democracy.[40] Reflecting on how the acceptance of middle-of-the-road positions can develop even in a system where extreme positions prevail in the beginning, this statement indeed seems obvious. People have seen that compromise as a strategy works and they are satisfied enough to leave the political system to their leaders. But is this assumption also true for consociational democracy in post-conflict societies? I do not think so, for the people in such societies have fought and suffered for their survival and were convinced by their political leaders to do so. Once the conflict is over, what is to say that the extremely salient ideological standpoints and the sacrifices made simply transform into a general political deference resulting in blind trust towards the leadership? The general public is likely to be in a grave situation after the conflict ends, confronted with a life in difficult circumstances, a weak or even non-existent economy, and little prospect for a bright future. At the same time, with the guns silent, the citizens' only possibility to express their views is through the political process. Is this kind of people likely to be deferent or apolitical? This assumption is hard to accept at the beginning of the consociational process, although there is some merit in its application for 'established' and 'functioning' consociations.

The 'imposed consociation' and the 'intervention prerogative'
Having established the inner workings of what I termed an 'ordinary consociation' applied to post-conflict societies, it seems obvious that this logic changes if we add the international aspect of peace implementation and maintenance of the consociational system to the model. Say that in order to maintain peace after a civil war, an international organisation, a state, or a group of states have decided to keep key governing functions in their hands while giving the local elites the consociational devices to regulate their conflicts. Let us assume that the external

---

[39]   Lijphart, *Politics of Accommodation*, 158.
[40]   Lijphart, "Consociational Democracy," 221.

actors have the power to override governmental and parliamentarian decisions and to enforce laws even without the consent of the government in question. This is what I shall call the external actor's 'intervention prerogative'. The actor can use it, but usually refrains from doing so if the local elites manage to achieve a compromise by themselves. (Naturally, this compromise has to be acceptable to the external actor with his or her own worldview and agenda.) These characteristics of international influence may seem exaggerated but they are not, for contemporary 'high commissioners appointed by great powers are undistinguishable from prefects of protectorates'.[41]

These kinds of consociations have been called 'complex' as they not only include the four consociational principles but, as Brendan O'Leary notes, 'they also invoke international efforts to resolve national self-determination disputes; international involvement in mediation, negotiation, arbitration, and implementation of peace settlements; and cross-border or confederal relationships (and sometimes institutions) for national minorities with their kin in other states'.[42] Contrary to 'ordinary consociations', the task in complex consociations is not only to achieve cooperation between different groups, but to 'heal the wounds' of the past and to prevent further violence through trust-building measures. In 'imposed consociations', this happens under the *supervision and with the active participation of international institutions*. Since widespread mutual trust is usually lacking after the signature of a peace agreement, international influence or, to put it slightly softer, 'help' is needed. The situation is furthermore complicated by the fact that in these consociations, state-building efforts have to be pursued together with nation-building efforts[43] augmenting the burden to the newly established political system; the state and its structures need to be legitimised. Since the crucial commitment of the elites to state and system maintenance cannot be ensured in the beginning, the establishment of controlling institutions (international missions or high commissioners) often seems a viable option to regulate the immediate post-conflict phase. This regulating body would give the local politicians as much freedom as possible in their daily work and only intervene when conflicts might endanger political stability or run against the norms of the international regulators. While its importance is evident, post-conflict models based on 'ordinary consociations' as described above fail to implement this kind of influence in their thinking and can therefore be deemed incomplete with respect to their applicability to this kind of post-conflict societies. The 'International Regulating Body' (IRB) and its 'intervention prerogative' are therefore crucial to the model of an 'imposed consociation'.

---

41   O'Leary, "Debating Consociational Politics," 35.
42   Ibid., 34.
43   Thorsten Gromes, "Democratisation of Post-War Societies: A Mission Impossible?," *European Journal of Political Science and Theory* 5 (2009): 418–41.

An 'imposed consociation', therefore, is by no means democratic, for it includes elements that cannot be altered or decided by the will of the people, which are subjected to the rules these elements pass and enforce. To paraphrase Abraham Lincoln's famous definition, while this form of government may be 'for' the people, it surely is not 'by' or 'from' the people. But the IRB is by no means a Hobbesian Leviathan either, for it is not equipped with absolute power; it rather is subject to conventions and norms of the international system, public international law, and (ideologically, at least) democracy. Its actions are directed not only towards the maintenance of peace, but towards the establishment of stable democratic rule. This, of course, reflects the temporary character of such institutions. A truly democratic state cannot exist if an IRB is present. That such a system needs to be abolished in the long run is therefore clear, yet the question of appropriate timing still remains unresolved.

The hope connected to the establishment of an 'imposed consociation' is that once the local elites have learned to trust each other and accepted the fact that in the new system only cooperation yields good outcomes, they will behave accordingly and the IRB could be abolished. Repeated interaction between the elites thereby performs the function of increasing trust-building measures. Unfortunately, this is not how this kind of system works. As I will argue, *the mere presence of an IRB, empowered by its 'intervention prerogative', decreases the willingness of the local politicians, i.e. the group leaders, to cooperate.*

Elite behaviour in 'imposed consociations'
To elaborate on this point, let us return to our previous ideal-type consociational thought experiment. There, we concluded that a general shift towards moderate positions is likely to happen. In contrast, the crucial point of an 'imposed consociation' is that once a candidate with extreme positions has been elected into government, he will *not* moderate his views in a consociation with an IRB. There will be *no general* shift towards middle-of-the-road positions, for the existence of an IRB changes the incentive structure for the political elites within the local political system. While in 'ordinary consociations' the inability of a group-leader to improve his group's situation is attributed to his lack of political skills, in 'imposed consociations' another excuse strategy becomes available as the leader can attribute his failure, in one way or another, to the IRB. In the process, he can also delegitimise the newly created state and prevent the emerging of the needed minimal consensus. Attacking the IRB thus becomes a potentially fruitful strategy, which makes the system itself an obstacle for the consociational setup to function.

There are various ways to imagine how a leader would behave in an 'imposed consociation'. Let us assume that after the first elections in a post-conflict society the extremist party of one group is elected into the government. Say that this party has fought for independence during the war and is thus not keen on cooperating in the new/old multi-group state. Consequently, its positions are designed towards achieving the war goals through the current system in which, to reverse Clausewitz's famous statement, politics becomes the continuation of war with other means. The party therefore tries to keep as much governing power as possible in its hands and, by using its veto possibilities, blocks any decisions aimed at making the central state functional. In 'ordinary consociations' such behaviour by the group elite would lead to a deadlock of the entire system and, consequently, would have to be abandoned over time. But in 'imposed consociations' the politician has no incentive to alter his position. Naturally, the IRB cannot accept such destructive policy and behaviour, for it threatens the maintenance of the entire system as well as the post-conflict stabilisation efforts. The reluctant group leader knows that important state legislation will be imposed despite his (and his group's) veto powers if the IRB deems it necessary. The IRB can thus circumvent the leader's veto, which means that despite his non-cooperation efforts the living situation of his electorate is bound to improve in one way or the other, say through the introduction of a stable economic system. There will thus be no deadlock, which does not allow the electorate to allocate responsibility appropriately. The latter will see an improvement of the situation and a fierce political leader that fights for their (extreme) cause against all odds.

Of course, the leader is in a delicate position during this process. He has to find the 'right degree' of non-cooperation; too much reluctance may lead to the IRB removing him from the political arena. He is thus likely to pick rather symbolic fights that are important for his group on a sentimental level and to which the electorate can relate. As long as he fights these issues, he can compromise on other things without looking weak. What is important is the *perception* that he fights for his group disregarding all obstacles. This is the platform on which he ensures his re-election and his actual performance during the legislative period becomes less important in order to get elected. This confortable situation furthermore allows the leader to gradually take on additional political issues on which he really is not keen to compromise. It also strengthens his negotiating positions towards the other groups and the IRB, which is likely to think twice before removing such a popular leader from office.

Nevertheless, in due time conflict between the IRB and the extremist group-leader can be expected. But it is the structural context of an 'imposed consociation' that allows the extremist politician to dominate the agenda and construct an argument against the IRB. In other words, he can blame the international actor for his own reluctance! The argument could be that his extreme positions, although not appreciated by the IRB, are simply necessary in order to safeguard the rights of his people and the accomplishments of the conflict. He simply cannot settle for less than his extreme position as compromise—in the areas he choses to fight— would directly threaten his people. Since in post-war societies fundamentally important laws need to be passed—e.g. the build-up of new security and financial systems—such reforms are almost always bound to weaken the positions of the groups, especially if those groups were never really willing to participate in the new state structure. As these decisions are deemed important, they are passed by the IRB thus allowing the extremist leaders to portray the IRB's involvement as designed against his group. In this case, *the maintenance of the status quo becomes a political victory and extreme positions the guiding rule*. We can thus expect that, with regards to intra-group competition, extremist parties will be contested by other extremist parties rather than moderate ones, if one assumes that representation in government is a party's main goal. This is the strategy that works and that in practical terms can easily be argued towards the electorate. This is, of course, not to say that other parties and strategies will have no success at all, but to argue that an extremist strategy remains an extremely viable option in an 'imposed consociation'.

One crucial conclusion from the mechanisms described above is the fact that once they have started working in an 'imposed consociation', the parameters guiding non-cooperative behaviour become stronger over time. This is due to the fact that more decisions have to be implemented and the perceived losses of the extremist politician's group become even more striking. However, the longer an 'imposed consociation' is in place, the lower is the 'fundamental' character of the generated decisions. In the beginning of the process, basically the entire state structure has to be defined and crucial state-building exercises are needed. Over time, the state is established and some of the decisions become part of the regular political process while others still keep their fundamental character, usually in a rather symbolic way. Decisions thus lose their immediate effect on the electorate.

Take the example of property rights and refugee return after a civil war. A decision whether or not refugees are entitled to their pre-conflict possessions (houses, apartments, land, etc.) in a territory that now belongs to another group is fundamental, both from a political and a societal point of view. The outcome of this decision directly affects thousands of people, not to speak of governmental institutions and international organisations that have to organise the return and establish the needed infrastructure. Such a debate, however, is typical for the first post-war period; but the longer the state exists the more distant the questions become so that they lose their immediate effect. This is not to suggest that the outcome of, say, a debate regarding appropriate procurement procedures for governmental institutions is of no public interest, but just to illustrate that the result of this debate has a lesser 'immediate effect' on the people's everyday lives. Consequently, this is the reason why the mechanisms of an 'imposed consociation' understood as an electoral strategy work better with some kinds of issues than with others. It is simply much more difficult to explain how one's group would be threatened by a procurement legislation than why it is threatened by, say, the establishment of a new state institution that takes competences away from the group level. This latter kind of argument is much more easily made and, consequently, the reason why one can expect the emergence of some symbolic debates within the context of an 'imposed consociation'.

The IRB's involvement is central to the argument regarding the inner workings of an 'imposed consociation'. But what happens if the IRB decides to intervene less often? This would be a defensible assumption since over time the decisions become less vital to the maintenance of the state. Even in this case, the workings of an 'ordinary consociation' with regards to electoral strategies and political behaviour cannot be assumed; in other words, the politician is likely to continue his extremist strategy. In due time, the strategy of external intervention will have become so powerful that it begins exerting influence outside the realm of actual usage. The actuality and potentiality of external intervention become interchangeable. In practical terms, the group leader has only to convince the voters that the IRB *may* intervene and that, as a consequence of this hypothetical intervention, the position of one's group within the common state will be weakened. If this claim is made with some repetitiveness, it may very well become the embodiment of successful electoral strategy within an 'imposed consociation'. In fact, having achieved a position of power, the politician can even deliberately provoke a conflict with the IRB thus strengthening his position within his own group. In such a situation, the IRB is confronted with a structural dilemma: it has to condemn the extremist positions by the group-leader and threaten to use its 'intervention prerogative' if consensus is not reached; but, at the same time, it is precisely such actions that help the reluctant group leaders to ensure their re-election.

It is of lesser importance that the leader only occasionally achieves desired outcomes as long as he can convincingly show that he is fighting for his group. It is important to note that the strategies of political leaders within an 'imposed consociation' are primarily aimed at one's own group. In essence they are perpetual electoral strategies and lack the traditional balance of consociational theory, where the ideological appeal to the group is balanced by a pragmatic policy in government. Continuance in government is dependent on election success, which advances extremist rhetoric. This rhetoric, however, should not be understood as factual statements and actual claims, but as the expression of the kind of ideas the electorate wants to hear. The guiding principle is not feasibility, but deeply rooted desirability. The politicians do not primarily act as honest brokers—as in the case of model 'ordinary consociations'—but as agitators and populists.

My elaborations on elite behaviour within 'imposed consociational systems' have an ideal-type character. The precise mechanisms are not to be expected in reality. Let me therefore sum up the proposed relationships in a more general way: My main hypothesis is that the IRB reverses the incentive structures in a consociational system since it prevents the emergence of real deadlocks and thus deprives the electorate of realising that the politician's behaviour is suboptimal for the achievement of stable democratic rule. Extremist rhetoric thus cannot be eradicated and non-cooperative behaviour prevails even if the IRB decides to intervene less often in the local system. The IRB becomes an integral part of the system, for its behaviour heavily influences the prevailing incentive structure within the consociational setting. As a result, the system is not bound to produce stable democracy, but challenging dependencies with respect to the IRB.

Changing the structural assumptions of 'imposed consociationalism'
In order to present the model of an 'imposed consociation', we introduced certain assumptions, most importantly the existence of an IRB with an intervention prerogative, but also a corporately designed electoral system. These characteristics of consociational post-conflict democracies are quite concrete, so that one may ask what would happen to the hypothesised relationships if one assumes different characteristics of the consociational build-up.

Brendan O'Leary distinguished between (a) *complete* consociations, where the leaders of all segments of an ethnically differentiated territory are represented in the executive; (b) *concurrent* consociations, where each significant segment is represented in the government and the executive (government) has at least majority support in each significant segment; and (c) *weak* consociations, where each segment has competitively elected political leaders in the government, but, in at least one segment, the relevant leadership has only plurality (rather than majority) support among voters.[44] These different categories may not only be applied to the composition of governments but also to the parliamentarian procedure. The mechanisms of 'imposed consociationalism' should work as expected in weak and concurrent consociations due to the competitive character of government formation. But I expect the logic to hold true in complete consociations as well, although here the competition is not for the representation in government *per se* but for the position of becoming the elite leading the group. Whether the mechanisms apply in this case depends on the salience of the dividing issues on which the elites base their strategies. If only one segment within the group can articulate these issues, challenging parties wishing to become the group leaders normally would not stand a chance against the existing 'ruling class'. This is what has happened in the Netherlands during the 'the politics of accommodation' when there was really an 'elite-cartel' running the country. However, even though the Dutch example proved to be very persistent, following the logic of consociationalism described above, competition within the segments needs to occur, especially in post-conflict societies. Therefore, the mechanisms of an 'imposed consociation' should also work within complete consociations. In fact, the distinction O'Leary

---

[44]   O'Leary, "Debating Consociational Politics," 12–15.

introduces is not as much a distinction in the *form* of consociation as it is an indicator for the *internal group cohesion* within the consociational system. As we have already established, the mere assumption of group cohesion within post-conflict societies has to be questioned.

Regarding the form of consociational democracies, one further distinction seems important: the difference in electoral systems. O'Leary distinguished between corporately designed consociations, in which the electoral system obliges the voters to vote only within their own group and for their own group parties, and liberal consociations, where all voters may vote for their own group parties but are not obliged to do so.[45] It is especially in this latter type that the logic of an 'imposed consociation' may change. Here, non-group parties with moderate views can offer solutions for every-day problems instead of involving themselves in 'group struggles'. Furthermore, leaders of moderate parties are themselves members of a group; moderate positions may weaken their status within their group but strengthen their position within the moderate members of the other groups thus leading to the mobilisation of an inter-group electorate. One precondition, however, would be the non-existence of territorial autonomy (or, at least, respective electoral boundaries) so that moderate, non-group-bound parties would have the possibility to actually influence policies in an environment not primarily defined through group memberships. Therefore, it can be expected that the model of an 'imposed consociation' is less likely to work where group autonomy is not fully established and a liberal electoral system is in place. Here, moderate parties may well be successful over time.

But also in cases where the ideal-type pre-conditions for an 'imposed consociation' are present, we cannot rule out the possibility of liberal, cross-group parties emerging. This is due to the fact that we have to abandon the consociational prejudice against the voter and not see him as some sort of 'ignorant follower' any more. He may well be tired of all the extremist rhetoric dominating the political system and realise that the improvements made are marginal, compared to the ones that would be possible if a coalescent behaviour were to be adopted by the leaders. In this case, he may give the moderates of his group his vote and let them try to solve the problems. For this scenario to happen, however, certain conditions need to be met. First, there need to be moderate parties the voter can choose from; following the expected path of development of parties in post-conflict societies, this is not always the case as existing extremist parties are as likely to be challenged by other nationalist as by moderate parties. Second, the cleavage that brought about the conflict needs to have lost some salience. It is only when the voter is sure that the extremist rhetoric regarding the position of his group and the threats to them are exaggerated that he can be expected to vote for a moderate

---

⁴⁵   Ibid., 15–6.

party. If those 'feelings' are as salient as during the conflict, moderate parties are not likely to succeed. Third, the voter needs to think that moderate positions do not weaken his group with respect to other groups. If he thinks that the members of the other groups are likely to vote for their extremist parties, he might see it as a danger to vote for a moderate party thus weakening his group's negotiating position. In this respect, it is probable that moderate parties have more chances of success when they are likely to achieve respectable results within the other groups as well. Fourth, the fact that an electorate choses to hand the government to a moderate party does not mean that extremist parties have lost their appeal forever. In fact, quite the contrary is true; if moderate parties fail to deliver results, the extremist parties always remain a fall-back option for the voter. These four points show that while a government with moderates is theoretically possible within the context of an 'imposed consociation', an extremist government is much more likely.

Until now, we have conceptualised external influence as direct influence of external actors into the domestic system through some kind of intervention prerogative. This is true as long as we are talking about state building in post-conflict societies and referring to the institutions or states that perform this exercise. But this is not the only form of external influence one has to take into account. As we have seen in Part I, when proposing the reframing of the nationalism discussion, Rogers Brubaker introduced three different categories of nationalisms, among them the nationalism of national minorities that hold the citizenship of one country and have ethnic ties to another historic origin. This drives the attention to neighbouring states with a similar cultural heritage as certain groups within the post-conflict state and poses the question how to conceptualise their influence.

Michael Kerr's book *Imposing Power-Sharing* has shown that the behaviour of the British and Irish governments in the case of Northern Ireland, and the behaviour of the Syrian government with respect to Lebanon were of crucial importance to success and failure of consociational experiments in those two cases. Kerr concludes that it 'was external intervention [i.e. by those states] that either strengthened or undermined the foundations of consociation, *depending on whether its influence was positive or negative*'.[46] This empirically founded statement can be used to infer that, in general terms, the influence of neighbouring states, not primarily charged with the nation-building experiment, depends on their strategic interests in the polity in question. A *general model* for the effects of intervention by neighbouring states can thus not be formulated. The goals of this intervention, unlike in the case of state building by recognised international actors, cannot be developed on a theoretical level to a degree that would allow the

---

[46]   Kerr, *Imposing Power-Sharing*, 198, my emphasis.

formulation of conclusions on elite behaviour. We can, however, state that local elites—especially when dependent in some form on the neighbouring state—are likely to act in a manner desired by the leaders of the neighbouring state as long as (a) they have no alternative and/or (b) their mutual goals are congruent.

6.4 Anticipated Critique of the Concept of the 'Imposed Consociation'

The concept of an 'imposed consociation' is, as of now, a theoretically deduced ideal-type model for implementing consociational democracy in divided post-conflict societies under conditions of external imposition. Before the model is strengthened through empirical evidence, there is a need to respond to certain critiques of the general assumptions and conclusions of the model. The two anticipated critiques presented in this section result from my own expectations as well as from comments received when presenting and discussing the idea as part of academic workshops and conferences.[47] In this section, only theoretical criticism will be addressed, whereas empirical criticism will be dealt with as part of the case study and the conclusions.

The first criticism concerns the role of the 'International Regulatory Body'. In the model, it was conceptualised as an institution that, while leaving much room for the local elites, intervenes in the system when it deems it necessary. This behaviour, it was argued, encourages extremist behaviour and the reluctance to compromise by the local elites. But could not the opposite be true as well? Could the 'intervention prerogative' of the IRB not be an incentive for cooperative rather than obstructionist behaviour as any uncooperative behaviour might lead to removal from office and, possibly, measures that punish the group as well? While such an effect cannot be excluded entirely, it seems rather unlikely that aggressive use of the 'intervention prerogative' would lead to more cooperative behaviour.

In order to explain this statement, let us return to our ideal-type 'imposed consociation' and recall that while each of the group leaderships has, at the beginning of the post-war system, some kind of legitimacy within its group, the IRB's legitimacy comes from the international community and the fact that it is

---

[47] Previous drafts of the model were *inter alia* presented at the PhD Colloquium of the Centre for Comparative and International Studies (Zurich, December 2011), the 44th Annual Convention of the Association for Slavic, East European, and Eurasian Studies (ASEEES, New Orleans, November 2012), the Colloquium of the Chair of Political Philosophy at the University of Zurich (March 2013), and the Young Researcher's Workshop 'Democracy in Plural Societies—Fresh Approaches' with invited guest Donald L. Horowitz (Zurich, April 2013). I thank the participants of these events, as well as many other colleagues with whom I had numerous private conversations, for their valuable comments.

backed by the powers that were responsible for bringing 'peace' to the system. As such, the IRB's role is distinct from the one of the local elites, while its powers and possibilities are much larger. But this does not mean that the IRB is in any way seen as a legitimate institution, especially within the groups that were not so keen with regards to the common state to start with. The IRB, just like any other post-conflict institution, has to prove itself useful and, as a result thereof, legitimate. This means that the IRB has to perform its duties carefully in order to either establish and/or not lose the support it has within the general public. This would mean the predominance of a policy designed to find compromise rather than imposed solutions. As Michael Kerr explains,

> While there is clearly the need for some form of coercive imposition of consociation in these cases [where external actors have an interest in regulating the conflict for the benefit of the society itself], its mishandling or selfish interpretation quickly deprives the formula of the legitimacy it needs for long-term success.[48]

The IRB is thus bound to act cautiously and cannot dismiss *all* public officials using an extremist rhetoric and condemn *all* such statements, especially considering the fact that the entire political elite is likely to be made up of such politicians. It is, after all, the consociational system itself that gave those war leaders the democratic legitimacy to represent their groups. However, this does not mean that in extreme cases where the foundation of the state is in danger the IRB should or would remain inactive. But would such action lead to more cooperative behaviour? Not necessarily, when, say, the politician removed from office enjoys support within his group; even though he may be gone his ideas need not be. Other candidates are likely to adopt a similar, yet slightly less extremist position in order to win this electorate over. Strong and repeated intervention by the IRB would thus have a balancing effect on the behaviour and rhetoric of the elites but not necessarily lead to more cooperative conduct. In certain cases, as we shall see in Bosnia, it can furthermore lead to the impression that the IRB is more benevolent to some groups than others thus, actually, enforcing the mechanisms of an 'imposed consociation'.

The second critique I would like to address is the issue of time, which was briefly introduced in the last chapter as well. It is, of course, impossible to dispute the argument that 'imposed consociations' will work in the same way as 'ordinary consociations' if one were to give the entire system some time to consolidate. Such arguments are often not theoretically or empirically founded and lack necessary precision. How much time should we give such a society? Five years? Twenty? Fifty? Furthermore, would international intervention not shorten the process instead of prolonging it?

---

[48]   Kerr, *Imposing Power-Sharing*, 199.

There is no doubt that consociational institutions need some time to start working, as Gerhard Lehmbruch has argued. Additionally, empirical studies suggest that the likelihood of a return to war decreases dramatically after a peace agreement has been in place for more than five years.[49] An 'imposed consociation' does not deny these findings, but embraces them. Yet it argues that the system itself does not provide enough incentives for cooperative elite behaviour. Given the fact that changes of a consociational system are hard to make, I fail to see the reason why time would change the incentive structure *per se.* Time can change the behaviour of the politicians, but if it fails to adapt the rewarding and punishing procedures connected to an 'imposed consociation', the same incentives remain virulent and strategically thinking politicians are likely to exploit them. This is especially true if the fundamental questions of the state have not been entirely solved in the first post-conflict period; those issues remain salient and can thus possibly be addressed in an extremist manner.

---

[49] Caroline A. Hartzell, Matthew Hoddie, and Donald Rothchild, "Stabilising the Peace after Civil War: An Investigation of Some Key Variables," *International Organization* 55, no. 1 (2001): 183–208.

Part III:
Bosnia
and Herzegovina

7 Consociationalism in Bosnia-Herzegovina

This short introductory chapter of Part III analyses the current political and legal system in Bosnia-Herzegovina. The latter originated with Annex IV of the Dayton Peace Agreement (DPA) and was further shaped through the 'constituent peoples' verdict of the Bosnian Constitutional Court and actions by the international community. This chapter serves as the background against which all political positions have to be compared in order to get an understanding of the country's contemporary challenges. Many of the themes and topics discussed as part of the constitutional structure shall recur in the next chapters when the positions of the local political leaders as well as the role of the High Representative will be further investigated.

7.1 The central state

Dayton envisions a central state with rather limited capacities. It is responsible for: foreign policy; foreign trade policy; customs policy; monetary policy; finances of its institutions and international obligations; immigration, refugee and asylum policy and regulation; international and inter-entity criminal law enforcement; common and international communication facilities; as well as inter-entity transportation and air traffic control.[1] All governmental functions and powers not specifically delegated to the central state remain those of the entities, as Bosnia's lower federal units are called (see below).[2] Effectively, this means that around eighty per cent of all state or institutional functions is located at entity level.[3] Bosnia is thus a highly decentralised country, even though the central state gained more competencies since 1995: 'In spring 2000, human rights and finance were added by the Bosnian Parliament; while in December 2002, justice, security and transportation were also included by the High Representative Paddy Ashdown in order to improve central governance and increase central state authority.'[4] Today, the central state also enjoys responsibility for the common armed forces and the state border agency.

The executive comprises two bodies whose competencies are, in practical terms, not always precisely distinguishable: the tripartite Presidency (see below) and the Council of Ministers, whose chairman is nominated by the Presidency

---

[1]   Constitution of Bosnia-Herzegovina, Art. 3, paragraph 1.

[2]   Ibid., Art. 3, paragraph 3.a.

[3]   Christophe Solioz, *Turning Points in Post-War Bosnia: Ownership Process and European Integration* (Baden-Baden: Nomos, 2007), 32.

[4]   Ibid., 88.

and approved by the House of Representatives.[5] In addition to the usual representation duties, the Presidency has the competencies to *conduct* Bosnia's foreign policy and to appoint ambassadors as well as to present an annual budget to the Parliamentary Assembly. It is also in charge of executing decisions of parliament,[6] which would technically make it *the* executive body. However, since the Presidency's duties are limited to areas specifically enumerated in the constitution, it is the Council of Ministers that is usually conceived of as the 'Bosnian government'. Its chairman is sometimes referred to as the country's Prime Minister.[7] The Council, in general, is responsible for 'carrying out the policies and decisions of Bosnia-Herzegovina' in accordance with the responsibilities of the central government or any other responsibilities the entities may delegate to the upper level. Its mandate is thus broader than the one of the Presidency. In addition, the Council is to report to the Parliamentary Assembly, including, at least annually, on expenditures of the state.[8]

The Parliamentary Assembly, as the legislative body, consists of two chambers. The (lower) House of Representatives is comprised of 42 members, two-thirds of which are *elected* in the Federation and one third in the Republika Srpska.[9] The (upper) House of Peoples has 15 members; two-thirds are *delegated* from the Federation (five Bosniaks and five Croats) and one third from the Republika Srpska (five Serbs).[10] All legislation requires approval from both parliamentary bodies,[11] following a qualified majority rule (see below). As statics show, it is the Council of Ministers that usually proposes legislation. In the legislative period 2006-2010, over seventy per cent of all adopted laws originated with this body. The parliament proposed some twenty per cent of the laws, while the Presidency submitted only a tiny fraction of legislation.[12]

---

[5]   Constitution of Bosnia-Herzegovina, Art. 5, paragraph 4.

[6]   Ibid., Art.5, paragraph 3.e.

[7]   This is especially true since the chair of the Council of Ministers is no longer rotating among different members, see Solioz, *Turning Points*, 111. Paddy Ashdown writes: 'On that day [20 December 2002], I met with the [sic] Bosnia's first non-rotating "Prime Minister" Adnan Terzić (his actual title was "Chairman of the Council of Ministers" but I insisted on calling him Prime Minister and the title has largely stuck).' See Paddy Ashdown, *Swords and Ploughshares: Building Peace to the 21st Century* (London: Weidenfeld & Nicolson, 2007), 257.

[8]   Constitution of Bosnia-Herzegovina, Art.5, paragraph 4.a.

[9]   Ibid., Art.4, paragraph 1.

[10] Ibid., Art.4, paragraph 2.

[11] Ibid., Art.4, paragraph 3.c.

[12] Nermina Saračević, "Parlamentarna Skupština Bosne I Hercegovine," in *Država, Politika I Društvo U Bosni I Hercegovini. Analiza Postdejtonskog Političkog Sistema* (Sarajevo: University Press Magistrat Izdanja, 2011), 244.

The Constitutional Court[13] and the state prosecutor[14] represent the judiciary branch of the central state.

7.2 The Entities

Post-Dayton Bosnia is composed of two federal units called 'entities': Republika Srpska (RS) and the Federation of Bosnia and Herzegovina (FBiH, see Figure 7.1). The relationship between these entities and the central state lies at the core of Bosnia's political and constitutional system. The entities have been declared the composing elements of the state,[15] and they are the reason for many discussions regarding Bosnia's constitutional character. Since the latter is nowhere defined in absolute terms, Bosnia has been termed an 'asymmetric confederation', a 'union', or even a 'federation *sui generis*' with regards to the competencies of the entities as opposed to those of the state.[16] We shall encounter the political discussions surrounding this relationship soon enough and can therefore concentrate on the legal structure for the moment.

As already mentioned, the entities are responsible for all policies not specifically deemed the competencies of the central government. As reminiscence of the war, the entities have the right to 'special parallel relationships with neighbouring states',[17] which concretely means that they can sign special relationship agreements with Croatia (for the FBiH) and Serbia (for the RS), respectively. They may also in general enter into international agreements with states and international organisation, provided the BiH Parliamentary Assembly approves it.[18] Despite this limited right to foreign policy, it is clear that only the central state enjoys subjectivity according to international law. Regardless of an ultimate determination of the state's character, the entities are lower federal units and not states, even though politicians, especially those from Republika Srpska, tend to conceive of them as such. The entities and their constitutions are subordinated to the constitution of the central state and must therefore not contradict it.[19] The Constitutional Court upheld this provision in its 'constituent peoples' verdict (see below).

---

[13] Constitution of Bosnia-Herzegovina, Art. 6.

[14] Maja Sahadžić, "Priroda političkog sistema u Bosni i Hercegovini," in *Država, Politika i Društvo u Bosni i Hercegovini. Analiza postdejtonskog političkog sistema* (Sarajevo: University Press Magistrat Izdanja, 2011), 16.

[15] Constitution of Bosnia-Herzegovina, Art. 1, paragraph 3.

[16] Sahadžić, "Priroda političkog sistema u Bosni i Hercegovini," 19.

[17] Constitution of Bosnia-Herzegovina, Art. 3, paragraph 2.a.

[18] Ibid., Art. 3, paragraph 2.d.

[19] Ibid., Art. 3, paragraph 3.b.

Figure 7.1 The Entities of Bosnia and Herzegovina

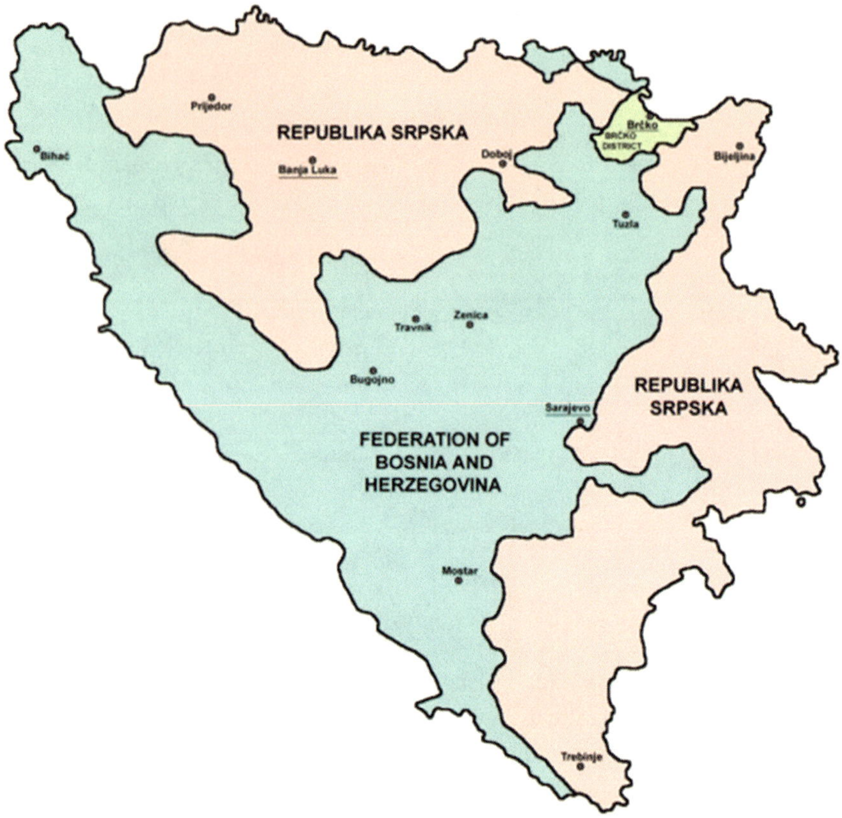

Source: Wikipedia, http://en.wikipedia.org/wiki/File:Map_Bih_entities.png, last accessed 20 Aug 2013.

From a legal perspective, it is therefore inaccurate when the president of RS, Milorad Dodik, claims that 'Serbs as a people have two countries, Serbia and Republika Srpska. RS has all the criteria of a state: territory, government, a people. And these are criteria from Montevideo'.[20] The references to the Montevideo-Convention of 1933 and to the 'three elements theory' of international law associated with Georg Jellinek may give the impression that Dodik has indeed a point. But while he is partially correct in his understanding of two of the three elements (people and territory), he is mistaken to think of the third, government, as simply meaning the existence of a body governing the country. What is rather meant is the prescription of sovereign governance (*Staatsgewalt*) over the territory and the people, which clearly excludes federal units from being full subjects of interna-

---

[20] *Oslobođenje*, "Dodik: Serbs Have Two Countries—Serbia and Republika Srpska," *Oslobođenje*, 15 May 2013, http://www.oslobodjenje.ba/daily-news/dodik-serbs-have-two-countries--serbia-and-republika-srpska. Accessed 17 August 2013.

tional law.[21] Otherwise all territorial units of a federal state could think of themselves as states, which can hardly be the intention of international law. Furthermore, states defined according to the Montevideo criteria must also fulfil a forth condition, namely the 'capacity to enter into relations with the other states'. While this prerequisite is not regarded as necessary according to international case law and practice,[22] the omission of this condition testifies to the political nature of the argument. The entities' foreign policy capacities are extremely limited, which makes it hard to argue for fulfilment of this criterion. But its omission implicitly admits the existence of another set of legal norms that may contradict, amend, or even nullify the Montevideo criteria. From a legal perspective, this makes the argument of RS's 'statehood', based on the (partial) fulfilment of the Montevideo criteria inherently flawed and inconsistent.

There can be no doubt that the RS decision makers are well aware of the legal inaccuracy of their argument. When Nebojša Radmanović, the Serb member in Bosnia's presidency between 2006 and 2014, says that, according to Dayton, 'Republika Srpska and the Federation [are] like states, apart from some common responsibilities, and [that] even the cantons in the Federation, which have absolute responsibility for education and health' can be regarded as 'statelets',[23] he implicitly agrees to the conceptual infinity of a statehood defined in terms of responsibility or government alone. After all, some responsibilities are those of the municipalities according to the principle of local self-government (see also below), which, if one were to follow Radmanović, would make them also some sort of states. But despite its obvious flaw, Radmanović's remark is especially important with regard to the way in which the argument is presented. He describes the entities as being 'like' states within the context of the academic interview, where he knows that his statements will be subject to scrutiny. His view could, for better or worse, be defended since he does not attribute sovereignty, i.e. ultimate governance, to the entities or the cantons as such. Instead, he simply suggests, with some reason, that we may think of entities as states with respect to those policy areas in which the DPA has awarded them ultimate responsibilities. Dodik on the other hand, presenting his argument to a supportive and, in matters of constitutional and international law largely uninformed audience, takes the argument further, to its most radical conclusion. It is doubtful that Radmanović would disapprove of such rhetoric, even though he is fully aware of its inaccuracy. What we are confronted with in this respect is not a legal argument; and, strictly speaking, it is not a political argument either. Rather it is an *act of political theatre*, performed in order to convince the masses of something that is inac-

---

[21]   Stephan Hobe and Otto Kimminich, *Einführung in das Völkerrecht*, 8. Auflage (Basel: A. Fracke Verlag, 2004), 67–70.

[22]   Ibid., 68.

[23]   Nebojša Radmanović, Personal Interview in Sarajevo (BiH), 7 November 2012.

curately presented as a matter of fact. Debating this reasoning briefly from a legal point of view was necessary, for here as well, we can see an important aspect of an 'imposed consociation' to which we shall return in chapter 8.

Figure 7.2 Bosnia's Executive and Legislative Bodies

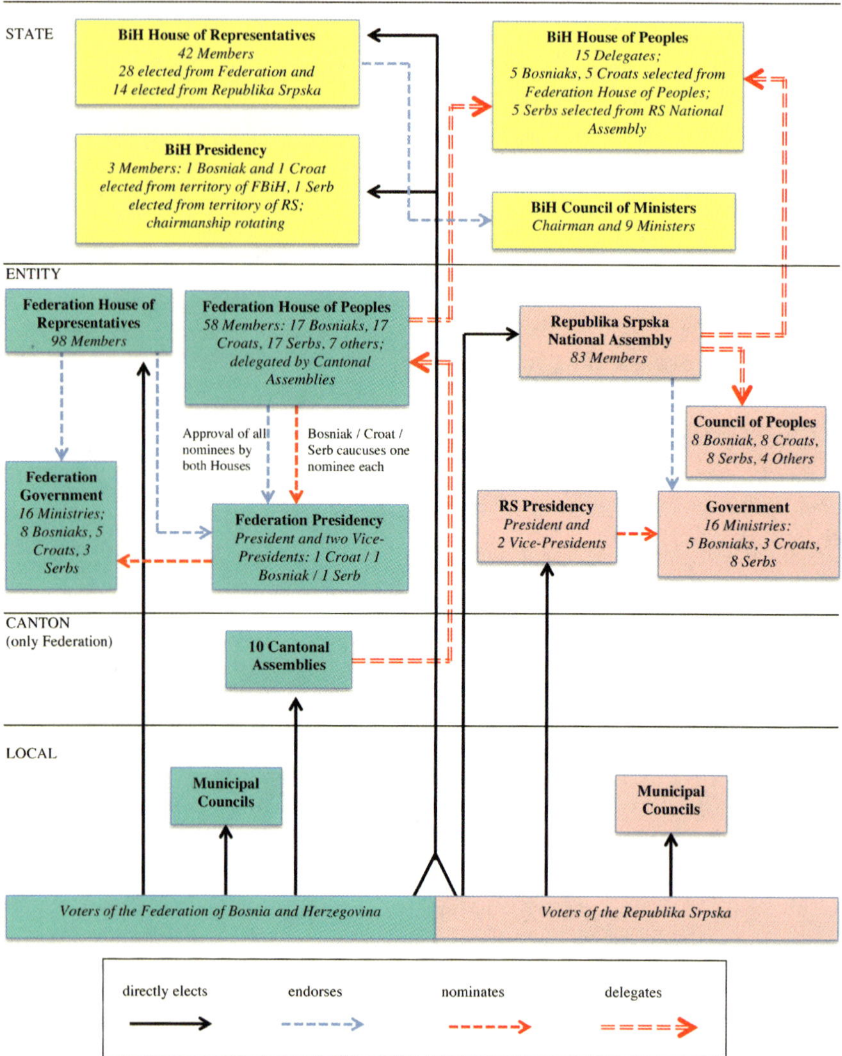

Source: Website Office of the High Representative, http://www.ohr.int/ohr-info/charts/images/legislative-and-exec-bodies.gif, accessed 15 August 2013.

The entities have their own political institutions comparable to the central state. They possess their own presidents, governments, parliaments, and courts. The FBiH is administratively divided into ten cantons, which can be described as 'territorial-political units of the dominant national communities'[24] and are responsible for education, culture, media, social and security policy, and, up to a certain extent, also for economic policy. The cantons, again, have their own institutions (parliaments, governments, courts) and their presidents are called prime ministers. Apart from managing daily politics, the cantons are important insofar as their parliaments delegate representatives to the Federation House of Peoples. And it is the latter body that delegates the 10 representatives from the Federation to the BiH House of Peoples. This mechanism sometimes prevented the central state parliament from being constituted until all the cantonal parliaments had taken up their work, since no representatives can be delegated if the cantonal parliaments are not in session. It is precisely for this reason that the implementation of any change to the nature or composition of the BiH House of Peoples (as requested by the *Sejdić and Finci* verdict of the European Court of Human Rights, see below) requires constitutional changes not only of the Dayton constitution, but also of the constitutions of the Federation and the cantons. Naturally, this results in a large number of possible vetoes that would make constitutional change difficult even if political will were present.

Contrary to the Federation, the RS is organised in a centralised manner and further divided into municipalities. The RS voters directly elect its president, whereas the FBiH president is selected by the FBiH parliament. Figure 7.2, provided by the Office of the High Representative, depicts the relationships between the different state levels and its bodies.

The established state structure shows thus a dual separation with two largely autonomous political and legal environments: While *territorial autonomy* is guaranteed to the Serbs in form of the RS, the Bosniaks' and Croats' autonomy is integrated into the cantonal structure of the FBiH. The territorial separation between RS and FBiH is as unfortunate as it is understandable. The Bosnian war was characterised by strategies to create strong territorial segregation as a result of absolutist nationalistic ideology.[25] Already in 1992, the three groups established their political influence spheres as geographic areas of direct control by forming para-governmental organisations. The most important were the '*Republika Srpska* of Bosnia and Herzegovina' (which was soon to drop 'Bosnia and Herzegovina' from its name) founded by the Serbs in January 1992, and the 'Croat Community of *Herceg-Bosna*' (HZ HB) established in summer 1992. The Bosnian Muslims largely, though never exclusively, took over the institutions of the newly independent Republic of Bosnia and Herzegovina (RBiH), while a small faction under the leadership of warlord Fikret Abdić established the 'Autonomous

---

24   Mirjana Kasapović, "Bosnia and Herzegovina: Consociational or Liberal Democracy?," *Politička Misao* XLII, no. 2 (2005): 4.

25   Adis Merdzanovic, "The Consequences of Ratko Mladić's Ideology for Today's Bosnia," *New Eastern Europe*, 2012, http://www.neweasterneurope.eu/node/332.

Province of Western Bosnia' in September 1993. Already by August 1992, the sovereignty of the common state of Bosnia was severely limited, since Serb and Croat para-governmental territorial arrangements occupied 80% of the territory.[26]

When the international actors sought their partners for peace negotiations, they had to start by paying tribute to the conditions on the ground. Territorial structures resulting from the agreement could hardly be more than a codification of the territorial *status quo*. The constitution, as Annex IV of the DPA, thus affirmed the basic territorial division of the country into the RS and the FBiH and established the inter-entity boundary by largely following the conditions on the ground, i.e. the territory held by the different armies. Notable exceptions are the unification of Sarajevo under FBiH control and the establishment of a corridor between FBiH territory and the enclave of Goražde. In return, RS was awarded some territory near Jajce, while the status of the city of Brčko was to be decided through arbitration later on (see below).

The (military) conditions on the ground thus forced international negotiators to accept a division of the country that would prove to be disastrous for inter-ethnic cooperation and that continues to undermine the legitimacy of the common state to this day. This is especially true since the return of refugees, foreseen in Annex VII of the DPA, was not fully accomplished. As a consequence, especially the RS remains an ethnically homogenous area.[27] The Bosnian territory was henceforth understood in 'categories of majority rule, where a dominant group determines rules of the game and excludes the minority from social and political participation'.[28] As a result of the 'constituent peoples' case before the Bosnian Constitutional Court, the entities had to change their own constitutions and incorporate the equality of all (constituent) people at the entity level. The Mrakovica-Sarajevo-Agreement[29] (see also chapter 9) granted 'the same status to all constituent peoples and citizens in the whole territory of Bosnia, thus ensuring that all peoples and citizens are proportionally represented at all levels of government and public administration in both entities; it create[d] mechanisms assuring the protection of the interest of each community, as well as their representation in the decision-making organs'.[30]

---

[26]   Calic, *Krieg und Frieden in Bosnien-Hercegovina*, 91.

[27]   Haris Silajdžić, Personal Interview in Sarajevo (BiH), 15 May 2012.

[28]   Eldar Sarajlić, "The Convenient Consociation," Francis Cheneval and Sylvie Ramel, ed., *From Peace to Shared Political Identities. Exploring Pathways in Contemporary Bosnia-Hercegovina. Special Volume of Transitions* 51, no. 1–2 (2011): 68.

[29]   The agreement can be found here: http://www.ohr.int/ohr-dept/legal/const/default.a sp?content_id=7273 (last accessed 20 August 2013).

[30]   Solioz, *Turning Points*, 96.

7.3   People vs. Citizens

The preamble of the constitution declares Bosniaks, Croats, and Serbs the 'constituent peoples' of Bosnia thereby entrusting them with special rights and privileges. The Constitutional Court strengthened their position of unquestioned equality through a decision in 2000,[31] which asserted the same rights to members of the 'constituent peoples' not only at the central but at the entity level as well. In general, this provision is in line with consociational theory, understood in its corporate form where the groups are pre-defined. Within the Bosnian context, its existence is hardly surprising. Already the resolution adopted in November 1943 by the communist 'National Anti-fascist Council of the People's Liberation of Bosnia and Herzegovina' (*Zemaljsko antifašističko vijeće narodnog oslobođenja Bosne i Hercegovine*, ZAVNOBiH) specifically mentioned those three groups by stating that the Bosnian state is 'neither Serb, nor Croat, nor Muslim, but Serb and Muslim and Croat'.[32] Similarly, the 1974 Constitution of the Socialist Republic of Bosnia-Herzegovina stated in its first article that the Republic belongs to the people of Bosnia-Herzegovina specifically including 'Muslims, Serbs and Croats, [as well as] members of other nations and national groups [*naroda i narodnosti*], who live in it'.[33] From this perspective, the Dayton formula— 'Bosniaks, Croats, as Serbs, as constituent peoples (along with Others), and the citizens of Bosnia-Herzegovina'[34]—is the continuation of an old tradition that establishes an interesting relationship between the concepts of a citizen, i.e. someone living within the premises of the state and being part of it, and his or her national belonging, i.e. group membership.

From a contemporary perspective, this practice clearly violates the democratic principle of equality, since members of certain minorities, like Roma or Jews, are treated differently than members of the constituent peoples. The former, for example, are barred from holding certain public offices like seats in the presidency or the BiH House of Peoples. Under certain circumstances, the same holds even true for constituent peoples. Since, according to the legal opinion by the Venice Commission, Bosnia's constitution mixes the ethnic and territorial principles of representation, only Serbs from the RS and Bosniaks and Croats from the

---

[31]   The English translation of the Constitutional Court verdict in case U 5/98 III is accessible through the Website of the Office of the High Representative, http://www.ohr.int/ohr-dept/legal/const/default.asp?content_id=5853, accessed 15 August 2013.

[32]   The significant parts of the resolution can be found in Omer Ibrahimagić, *Bosanski identitet i suverenitet* (Sarajevo: Univerzitet u Sarajevu, Institut za istraživanje zločina protiv čovječnosti i međunarodnog prava, 2012), 106–7.

[33]   Ibid., 124.

[34]   Preamble to the Constitution.

Federation may sit in the House of Peoples or the Presidency.[35] What the Commission had only hinted at in its legal opinion of 2005, the European Court of Human Rights has made clear in its famous *Sejdić and Finci* verdict in 2009:[36] such a practice violates the principle of non-discrimination with respect to participation in the political process. Bosnia is currently discussing options to change this undemocratic practice. But as we shall see, the position of the Others, i.e. the national minorities that the verdict had in mind, plays a secondary role in the discussions on how to implement the verdict.

7.4   Brčko District

An almost exotic element within Bosnia's state structure is the district of Brčko. Located in the northeastern part of the country, its strategic importance in military terms is evident (see Figure 7.1). It constitutes an important territorial connection between the eastern and northern parts of Republika Srpska as well as between the Posavina canton[37] and the rest of Federation territory. It is therefore hardly a surprise that it was among the most difficult things to negotiate at Dayton; in fact, it constituted one of these famous last-minute issues that threatened the entire agreement. Both entities wanted Brčko to be part of their respective territories. In order to save the agreement, Milošević proposed handing the issue over to an arbitrator, Lord Roberts Owen, who was supposed to deliver a final judgement within a year, after giving each side the chance to present its arguments. Tuđman and, more reluctantly, Izetbegović agreed and the Dayton agreement was saved.[38]

However, Lord Owen delivered his final judgement only in March 1999, when he presented a solution that awarded Brčko to neither of the entities. By making it a district, similar to the District of Columbia in the US, Brčko came

---

[35]   European Commission for Democracy through Law (Venice Commission), *Opinion on the Constitutional Situation in Bosnia and Herzegovina and the Powers of the High Representative* (Venice: CDL-AD (2005) 004, 11 March 2005), 16–20.

[36]   See judgements regarding applications 27996/06 and 34836/06 of the European Court on Human Rights. For an in-depth analysis of the judgement as well as a discussion of the subsequent political efforts to implement it, see Edin Hodžić and Nenad Stojanović, *New/Old Constitutional Engineering. Challenges and Implications of the European Court of Human Rights Decision in the Case of Sejdić and Finci v. BiH* (Sarajevo: Analitika, 2011). For the relevance of the case with regards to consociational theory, see Christopher McCrudden and Brendan O'Leary, "Courts and Consociations, or How Human Rights Courts May De-Stabilize Power-Sharing Settlements," *European Journal of International Law* 24, no. 2 (2013): 477–501.

[37]   In the Washington Agreement, the cantons were simply enumerated. With the exception of canton 10 (Livno) all cantons later received names based on their geographic location.

[38]   Holbrooke, *To End a War*, 305–309.

under the authority of the central state. Its statute[39] defines the town and its settlements as a 'single administrative unit of local self-government existing under the sovereignty of Bosnia and Herzegovina'. The statute furthermore states that '[t]he Entities shall exercise within the District only those functions and powers assigned to the Entities by this Statute' and that 'District authorities shall not assign or delegate to either Entity any governmental power or function not specifically assigned or delegated in this Statute'. In other words, the entities have no governing powers within the district other than those that the district is willing to grant them. The district is thus a politically independent unit, under its own authority and the sovereignty of the central state.

Consequently, Brčko has its own parliament, government, and courts. The district is responsible for a variety of policy areas, most of them corresponding to the principles of local self-government, i.e. the limited authority to decide based on the needs of the local populations. However, in some respects (police, judiciary, education), the statute awards powers to the district that, within the Bosnian legal context, are usually located at the entity level.[40] As such, the district is truly an entity *sui generis*. Its position vis-à-vis the central state was codified in an amendment to the Bosnian constitution passed by BiH's parliament in March 2009.[41] Technically, this amendment reaffirms Brčko's status by awarding the Constitutional Court the authority to decide legal matters between the central state and the district. With this act, the parliamentary assembly did in fact not clarify the status of the district with regards to the constitutional order of the country, but implicitly accepted the supremacy of the respective legal acts (final arbitration judgement and district statute) establishing the district.[42] In political (as well as legal) terms, the importance of this amendment lies less in the (non-)clarification of matters, but rather in the fact that it was the first and so far only change to the constitution Bosnia's political elites could agree upon.[43]

Unlike the central state and the entities, the philosophy of the district's political system does not follow the consociational logic (see next section). The statute does not prescribe any special representation formula (with regards to the constituent peoples) but simply states that the parliamentary assembly has 29 members.

---

[39]   Available at the OHR Website: http://www.ohr.int/ohr-offices/brcko/default.asp?content_id=5367, last accessed 20 August 2013.

[40]   Lejla Lijić, "Brčko distrikt," in *Država, Politika i Društvo u Bosni i Hercegovini. Analiza postdejtonskog političkog sistema* (Sarajevo: University Press Magistrat Izdanja, 2011), 426.

[41]   Amendment 1 to the Constitution of Bosnia and Herzegovina, *Official Gazette of BiH* No. 25/09.

[42]   Goran Marković, "Ustavne promjene u Bosni i Hercegovini," in *Država, Politika i Društvo u Bosni i Hercegovini. Analiza postdejtonskog političkog sistema* (Sarajevo: University Press Magistrat Izdanja, 2011), 92.

[43]   Ibid., 91.

Later, this provision was changed to 31 members in order to include two minority group representatives, in line with the new local electoral law.[44] The district is therefore a representative of the liberal democracy model, for decisions are taken by simple majority rule. In terms of political theory, the final verdict and the statute, respectively, reaffirmed 'the principle of equality (fairness, justice) by distributing it to all the citizens of a given polity' and the 'liberal-democratic principle of the rule of law, the rule of "generality" over the rule of "particularity"'.[45] This, again, contributes to the exotic character of the district.

7.5 Bosnian Consociation

Bosnia's distinctly consociational character was already implied in certain respects but deserves a deeper introduction within the context of an 'imposed consociation' model that guides the present study. Bosnia's consociational elements look as follows:

1. Grand coalition: The constitution prescribes certain mechanisms in order to ensure participation of all constituent peoples within state administration and government. The country possesses a three-person presidency consisting of one Bosniak, one Croat, and one Serb. Its members are directly elected in the Federation (for the Croat and Bosniak members) and the RS (for the Serb member).[46] Within the Council of Ministers no more than two thirds of all ministers can be appointed from Federation territory and the chair is to nominate deputy ministers for every ministry who are not supposed to be of the same constituent people as their ministers.[47] In essence, this provision means that every ministry—by now there are nine plus the chairman—has one minister and two deputies from the respective other groups. As Figure 7.2 illustrates, governments at the entity and cantonal levels have similar provisions regarding the composition of the governing bodies.

However, it is important to note that despite the provisions just cited, the Bosnian government is hardly a consensus government comparable with, for example, Switzerland's Federal Council. Since the parliament has to approve the government and its composition is only prescribed in terms of ethnic and not ideological belonging, the Council of Ministers' position resembles more the one of a government within a majoritarian democracy. In the immediate post-war period,

---

[44] Lijić, "Brčko distrikt," 427.

[45] Asim Mujkić, "Beyond Consociation: The Case of Brčko Arbitration," Francis Cheneval and Sylvie Ramel, ed., *Special Issue of Transitions: From Peace to Shared Political Identities. Exploring Pathways in Contemporary Bosnia-Herzegovina* 51, no. 1–2 (2011): 87.

[46] Constitution of Bosnia-Herzegovina, Art. 5.

[47] Ibid., Art. 5, paragraph 4.

it was a *de facto* law that the seats assigned to the groups were filled by the respective national(ist) parties (or people cooperating with them), since the national corpuses showed a remarkable cohesion. These parties had overwhelming majorities in parliament, which made confirmation of the Council of Ministers a formality. But when in 2000 the Alliance for Change, a rather diverse group of a large number of opposition parties, was able to secure a narrow majority in parliament, it naturally appointed its politicians to the Council. It had to respect the *ethnic* composition in terms of group membership, but the *political currents* each of the members represented differed significantly from the one of the previous nationalist governments. In this regard, the Bosnian system is rather flexible and prone to government-opposition mentality within the setup of a consociational system. (However, like elsewhere in Eastern Europe, the dividing line between government and opposition, or between nationalist and non-nationalist parties tends to be blurred when cooperation for political power is at stake. Following the principle that yesterday's enemy can without a problem be today's ally, Bosnia has witnessed some remarkable governing coalitions in its post-war period.) Similarly, the constitution furthermore only prescribes that the members of the presidency elected in the Federation are of Bosniak and Croat origins. In technical terms, it does not say that they have to be elected by the respective groups. Bosniaks, as long as they live in the Federation, could therefore vote for a Croat candidate and so could Croats with respect to a Bosniak candidate. This precise set of problems became apparent in 2006 with the election of Social Democratic candidate Željko Komšić as the Croat member of the presidency. Especially Bosnian Croats usually claimed that he was not a real representative of the Croats since, supposedly, Bosniaks had elected him (see discussion in next chapter).[48]

2. Proportional representation: Proportional representation, as a consociational tool, includes two aspects. The first one is representation in government and administration according to the share in population. With respect to political positions, the Bosnian constitution prescribes not proportionality but (usually) equality among the three constituent peoples. We have just seen what this means in terms of government composition. But the same principle is adhered to with respect to the parliament. The House of Peoples is composed of 15 members, five of each group. The House of Representatives has 42 members with one third coming from RS and two thirds from the Federation. Chairs and deputy chairs of the two chambers are distributed among the three groups. Equal representation is also the guiding principle with regards to administrative post. It also includes the judiciary branch: out of the nine members of the Constitutional Court, the Federa-

---

[48]   See Božo Ljubić, Personal Interview in Sarajevo (BiH), 20 June 2012; Dragan Čović, Personal interview in Mostar (BiH), 19 June 2012. But also Željko Komšić, Personal Interview in Sarajevo (BiH), 9 November 2012.

tion parliament selects four and RS parliament two judges.[49] With the changes implemented as part of the 'constituent peoples' verdict, national minorities (the 'Others') have also been designated representation in several bodies of the entities. However, the guiding principle at the entity level is proportionality rather than equality. The same holds true for administrative posts at lower levels.

The second aspect of the proportionality principle concerns the electoral system, which should follow the principle of proportional representation. Bosnia's current electoral law, passed in 2001 by the parliament, foresees the election of the House of Representatives following a party list system. The mandates are distributed according to the Sainte-Laguë method, which divides the total number of votes received by a party by 1, 3, 5, 7, 9 etc. until all the seats are allocated; as a correction, a system of compensation mandates is used.[50] This proportionality device tends to favour smaller parties, which helps explain the rather mixed picture within the Bosnian parliament. In the legislative period 2010-2014, no less than eleven parties had members in the House of Representatives.

3. Veto powers: The most striking features of the Bosnian consociation are the veto possibilities inherent in the system. There are three different types of veto rights the groups (constituent peoples) enjoy. First, the so-called entity voting relies on a qualified majority in parliament: for laws to pass in any of the two bodies they need to obtain not only an overall majority, but at least one third of the representatives from each entity must also vote in favour of them.[51] Second, all decisions require a majority in both parliamentary houses, which means that the groups possess significant veto powers through the House of Peoples. In this chamber, each group can easily block any legislation because the constitution requires a quorum of nine members in order for laws to pass, 'provided that at least three Bosniak, three Croat, and three Serb delegates are present'.[52] In other words, if three delegates within one group simply do not show up, the entire legislative system is blocked. Third, the delegates in the House of Peoples can declare a proposed decision by the parliament as 'destructive to a vital interest' of their respective group. In this case, such legislation requires a majority within each of the three group delegations present and voting.[53] If a majority of Bosniak, Serb, or Croat delegates objects to the invocation of the 'vital interest' clause, a joint commission is formed with the task to find a compromise within five days.

---

49   Constitution of Bosnia-Herzegovina, Art. 6, paragraph 1. After consultation with the BiH presidency, the President of the European Court of Human Rights selects the remaining three members of the Constitutional Court.

50   Maja Sahadžić, "Izbori i izborni sistem Bosne i Hercegovine," in *Država, Politika i Društvo u Bosni i Hercegovini. Analiza postdejtonskog političkog sistema* (Sarajevo: University Press Magistrat Izdanja, 2011), 408.

51   Constitution of Bosnia-Herzegovina, Art. 4, paragraph 3.d.

52   Constitution of Bosnia-Herzegovina, Art. 4, paragraph 1.b.

53   Constitution of Bosnia-Herzegovina, Article 5, paragraph 3.e.

If no such compromise is reached, the matter is referred to the Constitutional Court for a final decision whether or not the 'vital interest' is threatened. The political process is thus transformed into a legal decision.

4. Group autonomy: It has already been shown what group autonomy means in practice in the Bosnian example. It is, first and foremost, realised through the federal structure of the state, which includes the entities, but also the cantons. Since these have jurisdiction over a number of political issues, group autonomy is granted to a significant degree.

7.6   The High Representative

Concluding the DPA was a triumph of international negotiation efforts. The internationals had managed to end the war thus achieving 'the priority of priorities'.[54] However, they were fully aware of the fact that concluding an agreement is one thing, implementing it quite another. Their further obligations were twofold: first, they needed to enhance the security situation thereby guaranteeing the freedom of movement and the seizure of military actions. This task was mainly handled by the military parts of the DPA that *inter alia* established the so-called Implementation Force (IFOR), which later became the Stabilisation Force (SFOR) and, after the European Union took the lead with its operation Althea in 2004, the European Union Force (EUFOR).[55] On the other hand, Annex X of the DPA established the Office of the High Representative (OHR), which was charged with overseeing the civilian aspects of the DPA.

The mandate of the High Representative was to monitor the implementation of the peace settlement, ensure cooperation between the parties in order to implement the agreement, coordinate the activities of the civilian organisations and agencies on the field, facilitate the resolution of any difficulties arising in connection with the civilian implementation, participate in meetings of donor organisations, report periodically to the United Nations Security Council and the main stakeholders, and to provide guidance to the commissioner of the International Police Task Force (IPTF, supposed to train local police).[56] In legal terms, the High Representative is, according to Article V of Annex X of the DPA, the 'final authority in theatre regarding the interpretation of this agreement on the civilian implementation of the peace settlement'. The OHR thereby derives its powers directly from international law in a dual sense. In addition to originating as part of

---

[54]   Paddy Ashdown, "Statement by the High Representative, Lord Paddy Ashdown to the Venice Commission" (Appendix 1 of CDL-PV (2004) 003, Venice, 8 October 2004), 16.

[55]   Originally, IFOR was supposed to leave the country within a year, yet the security situation did not allow for this to happen.

[56]   DPA, Annex X, Art. 2.

an international treaty, its mandate was also approved by the UN Security Council in resolution 1031 (1995), passed in December 1995, and reaffirmed in resolution 1088 (1996) a year later.

Given the complexities of the job, the OHR's mandate was extremely large, especially taking into account how unprepared the international community was as it embarked on its journey. Paddy Ashdown, the forth High Representative (HR), writes that '[t]here were no plans for what would happen after NATO [SFOR] occupied Bosnia either, beyond sending the first High Representative in Bosnia, Carl Bildt, into Sarajevo with a suitcase full of money and instructions to get on with it'.[57] Bildt's own account is similar, in that, when arriving to Sarajevo in January 1996, he recalls having to borrow a car from the Swedish ambassador in order to get around, being forced to sleep on the ambassador's floor as NATO had occupied all the few hotels in town, and having to work in an office without electricity or heating.[58] Putting such personal inconveniences aside, this situation shows the lack of proper preparation by the international community as well as the clear focus on security rather than civilian concerns. Given the situation on the ground, such action was clearly justified. But what is more striking is that the international community lacked a clear concept regarding the post-war civilian implementation of the DPA. This was true, even though, as Ashdown explained in another context: 'I think everyone knew at the time that the constitutional structure Dayton created to end a very violent war would not be an easy one within which to build a functional state.'[59] The provisions of the 'Dayton monster'[60] set up a complicated state structure that had to be implemented in a highly unfavourable environment. And the person entrusted with this task, the High Representative, did not have any instruments in order to enforce cooperation between the different groups. At the same time, the local political elites, having been democratically legitimised by the premature elections held in 1996, embarked on a strategy of extreme reluctance (for the exact context, see chapter 9).

By the time the second High Representative, Carlos Westendorp, assumed office in 1997, the security situation had somewhat stabilised but no significant other progress could be reported. The only way to end the apparent stalemate, in the eyes of the international community, was to 'look into [the] Dayton Agreement and see what the flaws are'.[61] Even though publicly claiming that 'Bosnia is not a protectorate',[62] Westendorp and his team detected one of those flaws in the

---

57   Ashdown, *Swords and Ploughshares*, 125.
58   Carl Bildt, *Peace Journey: The Struggle for Peace in Bosnia* (London: Weidenfeld & Nicolson, 1999), 172–4.
59   Ashdown, "Statement by the High Representative," 16.
60   Ashdown, *Swords and Ploughshares*, 221.
61   Carlos Westendorp, Personal Interview in Madrid, 11 September 2012.
62   *Dnevni Avaz*, 19 August 1997, 5.

lack of final authority by the OHR. The Bonn Conference, held in December 1997, was therefore a turning point of the post-war Bosnian history. Here, the international community, in the words of Westendorp, 'managed to introduce a method by which the High Representative could take those decisions' on which the local politicians failed to reach a compromise. According to Westendorp, the granting of such authority was 'not very legal' but accepted by everybody within the international community, because the states 'knew that these things [i.e. the implementation of laws] were necessary but they [i.e. the Bosnian parties] were not able to accept [the proposed laws] by definition'.[63] He furthermore recalls that there was no significant resistance (apart from some concerns by Russia) to the introduction of the new method and that no alternative options or forms had been discussed. However, Christian Schwarz-Schilling, the fifth HR who was also involved in the Bonn conference negotiations, claims that, while approving of the need for those this kind of authority, he insisted that the decisions taken by the High Representative should be subject to review by some legal institution.[64] Even in retrospect, it is hard to determine what was really argued behind closed doors. But it is clear that such a proposal did not make it into the final document.

Concretely, the Peace Implementation Council (PIC), a body consisting of 55 countries and agencies responsible for the implementation of the DPA,[65] 'extensively interpreted'[66] the powers granted to the High Representative in Annex X. It stated in the conclusion of the 1997 Bonn summit:

> The Council welcomes the High Representative's intention to use his final authority in theatre regarding interpretation of the Agreement on the Civilian Implementation of the Peace Settlement in order to facilitate the resolution of difficulties by making binding decisions, as he judges necessary, on the following issues:
>
> a. timing, location and chairmanship of meetings of the common institutions;
>
> b. interim measures to take effect when parties are unable to reach agreement, which will remain in force until the Presidency or Council of Ministers has adopted a decision consistent with the Peace Agreement on the issue concerned;

---

[63] Westendorp, Personal Interview. When saying 'by definition', Westendorp refers to the nationalist character of the parties constituting the group elites at this moment. As a matter of principle, those could not engage in compromise with other parties since it ran counter to their nationalist ideologies.

[64] Christian Schwarz-Schilling, Personal Interview in Büdingen, Germany, 23 August 2012. The Venice Commission reached the same conclusion when examining the Bonn powers and stating that '[t]he continuation of such power being exercised by a non-elected political authority without any possibility of appeal and any input by an independent body is not acceptable.' See European Commission for Democracy through Law, *Opinion on the Constitutional Situation*, 24.

[65] For more information, see the website of the OHR, http://www.ohr.int/pic/default.a sp?content_id=38563, last accessed 28 September 2012.

[66] European Commission for Democracy through Law, *Opinion on the Constitutional Situation*, 21.

> c. other measures to ensure implementation of the Peace Agreement throughout Bosnia and Herzegovina and its Entities, as well as the smooth running of the common institutions. Such measures may include actions against persons holding public office or officials who are absent from meetings without good cause or who are found by the High Representative to be in violation of legal commitments made under Peace Agreement or the terms for its implementation.[67]

In other words, the Bonn conference gave the High Representative the authority 'to impose laws as he sees fit if Bosnia and Herzegovina's legislative bodies fail to do so' as well as the authority to 'remove from office public officials who violate legal commitments and the Dayton Peace Agreement'.[68] It is important to note that the OHR's 'Bonn powers' are, according to letter b of the excerpt just cited, limited in time. They are 'interim' measures as far as the OHR's capacity to impose laws is concerned. Accordingly, they can be changed or amended by decisions of the legislative branch. However, this seems possible in theory only, for legislative acts imposed by the OHR have often remained the law of the land for a substantial amount of time. The underlying reason is rather simple, since any action to change such a law would require consent by the parliamentary bodies and therefore be subject to the numerous possibilities of blockade and political quarrel. Furthermore, it is important to highlight the fact that, in a strict reading, the High Representative may not impose laws as he sees fit as a general rule. In fact, this authority is granted to him only in cases 'when parties are unable to reach agreement'. Again, this distinction, although undeniably important in a legal sense, has almost no relevance with regards to daily political practice. While it did admittedly contain OHR action in the first years after the introduction of the Bonn powers, later High Representatives would simply invoke the general sense of letter c of the cited excerpt and justify their legislative actions as necessary 'for the smooth running of the common institutions'.

As the Venice Commission rightly points out, it is 'not a normal situation that an unelected foreigner exercises such powers in a Council of Europe member state', which Bosnia has been since April 2002. The Commission goes on to qualify the Bonn powers as 'emergency powers', which '[b]y their very nature' have 'to cease together with the emergency originally justifying their use'.[69] However, within the Bosnian example, the 'emergency situation', if defined in terms of a state structure unable to function efficiently and a political system composed of politicians reluctant to cooperation, has continued ever since. It is questionable whether we can really conceive of those powers in terms of their 'emergency' ca-

---

[67]   Peace Implementation Council, *PIC Bonn Conclusions* (Bonn, 10 December 1997), http://www.ohr.int/pic/default.asp?content_id=5182. Last accessed 22 August 2013.

[68]   See the description of the OHR mandate on its website, http://www.ohr.int/ohr-info/gen-info/default.asp?content_id=38612, last accessed 28 September 2012.

[69]   European Commission for Democracy through Law, *Opinion on the Constitutional Situation*, 21.

pacities when, in fact, 'emergency' has become the new normal. In political terms, I believe, we have to come to exactly the opposite conclusion: The Bonn powers ultimately made the High Representative an *integral part of the political system*. Even though they were structured as a temporary means that presupposed a failure of domestic institution to pass laws, in practice they evolved to a *means of actual governing*.

We are in the lucky position to be able to exactly date when this evolution culminated. In 2002, the local politicians, with lots of cajoling and arm-twisting by the High Representative, managed to achieve a compromise on how to implement the 'constituent peoples' verdict of the Constitutional Court, i.e. what parts of the entity constitutions needed to be changed in what way. However, they did not have a sufficient majority in order pass all the respective changes in parliament. But since the compromise was so fundamental, the High Representative decided to impose those parts of the law despite the obvious shortcomings of due process. As Wolfgang Petritsch, the HR in question, recalls:

> The big issues were negotiated and agreed upon. But there were certain parts [of the Agreement] for which one would not have achieved a two third majority in parliament. That's when I said: I'll do it. And I had told them that before, when they were fighting: 'Look how far you get, I'll help you as good as I can, if it doesn't work. But it's up to you [to come to an agreement].' And I would say, they went three quarters of the way [by themselves]. And that's not bad for the first time.[70]

In this instance, which we shall analyse in chapter 9 in greater detail, the Bonn powers clearly became an instrument of actual governing. The locals knew that their compromises did not have to overcome the constitutional threshold of a qualified majority from the beginning, and they adapted to this initial position accordingly. In addition to being the mediator, the High Representative, due to the Bonn powers, became an integral part of the system. This is even more striking since, again in the words of the Venice Commission, 'such an arrangement is fundamentally incompatible with the democratic character of the state and the sovereignty of BiH'.[71]

In theory, the High Representative has to justify his actions and he is by no means a Hobbesian Leviathan. As the Venice Commission explains, he is politically responsible before the Peace Implementation Council. Legally, the Constitutional Court exercises 'control of the constitutionality of the content of legislation enacted by the High Representative in the same way as for legislation adopted by the Parliamentary Assembly of BiH. However, it does not examine whether there was enough justification for the High Representative to enact the legislation in-

---

[70] Wolfgang Petritsch, Personal Interview in Paris, 4 December 2012.
[71] European Commission for Democracy through Law, *Opinion on the Constitutional Situation*, 22.

stead of leaving it to the democratically elected organs of BiH.'[72] As we shall see in the next chapters in greater detail, the political control over the use of Bonn powers is dependent on the personalities inhabiting the post of High Representative. If the holders of this position are persons of great influence and charisma, the political oversight function of the PIC *de facto* ceases to exist. As far as the legal aspect is concerned, there is no mechanism to hold the High Representative accountable for any decision. Similarly, there are no public rules of procedure for taking such a decision. Especially in the first years, this process was entirely left to the discretion of the High Representative, who could almost do as he pleased. There is, however, evidence to suggest that this situation has changed. Nowadays, the political controls tend to work quite well, while the legal situation was not significantly improved with respect to Bosnia's constitutional order. It seems that even today, it is the High Representative's personal philosophy that puts limits to the usage of its intervention prerogative.

Given the characteristics of the OHR and its mandate after the introduction of the Bonn powers, it seems quite appropriate to designate the OHR the position of an 'International Regulating Body' in accordance with the theoretical assumption of 'imposed consociation'.

---

[72]   Ibid.

8   Political Elites and Political Quarrels[1]

The political elite of contemporary Bosnia and Herzegovina exhibits a seemingly contradictory behaviour. From the outset, the political representatives of the different groups argue radical standpoints and express an almost unimaginable reluctance to any collegiality or sympathy when the political adversary is concerned. Name-calling and the like are in this respect only minor offenses in a system that desperately tries to put together people that apparently have nothing in common apart from being forced to cooperate by some higher authority. But it is exactly this unity in non-cooperativeness that testifies to a deeply rooted unity in terms of behaviour and political motivation. Bosnia's political leaders are not a bunch of non-compromising political die-hards, for they have shown a remarkable capacity to adapt to changing circumstances. They are also not always hostile to each other, even though they do not often express respect or understanding for the adversary's positions. They are, in short, the product of the political system through which they try to articulate and implement their political visions and personal ambitions. This chapter shall elaborate on the latter from an intra-elite perspective; its goal is to shine a light on the complex incentive structure and the political debates dominating contemporary Bosnian politics.

To outline the context, we may start by stating that the main problem of Bosnia's political system is an unfortunate incentive structure for the political elites. As Mladen Ivanić, the president and founder of the Party of Democratic Progress and currently the Serb member of BiH's presidency, explains, 'political elites gain if they quarrel, but do not gain if they actually solve problems.' In this context, the concept of gain should be understood as winning elections thus becoming part of the governing coalition. This task is obviously made easier if one focuses on certain issues, and ignores others: 'I consider myself a politician who always repeats: economy, economy, economy. But I [i.e. my party] can never achieve more than ten per cent [at the elections]. But a politician who spits out some stupidity gains very much in our system.'[2] According to Ivanić, such stupid-

---

[1]   In this and the following chapters, I shall quote extensively from my personal interviews with Bosnia's political decision makers and former High Representatives. In order to avoid too many general references to these interviews, I shall use footnotes only when the interviewee is not clearly identifiable through the text, or when I refer to a statement that was not given within the context of these interviews. In all other cases, and as a general rule, the statements attributed to them are taken from my interviews.

[2]   This statement remains true even though Ivanić himself narrowly beat his opponent for the Serb seat in Bosnia's state presidency in October 2014. His party, the PDP, managed only to achieve some eight per cent of the votes for both the Serb seats in the BiH parliament as well as the National Assembly of the Republika Srpska.

ities include, for example, the demand for secession in Republika Srpska or the absolute affirmation of a strong, centralised state in the Federation. Due to systemic incentives, politicians are thus advised to pursue a strategy that concentrates on popular demands and stereotypes rather than on actual policies. In other words, they should become populists.

However, there is another layer to political behaviour as far as political vision is concerned. As Željko Komšić, member of the Bosnian presidency between 2006 and 2014 and recent founder of the political party *Demokratski Front* (Democratic Front), explains, within the Bosnian political spectrum, an 'essential war' is being waged about state resources, not state institutions. By resources, he understands the 'energetic infrastructure, telecommunication, and the control over large amounts of [foreign] loans', i.e. the enterprises still under national control as well as the large loans and financial benefits the central state and the entities receive from institutions like the European Union and the International Monetary Fund. Control over these resources is essential, for it means not only a substantial amount of personal financial and political gain but also access to a large pool of government jobs. The latter are usually distributed among one's supporters, often in order to fulfil campaign promises. This mechanism had an immediate consequence:

> What we have is not politics in the classical sense. Oftentimes disguised by those 'big' questions of national interest etc., the fact of the matter is that people who do what politicians are supposed to do—solving problems and achieving compromise in order to solve problems—are rare around here. Within the current political scene ... you cannot find anyone who is primarily concerned with politics as a general principle. Instead, we are fighting over resources. The contemporary political crisis ... is a war for resources instead of being what politics is supposed to be: a confrontation of concepts and the attempt at compromise.[3]

The system thus distorts the perception of the politician's main task. The latter is not understood anymore as 'doing good for the people' but instead as 'doing good for my people' which refers to a specific segment within the own national group. Such logic is perhaps not surprising for a divided society. However, intrinsically connected to it is the strange assumption that *my people* are best served if *I* remain in power to fight for their interests; after all, I am the only one who can truly represent them in the manner they deserve. It is in this way that, over time, my interests and the group's interests become interchangeable until, ultimately, personal interests prevail. Politics, understood as governing is thereby removed from the politician's job description. What counts are posts and personal gains—and winning elections so that posts and personal gains can be secured. In most simplified terms, this is the nucleus of the current Bosnian political system. Obvious deficiencies in terms of the quality of systemic outcomes are clearly secondary to the

---

[3]   Komšić, Personal Interview in Sarajevo (BiH). 9 November 2012.

political elite's primary *logic of self-perpetuation*. In a comparatively recent article, *New York Times* op-ed columnist Roger Cohen, from whom I borrowed the term, sums up the central paradigm of the 'Daytonians', as he calls the political elite, as follows:

> Daytonians came in various stripes: Bosnian Muslim (or Bosniak), Serb and Croat. They disagreed about many things and nursed bitter memories of a war that killed at least 100,000 people. But they agreed on the necessity of their self-perpetuation. They agreed that investigating the disappearance of hundreds of millions of dollars would be silly. They agreed on the need for political parties drawn on ethnic lines. They agreed on the efficacy of pre-election nationalist outbursts. And so a failed system endured.[4]

The mechanisms of this ideological unity among the group elites with regards to the political understanding of leadership have naturally not gone unnoticed by the local population. As Cohen writes in another op-ed, talking to ordinary people, one will 'hear complaints about abject governance, rampant corruption, the unworkable architecture of Dayton, political parties still drawn on ethnic lines, joblessness, drift, a dysfunctional judicial system, [and] the pettiness of sectarianism'.[5] This generalised view is supported by recent survey results. According to the 2010 Gallup Balkans Monitor Report, a 'majority of all three ethnic groups still do not feel that someone is speaking for them at the political level'. Ninety-two per cent of respondents in the Federation and eighty-two per cent of respondents in Republika Srpska describe the national governments' performance as 'poor' or only 'fair'; the entity governments get similar ratings.[6]

Given the relatively low trust in the state and its institutions as well as the fairly critical assessment of the governments' performance, it may surprise that twenty years after the conclusion of war the same people constitute large parts of the political elite. Let us look at a few examples. Between 2006 and 2010, Haris Silajdžić was the Bosniak member of the state presidency; during the war and in the late 1990s, he was the state's prime minister and co-Chairman of the Council of Ministers, respectively. Milorad Dodik, the president of Republika Srpska and previously this entity's prime minister held the latter function already in the late 1990s; he was furthermore a member of the Republika Srpska parliament during the war. Zlatko Lagumdžija, Bosnia's former foreign minister, was deputy prime

---

4   Roger Cohen, "Enough of the Daytonians," *The New York Times*, 18 July 2013, sec. Opinion / Global Opinion, http://www.nytimes.com/2013/07/19/opinion/global/roger-cohen-enough-of-the-daytonians.html. Accessed 3 August 2013.

5   Roger Cohen, "How Bosnia Heals," *The New York Times*, 15 July 2013, sec. Opinion / Global Opinion, http://www.nytimes.com/2013/07/16/opinion/global/roger-cohen-how-bosnia-heals.html. Accessed 3 August 2013.

6   Gallup Balkan Monitor, *The 2010 Gallup Balkan Monitor. Focus on Bosnia-Herzegovina*, 2010, 9, http://www.balkan-monitor.eu/files/Gallup_Balkan_Monitor-Focus_On_Bosnia_and_Herzegovina.pdf.

minister of the Republic of Bosnia-Herzegovina immediately following its independence in the early '90s; some ten years later, he led the famous Alliance for Change government. Dragan Čović, the Croat member of Bosnia's state presidency held this function already between 2002 and 2005—when Paddy Ashdown removed him due to alleged criminal charges; previously, he had been the Federation's minister of finance between 1998 and 2001. Similarly, Božo Ljubić, until very recently president of the Croat Democratic Union 1990 (*Hrvatska Demokratska Zajednica 1990,* or HDZ1990 as I shall call it henceforth), was minister of health in the Federation in the late '90s. The same trend can also be observed with regards to party functions. The late Sulejman Tihić for example, who until his death in September 2014 was president of the Party for Democratic Action (*Stranka Demokratske Akcije,* SDA) was only the second person to ever hold this position, even though the party was founded in March 1990. He succeeded Alija Izetbegović, the well-known first chairman of the presidency of the Republic of Bosnia-Herzegovina and wartime leader of the Bosnian state. Izetbegović's son, Bakir is the current Bosniak representative in Bosnia's state presidency, where he succeeded Haris Silajdžić—who, in turn, had succeeded Tihić. The only exception in this regard is found with the Serb Democratic Party (*Srpska Demokratska Stranka,* SDS). Founded by Radovan Karadžić in July 1990, its staff was decimated through an aggressive removal policy by the High Representative as part of the efforts conducted to capture and prosecute war criminals. SDS's wartime and late 1990s decision makers—Karadžić, Biljana Plavšić, and Momčilo Krajšnik—are either being tried or have been convicted by the International Criminal Tribunal for the former Yugoslavia (ICTY) in The Hague. With respect to the other major parties, the current presidents and key decision makers testify to the politicians' remarkable perfection of the system of self-perpetuation.

It belongs among the minor conundrums of the Bosnian story that such continuity is possible. The sometimes articulated frustration with the *people* that 'despite complaining about the politicians keep re-electing them'[7] is thereby a rather naïve statement that shifts the blame to where it does not really belong. In an idiosyncratic manner, politics (*politika*) has a negative connotation in Bosnian society. *Politika* is not only blamed for the war itself but also closely associated with criminal activity; in principle, it is generally mistrusted as both corrupt and uncertain.[8] Staying away from politics and the political process—which from the outset could be perceived as 'tolerance' of mediocrity and hypocrisy and, in the end, is undoubtedly conducive to the elite's stay in power—is thus a genuine feature of

---

[7]   I believe it was Miroslav Lajčák who once hinted at this relationship.

[8]   Julianne Funk Deckard, "'Invisible' Believers for Peace: Religion and Peacebuilding in Postwar Bosnia-Herzegovina" (Doctoral Dissertation, KU Leuven, 2012), 111. Funk relies on research provided by Torsten Kolind, *Post-War Identification. Everyday Muslim Counterdiscourse in Bosnia Herzegovina* (London: Verso, 2008).

the Bosnian *political* system as it currently unfolds. Lacking a strong civil society capable of influencing political developments, the political system itself is conducive to elite self-perpetuation and public deference in this regard.

One may question this claim by pointing to some recent events where popular dissatisfaction was publically voiced in an admittedly impressive and never before seen manner. In February 2014, protests by local workers who had not been paid for more than a year erupted in the city of Tuzla and soon after spread to other cities throughout Bosnia and Herzegovina. In what some commentators termed the 'Bosnian spring',[9] people everywhere in the country voiced their dissatisfaction with the local political elites and demanded substantial changes in the form of a responsive and responsible government. In open assemblies, which they called plena (plural of plenum), the protesters discussed and formulated concrete political demands that they put before the political leaderships, mostly on cantonal level. The international community as well as the local politicians, obviously surprised by the citizens' activism, did not really know how to respond to the protests. They had first experienced such public upheaval in summer of 2013 when the public physically blocked the parliament in Sarajevo so that the politicians could not leave until a law allowing identity numbers to be issued to new-borns was passed. This 'bebolucija'—a combination of the terms *'beba'* (baby) and *'revolucija'* (revolution)—as well as the 2014 protests constitute genuinely new phenomena within the Bosnian society and political landscape. *Their distinctive element is that they are social, not national in character.* They thus run against the entire spirit of the current political and societal system and target the entire political elite.

However, it seems that the organisational structure of the protests and plena, as it currently presents itself, lacks the necessary depth and institutional force to systematically alter the prevailing political dynamics. Since the plena constantly refused to become active *within* the political system by associating themselves to an existing party or forming a new party on their own, their opposition could not yield substantive political results at the last general elections in October 2014. Admittedly, some parties took certain of their demands seriously and tried to incorporate them into their political agendas. But for the most part, the political system was not responsive and the 'Bosnian spring' turned into an ordinary Bosnian autumn. While public opposition from outside of the system has undoubtedly its merits—especially in the Bosnian context where any association with politics or the political system may be deemed immoral—and even though there is undoubtedly something noble in the gesture of not joining a political system which one

---

9   Jasmin Mujanovic, "It's Spring at Last in Bosnia and Herzegovina," February 11, 2014, http://www.aljazeera.com/indepth/opinion/2014/02/it-spring-at-last-bosnia-her zegov-2014296537898443.html. Last accessed 14 October 2014.

opposes, it ultimately seems highly doubtful that such public forums can have a substantial effect on changing the system as such, at least in the short term.

The problem thereby is not theoretical but practical. Contrary to many Bosnian politicians, I believe that the citizen's plena do indeed enjoy some form of legitimacy, which stems from the wide public support for their demands. And since the necessity to address these demands, as well as the public dissatisfaction with the political elites and the political system in general persist, it would be analytically careless to conclude that such civic and civil unrest in Bosnia has run its course. Perhaps together with the international community, such public pressure from below may very well turn out to be the only driver of political and social change in the country. It therefore remains to be seen in what form the larger public will emerge in the political discussions of the future. But for the moment, at least, it seems that the plena were rather situational phenomena that could not (yet) deliver major results. In practical terms, they have not only failed to transform their demands into a larger and more lasting political concept but, in the general elections of October 2014, they also could not prevent the re-election of the same patronage networks that have dominated Bosnian politics in the two decades since the end of the war. The reason for the recent electoral successes of the familiar political elites is not so much that the people—especially those engaged in the protests, but also as a whole—'tolerate' or 'appreciate' the politician's earlier behaviour but rather that this kind of behaviour based on the logic of self-perpetuation is the only one the system tends to produce. As even some politicians agree, the people make their decisions based on the poor choices they are given,[10] while the candidates make sure that ethnic fear, however defined, remains a salient issue of contemporary politics.[11] This is a relatively easy task given the still existing lack of trust among the people.[12]

But even though the current political system is largely to blame for Bosnia's stagnation, the major culprit is not Dayton. Terming the political elites 'Daytonians', as the previously cited Roger Cohen does, is therefore inaccurate, for it presents them as some sort of strict adherents to the Dayton system. Such claims rest on a fundamental misconception about Bosnian state structure. The DPA provisions in Annex IV are indeed the foundation of the post-war political system. But the contemporary dynamics *within* the political system—in other words, the reasons for the state's dysfunction—are only *partially* the consequences of Dayton. They are rather the product of some important systemic changes as well as usually well-meaning international intervention and imposition.

The purpose of this chapter is to analyse the dynamics within the political system as it currently unfolds in Bosnia-Herzegovina and to reflect upon the na-

---

[10]   Ljubić, Personal Interview in Sarajevo (BiH), 20 June 2012.
[11]   Mladen Bosić, Personal Interview in Sarajevo (BiH), 15 May 2012.
[12]   Mladen Ivanić, Personal Interview in Banka Luka (BiH), 7 July 2012.

ture of some of its major shortcomings. These shortcomings are widely known in the literature, but, until now, they have mostly been presented from an outsider's perspective.[13] Following the elite-centred approach of this study, my intention is to shine a light on the system through the eyes of the people involved, the key decision makers. Their understandings regarding some of the current deadlocks yield interesting insight into the functional mechanisms of Bosnia's consociation. They also help understand some of the major incentives inherent to the system with all of its positive and negative consequences. The Office of the High Representative, an important aspect of Bosnia's contemporary political system shall be discussed in depth in the next chapter, while the 'imposed consociational' character of Bosnia will be the topic of chapter 10.

The present chapter will first look at the nature of Bosnia's historical statehood debate as well as the understanding of the relationship between the political elite and its people. It will then proceed to a discussion of three topics closely associated with constitutional reform, the keystone of Bosnia's problems: the relationship between the entities and the state, the modern Croat Question, and the misuse of the *Sejdić and Finci* verdict.

8.1 The Historical Statehood of Bosnia-Herzegovina

Democratic theoreticians Linz and Stepan describe the 'stateness' problem of newly established polities in terms of contested borders, contested functions, and contested structures of the state.[14] Within the Bosnian context, the 'stateness' problem lies at the heart of any discussion surrounding the political system. As a starting point, we may look at Article 1 of the Dayton constitution. It states that Bosnia-Herzegovina 'shall continue its legal existence under international law as a state, with its internal structure modified as provided herein and with its present internationally recognised borders'. The internal structure was *inter alia* modified in order to include the territorial division between RS and FBiH, the latter of which resulted from the cease-fire Washington Agreement between the Bosniaks and Croats signed in March 1995. In legal terms, this provision sufficiently answers all questions related to the 'stateness' problem. Bosnia, with its known borders, was internationally recognised as a sovereign state in 1992 when it became a member state of the United Nations. Since 1995, its legal foundation is the Day-

---

[13] See, e.g., Bieber, *Post-War Bosnia*; Bose, *Bosnia after Dayton*; Chandler, *Bosnia*; Florian Bieber, "Power Sharing after Yugoslavia: Functionality and Dysfunctionality of Power-Sharing Institutions in Post-War Bosnia, Macedonia, Kosovo," in *From Power Sharing to Democracy. Post-Conflict Institutions in Ethnically Divided Societies* (Montreal/Kingston: McGill-Queen's University Press, 2005), 85–103.

[14] Juan J. Linz and Alfred Stepan, *Problems of Democratic Transition and Consolidation: Southern Europe, South America, and Post-Communist Europe* (Baltimore: Johns Hopkins University Press, 1996), 29.

ton constitution, which clearly stipulates the powers and responsibilities of the central state and the entities. In legal terms, functions, borders, and structures are thus quite clear.

But the way in which the constitution was elaborated and some of the provisions it contains have led to different interpretations of the state's character. Bosnian Serbs and, perhaps to a lesser extent, Bosnian Croats claim that modern Bosnia-Herzegovina was in fact *founded* with the signature of the DPA by 'gluing together' the two existing structures of the Federation and the RS.[15] Before that, all three groups exercised administrative, political, and above all military control over certain areas within the territory of the state. Accordingly, this view concentrates on a specific reading of the *de facto* situation during the war. Bosniaks, on the other hand, refer to the *continued* existence clause of Article 1 in order to argue that modern Bosnia was founded in 1992 as a sovereign state and that the DPA simply re-affirmed the already existing sovereignty.[16] Their argument is thus concentrated on a *de jure* assessment of the situation during the war, with the Republic of Bosnia-Herzegovina being the legitimate representative of the internationally recognised Bosnian state. In fact, it is the Dayton Agreement itself that put together the *de facto* and the *de jure* arguments and made them conceptually compatible. In terms of practical politics, the continued existence clause was a way to preserve Bosnia's statehood (something that by no means seemed certain during the war) by accommodating the structure with regards to the actual situation on the ground. It was, in other words, one of those many compromises of international politics that so painfully characterise this state's history.

But the underlying problem is much more fundamental than the rather simplified argumentation lines of Bosnian Serbs, Bosnian Croats, or Bosniaks suggest. It centres on the all-important question of the legal and political origins of Bosnian statehood. If Bosnia was indeed founded in 1995 by the DPA, this means that the units founding the state, FBiH and RS, enjoyed sovereignty and chose to delegate it to a central state with regards to a narrowly defined set of policy fields. As it is the natural privilege of the sovereign to change its mind, this implies the entities' right to resume their sovereignty at any time. Because the FBiH was indeed some sort of paper-tiger confederation between territories controlled by the HZ HB and the RBiH, respectively,[17] some readings of this argument even imply that the sovereignty might be constituted on a lower level. Since these territorial

---

[15]   Ljubić, Personal Interview.

[16]   Silajdžić, Personal Interview in Sarajevo (BiH), 15 May 2012.

[17]   The applicable clause 1 of the Washington Framework Agreements for the Federation reads: 'Bosniaks and Croats, as constituent peoples (along with others) and citizens of the Republic of Bosnia and Herzegovina, in the exercise of their sovereign rights, transform the internal structure of the territories with a majority of Bosniak and Croat population in the Republic of Bosnia and Herzegovina into a Federation, which is composed of federal units with equal rights and responsibilities.'

entities were *de facto* ethnically homogenous areas of the respective peoples, one ends up with the understanding that every *people*, i.e. not the territorial units *per se*, has in fact the right to leave the Bosnian state and to resume its sovereignty, if it wishes to do so.

Contrary to this, if Bosnia's continued legal existence is accepted, this means that the Yugoslav Republic of Bosnia-Herzegovina is the root of Bosnian sovereignty. This reading, which is in line with the provisions of the Badinter Arbitration Commission, would effectively mean that despite their *de facto* rule over the territory, the territorial units of RS or HZ HB never actually possessed any sovereignty in a legal sense. As such, their or their peoples' right to resume it is inexistent; and, legally, they need to be regarded as entities under paramilitary control rather than internationally recognised body politics. While this later understanding is in line with the provisions of international law and true to the historical context of the situation surrounding Yugoslavia's dissolution, one is well advised to consider both historical and legal narratives carefully. Both are significant with regards to contemporary politics. It is a direct result of these narratives that all parts of Bosnia can attribute some form statehood and sovereignty to themselves, at least as part of their political and group-based narratives. This poses great problems to the common state, which, despite being the undisputable holder of subjectivity according to international law, sees itself confronted with a shady authority at best.[18]

While the legal argument centres on the question of entity vs. central state sovereignty, it is based on a peculiar historical argument that goes well beyond the events of the 1990s and focuses on the 'common idea of the state of Bosnia-Herzegovina'[19] and its historical character. Interestingly enough, such discussions are not left to the historians, despite some suggestions that they should be.[20] In fact, what we can observe is quite the opposite, namely history becoming an important part of daily politics. It is in this light that Božo Ljubić, when asked about the *current* political challenges in Bosnia, embarks on a lengthy explanation of what he calls the country's 'historical context'. As a representative of Bosnia's Croats, he stresses that, apart from the medieval Bosnian kingdom, Bosnia was 'always part of some supranational association, always under some sort of occupation'. As such, he argues, Bosnia has 'no experience with independent statehood until '92, when the referendum vote was held and it was recognized as an

---

[18]   One example of this general division within the country is the fact that, apart from New Year's Day and 1 May, there are no common holidays in the two entities. Most prominently, Statehood Day (25 November, remembering the declaration regarding the structure of the SR BiH by Tito's communists in 1943) and Independence Day (1 March, date of the independence referendum in 1992) are not generally accepted.

[19]   Ljubić, Personal Interview.

[20]   Dragan Čović, Personal Interview in Mostar (BiH), 19 June 2012; Nebojša Radmanović, Personal Interview in Sarajevo (BiH), 7 November 2012.

independent state'. By presenting Bosnia's pre-Yugoslav history in this way, Lju-bić implies that Bosnia's statehood has no historical foundation. But he goes even a step further and disputes the logical counter-argument wherein Bosnia's state-hood, just like the statehood of any other Yugoslav Republic, derives its legitima-cy from the mere fact of *being* a Yugoslav Republic. He does so by presenting Yugoslav Bosnia (SR BiH) as some sort of anomaly within the entire Yugoslav system that, consequentially, cannot be discussed by using the same conceptual framework:

> I think that the creation of Bosnia-Herzegovina as a [Yugoslav] Republic at that time was in essence some sort of compromise and an attempt to solve the national ques-tions of Bosnia and Yugoslavia. ... For this reason, Bosnia and Herzegovina was *neither* Serb, *nor* Croat, *nor* Muslim, but [Serb], *and* [Croat], *and* [Muslim]. ... It was said that Bosnia-Herzegovina is a small version of Yugoslavia. It was said that Bosnia-Herzegovina was the heart of Yugoslavia. And, in the end, [this system] worked as it did. [It worked] as long as there was some, if I may say so, supra-ethnic, supra-national dictatorship. And when Yugoslavia broke up and the question of what should be done with the Republics was put on the table, a majority of the citizens of Bosnia and Herzegovina—those were the Croats and the Muslims, as they were called at that time—chose independence.[21]

It is in this way that the historical and the legal narrative meet to form a rather in-separable unit. Presenting SR BiH as some sort of anomaly within the Yugoslav system is of course defensible, for Bosnia was indeed the only Yugoslav Republic that was not nationally determined. But the claim that SR BiH, as a political and social system, functioned only as long as there was some sort of dictatorship di-rectly puts the state's probability to exist under conditions of democracy into question. The practical implications of such reading are clear: the inefficiencies and challenges of the current system only reflect an alleged historical truth, name-ly that in its democratic form, the state as such is doomed to fail. But taken to its ultimate conclusion, Ljubić's argument is even more radical. For without a histor-ically rooted statehood, something Ljubić denies, an independent Bosnian state as such has no *right* to exist. From this angle, the obvious shortcomings of the cur-rent political system not only testify to the state's improbability, but in fact to its illegitimacy. Since the state is not able to justify its existence through the services it provides, advocates of Bosnian statehood are also deprived of the rather power-ful defence strategy of arguing the state's output-legitimacy. Consequently, Bos-nia as a sovereign state becomes practicably impossible and intellectually incon-ceivable.

However, Ljubić is not willing to take his statement this far: 'It is my belief that Bosnia and Herzegovina is possible and necessary as an independent state, in which the rights of every person are respected', he says. According to him, Bos-nia has a 'potential' in that its peoples are accustomed to living together. From a

---

[21]   Ljubić, Personal Interview.

purely logical standpoint, it seems hard to reconcile Ljubić's view about the 'possibility' and 'necessity' of the Bosnian state with his earlier remarks about the country's obvious deficiencies when it comes to statehood. But those two views are by no means contradictory, for according to Ljubić an independent Bosnian state is only (intellectually and practically) feasible if one starts with the assumption that Bosnia's plurality demands the rights of the individual to be secondary to those of the collective to which the individual belongs. In Ljubić's words: 'in a country like Bosnia-Herzegovina [has become] after the experience of war, individual rights cannot be realised without the protection of collective rights'. We shall discuss the immanent political implications of this view in the sections dedicated to the Croat Question and the implementation of the *Sejdić and Finci* verdict in greater detail. For now, it seems sufficient to say that according to this view, Bosnia's statehood is only acceptable if the state protects the rights of the constitutive peoples *in absolute terms*. A liberal Bosnia, on the other hand, is *a priori* doomed to fail.[22]

It is no surprise that liberal Bosnian voices come to a different conclusion with regards to Bosnia's statehood and character. But interestingly enough, in addition to specific and more modern arguments based on the principles of human rights and non-discrimination (see below), the historical narrative as well forms part of their general argument. As Komšić defines the central assumption of this view, 'Bosnia and Herzegovina is not a state that has come into being artificially. Nobody created it. Bosnia and Herzegovina was not created at Dayton.' Instead, the state as such has a long history that testifies not only to its probability but shows the people's remarkable resilience to foreign rule and their desire of being independent. Bosnia's history, understood in those terms, is a history that finds its teleological fulfilment in an independent state. As Komšić explains:

> Bosnia-Herzegovina has existed for many, many years. It has its historical justification regardless of one's impression that the people in Bosnia and Herzegovina are terribly divided in terms of its future. Bosnia and Herzegovina is, after all, a historical category ... with its own foundation. Once it was a kingdom, then it was some sort of a *corpus separatum*, to use the modern term, in the Ottoman and Austrian Empires. In Yugoslavia, it was a Republic on its own, equal to Croatia, Serbia, and Slovenia, regardless of the fact that it was not [a] national, but [a] multinational [Republic]. So, Bosnia and Herzegovina survived. It also survived the period between 1992 and 1995, which was the most brutal period; [Bosnia-Herzegovina] was attacked, the international environment was unfavourable, and they tried to divide it! ... Bosnia and Herzegovina always survived. It will survive, that's not the problem.

---

[22]   Interestingly enough, Ljubić seems apparently unaware of the central contradiction in his argument with respect to the liberal character. His argument would be convincing if the observed failures of the Bosnian state, on which he bases a substantial amount of his argument regarding the improbability of maintaining the polity, were indeed a product of too much liberalism.

> And we will survive. Whatever may come, the most important thing for us is to be Bosnians or Herzegovinians. We have this historical foundation, this historical justification.[23]

The primary difference between the historical arguments of Ljubić and Komšić lies in the interpretation of the historical circumstances. Whereas Ljubić denies Bosnia's historical uniqueness and sees it as merely an administrative part of bigger empires, Komšić refers to the country's distinct position within those empires by designating it the status of a *'corpus separatum'*. Komšić's strategy to defend Bosnia's historical statehood is twofold. First, he claims that Bosnia's historical predecessor was a Yugoslav Republic, just like Croatia's, Serbia's, or Slovenia's. It has therefore the same right to sovereignty and independence as the others do. In legal terms, Bosnia and Herzegovina is thus equally legitimate to participate in the international concert of nations. Second, for Komšić the achievement of Bosnian independence is the fulfilment of a historical path of the Bosnian people. The state derives its legitimacy from the *wish of the people*, and not only from its status as a Yugoslav Republic. In fact, Komšić expresses a strong critique with regard to Yugoslavia's legitimacy when he says: 'Bosnia and Herzegovina is [also] not [equal to] the former Yugoslavia, which was created at Versailles after the First World War in an artificial manner under the influence of some powers that had their own interests.' So, according to this view, Yugoslavia was an artificial product, for it was not the genuine wish of its citizens, while Bosnia-Herzegovina expresses the teleological achievement of a deeply rooted historical desire.

Even though the views of Ljubić and Komšić constitute intellectually opposing concepts, they are nevertheless quite similar in structure and intent. In fact, if we examine them closely, we may very well conclude that those two views constitute nothing less than modern versions of the well-known nationalist argument. The chief difference is that Komšić sees the 'nation' as being composed of all citizens of Bosnia-Herzegovina ('Whatever may come, the most important thing for us is to be Bosnians or Herzegovinians', as he says), while Ljubić denies the possibility of an all-encompassing citizenry on Bosnian soil and, for reasons of pragmatic politics, advocates a state based on the rights of the different peoples—autonomy, in other words. Both try to legitimise their claims through the re-interpretation of historical facts, also a well-known device of the nationalist argument.

Under normal circumstances, one may be well advised to leave such discussions to the respective national intellectuals in the Bosnian, Bosniak, Croat, or Serb camps. But it seems important to re-iterate the fact that these historical narratives were presented by leading Bosnian politicians within a discussion of the *contemporary* Bosnian political system. As such, they are articulations of a gen-

---

[23]   Željko Komšić, Personal Interview.

eral political quarrel determining not only the public debate but directing the actions of the individuals involved. In fact, all discussions at which we shall look are, in one way or another, connected to the central disagreements with regards to the character of the Bosnian state.

8.2   The People and the Society

As we have seen, the people generally mistrust their political representatives and deem the entire political system inherently corrupt. Interestingly enough, even leading politicians seem to share the peoples' dissatisfaction with their behaviour—or rather with the behaviour of 'the political elites', in which they generally do not include themselves. It is in this context that one has to understand Mladen Bosić's frustration with the current political system, which, in the opinion of the SDS president, is gradually turning into a *'partocracy'*, a rule of parties instead of a rule of democratic institutions: 'We think that it is absurd that six party presidents solve all the matters of the state when there are institutions with elected officials within the parliament that are supposed to do so.'[24] It seems a hardly convincing statement that Bosić is indeed troubled by the situation (for which he blames the international community, not without merit, as we shall see), simply because he is one of the six party presidents involved in those talks. What he is rather doing is *publicly distancing himself from a system in which he participates.* The same holds true for Nebojša Radmanović, an educated historian who is upset with the 'politicians' willingness to delve into historical discussions' despite having 'no clue about it'. Radmanović also accuses the 'political elites' of expressing the general attitude 'it will somehow work as long as I am here [*Dok sam ja, pa nek ide kako ide*]', implying that they do not care what happens afterwards.

Similar in intent, though slightly different in structure are remarks by Dragan Čović, Željko Komšić, and Mladen Ivanić in this regard. When Čović speaks of the existing ethnic tensions within the society, he says that the situation would be 'easier, if we politicians were to change our attitude towards everyday life [in cases] when the national [issue] is concerned'. And furthermore: 'If we politicians would put more emphasis on European integration, economy, social justice, and [concentrate] more on social stability, I think the dimensions [of ethnic tensions] would be lower than they are today'. Such statements are only superficially an admission of the political elites' responsibility for the general mistrust in politics and they are not significantly different to the ones presented before. In truth, the only difference is that Čović includes himself in this group, whereas the formers distanced themselves from it. But neither does he take any responsibility for

---

[24]   *Nezavisne Novine*, "Mladen Bosić: BiH se pretvara u partokratiju," *Nezavisne novine*, 5 March 2012, http://www.nezavisne.com/novosti/intervju/Mladen-Bosic-BiH-se-pretvara-u-partokratiju-131072.html. Accessed 26 August 2013.

the situation. In fact, one is almost tempted to ask why he, a member of the political elite, does not simply behave as he thinks politicians should behave. The answer, one may suppose, could either be similar to the one given by Ivanić with regards to the importance of economic issues within the context of gaining electoral majorities or something along the lines of 'I'll do it when you do it' with regards to other politicians.

Željko Komšić's general view of the corrupt elites concerned only with their own benefits was already introduced at the beginning of the chapter. But here again, his general frustration explicitly includes himself: 'We need to ask whether this generation of politicians—and I include myself here—even has the mental capacities to [bring Bosnia into NATO and the EU]. We are simply too burdened by our relations in the former Yugoslavia. We are burdened with war. Those are not things we can simply erase from our minds. … Perhaps it would be best if this generation of politicians, the current political elite in Bosnia, would be simply removed from the picture.' Komšić proposes giving the younger generations a chance at governing, but concedes that such thoughts 'may sound laughable'. But, in essence, they are anything but laughable, at least not under the assumption that the new generations possess the potential to look at the matters with fresh eyes and are more open towards compromises. Given the ethnically segregated educational systems that promote ethnic distinction within the younger cohorts, however, one may doubt this assumption (see also below). But the major problem with Komšić's argument lies not in its utopian character but in its own inconsequentiality. If his statement were taken seriously, it would also mean that Komšić himself, a decorated war veteran, should step down. In terms of political debate, nothing would be achieved if the only serious liberal voice were to vacate the political scene; but the argument still stands as far as its genuineness is concerned.

The last of this second group that simultaneously distance themselves from the political elites and participate in the current game of politics is Mladen Ivanić. Admittedly, Ivanić has some right to talk about the political elites in terms of an outsider, for he is somewhat of an exotic example within Bosnia's political spectrum. He sees himself as 'not a typical politician' because he 'was not always concerned with being re-elected' and 'voluntarily left the government twice'. He says: 'I believe this was the only case in BiH that someone left the government of his own will'. Of course, one may doubt the degree of 'his own will' connected to the abstention within governmental functions. As Paddy Ashdown recalls: 'I like [Mladen Ivanić] very much, he's a very good politician. But he didn't have much power, so I didn't pay much attention to him. You know, the truth is Mladen lost elections.' It was thus not always Ivanić's choice to abstain from the game of politics. But one may nevertheless assume that his situation also gives him some freedom to judge the existing political elites in honest terms. He is probably not mistaken when stating that 'for real political, economic or other changes [to happen] one needs completely new political elites'. Since he does not see any political figures capable of constituting this new elite, he is 'not a big optimist' with regards to Bosnia's political future.

Bosnia's divided society

The politicians' attempts to distance themselves from the political elite to which they so clearly belong are only fully understandable within the context of Bosnia's divided society. As Mladen Ivanić explains when discussing the international community's relations to Republika Srpska, the latter is not 'a product of political elites and [their] ideologies' but 'simply the result of all that happened in Bosnia-Herzegovina in this unfortunate war'. As such, it is deeply rooted within the people—and so are the respective concepts and worldviews prevailing within the other groups. Following Radmanović, we may not think of Bosnia in terms of a multicultural society, because the 'daily experience is different. We can observe daily how the political elites think—each one for itself, Bosniak, Serb, Croat. Despite this, they keep publicly claiming that we are a multicultural society.' There is some merit in Radmanović's assessment, for a *multicultural* society presupposes the existence of a 'society', i.e. some societal idea that binds the members together. Particularities within this context are only acceptable within the borders of the larger society itself. Acts committed against the general principle of tolerance are condemned by all of the members alike, for tolerance and acceptance are understood as the glue that binds such societies together. Contrary to this concept, the present study has so far used the concept and terminology of a *divided or heterogeneous* society that puts the aspect on the particularities of specific segments within a general societal framework. Admittedly, we may debate the use of the term 'society', for within the Bosnian context we are clearly not confronted with one society, but three largely independent societal units.[25] Nevertheless, social interaction, as the backbone of the political system, happens within the context of one state. As such, it inherits the potentiality of becoming a multicultural society and affirms a common political framework for all. In these terms and in relation to the space of interaction between the different groups, I think it is therefore analytically defensible to conceive of it in terms of a society, albeit a divided one.

It is indeed a significant, though probably not uncontested feature of the Bosnian society that 'everybody behaves nationally, everybody represents their own national interests, but everybody talks about multiculturalism'.[26] This was even true in the final days of the Yugoslav system, where everybody talked about supporting multi- or non-nationalist parties, but the nationalist parties nevertheless gained majorities in the elections. The deeper reason for this phenomenon is

---

[25]   For this reason, newer consociational literature proposes the use of the term 'divided places'. See O'Leary, "Power Sharing in Deeply Divided Places."

[26]   Radmanović, Personal Interview.

of course the still existing lack of trust between the members of the society; after all, 'if there were trust, institutional problems might be solved'[27] (see also below).

In principle, there are two ways out of this dilemma concerning the character of the Bosnian society. One would be to accept the societal division, which would also include the affirmation of the dividing mechanisms Dayton provides (following the principle articulated by Radmanović: 'when you know what [responsibility] is [located] where and what [competency] is whose, then you can more easily talk about common relations'). This would mean the strengthening of entities, perhaps even the introduction of a more decentralised system. Whereas this strategy puts the accent on diversity over unity, the second way would be to do exactly the opposite. As Haris Silajdžić, a former member of Bosnia's presidency and grey eminence in the country's politics since its independence, explains:

> Bosnia and Herzegovina becomes more and more a state of three separate entities, instead of being a plural, multicultural state. … It is a fact that Bosnia's multiculturalism and plurality are questioned constantly. … I believe Europe needs a country that is traditionally multicultural; where pluralism and multiculturalism were successful for hundreds of years, with admittedly some problems that one will always have. … It is in my interest that this hundreds-of-years-old model does not vanish while we are fighting for a unified Europe.[28]

Within the two models of understanding Bosnia's multiculturalism, one is reminded of the same discussion patterns already explained in the previous section dedicated to statehood. This is indeed no coincidence, as those two political spheres are highly interdependent. While Bosnian Serbs and Bosnian Croats mostly think that diversity (i.e. entities) should be strengthened, Bosniaks and people adhering to a Bosnian national concept see the future in strengthening the unity aspect of Bosnian existence (i.e. central state). These concepts translate into political action insofar as the Serbs and Croats demand a highly federalised state structure, whereas the Bosniaks and people conceiving of themselves as Bosnians fight for a more centralised state (or rather, a less federalised one, see below).

However, it is important to note that the societal situation is not ubiquitously regarded as prone to ethnic tension or to be on a verge of collapse. In fact, some political leaders think that, given the experience of war, the conditions of living together (*suživot*) are 'acceptable',[29] 'surprisingly good,[30] 'a big success story'[31], or 'good, because [they are] not as bad as I expected'.[32] Some even think it better than in other places often compared to Bosnia, like Northern Ireland. There, they

---

27 Ivanić, Personal Interview.
28 Silajdžić, Personal Interview.
29 Čović, Personal interview.
30 Ljubić, Personal Interview.
31 Bosić, Personal interview.
32 Ivanić, Personal Interview.

claim, 'it is still the case that Catholics have to accompany their children to school when they go to through Protestant quarters' and '[any sort of public] manifestation needs big police protection'; in Bosnia, 'this has not been the case for a long time'.[33] However, such analogies are hardly convincing, for the situation portrayed does in fact not refer to Northern Ireland, but rather to the city of Belfast. Since, as a result of ethnic cleansing and low minority return,[34] there are only few really divided cities in Bosnia (the best known of which is Mostar), ethnic confrontation equal to the one in Belfast is obviously less common. Nevertheless, it is astonishing how positive the politicians' assessment of the societal situation is.

The recent 2010 Balkan Monitor has some data to support the claim that, at least in the perception of the public, relations among the three ethnic groups are indeed improving. Around 60% of Bosniaks express trust in members of the two other communities. Similar numbers are also found for Bosnian Croats (73% trust Serbs and 63% Muslims) and Bosnian Serbs (67% trust Catholics and 62% Muslims).[35] However, given the everyday experience on the ground, we may question the sincerity of such statements. But more important is the fact that, as the report also notes, trust in the others group members does not *per se* imply agreement with the feasibility of the common state: 'While majorities of both Bosnian Croats and Bosniaks (63% and 80%, respectively) did not agree with a potential secession of Republika Srpska in the case of a referendum in that entity, 87% of interviewees in the Serb entity supported the creation of an independent state if a majority of its citizens voted that way.'[36] In a recent representative survey,[37] Bosnians were asked whether or not they thought compromise with people who have a different opinion was possible. Nationwide, the answers were almost equally split with one third thinking it was possible and one third doubting it; roughly a quarter of people were undecided. Within the ethnic groups, forty per cent of Serbs and roughly thirty per cent of Croats and Bosniaks, respectively, doubted the possibility of compromise, while thirty-five per cent of Bosniaks and Serbs, respectively, as well as twenty-five per cent of Croats thought it possible. These results show that much needs to be done in order to lay the ground for compromise as a default option for political and societal cooperation.

Two sets of arguments form the base for the political leaders' positive assessments of the societal situation. The first one is the factual absence of ethnical-

---

[33]   Ljubić, Personal Interview.

[34]   Minority return refers to refugees returning to areas in which their ethnic group does not constitute a majority.

[35]   It is unfortunate that the Balkan Monitor uses the religious rather than the national terms.

[36]   *The 2010 Gallup Balkan Monitor. Focus on Bosnia-Herzegovina.*, 4.

[37]   *Frontal.ba*, "Istraživanje stavova građana BiH," *Frontal.ba*, 28 August 2013, http://www.frontal.ba/novost/64739. Accessed 29 August 13.

ly motivated violence in recent years[38] and the fact that there is no obstruction of communication between the people or between their elected representatives.[39] However, these are relatively low hurdles to overcome; consequently, such examples are employed to demonstrate that societal co-existence has achieved the highest level one may expect in a society like Bosnia. As Mladen Bosić puts it: 'You cannot expect "brotherhood and unity", which was not even present before the war, [to prevail], or that there are no different political interests. But the level of tensions [in Bosnia] is lower than in mono-national societies. Accordingly, our political campaigns are fought more mildly than those between the political fronts in neighbouring Serbia and Croatia.' Of course, even if this were factually accurate, Bosić is wrong in thinking that mild political campaigns testify to a stable societal situation, when, in fact, exactly the opposite is true.

The second set of arguments underlining the positive assessment of societal co-existence is the high regard the politicians express for the 'wisdom of the people' and their capabilities to manage their daily situation. 'The people', Ivanić says, 'are the better part of Bosnia and Herzegovina. They are better than the politicians.' He is seconded by Željko Komšić who claims that '[t]he people are cleverer than the politicians give them credit for'. What we may observe in these statements is not so much trust in the people, but trust in a concept of community to which the politician attributes himself as well. This is the logical continuation of the previously observed attempt to distance oneself from the political elite, which, if the act is successful, puts one among the people. But subscribing to this view of the people as a collection of *citoyen* that are morally and factually superior to the corrupt *classe politique,* also means restating the classical conundrum raised in the beginning of this chapter: why does the people elect such politicians? Why is it prone to nationalist propaganda and dismisses politicians that try to find pragmatic solutions? And, consequentially, do the people not bear ultimate responsibility for their politicians?

One answer suggested for this 'absurd' situation[40] may lie in the lack of democratic experience. Previous experiments in democracy have led to war, which is why the people, as a general rule, do not trust the political system and live in constant fear of renewed ethnic violence: 'there are no rational decisions because there is no democratic experience', says Ivanić. 'The people, when they make their decisions, do not base them on real values, [on the needs of] real life, but on something completely different, something irrational.' This happens despite the fact that the needs of real life are well known, and do not significantly differ from other societies: 'The people want what they always want', explains Komšić, 'a little bit of peace, a little bit of safety, a stable economic situation—

---

[38]   Ivanić, Personal Interview.
[39]   Bosić, Personal interview.
[40]   Ivanić, Personal Interview.

and of course security in the sense that nobody physically threatens their environment. This is what the people want—like anywhere else in the world.' There is an apparent contradiction in such comments that seem to enjoy majority support among the interviewed politicians. It runs against the ideal-type concept of a *citoyen* as a well-informed and morally committed individual if he or she can be manipulated. Komšić is thus correct in his view when he says that '[t]he politicians think that they can manipulate the people, but they cannot'. However, there is also some merit in suggesting that politicians consciously use instruments like media of communication in order to cultivate ethnic fear, from which they benefit. Manipulation of the people is, contrary to the ideal-typical concept expressed by the politicians, not only a possibility but also a practical reality in Bosnia. It follows a 'clear strategy' and subscribes to 'propaganda' of the well-known formula from the 1990s.[41, 42]

The relationship between the political elites and their people is complex. On the one hand, the elites take their cues from the people. The latent fears of the other groups express themselves not so much in low levels of trust but rather in the conviction about the temporality of living together and in the questioning of Bosnia's multicultural character. On the other hand, the politicians consciously cultivate those fears. Ethnic tensions are kept at a substantial level, for example

---

[41] Silajdžić, Personal Interview.

[42] Of course, another answer consistent with the general situation in Bosnia lies in the multitude of peoples that is not analytically distinguishable in the interviews. In other words, it is hard to assess what the politicians mean when they speak of 'the people'. The way in which the respective questions were posed clearly aimed at the citizenry of Bosnia and Herzegovina and there is strong evidence to suggest that the interviewees made the same assumption. In fact, within most of the interviews, there can be no doubt about it. The politicians clearly distinguished between their assessment of the people, and their actions for their people within the political system. However, it is conceivable (and be it only in the realm of a hypothetical possibility) that when talking about the general concept the people, they primarily referred to their own ethnic group. This would indeed make their views of the people and their political actions in the name of their people quite consistent. But it would also mean subscribing to a concept of the other people that is characterised by something more than mere distrust. It would mean advocating a moral supremacy of one's own people over the other peoples. As such, it would be characteristic of a chauvinistic view of ethnic distinction. One may argue that such views still persist in Bosnia and Herzegovina, and perhaps there is even evidence to back up this claim. But the politicians' interviews show a remarkable amount of awareness that would be incompatible with the public expression of such views. No one made the distinction between 'my people' and 'the people' within such a context. But it is true that this view is quite often found when dealing with the fact that they see themselves as representatives of one people and feel therefore obliged to pursue a policy that primarily aims at their electorates.

through different historiographies[43] or the segregationist concept of 'two schools under one roof' that ethnically divides education in divided cities.[44] The results of such policies are quite shocking in that a 'nationally poisoned youth' is created that hates members of the other groups without in fact knowing them.[45] It is only under conditions of extremely salient ethnic cleavages that the people are willing to tolerate the elites' hypocrisy. Since this is a phenomenon that encompasses all ethnic groups, there must be some common origin. As I shall try to argue, it can be found in the systemic incentives of an 'imposed consociation'.

8.3   Debating the State

The analyses of the statehood argument and the perception of the people form an important part of understanding contemporary Bosnia's fascination with debating the existing political structure. In recent years, this debate has centred around three different problem sets that are all interconnected but need to be distinguished analytically. The first one concerns the relationship between the entities and the state and targets the fragile division of powers and responsibilities; the second one is concerned with one specific aspect of this relationship, the so-called Croat Question and alludes to the fact that Croats are not given their own entity as they perceive the Federation as some sort of Bosniak-dominated instrument of majority rule; the third one refers directly to the second one, for it presents the contemporary opportunity to discuss these issues, even though the actual target of the *Sejdić and Finci* verdict of the European Court of Human Rights was clearly a different one.

8.3.1   The relationship between the state and the entities: more or less federalism?

It appears as if nobody is happy with the present state structure of Bosnia and Herzegovina. Some deem it 'too complicated'[46] and 'unsustainable';[47] some believe that it is bad because it furthers ethnic segregation;[48] and some deem the foundations of the Dayton structure discriminatory since they are not based on in-

---

[43]   Radmanović, Personal Interview. See also "Writing the Past," *The Economist* (5 January 2013), http://www.economist.com/news/books-and-arts/21569007-teaching-children-about-history-nationalism-and-right-and-wrong-writing-past, accessed 30 August 2013.
[44]   Silajdžić, Personal Interview.
[45]   Radmanović, Personal Interview.
[46]   Čović, Personal Interview.
[47]   Ljubić, Personal Interview.
[48]   Silajdžić, Personal Interview.

dividual but on collective rights.[49] Each of those claims is of course not without merit. But this kind of unity within the political elite as to the general dysfunctionality of the system has a far more obvious downside than the contents of each of those claims. For unhappiness with the current political system always includes, or at least logically implies, the impulse to change the situation. But it is a real challenge to change a state structure that resulted from a compromise between warring parties. In the words of Mladen Bosić: 'It is very hard to deconstruct this compromise because it is uncertain whether there can be any other compromise.' Since according to the provisions of the Dayton constitution any new compromise would need approval by all groups through the respective consociational mechanisms, and since any suggestion for constitutional change to date has failed to secure such an approval, one may end up with an infinite discussion that, although unsolvable, overshadows everything else. As Bosić explains:

> The continuous talk about the European Union and about constitutional changes is responsible for a blockade of the system and, in practical terms, a worsening of the situation. Instead of turning our attention to real reforms—starting with health, education, police, judiciary, media, etc., i.e. all segments of society—we are circling around those two big topics, which ultimately will turn out to be counterproductive as the priorities of society.[50]

But there is a more important aspect to the constant debate about constitutional changes than the mere fact that this topic overshadows everything else. A deeply rooted conviction that the current system is doomed to fail, that it is dysfunctional, unsustainable, and too complicated to comprehend, may in fact turn into a self-fulfilling prophecy. The political leaders may very well become victims of their own propaganda. In order to make their claims of the system's dysfunctionality credible, the system has to constantly demonstrate its inappropriateness. This task is of course easily achievable within a consociational framework. A politician may easily prove his statement that the system is dysfunctional by vetoing any decision and thereby making the system unworkable indeed. But it is not due to consociationalism *per se*, but rather to the logic of 'imposed consociationalism' that this strategy appears viable.

What consequences a constant fixation on constitutional reform has in terms of practical politics is of course almost entirely detached from the question whether or not constitutional reform is objectively needed. There is evidence to suggest that Bosnia's present state structure is inappropriate for a state wishing to join the European Union. But this is a political argument, and furthermore one that can be easily refuted. In theory at least, there is nothing that prevents Bosnia from staying outside of the EU. The need for constitutional reform is therefore

---

49   Komšić, Personal Interview.
50   Bosić, Personal Interview.

better deduced from the largely out-dated and furthermore inefficient state structure itself. It is out-dated because it lags behind with regards to the basic standards of the contemporary European concert of nations. The still existing discrimination of the non-constituent peoples, i.e. the national minorities, is only one example of many one may cite in order to show that the Dayton constitution, despite the noblest of ideas inherent in its preamble, is not apt for a European state in the 21st century.

But the argument of the state's ineffectiveness is even a stronger one, for the citizens experience it every day. The major characteristic of this aspect is the overblown state administration. An allegedly common joke alludes to Bosnia's many ministers and deputy-ministers by stating that when you shout 'Minister' in the central street of Sarajevo, fifty heads turn. But it is not so much the existence of some 160 ministries[51] that mirrors the bloated public sector since such inflation in functions and titles is quite common for federal states. Just to illustrate the point, one may think of Switzerland's 26 cantonal executives that have between five and seven members, each one of which is formally the head of one cantonal ministry and is furthermore likely to preside in government at some point when he or she will be called 'President'. The same comparison can be made to refute the claim of Bosnia's 'too many constitutions'—one for the central state, two for the entities, 10 for the cantons, and the Statute for Brčko—since Switzerland has in fact 27 constitutions (federal plus 26 cantons).

The inefficiency of the state structure shows itself therefore less in these obvious terms than in, e.g., financial matters. In 2009, the complete state bureaucracy absorbed an estimated 50 per cent of the gross domestic product.[52] At the same time, the conditions to attract foreign investment are not the least bit favourable, as the World Bank explains: 'The business environment in BH is likely the least friendly in the region, as it is burdened by a large and complex public administration system and layers of administrative approval authorities. The maze of authorizations and approvals needed, the overlapping competencies among the approving authorities, and the lack of harmonization among the relevant laws give rise to increased costs and risks of doing business.'[53] This is readily admitted by politicians like Dragan Čović who claims that, when the Federation is concerned, 'you cannot find an honest jurist invested in these issues that really understands who is responsible for what, [i.e. what competencies belong to] the municipality, the

---

[51]   According to Dan Bilefsky, "War's Lingering Scars Slow Bosnia's Economic Growth," *The New York Times*, 8 February 2009, http://www.nytimes.com/2009/02/08/world/europe/08bosnia.html. Accessed 30 August 2013.

[52]   Ibid.

[53]   World Bank Group, *Bosnia and Herzegovina Partnership Country Program Snapshot* (Sarajevo: World Bank Country Office Bosnia and Herzegovina, April 2013), 3, http://www.worldbank.org/content/dam/Worldbank/document/eca/BH-Snapshot.pdf.

city, the canton, the Federation, [or] Bosnia and Herzegovina.' These configurations should make constitutional reform a political imperative, even though they influence different policy areas in a different manner. Thus, while the general need for reform is a given, need for reform in specific areas may not *a priori* be assumed and is subject to careful consideration.

The main line of division between the three groups with regards to constitutional reform lies in the dichotomy between a more federalised system, in which the entities or cantons would gain even more responsibilities, and a more centralised state, in which the central state would exercise more powers. But this terminology of federalism vs. centralism, even though it is extensively used in the interviews, is inaccurate insofar as especially the term 'centralism' gives the false impression of a state like France as the ideal outcome. Within the Bosnian context, however, such a centralised state is not even a theoretical possibility. The entire debate, therefore, is about the degree of federalism rather than the dichotomy of federalism vs. centralism.

The Bosniak side is closely associated with the centralist, or more accurately less federalist, position. They deem the current structure expensive, not only in financial but in societal terms. The entity system, in the words of Haris Silajdžić, creates 'some standards that are not the best for the promotion of Bosnia and Herzegovina' and 'undermines some victories' of the past. What Silajdžić alludes to is his frequently made claim that Republika Srpska is based on a genocide and that the Serbs, instead of being punished for the war and especially the events in Srebrenica, have been rewarded with their own state-like entity. As he has shown during his presidency, Silajdžić is a fierce supporter of a structure without entities, one with 'as few layers of government as possible'. He argues for a strong central state and a strong local community that 'possesses the necessary resources [i.e. financially and politically] to be held accountable by the citizens'. In his view, this would signify the introduction of real, locally based democracy instead of the current 'ethnic'-model democracy; he sees the latter as a contradiction in terms, for 'democracy is not founded on an ethnic group but on the individual'. Silajdžić's position, as well as those of the Bosniaks in general, would mean a fundamental restructuring of the state, preferably the abolishment of entities and their replacement by non-ethnically determined federal units that would have much less power than RS and FBiH have today. Interestingly enough, it seems as if it is not the principle of subsidiarity that should determine the division of power between the central state and the federal units, but some preconceived notion that the central state needs certain responsibilities in order to function efficiently.

Closely connected to the argument of increased efficiency is the claim for introducing the liberal principle 'one person, one vote' as the new standard. This is the reason why the demands of the Bosniaks are closely associated with those of the 'liberal group' to which Komšić belongs. The 'liberals' also demand a functional and strong central state without ethnic privileges, but argue their case not solely based on the inefficiency and destructive tendencies of the current system, but out of a deeply rooted conviction in liberal democracy and equality before the law. But even though Silajdžić articulates this claim as well, it may be doubted how sincere the Bosniak political elite really is with respect to the abolishment of the ethnic principle. The latter has also served them well in the past. The SDA, for example, has frequently claimed the infringement of Bosniak vital interests in the House of Peoples for purposes of political gains; it did so some years ago, when its ministers were to be removed from the central government, since the governing coalition had broken and the SDA members were supposed to be replaced by SBB members. Even though, in factual terms, the outgoing and the incoming ministers were all Bosniaks, the SDA referred the matter as a threat to the Bosniak vital interest to the Constitutional Court that, unsurprisingly, decided against them.[54] But such examples show rather the *modus vivendi* in the current system, and they are hardly indisputable proof of Bosniak elite intentions with regards to a future state structure.

It is a matter of fact, however, that the Bosniak side wishes to strengthen the central state and, thus, take away responsibilities from the entities. Since the EU has also pushed their pre-accession efforts in this direction, it provoked the perception of favouritism among representatives of the other groups. Bosnian Serbs and Bosnian Croats are clearly opposed to any strengthening of the central state, as they perceive these efforts as well as the liberal principle as instruments of 'majority rule' by the Bosniaks.[55] This view is of course based on the belief that Bosniaks constitute an overall majority in the country and would therefore be able to dictate decisions and dominate elections if they follow the majoritarian principle closely associated with 'one person, one vote'. However, since the data from the first post-war census of 2013 is not yet available and, in any case, may be questioned due to the process of its collection, it is unclear whether Bosniaks constitute indeed an overall majority. It is furthermore doubtful that the electorate as a whole would behave in the way Serbs and Croats fear, for the Bosniaks have been the only group in which multinational candidates and parties have managed to gain substantial support. In fact, it is often claimed that the SDP is not a multinational but rather a Bosniak party because it is dominated by Bosniaks and enjoys substantial Bosniak support. Moreover, the election of Željko Komšić as the Croat member of the presidency allegedly happened due to Bosniak votes (see below).

---

[54]   *Srna*, "Dom naroda danas glasa o smjeni ministara i zamjenika iz SDA," *Klix.ba* (22 October 2012), http://www.klix.ba/vijesti/bih/dom-naroda-danas-glasa-o-smjeni-ministara-i-zamjenika-iz-sda/121021085. Accessed 30 August 2013.

[55]   Ljubić, Personal Interview; Čović, Personal Interview; Bosić, Personal Interview; Radmanović, Personal Interview.

More important than such fluid fears is that Bosnian Serbs and Bosnian Croats claim that the current system is already too centralised and should therefore be reformed. While the former want to stick to a minimalist reading of the Dayton constitution and even reclaim all the responsibilities they already transferred to the central state in the past,[56] the latter express a certain readiness to negotiate the Dayton framework—but only if it leads to more territorially concentrated areas with clear Croat majorities, i.e. if they gain a third entity of sorts.

The Serb position is dictated by a specific interpretation of the Dayton constitution. Even though the Serbs originally opposed the Peace Agreement and did everything to crush it, they have come to see the advantages of the system it envisioned. The problem, in the Serb reading, is that the DPA was changed and wrongfully interpreted in the past, which led to Republika Srpska losing some of the competencies Dayton so clearly awarded to the entities.[57] Accordingly, there is need for constitutional reform; however, not to delegate competencies to the central state following the principle of subsidiarity or to come up with some new federal structure, but rather to take the responsibilities back that the entities have 'surrendered'. As Nebojša Radmanović explains, the 'easiest solution' would be to return to something he calls the 'original Dayton Agreement' (*osnovni Dayton*) because it 'already solved all those issues [of constitutional structure] in a specific form'. In his mind, subsequent changes of the DPA are the root of all the problems:

> [The problem blocking Bosnia's functioning] is that international representatives, with the help of us locals, have complicated the matter since [Dayton was signed]. And now they say that it can't work. Of course it can't! This attitude lends support to those who think a more centralised state would work better; but it also lends support to those who want more decentralisation and who think that a more decentralised or even separated state would work better. Those are our problems, out of which the daily non-compromises and other things develop.[58]

The Serb position rests on the central claim that the 'original' Dayton, one without a Bonn empowered High Representative and minimal functions for the central government would work well and that the current problems are the result of an abandonment of core Dayton principles. There is merit in this reading, for the actual Dayton arrangement, as we shall see in the next chapter, never really had a chance to start working before the High Representative assumed its Bonn powers. Radmanović alludes to this fact when he states that, without external interference, 'we in Bosnia-Herzegovina would surely have agreed upon some common responsibilities where it would have been beneficial; in those areas that are better

---

56   Radmanović, Personal Interview.
57   Ibid.
58   Ibid.

decided in Sarajevo than in Mostar, Banja Luka, Zenica or Tuzla. But we did not do so, because we came to more common responsibilities due to outside pressure, and now we are fighting against those.'[59] In this respect, we find ourselves in the middle of the chicken and the egg argument, for it is not clear whether the ineffectiveness of Dayton made the introduction of Bonn powers necessary or whether Dayton became only ineffective once the Bonn powers were introduced. There is evidence in support of both readings, as we shall see in the next chapter. However, it would be daring to conclude the failure of original Dayton after less than a year of actual working; at the same time, there is no way to convincingly prove that the original Dayton plan may have worked if given more time. We are thus left with the current, aptly termed post-Dayton system to analyse its dynamics; all other arguments belong to the realm of hypotheticals that defy falsification.

But despite such merits of Radmanović's argument, one may nevertheless question the sincerity of the Serb's wish to return to the 'original Dayton'. As the former member of the Presidency admits in passing, previous transfers of competencies to the central level did not always happen as a result of OHR imposition, but they were backed by legitimate claims and arguments to which the Serb side agreed in parliament. When Mladen Ivanić was in a position of power in the early 2000s, he agreed to the introduction of a state-wide value added tax system (VAT), because he knew that 'this VAT system would be beneficial for Republika Srpska'. And it is for the same reason that he agreed to the formation of the State Investigation and Protection Agency (SIPA), a state-wide secret service that was to replace respective bodies on the entity levels and that even today bears its English name and acronym. He also agreed to unify the armed forces under central command of the BiH presidency because 'it did not harm the Serbs in any way'. In other words, he supported those projects out of the conviction that they were necessary. As Ivanić explains his deciding principle: 'I am ready to make positive steps, if those do not run counter to the interests of the people that I represent [i.e. the Serbs] but may serve others. Why wouldn't I make such a decision? I think that's a correct manner of handling things and that is how I generally behave.' Of course, Ivanić's principle is open to interpretation insofar as it is unclear (in absolute terms) what the interests of the people really are. But his statement nevertheless shows that the current system, even though it clearly differs from the 'original Dayton', is also in part the product of a genuine evolution. Some of the changes were indeed part of what Radmanović proposed as a possible trajectory, namely that the local elites would agree to transfer certain competencies where they best belonged. The Serb political elite at that time supported

---

[59]   This optimistic view seems to contradict Radmanović's belief that the Bosnian political elites would not have been able to achieve compromise by themselves when the peace agreement was concerned.

those changes, including, as Radmanović admits, his SNSD. His claim of general outside imposition is, therefore, a half-truth.

The Serb demand to return to the 'original Dayton' is counterintuitive insofar as Dayton does not prohibit changes to the constitutional structures but makes them dependent on the agreement of the three groups. It is therefore logically incongruent to demand a return to the previous state of affairs based on a document according to the provisions of which the previous state was changed. This argument is of course more powerful for decisions made by the parliament than for those imposed by the High Representative. As far as the former are concerned, one may make the argument that, if one wishes to change the current structure, one needs to follow the Dayton procedure and overturn the respective laws accordingly. Since this is highly unlikely under the current circumstances and the established bodies on the central level have developed an institutional structure on their own, the Serb demand to regain competences is hardly a self-sustaining political position. Moreover, an inaccurate reading of the Dayton constitution delegitimises it. Radmanović, for example, in an effort to minimise central state competencies claims that 'according to Dayton, there are three ministries [on the central level] and the responsibilities [for governing] are divided between those three ministries and the Presidency'. While the latter part is true, as we have seen, the notion of only three ministries prescribed by Dayton is highly misleading. According to the constitution, the Chair of the Council of Ministers 'shall nominate a Foreign Minister, a Minister for Foreign Trade, *and other Ministers as may be appropriate*'.[60] Dayton therefore prescribes *at least* three ministers, not three at most. This goes to show that supporters of the 'original Dayton' and adherents of an allegedly 'strict reading' may also support interpretations in which, as the German proverb goes, the wish is the father to the thought.

The Bosnian Serb position to reclaim entity responsibilities is best understood as a political strategy directed against all further 'centralisation' efforts. The Serbs know very well that, in the words of Radmanović, 'what has been transferred [to the central level], has been transferred. There is no possibility to gain it back'. Nevertheless, any further delegation of competencies from the entities to the central state remains a red line.[61] This should, however, not prevent the political class to make the present arrangement work. As Mladen Bosić explains with regard to all the political communities: 'I may like it or not, but [Dayton] is the current framework that exists. Only when we accept this and when we agree that we need to find solutions within this framework will we be able to do something.'

---

60   Constitution of Bosnia and Herzegovina, Art. 5, paragraph 4, my italics.
61   Bosić, Personal Interview; Radmanović, Personal Interview.

The Croat position is highly determined by the experiences of war and a general unhappiness with the Dayton arrangement. In the Washington Agreement, the Croats and Bosniaks divided the Federation among themselves. In this setting, the partition of the country into ten cantons, eight of which have a clear national majority of either Bosniaks or Croats, put those two groups in a position of symmetry within a central state system. But when the Dayton Agreement took the Washington Agreement as its foundation, it degraded the position of the Federation to an entity within a new constitutional structure of the common state. As a result, the autonomy of the two groups was delegated one level further.

According to the Croat reading, their group is structurally discriminated against within the current system for, unlike the Serbs (RS) and the Bosniaks (FBiH), they do not have an entity on their own. It is for precisely this reason that the post-1995 establishment of the Federation took quite some time. Croats were not ready to delegate any competencies to the Federation, which they perceived as being dominated by the Bosniaks. Consequently, they held on to the instruments of self-government and autonomy within their parts of the entity; in other words, in the second half of the 1990s, they clung to the para-state structures of *Herceg-Bosna*. During this time of *Hrvatska samouprava* (Croat self-government), they masterfully played a double game: they pretended to be eager to participate in the Federation setting if their demands were met, but, with financial support from Croatia, they kept parallel structures alive in areas under their control. This double play, in which most of the current Bosnian Croat political elite participated, came to an end due to an aggressive removal policy by the High Representative. It culminated in the removal from office of Ante Jelavić, the Croat member of BiH presidency, in March 2001. Jelavić, a former Defence Minister of the Federation and president of HDZ, actively pursued a separatist agenda and tried to establish a third entity in areas where Croats were in the majority. To finance these efforts he used funds from Croatia, which were funnelled through the *Hercegovačka banka*. The international community, in the form of the OHR and SFOR, finally put an end to such activities that clearly ran counter to the DPA.[62] These events convinced the Bosnian Croats that they could not force the creation of a third entity by establishing a *fait accompli*. Additionally, after the revelations of the *Hercegovačka banka* scandal and the change in government in the early 2000s, Croatia significantly reduced its financial support to Bosnian Croats. They were henceforth forced to try their luck within the Dayton structures.

But subsequent events did not necessarily make them more eager to compromise. In 2002, Dragan Čović was elected Croat member of Bosnia's state presidency. However, when in 2005 the State Prosecutor indicted him for 'alleged

---

[62]   Anes Alic, "Influential Bosnian Croat Trio Arested," *Transitions Online*, 26 January 2004, http://www.tol.org/client/article/11490-influential-bosnian-croat-trio-arrested.html. Accessed 2 September 2013.

abuse of office or official authority, lack of commitment in office, conspiracy to perpetrate a criminal offence, organized crime and other counts', High Representative Paddy Ashdown decided to remove Čović from office.[63] The charges concerned his actions when he was Federation Minister of Finance between 1998 and 2001. As Čović recalls, Ashdown told him something along the lines of 'Dragan, you were an outstanding politician in my eyes, an outstanding president, etc. But, you know, there are certain allegations that you did some things, etc., and I therefore ask you to resign.'[64] Čović, according to his account, refused and proposed instead to let his mandate rest until the courts had come to a verdict. He did so because 'I knew very well what I had done and saw no need [to fear the courts] as I am absolutely clean'. But Ashdown was not willing to agree to such a solution and threatened to remove him. 'And that's when I said: "Use your Bonn powers and remove me!"'[65] Ashdown, who had no choice but to follow up on his earlier threats, based his decision to remove Čović on three arguments: first, the fear of international isolation if the official representative of the Bosnian state is facing criminal charges; second, the negative consequences to the reputation of the State presidency within Bosnia; and third, the possibility that the controversy over Čović's position might lead to political paralysis.[66] The judicial process against Čović—which consisted of several indictments on different federal levels and some convictions, which were later reversed by upper courts—came to an end only in May 2012 when Čović was formally cleared of any wrongdoing. The proposal to let his mandate rest would therefore hardly have been feasible, for the Croats would have been left without representation for an indefinite amount of time. Ashdown's arguments are quite compelling and his course of action was surely appropriate in a situation where Čović did not possess the dignity to resign himself.

But apart from the actual need for this removal, the High Representative's decision fuelled the conviction of some Bosnian Croats that the state and the international community was hostile towards them. As Čović explains, some Croats came to him and said: 'Dragan, if this can happen to you, what can my children and I expect? I can't live here.' It is against this background that the Croats' realignment to the Bosnian state has to be seen. It resulted first and foremost from a turn in the position of the Bosnian Croat elite who, despite the most recent events, had realised that their future lay within Bosnia.

---

63   See OHR, 'Decision Removing Dragan Čović from his Position as a Member of the Presidency of BiH', 29 March 2005, http://www.ohr.int/decisions/removalssdec/default.asp?content_id=34397, accessed 2 September 2013.

64   That is how Čović remembered Ashdown's words in the interview he gave me.

65   Čović, Personal Interview.

66   OHR, 'Decision Removing Dragan Čović'.

> Objectively speaking, these events provoked largely negative reactions among a large number of Croats—and I am talking about the positions of the people around me. There was no hatred, but [a negative perception] of this relationship. And it took me and us a great effort in the last four or five years to make the Croat Democratic Union [HDZ] a party in which no prominent member, i.e. no minister, director, representative, etc. advocates against Bosnia and Herzegovina as his country.[67]

That the Croat elites turned their attention to Bosnia is also understandable from another perspective. In general terms, they had three choices: to seek unification with Croatia, to try to establish a third entity by force, or to try to engage in the current system and thereby seek opportunities to reform it. After the second option was ended by the international community, they settled on the third one, which characterises their current position. But it is important to highlight that especially in the first post-war years the first was a rather powerful wish. Unification with Croatia was of course a practical impossibility, but it remained a political option in line with the dreams of nationalist unification and independence. This is the deeper reason why the Croatian government of Franjo Tuđman continued supporting the Bosnian Croats and even paying wages to Croat officials within Bosnia's state structure. When Tuđman died in 1999 and his party lost the elections of January 2000 to the opposing Social Democrats, this nationalist cooperation largely came to an end. At around the same time, the Bosnian Croats must have realised that being part of Bosnia, where they are granted special privileges due to their status as a constitutive nation, is a comparably better position than being part of Croatia, where they would just be another federal entity without any special privileges or reserved seats. Around that time, they decided to pursue the second strategy, which would eventually turn into the third and seek to strengthen the privileged positions of the Croats within Bosnia.

Within the discussions of the state structures, the Bosnian Croats are therefore found somewhere in the middle between the Bosnian Serbs and the Bosniaks. Like the Bosnian Serbs, they oppose any further centralisation efforts and the principle 'one person one vote'. Like the Bosniaks, they regard the Dayton structure as something that was supposed to be 'preliminary', a solution 'to end a war', as Božo Ljubić explains. He deems the present structure 'dysfunctional' because it is 'not self-sustainable'. Concretely, he demands the establishment of 'a different territorial [and] administrative structure' that would 'take into account the realities: that three constituent peoples live here, that [Bosnia] cannot be centralised, and that it can neither function nor survive on the principle of a dominant majority—not only on state, but also on entity level'. Implicit in these words is the critique of the current situation, where Croats 'suffer' from a Bosniak majority in the Federation. If his idea were realised, Bosnia would consist of a central state and several federal units. In the latter, 'one of the people will always be in

---

67   Čović, Personal Interview.

the majority', preferably in a relative rather than absolute one. It is therefore important to counter such territorial autonomy with what he calls 'institutional equality', namely the establishment of consociational elements within the central state and the federal units. In Ljubić's words: 'For some time, I advocated—I would not say naively, since I am not naïve—but I put much more emphasis on the institutional component of consociation; lately, I believe that equality in Bosnia and Herzegovina needs also a territorial foundation.' In accordance with Ljubić's view that the ethnic principle has to take precedent over the individual one, he seeks to establish the territorial units following the (relative) majority principle; and to counterweigh the thereby created potential for rule by the majority through consociational elements of veto powers and proportional representation.

Implicit in this proposal is something that only secondarily concerns the relationship between the state and the entities. Dragan Čović as well as Božo Ljubić agree that Bosnia's current state structure is complicated and ineffective and should therefore be reformed. That is what Čović means when he argues for only three levels of government—Bosnia and Herzegovina, entities, and local self-government—in order to make the governmental structure more rational. As he explains: 'Today, I believe we have two thirds more employees in the state apparatus than we really need and than we can pay.' But, in their view, far more important than actual ineffectiveness of the structures is the discriminatory element of the current state structure that left the Croats in a position where they cannot articulate their interests properly. This view is primarily based on something that has become known as the Croat Question.

8.3.2 The Croat Question

In its contemporary form, the Croat Question presented itself for the first time in 2006. At the general elections, SDP candidate Željko Komšić gained some 116,000 votes and was elected as the Croat Member of Bosnia's state presidency. He clearly beat his fiercest competitors—Ivo Miro Jović from HDZ (who achieved 76,700 votes) and Božo Ljubić from HDZ1990 (with 53,300 votes)—and secured almost forty per cent of the votes.[68] His election presented a novelty, for the elected Croat member to date had always been a representative from the major Croat parties, not one of a nominally multinational party. His achievement was suspicious to the Croat parties especially because Komšić managed to accumulate more votes than the coalitions of HDZ and HDZ1990, respectively. As the results for the BiH House of Representatives show, the former won some 68,200 votes, whereas the latter secured 52,000 of them; in other words, even combined, those two party coalitions achieved only some 4000 votes more than Komšić on

---

[68] For election results, see the Central Election Commission, available at www.izbori.ba, last accessed 3 September 2013.

his own. Even though it is, as Komšić rightly points out, impossible to say who voted for whom, for the Croat parties there was only one explanation for this kind of victory: the Bosniaks must have voted for Komšić, whereas the Croat electorate voted for HDZ and HDZ1990 candidates, respectively. In other words, the Bosniaks chose the Croat representative. Four years later, when Komšić was seeking a second term, he beat the Croat competitors even more impressively. He achieved some 337,000 votes (or 60 per cent), whereas HDZ candidate Bojana Krišto got 110,000 and HDZ1990 candidate Martin Raguž some 60,000. This time, even more Bosniaks must have voted for Komšić who gained twice as many votes as Bakir Izetbegović, the winner of the Bosniak seat.

If we remember the discussions of the constitutional structure (see previous chapter), the Bosniak and the Croat members of the state presidency are directly elected in the Federation. All voters get two lists and can therefore decide by themselves for which candidate they want to vote. It is therefore possible for a Bosniak to vote on the Croat presidency member ballot (and vice-versa); for national minorities, like Roma, Jews, or even the Serbs in the context of the Federation, voting for a non-group candidate is the only choice to voice their opinion on who is to govern them. Whatever the circumstances, Komšić's election was legal, for it was in full accordance with the constitution and the electoral law. However, it raises some questions of legitimacy. The constitution prescribes only that the Croat member of the state presidency is to be elected in the Federation and has to be a Croat. Among serious observers, there can be no doubt that Komšić fulfils both criteria. According to the quasi-liberal view, therefore, he is the legitimate representative of the Croats in the presidency. As Komšić says:

> If the Bosniaks mainly voted for me—let us say [for the sake of argument] that they most probably did—what is the problem? The constitution clearly states that this is [legally] possible. So, is it not the aim to trust each other in this country? If you have to prove that you are a good Croat by having Bosniaks or Serbs hate you—or that you are a good Serb if Bosniaks and Croats hate you—what country is that? I do not want to live in [such a country]! That is not the paradigm according to which I want to behave. Regardless of all the tragic experiences in this country, I do not accept to live like that. I do not want to live like that.[69]

Komšić, even though he does not want to discuss the issue at that level, nevertheless points out that nobody has ever said to him, which, if any, of his actions harmed Croat interests. He sees himself therefore as a legitimate representative of the Croats. However, according to the view of the Croat nationalist parties, HDZ and HDZ1990, the mere fact that he occupies the Croat seat in the presidency is harmful enough. As they claim, the legitimacy of a *Croat* member is ultimately rooted in the electorate that elects him, not in his personal characteristics. As Božo Ljubić puts it:

---

[69]   Komšić, Personal Interview.

> Željko Komšić is an ethnic Croat. Nobody denies his belonging to the Croat nation because he declares himself accordingly. That is enough for me. But Bosniaks elected him twice. That is the root of our frustration! I keep repeating it: I am born as a Croat in southern Herzegovina, in a region almost entirely inhabited by Croats. But this is not the reason why I am a political representative of the Croats—I am because of the people who voted for me.[70]

It would be outside the scope of the present thesis to discuss the different modes of representation and the philosophies on which they are grounded. Suffice it to say that the Croat position assumes the absolute congruity between the electorate and the elected, even if it is not said so directly. Hypothetically, if the entire Croat electoral corpus voted for a Bosniak, the Croat national parties would hardly see him as the representative of the Croats—because he is not a Croat. What they want is Croats electing those members of government and parliament whose position is nationally designated. In other words, Croat members elected by Croats should, e.g., occupy the Croat seat in the state presidency, the Croat positions in the House of Peoples, etc. While understandable enough, this position is dangerous within a democratic setting, for, ultimately, it makes multi-national candidates impossible. A multi-national candidate, by definition, recruits her electorate from different national groups even though she can only belong to one of those groups (or the 'others') at the same time. The congruity the Croat politicians demand is therefore a sectarian mean in order to further national cohesion. If taken to its ultimate conclusion, one ends up with a view according to which a true and legitimate Croat is only someone who comes from the Croat nationalist parties, in other words a member of this or that HDZ. (As Božo Ljubić claims, the HDZ and HDZ1990 coalitions combined achieved almost 90 per cent of the Croat electoral votes.[71])

But the Croats' discomfort with Komšić goes well beyond philosophical differences on the modes of representation. In their view, their national interests are harmed by the election of Komšić. As Čović explains, the Presidency is, for example, responsible for naming ambassadors and for conducting Bosnia's monetary and security policies. In addition, it is responsible for naming the Chairman of the Council of Ministers. 'So', Čović concludes, 'when you do not have your member of the presidency, none of your candidates will ever be named Chairman of the Council of Ministers. This is what we have experienced in the last eighteen months.' Čović refers to the fact that it took the Bosnian politicians around one and a half years to form a new coalition government after the general elections of 2010. Since the abolishment of the rotating chairmanship during the legislative period, this position is rotated between legislative periods. After Adnan Terzić

---

[70] Ljubić, Personal Interview.

[71] Božo Ljubić, "Croat Question—Key to the Stability of Bosnia and Herzegovina," speech at the National Federation of Croatian Americans, Pittsburgh, 4 June 2011.

(Bosniak, 2002-2007) and Nikola Špirić (Serb, 2007-2012), the position was to go to a Croat representative. But the government formation took such a long time because of different interpretations of who was a legitimate Croat representative. Was the SDP able to nominate a Croat from their ranks, or has this position to be occupied by a Croat from HDZ or HDZ1990? Finally, when the new government assumed office in January 2012, Vjekoslav Bevanda, a Croat from HDZ, became its chairman.

With respect to the present discussion, these events show, first, that Komšić's position did not prevent a Croat from HDZ being elected as head of government. Čović's fear thus turned out to be unsubstantiated, for even if the Presidency formally names the Chairman, the latter has to be confirmed by the parliament. Ultimately, the Presidency is deprived of all substantial powers in this matter as the selection of a Chairman and a governing coalition is a matter for parties. Second, this example shows a remarkable tendency to transform political disagreement into a discussion of legal matters. Disadvantages in the political area are thus explained by and presented as evidence of alleged legal discrimination that proves a larger point—in this case the discrimination against Croats by the state structure.

When Čović, in the just cited statement, refers to 'you' and 'your candidate', he does not mean a Croat representative; rather, he refers to what he perceives as a *legitimate* Croat representative. Accordingly, when such a representative is missing, the Croats' political influence is *de facto* marginalised. From this perspective, the election of Komšić can be seen as a deliberate attempt by the Bosniaks to secure more political power. As Mladen Bosić says: 'They [the Bosniaks] did not vote for Željko Komšić because he is some sort of intellectual or grand politician; they voted for him because they had enough political understanding to secure a bigger influence for the Bosniak political agenda.' What Bosić considers the 'Bosniak political agenda' is what is commonly referred to as the centralisation argument within the constitutional reform discussions. But rather than being the expression of a distinctively Bosniak agenda, this is actually, as we have seen, an area where liberal and Bosniak positions are congruent. We may also doubt the notion that the election of Komšić was completely detached from his personality, since he is among the few politicians that the people generally respect. As a decorated war veteran fighting for a unified Bosnia and as someone who repeatedly talks in frank terms to the people, he enjoys much credibility among the general public committed to the idea of a strong Bosnian state.

The election of Željko Komšić made the Croats question their general position within the structure of the Bosnian state. They came to the conclusion that they are structurally discriminated against, not only because they do not possess their own entity (as we have seen), but because the state itself is inherently designed to discriminate against them. In a speech to the National Federation of

Croatian Americans in the United States, Božo Ljubić developed this modern Croat Question in its entirety.[72] Accordingly, the Bosnian constitution contains the central antinomy of being a state of three constituent peoples while only possessing two entities that can be attributed to either the Serbs or the Bosniaks. This, in Ljubić's words, 'sealed the fate of the oldest, but also the least numerous Croat people'. It made them ask themselves, he claims: 'Did the great powers assigned [sic] us to be a "collateral damage" in the regional reshuffling of the "Balkan historical disorder" that began upon the disintegration of Yugoslavia'?

More to the point than such rather polemical questions is Ljubić's analysis of the Dayton system and especially its amendments. The 'critical impact on the constitutional position of the Croats in FBiH', in Ljubić's view, happened with the changes that Wolfgang Petritsch made to this entity's constitution: 'The consequence of his amendments was that the Croats have lost those minimum mechanisms for protection of their ethnic rights in the Federation BiH, envisaged by Dayton'. Concretely, Ljubić refers to the procedure of extending candidacies for presidents and vice-presidents of the FBiH presidency. Whereas until 2002, the Bosniak and Croat clubs in the FBiH House of Peoples proposed one candidate who had a majority of support in each club, afterwards one third of the support was enough. Similarly, a majority in the House of Representative and a majority within the group of representatives in the House of Peoples chose the president before. After 2002, this procedure applies only in the first round, whereas in the second round, the candidates only require a simple majority in the House of Representatives, in which, in Ljubić's words, 'the Bosniaks are the distinct majority'. Lastly, it constitutes an 'absurdity' to Ljubić that 'according to the Election Law more Croat delegates to the [House of Peoples] are elected by the cantons with [a] Bosniak majority than the cantons with Croat majority'. To sum up, these changes have left the Croats marginalised within Bosnia's political system: 'the ethnic structure of entity governments is prescribed in such a way that any decision of the RS government in Banja Luka can be made independently by Serb ministers and any decision of the Federation government can be made by Bosniak ministers. The Croats are, therefore, in both entities completely prevented from influencing important decisions.'

This characterisation of the situation is of course somewhat of a caricature, for the entity constitutions include the same consociational mechanisms as the central constitution does. The problem is not that Croats *per se* cannot influence the political process, but rather that new governing coalitions chose representatives from smaller Croat parties to fulfil the constitutional obligations of inclusion. For all their inaccuracies, the concerns raised by Ljubić remain important

---

[72]   Ibid. The quotes in this paragraph refer to the manuscript of this speech, which Ljubić was so kind to provide.

ones since they help understand the mind-set of the Croat political elite. That their fears are not illegitimate can be illustrated by the events following the 2010 election in the Federation (to which Ljubić refers in his speech as well). After election day, as the International Crisis Group explains—and as Ljubić does not mention—the two HDZs embarked on a strategy of non-cooperation in the cantons. Concretely, they 'violated the Federation constitution by blocking formation of governments and refusing to send delegates to the entity's House of Peoples from the four cantons they control.'[73] The SDP went ahead and formed a government without the approval of the Croat club in the House of Peoples, which clearly violated the entity constitution. Accordingly, the Central Election Commission (CEC) proclaimed the government formation illegal. But the High Representative, frustrated with the time it took to form *any* government, was not willing to let this compromise be disturbed by legal provisions. Consequently, on 27 March 2011, he 'temporarily suspended' the CEC decision and proclaimed the Federation government to be legal.[74] 'That suspension, which had the consequence of disrupting the normal appeal process, has undermined state bodies—most directly the CEC—and the rule of law.'[75] It is as a reaction to these events that those Croat politicians, who consider themselves the legitimate representatives of the Croat people, formed the Croat National Assembly as some sort of parallel organisation for defending the Croat interests. In Ljubić's words: 'The [Assembly's] Main Council that I personally chair is composed of eight departments, which is functioning on the principle of the *shadow cabinet* while considering all relevant issues from the spheres of economy and society.'[76] (This, in fact, is a more political form of another Croat non-governmental body established in the days of Croat self-government, see next chapter).

These events not only testify to the way in which the High Representative intervenes in the current Bosnian system (which will be analysed in the next chapter). They also showed the Croats that there is no guarantee that the constitutional mechanisms set out to protect their ethno-national interests will be respected. This adds a new layer to the discussion, for the potentiality of structural discrimination outlined above is completed by the actuality of discrimination and violation of constitutionally guaranteed protection. Within this context, it is of secondary importance that the Croats' behaviour provoked the unconstitutional acts

---

[73]   International Crisis Group, *Bosnia: State Institutions under Attack*, Europe Briefing (Sarajevo/Istanbul/Brussels: International Crisis Group, 6 May 2011), 1.

[74]   See the OHR decision 'Order Temporarily Suspending Certain Decisions of the Central Election Commission of Bosnia and Herzegovina Adopted at its 21st Session Held on 24 March 2011 and any Proceedings Concerning Said Decisions', 27 March 2011, available online: http://www.ohr.int/decisions/statemattersdec/default.asp?content_id=45890, last accessed 4 August 2013.

[75]   International Crisis Group, *Bosnia: State Institutions under Attack*, 1.

[76]   Ljubić, "Croat Question."

by the other groups and, ultimately, the High Representative. Their (mis-)use of the powers the entity and cantonal constitutions gave them can in no way serve as a legitimising principle for the later abuse of the rule of law by the SDP and the High Representative.

8.3.3 The misuse of the *Sejdić* and *Finci* verdict

When the European Court of Human Rights issued the *Sejdić and Finci* verdict in 2009, it made many observers of Bosnian politics hopeful that finally real constitutional reform would be possible. Bosnian politicians would not be able to ignore an assignment handed to them by Europe's most important court, some rejoiced. In an astonishing manner of ordinariness, however, the Bosnian political elite, despite many commissions and rounds of high-level negotiations,[77] has to date not managed to agree on the necessary changes, let alone pass the respective constitutional provisions. There are two primary reasons for this situation.

As outlined in the previous chapter, Bosnia's constitutional order is a patchwork of competencies and structures. So when the Court criticised the discrimination against Others with regards to their election to the Presidency and, even more importantly, the House of Peoples, it *de facto* gave the Bosnian state the task of changing its entire structure. Mere cosmetic changes, as some originally had hoped, were not feasible for even those present difficult questions and demand substantial change on all federal levels. Take for example the rather naïve proposal to just add another member of the Presidency that would represent the Others. From the outset, this seems like an easy fix, for it does not alter the present structure in a significant way. But the present members of the presidency are elected within the Federation and RS, respectively. Where would such a fourth member be elected? Obviously, she cannot be elected just in the Federation, or just in RS, for then again, some people would not be able to stand for elections. On the other hand, she cannot be elected from the entire territory of BiH, since this would give this member greater legitimacy than the other three possess. Simultaneously, this solution does not solve the problem that Serbs from the Federation as well as Bosniaks and Croats from Republika Srpska are currently ineligible to stand for elections to the BiH state presidency and are deprived of their right to vote for 'their' representative. As even this superficial examination shows, the question of reforming Bosnia's state presidency is no mere cosmetic change but demands serious alternation of the existing structures. The same holds true for the House of Peoples. Its members are delegated from entity parliaments; in the case of FBiH, the members delegating members to the House of Peoples are themselves delegated from cantonal parliaments. This means that introducing, e.g., more seats to the BiH House of Peoples would mean changing the Bosnian,

---

[77] Wonderfully outlined in Hodžić and Stojanović, *New/Old Constitutional Engineering.*

the entity, and the cantonal constitutions as well as coming up with a new mechanism on how the additional seats are filled. Even outside the context of a post-war society, this is an immense task for a state to handle.

But there is a far more important reason for the delay in implementing the verdict. *Sejdić and Finci* actually presents the practical culmination of our previous discussions regarding the divergent wishes for a new state structure and the Croat Question. The verdict's main task fell on fertile ground insofar as it echoed the claim to the necessity of constitutional reform. Since it added the aspect of urgency to the task, many among the political elites misused the issue in order to fight for their own political goals in this respect. Dragan Čović as well as Božo Ljubić, for example, mention *Sejdić and Finci* within the context of the Croat Question, where Čović concludes that one of the outcomes should put Croats in a position in which they can select their own political representatives autonomously. Similarly, Mladen Bosić thinks that 'there is no solution for *Sejdić and Finci* as long as this problem [i.e. the Croat Question] in the Federation is not agreed upon'. In fact, the fate of Dervo Sejdić and Jakub Finci, those two individuals whose rights to be candidates for the Presidency and to occupy seats in the House of Peoples are infringed upon, becomes secondary in the daily political debates. The verdict is misused to solve old and new questions surrounding the representation of the constituent peoples. The conviction that the verdict primarily targets individuals and *de facto* prescribes a new constitutional order following the liberal principle more closely is rarely expressed. In my interviews it was put forward only by Haris Silajdžić and, especially, Željko Komšić. As the latter explains:

> The *Sejdić and Finci* verdict tasked Bosnia and Herzegovina with changing its constitution in order to bring the individuals into the same position as the constituent peoples as far as political rights are concerned. But in our daily politics—mostly due to the biggest parties with ethnic connotation, but, unfortunately also the SDP—this task was turned into solving the problems of the collectives, most prominently the Croat Question. The essence of the international human rights court's decision is forgotten. The essence of this verdict is the individual and active and passive voting rights, in the sense that he can elect and be elected regardless of his national belonging [*narodna pripadnost*], regardless of whether or not he is a member of a majority or a minority.[78]

In one sense, the verdict opened a Pandora's box. Even though it did not contain all the evils of the world, it presented the perfect opportunity for the different groups to argue their points with regard to constitutional reform. Since time is generally a pressing matter the political elite is forced to engage in an active discussion regarding political stances. However, it remains an astonishing fact that in such an important area, there is no possible compromise in sight. Despite the objective urgency to find a solution, the political discussions remain blocked and

---

[78]   Komšić, Personal Interview.

centre on well-known patterns from the past. Rather than the exception that could break the rule of permanent crisis, *Sejdić and Finci* has so far proven to be another example of the logic behind the concept of 'imposed consociationalism'.

The question, then, is how Bosnia and Herzegovina arrived at this sorry state.

9 The Office of the High Representative from 1996 to 2013

In the months leading up to the Dayton negotiations, military options for intervention were on everybody's minds. But the international negotiators also knew that a peace agreement needed to follow a conceivable intervention scenario, and that the implementation of any such agreement would probably fall into the hands of NATO. Since this organisation is, by definition, primarily focused on military matters, the international community wished to establish some sort of political control over any NATO-led implementation efforts. Moreover, especially the European countries realised that there is a difference between bombing the parties into a cease-fire agreement and bringing real peace to the war-torn country of Bosnia-Herzegovina. They insisted that, despite the necessary focus on military issues, the civilian aspects of peace implementation should not be neglected, for it 'was thought that it would soon become apparent that civilian operations would prove the most difficult—and also the most important.'[1] Those two aspects culminated in the French proposal to appoint a High Representative (HR) as 'some kind of political representation and for civilian coordination'.[2] While other European countries supported this idea, the United States did not object on principle. However, the US insisted that the High Representative had nothing to do with the United Nations or the military efforts pursued by NATO.

During a flight from Paris to Moscow on 16 October 1995, Carl Bildt, who at that time was the European representative in the international peace negotiation team, presented a first outline on how a High Representative position could look. 'He, or she, must have a clear mandate, sufficient resources, and the opportunity to operate on both the Bosnian and the international level', Bildt wrote. 'It would be an enormous help to be able to rely on as much as possible of the civilian UN infrastructure in existence—offices, telephones, cars, interpreters, etc.'[3] This first outline already comprises some of the major structural shortcomings of what would become the Office of the High Representative (OHR). Its complete dependence on resources of other organisations testifies to the lack of a real concept and task. The international community conceived of the HR as some sort of trouble-shooter, someone who should be able to manage tensions and problems as they occurred, be it on the local or the international level. It did not sufficiently

---

[1]   Bildt, *Peace Journey*, 108.

[2]   Ibid., 109.

[3]   Ibid., 113.

reflect on the nature of the expectable problems—local reluctance to cooperate within the newly established structures being the most obvious one—but thought the issue solved with the mere existence of a 'referee' or 'facilitator' whose task was to find pragmatic solutions once problems presented themselves. Under such conditions, Bildt's 'clear mandate' was nothing more than an empty notion.

In addition, the United States, due to on-going discussions between the Clinton administration and the Republican-led US Congress as well as the general reluctance to put American NATO troops under the control of some international figure, opposed any real powers for the HR. As Bildt recalls, 'they wanted to get rid of the notion of a more powerful High Representative, with political powers, and have instead a "senior implementation coordinator" essentially working as some sort of local aid to the IFOR commander'.[4] Bildt's recollection may be biased by his later powerlessness, but, in this respect, Richard Holbrooke, the chief American negotiator, agrees with the presentation of the American position and even uses a similar terminology. Upon landing in Moscow, Holbrooke writes, the French representative 'announced that it had been "unanimously decided" that Carl Bildt would be *senior civilian representative* in Bosnia.'[5] However, having a person for the job did not mean that this person's job description had been finalised. The Americans continued their structural opposition well into the Dayton discussions, where, according to Bildt, 'the US delegation had clearly been instructed to do all it could to restrict the authority of the High Representative instead of giving him, or her, the authority necessary to safeguard the civilian and political implementation of the peace accords.'[6] Holbrooke admits that this observation is 'valid' but insists that 'the position [Bildt] criticises was not that of the negotiating team, which argued this point by phone with NATO throughout the first ten days of Dayton'.[7]

In hindsight, the two rationales do not appear equally defensible, even though they may be understandable. NATO's—and the official American—position was guided by a military understanding of the entire conflict and follows the paradigm that military conflicts need military solutions. Naturally, this would make NATO or IFOR the master in the field as far as implementation is concerned. The paradigm to which Bildt alludes years later, on the other hand, was focused on a political understanding of the conflict and the conviction that the underlying political struggles only expressed themselves in military ways. They therefore needed political solutions in order to be resolved. In essence, those two views depart from different concepts of peace: the 'military' one understands

---

4   Ibid., 117–8.

5   Holbrooke, *To End a War*, 209. My italics.

6   Bildt, *Peace Journey*, 131.

7   Holbrooke, *To End a War*, 364.

peace as the absence of conflict, which can be guaranteed by military might (negative peace), whereas the 'civilian' one focuses on the conditions necessary in order to maintain peace and, as a consequence thereof, requests the kind changes in the societal and political order that military force alone can hardly deliver (positive peace). This fundamental division in principle between the American and the European positions makes the final and weak structure of the High Representative's function comprehensive as yet another diplomatic compromise. From today's perspective, the fact that the Americans won the first round in this battle was clearly unfortunate, as even Holbrooke admits: 'Bildt's mandate should have been stronger.' But he is also eager to point out that the structure of Dayton was not as strict as Bildt makes it appear: 'On the other hand, when [in the first postwar years] Bosnian Serbs defied Dayton, the United States urged Bildt to interpret the authority granted him by Dayton more broadly, at which point, ironically, resistance came from the Europeans, who, having correctly criticized us initially for limiting Bildt's mandate, then reined him in.'[8]

This chapter traces the peace implementation efforts of the Office of the High Representative from its actual establishment in 1996 to date. It focuses on the general philosophical background of each HR, based on which their policies and strategies are analysed. Special emphasis is put on the need for what would later become known as the Bonn powers as well as the manner in which those powers were utilised ever since. A chronological structure to present these events is essential for understanding the post-conflict development of Bosnia and Herzegovina. Neither the internationals nor the locals stuck to their original strategies on how to operate within the newly established Bosnian political system. Instead, they adapted them gradually as they learned how the system functioned. For both, the *leitmotiv* could be describes as learning by doing. In 2005, Christophe Solioz proposed sequencing the post-war period in Bosnia-Herzegovina into four different phases: the first phase (1995-97) of humanitarian aid and reconstruction; the second phase (1997-2000) of strengthened authority for the OHR with the Bonn powers; the third phase (2001-2) of substantial policy changes in terms of new approaches to boost refugee return, to transform the socialist economy, and to improve the functioning of the state-level institutions; and, finally, the fourth phase (2002-5) of a gradual reduction of using the Bonn powers and the intensifying of Bosnia's EU integration process.[9] In light of later events, this sequencing appears not so much inaccurate as too optimistic. A turning point with regards to the use of Bonn powers was indeed reached during the fourth phase. But the im-

---

[8]   Ibid.

[9]   Solioz, *Turning Points in Post-War Bosnia*, 14.

plicit optimism that the OHR could therefore be closed soon[10] turned out to be a wish the locals were not willing to grant the international community. As we shall see, the structural importance of the Bonn powers became more apparent in the post-2005 phases, even though they were utilised less and less.

In fact, underlying Solioz' partition is the understanding that different High Representatives shaped policy in Bosnia in rather different ways. The substantial policy changes in his proposed phase three correspond to the policy priorities outlined by Wolfgang Petritsch, whereas the decrease in use of the Bonn powers after 2005 corresponds to the second half of Paddy Ashdown's mandate. Each High Representative, due to a unique philosophical understanding of its mandate and role, used the Bonn powers in a specific manner. In fact, the use of the Bonn powers depended not so much on the general situation in the country—or even in the international community, although, especially in the later periods, this factor cannot be neglected—but mostly on the person holding the office. My intention is to substantiate this general claim throughout this chapter. Yet for the moment, I am only interested in defending a chronological rather than thematic approach to the presentation of my argument. For this purpose, I think the following example should suffice: When Wolfgang Petritsch assumed the office of HR in 1999, he introduced a new paradigm by arguing for the concept of local ownership. The gist of it was that the locals, not the HR or the international community, should take responsibility for their country and implement much needed legislation on their own. Logically as well as practically, this approach would imply gradually reducing the use of the Bonn powers. However, since Paddy Ashdown, Petritsch's successor, had a completely different philosophical as well as practical understanding of the matter at hand, the use of Bonn powers subsequently increased. Thus, the situation evaluation of the person in the High Representative's office determined the strategy, whereas the international community followed its lead. Something similar (in terms of structure though not content) happened when Ashdown's successor, Christian Schwarz-Schilling, assumed office and once again revived Petritsch's concept of local ownership. His strategy was to refrain from using the Bonn powers. Unlike Ashdown, who had achieved some of his successes by simply decreeing the respective reforms, Schwarz-Schilling wanted the locals to achieve political compromises by themselves. Since such an approach naturally slowed the entire process, the international community, and es-

---

[10] Solioz' optimism is apparent in the following passage: 'There are other key turning points looming in the near future: the Office of the High Representative's (OHR) planned closure at the end of 2006, and its transition into a much smaller mission led by the European Union (EU); the formalisation of the overall Euro-Atlantic integration process by the start of negotiations for a Stabilisation and Association Agreement (SAA) with the EU; and entry into NATO's Partnership for Peace (PfP). However ... all of this will first require further reforms.' (Ibid.) As it turned out, the caveat Solioz introduces was a rather important one.

pecially the United States, disapproved of it. Unimpressed by such resistance, Schwarz-Schilling stubbornly clung to the idea of educating the locals on how to internally negotiate. He furthermore believed that his strategy delivered positive outcomes, which naturally increased his unwillingness to abandon this mediation-style approach. As the direct result of this confrontation, the international community did not extend the same courtesy to Schwarz-Schilling as they did to Ashdown; and ultimately, Schwarz-Schilling lost the battle with the Americans and had to leave the office after only 17 months—compared to the four-year term of Ashdown.

However, while he was in office, the international community, for many reasons, could neither make him use the Bonn powers nor change his general approach, which indicates the position of the High Representative. For the most part, his strategy, even though locals and observers alike sometimes inaccurately perceive of it as the strategy of the international community, is the result of his own philosophy, situation analysis, and style of governing. The same holds true for policy initiatives and priorities that can change abruptly from one High Representative to another. It is for this reason that I have chosen to structure the chapter according to the person holding the office. Such a chronological approach best serves my main purpose of analysing the structure and use of the intervention prerogative, i.e. the Bonn powers. The sections dedicated to each of the High Representatives will primarily focus on analysing the HR's understanding of his[11] task and philosophy as well as an assessment of the consequences of Bonn-power actions with regards to the local political system. As far as it seems necessary for understanding the latter, the sections will also include a discussion of the situation on the ground, which will gradually become briefer as we approach modern and better known times.

9.1 Carl Bildt (1996-1997)

Carl Bildt, until very recently the Swedish foreign minister, became closely involved with Bosnia in the spring of 1995 when he succeeded Lord Owen as the European representative in the international negotiating team. As the leader of the Moderate Party, Bildt had previously served as Sweden's prime minister, and it was under his leadership that Sweden negotiated its EU accession and furthermore started the process of modernising the IT sector.[12] Following his Co-Chairmanship at the Dayton negotiations, Bildt was appointed to serve as the first High Representative of the international community in Bosnia and Herzegovina.

---

[11] Since there have been no female High Representatives so far, I shall use the male formulation throughout the text.

[12] See Bildt's CV on the OHR website: http://www.ohr.int/ohr-info/hrs-dhrs/default.a sp?content_id=28041, last accessed 20 October 2013.

9.1.1   The political landscape before the first post-war elections

There are times when politics is quicker than one would appreciate. The months following the Dayton agreement were such a moment, for the warring parties had agreed to a strict timeline for setting up the new state. Crucial in this respect were elections that, according to Annex III of the DPA, had to be held within nine months of the agreement's signing, provided that the OSCE certified that elections were feasible under the current social conditions. Concretely, this meant elections no later than 14 September 1996. This is the reason why, immediately after signing the DPA, some sort of election campaign started—or rather a campaign to postpone the elections because the necessary conditions were obviously not met. As Zlatko Lagumdžija, member of the Social Democratic SDP BiH, exclaimed in January 1996: 'People in state functions have currently more important things to do than [engage in] a pre-election campaign.'[13] In the eyes of the international community, however, those functionaries were not legitimised to represent their people as long as they had not been democratically elected or confirmed.

The rationale behind such logic was not so much an insistence on democratic principles but rather pragmatism. For while the support for major nationalist parties within the three groups was rather strong at that time, the internationals wanted a fresh start, especially with regards to the newly established institutions of the central state. Integrating Serb (and Croat) representatives into the common state structures of the wartime Republic of Bosnia and Herzegovina—to which the new state was still intrinsically linked—without a democratic election would in a way have meant legitimising those structures by merely adapting them to changed circumstances. But even though post-Dayton Bosnia was *de jure* not a new state, one of its major elements was a completely new state structure that needed legitimisation in order to become recognised by the people. Consequently, quick elections became a *conditio sine qua non* of the new state.

This development was unfortunate, especially for the smaller parties. Not only had they to face the same obstacles as anyone else with the lack of security and freedom of movement when conducting their election 'campaigns', but they needed to establish a completely new internal organisational structure as well. As Mirnes Ajanović, president of the small party BOSS explained: 'We would appreciate a postponing of the elections for about a year; this would give us time to solve all the issues that need to be solved for establishing our organisational structure. Unlike other parties, we did not have the possibility to lead an active party life during the war.'[14] It seems clear that if elections were held under such circumstances, the established parties, i.e. the wartime leaderships within the

---

[13]   *Dnevni Avaz*, 4 January 1996, 5.
[14]   *Dnevni Avaz*, 7 January 1996, 6.

three electoral corpuses would win due to existing internal organisational structures that were additionally backed up by military and security forces. These three parties—the Bosniak *Stranka Demokratske Akcije* (SDA, Party of Democratic Action), the Bosnian Serb *Srpska Demokratska Stranka* (SDS, Serb Democratic Party), and the Bosnian Croat wing of the Croatian *Hrvatska Demokratska Zajednica* (HDZ, Croat Democratic Union)—almost exclusively represented the interests of the three groups. This initial position was not unwelcome from an external perspective. Holding elections in this manner meant that the already known negotiating partners would stay in power, with their representational capacities not only backed up by military mighty but by democratic legitimacy. Democracy could thus be introduced into the system without much fear of the result.

From a theoretical point of view, even the use of terms like 'democracy' or 'democratic legitimacy' in the present context is a travesty. The basic idea of democracy cannot be reduced to the mere element of elections, nor can true democratic legitimacy be achieved in a situation where, say, the freedoms of movement or expression are not guaranteed to a sufficient degree. Rather than being acceptable in terms of democratic theory, the insistence on early elections and especially the inherent 'legitimisation' of the wartime political elites is somewhat of a natural phenomenon for transitioning societies. After all, many communist elites became part of the post-communist state and helped induce democratic transitions in Eastern Europe. For post-war societies a similar logic may apply. The wartime elites, which usually also form part of the pre-war leadership, possess important insight into the functioning logics of a state and can, potentially, be a valid source of advice. Elections are the vehicle by which the people consent to this kind of involvement.

However, there is an important distinction between a peaceful transformation and a violent one. For the latter, the problem is not so much the *existence* of pre-war elites within the post-war state, but the potential *acceptance* of their wartime political programmes as valid within the newly democratic setup. Through elections, wartime goals may become democratically legitimate. During the transition to post-communism in Central and Eastern Europe, communism as such was delegitimised by history itself; the former elites had thus to adopt political stances that were compatible with democratic principles in order to play any role within the post-communist state. The same holds true for the ideology of Nazism that was delegitimised once Germany was defeated in World War II. Even though many of the former cadres became part of the post-1945 German state, they repelled their ideas on world leadership, the supremacy of the Arian race, and trust in a supposedly all-knowing leader. These transformations were successful only because the larger political programme was discredited. In Bosnia, the relationship between wartime ideologies and the post-war state was somewhat different. The war did not end with a victory but with a stalemate, and no ideology was clearly discredited, as had been the case with communism or Nazism. I would not like to second the views of those who, especially in recent years, have begun to claim that the war had ended too soon,[15] for I find such statements highly repugnant in light of the human sacrifice and suffering a continuation of war would have signified. But underlying such rather naïve statements is the generally valid conviction that a war that ends with a clear victor is much more likely to produce a stable post-war political system.[16] Peace-building practitioners alert us to the fact that 'you cannot built a sustainable peace until the "nomenklarura", the generation who had run the war, had left the political system'.[17] In post-war societies with no clear victor, there is no way of starting such a lustration process, which means that post-war state building is necessarily tainted by the wartime-elites and, ultimately, rests on their transition from war- to peace-makers.

In this process, elections perform a dual function. First, they reflect the existing political patterns within the respective groups. The way in which a candidate campaigns, her promises and general behaviour with regards to the other groups as well as to opposing parties within her own electorate, give external peace makers important insights into the conditions on the ground and help them come up with strategies to either support or combat existing tendencies. Second, elections also possess the potential to change the political landscape and to send important signals regarding the direction in which the country is to develop. If one assumes that, under the conditions of a stalemate-like end of the war, the old elites have rather good chances of winning the elections, this does not necessarily mean that other parties with a different, perhaps more cooperative agenda have no chances at all. Naturally, this latter potential rests on several conditions that, even when fulfilled, are unlikely to alter the political landscape dramatically. But the important point is that elections may also be a vice of change rather than simple confirmation.

This possibility would have been present in Bosnia as well, if the elections were held under slightly different circumstances—and, especially, if they had not been scheduled so early. For even though the three major group parties were the dominant forces in this immediate post-war period, one cannot assume complete group cohesion for two reasons. First, there existed other parties, even though not as powerful ones. Within the territory of the Federation, for example, there were two Social Democratic Parties (*Socijaldemokratska Partija Bosne i Hercegovine* SDP BiH and *Unija Bosanskih Socijaldemokrata* UBSD), the *Muslimanska*

---

[15]   Anes Alic, "The Bosnian War, My Way," *ISA Intel*, 24 April 2012, http://www.isa intel.com/2012/04/24/the-bosnian-war-my-way/. Accessed 22 November 2013.

[16]   This, of course, does not mean that a continuation of the Bosnian war would have ended with a clear victory, nor that it would have been the victory of the Bosniaks and Croats, as many of those proponents imply.

[17]   Paddy Ashdown, Personal Interview in London (UK), 23 October 2012.

Bošnjačka Organizacija (MBO, Muslim Bosniak Organisation), the *Hrvatska Seljačka Stranka* (HSS, Croat Peasants Party), the *Bosanska Stranka* (BOSS, Bosnian Party) or the Republican Party in addition to HDZ and SDA. On RS territory the main competition for the SDS, still led by Radovan Karadžić, came from the *Srpska Radikalna Stranka* (SRS, Serb Radical Party) and the *Socijalistička Partija Republike Srpske* (SPRS, Socialist Party of the Republic of Srpska).[18] Those two groups were the Bosnian wings of respective parties in Serbia/Yugoslavia, where Vojislav Šešelj led the former and Slobodan Milošević the latter. Furthermore, during the war, there existed a club of independents within the RS parliament, led by Milorad Dodik. The latter later became an important political figure, even though it would take some time for his party, the newly founded Party/Alliance of Independent Social Democrats SNSD,[19] to match his personal appeal. In neither Bosnian entity, therefore, was the political landscape as coherent as one may assume, for it bore at least the potentiality of intra-group opposition.

Second, even within the three main parties, there were soon splits into different factions. Most prominently, perhaps, Haris Silajdžić left the SDA soon after the end of the war and formed his own *Stranka za Bosnu i Hercegovinu* (SBiH, Party for Bosnia and Herzegovina). He nevertheless closely cooperated with the SDA in the following. In fact, together with Alija Izetbegović, as the leader of the SDA, Silajdžić came up a document called the 'Declaration for a Unified and Democratic Bosnia and Herzegovina' in April 1996, which was signed by many Bosniak parties and later transformed into an electoral coalition. The aim of the declaration was to strengthen a unified and sovereign Bosnia and Herzegovina as a democratic and multicultural society; concretely, it demanded the capture of war criminals, the return of refugees, and the reconstruction of the country.[20] The HDZ did not sign the declaration, officially because it was not introduced through the proper procedures (i.e. the parliament). Advocating similar reasons, several of the opposition parties abstained as well. It is as a reaction to this procedure that the SDP, the UBSD, the Republicans, the HSS, and the MBO formed the *Zadružena Lista* ('Common List') for the upcoming elections.[21] Silajdžić leaving the SDA thus signified not only a major rupture in this party's in-

---

[18]   Nina Caspersen, "Contingent Nationalist Dominance: Intra-Serb Challenges to the Serb Democratic Party," *Nationalities Papers: The Journal of Nationalism and Ethnicity* 34, no. 1 (2006): 51–69.

[19]   In the beginning, SNSD stood for '*Stranka nezavisnih Socijaldemokrata*' (Party of independent Social Democrats) alluding to their origins within the independent's club in the wartime RS parliament. But this party would soon merge with the party of Nebojša Radmanović and change its name into '*Savez nezavisnih Socijaldemokrata*' (Alliance of Independent Social Democrats) but keep the same abbreviation.

[20]   *Dnevni Avaz,* 3 April 1996, 1.

[21]   *Oslobođenje,* 16 June 1996, 4.

ternal structure, but also proved the catalysing agent for unifying the Bosniak opposition. In the Federation, therefore, the Bosniak electorate was clearly split, while the HDZ could still count on overwhelming support by Bosnia's Croats.

In the RS, the situation was also less coherent than one might expect. Immediately after the war, this entity was under firm control of the wartime Bosnian Serb leadership, which had its capital in Pale near Sarajevo. Radovan Karadžić, at that time president of the RS and of the SDS, had been indicted by the ICTY and could therefore not serve in any political function in post-Dayton Bosnia. The internationals therefore consistently refused to meet or talk to him, which, however, did not prevent him from playing a paramount political role within the entity. According to several reports, he was able to move freely within RS territory and even pass several IFOR checkpoints without being molested or arrested. At that time, IFOR commanders on the ground needed approval 'from above' in order to take action against alleged war criminals, for their political leaderships feared repercussions against their soldiers if a more aggressive strategy to apprehend war criminals were chosen. This situation, which changed only with the new government in Britain in 1997, threatened not only the commitment to international justice but also left an odd stain on the entire mission of the international community.[22]

The policy meant that Karadžić could remain the *de facto* leader of the RS entity even in the immediate post-Dayton period. Together with the leader of the RS parliament, Momčilo Krajšnik, Karadžić was heavily involved in unlawful activities on RS soil; he ran the entity more in the fashion of a large criminal organisation than a political unit. Naturally, this did not make him many friends. His position as the only true leader of the Bosnian Serbs was thus by no means unchallenged. But what really led to a split in the political leadership of the RS were antagonistic strategies relating to the commitment to Dayton. Prime minister Rajko Kasagić thereby represented the progressive Banja Luka faction that advocated full implementation of the Dayton Agreement and thus pursued a strategy of cooperation vis-à-vis the international community. At a session of RS parliament in the beginning of April 1996, Krajšnik and the Pale faction heavily attacked Kasagić for this strategy of 'exaggerated readiness to cooperate' [*pretjerana kooperativnost*], as they called it. They especially criticised the arrangement of official meetings in Banja Luka, instead of the wartime *de facto* capital Pale.[23] Karadžić himself accused Kasagić's government of 'too easily' accepting proposals that weakened the position of the entity with regards to the central state. As a result of these debates, the parliament created a special council for all relations with the international community whose task it was to 'secure the independence and sover-

---

[22]   Wolfgang Petritsch, *Bosnien und Herzegowina fünf Jahre nach Dayton - Hat der Friede eine Chance?*, Second Edition (Klagenfurt: Wieser Verlag, 2001), 80–81.

[23]   *Dnevni Avaz*, 4 April 1996, 9.

eignty that the RS received with Dayton'. In an act of sheer delusion, Karadžić also demanded the authority to be the sole representative of the RS in dealings with the international community.[24]

Throughout these debates, the international community clearly sided with what we may call the Banja Luka faction that, according to some reports, also enjoyed the support of Slobodan Milošević and Ratko Mladić, the chief of the RS army.[25] (The latter did not *per se* support a cooperative course but rather simply opposed Karadžić.) The international support was evident. For example, when Karadžić removed Kasagić from the post of RS prime minister in May 1996, Carl Bildt, NATO commander George Joulwan, and EU representative Javier Solana publicly visited the latter in his Banja Luka office.[26] The international community furthermore pressured Karadžić to resign and, at least on a political level, demanded his arrest and transfer to The Hague. By the end of July, after many rounds of diplomatic negotiations and political theatre,[27] Karadžić finally left both political offices he held, i.e. the RS presidency and the SDS party leadership, as part of an Agreement negotiated by Richard Holbrooke.[28] Vice-President Biljana Plavšić succeeded him and also became the SDS candidate for the RS presidency for the September 1996 elections. But for the time being, Karadžić's ousting could neither limit his *de facto* power in the entity, nor resolve the general antagonism between cooperation and opposition with regards to the Dayton implementation. Especially the latter would, during the tenure of Carlos Westendorp as the second High Representative, lead to a complete split in the RS.

Despite these two reasons for the non-existence of full group cohesion, it would be inaccurate to state that the three main parties were not the dominant political currents at this time. The SDA and the HDZ negotiated the makeup of the Federation on their own, while the SDA, the HDZ, and the SDS discussed among each other the main issues regarding the central state. They were the key players in immediate post-war Bosnia. The results of the first post-war general elections[29]

---

[24]   *Oslobođenje*, 9 April 1996, 8.

[25]   *Oslobođenje*, 9 April 1996, 8; *Dnevni Avaz*, 11 April 1996, 6.

[26]   *Oslobođenje,* 17 May 1996, 1-5.

[27]   Those included, *inter alia*, meetings with Milošević; threats against the entity and the SDS by Carl Bildt and OSCE chairman Robert Frowick; a subsequent threat of referendum in support of Karadžić in the RS; Karadžić's partial transfer of authority to Biljana Plavšić; a complete resignation from the RS presidency, combined with a candidacy for this post at the next elections; etc. Cf. *Dnevni Avaz*, 20 May 1996, 3; 24 May 1996, 2; 1 July 1996, 3; 20-21 July 1996, 1.

[28]   According to persistent rumours and Karadžić's own account during his opening statement at the Hague Tribunal, Karadžić was offered immunity from criminal prosecution in return for leaving politics. Holbrooke, however, always denied the existence of such a deal.

[29]   The local elections were postponed due to the conditions on the ground.

show no surprises in this regard.[30] The SDA was the strongest party, securing 19 out of 23 seats in national parliament. It furthermore dominated the FBiH parliament with 78 out of 140 seats, while Silajdžić's SBiH won 10 seats. The HDZ gained eight seats in national parliament and 36 seats in FBiH parliament. The SDS was the clear leader in the RS winning nine out of 14 seats in national parliament and around 60% of the seats in the National Assembly of the RS (NARS), the RS parliament. Consequently, the three people within the BiH state presidency came from the three main parties: Alija Izetbegović (SDA, 80% of votes), Krešimir Zubak (HDZ, 87%), and Momčilo Krajšnik (SDS, 67%).[31] Since he got the most votes in total, Alija Izetbegović became the Chairman of the BiH presidency for the first two years, for the rotation system had not yet been introduced. Biljana Plavšić was elected President of the RS. In line with the afore-mentioned fears regarding the incorporation of the pre-war leaders into the post-war setup, Bosnia's far too early elections clearly tell a cautionary tale.

9.1.2   Setting up the new state

In terms of setting up the new state, the first post-war year was characterised by a multitude of issues that had not been fully resolved at Dayton. These involved not only technical details—like where the different political representatives were to meet or which member of the BiH presidency was to speak first at which event, even though such issues took much time to be resolved and, compared to their relative unimportance, resulted in far too much press coverage—, but also concerned the foundations of the new state. Dayton had given Bosnia some guidelines, but how these would work in practice was anything but clear. The existing parliaments of the central state and the entities had their own constitutions that needed to be brought into accordance with Annex IV. New rules of procedure had to be established. The institutions of the central state could only be created in cooperation with RS representatives. Since these strongly opposed the mere idea of a central state, pressing issues that Dayton had left unspecified could only be really discussed once the Serb elites were elected by their people and thus also formally included in the Dayton process. In other words, the central state could only be properly set up after the September elections.

The Federation setup did not face similar challenges, for the Croats and Bosniaks did not oppose it on principle, but rather argued about the general character of their endeavour. Since its establishment as part of the Washington Agreement, the Federation had been nothing more than a dead letter. Conceptually, it was wrapped around the structures of the RBiH and the HZ HB, in combina-

---

[30]   Results according to the official Federation Gazette (*Službene Novine Federacije Bosne i Hercegovine,* 3 (20), 20 October 1996.

[31]   *Oslobođenje,* 19 September 1996, 1.

tion with the corresponding military organisations of the Bosnian Army (ABiH) and the Croat Defence Council (HVO). After Dayton, the main task was to combine those two separate political, administrative, and military structures into one general organisation. But since this unified administration was in itself a composition of ten different cantons whose exact borders and concrete competencies still needed to be negotiated, this was no easy assignment. The major obstacle for negotiating the Federation setup was the political elites' clear unwillingness to cooperate, as the international mediator, Christian Schwarz-Schilling, explained.[32] The later High Representative had been appointed to facilitate the dialogue between the two sides. It was only following a meeting in Geneva in March 1996, where Bosniak and Croat representatives met under international supervision, and a subsequent meeting with Schwarz-Schilling that an agreement regarding the inner workings of the Federation was reached; this agreement provided the platform for the actual creation of the cantonal structure.[33]

The problems between the Bosniaks and Croats in the Federation are exemplified by the events surrounding the integration of Mostar. The city on the Neretva River, which harbours Bosnia's most famous landmark, the Old Bridge, was at one time supposed to become the capital of the Croat 'Herceg-Bosna' para-state. Consequently, it was ethnically divided during the Croat-Bosniak war of 1993. The ABiH henceforth controlled the historical quarters on the eastern part of the city, whereas the HVO had control over the more modern quarters in the west. The local political structures corresponded to those military boundaries. In the Washington Agreement, which ended the Bosniak-Croat war in 1994, both parties agreed to the integration of the city under EU supervision. The German Social Democrat Hans Koschnick, a former mayor of Bremen, became the EU administrator in July 1994. His mandate, which should have lasted only two years, was no less ambitious than the later one of the OHR. He was to unite the city, establish a multinational administration, organise elections, ensure refugee return, guarantee the adherence of human rights, and, finally, organise humanitarian aid and economic recovery.[34] With an on-going war, these goals were impossible to achieve. But even after Dayton was signed, the two sides were not really eager to implement the provisions of the Washington Agreement. The unification of the city in particular was a contested issue, supposedly because it meant giving up certain prerogatives. But for Koschnick, a failure to unite Mostar was potentially the end of the entire Federation.[35] Putting his own political career on the line, he was determined not to let it happen: 'We want a multi-ethnic Federation and a multi-ethnic Mostar', he declared. 'I believe there is no need to negotiate

---

[32]   *Oslobođenje,* 28 March 1996, 3.
[33]   *Dnevni Avaz,* 26 March 1996, 1, 4; 1 April 1996, 4.
[34]   Petritsch, *Bosnien und Herzegowina fünf Jahre nach Dayton,* 45.
[35]   *Dnevni Avaz,* 8 January 1996, 1.

anymore. Instead we need to implement what we agreed. Peace in the Balkans is the task of the IFOR, but peace in Mostar is my personal obligation.' [36] Koschnick's personal commitment was put to test by the tenuous security situation in the city, which repeatedly erupted in violent outbursts. At one point, IFOR commander Leighton Smith had even to publicly assure Koschnick full military support to pacify the city, if needed.

Against this background, Koschnick tried to mediate between the Bosniaks and Croats with regards to the future political setup of the city. Since a real unification of Mostar seemed out of reach, the Bosniaks insisted on a rather large central district that would be ethnically mixed and thus open to all refugees. [37] The Croat leadership opposed this idea and advocated for the creation of ethnically homogenous districts. After all attempts to reach a compromise had failed, Koschnick delivered an arbitration judgement himself. He proclaimed Mostar to be a unified city with one ethnically mixed central zone and six municipalities, three of them with a Bosniak and three with a Croat majority. [38] The Bosniak mayor of eastern Mostar welcomed the judgement, while his Croat counterpart in southern Mostar was outraged and declared the end of all communication with the EU administration. [39] In the eyes of the Croat decision makers, the judgement was too favourable for the Bosniak side. They organised massive protests in opposition to the verdict, which even resulted in two assassination attempts on Koschnick. Following these events, and the decision of the internationals to accommodate the Croat position by reducing the size of the central district, Koschnick resigned his post. [40] In April, the Spanish Socialist Ricardo Pérez Casado replaced him. The central zone was put under EU control until the town's parliament and government were established.

Since Mostar followed a different timetable than the central state, municipal elections were held on 30 June 1996. The result confirmed the basic division of the city. The Bosniak 'List for a Unified Mostar' under the leadership of Safet Oručević came in first with 48.9% of the votes, closely followed by the Croat HDZ with 45.8%, while the opposition list secured only 3.3%. [41] The HDZ did not accept the results and subsequently boycotted the first session of the city parliament; they also protested against the renewal of the external administration mandate, which the EU had decided. After intensive negotiations in Brussels between

---

[36] *Oslobođenje,* 5 January 1996, 1.

[37] Petritsch, *Bosnien und Herzegowina fünf Jahre nach Dayton,* 45.

[38] *Oslobođenje,* 8 February 1996, 1,3.

[39] *Dnevni Avaz,* 8 February 1996, 1. The presidential council of the HZ HB later revoked this decision, see *Dnevni Avaz,* 14 February 1996, 2.

[40] Petritsch, *Bosnien und Herzegowina fünf Jahre nach Dayton,* 47.

[41] *Dnevni Avaz,* 2 July 1996, 1.

Ejup Ganić, Franjo Tuđman, and Alija Izetbegović, the HDZ finally ended its opposition in the beginning of August.[42]

The difficulties in establishing a unified Mostar are symptomatic for the entire situation in the Federation. Different concepts of what the Federation should be and how the political structures should look complicated the entire DPA implementation process. This period immediately following the signing of the DPA has also to be seen as the origin of the Croat Question that was discussed in the previous chapter. It was in March 1996, when the Croat Krešimir Zubak, President of the Federation, said:

> We entered the project called the Federation under time pressure. The principles and goals of neither the one nor the other people were predefined or redefined. The Croats can accept the Federation, but the problem is that the Muslim leadership did not accept the Federation as the ultimate model, but as a temporary solution in which one people dominates the other—all under the pretext of a civic option.[43]

In late August, HDZ president Božo Rajić explained that the Federation could only succeed if the 'liberal' principle is sacrificed for an ethnic one:

> For the Federation, the Croats sacrifice that degree of autonomy that they would have in a Republic on their own, and the Bosniaks sacrifice the concept of a unitary civic state that follows the principle of 'one man one vote'. None of the peoples [*narod*] should mourn this trade-off for it opens up perspectives for the Federation and the reintegration into a unified Bosnia and Herzegovina.[44]

Accusing the Bosniaks of pursuing a policy aimed at dominating the less numerous people in the Federation when they advocate the principle 'one person, one vote' has since become a standard tactic of Croat politicians, especially those with a nationalist agenda. In this immediate post-war period, however, such accusations had a different meaning. They were made in a situation when relapse to war was still a possibility, for all the sides still ruled over their armies. The only factor conditioning such actions was international military presence. In addition, the three political parties exercised a style of government that did not allow for much internal disagreement. Haris Silajdžić left the SDA for the precise reason that they did not give him enough room to fulfil his duties as the country's prime minister. In this respect, he later accused SDA and HDZ of pursuing a similar

---

42   *Dnevni Avaz* 24 July 1996, 3; 25 July 1996, 3; 29 July 1996, 1; *Oslobođenje,* 5 August 1996, 1; 6 August 1996, 1; 7 August 1996, 1.

43   *Oslobođenje,* 3 March 1996, 4. Zubak tried to substantiate his claim to alleged aspirations of Bosniak domination by referring to a statement by Alija Izetbegović who said: 'Bosnia will be as Muslim as France is Muslim, despite being the home of three million Arabs.' On another occasion, as Zubak explained, Izetbegović allegedly told Bosniak intellectuals that the president of Bosnia could only be someone of Bosniak origin and a member of the SDA. In the same article, Zubak also declared himself to be a nationalist, for 'I believe that a nation's rights are human rights'.

44   *Dnevni Avaz,* 24-25 August 1996, 4-5.

politics aimed at the creation of 'ethnic ghettos',[45] i.e. areas with clear national dominations so that party success could be guaranteed. This Bosnian form of 'gerrymandering' was based on the fundamental claim of nationalist parties to the right for sole representation of their group. But it has also to be seen as part of the on-going election campaign, for despite their factual dominance of the political landscape, the nationalist parties could not be sure that the electorate would not punish them for what they had agreed at Dayton.

The negotiations about the makeup of the Federation had certainly the character of those setting up new states, for nobody was sure how the central state would look in the end. When Croatian president Franjo Tuđman visited Bosnia in January 1996, for example, he promised visa liberalisations for the citizens of the Federation, but not for those of the Republika Srpska.[46] In itself, this is remarkable because it not only violates the international norm of treating all the citizens of an internationally recognised state equally but also expresses the deep mistrust of the common structures agreed upon in Dayton.

The exchange of territories between the two entities was a first major challenge in this respect. It especially concerned the areas in and around Sarajevo, which were held by the RS army but had been awarded to the FBiH. When the Serb authorities left Grbavica, Illijaš, or Ilidža, they set buildings on fire and took large parts of the economic infrastructure, i.e. factory equipment, with them. The leadership also pressured many Serbs against staying in the city and in Federation territory, so that around 100,000 Serbs left Sarajevo and others changed areas together with the Serb authorities.[47]

9.1.3   The efforts of the High Representative

The forum to discuss all issues related to the central state and the inter-entity relations was the Joint Interim Commission (JIC). It was composed of four representatives from the Federation, three from the RS, one from the central state, and chaired by the High Representative or someone he designated (usually his deputy Michael Steiner).[48] While the mere fact that JIC meetings took place was a success in the beginning of 1996, it soon became obvious that 'real' cooperation was hard to achieve. Even non-controversial projects like the reestablishment of telephone lines and inter-entity postal services, met with obstacles. Such were even bigger in areas when political changes were concerned, i.e. when the entity constitutions had to be brought in accordance with the Dayton provisions. While the NARS passed a set of laws without much debate, the FBiH parliament was not

---

[45]   *Oslobođenje*, 7 March 1996, 6.

[46]   *Dnevni Avaz* 5 January 1996, 1.

[47]   Petritsch, *Bosnien und Herzegowina fünf Jahre nach Dayton*, 75.

[48]   Annex 2 to Annex 4 of the DPA.

capable of doing the same.[49] Bildt and Steiner had to 'intervene' repeatedly, even though the only means they had at their disposal was personal commitment, as Michael Steiner explained at that time:

> In the military part of the [Dayton] Agreement, Bosnia is some sort of protectorate; in this part, some things can be done with pressure. But we do not have such mechanisms in the civilian parts of the Agreement because the Dayton Agreement foresaw that the parties would fulfil their obligations. If they do not do that, we have no effective means to force them to do that.[50]

The problem presented itself on a municipal level as well. As Christian Schwarz-Schilling, in his capacity as the international mediator for the Federation at that time, recalls:

> I visited mayors and in the negotiations [about refugee return], they told me: 'of course we have a lot of refugees that have submitted official requests for their former houses. We keep all of those [forms] in the basement, but have no intention of looking at them.' That is when I said: 'Beg your pardon?' So we had a big fight, and I told them: 'This is out of the question! Dayton is valid for you as well. There, refugee return is guaranteed and you have to obey, you cannot act like that…' … When I came back [some time later and saw that no progress had been made,] I asked them: 'what's happening here? Didn't I tell you that…' Already in those situations, I should have had the authority to remove those mayors from office based on their behaviour. But I did not. And it was like that everywhere.—And if I did not have the authority, the OHR should have had it. But [there was] nothing of that sort.[51]

Later on, Bildt named the same issues of non-compliance and non-cooperation as the basic shortcoming of the discussions with the local leaders, in this case the RS and FBiH prime ministers:

> My problem in all these discussions was that I did not really have much leverage against either of them. I could certainly argue with them, and I could try to find constructive solutions on complicated issues, guiding them through a terrain that they would not have been comfortable entering into on their own. But it was all dependent on a basic desire on their part to move the process forward. If there were more fundamental problems, I was more or less powerless. I had the moral authority of the international community behind me, but moral authority alone did not cut much ice in the hard political game over the future of Bosnia.[52]

Steiner, Schwarz-Schilling, and Bildt describe a phenomenon Carlos Westendorp, the second High Representative, later called the 'major flaw'[53] of the Dayton Agreement. Despite its fancy title, the international community's High Representative lacked final authority and the means to induce solutions against the will of the people involved. Compromises and agreements were needed, but hard to

---

49   *Dnevni Avaz*, 20-21 April 1996, 7.

50   *Dnevni Avaz*, 20-21 July 1996, 4,5.

51   Schwarz-Schilling, Personal Interview.

52   Bildt, *Peace Journey*, 202–3.

53   Westendorp, Personal Interview.

obtain. The experience of the first half-year had already proven that there were no agreements without high-level international pressure on the local leaders. As exemplified by the events in Mostar, the setup of the Federation, or the removal of Karadžić, this meant regular international summits in Brussels, Geneva, or Rome with representatives of the European Union, Croatia, Yugoslavia (Serbia), or the United States. Additionally, the Croats' and Serbs' *de facto* dependency on the respective structures in their 'other homelands' prevented the detachment of the Bosnian discussions from Croatia and Serbia, which is why Carl Bildt often looked for solutions to Bosnian problems in Belgrade or Zagreb.

The local political elite gradually understood these international mechanisms and started adapting. One may illustrate the general powerlessness of the High Representative and its dependence on international actors with the following example: After being elected as the Serb member of the Bosnian presidency, Momčilo Krajšnik refused to meet his presidential colleagues in Sarajevo due to 'security concerns'.[54] He was also unwilling to sign the presidential oath of office because it referred to 'the state of Bosnia'—a wording that the Serb side rightly saw as diminishing the 'sovereignty' of Republika Srpska. His reluctance meant effectively that the central state body could not start working and that all subsequent institutions were blocked as well. It took the visit of the American diplomat John Kornblum for Krajšnik to finally agree to sign the oath and take up his presidential office.[55]

But apart from such *ad hoc* visits and high-level dialogs in historic European cities, there was one powerful tool the High Representative could employ in order to induce cooperation: money. In this area, the HR used a strategy based on the principle of the carrot and the stick: cooperation was rewarded and non-cooperation punished through granting or withholding donors' money for the respective actors. Before a donors' meeting in May 1997, for example, the donations were conditional on the Council of Ministers' prior agreement on a package of laws, which included *inter alia* the law on the budget, the law on foreign debt, or the law on state tariffs.[56] This strategy of 'economic conditionality' had gradually developed since it was first employed in March 1996 in order to achieve the release of prisoners of war. There were, however, 'very strict limits on what could be achieved and what could not by wielding this particular weapon', for it depended on the international community as a whole. But as Bildt rightly points out, unwillingness on their part to use economic conditionality to induce cooperation would have sent 'a signal of weakness'.[57]

---

54   *Oslobođenje,* 9 October 1996, 1.
55   *Oslobođenje,* 10 October 1996, 4; 23 October 1996, 1.
56   *Dnevni Avaz,* 21 June 1997, 2; *Oslobođenje,* 6 May 1997, 1.
57   Bildt, *Peace Journey,* 203.

Highly dependent on international dynamics and equipped with no more than some sort of perceptional authority, the difficulties the High Representative faced in its daily work became obvious rather quickly. They primarily concerned the antagonism between the alleged omnipotence of what was usually referred to as the international community and the *de facto* rather limited powers granted to their representative on the ground. So it was no surprise that already in March 1996, Michael Steiner had to warn the local leaders not to use the international community as an excuse for their own omissions in achieving compromises.[58] But instead of taking Steiner's words seriously, the locals perfected a strategy that mercilessly exploited the High Representative's weaknesses. As one article remarked:

> Bildt is some sort of personification of the protectorate over Bosnia and Herzegovina, which *a priori* provokes indignation and stubborn determination [by the local leaders] to outlive him. ... Bildt is here with the task to do something. What exactly[?]—not even he knows that. But he does something...[59]

The assertion that Bildt did not know what should be done is of course an inadequate characterisation. Early on, the High Representative had defined his mission goals in terms of trust building, the establishment of dialogue, reconstruction, and setting up the new political system.[60] Nevertheless, the impression of desultoriness is not completely invalid either. Bildt's mandate, as we have seen, is nowhere defined in absolute terms. Moreover, the first year showed that the appropriate level and degree of HR involvement needed to be discussed. Bildt's actions included high-level dialogues on the European level as well as negotiations with the local political elite; but, for example, he was also involved in the comparatively banal task of finding a place for the common state presidency to meet. Even though tasks such as the latter could present rather difficult challenges in the Bosnian environment, they nevertheless diminished the efficacy of the High Representative's office.

All these weaknesses make us understand why the High Representative was determined to strengthen his mandate. But the Bonn powers, the ultimate instrument of strength for the office, did not come out of the blue; rather, it was the culmination of a gradual development that started already in March 1996 with the Sarajevo agreement. For the first time, this agreement, which regulated relations within the Federation, contained concrete penalties if parties failed to deliver on

---

58 *Dnevni Avaz*, 16 March 1996, 3.

59 *Dnevni Avaz*, 4-5 May 1996, 6.

60 The latter point also included the creation of a new TV station, the Open Broadcast Network (OBN, colloquially often referred to as 'Bildt's TV'). The aim was to provide a channel for all parties and thus be a competition to the official TV stations, which were controlled by HDZ, SDS, and SDA (*Oslobođenje*, 15 March 1996, 6). However, the station went on the air only after the September elections and was thus not able to fulfil its primary target.

their promises within the respective timeframe. Concretely, cantons unable to form governments should receive no financial support. The same was true for municipalities that obstructed refugee return. In addition, all representatives not fulfilling their obligations could be removed from office according to the earlier Geneva agreement, provided that the President and Vice-President of the Federation did not object.[61] Even though the conflict parties had still the possibilities to block the HR from taking concrete steps, the Sarajevo agreement, in combination with the Geneva agreement, already contained some of the main elements of the later Bonn powers.

One should note, however, that Bildt's mandate was not only characterised by the structural deficits of the OHR, but also by the first establishment of common state structures in post-war Bosnia. Once the elections were over and all the subsequent symbolic battles had been fought, the political process started as well. In the Federation, a government under the leadership of prime minister Edhem Bičakčić (SDA) and vice-prime minister Drago Bilandžija (HDZ) was formed in December 1996. In the RS, the SDS of President Biljana Plavšić nominated Gojko Klićković as RS prime minister and SDS interim president Aleksa Bruha became speaker of the NARS, thus succeeding to the position that Krajšnik had held. On the central state level, the three presidents discussed a new mechanism for the formation of the Council of Ministers. Zubak and Izetbegović wanted a council consisting of one prime minister and five ministries for foreign policy, finances, justice, refugees, foreign trade and communication plus one minister without a portfolio. But while the Croats insisted on parity in the composition of the government—i.e. two Bosniaks, two Croats, two Serbs—, the Bosniaks wished for a proportional formula—i.e. three Bosniaks, two Croats, one Serb. Krajšnik, on the other hand, sought to limit the central government as much as possible. He therefore argued for the creation of only two ministries (foreign policy and finances) plus one (Serb) chairman, i.e. for the minimum that Dayton foresaw. In Krajšnik's view, other ministries could be formed if needed, provided that the Council of Ministers deemed them necessary.[62] After two international conferences, one in Paris and one in London, failed to resolve the issues, Carl Bildt and Michael Steiner proposed a comprise acceptable to the BiH presidency. When the Council of Ministers was officially formed in January 1997, it consisted of two co-chairmen, Haris Silajdžić for the Bosniaks and Boro Bosić (SDS) for the Serbs, as well as one deputy, the Croat Neven Tomić (HDZ). In addition three ministries were created, responsible for foreign trade (headed by a Bosniak), foreign relations (headed by a Croat) and for civil issues and communications (headed by a Serb). Each minister had two deputies from the other two ethnic groups.[63]

---

61   Petritsch, *Bosnien und Herzegowina fünf Jahre nach Dayton*, 85.
62   *Oslobođenje*, 7 November 1996, 5; 9 November 1996, 1, 3.
63   *Dnevni Avaz*, 4-5 January 1997, 1-3.

Under the mediation of the international community, the locals had thus agreed to a consociational compromise based on a system of complete parity. In this respect it is a rather minor detail that the Croat representative had been formally degraded compared to the other two or that Haris Silajdžić did not formally belong to the SDA. This government was without doubt a coalition of the three national and nationalist elites.

A little more than a year after the signature of the Dayton agreement, the structures of the common state had formally been set up. This had been the 'strategic goal'[64] of the OHR's overall efforts for 1996 and it finally succeeded. The beginning of 1997 thus presented the opportunity to implement the Quick Start Packages (QSPs) that the OHR had been preparing. As Bildt explains: 'My idea was that, if we manage to set up the common institutions, we would have a ready made package of proposals for key decisions in a number of important areas to hand over to them.'[65] These QSPs became the central feature of the international community's efforts in 1997, as Bildt writes. They concerned two aspects: first, constitutional questions and rules for the way in which joint bodies were to function, and second the economic structures, i.e. the conditions to promoting the long-term economic development of the state.[66] The implementation of these QSPs was by no means an easy task, which heavily relied on economic conditionality. But it was a start and gave the locals a concrete agenda.

Carl Bildt decided to hand over his office to a successor before the local elections and the Brčko arbitration judgement, both foreseen for the fall of 1997. In his memoirs, he makes a positive overall summary of his struggles in Bosnia's first two years:

> When I completed my assignment in June 1997 and handed [it] over to my successor, the Office of the High Representative was seen no longer as something to be limited, representing a threat to the primacy of the military efforts, but instead, as the very key to the success of the overall peace implementation. I was particularly pleased finally to see the growing support in Washington for our work in turning around the political situation in key parts of the country. Particularly important has been its shift from efforts to restrict the mandate of the high representative to efforts to strengthen it.[67]

Bildt managed to convince the Americans to support a stronger mandate for the international community. He had, as one local journalist put it, also 'managed to balance the fine line between being a technocrat and a protector'.[68] In his one and a half years, he had encountered numerous instances of obstruction. And he had

---

[64]   Bildt, *Peace Journey*, 251.
[65]   Ibid.
[66]   Ibid., 252.
[67]   Ibid., 386.
[68]   *Dnevni Avaz*, 20 June 1997, 3.

experienced his powerlessness in a radical form. In a way, this powerlessness was the logical consequence not only of the different philosophies regarding the form of the OHR (from the American and European sides), but also regarding the basic experiment in democracy that they performed. Elections, even imperfect ones, provide political leaders not only with some form of legitimacy (again, even an imperfect one), but they also allow for certain independence. Democracies, as ideal-typical forms of political self-organisation, are designed as inwardly closed systems that tend to react rather unfavourably to outside intervention. It is therefore a conceptual and, as Bildt and also his successor Carlos Westendorp had to learn, a practical impossibility to impose a democracy or even induce a compromise within a quasi-democratic state without the support of the local leaders. This naturally presents a serious challenge to setting up new states through the tool of outside intervention. But in itself, it is a testimony to the strength of a democratic system.

9.2   Carlos Westendorp (1997-1999)

> The US Representative in charge of Bosnia at that time, Bob Gelbard, came and visited me at the embassy in New York and he asked me whether I was tough. 'Are you tough enough?' And I said: 'Well, what do you mean by tough? I can be—I am not tough by nature, but I can be if necessary.' And I didn't know that it would be so necessary to be tough.[69]

The way in which Carlos Westendorp was offered the position of High Representative is illuminating. Neither knowledge about the historical background of the conflict, nor an understanding for the complexities of inter-group relationships in the region but personal toughness and resolution qualified a person to hold the post. Presumably, toughness was deemed an effective tool for taming the prevailing nationalists in their efforts to disrupt a state the internationals fought so hard to sustain. But at that time, demanding toughness of the HR was nothing other than a mockery, for in order to be effective, toughness needs to be backed up by some form of power. And as we have seen in the previous section, this is exactly something of which the OHR still had only a limited amount. The choice of Westendorp furthermore testified to the still rather political nature of the mandate. Before he assumed the Office of the High Representative in June 1997, Westendorp served as Spain's ambassador to the United Nations; and before that, he was briefly this country's foreign minister. He fitted perfectly into the world of international politics unfolding in Bosnia, for he had been a member of the Spanish Diplomatic Service since 1965.[70] As a former ambassador, he knew how to behave on the diplomatic platform.

---

[69]   Westendorp, Personal Interview.

[70]   See Westendorp's CV on the OHR website: http://www.ohr.int/cv/cwestendorp.asp, last accessed 20 October 2013.

However, as the former quote suggests, his concrete task was outside of the realm of typical diplomacy, at least as far as it refers to the people on the ground. Rather than relying on soft power, the might of conviction and argument, or any specifically crafted protocol, Westendorp was the first HR to introduce a new instrument into the international community's dealings with the local political system: the Bonn powers. It is for precisely this reason that, analytically, one needs to distinguish two phases of Westendorp's engagement in Bosnia. The first and rather brief one covers the period between June and December 1997. During this time, Westendorp did not significantly alter the HR's general approach of economic conditionality and repeated high-level meetings, for he was preoccupied with assessing the situation on the ground. Like Carl Bildt, Westendorp identified the same lack of cooperation within the political elite as the major obstacle to renewing the country. As he gradually grew frustrated by it, he requested more powers from the international community. The granting of such powers at the Bonn PIC summit in December 1997 is the beginning of Westendorp's second phase. From then on, the High Representative could impose laws and remove people from office if they blocked the implementation of the Dayton Peace Agreement. These powers opened up new possibilities and approaches for organising the international efforts in the country. But they also provoked resistance for which the international forces had to be prepared. When Westendorp stepped down in July 1999, he had not only demonstrated the toughness his international masters had demanded, but also fundamentally transformed Bosnia's political system.

9.2.1   The pre-Bonn phase

When he assumed office, Carlos Westendorp found a country that was in many respects in a better shape than it had been one and a half years before. The most obvious improvement concerned the security situation; due to an impressive amount of military force, the international community had managed to stabilise the negative peace and restore some form of normalcy in many parts of the country. But, as the Peace Implementation Council (PIC) concluded at the very same conference in Sintra, Portugal, at which they appointed Westendorp to be the new High Representative, 'major problems and challenges remain[ed]'.[71] The major obstacle, according to paragraph five of the Sintra conclusions, was that 'the authorities of Bosnia and Herzegovina [were] failing to live up fully to their obligations under the Peace Agreement'. Echoing Michael Steiner's previous remarks,

---

[71]   Peace Implementation Council, *Communiqué: Political Declaration from Ministerial Meeting of the Steering Board of the Peace Implementation Council (Sintra Conference)* (Sintra: Office of the High Representative, 30 May 1997), http://www.ohr.int/ pic/default.asp?content_id=5180. Westendorp was appointed as Carl Bildt's successor at the Sintra conference.

the PIC chose strong and undiplomatic words in order to describe the on-going situation: 'the Steering Board urges the authorities of Bosnia and Herzegovina and its representatives to stop blaming each other, or the international community, for the problems they encounter, and to work together constructively and in a spirit of reconciliation for their common good.' Even though the PIC acknowledged some achievements regarding the setup of common state institutions, it also noted that much of this progress was made possible only through the active involvement of the HR. The Sintra conclusions thus sought to empower the local politicians to step up to the task by specifically supporting the politics of economic conditionality that Carl Bildt had introduced:

> The main responsibility for the future of the country rests with the elected and constitutional representatives of the country. The help they will receive from the international community will be dependent upon the commitment they demonstrate to the Peace Agreement.[72]

Bildt had developed his approach in an *ad hoc* manner, but he had managed to rally much international support around the initial idea. The Sintra conclusions, first and foremost, present one of the first codifications of a stronger role for the High Representative. In many aspects, the final document reads like a blueprint for a process that would end up with some major change. Repeatedly, the High Representative is tasked with assisting the locals in finding a solution to specific policy areas; but he is also given the clear mission to report back on measures that could be taken by the PIC if such assistance proved futile. It is in this manner that Sintra, like the Sarajevo and Geneva Agreements before it, laid the ground for the later introduction of the Bonn powers.

To the uninformed, the introduction of the Bonn powers may seem an overreaction. After all, the politics of economic conditionality proved rather successful in several areas. The parliaments on all levels started passing important laws and thus partially fulfilling their obligations: in June, and in anticipation of a donor's meeting the following month, for example, both chambers of the Bosnian parliament adopted a set of seven laws from the QSPs.[73] But more often than not, such efficiency was merely cosmetic, for real cooperation was still an illusion. Take the following examples: During a marathon session in May 1997, the FBiH parliament adopted legislation relating to fixing the borders of several municipalities that geographically lay in between cantons or entities. This was an important step in implementing the respective provisions of Dayton and Washington. Even though the proposals gained majority support and thus passed, the Croat members of parliament *and* government subsequently left the session because their pro-

---

⁷² Ibid.

⁷³ These laws included legislation on the Central Bank, customs policy, foreign trade policy, foreign debt, the budget for 1997 and the corresponding implementation legislation, as well as a law on immunity. Cf. *Dnevni Avaz*, 21 June 1997, 2.

posals had been outvoted.[74] Several days after the FBiH session, the Croats formed the 'Croat community of Herceg-Bosna', which was supposed to be of a cultural, not a political character. Nevertheless, its decisions should be 'morally binding for the political leaders of the Croats in Bosnia'.[75] The community's political significance was thus not hidden, and its existence proves the still fragile relationship between the Croats and Bosniaks in the Federation. In July, Serb politicians at the central state level boycotted sessions of the presidency and the council of ministers;[76] as a consequence, the much-needed citizenship law could not be adopted.[77] In August, the BiH presidency failed to reach an agreement on new ambassadors and thus did not fulfil a deadline set in Sintra. Following this failure, the HR declared all existing Bosnian ambassadors illegitimate and asked the international community not to extend to them the courtesy of genuine representatives of the state. This strategy succeeded, and ten days later, the members of the presidency finally agreed upon a proportional formula and named 13 Bosniak, 11 Serb, and nine Croat ambassadors.[78] The parties thus blocked more issues than they agreed upon, and a policy oriented towards some form of common good, as the Sintra declaration had demanded, was inexistent.

The larger political landscape made genuine efforts towards cooperation in 1997 almost impossible. In general, we can distinguish three reasons for a series of stalemates in the local political system: (1) the local elections; (2) the unfolding political divide in Republika Srpska; and (3) the emergence of evidence proving wide-spread corruption and conscious efforts to undermine the Dayton institutions. I shall discuss those in the remainder of this section, for it is the culmination of these experiences that ultimately convinced Carlos Westendorp to ask for a stronger mandate of the OHR.

Firstly: In 1996, conditions in the municipalities were not such that they allowed a free and fair electoral campaign. After a series of postponed deadlines, the OSCE finally declared 13 and 14 September 1997 as dates for the local elections. New elections presented the opportunity for the parties to adapt their strategies and reassess their coalition options. Interestingly, this not only concerned the opposition, but the governing parties as well. Under the somewhat cumbersome name '*Koalicija za cjelovitu i demokratsku Bosnu i Hercegovinu*' (CD BiH, Coalition for a unified and democratic BiH) the SDA entered into a coalition with four smaller Bosniak parties, namely Silajdžić's SBiH, the Liberal Party (LS), the Liberal Bosnian Organisation (LBO), and the Citizen's Democratic Party (GDO). As Izetbegović explained, this coalition was a pragmatic choice: 'the difference

---

[74]   *Oslobođenje*, 15 May 1997, 1.
[75]   *Oslobođenje*, 25 May 1997, 3.
[76]   *Dnevni Avaz*, 18 July 1997, 2.
[77]   *Oslobođenje*, 26 August 1997, 1.
[78]   *Oslobođenje*, 3 August 1997, 3; 4 August 1997, 1; 5 August 1997, 1; 9 August 1997, 1, 3.

between us is rooted in philosophy, not policy; and philosophy is not important here. Why should our forces not act in a coordinated manner so that our efforts may be successful?'[79] This coalition, which would become somewhat important due to the events unfolding in RS (see below), was by no means a surprise. It rather constituted the institutionalisation of the Unification Declaration that Silajdžić and Izetbegović had launched a year earlier. As one observer put it, the coalition aimed at improving SDA's tattered image and securing the survival of the other, smaller parties.[80] As far as the opposition was concerned, the SDP, now under the leadership of Zlatko Lagumdžija, tried to position itself as an independent party. In several municipalities, it wanted to run with its own candidate, while in others, it preferred an arrangement within the *Zadružena Lista ZL* coalition of the previous elections. But since the election law did not allow for such an approach, the SDP ultimately left the coalition, whereas the other parties stayed together under the new name *Zadružena Lista 97*. In RS, the Independent Social Democrats of Milorad Dodik, the National Party, the Democratic Party for Banja Luka and Krajna, also opted for a common coalition before the local elections. They ran under the name 'For Banja Luka', which, as Dodik explained, was 'the only city that had the potential of being the domicile for the RS institutions'.[81] This action, small as it was, reflected the general rift between the hard-line Pale and the moderate Banja Luka factions (see also below).

The key element in the elections was voter registration, which was especially important with regards to displaced persons. These had the possibility to choose to vote either where they currently lived or where they had lived in 1991. According to the International Crisis group, 'the nationalist parties attempted to pack key municipalities with voters from the "correct" ethnic group'; that they did so by methods of voter registration constitutes a genuine continuation of the Bosnian 'gerrymandering' tactics. Since the OSCE made a number of concessions to those parties in order to save the elections, the final result was not really surprising: the three ruling parties won around eighty per cent of council seats in the Federation and nearly sixty per cent in Republika Srpska; non-nationalist parties gained a majority of 63 per cent only in the municipality of Tuzla,[82] their traditional stronghold. In this way, the local elections confirmed the general picture and made attempts at cooperation even scarcer. That the nationalists had won over ethnically more or less homogenous municipalities directly threatened the possibility of refugee return, especially minority return.

---

[79]   *Dnevni Avaz*, 28 May 1997, 2.

[80]   *Oslobođenje*, 5 May 1997, 1.

[81]   *Oslobođenje*, 29 May 1997, 9.

[82]   International Crisis Group, *Dayton: Two Years On. A Review of Progress in Implementing the Dayton Peace Accords in Bosnia*, Bosnia Report (Brussels: International Crisis Group, 19 November 1997), 8.

Secondly, while the local elections can be seen as a setback in uniting the country, they were by no means as threatening to the future of the state as the events unfolding in Republika Srpska. Radovan Karadžić had formally left the political stage and Biljana Plavšić was in charge. Nevertheless, the former RS president, with the help of the Serb member in the Bosnian presidency, Momčilo Krajšnik, kept undermining Plavšić's authority and sabotaging any attempts of greater cooperation. The rifts in RS leadership became obvious already in March 1997, when Krajšnik—and not Plavšić—signed a treaty establishing special relations between RS and Milošević's Serbia. The possibility for such a treaty was left open to the entities as part of the Dayton Agreement. But it was clear that such agreements, even though they concerned the entities, were nevertheless international treaties for which the central state was responsible. Since neither the Bosnian presidency nor the Council of Ministers had been informed about the agreement, Izetbegović and Silajdžić deemed Krajšnik's actions unconstitutional.[83] The OHR did not go as far in its assessment but Michael Steiner made clear that the treaty was only valid once the Bosnian parliament ratified it.[84] The treaty, in its form at that moment, presented an important step back with regards to the unity of Bosnia, even though it contained several passages reaffirming Bosnia's territorial integrity. As the leader of the Socialist Party in the RS, Živko Radišić saw it, RS's statehood was formally confirmed by the document.[85] But apart from the concrete provisions, the treaty, in the eyes of the SDS had a 'historical' dimension for the Serb people, for it united them over the centuries-old barrier of the Drina River.[86] Even though the NARS ratified the treaty after long discussions, its evolution clearly proved a rift in RS leadership.

Superficially, the central question in the fight between Plavšić and Krajšnik concerned the legal matter of political authority. In Krajšnik's understanding, the Dayton agreement had given the Bosnian Serbs two presidents and it was anything but surprising that those two functions collided, as they did with the treaty.[87] In Plavšić's mind, she was the representative of the RS and thus entitled to sign such agreements. But underneath such legal discussions, which could have been easily resolved by the RS Constitutional Court, lay a fight for political power and survival. As mentioned in an article by the *International Herald Tribune*, Karadžić and Krajšnik *de facto* controlled two companies that had a monopoly on selling goods such as fuel or cigarettes in the RS.[88] So when Plavšić tried to con-

---

83   *Oslobođenje*, 3 March 1997, 1.

84   *Oslobođenje*, 6 March 1997, 5.

85   *Dnevni Avaz*, 4 March 1997, 4.

86   *Oslobođenje*, 4 March 1997, 4.

87   Michael Steiner recounted Krajšnik's argument in an interview with *Dnevni Avaz*, 31 March 1997, 5.

88   As reported in *Dnevni Avaz*, 10 April 1997, 3.

solidate her power, she naturally threatened the established monopolies of the Pale faction, particularly since she also ordered a special investigation of a company closely associated with Krajšnik and Karadžić. She publicly stated her intention to launch a 'crusade' against corruption in government and for the establishment of rule of law.[89] In general, she believed that the stubborn course of action against the Dayton institutions and the internationals threatened the mere survival of the RS. The situation escalated when Plavšić tried to relieve Dragan Kijac, RS's interior minister and close associate of Karadžić, from his duties in July 1997. The RS government, still under the control of the Pale faction, reversed her decision and a special session of the NARS was scheduled for Plavšić to explain herself. She subsequently dissolved the NARS altogether. While the opposition parties accepted this decision, the SDS and the SRS questioned Plavšić's authority to do so. At the session, which the opposition parties boycotted, Plavšić was called to resign. Despite some public rallies in support of the RS president in Banja Luka or Prijedor, the SDS kicked Plavšić out of the party and renewed its demand for her resignation. In her fight against the Pale faction, Plavšić received not only support from the international side, but also from the security apparatus of the RS. The police and large parts of the military supported her course of action. So when Karadžić supporters marched on Banja Luka, the police and the international forces were able to prevent any serious riots. An agreement brokered by Milošević in Belgrade finally resolved the tense situation. Both sides agreed to new elections for the NARS as well as for the RS presidency and the Serb member in the BiH presidency.

These elections dramatically changed the political landscape in the RS. During the election campaign, Karadžić was eager to portray Plavšić as a close ally of the internationals intending to crush the RS's sovereignty, whereas she accused the SDS of being too closely associated with Milošević. The international community was also deeply involved in the campaign, for in October, SFOR shut down a Pale-based TV station that served as a propaganda channel for the Karadžić faction. This action, in line with the Sintra conclusions that dedicated much space to media freedom, can be seen as a genuine, albeit stronger continuation of Carl Bildt's efforts of establishing a new TV channel that would give opposition parties the possibility of wider outreach. But Westendorp also feared that Plavšić, if denied access to the media, could lose the elections. The internationals thus clearly sided with the Banja Luka faction during the campaign, which was not very surprising, but naturally provoked reactions by the Pale faction that became even more uncooperative. When Westendorp called Krajšnik to quit his obstructionist behaviour in the BiH presidency and to resign, the latter responded quite tellingly: 'I am here to stay. Westendorp did not elect me, so he has not the

---

[89]   *Oslobođenje*, 15 July 1997, 3.

authority to remove me.'[90] In the RS parliamentary elections, which took place in November 1997, the SDS lost its absolute majority and, with the SRS RS, secured only 39 out of 83 seats. The Banja Luka faction—consisting of Plavšić's new party, the *Srpski Narodni Savez RS* (Serb national alliance, SNS) with 15 seats, the Socialist party with nine, and Dodik's SNSD with two mandates— secured altogether 26 mandates. Neither side had thus a majority, and the 'Federation coalition' CD BiH, which due to absentee voting won 16 seats, together with the SDP BiH with two mandates became the deciding factor.[91]

Thirdly: the criminal behaviour Plavšić had exposed with respect to the RS was not limited to the smaller entity. Throughout Bosnia, charges of corruption began surfacing. Already in January, FBiH Prime Minister Bičakčić had accused his Croat Deputy and FBiH's finance minister Bilandžija of unlawfully exempting the company Lijanović, which was and still is run by a Croat, from customs duties, thus damaging the federal budget for some 23 million German Marks. The justice ministry subsequently started an investigation into the claim, which the accused denied.[92] In July, Alija Izetbegović ordered an additional investigation after British Foreign Minister Robin Cook had accused the Bosnian government of widespread corruption.[93] Finally, in November, the OHR published a report from the Customs and Fiscal Assistance Office (CAFAO) that found widespread illegalities with regards to RS and FBiH budgets and, especially, the handling of imported goods. Instead of using the respective funds for the Dayton institutions, budgetary means went into parallel organisations that were not even supposed to exist any more (like the Herceg Bosna structures, for example).[94]

9.2.2 Towards the Bonn powers

All these events explain the general decrease in cooperation by local politicians. As Westendorp said at that time: 'Some problems originate within the Federation, more often they come from Krajšnik but we made clear to all of the people involved that those who obstruct the process should be removed.'[95] Following a meeting of the Steering Board, Westendorp tasked the locals with a list of eighteen items to be resolved until the Bonn PIC conference scheduled for 10 December. As the Steering Board explained, 'these items are a minimum requirement to signal to the international community in Bonn that the leadership of this country is taking its obligations seriously and is willing to cooperate with the international

---

90 *Oslobođenje*, 8 November 1997, 3.
91 Election results from *Oslobođenje*, 8 December 1997, 1.
92 *Dnevni Avaz*, 22 January 1997, 1, 6; 24 January 1997, 8; 27 January 1997, 1.
93 *Oslobođenje*, 27 July 1997, 1.
94 *Oslobođenje*, 1 November 1997, 1, 3; 7 November 1997, 3.
95 *Dnevni Avaz*, 7 November 1997, 1.

community in good faith.'[96] In the Joint Statement, the Steering Board also threatened selective sanctions against non-cooperative actors but it did not specify how such actions might look. However, at the corresponding press conference, apparently a concrete mechanism was discussed. As *Dnevni Avaz* reports, 'proposals to strengthen the mandate of the High Representative were supported but only with regards to those questions where, after a certain period of time, no progress is achieved.'[97] Concretely, the HR would have the power of issuing binding 'arbitration judgements' for issues where the locals could not find any solution.

Such a mandate, which anticipates the Bonn powers, was not so controversial. In fact, the Bosnian authorities themselves raised the possibility several months earlier. Because the Council of Ministers was unable to find an agreement with regards to the citizenship law, already in August Haris Silajdžić had asked the HR to arbitrate: 'We were not able to agree on some key issues so this would be the best solution.'[98] Jacques Klein, the Deputy HR, happily agreed to present his proposals for a new flag and the design of the new currency. In an interview with *Dnevni Avaz* in August, Westendorp explained his basic view of the Bosnian situation as follows:

> [Bosnia] is not a protectorate. Dayton did not conceive of the OHR as such. The Dayton Peace Agreement only conceived of us as the interpreter of the Agreement and that is the only thing we can do. It is our task to correctly interpret Dayton and to propose compromises on certain issues. Some proposals are accepted, like the ambassadors for examples, and some are not; sometimes we face obstruction forcing us to impose sanctions. But this is not a protectorate in the real sense of the word. If we had a protectorate, perhaps we could solve problems much quicker; but the question is how lasting these solutions would be once we leave. However, if the current situation is not radically improved in the next four or five months, I will ask the international community to strengthen the OHR mandate.[99]

The situation did not improve, and, according to Westendorp's understanding today, it could not have due to the parties involved in the government. He describes the Serb politicians as 'straight-forward, sometimes more primitive in thinking and very ultra-nationalist'; the Croat politicians as 'also very nationalistic, very openly nationalistic' due to the fundamental frustration of having to share a federation with the Bosniaks; and, ultimately, the Bosniaks as 'apparently easier to deal with—but not in [practice]', for they were 'very resilient'. In general, Westendorp describes the Bosnian politicians as: 'good politicians, but they were unable to avoid a catastrophe. And once they didn't avoid a catastrophe, they

---

[96]   Peace Implementation Council, *Joint Statement: Meeting of the Steering Board with the Presidency and the COM Chairs* (Sarajevo: Office of the High Representative, 6 November 1997), http://www.ohr.int/pic/default.asp?content_id=5181.

[97]   *Dnevni Avaz*, 7 November 1997, 2.

[98]   *Dnevni Avaz*, 8 August 1997, 2.

[99]   *Dnevni Avaz*, 19 August 1997, 5.

were also responsible for what had happened for the wrong reasons.' In his reading, the nationalist parties of the early '90s were the main culprits for the war as
such and, consequently, also responsible for the stalemates that he experienced in
daily political life. He thus unequivocally sided with the non-nationalist, opposition parties, as he explains:

> And this is why I tried very hard during my tenure to foster elections and non-
> nationalistic parties, more inter-ethnic parties, like the Social Democrats, Liberals—
> they were parties who were not nationalistic. One of the reasons why I decided, to-
> gether with SFOR, to take by force, to seize the TV of Republika Srpska and also to
> transform the TV in Sarajevo, BH, [which was] in the Bosniak[s'] hands, was pre-
> cisely because [of] the influence of TV over people, you know. And they were
> broadcasting programmes totally against Dayton['s] spirit, against reconciliation.[100]

Apart from providing moral and structural support, Westendorp was also actively
engaged in opposition politics. In May 1998, for example, he assembled the leaders of the opposing parties and tried to unite them. He urged them to form one coalition so that they could effectively counterbalance the nationalists.[101] Similar in
intent was the action by Heinz Fischer, then-president of the Austrian parliament,
and Robin Cook, the aforementioned British Foreign Minister, who tried to unite
the three Social Democratic parties in Bosnia (SDP BiH, UBSD, as well as
Dodik's SNSD).[102] But Westendorp and the internationals knew that such action
could, if at all, deliver results only in the long run. He needed immediate instruments, for he deeply believed that nationalist parties were not capable of compromise:

> When they [the Presidency of BiH] met, they did not agree on anything. Because
> agreeing among parties, political parties, who are not ideological parties in the sense
> of parties with a programme, parties with different points of views about reality,
> about economy, about … but, no, no, they are nationalistic parties. So, by essence,
> by definition, they cannot agree with the other group, because [their] nationalism is
> exclusive. So you're either with me or against me. So, what a compromise can be
> done between those three different parties? So this was one, the biggest problem.[103]

This deep conviction about the non-cooperative nature of nationalist parties was,
in Westendorp's understanding, proven by the reluctance towards cooperation
that he witnessed in his daily work. He and his team looked through the Dayton
agreement in the hope of finding some 'flaw', some possibility to strengthen the
OHR mandate in this respect. The HR was to be 'not just an advisor, a friendly
person, who tells you [that] you should do this and that' but someone who 'in the
absence of an agreement… will say: well, this is the law':

---

[100] Westendorp, Personal Interview.
[101] *Dnevni Avaz*, 4 March 1998, 5.
[102] *Oslobođenje*, 30 May 1998, 3.
[103] Westendorp, Personal Interview.

> At the Bonn conference, we managed to introduce a method by which the High Rep-
> resentative can take these decisions, which is not exactly in legal terms with Dayton.
> … It was not very legal, I have to admit; but I have to confess that everybody ac-
> cepted it. Nobody protested. Why? Because they [i.e. the members of the interna-
> tional community] knew that all these things [i.e. the implementation of laws] were
> necessary but they [i.e. the Bosnian parties] were not able to accept [the proposed
> laws] by definition, you know. And this was an important step forward, because we
> approved a lot of laws: the law on citizenship, etc. And even, even more, we did
> more things—that is to say to expel some of the elected officials, which were not in
> line with Dayton.[104]

From an international perspective, the introduction of the Bonn powers was a logical step with many historic predecessors. Referring to Germany and Japan after
the Second World War, El Salvador, Mozambique, or Eastern Slavonia, Paddy
Ashdown explains why it can be necessary to assume full governing power under
certain circumstances:

> There have been many cases in recent times when it has been necessary to assist a
> country to transition from war, especially a terrible war like that in Bosnia, to full
> democracy. In these circumstances and for a limited period of time, it is sometimes
> necessary to put democracy second to the imperative of ending the conflict and es-
> tablishing the institutions of justice and good governance upon which democracy de-
> pends.[105]

However, the nature of the introduction of the Bonn powers to Bosnia was different than in the other examples. For better or worse, Bosnia had already begun its
democratic path. It possessed a democratically elected government, repeated experiences with (imperfect) elections and a state that was finally gaining some
track. If the Bonn powers had been present in 1995, as many observers believe
they should have been, Ashdown's argument might be valid. But introducing
them into a system that was formally democratic and, despite of all its flaws, also
yielding results meant changing the character of the entire system. It cannot be
seen as a logical step in a process but rather as a break from it. The democratic
(and consociational) elements of the system could not be reversed, but they were
amended through an external presence that controlled the systemic dynamics. According to Schwarz-Schilling, who was present at the Bonn summit and who calls
himself 'one of the co-authors' of the Bonn powers, he insisted on some legal
provision that would distinguish Bosnia from a colonial administration. An idea,
which he kept repeating in the following years, was that an independent legal
body could examine decisions taken with the Bonn powers, especially when they
concern the removal of people. To the contrary, Westendorp does not recall any
discussions regarding the limits of the Bonn powers or their subjection under
some form of legal review. Nevertheless, he insists that those powers were not

---

[104]   Ibid.
[105]   Ashdown, *Swords and Ploughshares*, 19.

'unconditional' because 'all these decisions should be approved by the [PIC or Steering Board] conference[s] itself periodically. And also approved by the Security Council of the United Nations where the High Representative permanently went and explained and was supported. … So these powers were always under surveillance of the international community.' It was thus clear from the beginning that the HR's responsibility lay with the sphere of international law rather than with the institutions of the Bosnian state, which he was appointed to guard.

I have spent much space elaborating on the circumstances that led to the introduction of the Bonn powers for two reasons. First, I believe that the pre-Bonn phase of Bosnian history merits much more attention than it is currently given in political science literature. Too often the direct connection is made between local non-cooperation and the need for the Bonn powers, which, as I tried to show, is a simplistic but not completely invalid argument. But the nature of non-cooperation was not only based on a general reluctance towards cooperation, but has to be seen within the different context of internal power politics as well. Assuming a simplistic causality following the rather questionable logic of *post hoc ergo propter hoc* is misleading insofar as it neither allows us to clearly disentangle the different factions within the three ethnic groups (for they were by no means homogenous) nor to trace back the origins of several political issues, which hinder the progress of the country even today.

Second, the lengthy analysis of the pre-Bonn phase was necessary because I believe that the introduction of the Bonn powers was, for lack of a better term, justifiable. The international community had installed a rather powerless mediator that had found his only weapon of coercion in economic sanctions and threats of suspending certain politicians' travelling privileges. This could hardly serve as a coherent strategy because the Steering Board or the Peace Implementation Council had to authorise every action in one way or another and come up with new incentives and punishments for every policy area. The High Representative was tasked with assisting the locals, reporting about their progress, and suggesting possible courses of action if cooperation was not achieved. All of these tasks were part of a larger and internationally prescribed agenda that sought to sustain the Bosnian state. There was thus an overall strategy, even though it was only articulated through a number of concrete policy proposals: Bosnia should be transformed from a war-torn and divided polity into an efficient and modern state; its communist economy should be replaced by privatised market economy; and, finally, the communist system had to give way to a democratic one. These goals of international efforts constitute Bosnia's triple transition, as Papić called it.[106] Giving the High Representative the Bonn powers was a way to speed up the transi-

---

[106]   Žarko Papić, "The General Situation in B-H and International Support Policies," in *International Support Policies to South-East European Countries: Lessons (not) Learned in Bosnia and Herzegovina* (Sarajevo: Müller, 2001), 17–37.

tion and relieve the international community, especially the outside body, the PIC, of micro-managing functions. In addition, the solution corresponded to what Bosnians themselves had demanded before. In cases where compromise was needed but unobtainable, the HR could deliver arbitration judgements and thus provide a way of overcoming permanent blockades. The powers were a means of last resort and had clearly a subsidiary function, for they presupposed the failure of the local political system.

The problem of the Bonn powers lies less in the arguments that led to their introduction, but in the unintended consequences of the instrument itself. The Bonn powers altered the existing political system and added a new burden to the transitioning country: dependency. Their creators knew this danger very well, as Westendorp recalls: 'Of course, I knew that it was a temporary measure. It shouldn't be forever, because otherwise it creates a habit. This is the dependency syndrome, as they call it. It was in order to do the most important issues, the most important laws, the most important decisions.' But as we shall see, it is exactly this habit that developed, this unhealthy dependency on foreign intervention and, consequently, the relieving of the local political elites' responsibility. At Sintra, the PIC demanded the politicians to 'stop blaming each other, or the international community, for the problems they encounter[ed]'.[107] But rather than blaming the internationals for the problems, they could now blame them for not imposing the solutions—for with the Bonn powers, the HR clearly had the means to do so. It was in this manner that another task was put upon the Bosnian state, the transition from a dependent state into a self-governing and self-sustaining polity. The pre-disposition for this fourth transition was present during the first post-war years as well, but it is through the Bonn powers that it became the one transition that should incorporate all others. It is also the one that lasted until today.

9.2.3   The post-Bonn powers phase

The citizenship law was the first to be imposed using the Bonn powers. The parliament had managed to pass the laws on new travel documents and the Council of Minister by the international deadline of 16 December, but a new law on citizenship had not been adopted. One day after the deadline, Carlos Westendorp informed the members of the Bosnian presidency in a simple letter about his decision:

> In accordance with my authority under Annex 10 of the Peace Agreement and Article XI of the Bonn Document, I do hereby decide that the Law on Citizenship of Bosnia and Herzegovina shall enter into force by 1 January 1998 on [an] interim ba-

---

[107]   Peace Implementation Council, *Communiqué: Political Declaration from Ministerial Meeting of the Steering Board of the Peace Implementation Council (Sintra Conference).*

sis, until the Parliamentary Assembly adopts this law in due form, without amendments and no conditions attached. The text of the Law, submitted to Parliament and in accordance with Annex 1 of the Bonn Documents is attached hereto and must be published in the Official Gazette as well.

.... The Peace Process is, after Sintra and Bonn, entering a new and decisive phase. I am decided to fully use my authorities under Annex 10 of the Dayton peace Accord and Article 11 of the Bonn Document to insure an efficient implementation and fully count on your fully co-operation in this endeavour. [108]

This first imposition exemplifies the new strength of the High Representative. Not only can he adopt legislation with nothing more than a mere signature, he is also not obliged to justify his actions in any form. Regret about the parliament's failure to adopt the law sufficed in the present case. But it is important to highlight that the measures taken, in accordance with the philosophy at that time, had a temporary character. The HR proclaimed the law only on an 'interim basis, until the Parliamentary Assembly adopts this law in due form', as Westendorp wrote. In theory, the parliament, given certain conditions, could also adopt a different solution than the one proclaimed by the HR. However, this would imply that the chambers could reach a different agreement.

The citizenship law opened the door for a number of different decisions, which had been stuck for a long time. As Westendorp understood the situation, the main challenge was that the state did not exist, that it 'was to be made': 'there was no sense of state, no sense of unity. There were no symbols, no flag, nothing, no national anthem, no nationality/citizenship law', he recalls. Accordingly, he would use his powers to foster the exact same state structures that he deemed so important in order for the state to survive; in other words, he was engaged in the business of real state building. His usage of the Bonn powers in 1998 corresponds to this philosophy in a prototypical manner. After parliament failed to adopt any of the three different designs for the new state flag proposed by a commission, for example, the OHR settled on the alternatives that had secured the most votes in the House of Representatives. Later on, he would also decide under what circumstances the flag is to be displayed and how the Bosnian coat-of-arms would look. He also impacted a resolution of Bosnia's on-going currency debate. After the war, three different currencies were used: the Yugoslav Dinar in the RS, the Bosnian Dinar in ABiH areas, and the Kuna in the Herceg-Bosna territories, while the German Mark was accepted in all parts of the country. Bosnia's new currency, the 'Convertible Mark' (KM), symbolized the unification of the country, when it was introduced in June 1998. The KM was pegged to the German Mark with an exchange ratio of 1:1 and the High Representative decreed not only the time of its

---

[108]   Office of the High Representative, "Decision Imposing the Law on Citizenship of BiH," 16 December 1997, http://www.ohr.int/decisions/statemattersdec/default.asp?content_id=343. Accessed 22 October 2013.

introduction but also decided on its design, which features important personalities from all the three groups. Initially, only the Bosniaks used the new money; but since the salaries of politicians and state employees as well as the bills for electricity, gas, and administrative fees were all due in KM, the currency gained traction.[109] A new design was also necessary for the licence plates. Entity based plates, which had been used so far, effectively hindered the free movement throughout the Bosnian territory, for cars from one entity would systematically be controlled in the other. The new licence plates consisted of six numbers and a letter that were identical in the Cyrillic and the Latin alphabets. This simple measure, combined with the fact that the HR decreed a rather low fee for car registration, allowed people from one entity to travel to the other without the fear of being stopped due to their geographic origin. In the end, it was this measure that allowed the free movement of people.

One year later, in 1999, Westendorp also imposed a new national anthem after the respective law failed to gain majority support in parliament. Serbs and Croats opposed the anthem, which consisted only of an instrumental version, not because they did not like the music, but because they contested the name 'state anthem' (*'državna himna'*); instead, they argued, it should be called the 'anthem of BiH'.[110] The process leading up to the imposition of the state anthem illustrates the mechanism by which Westendorp made his decisions. As he recalls, an independent commission was established consisting of representatives from the different groups. An open contest was launched and different versions of the national anthem were presented to the commission. This was done anonymously, i.e. 'without knowing who the author was; if he was Serb or not, nobody knew.' The commission took a vote and agreed on one of the versions to be submitted to parliament. It was only after this procedure, which was similar to the one used for the licence plate and the state flag decisions, as well as the failure in parliament that the HR imposed a decision. As Westendorp wrote in the decision on the state flag, it is only after such an exhausting procedure that he thought his imposed decision legitimate.[111]

Such procedure, however, constrained Westendorp and his team as the case of travel documents illustrates. The parliament had passed a law regarding travel

---

[109]   Petritsch, *Bosnien und Herzegowina fünf Jahre nach Dayton*, 110.
[110]   *Dnevni Avaz*, 24 February 1999, 4.
[111]   'Following their statements made in the Parliamentary Assembly the abstention of the SDS and the HDZ Delegates can clearly not be seen as an expression of opposition to the flag proposals submitted. In the House of Representatives Alternative 1 for the flag secured 16 votes, 16 abstentions and only one vote against. On the basis of this I have decided that there is sufficient legitimacy for me to take a decision now.' Cf. Office of the High Representative, "Decision Imposing the Law on the Flag of BiH," 3 February 1998, http://www.ohr.int/decisions/statemattersdec/default.asp?content_id=344. Accessed 24 October 2013.

documentation, which foresaw that passports mention the holder's entity belonging on the cover. The internationals disliked this provision as it proved challenging for citizens of one or the other entity to enter the neighbouring states without fuss. Westendorp, supported by the international community, thus made an attempt to change the cover page and to indicate the entity belonging only inside the passport: 'I think the time has come when we can work on having a common passport cover', he said in February 1998.[112] But the Bonn powers, as they were interpreted at that time, did not allow for such an action, for Bosnia's legislative bodies had not failed; quite to the contrary, they had reached an agreement indicating the different origins on the cover. So, several days after Westendorp's statement, his Deputy, Hans Schumacher, had to take it back: even though the OHR would like a change in the respective law, Schumacher said, the HR lacked the authority to do so.[113] However, it seems that such a reading of local authority was employed rather eclectically. When in June 1999 the House of Representatives failed to formally adopt the laws on citizenship, flag, and coat-of-arms that the HR had imposed 'on temporary basis', Westendorp proclaimed that the imposed law nevertheless remained valid.[114] Even in this early phase, when the Bonn powers were constrained in a peculiar manner, the local authority of the political process remained extremely limited.

Westendorp's actions were designed to speed up the transition process and at first they succeeded. Even though after Bonn the behaviour of the local politicians did not change dramatically and reluctance to accept compromises and a general non-cooperation still prevailed, the OHR could now actively engage itself in removing the destructive elements. In his first decision of this kind, Carlos Westendorp dismissed Pero Raguž, the mayor of the southern Herzegovinian town of Stolac. This mayor, whom the Federation mediator Schwarz-Schilling still remembers years later as a very stubborn person posing a real obstacle to the return of non-Croats to the town, was only the first in a series of lower-level officials being removed due to a lack of cooperation in the area of refugee return. Local reluctance in this area is not really surprising, for refugee return by definition threatened the configuration of ethnically majoritarian territories that had been secured during the war. But as the internationals realised rather soon, a multi-ethnic Bosnia could only become a reality if the return of refugees and internally displaced persons could be achieved, particularly into areas where their group did not constitute a majority (so-called minority returns). Building on the provisions foreseen in Annex VII, refugee return thus became a major building block of international involvement.

---

[112] *Oslobođenje*, 6 February 1998, 1.
[113] *Dnevni Avaz*, 13 February 1998, 5; 19 February 1998, 8.
[114] *Oslobođenje*, 9 June 1999, 1, 3; 10 June 1999, 3.

The subject had not only a humanitarian or normative justification, but it was, in essence, highly connected to the political system. Take for example the Republika Srpska. If we neglect for a moment the unfortunate name and the history of its emergence and purely concentrate on the territorial aspect of the entity, it is not necessarily at odds with a modern state. Understood as just another federal unit, the RS becomes a representative of its citizens regardless of their national belonging. The entity voting provision in the Bosnian parliament—today considered one of the major obstacles and generally a bad idea—thus becomes an instrument of balancing federal competencies, not a means of one particular people to block legislation that runs counter to their 'national interests'. However, for such a reading to be accurate, the entity had to be multi-national. It is for precisely this reason that Haris Silajdžić demanded that Bosnian refugees be returned to Bosnia 'by force',[115] even though he meant that force should be applied to the RS in order to make returning feasible. It is therefore natural that pushing the process of refugee return forward became a major task of the HR. In order to be successful, it was important to ensure the safety of the returnees, but also decent conditions of living; houses and apartments had to be restored, rebuilt, or returned to their previous owners. By the end of December 1998, the respective laws had been adopted or imposed in both entities; Westendorp dedicated no less than 22 Bonn power decisions to the area of refugee return. But still only a few people returned, and minority return was especially low. By August 1999, after Westendorp had handed over the issue to his successor Wolfgang Petritsch, only 90,000 people had returned to areas where their group did not constitute the majority.[116] Like the capture and prosecution of war criminals, the return of refugees constituted both a clear benchmark for the success of international efforts as well as one of their basic challenges.

But any actions of the internationals had to confront the still provisional nature of the state. In the first half of 1998, the Bosnian Croats' commitment to the Federation and the central state was minimal and the structures of the Herceg Bosna para-state still in existence. The latter remained a viable option and the HDZ started to launch new proposals for re-negotiating the Federation's cantonal structure. Their approach aimed at a further 'cantonisation' based on the principle of ethnic majority. According to one draft proposal presented at a party conference in May 1998, the *srednjobosanski* and the *hercegovačko-neretvanski* cantons—both of which had proven to be roughly equally ethnically mixed between Croats and Bosniaks—were to be split into four cantons that had a clear national domination by one group or the other.[117] Unsurprisingly, this proposal—and such proposals in general—also found support within the radical elements of the Bos-

---

[115]   *Dnevni Avaz*, 15 June 1999, 3.
[116]   Petritsch, *Bosnien und Herzegowina fünf Jahre nach Dayton*, 117.
[117]   Oslobođenje, 5 May 1998, 1, 4.

nian Serbs. Krajšnik specifically praised the idea of further 'cantonisation' and furthermore expressed his conviction that the RS should not be turned into a multi-ethnic entity either.[118] For obvious reasons (especially since this would effectively mean the abandonment of Annex VII of the DPA), these proposals met severe resistance by the internationals. In a press statement, the OHR declared such ideas 'inconsistent with Dayton' and furthermore reminded the politicians that 'the Dayton agreement remains the only basis for discussion of borders, entities and cantonal division'. Consequently, the HR directed the politicians 'to readdress their attention to their commitments under Dayton to multi-ethnicity, freedom of movement, and the right of all citizens to return to their homes in an ethnically and culturally mixed BiH'.[119] The Bosniak side countered the Croat and Serb ideas. Their position varied between support for the existing structure and attempts to change it. In May 1999, for example, Haris Silajdžić launched an initiative to change the Dayton structure by getting rid of the entities. Instead, only a central state and the cantons would remain.[120] As with other ideas presented in the previous chapter, the origins of the Bosniak position can be traced back to this period where Dayton simultaneously seemed rigid and open to debate.

The lack of Croat commitment to the Federation and the central state become evident in 2001 when HR Wolfgang Petritsch removed Ante Jelavić from his post as Croat member of Bosnia's state presidency. When Jelavić became president of the HDZ in mid-1998, he defeated Božo Ljubić, who allegedly had been Tuđman's favourite.[121] This decision by the HDZ congress led to a split in Croat leadership, even though mediation by Tuđman prevented a major rupture. The Croatian president could exercise much power over the Bosnian Croat politicians not only because he was the intellectual father of their movement and in a sense the leader of the entire Croat people, but also because Croatia funded the operations of the local HDZ personnel. According to one report published in *Oslobođenje*, Croatia supported the logistical centre of the HVO—formally under the control of the Federation minister of defence, i.e. Jelavić—with some 32 million German Mark, which were *inter alia* used to pay the elected officials; allegedly, members of the Council of Ministers received some 1000 marks per month while Zubak as the Croat member of the Bosnian presidency got 2500 DM.[122] These numbers have to be taken with some caution since there is no independent way of showing their accuracy. Nevertheless, it seems not at all outrageous to as-

---

[118]   *Dnevni Avaz*, 15 May 1998, 3.

[119]   Office of the High Representative, "Comment by the High Representative on Re-Cantonisation in BiH," 24 April 1998, http://www.ohr.int/ohr-dept/presso/pressr/default.asp?content_id=4603. Accessed 24 October 2013.

[120]   *Oslobođenje*, 8 June 1999, 4.

[121]   *Oslobođenje*, 19 May 1998, 5.

[122]   *Oslobođenje*, 15 July 1998, 1, 7.

sume that Croatia, in addition to morally and politically supporting the Bosnian Croats, also helped them financially. After all, the Herceg Bosna institution had to be financed in one way or another. In this respect, the Croats were as dependent on Tuđman as the Serbs were on Milošević, even though both groups would soon emancipate themselves. For the Bosniaks, it can be assumed that much financial support, especially in the area of reconstruction of religious sites, came from the Islamic world, even though this support was probably not so clearly structured.

Tuđman's power, however, was not so weighty as to prevent a split within the HDZ structure. In June 1998, Krešimir Zubak left the HDZ and formed his own party called *Nova Hrvatska Inicijativa* (New Croat Initiative, NHI). His reasons were probably rather personal, for he knew that with Jelavić in charge, his chances of being nominated for a second term as member of the BiH presidency were slim. And the general election was just around the corner. Following the Dayton timetable, the first legislative period was only two years so that in September 1998, the Bosnians were called to the ballots once again in order to elect the representatives on all but the local level. HDZ did indeed nominate Jelavić as their candidate for the BiH presidency. Their election campaign was characterised by a high degree of national polemics. At one point, the OECD even removed several candidates from HDZ electoral lists because the party had inappropriately used the HRT TV channel and HVO officers had participated at one of the party's rallies. Deeming it an action of 'electoral engineering designed to ensure the result the OECD wants', both Tuđman and the HDZ protested this decision. The OECD, however, did not budge, despite the HDZ threat to boycott the elections.[123] Even though HDZ ultimately participated in the elections, the party's vice-president, Dragan Čović, said that 'in the case of any post-electoral engineering, a referendum on the fate of Croats in BiH will be called'.[124] In an ultranationalist talk in Čapljina, Jelavić even demanded the maintenance of the Herceg Bosna structures, for which the HR threatened him with dismissal.[125]

As far as the Federation side is concerned, the September 1998 elections did not alter the general outline of the political sphere. In the presidential elections, Alija Izetbegović was re-elected as the Bosniak member and Ante Jelavić succeeded Krešimir Zubak for the Croat side. Izetbegović's CD BiH coalition secured almost half the seats from the Federation in the Bosnian parliament, followed by HDZ with some 20 per cent and SDP with around 15. In the Federation parliament, the results were similar; Zubak's NHI only achieved around three per cent of the votes. The elections thus roughly confirmed the existing structure and Zubak's ousting testified to the still rather cohesive nature of the Croat electorate.

---

[123]   *Oslobođenje*, 8 October 1998, 1, 5.
[124]   *Oslobođenje*, 10 October 1998, 6.
[125]   *Dnevni Avaz*, 22 October 1998, 1.

Edhem Bičakčić of the SDA led the new Federation government, which consisted of members of SDA, HDZ, and SBiH.[126] On the central state level, Haris Silajdžić remained Co-Chairmen of the Council of Ministers, and Neven Tomić kept his post as Deputy. For the Serb side, Svetozar Mihajlović from SNS became Co-Chairman; the subsequently formed government remained largely unchanged.[127]

In the RS, a different pattern emerged throughout 1998, which has to be seen as the genuine continuation of the split between the Pale and the Banja Luka factions. Following the extraordinary elections in late 1997, a new government needed to be formed at the beginning of the year. Against the strong urging of the SDS and the SRS RS, Plavšić formally commissioned Mladen Ivanić, a Banja Luka based economics professor turned politician, to lead a new government. Ivanić's intention was to put together a 'government of national unity' equally composed of experts and party members as well as members of the Pale and Banja Luka factions.[128] However, without support from the Pale faction or the CD BiH, which opposed the idea of a unity government, Ivanić had no chance to secure a majority for his proposal in the NARS. After he withdrew his bid, Plavšić commissioned Milorad Dodik to be the RS Prime Minister. Unlike Ivanić, Dodik knew that he had to secure the votes of the CD BiH representatives if his government were to stand a chance in the NARS. Earlier, the OHR had informed the Serb side that the NARS could only be considered a legitimate body if a newly created, third vice-presidential post—in addition to one for each wing of the Serb political sphere—was given to the CD BiH, for they possessed twenty per cent of the seats. Since Dodik did not oppose a third vice-presidency on principle (given the new powers of the High Representative, he hardly could have opposed it in the long run), he was elected Prime Minister by the end of January despite strong objections from Pale nationalists. It soon became clear that the Pale faction had indeed something to fear, for as one of his first actions, Dodik blocked their financial institutions.[129] Nevertheless, after initially questioning Dodik's legitimacy because he was 'elected thanks to Muslim votes',[130] SDS and SRS RS had to accept his government.

This government consisted of non-aligned people as well as members of the SP RS, SNS, and SNSD, but it neither included anyone from the Pale faction nor a representative of CD BiH. As Petritsch explains, Dodik's position was a weak one, for he led an extremely heterogenic coalition and was furthermore confronted with a unified and rather strong opposition. This naturally limited his room for

---

126   *Oslobođenje*, 12 December 1998, 3.
127   *Oslobođenje*, 4 February 1999, 3; 5 February 1999, 3.
128   *Dnevni Avaz*, 7 February 1998, 3.
129   *Dnevni Avaz,* 21 January 1998, 9.
130   *Dnevni Avaz,* 21 January 1998, 9.

manoeuvre because he had not only to achieve progress in economic terms, but with regard to the 'Serbian cause' as well.[131] In an interview with *Oslobođenje*, Dodik explained his ambiguous role as follows: 'The most important thing right now is to ensure the uniqueness and unity of Republika Srpska. Naturally, we will strictly implement the Dayton agreement and thereby confirm and strengthen the position of Republika Srpska.'[132] Dodik presented himself thus as equally eager to strengthen the 'Serbian cause' as to implement the DPA, which many saw as a contradiction in terms. As we have seen, arguing for the strict implementation of Dayton is a conservative and nationalist strain of contemporary thought within the Bosnian Serbs; at the end of the 1990s, however, it was nothing less than a revolution, interpreted as a clear commitment to the new state and support for the international cause. As such, it was the sheer antithesis to the 'Serbian cause' as many Bosnian Serbs understood it. Dodik's contradictory behaviour resulted from this inherent antagonism, for he did not want to re-define the 'Serbian cause' altogether (nor could he have, since he was not yet its moral authority), but to position himself somewhere along the existing spectrum. This contradiction became fairly obvious when both Plavšić and Dodik threatened to resign if Brčko, the status of which had not yet been definitively decided, was not given to the RS. In the eyes of the Bosniaks and Croats, the internationally-backed candidate had thus proved to be just another Serb politician. Apparently unaware of the deeper complexities of his situation, *Dnevni Avaz* felt obliged to ask: 'Is Dodik the new fraud?'[133] Alija Izetbegović, paraphrasing Winston Churchill's famous remark about democracy, showed a much more pragmatic approach to the new RS leadership when he said: 'Plavšić and Dodik are a bad solution but all others are worse.'[134]

Dodik's government also sent mixed signals to the international community. The RS Prime Minister promised to arrest war criminals and make the SDS cadre resign in exchange for international loans for his entity.[135] He also signed several agreements of cooperation with the FBiH and was full of appreciation with regards to the cooperation with the internationals: 'I have to say that the cooperation with the Office of the High Representative is extremely good and perhaps this is the opportunity for me to thank Mr Westendorp and his team through your newspaper for the enormous efforts they undertook in order to stabilise the situation in the RS. I hope we shall continue such cooperation in the future.'[136] Dodik knew that his stay in politics largely depended on actions by the international

---

[131]   Petritsch, *Bosnien und Herzegowina fünf Jahre nach Dayton*, 104.
[132]   *Oslobođenje*, 22 January 1998, 7.
[133]   *Dnevni Avaz*, 12 January 1998, 3.
[134]   In an interview with *Le Monde*, reprinted in *Dnevni Avaz*, 8 April 1998, 8.
[135]   *Dnevni Avaz*, 7 May 1998, 9.
[136]   *Dnevni Avaz*, 6 May 1998, 5.

community that had so clearly sided with him during the interaction with the Pale faction. But he was also aware that the international community craved a politician with whom they could cooperate; the ousting of Karadžić and the Pale faction was only a success of international mediation if a concrete alternative could be presented. Dodik understood very well that much of his political capital stemmed exactly from this ambiguity. This is why his major tool in the negotiation with the internationals was to repeatedly threaten to resign.[137] The internationals soon realised that Dodik was not the sweet deal for which they had hoped. Deputy HR Hans Schumacher, for example, criticised Dodik for making a lot of promises but failing to deliver results.[138] How weak Dodik's position really was became clear rather soon. In the NARS, he was dependent on CD BiH support for passing any law since he faced opposition by the Pale faction on almost all issues. But the coalition was not happy with Dodik's actions either and criticised him in a similar manner as did Schumacher.[139] In addition, it still demanded an adequate representation in the executive bodies of the NARS. Through a series of blockades, abstentions, and threats, the CD was able to finally secure their third vice-presidential post. This success went along with a general restructuring of the NARS system through the ousting of the Pale cadres.

By the time the political situation in the RS had somehow stabilised, the new campaign for the October elections started. The Banja Luka faction, consisting of Plavšić's SNS, Dodik's SNSD, and Živko Radišić's Socialist Party (SP), formed an electoral coalition called '*Sloga*' (Unity) against the Pale faction of Krajšnik and Karadžić's SDS and the SRS. The election results testified to a divide among the Serb electorates. Radišić defeated Krajšnik in the bid for the Serb member of the BiH presidency, but Nikola Poplašen of SRS succeeded against Plavšić for the RS presidency. Both factions were thus successful in some respect. In the NARS, the general outline of the situation did not dramatically change, for neither the Pale (30 seats of 83) nor the Banja Luka (28 seats) faction secured a majority and the CD BiH (15 seats) remained the deciding factor. Naturally, this increased Dodik's chances to stay in government. But this time, the CD demanded more than the ear of the Prime Minister: they wanted to become members of government with their own ministers and deputy ministers. The internationals feared that this might end Dodik's run and the HR asked the Bosniaks to abstain from such demands[140] instead of pushing for a multi-national coalition governing the Serb entity.

---

[137]   Apart from the Brčko issue, he threatened to resign if the international community kept withholding financial aid for RS; see *Dnevni Avaz*, 21 February 1998, 7.

[138]   *Oslobođenje*, 1 July 1998, 5.

[139]   *Dnevni Avaz*, 16 May 1998, 1-2.

[140]   *Dnevni Avaz*, 31 October 1998, 3.

However, there was a bigger problem on the horizon. As the new RS president, it was Poplašen's prerogative to formally commission the new Prime Minister. Being from the Pale wing, he did not want to give the mandate to Dodik and chose Dragan Kalinić (SDS) instead. Surprised by the move, the OHR warned the Serbs that the election of Kalinić as Prime Minister would mean the cancelation of all financial aid to RS.[141] Even without this threat, Kalinić's chances for securing majority support in the NARS were inexistent, especially after the CD BiH dropped all demands and promised to support Dodik as long as he was committed to Dayton and refugee returns to the RS.[142] However, there still remained the technical issue that the RS president had to give the mandate to Dodik, which he consistently refused—even after 48 members of the NARS formally demanded it.[143] In a move of pseudo-cleverness, Poplašen dropped Kalinić and mandated Brano Miljuš instead, a member of Dodik's SNSD,[144] who was subsequently excluded from the party for accepting the offer.[145] Dodik formally remained Sloga's candidate and he still enjoyed the support of the international community, as Deputy OHR Jacques Klein explained: 'What Dodik's government has done so far was the most constructive thing that could have happened and we hope that RS President Poplašen will stop using parliamentary tricks to prevent what was the clear will of the people and what is the consensus in the parliament.'[146] In the eyes of the international community, the developments in RS testified to a 'presidential crisis' not a constitutional one.[147] Miljuš, supported by SDS and SRS, failed to gain majority support by the end of January 1999. Still reluctant to accept Dodik, Poplašen proceeded to mandate yet a third candidate, Petar Đokić from the SP, who would not stand a chance.[148] Supported by 26 SDS and SRS members of NARS, the RS president also started a procedure to remove Dodik from his post as RS Prime Minister, which he still held in a caretaker function.[149] This decision was a tipping point and Carlos Westendorp had to act: on 5 March 1999, the HR used its powers to remove the first high-level democratically elected politician in Bosnia-Herzegovina:

> President Nikola Poplašen has abused his power; blocked the will of the people of Republika Srpska by hindering the implementation of the elections results, refusing to abide by the decisions the National Assembly and consistently acting to impede the formation of a legitimate government with the support of the National Assembly;

---

[141]   *Dnevni Avaz*, 15 November 1998, 3.
[142]   *Oslobođenje*, 26 December 1998, 3.
[143]   *Dnevni Avaz*, 25 December 1998, 2.
[144]   *Oslobođenje*, 25 December 1998, 2.
[145]   *Dnevni Avaz*, 6 January 1999, 9.
[146]   *Dnevni Avaz*, 12 January 1999, 5.
[147]   *Dnevni Avaz*, 14 January 1999, 2.
[148]   *Oslobođenje*, 4 February 1999, 1.
[149]   *Oslobođenje*, 5 February 1999, 1.

obstructed the implementation of the General Framework Agreement for Peace, acted to trigger instability in the Republika Srpska and thus put peace into risk in the Republika Srpska and in the whole of Bosnia and Herzegovina.[150]

This decision constituted a major rupture in the political sphere of post-war Bosnia. For the first time, the HR had removed a high level official from his post: the president of the RS who had been elected with the majority of votes by the RS electorate. He had used the Bonn powers and shown his strength in a manner that was previously unknown; for even when the international community removed Karadžić, it was done in a more clandestine and negotiated manner than with Poplašen.

But the decision was also remarkable in terms of timing, for it was delivered the same day as the final verdict on the future of Brčko. In his arbitration judgement, Lord Owen awarded the municipality neither to RS nor to FBiH, but made it a sovereign district under BiH authority. For the Serbs, this constituted a major defeat and Dodik was forced to fulfil earlier promises: in an act that underlines the irony of realpolitik in an almost unimaginable way, Dodik resigned his post as caretaker RS Prime Minister on the very same day Westendorp removed the greatest obstacle to the future of his governing coalition.[151] In the following, both factions of the Serb leadership briefly united in protest of the two decisions by the internationals. Radišić stopped executing his functions in the BiH presidency, and the RS parliament passed a decision that all RS representatives in the BiH institutions were to do the same.[152] The OHR, knowing that without the Serb representatives the central state was *de facto* paralysed, was nevertheless determined to demonstrate strength. When Poplašen's Vice-President Mirko Šarović hesitated more than three days to assume the office of the President, Westendorp declared that he had missed his chance and would remain VP. Since the post of the President was vacant and only the president could name a new Prime Minister, Dodik's government would remain in charge until a new President was elected.[153] This course succeeded, for gradually all Serb officials went back to their posts and in June 1999, the NARS adopted a resolution demanding all Serb representatives to return to the common state institutions and to work towards the abolishment of the arbitration judgement on Brčko.[154] Later on, it also reversed his decision opposing the removal of Poplašen.[155] The crisis, one of the gravest since the end of the war, had ended.

---

150 Office of the High Representative, "Decision Removing Mr. Nikola Poplasen from the Office of President of Republika Srpska," 5 March 1999, http://www.ohr.int/de cisions/removalssdec/default.asp?content_id=267. Accessed 25 October 2013.

151 *Oslobođenje*, 6 March 1999, 1.

152 *Oslobođenje*, 7 March 1999, 1.

153 *Dnevni Avaz*, 26-27 March 1999, 3.

154 *Oslobođenje*, 5 June 1999, 8.

155 *Dnevni Avaz*, 15 July 1999, 1.

The unified Serb opposition to the actions of the international community was not surprising. The entire RS situation unfolded at a time when the war in Kosovo was in full swing. The respective events seemed to prove the general mistrust against the international community in large parts of the Serb population. The fact that the Poplašen decision coincided—and according to Westendorp it was a mere coincidence—with the Brčko verdict, naturally strengthened uncooperative tendencies. It put the 'moderate' Serb opposition on the same side as the hardliners. Personally, Westendorp did not support the Brčko decision, because 'it was my feeling at that time that we should have found a more balanced solution and not just this district without recognizing that the territory was also an enclave in Republika Srpska.' But according to him, the American pressure for this solution was so strong that everybody had to accept it. Apparently, the same holds true for the removal of Poplašen, which Westendorp describes as 'the most difficult decision I took'. The strong reaction by the Serb side, in his view, could have been avoided:

> I wanted to avoid that reaction. It could have been avoided. But, you know, sometimes when one of the main stakeholders, the United States, wants a solution, it's difficult to oppose. And it's never an exact science because this contestation and not-acceptance did not last too long. Everything settled down. And the main problem, the main problem over this problem, was the Kosovo war. ... When we were talking with Republika Srpska authorities, we heard the bombing and the planes coming over and bombing Kosovo. So, you can imagine that it was one of the most difficult times I had.[156]

In May 1999, Carlos Westendorp announced that he would step down as High Representative in summer. In one of his last interviews, he renewed his claim that the key to making Bosnia prosper was the removal of nationalist parties:

> I am convinced that mono-ethnic parties are responsible for the state of affairs in the country. I can understand why this is the case. They say that they are the only ones defending the interests of respective groups. That is why the people vote for them. But instead, they should defend themselves against those parties. We are always fighting for some symbols here, but nobody talks about unemployment, social security, or health care. Those are the real problems.[157]

Westendorp's analysis is of course accurate in its essence though not in structure. The issues he mentions were undeniably important, yet what lacked was the possibility to adequately address them within the existing system. The state had not yet been set up properly and it was furthermore prevented from working at all through a series of elections that kept coming. In the Federation, dreams of a new and better political structure still existed and produced reluctance to fully appreciate the Dayton system; in the RS, the two factions constantly engaged in a cam-

---

[156]   Westendorp, Personal Interview.
[157]   *Dnevni Avaz*, 7 May 1999, 5.

paign-like quarrel so that real issues could not be tackled even if the readiness were present. Through their engagement, the international community had hoped to move the process forward. As far as issues were concerned, the strategy succeeded. The High Representative's actions showed the people that progress was being made and his decisions—like licence plates or currency—started to positively impact their lives. However, they decoupled the actual policies from the political process, which was still a nightmare of non-cooperation and blockages. With regard to the political system, therefore, the situation had not improved very much—despite the 71 Bonn power decisions that Westendorp took. The international community had to decide what was more important: the socialisation of the local politicians within the political system or the prosperity of the new country. The first one would mean a decrease in the usage of the Bonn powers, whereas the second one would signify an increase. For Westendorp, it was clear that the big picture prevailed:

> When I took over from my predecessor, Carl Bildt, I quickly perceived the danger of getting lost in the day-to-day minutiae of peace implementation. This was why I pledged to identify the institutions that underpinned radical nationalism, and to transform them into the kind of institutions that exist in Western-style democracies. That is not to say that I ignored the minutiae. To have done so would have been irresponsible, since resistance to democratization can be seen (and will continue to be seen) at all levels of government and administration in Bosnia-Herzegovina.[158]

9.3   Wolfgang Petritsch (1999-2002)

The choice of Wolfgang Petritsch as High Representative represented a break with tradition, if that term can be applied for a process that was never really characterised by long-standing convictions. Petritsch's predecessors had been politicians who, either in the function of a negotiator or as a foreign minister, had become involved with Yugoslavia's dissolution process. But he was different. The career diplomat had previously served as secretary to Austrian chancellor Bruno Kreisky; he had been Austria's ambassador in Belgrade between 1997 and 1999; and since 1998, he was the Special Envoy of the European Commission for Kosovo. In the latter function, he was also the EU's chief negotiator at the Rambouillet peace talks of March 1999. This position, which naturally put Petritsch in close contact with the German EU presidency at that time, also made him a player within the larger European personnel pool in the region. So when the question of Westendorp's succession presented itself, the Germans approached the Austrian—who hesitated. 'I told them clearly that this was a position for a politician,

---

[158]   Carlos Westendorp, "Lessons From Bosnia," *Wall Street Journal Europe*, 29 July 1999, http://www.ohr.int/ohr-dept/presso/pressa/default.asp?content_id=3186. Accessed 28 October 2013.

not a civil servant', Petritsch recalls. 'But they said: we would like to have an expert.'

Petritsch was indeed an expert for the region. Apart from his diplomatic credentials, he had a PhD in South-Eastern European History and Politics from the University of Vienna and had been a Fulbright Scholar in Political Science and International Relations at the University of Southern California between 1972 and 1973. In an academic sense, he understood the general dynamics in the region as well as their historical roots. His views were thus informed by an academic as well as practical experience with the Western Balkans. Most important among those views was Petritsch's conviction that 'one of the crucial political problems of the region' was 'the lack of a culture of political compromise', which he formed after the experiences of Rambouillet:

> Compromise is perceived negatively in the region—it is seen to mean giving in to the oppressor. I have noticed that politicians in the former Yugoslavia are still aiming for 'win-or-lose' scenarios. They would rather be defeated than compromise. The concept of a 'win–win situation' simply does not exist. For me, this is the single most important reason why negotiations in this region almost invariably fail without outside help.[159]

In Petritsch's understanding, these cultural concepts were also applicable to Bosnia—not only because Bosnia formed part of the same geographical context, but because the state was in essence a smaller version of Yugoslavia, so that the mentioned challenges presented themselves even more acutely.[160] In other words: compromise was even more difficult to achieve in Bosnia because of a combination of the general regional predisposition and the structures and experiences leading up and following the most recent war. This understanding of the Bosnian complexities forms a corner stone of Petritsch's philosophy as High Representative. Moreover, it helps explain the central ambiguity of his actions. He knew about the paramount importance of strengthening local leadership and inducing locally based compromises, for only these two factors could sustain the state in the long run. His doctrine of 'ownership' aimed precisely at strengthening these dynamics within the existing political system. But due to his understanding of the prevailing political culture, Petritsch was also convinced that local compromise was often simply out of reach. He therefore did not hesitate to impose certain laws by using the Bonn powers in situations where a solution was desperately needed but seemed unobtainable. He understood such imposition as 'assistance', and was also well aware of the fact that every use of the Bonn powers *de facto*

---

159   Christophe Solioz and Wolfgang Petritsch, "The Interview: The Fate of Bosnia and Herzegovina: An Exclusive Interview of Christophe Solioz with Wolfgang Petritsch," *Journal of Southern Europe and the Balkans Online* 5, no. 3 (2003): 357.
160   Petritsch, Personal Interview.

'disavowed' his own concept of ownership.[161] This antagonism between local ownership and international imposition would characterise the forthcoming period of international engagement in Bosnia. Like a pendulum, it would swing in one or the other direction depending on certain conditions that will be elaborated throughout the chapter. Before that, however, the two different poles of this debate merit detailed examination.

9.3.1 Dependency vs. ownership

Wolfgang Petritsch was fully aware of the dangers of the Bonn powers. The latter had proven to be an effective instrument in many areas, but had also hindered locals taking political responsibility: 'When uneasy decisions [were] concerned, the governing parties still rely[ed] on the High Representative to take them.'[162] As Petritsch saw it, this reluctance was rooted in two features of the Bosnian system: the nature of party politics and the actions of the internationals.

The first factor expressed itself in a specific reluctance towards accepting any compromises when the so-called national interests were concerned. But to Petritsch, those national interests were anything but national; instead, what was at stake were 'the interests of retaining power and control.'[163] Beneath the official lines of argument thus lay a fight for political power, which made certain compromises hard to achieve. If we recall the way in which the Pale faction was ousted from power in the RS, this argument becomes evident. But there is an even larger dynamic at play, which is not limited to the experience in Bosnia. Transforming a state structure that emerged during a war into a democratic post-war system usually threatens established power alliances and privileges. Reluctance towards this transformation is thus more likely, provided that the concerned political actors possess effective possibilities of slowing down the process. Within a negotiated post-war settlement with the wartime elite, such reluctance is merely the logical consequence of the peace treaty itself. As an external peacemaker, one is thus confronted with the often times unrealistic need for new elites and the *de facto* perseverance of the old guard. This is when one is often inclined to take 'the easy deal', as Ashdown explains:

> If you ask me to choose between having an elite, and it was inevitably the same elite from around the war, or having a charge of people unconnected to the war but less elite in their experience, I'd choose the second. [But when we go into a country] ... we, the international community, do an immediate deal with the people in charge because it makes it easier for us to rule the country—and, by the way, solves the problem of legitimacy as well. But what [you] do then is that you buy in the very people who brought the war. In almost all the cases they are the corrupt people because

---

[161]   Ibid.
[162]   Petritsch, *Bosnien und Herzegowina fünf Jahre nach Dayton*, 125.
[163]   Ibid.

that's what wars produce. You can see it in Bosnia, you can see it in Britain after the Second World War—read 'The Third Man' and you see it very clearly. So, we do the easy deal, the quick deal: you're in charge, you're the legitimate representative of the Bosniaks I will now have you as my primary partner.[164]

As a consequence of this 'easy deal', the wartime elites become the post-war elites and their wartime goals transform into valid post-war arguments under the condition that they are articulated within the framework of the new state. If this framework allows for its own undermining—as consociational systems tend to do due to the incorporation of veto powers—, the current elites are very likely to obstruct the state in order to push for their wartime agenda. But since the democratic post-war state also aims at overcoming the rather informal loyalty structures that emerged during the war through the introduction of an all-encompassing framework based on the rule of law, it threatens the pure base of the existing party system and thus results in general reluctance to abandon privileges based on mere party membership. In this context, party politics necessarily becomes some kind of patronage politics for the cadres of the nationalist and supposedly mass parties. As a consequence, the observed reluctance of the political elites within the transition process is rooted in defensible, democratically legitimate resistance to certain aspects of the transition, but also in the mere fear of losing control or power.

The Bonn powers present a natural way out of this dilemma that the international community put itself into by accepting the 'easy deal'. The international community's action, Petritsch's second feature of the Bosnian situation, and especially the Bonn powers, exposed the disingenuousness of the local politicians. As Petritsch explained in an article published in the *Wall Street Journal Europe* in September 1999:

> Imposition [by Bonn powers] has always been used as a final resort, when every avenue of negotiation has been exhausted. But interestingly, despite the sound and the fury that always preceded these impositions, each and every one of the high representative's decisions has been accepted without major fuss once it has been taken. This is because, at heart, the leaders of the three ethnic groups—the Bosniacs, the Croats and the Serbs—know what needs to be done to secure a future for their country. But our presence here has inadvertently absolved them of their responsibilities as democratically elected leaders. We enable the local politicians to fight their tribalistic battles, and then to place the blame for potentially unpopular compromises squarely on the shoulders of foreigners. I call this the 'dependency syndrome'.[165]

From an analytical point of view, the concept of 'dependency' is somehow difficult to grasp, for there seems to be no commonly agreed upon definition of 'dependency syndrome' or what categorisation could be used to mark a concrete po-

---

[164]   Ashdown, Personal Interview.

[165]   Wolfgang Petritsch, "The Future of Bosnia Lies with Its People," *Wall Street Journal Europe*, 17 September 1999, http://www.ohr.int/ohr-dept/presso/pressa/default.a sp?content_id=3188.

litical action as a symptom of dependency.[166] While regrettable in general, such a lack of analytical precision is of lesser importance in the present context. For our purposes, it suffices to focus on how the key stakeholders understood dependency; in other words, we are concerned with what dependency was aimed at preventing and what it aspired to be in the Bosnian case rather than with the analytical sustainability of the concept in general. This approach, I believe, allows us to understand the contradictions between the concept of ownership and its practical application in Bosnia-Herzegovina.

Petritsch's analysis of the Bosnian situation rests on an important assumption. To use the consociational terminology, it presupposes the existence of a minimal consensus with regards to the future of the common state. As we have seen previously, and as will become more evident soon, one may doubt whether such commitment was present within the local political group elites. The Croats only reluctantly dismantled the structures of Herceg Bosna and their president Ante Jelavić was removed from office for undermining the authority of the central state. The Serbs still quarrelled among themselves and were preoccupied with getting rid of the heritage of Karadžić and Krajšnik. Owing to their position between the still rather nationalistically minded electorate and their dependence on international funding and influence, the allegedly pro-Western opposition (the Sloga coalition) chose an ambivalent course with regards to cooperation with the central state. Consequently, the Serb side was in essence highly critical with regards to the future of the common state. The Bosniak electoral corpus had clearly started breaking up and the nationalists were primarily concerned with securing their power base; their commitment to the central state was absolute, but it was combined with efforts to establish a state that would not only safeguard their group interests, but their party interests as well. Finally, multi-ethnic parties, even though they would soon manage to gain a majority, remained a split, heterogeneous association with diverging ideas and perspectives. As such, they were hardly able to influence the political arena, at least at this time. In general, therefore, commitment to the central state was more a necessity of political perception or, at best, a normative aspiration rather than a matter of fact, which puts into question Petritsch's assertion that the politicians genuinely wanted to 'secure a future for their country'. The acceptance of Bonn power impositions can better be explained, I believe, with the power of the internationals to back their actions up

---

[166] Take for example the collection of works edited by Wolfgang Petritsch and Christophe Solioz about the ownership paradigm where authors understand the concepts of ownership and dependency quite differently. Cf. Wolfgang Petritsch and Christophe Solioz, ed., *Ownership Process in Bosnia and Herzegovina : Contributions on the International Dimensions of Democratization in the Balkans*, vol. 159 (Baden-Baden: Nomos, 2003).

with concrete threats, i.e. military interventions and the politics of economic conditionality.

Being the international community's representative, Petritsch could of course not question the local elites' commitment to the central state, for it would have meant that all international efforts to pacify and integrate the country in the previous years had failed. One may therefore excuse his flawed presentation of the reasons for the continuous political deadlock as strategic. In fact, Petritsch was very well aware that not only central state institutions needed strengthening but also the mere idea of a Bosnian state. Trying to restore the centuries-old compatibility between being a Croat and/or Serb on the one and being a Bosnian on the other hand was a major characteristic of his tenure. He advocated a somewhat republican concept of Bosnian identity whereby it would be possible to be both a 'good' Croat or Serb and a loyal citizen of the state of Bosnia-Herzegovina.[167] The mere fact that he needed to urge such a concept testifies to the lack of layers to Bosnian national identity. He was furthermore well aware that this exercise was doomed to fail with the current political elites: 'you cannot make a common state with ethno-nationalist parties. Those two concepts exclude each other *per definitionem*.'[168] In addition to being strategic, Petritsch's omission in the above quotation may thus be rooted in a teleological wish—and as such are political in nature—than a testimony of his factual unawareness. His general analysis therefore remains accurate, for the international actions relieved the locals of their responsibility to act and decide by themselves. What is more, they relieved them of any accountability with regards to the political system and their voters.

Petritsch was determined to present a counter-argument to such tendencies, a different philosophical and practical approach to the international community's handling of issues that desperately needed solving but that the locals were unable to solve. This is the essence of what he called 'ownership', a 'local ownership not just of assets but of the problems inherited from communism and the war. Indeed, [the ownership approach] implies the entire process of Dayton['s] implementation, the very future of Bosnia-Herzegovina itself'.[169] Taking the example of corruption, where especially Alija Izetbegović had demanded the internationals 'do something', 'investigate', and 'compile a report' after the newest set of allegations, Petritsch explained the essence of his concept:

> Well, no we won't. We can and will assist [Izetbegović] and other leaders to the best of our ability, but the primary responsibility for dealing with issues like corruption lies with the elected leaders of Bosnia. We can help them develop necessary instruments, such as modern law enforcement agencies and an independent judiciary. We can remove corrupt officials forever, and document instances of corruption until we

---

[167]   *Oslobođenje*, 3 April 2000, 3; cf. also. Petritsch, Personal Interview.
[168]   Ibid.
[169]   Petritsch, "The Future of Bosnia Lies with Its People."

are blue in the face, but it will do no good without the political impetus from the top. That is the essence of the concept of ownership.[170]

Petritsch did not 'invent' the concept of ownership, even though he gave special distinction to it within the Bosnian context. Ownership has its historical roots in the 1970s and 1980s. In 1981, Petritsch encountered it as he was involved in the organisation of an international summit dedicated to the so-called North-South conflict. The Cancún conference highlighted several areas where the South could contribute to improving the situation of its people: good governance, transparency, accountability, the fight against corruption, and the rule of law.[171] To be effective, ownership conceptually implied 'the engagement of civil society in political life.'[172] Within the Bosnian context, however, such civil society was still missing, which in conceptual terms meant that ownership could not succeed. Despite constantly advocating for ownership in absolute, i.e. conceptually coherent terms, Petritsch understood ownership quite differently. In practical terms, ownership was nothing more than a 'euphemism', since the internationals did far more to sustain the state than the locals. In conceptual terms, Petritsch saw ownership as a 'dialectic process' between intervention and local responsibility, which had practical implications insofar as it guided his actions as High Representative:

> Dialectic means on the one hand [imposition] and on the other hand [ownership]—but something has to grow out of it that is more than what was there before. It is in this sense that I said: I intervene, but ideally only in those cases that contribute to the success of the general project and that, *peu à peu*, step by step, will lead to some form of identification and, well, ownership.[173]

Petritsch's Bosnian version of ownership had thus a dual aspiration: the Bonn powers were to create a political momentum through some form of common identification that would, if successful, allow real ownership to happen. In essence, the ownership *process*—rather than the mere concept of ownership—tried to square the circle between imposition and ownership; but as Petritsch admits, 'to my mind, "imposing" democracy and civil society seemed a contradiction in terms'.[174] And he was hardly the only one, for it took him some time to make his concept understandable to the locals. For one, his actions allowed serious doubts about his willingness to step back and hand the process over to the locals. He admits that in the first one and a half years of his mandate, he 'had to act as the most interventionist High Representative ever' because ownership 'is a process that requires a framework, and I first had to lay solid foundations to get this process go-

---

[170]   Ibid.
[171]   As described in Solioz and Petritsch, "The Interview," 359–360.
[172]   Ibid., 359.
[173]   Petritsch, Personal Interview.
[174]   Solioz and Petritsch, "The Interview," 361.

ing and create the conditions for ownership to take root.'[175] Following this logic, in the second half of 1999, Petritsch imposed no less than 48 decisions, 24 of them in the category of removals; and in 2000, he used the Bonn powers 86 times.

His understanding of ownership presented also the only guidelines for the usage of the Bonn powers. In the area of removals, Petritsch had initially used the Bonn powers without any structural or corrective framework—'relatively free-handedly', as he says.[176] But over time, he and his team developed a two-step system to handle such situations. He declared that he was 'not going to remove someone from office only because an employee says so, or the UN says so', or, for that matter, any of the numerous international organisations present in the field asked him to do so. Instead, Petritsch decided to introduce a warning system, by which the person in question would be informed that the HR was aware of their conduct and given a chance to explain himself and alter his behaviour. This 'parley' was combined with a clear warning, for Petritsch also reminded the politicians of the OHR's competencies. If the politician still continued to obstruct the process, he would receive a second warning in the form of a letter. Only when both warnings failed was the politician removed using the Bonn powers. Everything in this system, in the eyes of Petritsch, 'was rather transparent. I always tried to give all the people involved a chance—including the person concerned; [I tried] to reason with them'.[177]

As far as the imposition of laws was concerned, Petritsch's intervention policy was also founded on a careful examination of the reasons for the deadlock. But he also had the consequences of continued blockades in mind when he debated whether or not to simply impose a solution. As he explains:

> Take for example the laws concerning phytosanitary regulations: Bosnia was not able to export anything as a consequence of [the failure to adopt] these things. So I said: If we want to get the economy going... the farmers can produce, but if they cannot sell, what is the point? So, since there was no law after, say, two years, I said: I will now impose this law.[178]

Petritsch tried to make the locals understand the ways in which his office worked and make the evolution of his decisions, in his words, more 'transparent'. It was clear that this strategy could not be implemented in a vacuum but had systemic consequences inherent in the sum of its actions:

> Through these actions, we tried—and I mention this not without self critique—to establish some kind of *parallel rule of law or legal system*, that was perhaps implemented more speedily than would correspond to the normal political, the normal

---

[175]   Ibid.
[176]   Petritsch, Personal Interview.
[177]   Ibid.
[178]   Ibid.

> democratic process. But [such circumvention] was necessary because it was not a
> normal situation. It was a grave situation. There was the danger of conflicts and
> fights flaming up. … This is something extraordinary. And in such situations, there
> are, so to speak, no normal and regulatory rules to be applied: as far as possible [they
> should be applied], yes; but there where it is absolutely necessary, you have to leave
> this path. But you have to make clear: this is not normal.[179]

Petritsch's philosophical defence for the usage of Bonn powers contains two levels that are conceptually detached. The first and fundamental one concerns his reasoning for using the Bonn powers, which is found in the extraordinary character of the current situation. Bosnia as a transitional state provides all the justification necessary for the infringement of the democratic process and the circumvention of the legal political setup. The second level concerns the mechanism by which the Bonn powers are used. Petritsch claims that through the introduction of a process consisting of warning, discussion, and, as *ultima ratio*, removal or imposition, the OHR created a second layer of 'rule of law' that is adjacent to the existing one, but that functions more efficiently than the latter. Yet it remains doubtful whether one can conceive of this secondary set of rules as some form of a modern legal system, for it did not evolve out of a transparent and well-regulated process nor were its rules known to anybody from the outside. The transparency Petritsch mentions primarily concerned the people involved, who were—more as a matter of principle than as a generally binding rule—given warnings that they may be sacked. The notion of a secondary legal system is also questionable since Petritsch only mentions the *process* to substantiate his claim. While procedural provisions form an important part of substantiating legal norms, they can hardly be seen as legal norms themselves—and legal norms are, after all, the foundation of any legal system. So, rather than conceiving of the Bonn powers as a system restricted by a set of legal provisions, one should understand it as some form of 'rules of engagement' that guide and potentially restrict the High Representative's actions, but whose interpretation lies strictly with the High Representative himself. Not unlike a Hobbesian Leviathan, the HR cannot, *per definitionem*, overstep his boundaries nor legally violate any norm; conceptually, this puts into question the norm itself.

Apart from philosophical and logical problems that one may deem of lesser importance, Petritsch's approach towards the Bonn powers also contains practical concerns. The necessity condition mentioned earlier was omnipresent in early 2000 Bosnia, so that the Bonn powers were frequently used. As far as the general public was concerned, Petritsch's numerous Bonn power decisions left the impression that his commitment to ownership was purely cosmetic. It is therefore no surprise that the editorial board of the news magazine *Dani* published an article—written in the form of a political manifesto—containing ten hypotheses for Bosnia

---

[179]   Ibid. My italics.

and Herzegovina,[180] in which the authors demanded nothing less than the abolition of the current political system and the introduction of a full-fledged international protectorate, limited for one year. During this time, the HR was to bring the structure of the military organisation in accordance with NATO provisions, and the state constitution and organisation in line with the provisions of European integration and the principle of effective governance. In his response, published in March 2000 and entitled 'This is not our country', Petritsch rejected any notion of establishing a protectorate. Bosnia's problems, he argued, are of a societal character and rooted in complex history and a political caste that, like the one in communist times, is first and foremost interested in personal gain and has never learned to be held accountable for its actions. Impositions could not change that particular problem: 'democracy, good governance, political maturity, and a civil society can neither be ordered nor imposed by decree; they are the result of a process. Democracy and civil virtues must be learned.'[181] Politicians could only learn them if they were given the chance—and ownership indeed aimed at this, despite many shortcomings in its implementation.

Petritsch knew that with the current nationalistically minded elite, his concept of local ownership was doomed to fail. Bringing those leaders together and making them agree to a democratic compromise was 'in some sense utopian', as he admits.[182] Therefore, in addition to pushing for more local responsibility and promoting a new sense of national belonging among the Bosnian Serbs and Bosnian Croats, Petritsch also hoped that a new electoral law, which introduced open voting lists and allowed the people to vote for individual candidates and not only parties, would give the international community new partners after the local elections in April 2000 and the general elections in November of the same year. [183] His wish was to come true.

9.3.2   The Alliance for Change

Petritsch declared three priorities for his mandate: strengthening the common state institutions, accelerating refugee return, and, finally, economic reform: 'These three pillars of my tenure were, so to speak, grounded in my concept of

---

[180]   The article "Ten Hypotheses for Bosnia and Herzegovina", originally published in *Dani* on 28 January 2000, as well as Petritsch's response entitled "This is not our country", are reprinted in: Petritsch, *Bosnien und Herzegowina fünf Jahre nach Dayton*, 235–245. Concretely, the authors demanded a suspension of all local political institutions, i.e. parliaments on all state levels, the presidency, etc., and the transfer of these institution's authority to the High Representative, who was to exercise all political and administrative powers in Bosnia until the elections, which were to be postponed until the following year.

[181]   Ibid., 240.

[182]   Petritsch, Personal Interview.

[183]   Petritsch, "The Future of Bosnia Lies with Its People." Accessed 28 October 2013.

ownership. We would establish the framework and get the process going and then hand over to the local elected leaders as soon as possible.'[184] However, the local elite was anything but eager to take on the issues Petritsch proposed, so that he was forced to implement his priorities 'more with relative imposition and political force than with political arguments'.[185] Like Westendorp, Petritsch located the main problem in the nationalist ideology of the current political elite. In September 2000, he chose strong words to describe his discontent: 'The political leaders of this country—and this is the unanimous opinion of the Steering Board—work in an irresponsible way, which cannot simply be explained with the [on-going] election campaign. This is sheer irresponsibility.'[186] Petritsch's desperation was rooted in a deep frustration with the factual political deadlock that he encountered prior to the general elections in November 2000.

There were various instances of non-cooperation that severely damaged the state's capacity to act. They all had their roots in the different attitudes towards the state, which were explained in the previous section. Perhaps most illuminating are the events surrounding the reform of the Council of Ministers. After the Constitutional Court found the existing law unconstitutional and the parliament failed to adopt a new law within a three-month period, the provisions in question, which targeted the composition of the government, were nullified by judicial fiat. In February 2000, Bosnia thus did not possess a legitimate government any more.[187] Even though the presidency reached an agreement on the new composition of the Council of Ministers—which foresaw the creation of additional ministries, the introduction of a general rule stating that ministers from one group should have deputies from the other two, and a rotating chairmanship—and even though the parliament passed the agreement in April, the presidency repeatedly failed to agree on a new Chairman.[188] So it was only at the end of June that a new Council of Ministers was formed. Due to the scheduled general elections in November, this Council could hardly do any real governing—even if the people involved had been eager to do so. But since they were not, what prevailed was a similar situation that Petritsch had encountered when assuming his post: 'a complete stand still with regards to state building'.[189]

The next general elections would prove to be decisive in many ways for Petritsch's mandate. Already the local elections in April had shown that parties with a non-nationalistic outreach could be successful. The SDP, like Mladen Ivanić's

---

[184]   Solioz and Petritsch, "The Interview," 361.

[185]   Petritsch, Personal Interview.

[186]   *Oslobođenje*, 30 September 2000, 3.

[187]   *Oslobođenje*, 30 January 2000, 2.

[188]   *Dnevni Avaz*, 10 February 2000, 2. Petritsch, *Bosnien und Herzegowina fünf Jahre nach Dayton*, 159–60.

[189]   Petritsch, Personal Interview.

newly founded Party of Democratic Progress (PDP) and Dodik's SNSD put the economy in the foreground of their campaigns. Even though the nationalist parties still achieved relatively good results, the SDP became the strongest party in the Federation with 30 per cent of the votes compared to 28 of the SDA; in the RS, SNSD secured 14 per cent and, surprisingly, PDP eight per cent. In all municipalities, moderate parties were now a substantial part of the local parliaments.[190] The general elections confirmed this trend, for the nationalist parties lost their majority in the state's parliament. In the Federation, the SDP and the SDA both achieved 27 per cent of the votes, the HDZ 18 and the SBiH 15. In the RS, the SDS gained some 38 per cent, while the PDP secured 14 per cent and the SNSD 12—followed by the SDA with eight and the SP RS with five per cent.[191] For the first time in Bosnia's post-war history, non-nationalist parties thus had the numerical majority to form a government.

In parts, this result was the success of the internationals, for they had started a rigorous campaign to convince Bosnians to vote for change already before the local elections. The internationals decided to continue this strategy for the general elections, which excluded BiH presidential elections since the presidential mandate lasted four years. In addition to the locally present internationals, prominent international figures openly supported the opposition that they deemed non-nationalistic. For example, NATO Secretary General George Robertson publicly expressed his hope that 'the people of BiH will elect change and turn their backs on a politics of the past that is based on ethnic belonging;'[192] and US President Bill Clinton described Milorad Dodik as a leader that had managed to 'put a barrier between the nationalists that were leading the Bosnian Serbs [thus far]' and Zlatko Lagumdžija as an 'outstanding opposition leader and leader of the biggest multi-ethnic party that without doubt presents the future of BiH'.[193] While one may condemn such open expressions of support as an infringement of the democratic process as such (rightfully, I might add), they do not violate the inherent logic of the Bosnian political system at that time, but exemplify its hybrid nature between international imposition and a minimalist version of democracy that only includes the element of elections. The international's 'problem' in this setting is of course that they cannot control the democratic process and its outcome since they only have the means to deal with the consequences. But even in doing so, they are nevertheless limited by what we have so far described as a non-ideal form of democratic legitimacy that is necessarily associated with elections, however imperfect they may be.

---

[190]   Petritsch, *Bosnien und Herzegowina fünf Jahre nach Dayton* 161–2.
[191]   Ibid.
[192]   *Dnevni Avaz*, 20 July 2000, 2.
[193]   *Oslobođenje*, 16 August 2000, 2.

Apart from a general orientation towards economic issues by the candidates and the immense campaign of the internationals for change, the non-nationalist parties triumphed in November also because of an altered overall setting in the neighbouring countries. In Croatia, President Franjo Tuđman, one of the main supporters of the Bosnian Croat's obstructionist policies, died on 10 December 1999. In February 2000, Stjepan Mesić, who had broken with the HDZ over its politics with regards to Bosnia-Herzegovina during the war, was elected as Tuđman's successor. Already in January 2000, the HDZ had lost its majority in Croatian parliament and the Social Democrats of Ivica Račan took charge. As a result of these events, the Bosnian Croats lost a major part of their support from Croatia, and Mesić specifically told them that Sarajevo and not Zagreb was their capital. The new Croatian leadership was thus clearly willing to respect Bosnia's sovereignty and to limit cooperation with Bosnian Croats to cultural and economic ties.[194] Due to this change in attitude, the interests of Croatia and the international community in Bosnia aligned.

The Bosnian Croats soon realised that their relations with Croatia had changed. In June, they adopted a new party statute effectively establishing the HDZ BiH as an independent party, which ought to have special relations with its Croatian counterpart.[195] However, the Bosnian Croat elites were not yet ready to fully support the Bosnian state. Instead of working within the given setup, HDZ President and Croat Member of Bosnia's state presidency, Ante Jelavić kept complaining about the current structure. Especially in the Federation, he claimed the Croat's 'national, political, and religious'[196] rights to be in jeopardy. In February 2000, the Croat National Council once again presented a proposal for a further cantonisation of the state along the principle of territorial ethnic majorities.[197] That the Croats deeply mistrusted the Federation construct became evident when HDZ showed its readiness to transfer some Federation competencies to the central state under the condition that the canton's competencies remained untouched.[198] Naturally, Petritsch opposed any such attempts to renegotiate the Dayton structure. At first, the HDZ seemed to comply. At the sixth party congress held in July 2000, Jelavić specifically declared the Bosnian Croats' commitment to the Bosnian state and its intent to work for its progress.[199] But before the elections, it became gradually clear that the HDZ was gearing up for a serious confrontation with the international community.

---

194   Petritsch believes that Croatia's changed policy had also something to do with the new leadership's unwillingness to keep sending large sums of money to a small portion of Bosnian Croat officials. Cf. Petritsch, Personal Interview.

195   *Dnevni Avaz*, 6 June 2000, 9.

196   *Oslobođenje*, 24 October 1999, 3.

197   *Dnevni Avaz*, 6 February 2000, 5.

198   *Dnevni Avaz*, 25 February 2000, 3.

199   *Oslobođenje*, 16 July 2000, 2, 3.

About a month before the election date, Jelavić complained about the rules for the election of the Croat members in the FBiH House of Peoples. In his view, the rules—that placed the elections of representatives within the cantonal parliaments—led to a situation where twenty or thirty Croat representatives, which were to be sent to the House of Peoples, were elected by non-Croat members of the cantonal parliaments; he feared that this provision was aimed at 'eliminating HDZ and other Croat political parties'. Consequently, HDZ not only threatened to boycott the general elections, but to fight the decision by, as Jelavić called it, 'non-institutional means'.[200] His fear, of course, was not so much a general discrimination against Croats but that those non-Croat members of cantonal parliaments might elect Croat representatives from moderate parties, i.e. not HDZ. This, however, was exactly the opportunity the new system presented: 'That is precisely the point', OSCE ambassador Robert Barry explained, 'since we do not think that HDZ is the only party that has the exclusive right to represent the Croat people. The fact that there are Croats that are not members of HDZ does not make these people less legitimate [to represent the Croat people].'[201] The Preliminary Election Commission under the leadership of the OSCE was thus not inclined to change the rules. The latter clearly stated that 30 representatives in the FBiH House of Peoples had to be Croats, which means that there was no formal breach of the non-discrimination principle. This discussion presents the core of what contemporary Croat representatives call the Croat Question, which was discussed in the previous chapter.

In a manoeuvre that can only be understood as the ultimate provocation, the HDZ and the Croat National Assembly decided to hold a referendum among Bosnian Croats with regards to their rights in Bosnia and Herzegovina on election day.[202] Even though this referendum had 'no legal foundation', as the OHR termed it,[203] it remained a clear signal aimed at de-legitimising the entire state and the electoral process. The declaration, which was the subject matter of the referendum, clearly stated that the equality of the constitutive peoples can only be achieved through an adaptation of the existing state structure in an 'administrative and territorial' manner, which is why some observers claimed that the Croats in fact demanded a third entity.[204] But it was also some form of electoral strategy in order to mobilise HDZ supporters; ultimately, it failed.

The formation of the 'Alliance for Change' government in January 2001 (see below) presented the ultimate defeat for the HDZ and made them even more eager to support parallel structures. After the election, they boycotted the Federa-

---

[200]   *Oslobođenje,* 14 October 2000, 7.
[201]   *Oslobođenje,* 18 October 2000, 3.
[202]   *Oslobođenje,* 29 October 2000, 1, 4, 5.
[203]   *Dnevni Avaz,* 19 October 2000, 9
[204]   *Nezavisne Novine,* 30 October 2000, 2.

tion parliament, demanding the establishment of a 'Croat Republic' analogue to the RS,[205] and on 3 March 2001—after the Constitutional Court refused to give an opinion on the constitutionality of the OSCE rules with regards to the election of the Federation House of Peoples, since it deemed such rules in accordance with the powers granted to the OSCE by the international mandate—Ante Jelavić and the Croat National Assembly declared Croat 'self-rule' and the formal establishment of parallel structures.[206] The High Representative, rightfully deeming such actions a violation of the Dayton Peace Agreement and presumably also reminded of the fact that the establishment of autonomous, self-ruled regions played an important role in the outbreak of the war in 1992, was forced to act. After publicly warning Jelavić, on 7 March 2001 he dismissed him from office,[207] together with other leaders of HDZ.[208] Even though such action angered many supporters of the HDZ, it also provided an opportunity for the more moderate forces that were either willing to accept the current state structure or pledged to fight for its adaptation from within. Moreover, the HDZ itself returned to the negotiating table soon after the public outrage had settled.

But the relative success of non-nationalist parties in the general elections also had something to do with the events in neighbouring Serbia, where the rule of Slobodan Milošević came to an end. His downfall on 5 October 2000 happened only a month before the Bosnian elections and was preceded by the electoral win of Vojislav Koštunica from the Democratic Opposition of Serbia. In the same month, Alija Izetbegović stepped down as the Bosniak member of the BiH presidency, which meant that by October 2000 all three of the Bosnian war's main protagonists had disappeared from the political stage. In Serbia and Croatia, opposition groups had replaced their respective parties in power. These events created a window of opportunity, which proved decisive for the Bosnian elections.

It would be an overstatement to claim that the nationalist parties had clearly lost in Bosnia, for they only missed the majority by a narrow margin. This also meant that the opposition groups aspiring to govern the country had to create a coalition that included almost all other parties in order to secure a majority. Once again the internationals stepped in and, as a result of 'energetic lobbying and arm-twisting by the then American and British ambassadors to Bosnia & Herzegovina' in January 2001 a ten-party coalition was formed under the name 'Demo-

---

[205] *Oslobođenje,* 2 January 2001, 1.

[206] International Crisis Group, *Bosnia's Alliance for (Smallish) Change*, Balkans Report (Sarajevo/Brussels: International Crisis Group, 2 August 2002), 6.

[207] Office of the High Representative, "Decision Removing Ante Jelavic from His Position as the Croat Member of the BiH Presidency," 7 March 2001, http://www.ohr.int /decisions/removalssdec/default.asp?content_id=328. Accessed 6 November 2013.

[208] *Oslobođenje,* 8 March 2001, 1.

cratic Alliance for Change'.[209] In the Federation, this Alliance was led by the Social Democrats (SDP), the Party for Bosnia-Herzegovina (SBiH) and the New Croat Initiative of Krešimir Zubak (NHI) and furthermore included smaller parties such as the GDS, BPS, HSS, LDS, and two pensioner's parties that subsequently merged. The Alliance also had a working arrangement with the Croat NSRzB and, on state level, four parties from the RS: PDP, SNSD, SPSR and SNS. Three out of those four RS parties also shared power in the new RS government, which was dominated by the SDS but led by PDP's Mladen Ivanić (though the SNS later joined the SNSD in opposition).[210] The governing coalition in the Federation and in the state was thus highly heterogeneous, while the SDS once again effectively controlled the RS structures. It is therefore no surprise that finding common ground with regards to political proposals remained a difficult task, despite good will and international backing. The Alliance was 'a marriage of convenience between parties of disparate size, ideological hue and history and national composition'.[211] It was furthermore led by personalities that Petritsch recalls as being 'difficult' and not prone to 'the virtue of integration' but to the 'non-virtue of exclusion'.[212] This naturally made cooperation difficult, especially between Haris Silajdžić and Zlatko Lagumdžija. Those two figures were almost antagonistic ones with Silajdžić being politically and ideologically close to the SDA cadres and Lagumdžija being the representative of the biggest opposition group. But one also needs to take into account that most of the parties had no real governing experiences and that, for some of the RS parties, it was a completely new role to be an opposition party in the entity and *de facto* part of the central state government. That these issues produced difficulties in every-day politics is all too understandable.

Despite these unfavourable circumstances, the legacy of the Alliance is not ubiquitously bad.[213] Especially in the Federation, it managed to partially overcome the divisions among the parallel structures of Bosniak and Croat leadership. Following the attacks on New York and Washington, D.C., on 11 September 2001, the two respective intelligence services were merged. After Jelavić's removal, the Alliance seized the opportunity to merge and reorganise the pension and health care funds, impose its authority on police and customs officers unwilling to participate in the FBiH structures, unify the previously separate budgets in

---

[209]   International Crisis Group, *Bosnia's Alliance for (Smallish) Change*, 1.
[210]   Ibid.
[211]   Ibid., 3.
[212]   Petritsch, Personal Interview. He specifically mentions Zlatko Lagumdžija in this context.
[213]   In the following, I rely on the superb report regarding the accomplishments of the Alliance presented by the International Crisis Group, for it largely corresponds with my own observations gained through newspaper analysis. Cf. International Crisis Group, *Bosnia's Alliance for (Smallish) Change*.

the Federation (especially with regards to intelligence services, pensions, health care funds, government institutions, and publicly owned companies), and to downsize the Federation army and investigate the malfeasance of former defence ministers.[214] However, many of these improvements were only possible due to an ill-advised blockade tactic of the Federation parliament by the HDZ. At central state level, the Alliance managed to improve matters considerably, especially as far as the setup of the state was concerned. The Council of Ministers was able to put forward pragmatic compromises as its members shared some common ground; they were united by the short-term virtue of pragmatism and the long-term prospect of European integration. The six existing ministries were consolidated and a new formula was found by which the constituent peoples ought to have equal number of ministries whose leaders do not need to rotate every six months.[215] The Bosnian presidency partially abandoned the practice of separate offices and established a common secretariat to service all three members equally.[216]

Policy-wise, the Alliance—with the help of the help of the internationals—managed to secure Bosnia's membership in the Council of Europe and the parliament passed many laws that had been imposed years earlier. Of course, such improvements were remarkable, but they hardly changed the general outline of politics in Bosnia. Obstructionist politics still prevailed—be it in parliament, where obstruction remained the MPs 'weapon of first and last resort',[217] or with regards to the nationalist parties, for who 'politics remain[ed] a zero-sum game'. As the International Crisis Group further notes, as far as the RS is concerned, 'virtually every initiative to equip BiH with state-like powers, responsibilities and dignities is denounced as unconstitutional and resisted to the last semi-colon in order to stop it in its procedural tracks'.[218]

For these reasons, progress towards European integration and state building in general was stalled, so that the High Representative had to keep imposing laws. In 2001 and 2002, Wolfgang Petritsch issued no less than 116 Bonn power decisions, 74 of them imposing or amending laws and regulations. These decisions *inter alia* included the establishment of the State Court, a law on the Civil Service Agency, or a conflict of interest law for the central state. The High Representative furthermore imposed several changes to the entity constitutions (see also below). In their dealings with the international community and the High Representative, the Alliance tried to reframe Petritsch's paradigm of 'ownership' into one of 'partnership', which naturally did not go without confrontation, especially when

---

214   Ibid., 4, 6, 10.
215   Ibid., 16.
216   Ibid., 17.
217   Ibid., 18.
218   Ibid., 16.

public tenders were concerned (as in the cases of the Citizen Information Protection System [CIPS] or the third mobile telephone operator).[219] But even though such rhetoric served to show the Alliance's independence with regards to the international community, the reality was that the High Representative was still the main stakeholder in the process.

Nevertheless, the Alliance government presented the first opportunity in post-war Bosnia for real political bargaining within a generally favourable framework. For the first time, Bosnia as a state became more than a mere fiction or a hope of the internationals, even though it was still far away from being an ideal or functioning state. Unfortunately, much of the political successes were limited to strengthening state structures and making its institutions more efficient, which, in terms of electorate perception, was hardly enough to sustain the impression of real progress. Combined with the rather slim majority that the Alliance relied on in the first place, it was improbable that this would be enough to continue this kind of cooperation beyond the general elections of October 2002. Moreover, during only two years in power, 'no government can really produce a convincing track record' so that 'some disappointment' among the voters was inevitable.[220] The Alliance's temporary character was thus inherent in its foundation.

9.3.3   The Mrakovica-Sarajevo Agreement and its implications

Even though Petritsch's successor Paddy Ashdown substantially modified the state and issued more Bonn power decisions than any High Representative before or after him, Petritsch changed the *structural* character of the Bosnian state more profoundly than Ashdown. This was mostly due to his role in the implementation process of the Constitutional Court's 'constituent peoples' verdict. The Court was invited to decide the constitutive character of the three groups recognised as constitutive peoples in the Bosnian constitution with regards to the entities. In April 1997, the Serb Civic Council [*Srpsko Građansko Vjeće*] in the Federation had issued a declaration demanding the constitutionally equal treatment of all constitutive peoples on all levels of the state. Concretely, the declaration demanded constitutional amendments to the entity constitutions so that Bosniaks and Croats would gain constitutive character in the RS and Serbs in the FBiH.[221] Eventually, the request reached Alija Izetbegović, the chairman of the BiH presidency, who in early 1998 instituted proceedings before the Constitutional Court for an evaluation of the consistency of the entity constitutions with the state constitutions.[222] In several partial decisions between January and August 2000, the Constitutional

---

[219]   Ibid., 7. See also *Dnevni Avaz,* 22 July 2001, 5.
[220]   Petritsch, Personal Interview.
[221]   *Dnevni Avaz,* 4 June 1997, 2.
[222]   Cf. Constitutional Court of Bosnia and Herzegovina, Decision in case U5/98.

Court came to the conclusion that the current entity constitutions needed to be adapted in order to incorporate the constitutionality of the three constituent peoples.

The implementation of the verdict proved particularly difficult, however. Faced with inactivity by the local politicians, in January 2001 the High Representative established a temporary constitutional commission in each entity 'whose mandate it was to eliminate all discriminatory elements'.[223] Based on the proposals by these commissions, the local politicians succeeded to negotiate a common solution in form of the Mrakovica-Sarajevo Agreement on 27 March 2002: 'This agreement grants the same status to all constituent peoples in the whole territory of Bosnia, thus ensuring that all constituent peoples and citizens are proportionally represented at all levels of government and public administration in both entities; it creates mechanisms assuring the protection of the interests of each community, as well as their representation in the decision making organs.'[224]

The Mrakovica-Sarajevo agreement ultimately meant that the consociational structure of the state was to be implemented in the entities as well. As a consequence of the Agreement and the Constitutional Court decision, 'the institutional structure in both entities is a rigid power-sharing arrangement, with a constitutionally required grand coalition, veto rights and proportional representation. The only thing lacking in the entities is autonomy for the communities'.[225] This reform thus fundamentally changed the character of the state, for it is only through this action that Bosnia became a consociation (in an empirical sense) on all of its levels. Importantly, the agreement used the 1991 census rather than the actual, post-war situation, as the foundation for determining the proportional quota, at least until the fulfilment of Annex VII of the DPA, i.e. full refugee return. Since this meant that the share of Bosniaks and Croats would be much higher in RS institutions than 'on the ground' at the time, the parties that signed the agreement from the RS did so with two reservations.[226] As Florian Bieber explains, the NARS, upon debate, adopted a different version of the amendments, which was in line with the Constituent People's verdict but departed form the agreement. The changes foresaw no specific numerical requirement for the representation of Bosniaks and Croats in government but merely a 15 per cent minimum threshold for each group. 'In light of the decision of the RS, the government of the Federation failed to secure the support from the opposing HDZ and SDA for passing the

---

[223]   Solioz, *Turning Points in Post-War Bosnia*, 96.

[224]   Ibid.

[225]   Bieber, *Post-War Bosnia*, 131.

[226]   *Nezavisne Novine*, 28 March 2002, 3. Concretely, the RS parties objected to the provision that 2/3 of members of one club in the Entity Houses of People could deem a law as a threat to their group's vital interests and the provision on how the government was to be composed, cf. *Nezavisne Novine*, 28 March 2002, 4.

amendments in the Federation House of Peoples. In order to resolve the deadlock, Wolfgang Petritsch imposed the constitutional amendments in both entities on 19 April 2002.'[227]

For the present context, the nature of its emergence is more interesting than the precise content of the agreement. It was a process that, for the first time since the war, was determined within the local political system. All the major parties, 'national, moderate, and multi-ethnic, met independently of international supervision'[228] and managed to broker an agreement that was, ultimately, fully signed by three parties (SDP, SBiH, NHI) and signed with reservations by four parties from the RS (PDP, SNSD, SDS, SPSR).[229] The Alliance had managed to agree on a fundamental restructuring of the entities, while the nationalist parties stayed outside of the agreement and heavily criticised it in the upcoming October election campaign. As Solioz points out, the importance of the agreement was also that the outcome 'was not imposed by the High Representative, but was the result of negotiations among the country's political leadership, including the two entities and the state'.[230] The agreement naturally belongs to Wolfgang Petritsch's major achievements, as he was eager to point out: 'Personally, I think that the Mrakovica–Sarajevo Agreement, this historic constitutional compromise between Bosnia and Herzegovina's peoples, has the potential to become the turning point on the way to a self-sustaining country.'[231] Similarly—and probably not independent of Petritsch's assertion—Solioz deems the agreement 'one of the outstanding results of the politics of Wolfgang Petritsch, who banked on the responsibility of the Bosnian leaders'.[232]

However, it is important not to overestimate the importance of the Mrakovica-Sarajevo Agreement in terms of its significance for the political process. Admittedly, the fact that the local leaders managed to achieve a compromise 'in which everybody had to give something up' was indeed an unknown feature in Bosnia's post-war history, as Petritsch points out: 'It was fascinating to see how proud the people involved were that they had come to a compromise. That must have been a completely new experience for them.' For the first time, they as well as the internationals saw 'a sparkle of community'. But this compromise was by no means an achievement of the local politicians alone. Through formal and informal meetings and the instrument of 'cajoling', the internationals had 'managed to create a situation, where the locals could not get out [without finding a compromise] but did not feel trapped'. A major catalyst for the agreement was Pe-

---

[227]   Bieber, *Post-War Bosnia*, 129.

[228]   Ibid., 128.

[229]   Solioz, *Turning Points in Post-War Bosnia*, 96 fn. 40.

[230]   Ibid., 97.

[231]   Solioz and Petritsch, "The Interview," 365.

[232]   Solioz, *Turning Points in Post-War Bosnia*, 97.

tritsch's promise to assist the locals *however he could.* Concretely, this meant that he would make sure that any agreement between them would become law. That he had finally to impose the agreement through the Bonn powers was, in Petritsch's view, not the ultimate failure of the process, but rather its ultimate conclusion:

> [I only had to impose] certain parts of the Agreement. For the most part, the terms were fully negotiated. But there were certain areas where it would have been impossible to secure a two-third majority in parliament. This is when I said: ok, I will do this now. And that was also what I had told them before, when they were still fighting: 'Look how far you can get; I will help you with all my powers, if it does not work. But it's up to you…' And I would say that they went three quarters of the way [by themselves]. This is not bad for the first time. Again: ownership-process—and not ownership in perfection.[233]

The process Petritsch employed thus corresponded to his understanding of the ownership paradigm. But in this concrete case, it also meant that the blockades encountered with regards to the formal acceptance of the agreement were simply moved aside by the High Representative's institutional prerogatives. The failure to adopt the provisions testified once again to systemic shortcomings that were, when the negotiations had stalled, removed by international fiat. It is through this action that the two political systems in Bosnia, which until now had existed in two separate realms were for the first time *merged into one coherent structure.* The Bonn powers *de facto* did not serve any more to overcome the blockades of the local political system in areas where agreement was necessary but unobtainable, but as an instrument that anticipated the likely blockades and presented an option to overcome them. Rather than the exception justified by the abnormality of the current situation, the Bonn powers became part of the *local* political system comparable to any institutional rule foreseen in a constitution. Whereas the internationals had used the international prerogative to govern the country for some time, I believe this was the moment when the local political elite came to realise its potential for the same purpose.

At that time, however, this kind of merger between the international and local political systems remained a unique event. It was only made possible by the simultaneous existence of a government composed of moderate parties and a High Representative committed to the ownership paradigm. However, with a nationalist government pursuing an obstructionist politics and a High Representative keen on imposition rather than cooperation, the two systems by no means remained detached. Quite to the contrary: the seed that Petritsch had planted continuously grew until it was too late to weed out.

---

233   Petritsch, Personal Interview.

Wolfgang Petritsch left the office of the High Representative in May 2002. His mandate was characterised by the implementation of a new paradigm of ownership that contrasted harshly with the realities of international imposition as well as by the emergence of a government that was, for the first time, able to make the state work and consolidate its institutions. In general, Petritsch proved to be an ambivalent figure. He knew the geographical and historical determinants of the area much better than any High Representative before or after him and he perfectly assessed the major shortcomings in the international involvement. At the same time, he failed to make his concept of ownership understandable and thus did not convince either the internationals or the locals to take it sufficiently seriously. His actions contradicted too harshly the self-imposed paradigm of ownership, even if understood as process. In the end, it was the political reality that prevented him from staying true to these principles:

> You know, it all sounds well in theory, or in a schoolbook where you say: you do this, then this, then this. In reality, everything—and more—has to be done at the same time. This may be the reason for what was probably the most frustrating aspect of the job: You have a plan, you have a strategy, but acute developments always force you to abandon both. [234]

9.4   Paddy Ashdown (2002-2006)

> A senior member of the Foreign Office told me he was present when Tony Blair sought support for my candidature [as High Representative] from his fellow European leaders. One of them asked who I was and whether I was really up to such a difficult post, to which Blair replied, 'Look, this guy led the British Liberal Democrats for eleven years. After that, Bosnia will be a doodle!'[235]

The choice of Lord Paddy Ashdown as the High Representative in Bosnia and Herzegovina signified a major shift in the international community's approach towards post-war state building in the country. First of all, the choice itself was remarkable. Compared to Wolfgang Petritsch, a bureaucrat and historian whose actions were based on intense knowledge of the region, Ashdown seemed the antithesis. Born in what still was British India in 1941, he grew up in Northern Ireland and joined the Royal Marines in 1959. During his military service, he entered the prestigious Special Boat Service, and, in 1970, commanded a unit on the streets of Belfast. After leaving the military, he officially joined the Foreign Service and was assigned to the UK's mission in Geneva; unofficially, however, his duties were not so much diplomatic but rather belonged to the realm of the intelligence community. He subsequently became involved with politics and learned how to organise a campaign from the bottom up; in 1983 he was elected to the House of Commons and in 1989, became the first leader of the newly founded

---

234   Ibid.
235   Paddy Ashdown, *A Fortunate Life* (London: Aurum, 2009), 336.

Liberal Democrats. When the events in Yugoslavia started filling the newspapers in mid-1991, Ashdown, as he recalls, 'asked for a briefing and had to be shown where the various "countries" of Yugoslavia were, after which I dismissed it all as too complex and, anyway, not something for me to bother about, because it wasn't going to amount to anything important'.[236]

In fact, his involvement with the Balkans was rather accidental and began during the honeymoon period after the 1992 British elections, when the opposition could not really criticise the government, for it had not yet done anything. It is at this point that one of his aides suggested: 'You know a bit about wars, Paddy. If you are so bored, why don't you go out and have a look at the one that has just started in Yugoslavia.'[237] So Ashdown visited the war zone, and Sarajevo in particular. His interest in the conflict was thus based on a mixture of boredom and military experience, while his historical understanding of the matter was highly influenced by the British government's official position that regarded the war as a the logical consequence of 'ancient hatreds' of the peoples of Bosnia.[238] Consequently, even though he assigned the major part of the atrocities to the Serbs, he was convinced that what was going on was a 'war of minorities between three warring parties', a 'bewildering conflict, and one in which nobody (presumably least of all himself) actually understands'.[239] The choice of Ashdown as High Representative, therefore, was the return of people skilled in the art of politics, well-versed *politicians*, in other words. By his own admission, despite being involved with the conflict since the early 1990s, Ashdown 'knew so little' about Bosnia.[240]

Secondly, as far as his approach towards the mandate of the HR is concerned, Ashdown was, for the lack of more appropriate terms, a hands-on pragmatist rather than an ideologue or theoretician. Presumably as a result of his leadership positions in the military and his party, he exercised a style of governing that was aimed at results rather than being an educational process. For him, the progress of the country in *absolute* terms was the guiding mark, whereas Petritsch had always focused on a *relative* concept of progress. The latter, based on a dialectic understanding of advancement, meant that slow progress was qualitatively better, provided it was rooted in a genuine development within the existing political structure. For Ashdown, however, concrete outcomes represented the justification for his actions and, thusly, the ultimate tool for sustaining the country. De-

---

[236]   Ibid., 256.

[237]   Ibid., 264.

[238]   Jonathan May has recently presented an in-depth study of Ashdown's evolution and interaction with Bosnia upon which I rely in this segment. Cf. Jonathan May, "How Bosnia Changed Paddy," *East European Politics and Societies and Cultures* 27, no. 4 (2013): 593–618.

[239]   Ibid., 597.

[240]   Ashdown, *A Fortunate Life*, 347.

pending on the kind of progress one prefers, Ashdown's four-year mandate can be described as the best or the worst phase of Bosnia's post-war development without any contradiction; the important point is simply to acknowledge that different standards are applied in the assessment. One should also note that these two kinds of progress overlap, for even Petritsch, despite a different philosophical understanding, saw the practical need for imposition in order to create a framework for local ownership. Nevertheless, I believe that there are important differences between the two approaches that become evident not only through the analysis of their philosophical backgrounds but also by looking at their intended and unintended practical consequences.

9.4.1   The end of ownership and the African chief approach

Consistent with the absolute concept of progress, Paddy Ashdown elaborated a clear plan with regards to what he wanted to achieve during his first hundred days in office. Even apart from the content, this approach to the task already testifies to his understanding of the High Representative's role, i.e. as equal to the one of a new government rather then the friendly, external supporter.

The plan he outlined contained ten concrete steps, which included: grabbing the initiative for the state-building programme; a 'series of small victories' that would foster the way for later, bigger successes; a long-term concentration on specific reforms in the rule of law and economic sectors; a concentration of OHR activities into specific areas with the understanding of slowly shutting the office down; a stronger involvement of the overall international community and other international organisations; a close relationship with NATO; regular meetings with the ambassadors of the Steering Board countries and members from other international organisations; a new OHR structure; a concentrated media strategy to communicate the strategic goals; and, finally, a soft renunciation of the Sarajevo intellectuals (the so-called *čaršija*) and the dedication of more time to other regions of the country.[241] In his inaugural speech on 27 May 2002 before the Bosnian parliament, Ashdown outlined his strategy in greater detail. As he told the representatives, his aim was 'to work with the people of Bosnia and Herzegovina to put this country irreversibly onto the road to statehood and membership of Europe'. Paraphrasing Kennedy's famous remark, Ashdown warned the locals: 'do not ask what the international community can do for you. Ask what you can do for yourselves.' At least rhetorically, he wanted to put them in charge of Bosnia's future. But he also reminded the politicians of his powers to punish destructive behaviour by pledging to 'never permit any constitutional change that fundamentally threatens the identity or security of any of Bosnia and Herzegovina's constituent peoples'. Nevertheless, he made clear that this would not exclude the pos-

---

[241]   Ashdown, *Swords and Ploughshares*, 226–231.

sibility for a negotiated constitutional reform; in this respect, Dayton was 'the floor, not the ceiling'. In terms of key policy priorities, he wanted to concentrate on justice reform—'because the rule of law is the starting point—the essential requirement for a decent life for the people of BiH and for progress in everything we do'—and the creation of jobs.

While all these statements in themselves do not present something new, Ashdown's approach to the partnership and ownership paradigms has in retrospect to be seen as the core of his philosophy as High Representative. He departed from the ownership paradigm even though he assessed it as 'reaching towards the right solution'. But 'looking at what [Petritsch] did, my iteration on his policy, was to use the European Union to persuade the Bosnians to take responsibility for institutions rather than issues—institutions of the state, in this case the High Judicial Constitutional Council, the Customs Service ... that was that form of ownership.'[242] Rather than concentrating purely on institutional design, Ashdown tried a holistic approach that concentrated on issues as well as on structure. This form of 'partnership'—a term the Alliance government had already established as part of their dealings with Petritsch—was based on a fundamental re-interpretation of the High Representative's approach to the locals and the local political system. As Ashdown explained in his inaugural speech:

> To me, partnership means a more open relationship between the international organizations here and the people of Bosnia and Herzegovina. I see myself not just as a representative of the International Community. I am also a *servant of Bosnia and Herzegovina*. And that applies to all my colleagues as well. I have therefore asked that the BiH flag will be flown on all OHR buildings—and I hope that other international organizations will follow suit. And when I have to travel abroad I shall wish to do so as a representative, not just of the international community, but of Bosnia and Herzegovina, under the BiH flag. I want the Office of the High Representative to be open and accessible to the people of Bosnia and Herzegovina. So, starting today, I will be spending more time out of Sarajevo, meeting people from across the country, and listening to their views. And I have given instructions today, that the iron gates at the front of OHR Sarajevo will be opened, and left open, except when a specific security threat requires otherwise. I will also be increasing the number of Bosnians working within the OHR—including at senior level—as part of a broader drive to create a cadre of young professionals who will serve Bosnia and Herzegovina and push forward the reform agenda.[243]

The notion of being a 'servant' of the people of Bosnia and Herzegovina was rooted in a belief that even the usage of an instrument such as the Bonn powers depended, 'on the ultimate acceptance of the people to whom it was being applied'; Ashdown believed that '[i]f any of the Bonn power decisions taken by

---

[242] Ashdown, Personal Interview.

[243] Paddy Ashdown, *Inaugural Speech by Paddy Ashdown, the New High Representative for Bosnia & Herzegovina* (Sarajevo: Office of the High Representative, 27 May 2002), http://www.ohr.int/ohr-dept/presso/presssp/default.asp?content_id=8417. Accessed 8 November 2013. My emphasis.

myself or my predecessors had been rejected outright by the people of Bosnia, or by their politicians, there was no way the decision could have stood and the powers themselves would have de facto vanished over night.'[244] However, if one, e.g., recalls the unhappiness with the Brčko arbitration verdict and the subsequent events in Republika Srpska, Ashdown's conviction appears questionable. The international community possessed the powers to implement its decisions, not only in political and economic but also in military terms. It could rely on both hard and soft power in its approach to the state. Ashdown must have been well aware of this fact, which is why one has to understand his belief not necessarily in practical, but rather in normative terms. As such, the effort to re-attach the usage of the Bonn powers to the consent of the people testifies more to Ashdown's philosophy than to the actuality of the claim's content.[245]

Understood as the foundation of his philosophy, Ashdown's notion of being a public servant serves as a justification not only for his absolute concept of progress but also for the means that he employed to achieve such progress, i.e. the Bonn powers. Crucial in this respect is public support as the sole currency in which public approval for decisions is measured. In simplified terms, one might say that only a High Representative enjoying high public support can be an effective High Representative. However, it is important to analytically detach public support from the actual policies implemented, for, according to Ashdown, these two concepts were not necessarily linked. Public support was the means in order to push for an agenda deemed appropriate and *not* the substrate out of which concrete policy proposals were to evolve. In other words, public support determined the 'how' rather than the 'what', as Ashdown himself explains:

> So, the crucial battlefield that I had to win on was the battlefield of public opinion. What this meant was that I would have to behave like a politician myself and build up public support for the measures we needed to get through. I have always thought that popularity should be to the politician what cattle are to the African chief. You built up your stock when you can, so that you can sell it when you need to in order to obtain the things you want.[246]

Leaving aside the somewhat irritating notion that public support can be 'bought' and 'sold off' like cattle, Ashdown's concept of the 'African chief' suffers from a basic contradiction as far as the public is concerned. If the validity of any law— and Ashdown conceived of Bonn power decisions as philosophically equal to laws—really rests on the consent of the people, why are the people not the ones to judge which laws are to be passed? How can one justify involving the people at

---

[244] Ashdown, *Swords and Ploughshares*, 219.

[245] But as we shall see during the term of Miroslav Lajčák, international involvement was gradually subject to public scrutiny, which also affected the international community's ability to impose laws. For the time being, however, such concerns were rather theoretical, for the international community remained the sole 'sheriff in town'.

[246] Ashdown, *Swords and Ploughshares*, 225.

the outcome-stage of the political process while giving them no say in the input-phase? One may recall that Ashdown and his team elaborated their 100-day-programme and the long-term policy goals prior to coming to Bosnia, i.e. independently of the local political institutions and the people; those were measures that '*we* needed to get through', as Ashdown writes in the above quotation. While I do not wish to imply that it is generally impossible to justify one's policies based on the outcomes generated, I believe that such an approach is conceptually almost impossible if one measures the legitimacy of certain outcomes not by concrete principles on which the institution taking such decisions is founded but on the somewhat general notion of public consent. If public consent is the guideline, limiting it to the outcome phase seems highly problematic. Therefore, what Ashdown understood as some form of 'rule by public consent' is nothing else than rule by guardianship, in which agents of the international community have replaced Plato's philosophers. In this notion, consent of the people is reduced to its negative form, in the sense that one cannot constantly govern against large parts of the population. In itself, this is by no means a democratic idea, for even dictatorships have proven unstable when confronted by massive public disapproval. To once again paraphrase Abraham Lincoln, this form of governing, contrary to its superficial claim, is neither 'of' nor 'by' the people; at most, it is 'for' the people. This is, of course, not to say that the people might not have approved of Ashdown's agenda, but simply to illustrate that within the boundaries of his conceptual approach, the people played an instrumental rather than substantial role.

Despite such conceptual incongruences, Ashdown's 'African chief' approach was based on the novel and also noble notion that the international community needed to justify its involvement in Bosnia not only through the abnormality of the current situation but through concrete benefits of the engagement. Since benefits lead to, and can only be measured in public support, Ashdown's style of governing had necessarily to be based on personal popularity. Consequently, all actions not primary aimed at significantly influencing a course of political action became opportunities to 'stock up' on public approval, i.e. popularity. Conceptually and practically, this was a completely new approach. Popularity, in this form, had never been an issue for the High Representatives before. Quite to the contrary: Petritsch, for example, consciously tried to withdraw himself from the public political process and let the locals play the important roles in selling the policies, even when he imposed them. Even though he recalls having approval ratings of around eighty per cent, Petritsch never thought to use his popularity as a commodity in the everyday political mongering.[247]

At this point an important clarification deserves to be stated plainly so as to avoid a potential misunderstanding of my assessment and analysis: in no way do I

---

[247]   Petritsch, Personal Interview.

wish to imply that Ashdown's behaviour as High Representative was somehow disingenuous. In fact, I believe that quite the contrary is true. Ashdown's stay with an older refugee couple near Višegrad in June 2003, for example, seems to have had a deep impact on his understanding of the refugee situation, which makes such visits, even if publicised, anything but dishonest or simply opportunistic.[248] As he convincingly explains, his understanding of being a *public servant* of the people was based on a *genuine* love for Bosnia and the personal will 'to do the right thing':

> I love the Bosnian people, in all of their forms. They remind me so much of my own people. ... I just wanted to make the place better. It was a genuine thing. And unless you have that instinct, you can go terribly easy wrong. Unless you have the instincts that all are slightly romantics, unless you have that instinct to want to do the right thing, I think you are terribly wrong in the business.[249]

In any case, we are *not* concerned with this kind of personal assessments, for the subject matter of this study is the *strategic* behaviour of the political elite within a specific political framework. As Ashdown himself has explained in the second to last quote, he consciously chose 'the battlefield of public opinion' in order to create some form of momentum for much needed legislation. In this respect, visits to refugee camps remain important photo-ops for increasing one's popularity. In terms of political strategy, it seem that, if popularity is understood as the fuel that keeps the HR engine running, it would be unwise to ignore such opportunities.

From an analytical point of view, there are several dangers in linking one's actions to popular approval. Seeking public approval may lead to the neglect of certain unpopular measures necessary within a greater context. For Ashdown, this seems never to have been the case, for he defined his agenda largely independent of the public notion. However, there is a more substantial threat with regards to the political system. If the High Representative has to 'behave like a politician', he automatically enters into competition with other politicians, i.e. the locals. This competition is not necessarily based on policy differences but solely on the perception of public appeal. As a well-experienced politician, who at one time even ran some sort of a public complaints office in his own electoral district, Ashdown undeniably knew better how to communicate to the people than the local politicians, many of whom were the products of communist times. In addition, Ashdown possessed the political influence and power to actually put into action what he publicly promised, whereas the local politicians were burdened by the consociational mechanisms of veto powers and group negotiations. All this means that in the competition for public approval, the playing field was anything but level.

---

248   The encounter in Višegrad is described in Ashdown, *Swords and Ploughshares*, 287–291.

249   Ashdown, Personal Interview.

Ashdown's charismatic personality, his substantial experience with campaigning, and his political powers gave him all he needed to outact the local politicians. A poll in May 2003 found a nearly ninety per cent approval rating for Ashdown, while the local politicians ranked somewhere in the single-digits.[250] A British journalist who accompanied Ashdown on one of his visits described the experience as follows:

> In a convoy of cars we head for the local high school where Lord Ashdown wants to meet the teachers and see education at the sharp end. There is spontaneous applause from the students as he strides in. "Ashdown is cool," one of them says. "He is a good man," another says. "He wants to do something for us, for Bosnia. He wants to help us." They are not the first in Bosnia to have more faith in Paddy Ashdown than in their own politicians. There are more visits and meetings until finally, in the evening we arrive at the refugee transit centre a few miles outside Bihac. It is the last stop of the day and the Ashdowns will be spending the night in the rundown building, reminiscent of a Victorian workhouse without the frills. Lord Ashdown is here, he says, to listen to the problems of the "flotsam and jetsam of Bosnian society, of those washed up by war and conflict". After changing into jeans and jumper he spends three hours talking to the residents, visiting each of their pathetic little rooms. To each one he says that he can do very little. But then quietly, later, he has a word with his assistant, telling her to take their names and do what she can.[251]

The high personal popularity that Ashdown enjoyed is problematic insofar as it gradually made the High Representative an integral part of the political system *in the public's perception*. While Petritsch's imposition of key parts of the Mrakovica-Sarajevo Agreement melded the Bonn powers and the political system in structural terms, Ashdown's 'new' role made this structure evident to everybody; and it also showed the asymmetry in the relations between the High Representative and the local political system more clearly than before. As I have tried to argue throughout this book, it is the combination of those two elements that ultimately resulted in the unhealthy incentive structure that the model of an 'imposed consociation' foresees.

9.4.2   The push and pull of Euro-Atlantic integration

Lord Ashdown set out an agenda for Bosnia-Herzegovina that, if successful, would conclude the transition 'from Dayton to Brussels', as one analyst put it.[252] The establishment of the Stability Pact as well as Bosnia's accession to the Council of Europe were the first steps in this direction. Wolfgang Petritsch, in the reading of Ashdown, had 'declared that the international community's exit strategy

---

250   *Dnevni Avaz*, 14 May 2003, 3.

251   Nick Hawton, "Ashdown Strives to Atone for the West's Sins over Bosnia," *The Times*, 26 December 2002, http://www.ohr.int/ohr-dept/presso/pressa/default.asp?content_id=28812. Accessed 13 November 2013.

252   Emir Hadžikadunić, *Od Dejtona Do Brisela (From Dayton to Brussels)* (Sarajevo: ACIPS, 2005).

should be to transit Bosnia into Europe, so it was clear to me that our destination should be ultimate membership of the EU and NATO—the so-called Euro-Atlantic structures'.[253]

This approach was possible because, by the time Ashdown arrived in Bosnia, international engagement was entering a new phase. Before him, the efforts of the international community had focused on what he termed the stabilisation aspect of post-conflict reconstruction; Ashdown therefore now sought to highlight the state-building aspect. As he understood state building in Bosnia, it meant to create 'the outline structure of a modern, light-level state, governing a highly decentralised country'.[254] This situation analysis is slightly anachronistic, for international intervention did not neglect this aspect before Ashdown's tenure, nor was it purely concerned with reconstructive programmes. In fact, at least since the times of Carlos Westendorp, the internationals consciously focused on state building as part of their overall transition strategy. I believe it is this slight misconception about the nature of international involvement that makes understandable Ashdown's abandonment of the ownership paradigm. In its most simplified terms, Ashdown's approach would have been much more appropriate for the mid-1990s than it was for the early to mid-2000s. But since Ashdown believed that international politics had so far largely failed in establishing the rule of law, i.e. one of the central cornerstones of any democratic state, he was convinced that the state-building efforts preceding him lacked the necessary depth. Consequently, state building—understood not only as efficiency in terms of functioning but, first and foremost, as a duty to create a state structure—gained extreme importance.

As part of his state building, Ashdown distilled three priorities for his engagement: the establishment of the rule of law, getting the economy moving, and beginning to tackle high-level corruption in the country.[255] The method for achieving these goals was reminiscent of the older days when international involvement had followed the carrot-and-stick approach. Whereas in the days of economic conditionality, financial aid was both the carrot and the stick, Ashdown based his strategy on another kind of push and pull, namely the Bonn powers and the prospect of Euro-Atlantic integration:

> The paradox about Dayton is: it was at once the most important instrument for stabilisation as well as being the most important roadblock for moving towards a sustainable state. And that's why we have to move beyond Dayton. And I think if we were going to persuade people to work together in a sustainable, post-stabilisation state, Dayton was the enemy. But the European Union should have been the driver. I did use the European Union ruthlessly as the driver. I said: ok, if you want to belong to NATO, you've got to go through these processes; you've got to unify the army. They did want to belong to NATO. You want to belong to the European Union? You have

---

253   Ashdown, *Swords and Ploughshares*, 221.
254   Ibid., 100.
255   Ashdown, *A Fortunate Life*, 338.

> to get rid of your sales taxes and you have to let a VAT system in. I think it was the
> attraction, the carrot and the stick, of the Brussels institutions—NATO and the Euro-
> pean Union—which was the driver for moving towards a sustainable state.[256]

Consistent with these goals, Ashdown embarked on an agenda focused on economic progress and the rule of law. With regards to the latter, his approach was twofold. First, he intensified the cooperation with the ICTY and made sure that local institutions possessed the authority to prosecute war and other criminals. He broadened the authority of the State Court to indict such people and also pushed for stronger action against the most well known fugitives. Quite frequently, he publically referenced the need to arrest Radovan Karadžić and Ratko Mladić,[257] while SFOR operations to do so increased as well.[258] Throughout his mandate, Ashdown also tried to abolish the financial and personal support networks such criminals relied upon in order to remain at large. In fact, out of 345 Bonn power decisions between assuming office in May 2002 and the end of 2004, 103 of them belong to the category of ICTY cooperation and prosecution of war crimes. It is on the issue of 'getting the Bosnians to ... cooperate with the war crimes tribunal' that Ashdown saw the Bonn powers as the key instrument:

> Yes, I've used the Bonn powers a lot for that. And the consequence was that 13 of
> the outstanding Hague indictees were in my time sent to The Hague. So, I closed
> down their support structures; I used the Bonn powers to shut off their supply of
> money. Up until then, the whole Hague tribunal effort was... 'justice' descending in
> form of an IFOR/SFOR helicopter into a clearing on [a mountain] to lift said war
> criminal. That was the case. I said we['ve] got to attack the structure, the political
> structure, and I used the Bonn powers to do that.[259]

But Ashdown's commitment to the rule of law went further than ICTY cooperation. Apart from changes to the current legal structure aimed at strengthening the state prosecutor's mandate, the High Representative also introduced the principle of what he called 'ministerial responsibility'.[260] So when evidence of high-level corruption and illegal activities surfaced in June 2002 in both the RS and the FBiH, Ashdown did not hesitate. The involved RS minister of finance resigned, while the Federation minister of finance refused to do so and had to be removed.[261] Ashdown had thus shown his willingness to act, and, in fact, during his first one hundred days in office, he removed six people in total;[262] during his entire mandate, he issued 62 decisions belonging to the category 'removals or sus-

---

[256] Ashdown, Personal Interview.

[257] Cf, e.g., *Dnevni Avaz*, 1 June 2002, 2; 15 January 2003, 5.

[258] Ashdown, *Swords and Ploughshares*, 237.

[259] Ashdown, Personal Interview.

[260] Ashdown, *Swords and Ploughshares*, 237.

[261] *Dnevni Avaz*, 15 June 2002, 2.

[262] *Oslobođenje*, 11 September 2002, 6.

pensions from office', even though 24 of these decisions concerned lifts of bans, i.e. not actual removals.

A second pillar of Ashdown's engagement was dedicated to boosting the economy. Consistent with the paradigm of absolute progress, the High Representative tried a bold approach at first. According to a secret plan elaborated together with Peter Nicholl, the Chief of the Central Bank, Bosnia was to abandon its currency and join the Euro. As Nicholl and Ashdown saw it, this action would have had several advantages: 'the currency would have been permanently protected against manipulation by local politicians; transaction costs to the country's main potential markets would have been reduced and it would encourage investment'.[263] But, as Ashdown also mentions, there was a tactical component to the plan as well, for the next general elections were around the corner and the Alliance was losing momentum. This is why introducing the Euro should not be imposed, but subjected to a public referendum which would require a double majority in the state and the entities to pass. 'This, we believed, would add political advantage to economic gain.... A referendum on the Euro (which we judged would have overwhelming support) would have raised turnout, identified European reform as the key subject of the elections and helped the Alliance.'[264] Eventually, this plan was turned down due to severe opposition from the political leaderships in Paris and Berlin.

With the anticipated difficulties of the Alliance government to stay in power, the international community's agenda was in danger as well—or, to be more accurate, its agenda in its form at that time, which still mingled somewhere between partnership, ownership, and imposition. Even though the nationalist parties adopted their rhetoric during the electoral campaign in order to reflect their commitment to the central state—Dragan Čović for example, the HDZ candidate for the state presidency, clearly rejected any notion of 'a third entity' or 'Croat self-government' as part of HDZ's electoral campaign[265]—their true allegiances naturally remained with their own national electorates. According to the paradigm adopted by the international community at least since Westendorp, this made them by definition more difficult to cooperate with. Paddy Ashdown, despite reiterating the old song and dance that the international community had no favourites as far as elections were concerned, clearly urged the people to vote for reforms and the Euro-Atlantic agenda.[266] The Peace Implementation Council seconded Ashdown in his efforts by calling Bosnians to 'vote for the reforms that will put

---

[263]   Ashdown, *Swords and Ploughshares*, 239.
[264]   Ibid.
[265]   *Dnevni Avaz*, 21 August 2002, 6.
[266]   *Oslobođenje*, 11 September 2002, 6.

BiH decisively on the path to Europe'.[267] Shortly before the elections, the HR even sent a personal letter to Bosnian households encouraging them to vote for reforms and the parties that support EU accession.[268] (Note that there was no talk of political change as such, as had been the major line of argument in the previous elections.)

But the international community was fully aware of the fact that the Alliance government had been some sort of a lucky punch—an event unlikely to happen in the first place, and even more unlikely to be repeated. The majority in parliament was slim and the majority in the presidency was only the result of parliamentary replacements, not elections. So, with this in mind, the internationals needed

> some insurance for ourselves that the reform agenda would survive a change of government by getting buy-in from all parties for the reform programme. To do this we drew up a document called 'Jobs and Justice' which listed the reforms needed for BiH to start the journey to Europe. The document was the first to be drawn up jointly by the OHR and the government and became, during the campaign, more or less the manifesto for the re-election of the Alliance government. Before the campaign started, however, we were able to gain the formal acceptance of all parties to the 'Justice and Jobs' package, who declared publicly that this would be their programme, if elected.[269]

There is an obvious contradiction in Ashdown's account of the 'Justice and Jobs' package: If all the parties, even only formally, supported the package how could it serve as a manifesto of the Alliance's re-election? The fact of the matter was that the commitment of the nationalist parties was purely cosmetic, just as the 'cooperation' between the government and the OHR in producing the document had probably not been a partnership. The 'Justice and Jobs' programme corresponded so clearly to the objectives advocated by the international community— the introduction of the rule of law, making parliament more functional, attracting foreign investment, reducing the administrative burden to start a new business, unification of customs administration, the introduction of a common VAT system, etc.[270]—that one may very well doubt local involvement in drafting the agenda at all. Be that as it may, the 'Jobs and Justice' package was in the true sense an insurance policy for the international agenda. Since all parties had pub-

---

267   Peace Implementation Council, *Declaration of the Political Directors of the Peace Implementation Council Steering Board* (Sarajevo: Office of the High Representative, 24 September 2002), http://www.ohr.int/pic/default.asp?content_id=27982. Accessed 19 November 2013.

268   *Dnevni Avaz*, 26 September 2002, 3.

269   Ashdown, *Swords and Ploughshares: Building Peace to the 21st Century*, 243.

270   Paddy Ashdown, *Speech by the High Representative for Bosnia and Herzegovina Paddy Ashdown to the BiH House of Representatives* (Sarajevo: Office of the High Representative, December 17, 2002), http://www.ohr.int/ohr-dept/presso/presssp/default.asp?content_id=28736. Accessed 19 November 2013.

licly accepted it, the demands the document contained could be used against anyone who tried to block corresponding legislation, be it the Alliance or the nationalist opposition. In this sense, the 'Jobs and Justice' package was a bullet-proof strategy that would either serve as the foundation for the common work (in case the Alliance won), or as a blueprint for the path on which the government would have to be forced (in the case of a nationalist electoral win).

There are diverging interpretations of the results of the 5 October 2002 general elections. For some, the result was the definitive proof of 'a return to the 1990s'[271] while for others, including the international community, it exemplified 'a protest against an inactive government'.[272] In any case, nationalist parties clearly won the elections while the Alliance lost its narrow majority in parliament. Sulejman Tihić (SDA), Dragan Čović (HDZ) and Mirko Šarović (SDS) were elected to the BiH Presidency, while in the House of Representatives, SDA secured 16 seats, and HDZ and SDS five seats each. The close ally of SDA, the SBiH, won six seats, while the SDP (four), the SNSD (three), and the PDP (two) came in well under the expectations of the internationals. The nationalists had thus control over the Presidency, but, by themselves, had no majority in parliament. While the SDA and the HDZ agreed to a general coalition on all levels of government rather quickly,[273] the actual formation of a new government took some time since the nationalists needed a coalition partner. By the end of December, three months after the elections, the new government was finally assembled. Led by the Bosniak Adnan Terzić (SDA), the governing coalition consisted of SDA, SDS, HDZ, SBiH, and PDP (with PDP-President Mladen Ivanić becoming Bosnia's Foreign Minister). That the nationalists were clearly back in business became evident in April 2003, when Mirko Šarović resigned from the BH presidency. Šarović's resignation—which has to be seen against the alternative to being removed by the HR—meant that he took political responsibility for actions that happened during his term as RS president. Concretely, the RS controlled company *'Orao'* ('Eagle') had violated UN sanctions by trading knowhow and areal equipment to Iraq. With Boris Paravac, also a member of the SDS, subsequently succeeding Šarović, the nationalist coalition showed its unity in parliament, where such elections were held. The same would hold true in 2005, when Dragan Čović was removed from office based on alleged corruption during his term as FBiH Minister of Finance (see previous chapter). With the election of Ivo Miro Jović, another member of HDZ succeeded him.

---

[271]   *Nezavisne Novine*, 7 October 2002, 1.
[272]   *Dnevni Avaz*, 6 October 2002, 3.
[273]   *Nezavisne Novine*, 19-20 October 2002, 2.

9.4.3   The assumption of full gubernatorial power

With the return of the nationalists, who constituted the Bosnian government for the next four years, the international community's expected, but nevertheless worst-case scenario had become reality. Paddy Ashdown, however, was not willing to go through the same bickering with the nationalists that Bildt, Westendorp, and even Petritsch had experienced. Instead, he relied on his insurance policy and proclaimed the 'Justice and Jobs' programme to be the guideline for the new legislative period.

Immediately after the elections, Ashdown presented the Bosnian politicians with an 'ambitious package of reforms, on which we had previously secured agreement from Solana and Patten and the PIC countries'.[274] Consistent with my previous suspicion that the locals were hardly involved in drafting the 'Justice and Jobs' programme, the first steps of its implementation were agreed between the HR and representatives of the Peace Implementation Council; they also included Javier Solana, the EU's High Representative of the Common and Security Policy, and Chris Patten, the EU's Commissioner for External Relations. Thus, immediately after the elections, Ashdown presented the locals with concrete issues that needed to be addressed:[275] reform of the Council of Ministers, which included the abolishment of the rotation system; the introduction of a VAT instead of the complex and inefficient sales tax; the establishment of an ethics committee with corresponding laws on conflicts of interest; a reform of the criminal law so that the State Court could start working properly; ensuring better qualified personnel in the civil service by limiting the influence of politicians; the abolishment of the country's two customs systems and their combination into a single one. Ashdown furthermore planned 'to narrow significantly the scope of immunity provisions and replace them with provisions in line with the standards in other democratic countries'; to 'strengthen our capacity to carry out audits, especially in public utilities, where high-level political corruption was rife'; and undertook measures 'aimed at liberalising the Bosnian economy and creating a single economic space in the country'.[276] In November 2002, he set up the so-called Bulldozer commission, which in the end included some twenty-odd business organisations from all over the territory. Its task was to detect the most obvious obstacles to doing business in Bosnia and to present the parliament a list of provisions that needed to be abolished in order for the economy to thrive.

When analysing this package, one needs to distinguish between its content and its process. As far as the former is concerned, I believe nobody can doubt the usefulness of the proposed reforms, for they reflect well-established policies in

---

[274]   Ashdown, *Swords and Ploughshares*, 244.
[275]   Ibid., 244–5. Supplemented by *Nezavisne Novine*, 10 October 2002, 3.
[276]   Ibid., 245.

Western Europe that, since the fall of the Iron Curtain, have also helped restructure the political scene and the economy in Eastern Europe. But there is something to be said about the process by which the international community pushed the reforms through. If, as Ashdown alleges, the 'Justice and Jobs' package represented the Alliance's manifesto, and the Alliance had lost the elections with, for example, the SDP losing some 15 per cent of its share in electoral votes, was the package as such not discredited? How can one possibly legitimise the introduction of said policies when the people so clearly voted against those backing the reforms? Taking Ashdown's insurance policy seriously, and justifying later actions with the *pro forma* agreement of all parties, essentially means negating the importance of elections altogether. After all, if the governmental policy is established beforehand and the people cannot influence it, do the elections not become merely cosmetic?

Interestingly enough, it is within this context that we find ourselves reminded of the consociational claim with regards to the relative unimportance of elections, for due to the rule by elite cartel the result is highly unlikely to change the general outline of the pursued policies. But this part of the consociational argument rested on the assumption of coherent group structures, which largely prevent volatility in the electoral corpuses. Consequently, it cannot serve as an adequate interpretation of the Bosnian model where group cohesion has been absent since around the year 2000. In fact, the formation of the Alliance government provided ultimate proof of the non-existence of intra-group cohesion. Moreover, since the Mrakovica-Sarajevo Agreement, Bosnia cannot be understood merely in terms of a consociational democracy; rather, it should be conceived as something between a consociational democracy and a system based on international imposition. In other words, a dynamic space in which the pendulum can swing in either direction at any time. But given the strong imperative of contemporary political thought in Europe, this hybrid situation could not be sustained for very long. As we have already seen with Ashdown's philosophy regarding public support, the international community gradually needed more justifications for imposing decisions in a nominally democratic country, which was furthermore a member state of the Council of Europe.

Ashdown's approach towards the 'Justice and Jobs' package implementation, and to reforms in general, can be seen as the prototype of a new kind of OHR involvement. Whereas Petritsch had thought of the Bonn powers as a legal system that took effect once the domestic system had failed, Ashdown understood these systems as conceptually and practically interlinked, meaning that it was pragmatism, not ideology, which was to be employed in order to secure the desired outcome. In a speech to the newly elected Bosnian Parliament on 17 December 2002, Ashdown explained his approach in frank terms:

So the choice is not whether to reform. But how fast, how soon and, above all, who will drive the process of reform—you or me? I do not have the monopoly of wisdom on what is right for this country. There will always be room for compromise between us if this parliament comes up with sensible and workable solutions that push the reform agenda forward. Donors and investors don't think High Representative impositions are a sustainable way to build a country in the long term. Increasingly their assistance to this country will be conditioned on BiH institutions passing and implementing reforms themselves. I will act if I have to. But let's be clear. Every time I have to use my powers, it represents a failure of the system—your system. My job is to get rid of my job. But the pace at which that happens will be decided not by me, not by the international community, but by you. The more you reform, the less I will have to. The less you reform, the more I will have to.[277]

This speech, indeed a 'striking document',[278] testifies to the international community's approach during the first Ashdown years more clearly than any other act. First of all, it follows the central paradigm that imposition not only *presupposes*, but, in fact, *equals* a failure of the Bosnian system. Let me be clear: while one may be reminded of Petritsch's similar assertion, there is an important difference between the concept of failure in Petritsch's and Ashdown's understandings. For Petritsch, a failure of the system to come to an agreement on a specific issue justified the invocation of the parallel system, which contained the Bonn powers. The usage of the Bonn powers was thus *a consequence* of the local political system's failure and something out of the ordinary. For Ashdown, on the other hand, imposition was *integral part* of the local system, not unlike any other institution that is employed once a certain institution has run its course. What Ashdown said to the parliamentarians was simple enough: reform, within a certain range, is a given—and if you do not do it, I will have to. Maintaining the perception of local responsibility effectively emphasises the integration of the Bonn powers into the existing political system. The latter can no longer be understood as a hybrid between guardianship-rule and pseudo-democracy, but becomes a particular form of consociational rule. The primary characteristic of such a political system is thus its consociational democratic character, in which the most important element is outside intervention in the form of imposition. In other words, it was during Ashdown's mandate that Bosnia structurally became an 'imposed consociational' system that then developed the corresponding incentive structures determining elite behaviour.

That Ashdown understood the Bonn powers as part of the system became evident in the aftermath of the 2002 elections. Between the elections and the formation of the Bosnian government in December 2002/January 2003, Ashdown issued no less than 56 Bonn power decisions, only two of which concerned removals from office. The others were dedicated at enacting several laws that had either

---

[277] Ashdown, *Speech by the High Representative.*

[278] Gerhard Knaus and Felix Martin, "Travails of the European Raj," *Journal of Democracy* 14, no. 3 (2003): 60

become necessary as part of Ashdown's larger strategy, had failed in parliament, or had not yet been presented to parliament but adopted by the Council of Ministers. Among the more important impositions belonged a new law on immunity; a reform of the Council of Ministers establishing one Chairman for four years who could also be called 'Prime Minister' (even though this is not part of the actual law, just the preamble of the HR decision); banking and land registry laws in RS and FBiH; a law on statistics in BiH; several amendments to the judicial organisation in the cantons and the entities; the law on the Federation budget (which, if not passed by mid-December, would have stalled an IMF standby arrangement); and, finally, a ten-year moratorium on a clause in the citizenship law, which meant that dual citizens would not lose their Bosnian citizenship if no dual citizenship agreement with their new home state existed.

These impositions presented the first steps towards much further-reaching changes in the state structure. The latter reforms, however, could *not* be pushed through without the newly elected leaders, since they went beyond what had previously been part of governmental decision or was of paramount significance for the state's advancement. The issues included the unification of the customs system and the intelligence services, the introduction of a VAT system, the unification of the army under the control of the presidency, and the reform of the police. Cooperation with the locals was essential in these areas, as Ashdown explains:

> All of those things that I think were important because of my mandate there—they all had to be done with the agreement of the local politicians. I may have cajoled, I may have used European resources, assistance, for instance in establishing a VAT system as a leaver on the one hand and a reward on the other. Essentially, all of these had to be done by the local politicians. In fact, I think if you speak to my major partners—and my major partners were not in the international community, they were Prime Minister Adnan Terzić and President Dragan Čavić in Republika Srpska—we saw ourselves very much as a team, we worked together. And one of the tragedies, I think, of Bosnia is that as a result of their working with me, they ended—they set to sacrifice their political careers in the coming elections and afterwards. And I think that is a great shame.[279]

In a recent speech before the House of Lords in the British parliament, Ashdown reiterated the same point by referencing the same political issues mentioned above but furthermore including steps towards uniting the city of Mostar:

> I do not claim these as successes for those who were high representatives in Bosnia and Herzegovina, for we played but a small part in them. *None of these things was done, as the legend now says, by the use of the Bonn powers or by coercion; all of them were done by persuasion.* All of them were done by having a co-ordinated policy from the European Union and Washington to drive the process of state functionality. All of them were done not by me but by brave Bosnian politicians such as Adnan

---

279   Ashdown, Personal Interview.

Terzic and Dragan Covic,[280] who were my partners in my days there and who took great risks to themselves and believed in the Bosnian state. These were achievements by the Bosnian politicians; they passed through the Bosnian state democratic institutions; *they were not imposed by outsiders*. And then, in 2007, sadly, the European Union adopted a policy to stand back and take no further action. It would leave it to the policy of ownership.[281]

We can indeed detect a different approach in these areas than in the policy fields analysed so far and, correspondingly, a decrease in the general usage of the Bonn powers in the second half of Ashdown's term. The combination of seemingly cooperative politicians, a coherent international strategy, and the pull of Euro-Atlantic integration now allowed for a finer approach and a larger involvement of local politicians. However, this does not contradict my major claim that the High Representative became increasingly involved *within* the political system. That the major instrument of the Bonn powers—which would remain in use in the area of ICTY cooperation—was not applied for these major reforms, does not change the fact that the High Representative gradually became a *constituent part of the local political system* and that this institution remained closely attached to the experiences of Bonn power impositions. In fact, the notion of close cooperation—or partnership—between the international body and the locals precisely testifies to the fact that the HR was still perceived as the major driver of reforms, which indeed he was. But in this sense, the cooperation could hardly have been as harmonious as Ashdown now seems to think. The admittedly achieved political successes were probably not the result of mere persuasion, as Ashdown claims, but also of a specific form of political coercion—even though Ashdown does object to this labelling. The latter consisted of the simple conviction that, short of Bonn power imposition, the High Representative was ready to use all political leverage in his arsenal to get the reforms through.

In this respect, the treatment of 'critics' of the international course of action testifies to the arguably euphemistic character of the cooperation that Ashdown described. Take the following example: During his term as Foreign Minister, Mladen Ivanić strongly opposed the proposed police reform, even though he was not totally against the introduction of the VAT, for he thought that it would benefit the RS—under the condition that the respective revenues were put at the disposal of the entities, not the central state. The situation in which he found himself shows the highly asymmetric character of the relationship between the HR and uncooperative locals. As Ivanić recalls:

---

[280]   While the official record says Dragan Čović, it is more probable that Ashdown means Dragan Čavić, as in the quote above.

[281]   Question regarding Bosnia and Herzegovina for short debate, asked by Lord Ashdown of Norton-sub-Hamdon in the House of Lords, 21 October 2014, the transcript is available online: http://www.publications.parliament.uk/pa/ld201415/ldhansrd/text/141021-0002.htm#14102193000107, accessed 22 October 2014. My emphasis.

> Most often, the pressures I experienced belonged to the realm of power politics. And this was, to be perfectly honest, a period in which I became strongly disappointed with the values of democracy. Here, we were subject to a misuse of democratic powers never seen before—never before! During my time [as Foreign Minister], I thought this to be awful and completely inappropriate. To be perfectly frank, I still hold a grudge with regards to what was done in a democracy, in Bosnia and Herzegovina, and, if you wish, what was done to some people. ... I always thought myself a democrat and I know of, say, no Bosniak who would say that I ever said something harsh or bad to him. But at one time during my term as Foreign Minister, I was prohibited from visiting the United States—simply because I refused certain policies, like the police reform. On this issue, I believed a decentralised state like Bosnia needed a decentralised police organisation, so that is why I opposed the establishment of a central police on state level. But I was for the granting of more authority for the State and Intelligence Protection Agency, which was located on state level. But [my opposition to police reform] was interpreted as an obstruction to progress in Bosnia and Herzegovina and I was thus under a lot of different pressure. But whoever is not up to this, especially as a Serb politician, should not start with politics in Bosnia and Herzegovina.[282]

Ivanić believes that, especially during Paddy Ashdown's mandate, the international community was hostile towards the Republika Srpska and its representatives. In his belief, the internationals perceived of the RS as some sort of elitist project that did not actually reflect the desires of the peoples. If they had accepted that the RS was grounded in the will of the people as well as being a consequence of the most recent war, Ivanić claims, cooperation on equal footing might have been possible.

Ivanić's interpretation in general has to be taken with serious caution. For one, Ashdown's acts were not characterised by a special hostility towards the Serb side; rather, the actions he undertook in the area of ICTY cooperation were primarily aimed at the RS because this entity, for obvious reasons, was primarily harbouring war criminals. Furthermore, the prime opponents to any strengthening of the central state came from the RS. Naturally, this put the Serbs at odds with the reform agenda of the international community. As Ashdown puts it: 'you won't find the Serbs thinking I was a very good High Representative? Well, of course not. They wanted to hang on to Republika Srpska and I wanted to make sure that they lived in a state, not in an entity.'[283] Additionally, it is simply not true that cooperation between the Serb side and Ashdown was in general characterised by hostility. With Dragan Čavić, for example, the High Representative had very good cooperation and still thinks of him as someone 'whom I admire very much'—not least for his admission of Serb responsibility for the events in Srebrenica. Ashdown perceived this as a 'very, very, very brave act, and a necessary act' equal to Willy Brandt's visit to Auschwitz.[284] In fact, it was this cooperation

---

[282] Ivanić, Personal Interview.
[283] Ashdown, Personal Interview.
[284] Ibid.

with the internationals among parts of the Serb elites, to which Ivanić was not immune, that allowed a nationalist opposition to be formed in the next years. Lastly, there is a danger in equating the actions of the High Representative with the general mood of the international community. As Ashdown describes in one of his recollections, some of his actions or plans were criticised by the representatives of the Russian government, especially when the use of Bonn powers was concerned.[285] After all, let us not forget that this was the time when the international community started turning their attention to events in Iraq and the geopolitical landscape adjusted accordingly. And it was probably only the grandeur of Paddy Ashdown, his political stature perhaps, which in light of these international configurations allowed the Office of the High Representative to function as actively and effectively as it did. For all these reasons, the interpretation of Ashdown's actions and the international community's approach towards Bosnia as being 'hostile to the Serb side' is inaccurate, or, at the very least, a wonderful exhibit of a nonsense correlation.

Nevertheless, despite all of these flaws in Ivanić's argument, it shows that the relationship between the High Representative and the locals was by no means a partnership but rather a highly asymmetric dependency. With the help of the international community, the High Representative could impose not only laws but also personal sanctions on the non-cooperative politicians that did not yet amount to the threshold of removal. In other words, Ashdown used all available leverage, as he admits: 'I'm sorry, but politics is about using influence and using leverage. That's why I think the people who are doing these jobs are far better politicians than they are diplomats—there are exceptions to that.'[286]

Ashdown's term, which lasted until January 2006, should be judged on two accounts. The first one concerns the achievement in terms of political reform. In the end, he is responsible for substantial progress in the country. The introduction of a state-wide VAT, significant progress in terms of the establishment of rule of law, the handing over of responsibility for refugee and property return to the Bosnians, the unification of the armed forces under the command of the central state presidency, or the general strengthening of the common state structures; all these issues belong among the major achievements of his term. On the other hand, police reform, i.e. the attempt to introduce a centralised police force, has to be listed among his major failures. As Ana E. Juncos has convincingly shown, Ashdown tried to impose police reform (in general as well as in particular, i.e. the structure of the new police force), through highly coercive means, by which he monopolised the Europeanisation discourse and failed to make the locals understand the

---

[285]   Ashdown, *Swords and Ploughshares*, 252.
[286]   Ashdown, Personal Interview.

need for such adaptation.[287] This was only possible because, since Ashdown's mandate, the High Representative was also the EU Special Representative to Bosnia, which made the separation between EU agenda and post-conflict state building in practical terms impossible. Even though Ashdown changed his role throughout his mandate and started relying more on local political elites as time went by, imposition always remained an important tool in his arsenal. Compared to 158 Bonn power decision in 2004 (84 of them in the area of ICTY cooperation), he issued 91 such decisions in 2005; however, 31 of them constituted lifts of bans for people previously removed from office. In 2006, he issued 11 decisions, seven of which concerned lifts of bans as well.

Therein lays the second aspect by which to judge Ashdown's term. As a result of his 'governing by public support' and the perception of the Bonn empowered High Representative as an integral part of the Bosnian system, he managed to structurally link the OHR and the Bosnian institutions, which, in turn, relied on the political elite. This is the root of what Eldar Sarajlić has called Bosnia's 'convenient consociation', i.e. a consociational system that relies on direct interaction between the internationals and the local political elites; it thus circumvents the institutional arrangement of the state, which naturally makes negotiations with Bosnia more convenient from an outsider's perspective. Those elites, in Sarajlić's understanding, necessarily behave ethno-nationalistically, for consociational democracy, as a general rule, tends to lead to ethno-nationalistically oriented parties.[288] This pattern, which only unfolded after the OHR loosened its grip on the system and used the Bonn powers less often, has its origins in the Ashdown era. But, contrary to Sarajlić, I put forward the argument that it is not the consociational system *per se* that creates ethno-nationalistically oriented parties; rather, the ethno-nationalist orientation of Bosnia's political elites is the result of experiencing a high degree of international intervention through the usage of Bonn powers during Petritsch's and, more clearly, the first part of Ashdown's mandates. These events have convinced the political elites that the internationals have both the capacity and the willingness to impose solutions if they deem it necessary. As long as the High Representative keeps all the governing power *de facto* in his hands, the effect of this belief is limited. But once such international intervention loosens its grip and local politics starts having an impact again, it is precisely this belief that becomes part of the incentive structure in a consociational system. Since it removes the need to compromise with the other groups on actual policies as a general strategy, the elites may concentrate on the course of action that secures their stay in government. Within a society like Bosnia, this is naturally a nationalistically minded orientation. The pre-determination of a European

---

[287]   Ana E. Juncos, "Europeanization by Decree? The Case of Police Reform in Bosnia," *Journal of Common Market Studies* 49, no. 2 (2011): 367–89.

[288]   Sarajlić, "The Convenient Consociation."

agenda, which absolves the politicians of their input responsibilities, serves as a catalyst agent in this process. In sum, the OHR becoming a crucial element of daily political business was not a mere possibility or intellectual fear, but a fact during Ashdown's term. In other words, dependency became part of the system. As Ashdown says today:

> Every time the High Representative uses his powers—and by the way, that applies to Dayton but it also uses the leverage—he or she needs to be aware that in getting things done, they're also creating dependencies. And that is the calculation you always must make. The temptation for somebody in Bosnia with those [sic] kind of powers is to use the powers to get things done quickly. And I always used to ask: if I do this, is the advantage of getting things done quickly worth the price I have to pay, which is creating dependencies within the structure? Perfectly fair argument. And the whole thing comes down—and I'm not saying I always got the balance right—but the whole thing comes down to a careful judgement about those two things.[289]

9.5   Christian Schwarz-Schilling (2006-2007)

Within the group of High Representatives, Christian Schwarz-Schilling is a unique as well as tragic figure. Unlike with Westendorp, Petritsch, or Ashdown, the Bosnian public actually knew who Schwarz-Schilling was before he assumed the office of High Representative. In an act of protest against his government's passivity during the early days of the Bosnian war, the German had resigned his ministerial post in December 1992 explicitly stating that he would be ashamed to be part of Helmut Kohl's cabinet if inactivity prevailed.[290] While the politically proclaimed 'Hour of Europe' had turned into a political and moral disaster, Schwarz-Schilling had managed to stay faithful to his own morality, which did not allow for German passivity in the face of human suffering on the European continent. His subsequent humanitarian engagement during the war, the participation at the Dayton negotiations, and the tenure as the international community's mediator for the Federation between 1995 and 2004—during which he focused on the re-integration of the now segregated municipalities—made Schwarz-Schilling a moral authority as well as an expert in the country in the eyes of many Bosnians. And even though he had always seen Serb nationalism as the main cause of the Bosnian war, his expertise and qualifications were not put into question by the Bosnian Serb politicians either. Schwarz-Schilling, who had once declared Bosnia his second home, was perceived as an older statesman who had only the good of the country in mind. It is thus of little surprise that one media outlet comment-

---

289   Ashdown, Personal Interview.

290   Dževada Šuško, "Reaktionen der bosnischen Öffentlichkeit auf Christian Schwarz-Schilling als Hoher Repräsentant," in *Bosnien im Fokus. Die zweite politische Herausforderung des Christian Schwarz-Schilling*, Erich Rathfelder and Carl Bethke, ed. (Berlin/Tübingen: Verlag Hans Schiler, 2010), 299.

ed the change from Ashdown to Schwarz-Schilling by stating that 'the administrator goes, the friend comes'.[291]

But with the friend came also a new approach towards international engagement. Like Petritsch, Schwarz-Schilling understood his mission in Bosnia in educational and dialectic terms; he was there not to decide but to induce local decisions. Whereas Ashdown had ended the paradigm of ownership, Schwarz-Schilling sought to revive it. The notion of absolute success was once again replaced by one of relative success, which put the German's approach at odds with the needs of the international community at that moment. Somewhat misled by Ashdown's impressive achievements, which however had not been based the evolution of a cooperative spirit by the locals, the international community had come to an agreement to close down the OHR by the end of 2006. Such a decision would have meant that Bosnia had become a self-sustaining country and ultimately proved the success of international intervention—at a time when the entire world questioned this very same approach in Iraq or Afghanistan.

Schwarz-Schilling had agreed to act as the last High Representative, provided that the conditions on the ground matched an international assessment and a closure of the OHR could be performed. However, he rather soon realised that this was not the case and that Bosnia was by no means a self-sustaining country. Consequently, Schwarz-Schilling refused to comply with an obviously nonsense international policy. For the first time in OHR history, the international agenda and the one of the HR were not in accord; and for the first time, the High Representative refused to take the instructions from Washington as direct commands. 'During personal talks in Sarajevo', Schwarz-Schilling recalls, 'the American ambassador thought he could scold me like a school boy, for he apparently took it for granted that American wishes were offhandedly executed.'[292] Missing support from his own government in Berlin (that sought to establish a good working relation with the US after the rifts of the Iraq war), Schwarz-Schilling fought a lost cause. In the end, he managed to prevent the OHR closure, not least due to a shift in the American position after the mid-term elections. But in the process he became a *persona non grata*. Therein lies one of the many tragedies of international post-war engagement in Bosnia-Herzegovina.

---

[291] *Slobodna Bosna*, 12 January 2006, quoted in Ibid., 302.

[292] Christian Schwarz-Schilling, "Europa und Deutschland müssen sich ihrer Verantwortung stellen," in *Bosnien im Fokus. Die zweite politische Herausforderung des Christian Schwarz-Schilling*, Erich Rathfelder and Carl Bethke, ed. (Berlin/Tübingen: Verlag Hans Schiler, 2010), 263.

9.5.1 Taking ownership seriously once again

The change from Ashdown to Schwarz-Schilling was not just a change in personnel, as would be the case with later High Representatives, but a fundamental rupture in governing style and philosophy. Qualifying Ashdown's approach to his office as equal to the position of a 'European raj', as some have suggested,[293] of course fits the superficial line of argument that links the lord to the colonial rule of the British Empire. While some of his actions could indeed be characterised as somewhat 'imperial', his general approach was far too sophisticated for such condescending explanations. Judging by the actions and style of behaviour, I think it is more illuminating to understand Ashdown's actions as part of a mind-set that allows for intervention into democratic orders in the pursuit of a greater good. If one accepts such an illustrative characterisation—just for the sake of the argument—Christian Schwarz-Schilling would be a prime example of a different mind-set that regards international intervention in a formally democratic system much more critically—without, however, being completely opposed to it. From the get-go, Christian Schwarz-Schilling was burdened by the overwhelming contradiction in the international community's Bosnia policy. As the result of international efforts, the state had joined the Council of Europe and made significant progress with regards to its membership application in the European Union. The conditions of a Road Map were assessed as substantially completed in October 2003, and in November of the same year, a Feasibility Study outlined priorities that needed to be addressed before initialling the Stabilisation and Association Agreement (SAA). When Schwarz-Schilling assumed office, Bosnia was in the middle of such negotiations, which also included police reform. But presumably due to his personal experiences, the German understood the process of European integration as a transition towards democracy, which necessarily contradicted the way in which it had been handled in Bosnia. A transition from Dayton to Brussels was not possible through the use of Bonn powers, as Schwarz-Schilling had explained before taking office: 'It cannot be that that the High Representative is legislature, executive, and judge on his own behalf while Europe preaches separation of powers.'[294]

This fundamental contradiction could only be resolved if the use of the Bonn powers was curtailed to an absolute minimum. This meant not only establishing a new paradigm for future utilisation but also a re-assessment of how the powers had been used in the past. Schwarz-Schilling, who at the Bonn conference had argued for putting such powers under the control of judicial review, started

---

293   Knaus and Martin, "Travails of the European Raj."

294   Michael Martens, "Schwarz-Schillings nicht ganz freiwilliger Abschied," *FAZ.NET*, 25 January 2007, http://www.faz.net/aktuell/politik/ausland/bosnien-hercegovina-schwarz-schillings-nicht-ganz-freiwilliger-abschied-1409649.html. Accessed 29 November 13.

by reformulating the policy on people removed from office. In April, he issued a decision limiting the scope of the HR's capacity to remove people from public office, which in effect reinstated the right of banned people to once again hold offices only indirectly connected to the government (i.e. offices in public enterprises, public institutions (*javne ustanove*) or any other institutions to which the respective laws regulating civil service did not apply but which were partly or fully financed from a budget at any level of government in Bosnia and Herzegovina).[295] In June, he lifted the ban from office within political parties, which had been included in previous removal decisions by the High Representative.[296] Exempted in such decisions were only people whose removals had been connected to ICTY cooperation.

These decisions were part of a new understanding, which saw removals as an extraordinary measure in the true sense of the word. Within a country that had started European integration negotiations and had thus been attested a sufficient degree of democratic functionality, the circumstances naturally imposed strict limits on the legitimacy of such intervention. As explained in the preamble of the April decision, Schwarz-Schilling understood those limits as follows:

> Mindful, however, that the sanction of removal imposed against public officials pursuant to the powers vested in the High Representative constitutes an extraordinary measure interfering with certain rights of the persons concerned, and that, given its comprehensive nature, such a sanction can only be justified if: (1) deemed a provisional remedy, deployed at a period and for a period during which it advances the legitimate aims specified in the GFAP and the Conclusions; and (2) issued sparingly and judiciously, following due consideration of all relevant facts and factors.[297]

These two conditions for removals significantly restricted the ways in which this instrument could function. They were based on Schwarz-Schilling's conviction that the international community's representative has to lead by example in terms of rule of law. And so he declared that, if people had been removed from office due to criminal charges, their cases were to be processed through the local judicial system; if the decision had been taken on other grounds, Schwarz-Schilling demanded to be informed on the precise reasons and to be presented the respective evidence. Lacking any compelling proofs, the High Representative decided to lift the respective bans: 'The so-called evidence I was presented consisted of big

---

[295]   Office of the High Representative, "Decision Further Limiting the Scope of the Ban from Public Office in the Removal Decisions Issued by the High Representative," 4 April 2006, http://www.ohr.int/decisions/removalssdec/default.asp?content_id=36919. Accessed 29 November 2013.

[296]   Office of the High Representative, "Decision Lifting the Ban from Office within Political Parties in the Removal Decisions Issued by the High Representative," 7 June 2006, http://www.ohr.int/decisions/removalssdec/default.asp?content_id=37615. Accessed 29 November 2013.

[297]   Office of the High Representative, "Decision Further Limiting the Scope of the Ban from Public Office."

words, involving intelligence gathered by clandestine agencies, mostly located in England and the United States; but the OHR was never actually provided with the respective documents, which is why I said: if we do not have the evidence [for their alleged activities], there is no ground not to pardon [these people].'[298] Following this logic, Schwarz-Schilling pardoned 15 people that were targeted by HR decision, in addition to substantially limiting the applicability of previous decisions. (Such pardons could not be enacted retroactively, for this would have made the OHR legally liable for any potential damage that they had caused.)

Schwarz-Schilling's general approach with regards to the Bonn powers consisted in a return to what 'everybody had always stated but what nobody had actually done', as he says, i.e. ownership. In his inaugural speech to the Bosnian parliament, which he held in May 2006, i.e. 100 days after his mandate started, he declared:

> I made it clear on day one when I addressed the citizens of Bosnia and Herzegovina that I have come to assist, advise and advocate. I have kept that promise. I will not take decisions for those who do not have the courage to take them—this is a democracy, and Parliament must make up its own mind; I will not intervene every time the authorities fail to take up their responsibilities; In short, I will not do the jobs that the institutions and elected leaders of this country must do.[299]

Behind his remarks stood a clear political strategy:

> I said to the local politicians: 'Ownership is the rule! You are the ones [to decide] and I will only intervene if there is a danger for the people, or if some issue becomes so big that I deem it necessary to prevent further harm. But [I will] always [intervene] in a way, which allows you to correct my decisions if you deem them wrong.' As you see, I thought of such intervention always as some sort of educational process. And such a process was badly needed in my opinion. But the international community was unable to understand what that meant.[300]

The contrast to Ashdown's 'either you do it or I will' approach could not be stronger. Rather than imposing concrete political decisions, Schwarz-Schilling's most invasive decisions mainly targeted structural issues that hindered progress. It was rare that he directly intervened in the political process. Disregarding some decisions of minor importance, he did so only once and in a rather clever way. Eight months after the 2006 elections (see below), there was still no government in the *Hercegovačko-Neretvanski* Canton (Mostar), which Schwarz-Schilling deemed irresponsible. Consistent with his educative approach, he issued a decision 'suspending all disbursement of budgetary itemisations for party funding to the HDZ BiH, SDA, HDZ 1990–HZ and SBiH from the budget of Bosnia and Herzegovina, the budget of the Federation of Bosnia and Herzegovina and the

---

[298]   Schwarz-Schilling, Personal Interview.

[299]   Christian Schwarz-Schilling, *Speech by the High Representative, Christian Schwarz-Schilling, to the BiH Parliament* (Sarajevo: Office of the High Representative, 05 2006), http://www.ohr.int/ohr-dept/presso/presssp/default.asp?content_id=37224.

[300]   Schwarz-Schilling, Personal Interview.

budget of the Herzegovina-Neretva Canton and reducing party funding to the HDZ BiH, SDA, HDZ 1990–HZ and SBiH from the budget of the Herzegovina-Neretva Canton'. The decision suspended the funding of the main stakeholders with immediate effect, but also reduced it by forty per cent for the major parties and twenty per cent for the smaller ones (SBiH, HDZ1990) for the rest of the year as some sort of punishment for political inactivity. Additionally, the decision contained a provision that party funding would be further reduced by twenty per cent if a new government were not confirmed within a ten-day period.[301]

While Ashdown had understood the Bonn powers as a means of actual governing, Schwarz-Schilling saw them as a way to induce local cooperation. In this respect, the existence of the instrument and the fact that impositions could be threatened meant more than its actual usage, which always equalled a strategic failure. As such, the Bonn powers were an integral part of Schwarz-Schilling's strategy as well. Like the OHR, they could not be suspended, even though the HR did not use them very often. But for Schwarz-Schilling, it made 'a big difference whether the OHR has the powers to intervene but refrains from doing so, or whether he is deprived of such possibilities'.[302] Only the former structure would prevent locals from not taking the High Representative and the international community seriously, which also ensured that they took their responsibilities for Euro-Atlantic integration seriously. Unlike previously, when the Bonn power decisions had presented the Bosnians with more or less definitive solutions to be implemented, Schwarz-Schilling allowed for substantial local discussion before making many of his decisions: 'I believe deeply in democracy with a separation of powers. But if you do not respect these structures and consistently act against them, you cannot have a pedagogic effect in the sense that [the local politicians] begin to act within this framework.'[303] Consequently, Schwarz-Schilling only intervened when he detected immanent danger. This was the case when, in his last week in office, he feared for the future of the Srebrenica genocide memorial in Potočari if it were to remain under RS authority. Against the advice of many in the OHR office, he thus imposed a respective law on central state level.[304]

---

[301]   Office of the High Representative, "Decision Suspending All Disbursement of Budgetary Itemisations for Party Funding to the HDZ BiH, the SDA, the HDZ 1990—HZ and the SBiH from the Budget of the Bosnia and Herzegovina, the Budget of the Federation of Bosnia and Herzegovina and the Budget of the Herzegovina-Neretva Canton and Reducing Party Funding to the HDZ BiH, the SDA, the HDZ 1990—HZ and the SBiH from the Budget of the Herzegovina-Neretva Canton," 29 May 2007, http://www.ohr.int/decisions/mo-hncantdec/default.asp?content_id=39853. Accessed 29 November 2013.

[302]   Schwarz-Schilling, Personal Interview.

[303]   Ibid.

[304]   Office of the High Representative, "Decision Enacting the Law on the Center for the Srebrenica-Potocari Memorial and Cemetery for the Victims of the 1995 Genocide," 25 June 2007, http://www.ohr.int/decisions/plipdec/default.asp?content_id=40028. Accessed 29 November 2013.

Schwarz-Schilling's short mandate was characterised by two issues that shall be discussed in the next two sections. The first issue concerns the already mentioned discussion with regards to the closure of the OHR, while the second one is aimed at the situation on the ground before and after the 2006 general elections. Interestingly enough, those two issues were only interconnected through Schwarz-Schilling's insistence on their interdependence, not by the design of international policy.

9.5.2   The closure of the OHR

The decision to end the rule of the OHR in Bosnia was one of the few international agreements at a time when the international community and especially the transatlantic relationships had been deeply harmed by the aftermath of the Iraq war controversy. The Russians who began playing a more important role in the Balkans, supported closure, as did the French, Germans, Brits, and the Americans.[305] The latter had a particular interest in wrapping up the Bosnian project, for it would have provided the George W. Bush administration with an opportunity to portray Bosnia as a success story of international intervention. Ashdown's successes convinced the international community that the situation in Bosnia was indeed improving, which made the closure of the OHR a logical outcome. Not realising that those successes had little foundation within the local political system but were mostly based on Bonn-power impositions, the Canadian, Japanese, and some German officials even argued for some form of voluntary suspension of the Bonn powers after Schwarz-Schilling assumed office.[306]

On his first formal meeting with the Steering Board of the Peace Implementation Council in Vienna in March 2006, Christian Schwarz-Schilling expressed his commitment to closing the OHR:

> The High Representative said his office will continue the process of transferring responsibilities to the BiH Authorities in order to prepare for the transition to an Office of the EU Special Representative next year, taking into account progress towards Euro-Atlantic integration. In this respect, he said that the OHR will no longer take on new commitments and will focus on meeting existing tasks. He highlighted the need to address a range of issues to prepare for transition allowing OHR to be phased out in an orderly manner. He explained that he was considering the first or second quarter of 2007 as a possible timeframe for transition to occur.[307]

---

[305]   When I use such categorisations, I always refer to the political leaderships, not the peoples within those countries.

[306]   Schwarz-Schilling, "Europa und Deutschland müssen sich ihrer Verantwortung stellen," 260.

[307]   Peace Implementation Council, *Communique by the PIC Steering Board* (Vienna: Office of the High Representative, 15 March 2006), http://www.ohr.int/pic/default.asp?content_id=36760. Accessed 29 November 2013.

Schwarz-Schilling thus outlined a timeframe, which slightly differed from the one of the internationals. The latter would have preferred a closure already by the end of 2006. However, even when he was still only a HR candidate, Schwarz-Schilling had made his commitment on closure dependent on the validity of the international community's situation assessment: 'I said: if it is true that the preconditions [for closing the OHR] were fulfilled, I would be more than happy to call it a day and extinguish the lights'.[308] But he soon realised that the international assessment was inaccurate. The police reform, which had been declared some sort of precondition for both the SAA and the end of the OHR, existed only 'on paper'.[309] There was no agreement within the local political elite. Especially the Serb side resisted any attempts to establish a common police force, i.e. to delegate competencies to the central state. Moreover, in April, constitutional reform (see below), whose adaptation the Americans had assured Schwarz-Schilling to be a mere formality, failed in parliament due to severe opposition by Haris Silajdžić's SBiH and parts of the Croat HDZ. On top of this, Milorad Dodik, who had come back to the post of RS prime minister as part of a coalition change in May 2006, started threatening a secession referendum following similar proceedings in Montenegro.

In his inaugural speech before BiH's parliament, Schwarz-Schilling outlined a number of laws that needed to be implemented before the next elections, i.e. within 100 days. If such major political reform succeeded, Schwarz-Schilling told the representatives, Bosnia would be rewarded with the completion of the SAA negotiations by the end of the year, which would pave the way for European Integration and the closure of the OHR.[310] But the respective laws were not adopted, for the politicians had switched to campaign mode. Moreover, Schwarz-Schilling detected a genuine reliance on the OHR as part of a wider political strategy. While all the parties abstained from engaging in hard negotiations and compromises, some of them saw the High Representative as a means to push their own agendas. Schwarz-Schilling mentioned the example of the SDA that opposed a closure of the OHR because it deemed it a useful instrument to prevent any far-reaching agenda of the RS entity. Others, like Milorad Dodik or Zlatko Lagumdžija, for example, supported a closure of the HR with the argument that the local politicians were capable of taking full responsibility. 'But in reality', so Schwarz-Schilling says, 'they behaved in a way that made it irresponsible to leave them alone.'[311]

---

[308]   Schwarz-Schilling, Personal Interview.

[309]   Schwarz-Schilling, "Europa und Deutschland müssen sich ihrer Verantwortung stellen," 261.

[310]   Schwarz-Schilling, *Speech by the High Representative, Christian Schwarz-Schilling, to the BiH Parliament.*

[311]   Schwarz-Schilling, Personal Interview.

The passivity of the Bosnian parliament, the 'shock' of a non-existent police reform strategy, and the failure of constitutional reform, made Schwarz-Schilling realise the true state of Bosnia. The country was 'under no circumstances' able to function independently of the OHR structure: 'I thought it would have been absolutely irresponsible to let the things play out by themselves, which is why my opposition against OHR closure grew stronger and stronger.'[312]

Naturally, this realisation put the High Representative at odds with the international agenda. In October 2006, Schwarz-Schilling informed the Americans, the biggest supporters of a closure, that the deadline had to be postponed—something the US administration strongly rejected. The Europeans supported the American position, for due to the on-going situation in Kosovo, they needed not be occupied with Bosnia. Schwarz-Schilling prepared two plans on how to proceed: one involved the closure of the OHR as the Americans wished, the second some form of a transitional arrangement where the OHR would be closed, but certain aspects of the Bonn powers would remain with the EU Special Representative.[313] Since the EU Commission rejected this alternative plan because the Bonn powers were incompatible with the mandate of the EUSR, only the closure option remained. Schwarz-Schilling, who even threatened to resign if the international community insisted on immediate closure, realised that the only way to save the OHR was to convince the Americans to change their position. Through backchannels he contacted Richard Holbrooke and Madeline Albright, both of whom deemed a closure irresponsible. They subsequently started pressuring the US Democrats to fight for the maintenance of the OHR. The position of the Republican administration was thus no longer uncontested. So after they lost their majority in Congress in the mid-term 2006 elections, the Republicans reconfigured their strategy and came to an agreement with the Democrats not to push for closure. With presidential elections in 2008, President Bush's successor should have the possibility to make up his own strategy for Bosnia. In return, the Democrats would refrain from campaigning on the Republican's failed attempts at closing the OHR in the presidential election.[314] The other PIC members, who had already started questioning the official timetable before the Americans reversed their position, were surprised by such a development but nevertheless agreed to refrain from closing the OHR at the present time. However, even though everybody knew that the OHR had to close eventually, the international community lacked a coherent strategy on when and under what conditions this was to happen.

It was clearly a success of Schwarz-Schilling that a closure of OHR was not on the immediate international agenda anymore. But this success came at a price,

---

[312]   Ibid.

[313]   Schwarz-Schilling, "Europa und Deutschland müssen sich ihrer Verantwortung stellen," 268–9.

[314]   Ibid., 270.

for the Americans demanded his mandate not be renewed. He had proved to be stubborn and, perhaps more importantly, hard to control. Moreover, he had refused to use the Bonn powers in order to intervene in internal matters, which had slowed down the progress of Bosnia. The reassessment of the OHR strategy presented a welcome opportunity to get rid of him. Lacking substantial support from Berlin—something, which Schwarz-Schilling is still very angry about—his departure from office by the end of June 2007 was a done deal. But what really presented the ultimate humiliation was that his departure date was leaked to a Bosnian newspaper in January 2007, which made Schwarz-Schilling a lame duck for most of his term.[315]

9.5.3   The April package and the 2006 elections

The first serious attempt to reform the constitution, the so-called April package, constitutes the prelude to the 2006 general elections. The reform process had been launched on the occasion of Dayton's tenth anniversary. The US Institute of Peace and the former Deputy High Representative Donald Hayes led the negotiations. The entire reform effort was thus an American attempt to bring Bosnia to order before closing down the OHR. The Europeans supported the goals but were only partially involved in the negotiations. The goal was to create an efficient state with legislative structures capable of adopting laws rather quickly; an efficient executive; a mechanism to prevent political deadlocks; to introduce local self-government following the European principle; and, in general, to reform those parts of the current constitution that were at odds with the European Convention on Human Rights.[316] Open to discussion was thus not only the state structure itself, but all the bodies constituting it: both houses of parliament, the council of ministers, the presidency, etc.

When the negotiations began, the eight biggest parties in Bosnia—SDA, HDZ BiH, SDS, HNZ, PDP, SBiH, SNSD, SDP—participated. They basically discussed two antagonistic models for the future of the state. The first one, which we may call the entity model, presupposed that the central state's legitimacy stems from the entities and thus concluded that the entities needed to be represented in central state institutions. Based on this understanding, the parties from the RS fought for keeping the entity voting mechanism in the House of Representatives. The HDZ, whose president Dragan Čović saw the dangers of such a model for the Croats that did not possess an entity on their own, demanded a quota of 25% Croat representatives in the lower house of parliament.[317] Contrary to this position stood the model of a 'civic' state whose central institutions are based

---

[315]   Martens, "Schwarz-Schillings nicht ganz freiwilliger Abschied."
[316]   *Nezavisne Novine*, 8 January 2006, 8.
[317]   *Nezavisne Novine*, 16 January 2006, 6.

on the will of the people rather than the one of the entities or ethnicities. Consequently, this side argued for the abolition of the entity voting and the general strengthening of the House of Representatives as the aggregated form of the people's will. The fact that a solution would necessarily take the form of a constitutional reform package, as opposed to singular reform acts, facilitated the negotiations because it allowed for compensations across different political fields.

The negotiations also presented the first real opportunity for Milorad Dodik to re-enter the political stage. Since the previous elections, he had been the vocal leader of the opposition in the RS. But by the end of January 2006, the SDS government had lost a vote of confidence in the RS National Assembly, which was initiated by the SNSD. Even though it would take Dodik until May to formally assume the position of RS prime minister, his candidacy enjoyed support by PDP, DNS, DSS, SDP BiH, NHI, SBiH, and SDA[318]—even though the latter two parties soon revoked their original support.[319] Even before the elections, Dodik rose to the ranks of political leaders in the RS, while the SDS of president Čavić opposed him. Dodik did however conclude that in order to differentiate himself from the SDS and Čavić's cooperative course with respect to the internationals, a nationalist agenda was key. The failure of the April package gave him all the cover he needed to start this line of argument.

The constitutional reform negotiations also presented the opportunity for another politician to re-enter the stage, from which he, like Dodik, had never really been absent. Haris Silajdžić, who became Dodik's main political rival in the next years, rightly detected one of the major flaws of the current system in the entity voting principle. If not circumvented by an OHR decision, this mechanism led to perpetual deadlocks. This is why the SBiH, still formally led by its president Safet Halilović, strongly opposed the retention of entity voting in the House of Representatives. The SBiH proposal for a new constitution, based on a truly civic orientation, foresaw the abolishment of the entities and the introduction of economic regions as the middle layer of a genuinely federal system. Those regions would send equal numbers of representatives to the central state parliament whose task would be to defend the interests of their region rather than their national group.[320] In fact, this proposal was not really new, for the SBiH had argued for it at least since the early 2000s. But within the discussions in this context, such demands had a new dimension. When it became clear that the entity model would prevail and that entity voting would remain, the SBiH left the negotiations and Silajdžić began his harsh rhetoric: 'Such an arrangement is an embargo on the democratic future of Bosnia', he proclaimed. 'It is also an embargo on truth regarding the past, for [it] presents the undeniable legitimisation of genocide and

---

318   *Nezavisne Novine,* 5 February 2006, 3.
319   *Nezavisne Novine,* 9 May 2006, 6.
320   *Oslobođenje,* 25 February 2006, 6.

ethnic cleansing.'[321] Along these lines of argument, Silajdžić continued to oppose not only the constitutional reform package on which the other parties finally settled, but also the current Bosnian constitution, which is also based on entities. The RS representatives rightly understood his words as an offence and an undisguised threat to their entity, while Silajdžić, rightly as well, regarded them as an expression of the truth in light of Bosnia's recent history.

In fact, the antagonistic battle between Dodik and Silajdžić that developed as part of the electoral campaign and lasted for the next years is based on two different interpretations of the post-war Bosnian state. Silajdžić, who had been one of the main fighters for Bosnia's survival in the 1990s, put the central state—and the Bosniak interest in this state—at the forefront of his ideology, whereas Dodik, even in his more moderate days as the international community's darling, stood firm in his fight for the RS. In light of Dodik's on-going quarrel with the SDS, Silajdžić's proposal to abandon the entities and his *de facto* de-legitimisation of the RS entity as a creation of genocide, presented the perfect opportunity for a populist battle between those two antagonistic figures. Silajdžić, whose motives may have been more principled than Dodik's, nevertheless employed the same tactic in the coming years. It is thus only partially accurate when Silajdžić accused the international community of inaccurately equating him, who 'had always defended Bosnia and Herzegovina against partitions'[322] with Dodik, who regarded the war in Bosnia as a civil war and attributed equal guilt for it to Milošević, Tuđman, and Izetbegović. The latter furthermore saw the DPA as the origin of Bosnia's statehood, since in 1992, 'Bosnia may have been recognised by some states, but it was not a state in the formal and judicial way'.[323] Such historically—and legally—questionable arguments soon transformed into secessionist claims for the RS entity and, ultimately, led to the legally and practically unsustainable notion of the RS being a state in the sense of the international law, which was discussed in the previous chapter. Naturally, Silajdžić and Dodik argued based on different ideologies. But when they simplified their positions for public consumption they consciously created the impression of an unbridgeable divide. Since political action, even when based on flawed perceptions, has real consequences, such simplified lines of arguments necessarily posed a threat to the entire state-building project.

That the April package ultimately failed was also due to resistance from some Croat members of parliament. They regarded any compromise of the ruling parties as illegitimate since it *de facto* bypassed the legislature. As one representative remarked, the HDZ club in parliament had already introduced a parliamentary initiative to reform the constitution in 2004, which the party leaders were

---

[321]   *Dnevni Avaz*, 28 February 2006, 4.
[322]   Silajdžić, Personal Interview.
[323]   *Oslobođenje*, 17 March 2006, 9.

about to 'put out of action'.[324] But Croat resistance was also based on the content of the negotiations. They especially opposed the entity voting, which in their views put the Croats on an unequal footing with respect to the other constituent peoples and allowed a continuation of deadlock. A possible transformation of the House of Peoples into a 'House of Entities' would be disadvantageous for the Croats, for 'it is clear who governs in the entities', as HDZ representative Martin Raguž put it, alluding to the assumed numerical majority of the Bosniaks in the Federation.[325] Given such reservations among the Croat delegates in parliament, Čović's signature on the finalised April package had to be taken with caution. As a direct result of these different views, some HDZ members abandoned their party to form the HDZ1990 under the leadership of Božo Ljubić.

The final version of the constitutional reform package consisted of four concrete amendments.[326] The first one essentially legalised the responsibility of the central state in the areas of defence and security as well as the State Court, which *de facto* had been present since the respective OHR impositions. The second reformed the parliament by increasing the number of representatives in both chambers, with the members of the House of Peoples being elected in the House of Representatives. The competencies of the House of Peoples would be reduced, for it would only be involved in the political process when the national interest of a group is at stake, an amendment to the constitution is discussed, or the president and vice-presidents of Bosnia are being elected. The instrument of entity voting remained as a mechanism. Amendment three foresaw a new structure for the presidency. It still would consist of three members from the three constituent peoples, but the chairman would be the president of Bosnia. The members were to be elected by parliament. Finally, the forth amendment was dedicated to the Council of Ministers and its competencies.

These four amendments presented a compromise that enjoyed far-reaching support among the now seven parties involved, even though not all of them regarded the changes as the final solution. Interestingly enough, there seems to have been some 'pride' in reaching the compromises equal to the one Petritsch experienced when the Mrakovica-Sarajevo Agreement was finalised. Dragan Čavić, apparently unaware of the inherent irony in uttering such a statement after the final five-hour meeting at the residence of the US ambassador, said that the biggest quality of the package was that 'this is an agreement among us in BiH, without any inference of the High Representative or the international community'. Zlatko Lagumdžija deemed the package 'far from what we wanted but a first step after

---

[324]   *Oslobođenje*, 8 March 2006, 7.
[325]   Ibid.
[326]   Marković, "Ustavne promjene u Bosni i Hercegovini," 99–101.

so many years', while Dodik expressed his content that 'after many painful meetings a final solution could be reached'.[327]

SBiH, SDU, and BOSS opposed the package since it included entity voting and strengthened the entities thus incorporating the risks of continued deadlocks.[328] The HDZ representatives, who had opposed Čović even before the final agreement had been reached, continued to criticise the April package as contrary to the interests of the Croats. Since the agreement still foresaw two entities and entity voting, Božo Ljubić concluded that the goal of creating an efficient and economic state had not been achieved. Furthermore, the proposed amendments harmed the position of the Croats within the state structure.[329] Interestingly enough, the Catholic Church in Bosnia supported this interpretation. Cardinal Vinko Puljić said that 'a constitution must ensure equality among the people and not legalise ethnic cleansing and confirm the results of wartime gains'.[330] The combined opposition of SBiH, five HDZ members and some additional representatives (one of which belonged to the SDA) prevented the adoption of the April package in the House of Representatives; with 16 votes against and 26 in favour,[331] the necessary qualified majority was not obtained.

Christian Schwarz-Schilling had not been directly involved in the negotiations of the April package, even though he had tried to secure agreement from the opposing parties once the package was finalised. Unlike Petritsch, who had resolved the lack of a qualified majority with imposing the solution, he was neither inclined to use the Bonn powers due his own philosophy nor was there international support for such action. In any case, it would have been legally challenging, to say the least, to impose constitutional changes on the state level. What he could do, however, was to address the parliament and remind the politicians of their duties with regards to the state (see above). But such action was doomed to fail as well, for the politicians were already engaged in the electoral campaign. 'It was understandable that this was not the time for consensus building in parliament', Schwarz-Schilling remembers. 'We experience the same pattern in our countries;

---

[327]   *Dnevni Avaz*, 19 March 2006, 2.
[328]   *Oslobođenje*, 21 March 2006, 4.
[329]   *Dnevni Avaz*, 13 April 2006, 3. The HDZ1990 also presented its own proposals on how to reform the constitution.
[330]   *Nezavisne Novine*, 30 March 2006, 4. What both Puljić and Silajdžić seem to have forgotten in this context is that the DPA itself confirmed wartime gains based on ethnic cleansing. Without an overwhelming majority distancing themselves from their wartime agenda, a reform of the DPA constitution is subject to the same constraints of political compromise that Dayton was. Expecting a complete abandonment of this basic principle belongs therefore more to the realm of wishful thinking than actually achievable political results.
[331]   *Dnevni Avaz*, 27 April 2006, 2.

it is thus not the case that the behaviour of Bosnian politicians was somehow bizarre in this respect.'[332]

The election campaign itself was characterised by a multitude of issues, some of which could be traced back to the April package. Let us start with the Croat electorate that, for the first time since 1996 (if we neglect Krešimir Zubak's NHI), had two HDZs to chose from—in other words: two genuinely Croat nationalist parties. In any case, the goal of both party presidents, Ljubić and Čović, was to assure a high turnout.[333] As reminiscent to the old days, Čović tried to portray the upcoming elections as a 'referendum': 'The Serbs want to confirm the reality of RS, while the Bosniaks long for the establishment of a civic state.' A first step in these efforts, according to Čović, were the attempts of Bosniak parties (into which he included the SDP) to 'attack the Croat political space' in their wish to assimilate and evacuate the Croats. As he continued: 'If we do not reject the possibility of Bosniaks electing the Croat member of BiH presidency, we will become a national minority.' In this respect, the rift among the Croats was understandably regrettable: 'We have to understand: what is going on is the final phase of mapping the Balkans. Decisions are made outside the country. Without a clear signal that the Croats are a political force in BiH, the process of creating a state will begin without us.'[334] These statements clearly testify to the constituency of the Croat political elite. Not only did it feel threatened by an internal rift that could potentially marginalise HDZ's political influence but it was also afraid of the realistic possibility that the new Croat member of presidency would not come from the HDZ. When you have an internal enemy that is nationalistic as well as a potential enemy from the multi-national front, the adoption of an even more nationalistic and overheated rhetoric is hardly surprising. We have analysed the respective consequences in the previous chapter, so that it is sufficient to restate the result: SDP candidate Željko Komšić won the seat as Croat member of the presidency with some 40 per cent of the votes. In parliament, HDZ and HDZ1990 combined secured the same amount of seats as the SDP did alone, namely five.

On the Serb side, Milorad Dodik found himself in a similar position as the HDZs. As former opposition leader turned prime minister, his main competition came from the SDS. Due to the moderate course of its president Dragan Čavić and a lustration campaign pursued by Paddy Ashdown, the SDS had become a partner of the international community. Since both the SDS and the SNSD had supported the April package, this issue could not serve as a distinguishing feature. Dodik therefore chose to out-nationalist the former nationalists. His major claim in this respect was the public contemplation of a possible secession of the RS in

---

[332]   Schwarz-Schilling, Personal Interview.
[333]   For Ljubić, see *Oslobođenje*, 20 May 2006, 7; for Čović, see *Dnevni Avaz*, 6 June 2006, 8.
[334]   *Dnevni Avaz*, 6 June 2006, 8.

the case that this entity's abolition was discussed. Some politicians, like Halid Genjac, realised that the best way to counter the respective referendum threats was to mobilise Bosniaks and Croats living in the RS to participate in the elections.[335] However, others chose a strategy of lesser wisdom. When Federation politicians publicly asked the High Representative to remove Dodik due to his clearly anti-Dayton statements undermining the state, it effectively made him look like a strong political figure fighting for some noble principle. One commentary published in *Nezavisne Novine* illustrates the effect such requests had on the Serb side quite well.

> If one carefully reads the newspapers these days, starting with the assumption of the famous 'right to a democratic referendum', one cannot but wonder: what was so bad [*anatemično*] in Dodik's statement that would make one seek his removal from the electoral list? He spoke of the theoretical possibility of a referendum if a discussion about the abolition of the Republika Srpska were opened. What is anti-Dayton about that? What kind of undermining of the state is that? The 'Dodik' case exemplifies how upside down things are in this country. His statement about a referendum as a possibility is met with the demand to have him removed—initiated by those who constantly try to scatter the constitutional foundation of the state!? *In this case, actually, Dodik is not important; it's about a principle.* If one man were punished for theorising about a referendum, what would happen to all those state builders who do not theorise but literally demand the abolition of the Dayton constitution?[336]

The demand to have him removed thus made Dodik more powerful than the mere threat of secession could ever have done. He became an example, a principle around which one must align for the greater good. He became the personification of the Serbs' quarrels with the Bosniaks and Croats but also with the international community. The latter was not essentially opposed to removing Dodik from his post. The American side especially urged Schwarz-Schilling to take such an action, but the High Representative, in line with his previously outlined philosophy, deemed it inconsistent to preach ownership and discuss the closure of the OHR and simultaneously intervene when someone threatens with secession at an electoral rally. He chose to warn Dodik, but to postpone any real action. In an interview with the Austrian newspaper *Der Standard* he said that 'if Dodik were to continue his polemic and pursue just one real measure towards organising a referendum, I will use the full extent of the Bonn powers'.[337] This statement established a clear line of action: if Dodik were to take any concrete steps towards realising his referendum threat, he would be removed; mere talk about it, however, would not result in any such action. Upon reading this, Dodik called Schwarz-Schilling to inquire whether he would be removed any time soon; when the High

---

[335]   *Dnevni Avaz*, 18 June 2006, 8.

[336]   *Nezavisne Novine*, 9 June 2006, 7. Emphasis added.

[337]   Schwarz-Schilling, "Europa und Deutschland müssen sich ihrer Verantwortung stellen," 264–266.

Representative refused to elaborate on his comments, Dodik supposedly felt threatened. Choosing not to test the fine line between talk and action, he completely abandoned the mention of a referendum for the remainder of the electoral campaign. He could do so since his general statements and views were already publicly known. If the story ended here we could deem Schwarz-Schilling's action a model for international intervention. He had used the threat of the Bonn powers to make Dodik stop his destructive course.

But as is always the case in these situations, election day is what really counts. So when the SNSD gained an absolute majority in the NARS (43 per cent of votes or 41 seats) and Nebojša Radmanović was elected as the Serb member of Bosnia's presidency with 53 per cent of the votes, Dodik was surer than ever in his political course of action. In the form of an absolute majority the people had legitimised his stance. So when he was formally re-elected as prime minister, he renewed his claim that there would be a referendum if the abolition of the RS remained on the table.[338] The NARS passed a respective resolution, which Schwarz-Schilling deemed as an action towards organising the referendum. Following an already outlined plan of action, the German sought support from the Steering Board to take action against Dodik. At first, the American and British members concurred. They invited Dodik to London to allegedly convince him to abandon his position. Schwarz-Schilling, however, doubts that such efforts were genuine, for 'Dodik suddenly said: "The OHR should try and remove me", so he must have received some form of support [in London].'[339] In a subsequent meeting of the Steering Board, the Russian members opposed any action against Dodik while the American ambassador asked for time to contact the State Department:

> So we waited until the following week. Then the American ambassador informed us that the US 'did not wish any measures against Dodik at this point'. The Brits and Americans had thus gotten cold feet. … They claimed that the situation had changed. The election had given Dodik clear support. But, even more importantly, they said that they could not afford a confrontation with Dodik due to developments in Kosovo. If one wanted to make progress there, one could not open a new front here.[340]

Schwarz-Schilling's counterargument that this position was inconsistent did not succeed in changing the American view. So one after the other, all the European countries opposed any action on this front and Dodik was safely installed. This episode exemplifies the dilemma of international action in the years following. First of all, since 9/11 and the invasions of Afghanistan and Iraq that followed, other issues dominated the international geopolitical agenda. Actions in Bosnia

---

338   *Nezavisne Novine*, 1 December 2006, 2.

339   Schwarz-Schilling, "Europa und Deutschland müssen sich ihrer Verantwortung stellen," 265.

340   Ibid.

were thus reduced to a minimum, with geopolitical considerations determining the course of action. Second, elections, as the cornerstone of any democratic system, were perceived as the litmus test of political stability and legitimacy. Consequently, international action against clear winners of elections ceased to be a possible opportunity to overcome political deadlocks. As a consequence of those two issues, Dodik came to the only conclusion he could have come to: as long as he wins elections, he would not be removed due to the international configurations that constrained the High Representative in this respect. Given that his electoral success was based on nationalistic stances *as well as the international community's reaction to his secessionist threat*, he continued not only to repeat the secessionist threats in the subsequent years, but actively sought to pick quarrels with the High Representative (see the renewed referendum threat in 2011 below, or the declaration that the RS is, in fact, a state that was discussed in chapter seven). His majority in the RS allowed him to run the smaller entity as he wished so that the effects of continued deadlock on central state level could be mitigated.

Haris Silajdžić also picked a fight with the internationals by openly opposing the April package. Even though the Council of Europe supported the abolition of entity voting in a resolution aimed at inducing a new round of negotiations after the elections,[341] Silajdžić's opposition remained the main issue on which the SDA attacked him. In a fight for dominance among the Bosniak electorate, SDA president Tihić, himself a candidate for the Bosniak seat in the BiH presidency, accused Silajdžić, his main opponent for the seat, of endangering the future of the state. Because of Silajdžić and his party, he argued, the conclusion of a Stabilisation and Association Agreement with the EU was in danger. And furthermore: 'According to Tihić, Silajdžić and the parties associated to him as part of the patriotic block are not patriots, for they are not fighting for the cause of the country but for personal and party interests instead.'[342] Since in a battle of patriots the nationalist is always king, Silajdžić continued attacking the SDA for selling out the country with its agreement to the April package and renewed his attacks on the RS as a creation based on ethnic cleansing. He won the Bosniak seat in the presidency with around 60 per cent of the votes, while Tihić gained less then 30. With seven seats, the SBiH secured only one seat less in the House of Representatives than the SDA. This result could thus not do anything else than to encourage Silajdžić in his extreme positions. Given the same type of legitimisation that Dodik enjoyed, the international community was trapped in a seemingly unsolvable dilemma.

---

[341]   *Oslobođenje*, 30 June 2006, 4.
[342]   *Nezavisne Novine*, 28 May 2006, 8.

Be that as it may, the resolution of this situation was no longer Christian Schwarz-Schilling's concern. A lame duck for his entire term in 2007, he could do little to actually influence the political scene. His authority had been undermined not only through the premature announcement of his departure but also by the substantial lack of support and courtesy he received from the international community. On a personal level, the German government's inaction was most frustrating in this respect. But Schwarz-Schilling also genuinely felt sabotaged, for he tried to make the international community a coherent and transparent player in the country's political system. He wanted to abolish the usual zigzagging of international politics and to take the internationally proclaimed norms of local ownership seriously. After the failure of the April package, for example, Schwarz-Schilling started secret discussions with all political leaders regarding a new constitutional reform package. Assisted by an expert body, he tried to avoid the mistakes that the American negotiators had previously made and sought to put a new reform proposal on better foundations. After holding many bilateral discussions, Schwarz-Schilling organised common meetings with all party representatives. In his recollection, a deal seemed possible, provided that the entire process was duly managed. But after his departure became known, the locals no longer took him seriously and the project failed.[343] Had he had international support for his actions, many things might have turned out differently. Or, in his words: 'Stupid as it may be to say this now: the country of Bosnia and Herzegovina would have become a different one if I had had three more years.'[344]

9.6   Miroslav Lajčák (2007-2009)

Like Petritsch and Westendorp, Miroslav Lajčák, the current Slovak Foreign Minister, had a diplomatic career that preceded his appointment as High Representative. Between 1999 and 2001 he had been special assistant to Foreign Minister Eduard Kukan while the latter was the UN's Special Envoy for the Balkans. He subsequently served four years as Slovakia's ambassador in Belgrade until, in 2006, he became Javier Solana's special envoy for the Montenegrin independence and the respective referendum. He was thus, as he explains, 'quite well acquainted with the region'.[345] But unlike Petritsch, Lajčák had no academic background specific to the region. As a graduate in law, international relations, and security studies, he had joined the (Czecho-)Slovak foreign service in 1988 and served as ambassador in Moscow and Japan as well as *chef de cabinet* in the Foreign Minis-

---

343   Schwarz-Schilling, "Europa und Deutschland müssen sich ihrer Verantwortung stellen"; Schwarz-Schilling, Personal Interview.

344   Schwarz-Schilling, Personal Interview.

345   Miroslav Lajčák, Personal Interview in Bratislava, 17 December 2012.

try. His experiences with the Balkans were thus all mostly based on practical con-stellations. But he nevertheless was fluent in the local language(s).

9.6.1   The doctrine of non-intervention

Miroslav Lajčák's approach towards the Bonn powers was guided by pragma-tism, not some idealised form of a stringent philosophy. We thus cannot analyse his views and actions without reference to the situation on the ground. When La-jčák assumed office, the political configurations were quite different from what Schwarz-Schilling had encountered. The failure of the April package had led to a profound stalemate; 'you could feel it everywhere', Lajčák recalls. 'Many of those who invested a lot of their political credibility felt betrayed.' Especially the Serbs used the failure as an excuse for their activities against the common state. 'They said: "We were participating *bona fide* in this effort but it was the last time that we were ready to give as much power to the state"'.[346] Of course, the Serbs' reluctance was, as we have seen, not purely based on some feeling of betrayal but rather the logical consequence of an electoral strategy that fuelled itself from re-sistance to the international community and the central state.

In addition to constitutional reform visibly hindering the state, police re-form, since Paddy Ashdown's times a pre-condition in the EU accession package, was still not agreed upon. Interestingly enough, Lajčák was told the same fairy tale as Schwarz-Schilling in this respect: 'When I had my consultations and my preparations, the overall feeling was [that] like ninety per cent of the reform was completed. But when I arrived and had my briefings by the OHR staff I realised that, in reality, nothing is agreed because the key principles of the reform were not agreed.' So once again, the situation presented itself rather differently than what the international community had hoped or believed. Interestingly enough, Lajčák, despite explicitly denying such interpretation, seems nevertheless to be-lieve that Schwarz-Schilling's reluctance to pursue a more interventionist policy allowed the re-emergence of Dodik and his extreme rhetoric:

> The problem was that the political atmosphere was changing because the Serbs, with the arrival of Milorad Dodik, were becoming more and more vocal—and there was no reaction from the OHR. But I do not want to follow the usual pattern of criticising Christian Schwarz-Schilling because the fact is that he had his views about Bosnia-Herzegovina and he made no secret of what he thought. He was really of the opinion that the country is ready to take responsibility into its own hands. The problem was that the approach of the international community looked very inconsistent because you had Paddy Ashdown's approach, which was very heavy, and then he was imme-diately replaced by Schwarz-Schilling, whose approach was extremely soft. There-fore he [i.e. Schwarz-Schilling] decided not to intervene and the Serbs had used it. They also used the failure of the April package and, by the time that I arrived, it was quite clear that the point of no return was crossed. That means that the international

---

[346]   Ibid.

community was no longer in a position to continue acting as during Paddy Ashdown's times—let alone the fact that, at the same time I was arriving, the EUFOR forces were limited from 7000 to 2000, so to a very symbolic presence.[347]

As we have seen, Schwarz-Schilling was not 'really of the opinion that the country is ready to take the responsibility into its own hands', as Lajčák seemed to think. In fact, his fight against the closure of the OHR is precisely the antithesis to any such interpretation. But it is true that he acted as if the local politicians were responsible enough, for he saw such action as educative and consistent with the continuous international talk of local ownership. Lajčák thus slightly misrepresents his predecessor's position. Similarly, while there is no doubt that the OHR's soft approach created a window of opportunity for Milorad Dodik, it is doubtful that Schwarz-Schilling's own philosophy was responsible for the international community's non-action in this particular area.

Be that as it may, the political climate was quite unfavourable when Lajčák assumed office. A Steering Board communiqué sums it up as follows:

> The current political situation in Bosnia and Herzegovina is of grave concern to the Steering Board. There has been a severe deterioration in the political atmosphere, as well as threats by some non-state actors to take security into their own hands. Responsibility lies with those political leaders who have blocked progress and undermined the political situation with their aggressive rhetoric. The International Community stands united: It will not tolerate any attempts to undermine the Dayton Peace Agreement and it will not remain passive in the face of provocative statements and acts.[348]

So while the international community diplomatically condemned any actions or threats against the Dayton system, there was little they could do with regards to general political reluctance. Of course, employing the Bonn powers was a way out of perpetual deadlock. For Lajčák, however, this was only the 'the ultimate instrument', one whose usage should be avoided for two reasons. The first was the existence of democratic structures in Bosnia: 'You have a democratic process, which is accepted by democratic Europe. You cannot just come and remove a politician because you do not like what he did or what he said. This politician does have democratic credibility.'[349] Elections had thus legitimised the local political elite and the internationals' task was to accept the decisions by the people, however unhappy they may be.

The second reason was the adaptation of the local politicians to the instrument itself. As Lajčák recalls, 'the politicians got used to the Bonn powers and they learnt how to live with it. Namely, whenever they wanted to agree, they al-

---

[347]   Ibid.

[348]   Peace Implementation Council, *Declaration by the Steering Board of the Peace Implementation Council* (Sarajevo: Office of the High Representative, June 19, 2007), http://www.ohr.int/pic/default.asp?content_id=39997. Accessed 16 December 2013.

[349]   Lajčák, Personal Interview in Bratislava (SK).

ways agreed. Whenever they had to deal with difficult situations, they asked the High Representative to intervene so as to accept the responsibility for negative consequences. That was also quite clear. There were moments when they would never allow the High Representative to intervene and there were opposite [situations].' There is hardly a better sentiment to emphasise the deep rootedness of the OHR within Bosnia's political system and its role within the local politicians' strategies. Depending on the issue at hand, they could either choose to be cooperative and compromise, or they could take their chances and provoke a decision by the High Representative. This is quite a different kind of dependency than we have witnessed before. When Petritsch first detected this condition, it testified to the general impossibility of local compromise. In Lajčák's times, it became the expression of strategic thinking rather than mere incapability. So when Lajčák says that the 'political culture of dependency is a reality, particularly with the Bosniaks, while the Serbs were on the opposite side' he does not mean that Serbs were more prone to particular action or compromise. Rather, he refers to the fact that the Bosniaks' positions were more in line with the course of action pursued by the international community; since they could be pretty sure that an eventual OHR imposition would result in a solution to which they could agree in principle, they had no need to compromise with the others for anything less. Similarly, the Serbs were only eager to compromise on those issues where they felt an OHR decision would be less beneficial for them. There was thus no inherent, systemic need for cooperation. The problem with this reasoning, of course, is that it only works if the OHR is actually prone to intervene. If no OHR decision on an issue is expected, the Serb side, for example, has no need to seek compromise on those issues that it does not want to change.

In addition to democratic legitimacy preventing the removal of uncooperative politicians, the international constellation limited the scope of intervention by the OHR as well (see also below). Lajčák was thus forced to introduce new guidelines for the usage of the Bonn powers. He did so in a negative manner:

> They will not be used to impose political solutions, to impose laws, to push the country into certain directions. But they would rather be used to protect institutions of state that have been established since Dayton, the internal integrity of the state, and reforms that were implemented since Dayton. So, I was proposing that we keep the Bonn powers but as a clear instrument to prevent the already achieved results from being dismantled.[350]

While Lajčák intervened frequently in the area of ICTY cooperation—for example by issuing an order seizing travel documents of many persons connected to war crimes[351]—he was thus rather cautious in using this instrument in the area of

---

[350] Ibid.

[351] Office of the High Representative, "Order Seizing Travel Documents of Persons Who Obstruct or Threaten to Obstruct the Peace Implementation Process," 10 July

politics. He discussed any action within the OHR in order to analyse the purpose and process of how an imposition would help; sought consultations with the key international players and, more informally, with local politicians. Only after such a process was a Bonn power decision an option—and more often than not, the process ended with the conclusion that there was either no support for imposing a solution or that an imposition would not have the expected result. So, even though Lajčák criticised Schwarz-Schilling earlier for allowing the emergence of a radical Serb position, he unknowingly arrived at the same doctrine of non-intervention into political manners. But unlike Schwarz-Schilling, his reluctance was not so much based on a philosophical approach, as it was the result of a sin-gular event in October 2007.

9.6.2   The showdown of 2007

Frustrated with the ultimate failure of police reform negotiations, Miroslav La-jčák decided on 19 October 2007 to issue a decision 'on changes and amendments to the law on the Council of Ministers'[352] and to furthermore alter the procedures concerning decision making in parliament. These changes were designed to pre-vent obstruction by non-participation as well as making it more difficult to ob-struct the work of these bodies in general.[353] While the Bosniaks supported such actions, the Serb side opposed them in surprisingly strong terms. Milorad Dodik called the decision 'absolutely unacceptable': 'I believe that Mr Lajčák made a huge mistake. He made a decision that was not needed in order to mark strength. He created completely new relations in Bosnia; [his action] decreased our trust in BiH and renewed our view about the way in which we need to talk to the interna-tional community and the others in BiH.' Dodik deemed the decision the confir-mation of an 'arrogance that seeks to change the BiH constitution and that neither recognised any of our positions nor accepts that the RS is a part of BiH.'[354] Deeming Lajčák's action incompatible with his powers according to the Dayton Agreement, Dodik called upon the masses to protest it peacefully.[355] He further-more threatened to resign and to withdraw all of his party's representatives from the common institutions,[356] which would effectively stymie the entire state. Other

---

[illegible] 2007,   http://www.ohr.int/decisions/war-crimes-decs/default.asp?content_id=41138. Accessed 16 December 2013.

[352] Office of the High Representative, "Decision Enacting the Law on Changes and Amendments to the Law on the Council of Ministers of Bosnia and Herzegovina," 19 October 2007, http://www.ohr.int/decisions/statemattersdec/default.asp?content_ id=40687. Accessed 16 December 2013.

[353] Lajčák, Personal Interview.

[354] *Dnevni Avaz*, 20 October 2007, 2.

[355] *Dnevni Avaz*, 21 October 2007, 4.

[356] *Dnevni Avaz*, 23 October 2007, 2.

parties from the RS, like the PDP, decided to follow Dodik's lead in this matter[357] and accused Lajčák of favouritism to certain groups while completely ignoring the Serb positions.[358] Support came also from several non-governmental groups, like the union of train employees in RS that, in an 'act of civil disobedience', as they claimed, stopped all trains until Lajčák withdrew his decision.[359] Union members, students, and retirees took to the streets all over RS territory to protest the decision.[360] In total, protests were registered in 63 RS municipalities, with some 5000 people and all RS political parties protesting in Banja Luka.[361] On a political level, the NARS adopted a resolution calling Lajčák's decision incompatible with Dayton. If the decision were not changed 'in due time', the RS parliament would call upon the Constitutional Court to decide the constitutionality of Lajčák's actions.[362] Nikola Špirić, the SNSD Chairman of the BiH Council of Ministers, even resigned his post.[363]

Such public resistance took the OHR, the international community, and Miroslav Lajčák in particular by surprise: 'I think it was a professional mistake of the OHR apparatus that they did not anticipate the Serb reaction in October 2007. … They totally miscalculated the reaction by the Serbs—as well as the reaction by most of the European members of the Steering Board.'[364] While the Steering Board initially supported Lajčák's imposition, the strong reaction from the RS made them re-examine their position. A familiar constellation emerged. The Russian members opposed actions against the Serbs, while the British and American members supported them; the other Europeans generally regarded the Bonn powers with suspicion. The strong reaction by the Bosnian Serbs united those three groups and made them abandon their original position. Despite numerous public statements in support of his action,[365] they asked Lajčák not to implement the decision: 'And I had to find a way out of this even though it was not my individual decision.'[366] But there was no obvious way out because Lajčák could not allow the legitimacy of the Bonn powers to be directly questioned, while the people in the RS would hardly have understood a complete reversal of their government's position. Luckily, the RS authorities did not break up all contacts with the OHR, as they had done on previous occasions. Quite the contrary, by the end of Octo-

---

[357]   *Nezavisne Novine*, 22 October 2007, 3.
[358]   *Nezavisne Novine*, 24 October 2007, 2.
[359]   *Oslobođenje*, 23 October 2007, 3.
[360]   *Nezavisne Novine*, 24 October 2007, 3.
[361]   *Dnevni Avaz*, 30 October 2007, 2.
[362]   *Nezavisne Novine*, 31 October 2007, 3.
[363]   *Dnevni Avaz*, 2 November 2007, 2.
[364]   Lajčák, Personal Interview.
[365]   Cf., for example, *Dnevni Avaz*, 23 October 2007, 2; *Nezavisne Novine*, 26 October 2007, 2; *Dnevni Avaz*, 17 November 2007, 2.
[366]   Lajčák, Personal Interview.

ber, Dodik and Ivanić participated at a meeting in Mostar with the HR and the leaders of HDZ BiH, HDZ 1990, SBiH, and SDA, i.e. the governing coalition. They even signed a declaration obliging them to hold regular meetings in order to find a solution to police reform.[367] One month later, they even had a concrete plan of action and basically agreed to the formation of a police body at the central state level.[368]

Meanwhile, presumably in order to buy time, the OHR engaged in a formal debate with legal experts from RS that presented their views on the legality of Lajčák's imposition. While there can be no doubt that the OHR would never have admitted any wrongdoing in this area, this opened up the political space for other ways out of the acute crisis. The 'way out', as Lajčák called it, was to be European integration. EU commissioner Olli Rehn agreed that, if a compromise can be found by which the RS leadership would accept Lajčák's imposition, the EU was ready to initial the Stabilisation and Association Agreement (SAA). Dodik agreed to this trade-off after a meeting in Banja Luka,[369] and the BiH parliament adopted a change of its rules of procedure reflecting Lajčák's proposals.[370] Four days later, on 4 December 2007, the SAA was initialled. (The SAA itself was signed in June 2008.) Lajčák had thus managed to turn the situation around, 'from deepest crisis into a moment of glory',[371] as he says.

But in reality, the solution was anything but glorious—and Lajčák understood it very well. The Bosnian Serbs had demonstrated their strength and willingness not to play by the rules any more. Despite disagreement and frustration, Bonn power impositions had always been respected previously, but no longer. What made matters worse was the realisation that the international community had no way to make the locals accept the decisions if they simply disobeyed and mobilised their electorates in protest. The same must have been true for the local leaders who suddenly realised that they could survive the toughest confrontation with the international community—and even get something out of it. While the Bonn powers had always been the stick to different forms of the carrot, this quality was now completely lost. As Miroslav Lajčák explains:

> Many people did not want to understand it [at that time] and they still do not want to understand it, but that was the moment when you realised that it was actually the European perspective that is more powerful than the Bonn powers…. And it was very clear from that moment that you cannot be using Bonn powers to change the political life, because the Serbs would say 'no'—and you would have no authority to impose,

---

[367] *Nezavisne Novine*, 29 October 2007, 3.

[368] *Dnevni Avaz*, 23 November 2007, 3.

[369] *Dnevni Avaz*, 30 November 2007, 3.

[370] *Nezavisne Novine*, 1 December 2007, 3.

[371] Lajčák, Personal Interview.

> to enforce your decision. Therefore I said: formally you keep supporting the Bonn powers, but deep down you understand that you are a paper tiger.[372]

So the moment of glory was in fact the moment of clearest defeat: the moment when the Bonn powers died. As far as Lajčák was concerned, 'they [did] not really exist' anymore. While the Serbs had assured that they would not oppose Bonn power decisions in the area of ICTY cooperation, any other use was out of question. The only incentive to induce cooperation thus remained the European perspective on which the OHR campaigned:

> As a result of this autumn 2007, I started very actively promoting the European idea. We created this whole activity called 'reci.ba', the website. I was talking directly to citizens through the media stream, conferences, and visits to many cities across the country. And for six months we kept ourselves very busy with this and talking to people and mapping the atmosphere and promoting European agenda. And it was much more satisfactory for me than to think about how to use the Bonn powers knowing that it will not work.[373]

Apart from such activities to promote the European idea, Lajčák initialled regular gatherings between representatives of the leading six parties—the governing coalition—and the HR. These 6+1 meetings had the purpose of establishing personal ties between the different leaders thus inducing cooperation in the long run. Lajčák sees those meetings as his 'biggest achievement or something I am most proud of' since the leaders met and started 'building a normal, civilised relationship'. However, 'unfortunately' such successes were 'later destroyed because some people got too scared that this might be working'. So even regular meetings (that in one way or another continue to this day) were not able to solve the basic dilemma of the Bosnian system: 'On the human, personal level, the relationship between the politicians was good. They were just playing their role; and the role was to treat the others as enemies, which was the consequence of the political system in Bosnia-Herzegovina.'[374]

The people embodying these dilemmas were Milorad Dodik and Haris Silajdžić who continued their non-cooperation and extreme rhetoric. In a communiqué in November 2008, the Steering Board expressed 'its deep concern about the frequent challenges to the constitutional order of BiH and, in particular, to the sovereignty and territorial integrity of BiH or the existence of the Republika Srpska as one of the two entities under the Constitution of BiH'.[375] As Lajčák confirms, the first accusation was directed against Dodik and the second against

---

[372]   Ibid.
[373]   Ibid.
[374]   Ibid.
[375]   Peace Implementation Council, *Communiqué of the Steering Board of the Peace Implementation Council* (Sarajevo: Office of the High Representative, 20 November 2008), http://www.ohr.int/pic/default.asp?content_id=42667. Accessed 16 December 2013.

Silajdžić. The Slovak was convinced that those two people 'respected each other' but 'represented opposite concepts' of the state's future, i.e. 'the fight for a stronger state versus the fight against the state and for stronger entities'.[376] As the events with the police reform declaration and the action plan demonstrated, those two figures were not principally opposed to cooperation. Nevertheless, as far as their public standing was concerned, they probably needed the confrontation with each other to grow stronger.

9.6.3 International divisions and the 5+2 agenda

Miroslav Lajčák had decided early on not to react to every secessionist or nationalist statement made by Dodik (or, presumably, any comment directed against the RS by Silajdžić, even though he does not mention him specifically). Here again, he was unconsciously following the same practice as Schwarz-Schilling. But apart from his conviction that 'we are not here to react or issue a statement; we are here to shape the political life in this country and to set a political agenda', there was another issue that hindered him from taking a firm stand against the Bosnian Serbs. The international constellation in 2007 had changed, so that the Steering Board was quite divided. Naturally, this did not make Lajčák's task much easier:

> The Turks were strongly supporting the Bosniaks. And there were moments when I informed the Steering Board about my decisions and the Turkish ambassador informed me: 'Well, that was not enough', [i.e. when I did] something with regards to the Serbs. So, the Turkish ambassador said: 'But this was not enough, you should have gone further'. And the Russian ambassador said: 'No, you went too far.' I said: 'Guys, you are not serious! How do you want me to operate with this division?' This division of the international community has been for years a big problem and one of the reasons why the international community was not able to deal with the problem of Bosnia-Herzegovina.[377]

So, in addition to the general fecklessness of the Bonn powers after the events of October 2007, it was the international constellation that prevented Lajčák from taking any serious action. That the Russians sided with the Bosnian Serbs was in no way surprising due to well-known historical constellations. Rather more interesting was the fact that the 'Western' partners cared about Russia's position. The reason is well known and did not significantly change since the times of Christian Schwarz-Schilling: Kosovo. Russia had prevented the Ahtisaari plan from being discussed in the UN Security Council, which, according to Lajčák, presented 'the very first time after the whole period of the '90s that Russia said no'. Its international partners had thus to take the Russian diplomats seriously again, for the issues of Kosovo and Bosnia were interconnected precisely through the Serb com-

---

[376] Lajčák, Personal Interview.
[377] Ibid.

ponent. But while the internationals had more than ten years to accommodate themselves to the RS, the Kosovo situation was acute due to the prospect of independence. So, when the international community, especially the Steering Board ambassadors, silenced Miroslav Lajčák with respect to the Bosnian Serbs, they did so for the same reason with which the Americans and Brits had prevented Schwarz-Schilling from taking action against Dodik after the 2006 election:

> The problem I discovered when I arrived in Bosnia-Herzegovina: there was very little interest in Bosnia-Herzegovina in [the] countries of the Steering Board. When I was visiting the capitals and I was trying to talk about Bosnia-Herzegovina, the reaction I received was, if I have to put it simply: 'We are too busy with Kosovo now. We have no time to deal with Bosnia-Herzegovina.' And secondly, when I was directing part of my attention to some activities done by the Serbs, they said: 'Ok, but we are fighting with the Serbs in Belgrade. We are fighting with Serbs in Kosovo. We cannot open a third front with the Serbs in Bosnia-Herzegovina.' This was the problem because there was very little attention. It was during my mandate that Kosovo acquired independence and of course everybody was really very much focused on this—and capacities in the Foreign Ministries, the Balkan capacities were really absorbed by Kosovo. ... It was a period when I clearly saw that Serbia lost Kosovo but won Republika Srpska by the fact that the Serbs were cleverly using this lack of attention.[378]

Lajčák describes his relationship with the Steering Board as 'good', even though he soon realised that the Steering Board ambassadors were more radical in some respects than their ministries at home. Such incongruence in political position is of course hard to quantify and probably explainable through the general lack of interest in the Bosnian situation in the higher echelons of the diplomatic service. Be that as it may, there was one issue where a united position from the international community was needed and it concerned the future of the OHR. That the OHR would eventually close and be replaced by some form of EU presence was clear since the times of Paddy Ashdown, or even before. Schwarz-Schilling had managed to prevent a premature closure, but his success was minimal as it only postponed the seemingly unavoidable for a year or two. Without a clear concept on the institution's future, the international community ran the risk of prolonging local dependence and raising doubts about the seriousness of the stated intentions. This is what Miroslav Lajčák wanted to avoid: 'I tried to show that [the intent to close the OHR] is credible; and [I] tried to identify the conditions for the closure of the OHR so as to motivate all factors to meet all those objectives and conditions.' Had the decision to close the OHR in 2006 largely been the result of geopolitical considerations (especially the Bush administration's that sought an intervention success story), Lajčák's approach in 2008 put the emphasis on the conditions in the country.

---

[378]   Ibid.

Already in April 2007, the OHR had elaborated a Working Plan containing 'a number of longstanding objectives that the PIC Steering Board considers to be essential for the creation of … a peaceful, viable state'. In February 2008, the Steering Board decided that 'the most critical' of those issues 'be considered objectives that need to be achieved by the BiH authorities prior to transition.'[379] With this list, the internationals had now a clear policy, a precise outline on the situation under which they could consider closing the OHR. Concretely, the list, which was adopted unanimously and is since known as the '5+2 agenda', contained the following five objectives that needed to be fulfilled prior to 'transition', as the Steering Board called it in its declaration:[380] (1) acceptable and sustainable resolution of the issue of apportionment of property between State and other levels of government;(2) acceptable and sustainable resolution of defence property; (3) completion of the Brčko final award; (4) fiscal sustainability (promoted through an agreement on a Permanent ITA Coefficient methodology and establishment of a National Fiscal Council); and, finally, (5) entrenchment of the rule of law (demonstrated through adoption of national War Crimes Strategy, passage of Law on Aliens and Asylum, and adoption of National Justice Sector Reform Strategy). Additionally, the declaration contained two conditions for OHR closure: (a) signing of the SAA, and (b) a positive assessment of the situation in BiH by the PIC SB based on full compliance with the Dayton Peace Agreement.

Since its establishment, the 5+2 agenda has served two purposes. On the one hand, its goal was to show the local politicians what kind of effort is needed in order to sustain the state of Bosnia and Herzegovina. In this respect, it was perceived as a genuinely European agenda, for it outlines the conditions and objectives to be fulfilled prior to entering membership negotiations. But on the other hand and much more importantly, the policy was conceived as an exit strategy for the international community. As I hope to have convincingly shown, the main goal of this agenda was not European integration but the establishment of a clear-cut concept regarding the closure of the OHR. All these conditions were already contained in the earlier OHR Working Plan; but now, their significance increased as the international community elevated them from objectives and goals to conditions *sine quibus non* of any further international strategy in the country. Needless to say, the agenda itself is highly asymmetrical, i.e. clearly advantageous to the international community. While fulfilment of some of the objectives and conditions—like, e.g. signing of the SAA—can be objectively established, some of the points remain largely open to interpretation and the internationals' assessment. As

---

379   Peace Implementation Council, *Declaration by the Steering Board of the Peace Implementation Council* (Sarajevo: Office of the High Representative, 27 February 2008), http://www.ohr.int/pic/default.asp?content_id=41352. Accessed 18 December 2013. The following points are quoted verbatim from the document.

380   Ibid

such, the 5+2 agenda served more to calm the international actors than to really guide the locals through the maze of transitional efforts.

After the events of October 2007 ended with the initialisation of SAA negotiations, the establishment of the 5+2 agenda in February 2008 underlined the perception of Bosnia's gradual integration into the European structures. Since Lajčák put much emphasis on 'the European issue' as part of his general post-2007 strategy, the local political elites primarily and rightfully understood the 5+2 agenda as a tool towards European integration, whereas they were largely uninterested in (or perhaps unaware of) the international reasons for adopting this approach. In fact, it is the great strength of the 5+2 agenda that it gives the locals clear guidelines while, implicitly at least, also naming the goal. However, such a policy of conditionality suffers from two rather large disadvantages. The first one is that it limits the scope of EU engagement in the country, for it effectively excluded any amendment of the conditions and objectives. Given that the local political system is rather slow and inefficient, the internationals must have known that fulfilment of 5+2 would take quite some time. Even though it is likely that new issues will arise during this period, their inclusion would once again raise doubts about the credibility of the international intent to close the OHR. This disadvantage can be countered by referring to the genuine fact that the 5+2 agenda is not *de facto* a European but an international agenda. As such, it is actually not aimed at EU integration, but towards creating a sustainable and stable state. Of course, such an approach is highly dubious; one cannot motivate an actor with a specific prize to perform certain actions, then change the rules in the middle of the game and tell him, in the end, that the prize with which one lured him into playing was actually never there. Rather than expressing partnership and credibility, such a course of action reminds one of thimblerig.

But while it is not unthinkable that this first disadvantage can be overcome through certain mechanisms and diplomatic channels (as, in fact, it was with the *Sejdić and Finci* verdict, which imposed itself by some form of higher authority), this cannot be said for the second negative aspect: using the European agenda as the carrot for implementing certain policies is suitable only if EU membership or partnership is a goal of the locals as well. Thus, only with a true commitment on their part can the 5+2 agenda deliver what it implicitly promises. If, however, one were to doubt such a commitment, any effect of this kind of international policy disappears (apart from laying to rest the discussions about OHR closure). Admittedly, such considerations would have been anachronistic in 2008, for the EU was the only prospect around which the political elites could unite. After all, the crisis following October 2007 had been resolved by promising advancement in the area of EU integration. In Lajčák's view, it is anything but a disadvantage that the 5+2 policy relies on credible commitment by the local political elites: 'European policy is always built on the interest of partners to join the European Union, which means to meet the conditions and criteria for joining the European Union. There is no other way.' But as is so often the case, this simple statement has a different connotation within the Bosnian context:

> I was confronted many times in Bosnia-Herzegovina with [the] people's wish: 'you should be tougher with us, you should impose sanctions, etc.' Well, my answer was: no one has ever joined the European Union as a result of sanctions. We cannot force you because [the only] punishment you can get from the European Union is that you are deprived of your European perspective, which you do not understand now. You do not see this as a punishment, but it is a punishment. [The] EU is not pushing candidates into membership against their will. We believed, and I still believe, that the only realistic way forward for Bosnia-Herzegovina is to get seriously into the European Union integration process. But the fact is that the citizens wish it instinctively, but [the] political leaders do not really understand and they are not really interested because it means more accountability, more transparency, more openness. That is not how the political system in Bosnia-Herzegovina operates.[381]

The political system in Bosnia indeed operates on a different level. Because the people perceive EU integration as beneficial, they support policies that would bring their country closer to the glorious club. But the political elites have different incentives. Their logic of self-perpetuation is closely associated with the current system, as Lajčák has experienced as well:

> The political leadership divides the country into three parts—let us face it. They have absolute control over the political process, appointments, economic life, and other things. The philosophy is: I do not touch you—you do not touch me. Obviously, any process of European integration would limit the freedom in dealing with their part of Bosnia-Herzegovina. So they are not really interested, that is clear. What we need is to generate stronger pressure by the citizens and to limit the space of fighting against each other as a way of driving the attention away from the real problems of Bosnia-Herzegovina. And here, I would say, [the] European Union on the top and public support on the bottom should sandwich the local leaders and not allow them to resort to [the] usual propaganda, as they always do. I see no other way forward.[382]

By the end of January 2009, Lajčák assumed the position of Foreign Minister in the Slovak government under the leadership of Prime Minister Robert Fico. He continued preforming his duties as High Representative until March of that year, which in itself constituted a novelty. His term in office was thus rather short but nevertheless undoubtedly influential. As a result of the October 2007 events, the internationals became aware of the actual limits of the Bonn powers—as opposed to the potential limits presented by considerations based on democratic legitimacy and the like. At least since the return of Dodik, the Bosnian Serbs had a superb relationship with certain elements within the international community and the OHR staff; they were therefore well informed with regard to the prevailing positions,

---

[381]   Lajčák, Personal Interview.

[382]   Ibid.

demands, and opinions.[383] In Lajčák's term they managed not only to resist a first-level order but also to end the subsequent confrontation with a political win in the form of SAA initialisation.

It is not unique that the locals resist international pressure; the example of Silajdžić and Ljubić bringing down the April package comes to mind. But this constituted something we may see as 'ordinary resistance', for it was uttered and performed in parliament following the usual procedures. Dodik's resistance was structurally different. Lajčák's Bonn power decision could not be countered by ordinary mechanisms of the political system, for the Bonn powers supersede the latter. So by definition, the resistance had to be out of the ordinary or non-parliamentarian; its nature had to be rather diplomatic than legal or political (in the narrow sense). But what the international community, and Lajčák in particular, did not see was that by accepting this kind of local resistance they created a precedent of immense magnitude. They effectively showed that, given the right circumstances, the international community, and the European Union in particular, would give in to public upheaval, political demands, or threats by the local political elite. It is this unhealthy combination of a system that supports such behaviour and the international readiness to tolerate the same that in a nutshell explains the circumference of the Bosnian political system and its incentive structures.

9.7   Valentin Inzko (2009-present)

Like Miroslav Lajčák, Valentin Inzko comes from the diplomatic corps. The Austrian had been ambassador in Belgrade when Yugoslavia still existed (1982-1986); he had headed the OSCE mission in Sandžak in 1992; and he was the first resident ambassador to Bosnia-Herzegovina after the war (1996-1999). In 1999, he assumed a position in Vienna within the Foreign Ministry's departments for Central, Eastern, and Southern Europe as well as Central Asia and the Southern Caucasus. Before being nominated as the international community's representative in Bosnia, Inzko served four years as his country's ambassador to Slovenia to which he had a personal connection as well. As a member of the Slovenian minority in his home-region of Carinthia, Inzko, who studied law and languages (Russian and Serbo-Croat), is well accustomed to minority politics and minority demands. Since 2010, he serves as the Head of the Council of Slovenes in the Austrian province of Carinthia, a Christian organization dedicated to promoting the identity of Carinthia's Slovenes and to contribute to a 'fruitful coexistence' of

---

[383]   See also Schwarz-Schilling, "Europa und Deutschland müssen sich ihrer Verantwortung stellen."

Austrians and Slovenes in the province.[384] In his function as the main advocate of Slovene interest, Inzko was also involved in the famous Carinthian *Ortstafelstreit*.

In analysing Inzko's approach towards the Bonn powers and Bosnia in general, I face a slight disadvantage, since I was not able to interview to him personally. I am furthermore not aware of any personal recollections or analyses he has produced in writing that would help bridge the divide between the publicly stated and the personally felt as far as the Bosnian case is concerned. This is not as unfortunate as it may seem at first glance, for a deep analysis of Inzko's mandate is not needed in the present context. As will be shown in the next chapter with greater precision, the elements of 'imposed consociationalism' at which I am implicitly aiming since the beginning of this chapter, were already fully developed before Inzko assumed office. From the perspective of political systems theory, the events during his mandate exemplify solely the reality of the institutional interplay and do not significantly alter the existing incentive system. It is for this reason that I will keep this final section rather brief. Additionally, many of the contemporary issues were already discussed in the previous chapter.

9.7.1   The contemporary role of the OHR and the Bonn powers

In practical terms, Valentin Inzko continued the OHR policy that Miroslav Lajčák had established. In his first address to the Bosnian parliament,[385] he emphasised the links between the 5+2 agenda, the closure of the OHR, and the European future of Bosnia-Herzegovina. He furthermore urged the parliamentarians to 'find new and concrete ways to broker agreements and expedite adoption of laws crucial to Bosnia and Herzegovina's European path'. He repeated the international community's commitment not to tolerate any secessionist movements and emphasised once again the need for constitutional reform: 'the system has to be changed because the country needs efficient and representative government that can start helping to raise living standards'. In terms of rhetoric, as well as practice, there was nothing new in Inzko's understanding of his role. After Lajčák had stated the death of the Bonn powers, OHR policy concentrated first and foremost on the European agenda. Since the latter is indeed a choice rather than a necessity for a country, it is conceptually immune to real pressure or the usage of Bonn powers.

That the High Representative embodied the European agenda had always been a conceptual incongruence. But once the state was stabilised and the locals

---

[384]   See the Council's website: http://nsks.at/deutsch/?page_id=236, accessed 19 December 2013.

[385]   Valentin Inzko, *Address by High Representative and EU Special Representative Valentin Inzko to the BiH Parliamentary Assembly* (Sarajevo: Office of the High Representative, 5 December 2009), http://www.ohr.int/ohr-dept/presso/presssp/default.asp?content_id= 43453. Accessed 19 December 2013.

needed to be tasked with their share of responsibility, this incongruence became too contradictory to uphold. As Lajčák explained, one cannot force a country into becoming a member state. The Bonn powers as the prime characteristic of the High Representative, however, were precisely an instrument of force, even when they are not used. In Lajčák's terms: 'The fact that they exist was more important than the actual using of the Bonn powers.'[386] They had served well when aimed at state building but proved utterly useless when the European agenda was concerned. The contradiction became obvious during Inzko's mandate. When he demanded constitutional reform, for example, did he do so as the international community's High Representative seeking to build a self-sustaining state? Or did he do so as EU Special Representative explaining the locals that constitutional reform is necessary condition for European integration? Aware of such ambiguity in the person of the High Representative, the European Union decided to end the double hatting and, in September 2011, named Peter Sørensen EU Special Representative. The two issues were thus decoupled, with the EUSR being responsible for the EU agenda and the OHR assisting those efforts and intervening only when the sustainability of the state itself was at stake.

The High Representative's task was thus formally deprived of its most notable component. Naturally, this decreased the potential usage of the Bonn powers even further. Apart from the one instance described in the previous chapter, Inzko did never intervene in political processes and concentrated his limited attention more on administrative and judicial issues that were not of great importance. His usage of the Bonn powers has thus gone largely unnoticed: in 2009, he used the Bonn powers 28 times, but 9 of those decisions actually repealed former acts. In 2010 and 2011, we count ten decisions per year, eight and five of which, respectively, were repeals. Finally, 2012 and 2013 give us with four and one decision, respectively, all of which were repeals.

The major political issue of Inzko's term was the *Sejdić and Finci* verdict, whose misuse by the political elites has been described in the previous chapter. While former attempts at reforming the constitution were initialled by representatives of the international community, this demand came by a widely respected international body dedicated at the protection and interpretation of human rights. Even though such demands had higher credibility and came with seemingly higher urgency, a solution imposed by the High Representative was in no way conceivable. Furthermore, the EU adapted its pre-membership agenda with regards to Bosnia to include an implementation of the verdict. Since 2011, the issue was thus primarily handled by the EUSR, not the OHR. Combined with the non-effectiveness of the Bonn powers, these events dramatically decreased the importance of the OHR with regards to the Bosnian political system. Even though

---

[386]   Lajčák, Personal Interview in Bratislava (SK).

its legal structure did not change in any way and the High Representative still enjoyed some form of absolute powers, he did not exert much influence on the practical level.

These changes in the role and the actions of the HR did not go unnoticed by the local political elite. As Božo Ljubić explains: 'There was a time when [politicians] polished their statements based on how they would sound in the ears of the internationals. Today, nobody cares about that.'[387] Similarly, Dragan Čović states: 'Once, it looked like everything was in the hands of the internationals. Surely, when someone from the OHR would call anybody in the local administration—be that on an executive, legislative, or judicial level—the latter would follow the request in a military manner. Today, this is not the case any more.' While Čović does not doubt that the OHR's large administration still has some impact (since large administrations always exert some influence), he does not believe that the effect is in any way decisive for the policy of the locals. He is rather convinced that the current OHR has become an end in itself and could therefore be abolished.[388] A similar view is expressed by the Bosnian Serbs, historically the fiercest critics of the OHR. Mladen Bosić explains that the strategy of the SDS is in no ways concerned with the likes and dislikes of the international community or the OHR.[389] Mladen Ivanić thinks that the 'international community has learnt its lesson' in the past so that it now abstains from direct threats and pressures against certain people. The internationals, he believes, 'have realised that nothing will be solved by the use of pressure; instead, a solution can only be reached when a proposal is presented that is acceptable to all the peoples in BiH.' As far as he is concerned, 'such an OHR', i.e. an inactive and mute one, can stay 'forever' in Bosnia.[390]

But the OHR is not the only representative of the international community that has lost its influence as far as the local politicians are concerned—it is merely the most visible one. Željko Komšić summarises the feelings of the local politicians, when asked about the influence of the international community in Bosnia:

> Look, let me be frank: Nobody among Bosnia's politicians takes any representative of the international community seriously any more. They play and ridicule them, because they see what the latter are. Political leaders in Bosnia respect nothing but pure force and pure pressure—and only [if it comes] from powerful actors. Surely, neither the OHR, nor the European Commission has such power. … The only political factor that we take seriously is the policy of the United States—but only if one recognises it as a pragmatic approach. So, only when one sees that a certain action is coming from Washington and not some local diplomat, that's when there's respect. But on all other issues? We laugh about the High Representative or ambassador Sørensen, or cer-

---

[387]   Ljubić, Personal Interview.

[388]   Čović, Personal interview.

[389]   Bosić, Personal Interview.

[390]   Ivanić, Personal Interview.

tain other ambassadors. Nobody takes them seriously any more as far as our political life is concerned. We may take them seriously when they come with money or some project. Then we talk seriously about money. But as far as their political influence in general is concerned? Nobody takes them seriously.[391]

That the political elites no longer take the internationals seriously is thus only a half-truth, just as is the statement that the internationals have stopped exerting influence altogether. As Mladen Ivanić explains, there is still regular contact between certain ambassadors and the political elite: 'You know, sometimes an ambassador comes to you. He does not say you have to do this or that on the record, but he gives you his opinion, he makes suggestions, and he is usually well informed.' So while the internationals still try to influence the local politicians, they do so with diplomatic means and behind closed doors.

This raises the question of the relevance of the OHR in the contemporary Bosnian system. If it no longer serves a function, why is it still there? There are two answers to this question. The first one comes from advocates of the OHR, like the Bosniaks. This group sees its interests aligned with the ones of the international community and has thus been rather positive about the entire OHR policy so far. It still believes that, given the right amount of political pressure from the right addressor, the international policy priorities can still be decisive. As Haris Silajdžić says: In the past, the effect of international pressure 'depended on the intensity of this pressure and the true goals of the international community; whether the internationals wanted simply to say "we told them", or whether they really wanted to get the job done. History tells us: when they opted for the latter, they were able to get the job done.' This logic still applies; the problem is just that the internationals have stopped caring about the Bosnian situation. Therefore, Silajdžić deems an eventual closure of the OHR as the ultimate surrender of the international community: 'If they want to leave, this means that the job is done. But far from it! ... If they leave now, they will leave behind a country that is not based on the rule of law.'[392]

The second answer lies in the political reality. The existence of the OHR still has practical implications. Mladen Bosić, for example, blames the High Representative for the shortcomings of the political system. Referring to certain contested provisions within the electoral law that prevented absentee voting in the municipality of Srebrenica in the 2012 local elections (thus ensuring that the mayor of Srebrenica would be a Serb), Bosić says:

The expectation that the international community will solve this issue—instead of finding a solution through local discussions—is something that practically hinders compromise. You cannot have discussions if you think that somebody else will do the job for you. I suppose that Tihić [i.e. the then-president of the SDA], instead of

---

[391]   Komšić, Personal Interview.
[392]   Silajdžić, Personal Interview.

> calling the international community to intervene, would, if this factor [i.e. the OHR] were not here, have called us to discuss these issues.[393]

Leaving aside speculations about Tihić's intention to involve the internationals in an internal dispute, the example shows that the OHR still plays a role in contemporary politics. What Bosić is effectively saying, is that without the OHR, the locals would be forced to find compromises among themselves. It is in this way that the locals use the OHR as a scapegoat for own misconduct. Whereas in the old days, the High Representative's Office served as a framework for structuring debate and demands, it is nowadays employed as a tool of political struggle. The local politicians treat the international community and the OHR as some sort of a barking dog of which they know that it will never bite.

To close this chapter, I would like to exemplify this new role of the internationals with one rather short example in recent times. In 2011, Milorad Dodik, as part of a larger effort to discredit the central state and ensure more autonomy for the RS, announced a referendum regarding the judicial authority of central state organs and the OHR on RS territory. The Bosnian Serbs deemed actions by both institutions as specifically targeting their co-nationals and opposed it on that ground. The NARS adopted a resolution that foresaw a referendum to be held in June 2011. This inherently counter-Daytonist plan naturally stirred some controversy in the country and on the international level. In May, however, Dodik suddenly dropped the plan after a surprise visit by Catherine Ashton, the EU's High Representative for Foreign Affairs, who promised the establishment of a commission to review the legal framework of central state institutions.[394] So, in the end, the entire 'referendum threat' turned out to be only hot air—a populist claim aimed at Dodik's own electorate. Nevertheless, it fulfilled a function, for it was Dodik who had managed to defend Serb interests and provoke direct negotiations with the EU's chief diplomat on equal footing. Once again, he was able to present himself as the *de facto* leader of a state, not merely the representative of some federal entity. That the European Union played along and offered him a face-saving way out embodies the unhealthy incentive structure of the current Bosnian system. Its targets are locals and internationals alike, but its primary victim is the Bosnian people.

---

[393]   Bosić, Personal Interview.

[394]   Thomas Fuster, "Bosniens Serben krebsen zurück: Verzicht auf das umstrittene Volksreferendum nach einem Überraschungsbesuch der EU-Aussenbeauftragten Ashton," *Neue Zürcher Zeitung*, 14 May 2011, sec. International, http://www.nzz.ch/aktuell/international/bosniens-serben-krebsen-zurueck-1.10571555.   Accessed   19   December 2013.

10 Bosnia-Herzegovina as an 'Imposed Consociation'

While chapter eight presented the views of the political elites and elaborated on the dynamics within the contemporary Bosnian political system and chapter nine was dedicated to the development of OHR policy since the establishment of the institution, this concluding chapter of part III shall focus on the interpretation of those findings using the theoretical model of 'imposed consociationalism'. Since the latter was already implied in the previous two chapters, I shall be brief as far as the actual content is concerned and primarily try to present the previous findings in a more structured manner. The first section is dedicated to the central assumption of 'imposed consociationalism' and its presence in the Bosnian context, i.e. the non-existence of group cohesion within a fully consociational system. The second section deals with the Office of the High Representative as the prototypical example of an 'International Regulating Body' (IRB). The third and concluding section addresses the assumed relationships and incentive structures that characterise the 'imposed consociational' model.

To remind the reader, let me quickly restate the central hypothesis of 'imposed consociationalism'. In a fully consociational system that incorporates an IRB with the prerogative to intervene in political decision making, the positive incentive structure of consociationalism is reversed. The possibility of deadlocks is circumvented by IRB interventions and the politicians are deprived of their need to compromise among themselves. Thus, the extreme rhetoric that usually characterises consociational electoral campaigns is not countered by a pragmatic approach once participation in government is secured. Instead, even more extreme rhetoric is likely to occur since, without really governing, the political elite's main goal becomes keeping their governmental positions. Over time, one can expect a race to the extremes instead of middle-of-the-road positions. The entire system, furthermore, has a long-term effect in that uncooperative behaviour prevails even if the IRB decides to intervene less often. The ultimate result, therefore, is not stable democratic rule but a challenging dependency with respect to the IRB and the international community it represents.

10.1 The Assumptions of 'Imposed Consociation' in the Bosnian Context

I defined an 'imposed consociation' as a full-fledged consociational system that owes its mere existence to some sort of external actors, and in which this kind of actors still influence the newly created political system. This latter condition was further clarified through the conceptual introduction of an 'International Regulating Body' that possesses what I have termed an 'intervention prerogative' in the form of the power to circumvent the local legal and democratic system by imposing decisions as it deems necessary in order to maintain a stable political rule. While I shall deal with the IRB in the next section, I would like first to address the other assumptions on which this construct relies.

In order to explain the drift towards extremist political stances, the 'imposed consociation' relied on the assumption of intra-group competition. Only with different parties targeting the same electorate within a corporately designed electoral system does the assumption of non-group cohesion become defendable. As the previous chapter has shown, Bosnia never relied on a fully cohesive group structure if one understands the latter as the existence of merely one political current within the different groups. Admittedly, there was a high level of cohesion during the war and in the first post-war years. But the period immediately preceding the first elections in 1996 also contained the potentiality of intra-group quarrels. On the territory of the Federation, one could count six parties in addition to SDA and HDZ, whereas in the RS two parties and an independent club within the wartime parliament countered the dominance of the SDS. In the subsequent years, this potentiality of intra-group competition became a reality.

In the RS, the SDS split into 'progressive' and nationalist wings, while changing circumstances led to new political demands and the formation of new parties like the PDP, which was naturally conservative but whose political programme put(s) economic demands at the forefront. The first RS opposition government of Biljana Plavšić and Milorad Dodik resulted mostly from a divide within the still rather nationalistic RS leadership. But the true culmination of opposition activity, i.e. the true state of non-cohesiveness, happened only with the *de facto* participation of RS-based parties in the Alliance government in 2000. This experiment ended two years later with the return to power by the nationalists. However, the latter became softer in their demands and tone—not least due to the unforgiving activity of the OHR in the area of ICTY cooperation. This (relatively speaking) cooperative course of action towards international demands presented the opportunity for a new kind of opposition and competition. In 2006, it culminated in the return to power of Milorad Dodik, who had adopted a populist and nationalist agenda. Since then, we can once again observe a trend towards higher cohesion in Bosnia's smaller entity. Dodik styled himself the bearer of Serb interest and the beacon of Serb hopes, which has made Serb opposition to him almost blasphemy. Days before the general elections of October 2014, patriarch Irinej, the head of the Serbian Orthodox Church publicly expressed his support for Dodik's re-election.[1] However, as history tells us, such absolute positions are not sustainable in the long run. While Milorad Dodik continues to dominate RS and BiH politics, the local elections of 2012 and, even more clearly, the most recent general elections of October 2014 can be seen as the beginning of a gradual erosion of the SNSD monopoly. The opposition, united in a unified coalition, managed to truly challenge Dodik's position and achieve quite impressive results (see also below). The opposition candidate for the Serb seat in BiH's presidency, Mladen Ivanić, narrowly beat the SNSD candidate of Dodik's choosing, Željka Cvijanović; Dodik's opponent for the RS presidency, Ognjen Tadić of SDS, came rather close to beating him as well, but ultimately failed. The opposition is thus clearly getting stronger in the RS.

In the Federation, we can observe another kind of evolution. Within the Bosniak electoral corpus, the early secession of Silajdžić from the SDA was not so much a demonstration of the group's non-cohesion but rather an example of diverging political views that could not be fitted into the framework of existing party structures. This is the reason why Silajdžić closely cooperated with his ex-party, and by the grace of the SDA even served as Co-Chairman of the Council of Ministers. Neglecting some smaller parties that never enjoyed much electoral support, the more important split within the Bosniak electoral corpus is likely the one between traditional Bosniak parties of SDA and SBiH and the nominally multinational parties, such as the UBSD and the SDP. Here as well, the point of no return with regards to ending intra-group cohesion was crossed with the Alliance for Change government between 2000 and 2002. For the first time, the highly eclectic and internally non-cohesive and non-nationalist opposition parties managed to secure a majority, which not only potentially threatened but actually ended the dominance of SDA, HDZ, and SDS. This opposition cooperation furthermore broke the *de facto* alliance between SBiH and SDA, so that those two parties would henceforth compete for the nominally Bosniak representation.

The Croat national corpus, on the other hand, remained largely intact in the first post-war years, despite the efforts of Krešimir Zubak to form his own party as a viable alternative. The maintenance of illegal self-rule within the Federation and the international community's harsh approach towards those Croat officials who supported the continuation of such structures, combined with the minority position of the Croats in general and perhaps even the ever-existent dream of unification with Croatia, presumably proved to be factors favouring unified stances among the Bosnian Croats. Even though smaller and more liberal parties existed after the end of the war, the real political divide in this electorate happened only

---

[1]   *Nezavisne Novine*, "Patrijarh Irinej poželio da Dodik i dalje vodi narod RS", *Nezavisne Novine Online,* 10 October 2014, http://www.nezavisne.com/novosti/bih/ Patrijarh-Irinej-pozelio-da-Dodik-i-dalje-vodi-narod-RS-267383.html. Accessed 10 October 2014.

in 2006 when the HDZ itself split into two parties. This instance presented the local Croats with the possibility of staying true to their perceived national values while choosing who would represent those values in different parties.

Interestingly enough, it was at the same time that Željko Komšić of the multi-national SDP won the Croat seat in Bosnia's presidency. The intricacies of this election have been stressed in chapter eight and shall not be repeated here. I mention it only to demonstrate that always above the group structures lurks the possibility of supporting a multi-national candidate. Within the Bosnian system, this candidate is in almost all cases bound to be a member of some particular group but in his comportment and policy he may well express the multi-national conviction that corporate consociations tend to silence. The emblematic problem of such a candidate is his party, for there is no party with significant support that is truly perceived as multi-national. The only possible choice for fitting this characteristic, the SDP, is often accused and surely even more often perceived as a Bosniak rather than multi-national party. The future of Komšić's own party, the Democratic Front, remains to be seen. Due to its impressive election results, the party is likely to play an important role in the political arena; however, it runs the risk of being too closely associated with Komšić and thus too dependent on his personal appeal, statements, and behaviour. Just as the future of the SNSD after Dodik is anything but secure, the sustainability of the DF is likely to largely depend on Komšić.

Not least due to the consociational device of proportional representation, Bosnia thus possesses a highly fragmented party system that is primarily organised on the state and entity levels. Reminiscence of the early post-war years when local elections were rushed, the municipalities play a minor part in the entire system. Party leaders and presidents decide the local electoral strategy, i.e. what candidates to support and what alliances to form. As such, local elections have always an entity or state overtone and are usually not really based on local demands and issues. As a slight exception to this rule, the direct election of mayors may serve as a positive example. In order to secure majorities, these need to bridge the group-based divide, and especially in largely homogenous municipalities, minority votes may give one candidate the pivotal advantage over the other. An analysis of local level politics is thus likely to lead to rather interesting findings and should be pursued.

Bosnia thus fulfils the assumption of the non-existence of group cohesion, for since the early 2000s (or 2006 in the case of the Bosnian Croats) all three groups are internally divided into parties that enjoy non-negligible support among the respective electorates. Consequently, the voters themselves are divided into different factions and, as a consequence, the groups are non-cohesive. But Bosnia also fulfils an unmentioned assumption within consociational theory, namely the readiness to make coalitions among very unlikely partners representing the groups. Since the Bosnian system *de facto* relies on the majoritarian method of government formation, party coalitions need parliamentary majorities. In the past, this has led to rather surprising alliances. The PDP, for example, participated in nationalist governments as well as the Alliance government in 2000. After the general elections of 2010, the SDP entered into a coalition with the SDA; when this cooperation ended due to differences on an important political issue, the SDP had no problems in replacing the SDA with the SBB. Political coalitions between nationalists and multi-nationalists are thus a reality in Bosnia. But contrary to what consociational theory assumes, these coalitions do not exemplify pragmatism with regards to governing as the natural counterbalance to the nationalist rhetoric that dominated the electoral campaigns; rather, they emphasise the fact that the political elite as such is unified in its pursuit of governmental positions and the logic of self-perpetuation.

The second part of the assumption is dedicated to the existence of a fully-fledged consociational system. Bosnia's consociational character has been described in-depth in chapter seven and shall not be repeated here. Suffice it to say that contemporary Bosnia has all the elements demanded by an empirical definition of a consociation, i.e. grand coalition, group autonomy, proportionality, and group veto. However, even though Dayton itself foresaw a consociational state structure, it would be wrong to assume that this has been the case since the end of the war. First, the establishment of the state structures took quite some time. The provisions of Annex IV needed amending in the sense that the rules of procedures for the foreseen institutions had to be established. The process of making the state work characterised the mandates of the first four High Representatives. Institutionally, I would argue, the process was largely completed after the implementation of the 'constituent peoples' verdict in 2002, which provided the Bosnian state with many of the consociational institutions and mechanisms that exist today. Even though these changes primarily concerned the entities, they nevertheless had a national significance due to the highly interconnected political system. In the empirical sense, I believe, one may conceive of the Bosnian state as a consociation only after the implementation of this verdict and Petritsch's impositions, respectively.

Second, if one looks behind an empirical definition of a consociation, we may recall Lehmbruch's argument according to which a consociation is more than the sum of its institutional parts; it consists of a process characterised by the principle of learning through success. Provided that the local elites realise the benefits of cooperation, over time a sense of mutual trust amongst themselves and in the system may develop. Only when this process is completed are we truly allowed to speak of a consociation. If we follow this reading, it seems highly unlikely that the political elites clearly understood the consociational system and its peculiarities when it was established in 1996. More suitable is the assumption that they needed time to adjust to the mechanisms that would later guide their political endeavours. A mutual lack of trust hindered this process; if we recall the times of the Co-Chairmanship of the Council of Ministers, we find that the two chairmen only met during the sessions and had no other contact whatsoever. They designed their policies thus largely independently of each other and of the institutions in which they participated. In fact, it was only with the establishment of the Alliance government that the central state structures became 'workable', for, even though the parties differed on many issues, they all nevertheless expressed the political will to work within the established institutional framework. This cooperation served as an important experience in the Bosnian political sphere, for the subsequent nationalist governments continued to use the existing system to advance political initiatives or block their attempts. Even though it would be highly exaggerated to state that the locals began trusting each other after 2002, it surely is true that by then they understood the working mechanisms of the system. Instead of opposing it, they began using it to their advantage.

For the model of an 'imposed consociation', this means that the assumptions on which it is based were probably fully fulfilled somewhere after 2002/2003. Non-group cohesion was fully established in at least two groups—probably even all three of them, if we add the option of supporting multi-national parties—and the political system was not only set up properly but its mechanisms were also fully understandable to the politicians involved.

10.2 The OHR as the Prototypical International Regulating Body (IRB)

The 'imposed consociational' model relies on an institution that is not common to other forms of consociation or to the democratic state as such: the existence of an International Regulating Body that possesses the prerogative to intervene in the local system by the grace of some higher authority. This authority is deemed legitimate, for the goal of the IRB is not only the maintenance of peace after the end of violent conflict, but the establishment of stable democratic rule. Within this mind-set, such stability in terms of political institutions is only achievable through the punctual suspension of the democratic system itself, which is perceived as messy, complicated, and prone to continued group-based conflict. However, the actions of the IRB do not happen in a vacuum, for its guiding principles are located on the international level and, consequently, the institution itself is subject to those international norms and regulations.

Figure 10.1 Intervention Quota by High Representative

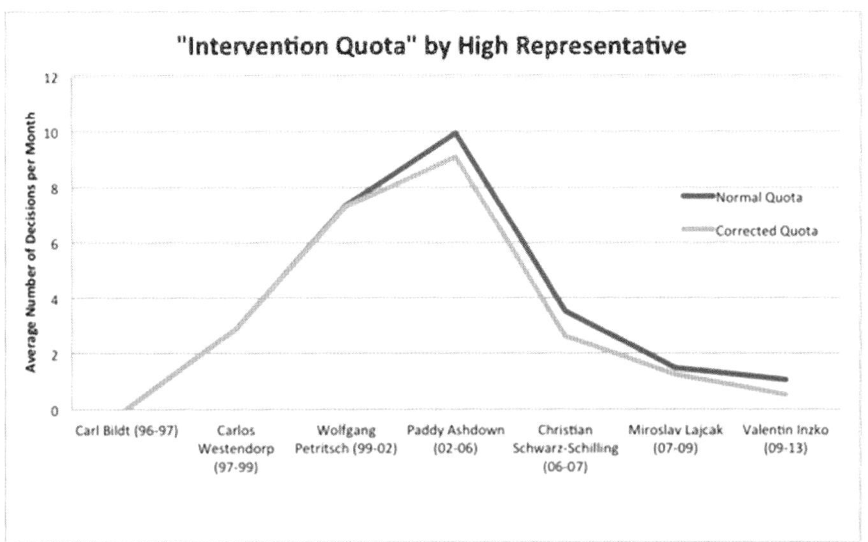

There can be no doubt that the Office of the High Representative in Bosnia-Herzegovina constitutes the prime example of this kind of international intervention in a post-war state. Conceived as part of an international agreement and legally founded on a UN Security Council resolution, the OHR is a purely international body. Originally equipped with a far-reaching mandate stretching from inducing local cooperation to the coordination of the numerous international organisations involved in post-war reconstruction, the High Representative soon realised the limits of its mandate. At the Bonn conference in 1997, he thus demanded, and was granted, the powers that constitute the OHR's intervention prerogatives. Henceforth, he could not only impose laws circumventing the entire local political system, but also remove people from political positions if they in any form violated the provisions of the DPA. One year later, at the Madrid conference, the HR was furthermore given the authority to remove people from positions within political parties, if he deemed it necessary. In the subsequent years, the original provision that the local system must have failed in order for the Bonn powers to be used, i.e. that the local politicians must have failed to achieve some kind of agreement, was simply abandoned in practice. Especially after the mandates of Petritsch and, in particular, Ashdown, we find ourselves confronted with a system of high-level impositions that deliberately circumvent the existing political structures.

Figure 10.1 shows the usage of the Bonn powers by each High Representative. The 'intervention quota' that it depicts is calculated by dividing the total number of decisions by the total amount of months in office; in this respect, it gives an average of Bonn-power usage per month, so that actions by the different

High Representatives, whose terms were not equal in length, can be compared. The figure distinguishes between a 'normal quota' and a 'corrected quota'. The former includes all Bonn power based decisions by the High Representative, whereas in the latter, decisions repealing former decisions are subtracted from the total amount of decisions. This 'corrected quota' is therefore always a little bit lower than the 'normal quota' and makes an appearance only in the second half of the analysed timeframe.[2] In any case, the differences between the two quotas are marginal and do not change the general picture.

We can observe a rather steep increase in the usage of Bonn powers until the mandate of Paddy Ashdown and an even steeper decrease in the subsequent years. The detailed reasons for these changes have been explained in the previous chapter, which is why I shall now concentrate on a more generalised interpretation of the events. In the first years of Bonn-power usage, international imposition in Bosnia has to be understood as a protectorate-like rule over a non-sovereign country. Even though Westendorp's approach may be deemed a counter-argument to this characterisation, it simply reflected the general concept of the instrument at that time. When the international community decided not to care any more about the condition of previous local failure, the OHR became undeniably the most important institution to push the political process forward. Knaus and Martin, therefore, compare the position of the High Representative in Bosnia, especially during the time of Paddy Ashdown, to imperial rule over colonies. They write that in Bosnia 'outsiders actually *set* that agenda, *impose[d]* it, and *punish[ed] with sanctions* those who refuse[d] to implement it'.[3] But the equivalence between colonial rule and imposition in Bosnia, as Knaus and Martin admit, is subject to some constraints:

> Of course, there are obvious differences between Bosnia and the imperial colonies of the nineteenth century—chief among them the fact that Bosnia's international administration was established with the agreement of the Bosnians as part of a peace treaty. Nevertheless, the similarities of style and substance are astonishing. Vast ambitions, the fervent belief in progress, the assumption that outsiders can best interpret the true interest of a subject people—all these are hallmarks that the international administra-

---

[2]   Such decisions repealing former decisions have most often concerned people who have been banned from holding public office. Several years after the ban was installed, it was usually lifted again. Since there is no clear procedure on how to lift bans, the High Representative simply issues another Bonn-power decision reinstating this person's civil and political rights. However, the latter can hardly be counted as a new decision intending to exercise influence on the political system since by the time it is issued, the individual concerned is usually a private citizen again with no political significance. This is why I removed such decisions from the calculations in the 'corrected quota'.

[3]   Knaus and Martin, "Travails of the European Raj," 61. Original italics.

tion in Bosnia shares with the British East India Company and the Utilitarian philosophers who staffed it in the early nineteenth century.[4]

Despite such similarities, there is a clear difference between colonial rule and international imposition in Bosnia that does not belong to the peace agreement and its aftermath. Rather, it is to be found in the European and American context, which aimed at the proliferation of democracy. Effectively, this means that the international community could not establish a colonial protectorate equivalent to former British rule over India any more. Far from being technical, this difference is an actual constraint to international imposition. While it does not necessarily change the action itself, this surely determines the public representation of the matter; it also means that the local political system cannot be wholly circumvented. Imposition thus remains intrinsically linked to the existing political system, despite often appearing factually detached from it. Knaus and Martin are thus right in observing that the actions of the High Representatives stem from outside the local political system and are largely not responsible to it, but their analysis underestimates the constraints under which the internationals have intervened in the system. This is not a critique *per se*, for the larger context of such constraints becomes evident only in retrospect and only in light of subsequent developments.

Nevertheless, it would be wrong to underestimate the influence of the internationals or to overemphasise the constraints that the philosophical adherence to democracy presents. To this day, the internationals do not perceive the locals as equals, which consequently means that their input with regards to the general development of the country remains extremely limited. Especially in the first postwar years, the locals were merely the executors of an internationally imposed and agreed upon agenda—and the HR had to make them stick to the respective goals and timetables. This is not to say that they deserved any other treatment, for they kept proving their general reluctance towards any form of cooperation or common political ideal. But it is to illustrate that the experiment in democracy, and in consociational democracy in particular, had not properly begun and was thus unable to deliver the results that consociational theory promises. In a situation where the political agenda is imposed (beginning with the QSPs of Bildt and ending with the process of European integration advocated today) and the internationals *de facto* keep all the decision powers to themselves (in earlier times through donor's money, today through assessing progress towards EU integration and related funds), one cannot assume that the political system as such has any effect on legislative decision-making. Consequently, the system is not a democracy, and especially not a consociational one; neither is it some form of a hybrid in which democratic elements are mixed with non-democratic features. Lastly, it is also not a purely non-democratic protectorate, in which the internationals margin-

---

[4]　　Ibid., 62.

alise the locals, even though the former might sometime have perceived of it as such.

Instead, I believe, a nuanced and developmental picture would best characterise the development of the Bosnian political system. Between 1996 and 2002, politics in Bosnia-Herzegovina operated on two distinct systems that functioned not independently of each other but that had only few points of contact. On the one hand, we have the formally democratic state, which possessed its own institutions built around the basic idea of a consociational democratic setup. Its members were elected to the presidency and both houses of parliament, and they adopted or started to adopt required procedures that allowed them to handle the political workload. On the other hand, this democratic setup formed the mere façade for a system of external decision making. The local agenda was the result of international priorities and the means to pursue it remained largely dependent on international commitment and readiness. Local politics was thus only *pro forma* in charge. But precisely because international pressures of this kind happened in a system that was also democratic, the locals nevertheless had an inherent right to oppose the external forces. For determining the nature of this system, the reasons for such opposition were less important than the fact that this opposition can be deemed legitimate if the democratic system itself is legitimate (within the usual constraints of a post-war societies). International involvement in Bosnia at this time thus suffered from a basic contradiction. It fought tirelessly to make Bosnia's state structure work, which in itself is a testimony to the democratically illegitimate nature of the endeavour. At the same time, however, the international post-war involvement aimed at creating the illusion of independent decision making by the local political elite within a democratic, and thus legitimate, political system; in other words, the internationals faked democracy, to re-use David Chandler's famous formula.[5]

With the introduction of the Bonn powers, the superiority of the international over the local political system was formally established. Moreover, the internationals introduced the principle of subsidiarity in order to pay tribute to the democratic character of the polity. But with the impositions surrounding the Mrakovica-Sarajevo Agreement, it became clear that this tribute was only lip service. The Bonn powers became an integral part of the local system that, in the time of Paddy Ashdown, ultimately merged to form a new kind of system in which the intervention prerogative constituted just another instrument of political decision making.

In essence, the system that Ashdown's 'either you do it or I will' doctrine established is not very different from guardianship rule. Following the Platonic idea of philosopher kings, Robert Dahl defines guardianship as 'a regime in

---

[5]   Chandler, *Bosnia*.

which the state is governed by meritorious ruler who consist of a minority of adults, quite likely a small minority, *and who are not subject to the democratic process.*'[6] While one can debate the meritorious qualities of external actors in the Bosnian example, the structure of OHR rule, especially during the times of Petritsch and Ashdown, would clearly correspond to the rule of a few not bound by the democratic process (in its narrower sense). For precisely this reason, Dahl conceives of guardianship rule not as 'a mere modification of a democratic regime' but as 'an alternative to democracy, a fundamentally different *kind* of regime'.[7] But it would be nevertheless inaccurate to call the Bosnian system guardianship rule, for the internationals have indeed been bound by the democratic principle and the perception of autonomous local self-government. These constraints were ultimately responsible for the abandonment of large-scale government by Bonn powers in the latter third of Ashdown's and especially Schwarz-Schilling's term. Lajčák's realisation of the non-effectiveness of the Bonn powers signified the ultimate death of this kind of intervention—and the ultimate victory of the local political system, however ill-adapted it was. Neither guardianship rule nor pure consociational democracy possesses the conceptual flexibility to capture this broad development. But the model of an 'imposed consociation', I believe, helps us structure and understand the different dynamics that characterise this sort of consociational democracy.

There is, however, one aspect that the theoretical model underestimated. In chapter six we conceived of the IRB as a singular actor guided by international norms and practices. While not precisely inaccurate, this statement needs to be amended to reflect the factual non-cohesiveness of such norms and practices. The empirical analysis suggests that we need to conceive of the IRB as an actor equal to any other international organisation and therefore subject to the same constraints. Especially since the mandate of Christian Schwarz-Schilling, we could observe an international divide that significantly limited the scope of OHR action. With the return of the Russians to the international stage, the diverging interests of the Americans and Brits after the invasion of Iraq, and the re-emergence of the Kosovo issue, the position of the Bosnian High Representative came to mirror the goals and strategies of the international actors involved. This put the OHR in an interesting position, for despite possessing the powers to decide matters, the HR in fact became powerless. As Miroslav Lajčák put it to the Steering Board: 'How do you want me to operate with this division?' This means that the position of the OHR was still absolute in terms of the consociational system, which is what the model foresaw; however, there were other factors influencing and limiting the arsenal of policies at the OHR's disposal that stemmed *not* from any systemic con-

---

6   Robert A Dahl, *Democracy and Its Critics* (New Haven: Yale University Press, 1989), 57. Original italics.
7   Ibid. orginal italics.

straints but from the nature of the institution itself. Such conceptual incongruity may be overcome by strong personalities, but not by systemic changes. With the performed change in personnel—from charismatic politicians and experts to knowledgeable diplomats filling the seat of HR—the dependency of the OHR vis-à-vis the international community deepened. Since this also limited the potential use of Bonn powers, it contributed to the proliferation of extreme rhetoric by the local political actors. As such, it increased the negative incentive structures that one can find in contemporary Bosnia.

10.3 The Incentive Structures in Contemporary Bosnia-Herzegovina

The model of an 'imposed consociation' assumes a causal relationship between the political system and the behaviour of political elites. In itself, this statement is tautological, for any political system constitutes the foundation for political action so that the individuals performing such an action, i.e. the political elites, are always bound by systemic constraints when pursuing their political visions. But an 'imposed consociation' foresees a specific kind of relation between the system and the politician that is quite different than the one ordinary consociational theory generally advocates. Under the condition of non-cohesive groups, an ordinary consociation assumes electoral campaigns that are dominated by extreme rhetoric, but a cooperative course of action once the government is formed; over time, this cooperation will grow to the entire population so that middle-of-the-road positions are likely to be assumed. Due to these centripetal effects, the entire system will lead to stable democratic rule in heterogeneous societies. The 'imposed consociation' model, on the other hand, does not so much doubt this sequence of events as it points to the necessary condition of full sovereignty in order for it to be even theoretically conceivable. Only when the political elites possess the ultimate decision-making capacity is the electorate capable of attributing action and consequence to some political parties and thus realise the benefits of compromise—and attribute political deadlocks to the appropriate politician and his non-cooperative stances. If this capacity is lacking, such attribution is impossible to make and other factors determine the behaviour of the politician and the electorate. Extremist positions prevail and since deadlocks are resolved by the IRB through its intervention prerogative, the local political elites are deprived of their need to govern.

The assumed mechanisms are present in contemporary Bosnia and Herzegovina. They evolved naturally due to the post-war situation of the state, the characteristics of the political elites, and the existence of an international body tasked with building the state. Carl Bildt not only led the necessary negotiations in order to set up the political structure to which the parties had agreed, he also presented the local elites with their first legislative package that international institutions had designed. Due to a lack of trust and a general reluctance to engage in meaningful dialogue with the former enemies, the local elite proved a tough partner given the internationals' wish to quickly implement the needed reforms. It was only gradually that the locals themselves started seeing the benefits of international involvement. Even before the OHR was formally granted the Bonn powers, the Bosnian government approached Westendorp with a plea to deliver an arbitration judgement for the citizenship law—a task the HR gladly accepted. The Bonn powers institutionalised this possibility and helped overcome serious deadlocks that the locals were unable to resolve. So, even though the locals did not significantly alter their behaviour or their political stances, the first results were visible in the form of a new currency, a new citizenship law, or, perhaps most importantly, the freedom of movement granted through the introduction of neutral licence plates. Nationalist stances and progress were thus not mutually exclusive, even though the internationals continued to attribute the lack of larger progress to the nationalist leaders and sought to support non-national opposition parties. However, the Alliance government of 2000 does not demonstrate this strategy's success, for it owed its emergence to a specific constellation in the region. With the death of Tuđman, the subsequent change in Croatian government, and the end of Milošević in Serbia, a window of opportunity was created that helped the Bosnian opposition parties. That the nationalist narrative was still powerful became clear two years later when the nationalists re-assumed power.

This was precisely the time when Paddy Ashdown's 'either you do it or I will' doctrine started and ultimately unified the Bonn powers and the local system. Given such assurances that progress would be made either way, the local elites could selectively cooperate with the HR on non-problematic issues, while still engage in their non-compromising politics with regards to the other leaders and, more importantly, the public. However, it was still unclear which of those two strategies would prevail, and the April package presented another window of opportunity that directly targeted the local elite's capabilities to show that kind of pragmatism on which consociational theory so desperately relies. In fact, this was successfully achieved, even though the content of the package was never an issue of the locals alone and the internationals were highly involved in the process. But the April package also showed how difficult negotiations among such diverse political parties truly are. Its failure absolved all the leaders from the necessity to seriously retry the experiment in compromise and, due to the specific constellation of the next general elections, furthered extreme rhetoric and uncompromising stances. That Milorad Dodik returned to the political stage with public contemplations of RS secession; that Haris Silajdžić questioned the moral character of the RS as a creation based on genocide; that Sulejman Tihić accused Silajdžić of lacking patriotism; that the two HDZs tried to present the elections as the ultimate referendum of the Croats' future in Bosnia; and that the multi-national SDP managed to win its first truly elected seat in the Bosnian presidency—all those instances were direct consequences of the failure of the April package and the re-emergence of uncompromising stances, with the last point being the exception that proves the rule. Henceforth, nationalist attacks and non-cooperative behaviour in government was the default option of any Bosnian politician. Unlike earlier days, when such behaviour simply testified to the genuine impossibility of compromise, the post-2006 era has been characterised by the conscious usage of non-cooperation as a strategic device. To restate Miroslav Lajčák's observation:

> The politicians got used to the Bonn powers and they learnt how to live with it. Namely, whenever they wanted to agree, they always agreed. Whenever they had to deal with difficult situations, they asked the High Representative to intervene so as to accept the responsibility for negative consequences. That was also quite clear. There were moments when they would never allow the High Representative to intervene and there were opposite [situations].[8]

In other words, cooperation depended on the issue and was not, as it is usually the case with democratic systems, the result of the willingness to govern within the given structures. In general, the Bosnian Serbs clung to the far-reaching autonomy that Dayton had granted them and even contemplated the option of returning to 'original Dayton' thus revoking the changes since that agreement. The Croats kept advocating systemic changes to the Dayton structures so as to prevent the assumption of Croat positions by allegedly illegitimate Croats. The Bosniaks fought to strengthen the central state while keeping their group-based privileges, while the liberals advocated a system based on the principle 'one person, one vote'. Even though there seems hardly any common ground between those different stances, coalitions between the respective parties were rather the rule than the exception. However, the impossibility to square the circle in terms of policy content also meant that the government as such remained divided. Since almost all the proposed laws touched upon this general outline, the country became *de facto* ungovernable on it own terms. Once again, international involvement was needed. But whereas the international community had previously resolved such deadlocks with Bonn-power impositions, it now abstained from such actions due to philosophical (since Schwarz-Schilling) and practical (since Lajčák) considerations. Effectively, this led to the perpetual deadlock in which Bosnia finds itself today.

However, it is interesting that the same parties who proved incapable to govern properly nevertheless did not lose significant support among their electorates in the elections. Let us first look at the 2010 general elections. Admittedly, that Bakir Izetbegović of the SDA replaced Haris Silajdžić as the Bosniak member of the presidency and that the SDP won the most seats in the Federation may be interpreted as the Bosniak punishment for his extreme behaviour. But since the

---

[8]   Lajčák, Personal Interview.

Bosniak electorate is probably the most volatile among the three groups and many Bosniaks probably participated in the election of the Croat member of the presidency, Željko Komšić, these results are hardly the genuine proof that the nationalist strategy has run its course. After all, Milorad Dodik's party confirmed its dominant position within the smaller entity. The more interesting development, however, happened when, after more than a year without a government, the SDP and the SDA entered into a coalition together. This move testifies to the prevailing systemic incentives, in which extreme stances in electoral campaigns are largely detached from the task of government formation so that, as already mentioned, all coalitions become possible—precisely because governing as such is no longer either an option nor a necessity. What counts is electoral support, for it determines whether one participates in the allocation of government seats and state funds. Naturally, this reinforces the dynamics of an 'imposed consociation' in that all the leaders have to present themselves as the bearers of the national interest and the only true defenders against the unreasonable and supposedly dangerous claims of the other groups. They thus may be well advised even to provoke fights, as Milorad Dodik did in 2011 when he managed to pressure Catherine Ashton into direct EU talks. Even though he did not succeed in his original demand (something he could never truly have hoped to do), he was the clear winner of that round.

But the results of the 2014 general elections show that the electorate is not entirely immune to policy content. Admittedly, the general picture did not change much in this last election; Bakir Izetbegović clearly won the Bosniak seat in the state presidency and Dragan Čović got comfortably elected as its Croat member, thus putting an end to the, in his eyes, illegitimate representation of the Croats in the presidency (after two terms, Komšić was not eligible to run). In the Federation and in the RS, the SDA and the SNSD, respectively, gained relative majorities, while the HDZ did relatively well with the Croat electorate. However, concluding that the nationalists won is only a half-truth, for it neglects important developments within both entities. Let us start with the Republika Srpska, where the opposition united in a single coalition before the elections. This strategy definitively prevented the opposing votes from being split between different parties and thus allowed a true alternative to Milorad Dodik and his SNSD. In addition—and this is where actual political content comes in—there was a substantial discontent with the RS government's policy after the massive floods that Bosnia experienced in May 2014. Especially the eastern part of the RS voiced discontent with the way in which the government had responded. This opened up a window of opportunity for the SDS-PDP-led opposition that, as already mentioned, was able to get Ivanić elected to the BiH presidency and furthermore seriously challenge Dodik for the RS presidency. Nevertheless, the importance of this development should not be overstated for two reasons. First, the decision was rather close and could have gone either way: Ivanić received about 7'500 votes more than his SNSD opponent, while Dodik beat his SDS opponent with a margin of roughly 6'900 votes. In the RS parliament, the SNSD remained the strongest party with 32 per cent of the votes, followed by the SDS with 26 per cent. These numbers hardly suggest a major shift in the political scene. Second, it would be incorrect to *a priori* assume that this opposition, whose main components are the PDP and the SDS, is 'better' than the SNSD government in terms of compromising stances. In this respect, it remains to be seen whether the opposition turns out to be 'the real deal' or just 'old wine in new bottles'.

The events in the Federation are also largely in line with the general tendencies explained so far. Yet the most astonishing, though not entirely surprising development was that Željko Komšić's DF marginalised the SDP and achieved superb results on the latter's expenses. Apparently, Komšić was able to convince the electorate that he represents a real alternative to the corrupt system that had governed the country so far; whether this public goodwill lasts and whether the DF is really capable to resist the temptations of the systemic incentives remains to be seen. In any case, it would be premature to see this development as a genuine transformation within the electorate towards more liberal values, especially since the transfer of votes seems to have happened between the SDP and the DP; combined these two parties have around the same share of votes as the SDP had in 2010.[9] Taken together with the fact that the nationalist parties still did rather well, it is doubtful that Bosnia will become easier to govern after the latest elections. Without entering into clairvoyance, we may assume similar dynamics as in the last eight years to prevail.

As the negotiations of the *Sejdić and Finci* implementation exemplify, the international community is trapped in this situation of nationalist outreach, patronage politics, and unhealthy systemic incentives. This is particularly true for the European Union who cannot abandon ship as the Americans or the United Nations have already done. With Bonn-power impositions off the table and accession conditionality not delivering any real results due to perceived accession fatigue, there seems to be little that the EU can do to resolve the situation. The European Commission's postponement of implementing the SAA, which Bosnia as well as all EU member states have already ratified, until *Sejdić and Finci* is implemented, testifies to the lack of any real strategy on the part of the European Union. It is for this reason that Paddy Ashdown finds frank words to describe the EU policy:

> I mean Europe has totally failed since 2006. ... I have to say that Brussels is being responsible for this reversal of dynamics in Bosnia. ... The European Union has more instruments and leverage in Bosnia, the High Representative, plus a European

---

[9]   This statement concerns votes for the state parliament coming from the FBiH.

Special Representative, a vast amount of money, a police mission—comparable to no other countries. And yet, it's done almost nothing to influence the direction of Bosnia. … 1992 seems to be repeated as well: Europe speaking but not acting dramatically.[10]

In a similar tone, Wolfgang Petritsch predicts that Bosnia is likely to remain a 'weak, relatively dysfunctional state' for the time being:

The danger of dissolution is a given and it can only be stopped by a quick and decisive integration into the European framework. By that, I do not mean an immediate accession to the EU but simply a more active policy that through the use of a more creative policy makes the perspectives of this country clearer—also in regional connection to Serbia and Croatia.[11]

It seems clear that Europe in general, and the European Union in particular have failed to present this overarching vision and have stopped exerting the kind of influence that they (may) still possess. Through their reliance on local party leaders—most visibly shown by the High Level Dialogue as part of the *Sejdić and Finci* implementation negotiations, but existent well before that in, e.g. the structure of the April package negotiations, Schwarz-Schilling's shadow dialogues, or Miroslav Lajčák's 6+1 meetings—they have not only given political legitimacy to this kind of rule by elite cartel or 'partocracy' but also de-legitimised the existing democratic institutions. Even though there is no alternative to the European way for Bosnia, as Miroslav Lajčák says, it seems highly unlikely that Bosnia in its current state will be able to perform the duties necessary for this perspective to become a reality. Christian Schwarz-Schilling captures not only the current Bosnian tragedy, but gives also a concentrated argument of an 'imposed consociation':

The fatal thing is, in my opinion, that in reality the destiny of this country and the region depends as much on the behaviour of the international community as it does on the comportment of the Bosnian politicians.[12]

---

[10]　　Ashdown, Personal Interview.
[11]　　Petritsch, Personal Interview.
[12]　　Schwarz-Schilling, Personal Interview.

Part IV:
Concluding Remarks

11 Conclusion

This study set out to investigate the relationship between consociational democratic systems and the international sphere of influence. It sought to describe the effects of continued international intervention on a seemingly sovereign and democratic political system. While it did so for the case of Bosnia and Herzegovina, its further reaching goals were to enrich the field of consociational theory and to narrow the existing research gap between international studies, comparative politics, and history through a particular understanding of political theory. Given this outline, the concluding remarks are necessarily situated on different levels.

Let us start with the obvious, the conclusions with regard to the Bosnian case. First, in order to understand contemporary politics in Bosnia-Herzegovina, we need a deeper knowledge of the historical context, in particular the nationalist debates. The Croats' insistence on their autochthonous character that should legitimise their claim for a third entity, the Bosniaks' adherence to a strong central state which nevertheless accommodates their group interests, or the Serbs' constant public contemplation of possible secession and the nature of the smaller entity are the contemporary forms of a nationalist argument to which the Bosnian peoples were subjected since the nineteenth century. Conversely, the historicity of such claims helps explain the difficulties multi-nationalist or liberal parties have in attracting public support. Whether we like it or not, the current Bosnian society is deeply shaped by ethno-national belonging, both internally and externally. Internally, the people still value their respective group-based identity and tend to select their societal networks accordingly. Presumably, this development is explainable through the 'chronological overlap' of historical developments[1] as well as through the most recent experiences of war and slaughter that helped foster the ethno-national identity. Externally, the political system and its consociational devices increase the salience of ethno-national cleavages. When the system solely accommodates one (ascribed) kind of belonging, as corporate consociations tend to do, civil society actors and the general population adjust to the prevailing political narrative. As a consequence, the historical argument as such is unlikely to be eradicated; political scientists, therefore, need to study it.

In contrast to integrationist arguments, which tend to respect societal heterogeneity but seek to bar minority cultures and demands from the political and public spheres, advocates of power sharing acknowledge the deep-rootedness of ethnic, religious, national, or linguistic identities. They do so not out of a general-

---

[1]   Bardoš, "Balkan Ethnoconfessional Nationalism."

ly primordialist orientation but because such divisions are 'a matter of empirical verification and judgement, not to be dismissed through slogans such as "the myth of ancient hatreds"'.[2] The same holds true for the Bosnian context. There is indeed little merit in the thesis of ancient hatreds in historical terms; the wars surrounding the dissolution of Yugoslavia were the deliberate result of nationalist aspirations and advocated by the strategic considerations of certain individuals. The main culprit for the war, Slobodan Milošević, was originally a lower ranking communist party cadre before he realised the potential of nationalistic rhetoric for his own purposes. The Yugoslav wars, therefore, were part of a specific strategy to enhance power and control and not the unavoidable result of historical determinism. However, in no way does this contradict the salience of ethno-national group identities after the war, or make their incorporation as the foundation of the new political system in Bosnia morally reprehensible. For reasons of historical continuity, ethno-national identities, which are based on a peculiar combination of national, religious, ethnic, and even linguistic elements, are the most important kind of group membership in contemporary Bosnia-Herzegovina. Consociationalism accepts this reality and merely seeks to accommodate the respective identities within the political system, for it deems alternative approaches less viable due to the nature of the society and the people in question.

But while consociationalism neither adheres to the primordialist character of group distinctions nor in effect creates the respective group memberships, it nevertheless strengthens such identification. Their reproduction as the essence of a political system leads to respective differentiation on all levels of social and political engagement. By promoting this kind of action, consociationalism in effect strengthens the respective historical narratives upon which such identification, rightly or wrongly, is based. It is therefore not at all surprising that Bosnian politicians, when asked about the current political issues, embark on lengthy explanations of the historical statehood argument; or when they try to link political demands to alleged historical laws or the larger principles of a people's right to self-determination; or when they try to convince their electorate that statehood was in fact already achieved by upgrading territorial autonomy through false interpretations of international legal standards. Just as the societal division of Bosnia is a fact to be accepted, the historical connotation of such current political demands must not be neglected within the analysis of the Bosnian case. In fact, there may be a farther reaching truth in this realisation, for it is anything but unlikely that group-based identities in other contexts also have a historical connotation justifying and determining current political demands and claims. As such, political scientists need to pay more attention to the historical context and try to incorporate respective variables in their quantitative or qualitative research settings.

---

[2]   O'Leary, "Power Sharing in Deeply Divided Places," 16; 33.

Second, despite its ideal-typical character in terms of political structure, we may not conceive of the Bosnian case as a pure example of consociational democracy. Brendan O'Leary is both too modest and incorrect when stating that the absence of violence in Bosnia-Herzegovina since 1995 is evidence for consociational success.[3] It is overly modest to point to the lack of large-scale murder in a specific case to prove that consociationalism is not as bad as critics would have it. O'Leary seems to unnecessarily subscribe to a rather minimalist notion with regards to the merits of a model whose general usefulness he constantly keeps advocating. The statement is also incorrect because the lack of violence in Bosnia is probably more due to the immense military presence in the immediate post-war years than to the initially inexistent consociational structures. Generally speaking, security, in a narrow sense, is hardly the result of any consociational system but a necessary precondition for the merits of the latter to develop.

O'Leary's modesty is therefore ill advised, especially since the Bosnian example does in fact not prove the inadequacy of the consociational model as such. Admittedly, the Dayton Peace Agreement envisioned a consociational system, based not on proportionality but on parity between the three constituent peoples. Furthermore, with the implementation of the 'constituent peoples' verdict of the Bosnian Constitutional Court the political system within the entities was brought up to the same consociational standards to which the central state already adhered. In structural terms, Bosnia is thus a fully-fledged, almost ideal-typical consociation. But consociationalists do not recommend consociational institutions for their own sake; instead, they advocate the increased likelihood of a specific outcome, i.e. stable democratic rule, as a reason for the introduction of such institutions. However, this outcome is only achievable if the systemic incentive structures induce a specific kind of behaviour within the political elite. If, on the other hand, other institutions alter the systemic incentive structures that the concert of consociational institutions provides, the intended outcome can no longer be ensured. The Bosnian consociation derailed in precisely this manner from the consociationalist ideal. With the incorporation of the Office of the High Representative into the local political system the prevailing incentive structures adjusted to the changed circumstances. This process was not straightforward and, in fact, included several distinct outside impulses, some of which were done simultaneously to the establishment of the consociational system while others happened only after the local system had already been formed. Nevertheless, in their totality, such actions heavily influenced the existing system and its structures. Being the goal-oriented humans that they are, the Bosnian politicians adjusted to the changed circumstances, which ultimately explains the failure of the imposed po-

---

[3]   Ibid., 34.

litical system in Bosnia-Herzegovina. Its end product could not be stable democratic rule, but a challenging dependency upon international actors.

To attribute the failure to produce a self-sustaining political system in postwar Bosnia and Herzegovina to the consociational democratic model, therefore, is not only disreputable but inaccurate as well. In the Bosnian case, we are confronted with a specific kind of consociational model that distinguishes itself from the consociational ideal probably as much as it does from the ideal of democratic theory. Neglecting this fundamental difference is impermissible, and consociationalists are not innocent for the fact that it has constantly happened in the past. Presumably as a result of contemporary consociationalism's tendency to merely emphasise the empirical component of the theory, consociationalists too easily accepted the claim of Bosnia's ideal-typical consociational character and felt the need to justify the merits of their theory under the constraints such acceptance implied. But instead of pointing to the rather shallow argument of no large-scale violence, as O'Leary does in the instance quoted above, or to the cursory argument that more time is needed before the consociational mechanisms start working properly, as Lijphart does in correspondence with Roberto Belloni,[4] advocates of consociationalism would better question the proposition of the critic's statement by referring to the distinct character of the Bosnian consociation. For without the international component, the Bosnian case is inexplicable.

Therein lies a third conclusion of the present thesis: When analysing the Bosnian case, we absolutely have to account for international influence. Well before the processes of global interdependence connected local and international decision making to an almost undistinguishable degree, the experiment in internationally supervised peace implementation in Bosnia provided us with various examples of what such a connection actually means. Without reference to goals and strategies of international actors, the case as such is incomprehensible. With regards to international actors, we may first and foremost think of the Office of the High Representative, the spokesperson and deciding agent of the international community in the field. That its impositions and intrusions into the local political system have been immense is not necessarily a novel conclusion of the present study. But I nevertheless hope to have provided a novel insight with regards to the quality and consequences of such intervention. Without the OHR, Bosnia would definitively be a different country today; given the unpredictable character of human nature, no analyst can tell us with certainty whether the Bosnian people would have been better off had the OHR not existed. Since all such arguments based on a hypothetical development without OHR interference are not falsifiable, they are in analytical terms useless.

---

[4]   See chapter 5.

But the OHR is just the most obvious form of outside intervention into the system within the Bosnian case. In fact, the multitude of international organisations engaged in the field changed the outline of the case in ways that are not yet fully understandable. While we have a rather clear idea how access to international funds induced cooperation among the political elites (under the condition that the benefits are justly distributed, whatever that may mean within the perception of the elites), we are still far away from mapping out the consequences of such influence with regards to the society and the individuals. Given the fact that much of the reconstruction efforts in the second half of the 1990s were directly organised by international organisations, it would be not surprising to find a specific kind of dependency within the society as such. Anthropological studies, therefore, need to be aware of the intrinsic connection between the Bosnian postwar society and the international sphere. In this respect, the culture of dependency in contemporary Bosnia is not a phenomenon limited to the political system, even though this is where it is most visible.

But when thinking about international actors, we must not neglect two specific features those actors possess. First of all, they are usually products of the international sphere and subject to the respective norms. International organisations, in particular, are prone to inactivity, for a plan of action requires agreement among the members, often unanimity or a qualified majority of sorts. When Bosnia vanished from the priority list of the international community and the rifts within the international sphere became visible, the OHR was put in a delicate position. Lacking international agreement on a course of action, the High Representative's options were highly constrained. In principle, the same constraints apply to all international actors constituting more than one state. Second, we need to acknowledge that international actors are not impartial. They usually have a specific belief system providing the philosophical background for their actions. More importantly, they have own goals and interests that they wish to accomplish through specific actions. When international organisations are concerned, the respective goals are usually known; but when dealing with *ad hoc* groups of states, we are usually left with a statement that is as open to interpretation as the sea is wide. The Peace Implementation Council that determines the policy of the OHR, for example, is a body of 55 countries and agencies that 'support the [Bosnian] peace process in many different ways—by assisting financially, providing troops for EUFOR, or directly running operations in Bosnia and Herzegovina'.[5] While such support is open to many interpretations, one is probably best advised to conceive of the interests of the PIC's *de facto* executive body, the Steering Board, in terms of the interests of the states which participating ambassadors represent. The

---

[5]   According to the description provided on the website of the OHR, http://www.ohr.int/pic/default.asp?content_id=38563, accessed 27 December 2013.

importance of acknowledging specific interests and agendas of international actors is far clearer when such actors are not the product of the international sphere, but its constitutive element. Nobody would dare to *prima facie* think of neutral involvement when, say, Serbia tries to influence Bosnian politics. We have no problem in accepting the existence of interests and agendas when particular states are concerned; yet we tend to hold international bodies like the OHR to some form of higher standard. Instead, we need to accept a simple truth: there are no neutral actors coming from the international sphere. Consequently, if the primary task of the OHR, i.e. to make the Bosnian polity functional, were conceived on neutral grounds, the institution's position would have to be comparable to the one, say, of a Constitutional Court—the main point being that it would have to be a genuine product of the local constitutional order subject to the usual constraints of a democratic state. If those conditions are not fulfilled, the OHR is a partisan body with all the implications this position entails.

The importance of international actors within the analysis of the Bosnian case brings us to the most important conclusion of the present study regarding consociational theory: we are capable of modelling international influence into an ideal-typical consociational system and accurately hypothesise the consequences of such adaptation. The model of an 'imposed consociation' is a specific kind of consociation system whose main characteristic is the dysfunctionality of the polity in which it is established. While the model itself is closely connected to the Bosnian case, its adaptation to other contexts is neither unthinkable nor undesirable. In the epilogue, I include some tentative remarks with regards to the usefulness of the 'imposed consociational' analytical framework in the cases of Kosovo and Macedonia. Naturally, such adaptation cannot happen without loosening the theoretical framework. However, I believe that such an action does not concern the nucleus of the model itself.

The model tries to explain how international actors influence consociational systems and under what circumstances the advantages of this kind of power sharing may become disadvantages. As an explanatory model it is based on the assumption of a (corporately or liberally designed) consociational setting and the non-existence of group cohesion as well as the presence of international influences. While International Regulating Bodies constitute the ideal type of such influences and the intervention prerogative equals the most radical form of international imposition, the model is not confined to these particular settings. I have used those to exhibit the Bosnian dynamic and to make the underlying theoretical mechanisms as visible as possible. There is nothing in the model, however, to suggest that a similar dynamic could not be expected if those two aspects were present in some softer form. For example, if instead of an IRB we simply have a particular international super power, like the United States, and instead of a

Bonn-power style intervention prerogative some form of financial or military dependence. In such cases, the quality of influence and the negative consequences in terms of the consociational design may well be similar to the ones hypothesised by the model of the 'imposed consociation'. The problem is, of course, that we cannot model all those kinds of influences into a single and coherent theoretical construct. Moreover, while we were in the lucky position of having all intrusions by the OHR into the local system well documented and easily accessible, the challenges for analytically counterweighing theoretical expectations with empirical findings are much bigger when the ideal-type scenario is abandoned. Naturally, this puts certain constraints on the applicability of the 'imposed consociational' model with respect to other cases; nevertheless, I believe that it should be attempted and could succeed with the necessary determination.

While I generally do not need to insist on the applicability of the model outside the confines of the present case study, I believe that there is a more important tendency at stake here. It comes in the form of a second conclusion with respect to consociational theory: we need to abandon the tendency of conceiving of consociational systems as inwardly closed political spheres. In this respect I second John McGarry and Brendan O'Leary's acknowledgement that early consociationalism downplayed the importance of international factors for emergence and promotion of consociational arrangements and furthermore neglected the possibilities of positive roles that outsiders can play in implementing and operationalising power-sharing settlements.[6] However, as they also note, outside intervention does not always have to be positive and may also have a negative impact on the sustainability of the consociational settlement. Given such diverse effects, it seems highly careless to exclude the international context as a variable when analysing the internal setting. International factors have not only proven key for understanding the establishment and maintenance of consociational democracy but, as the Bosnian case clearly shows, they can also explain specific aspects of the systemic logics. For precisely this reason, we need more studies that cross the divide between comparative systems analysis and international studies. The accomplishments of globalisation and the steady inclusion of post-war societies into the worldwide system of interdependence is likely to make the inclusion of international variables into the analytical context an imperative in the near future.

Implicit in the present study is the belief that deeply divided societies are probably better off with a power-sharing than an integrationist constitutional model. Purposefully, I have refrained from taking a specific position in the ongoing debate *within* the power-sharing spectrum, probably most vividly exemplified in the decade-old academic rivalry between Donald Horowitz and Arend Lijphart. While Horowitz and his followers advocate a centripetal model of power

---

[6] McGarry and O'Leary, "Power Shared after the Death of Thousands," 37–44.

sharing based on electoral systems that favour moderate candidates and encourage 'vote pooling', Lijphart and his supporters fight for consociational devices and proportional representation in order to induce cooperation between extremist politicians.[7] My hesitation in engaging in this debate stems from the simple fact that the present analysis cannot contribute towards resolving the underlying issues. Since Bosnia cannot be used as an example of consociational democracy, the respective failure does not discredit the consociational approach towards post-conflict state building. Similarly, since the centripetal devices in the Bosnian system are punctual at best and were furthermore not investigated in the present context, I see no possible way to conclude anything with respect to the merits of Horowitz's approach. Nevertheless, the present study clearly suggests that each case is different; too much theoretical strictness may therefore be counterproductive when arguing for one or the other approach to be applied in a concrete case.

The consequences of the 'imposed consociational' model are negative, for it does not lead to stable democratic rule. Consequently, if one wants to defend consociational democracy as an internationally imposed and managed method for peace in deeply divided post-war societies, one needs to be aware of the implications suggested by the model. It has been shown how difficult it is for Bosnia to escape the vicious circle in which it is currently stuck; therefore, international negotiators are well advised to anticipate the negative consequences and to avoid planting their seeds early on in the peace implementation process.

This brings us to practical recommendations that the present study may have. All of the following points are derived from theoretical and empirical considerations mentioned in the study and furthermore assume that, for whatever reason, a consociational setting has been chosen as the foundation of a post-war state (even though this choice is not necessarily part of the peace agreement).

First, while there is an obvious necessity to negotiate a peace agreement with the wartime leaders of the different factions, the staying in power of this political elite during the post-war period should be avoided. The international community should not take 'the easy deal', as Paddy Ashdown has called it, because wartime elites tend to exhibit wartime attitudes and their political stances tend to correspond to their wartime goals. Only in the best of circumstances are such politicians able to renounce their previous behaviour and to truly work towards reconciliation. Internationals should therefore encourage some kind of lustration process well before the new political system is established. For when the latter has already happened, consociationalism tends to have a self-enforcing effect, which effectively makes societal and political progress less likely.

---

[7]   For an overview of power-sharing and integrationist approaches, see O'Leary, "Power Sharing in Deeply Divided Places." See also: Horowitz, *Ethnic Groups in Conflict*; Lijphart, *Democracy in Plural Societies*.

Second, while the goal of a peace agreement has to be the establishment of a common state, the peace agreement should probably not already include a constitution as well. Much of the Bosnian tragedy is due to the fact that the constitution was part of the DPA and is as such intrinsically connected to the peace that the agreement brought. Accordingly, changes to the constitution are perceived as attempts to alter the foundation on which peace itself is based. This is an unhealthy tendency, for constitutions should always be living documents that are adapted as the circumstances demand. Such a process is next to impossible when everything is part of one major document that at least some groups regard as sacrosanct. A better alternative would be to put the locals in charge of writing a constitution on their own terms, naturally with the help of prominent constitutional scholars. Since this can hardly happen as part of the peace negotiations, it should be the first task of the (post-lustration) political elites after the war. Constitutional assemblies seem a viable option in this regard. By decoupling actual peace and the constitution, the latter can be adapted if need be without threatening the stability of the state. Such a course of action naturally entails risks and the international forces should ensure that harm is prevented as a result of negotiations.

Third, while international actors should assist the locals in making peace and writing the constitution, they should not hoist the 'mission accomplished' banner too soon. By now, I believe, it is a widely acknowledged fact that elections should not be rushed in post-war societies. After intervening in an on-going conflict, international actors, presumably in an effort to demonstrate that they have no ulterior motives, quickly proclaim the establishment of a democracy and the *pro forma* return of sovereignty to the people of the state in which they just intervened. Both theoretically and practically, such statements most often do not bear up to scrutiny. International actors remain pivotal to the development of the country and the local political (or democratic) institutions are usually merely a façade. Additionally, early elections provide political elites with legitimacy, which may not always be the best course of action. Especially unfortunate about this development is the fact that this precise situation is the beginning of a dependency that can culminate in an 'imposed consociation'. International actors are needed to ensure security and adherence to peace treaties; such security actions are not distinguishable from the task to build new political institutions. International actors, therefore, should assume full political power and responsibility of the peace implementation process in the first years. Rather than faking democracy, as David Chandler has so wonderfully put it, they should establish clear-cut protectorates. At the same time, when they hand over the responsibility to the locals, they should not keep any political governing power to themselves (however, military supervision may still be permissible, as it does not target the political system directly). Only under the condition of full local decision-making powers are the local elites under the pressures that make consociational theory workable and successful. The introduction of democracy has to mean true democracy.

Fourth, closely connected to the establishment of the political system is the rule of law. Given that corruption is one of the major obstacles to a democratically stable state and that international criminal justice is as necessary as it is difficult, the internationals should quickly introduce the respective mechanisms even before sovereignty is handed over to the locals. In this respect, I agree with Paddy Ashdown's assessment that the rule of law has to be a priority on day one.[8] Otherwise, the state as such lacks necessary credibility, which may hinder its acceptance among the people. Furthermore, one needs to be aware that the state in question is usually involved in a larger transition process. The restructuring of state industries and the redistribution of state resources through methods like privatisation is inherently prone to malfeasance, especially if handled by local political elites. The same holds true for the large amounts of reconstruction money that pours into a state that largely relies on informal networks. If local misconduct in these situations remains unprosecuted, the state is usually off to a very bad start.

Fifth, the established consociational system should not follow the corporate but rather the liberal model. In this respect, I concur with the respective findings of recent studies and the consociational recommendation that prefers self-determination to predetermination.[9] While the accommodation of group identities probably cannot be avoided immediately after the end of the war, the political system should nevertheless allow for new kinds of identities to enter the political arena on equal footing. As such, it has to be as rigid as necessary and as flexible as possible; liberal consociationalism seems to fulfil this condition. And even though the groups are more likely to agree to formalised rules in terms of quota or veto possibilities due to deep mistrust of each other, outside actors should urge them to accept more informal political institutions.[10] In general, the state should

---

[8]   Ashdown, *Swords and Ploughshares*.

[9]   Schneckener, "Making Power-Sharing Work"; McGarry and O'Leary, "Iraq's Constitution of 2005"; Rupert Taylor, ed., *Consociational Theory: McGarry and O-Leary and the Northern Ireland Conflict: McGarry and O'Leary and the Northern Ireland Conflict*, 1st ed. (London: Routledge, 2009).

[10]   See also the related research done by Nenad Stojanović in this area: Stojanović, *Dialogue*; Nenad Stojanović, "The Dilemma of Ethnic Quotas in Power Sharing Theory: The Case of Bosnia and Herzegovina," in *The Western Balkans: A European Challenge*, Milan Bufon et al., ed. (Koper: Publishing House Annales, 2006), 331–347. However, I am rather sceptical with respect to Stojanović's proposal of direct democracy in divided societies, for I believe that even clearly non-group issues may be politicised along the respective group cleavage and thus have the reverse effects. Additionally, I refer the reader to the respective counter-arguments outlined by Daniel Bochsler. See Nenad Stojanović, "Limits of Consociationalism and Possible Alternatives: Centripetal Effects of Direct Democracy in a Multiethnic Society," Francis Cheneval and Sylvie Ramel, ed. *From Peace to Shared Political Identities. Ex-*

have viable options to deal with non-cooperative groups that misuse the consociational veto possibilities. I believe that the potential of political deadlocks is the main challenge to the feasibility of a consociational post-war design. In this respect, one may think of limiting the veto possibilities to specific areas, as the Macedonian system does (see epilogue); an alternative would be to introduce new institutions that possess the procedural powers to resolve unnecessary deadlocks and induce local cooperation.

Sixth, a major problem of international involvement in the Bosnian context has been its inconsequentiality. International actors should therefore openly state their policy goals and respective demands and act accordingly. In Bosnia, the kind of zigzagging that the OHR and the international community performed not only with respect to using Bonn powers, but to its politics in general testifies to a lack of any clear strategy. Peace implementation processes cannot be sacrosanct as they always need to be adaptable to changing circumstances; but there are certain outlines in terms of content and means to be employed that need to be clear to all participants. Only when the locals can predict the course of international action are they likely to take their part of the bargain seriously.

All these practical recommendations come too late for Bosnia-Herzegovina. The present study has hopefully contributed to a better understanding of the mistakes made in the past. Since political scientists tend to be rather bad prognosticators, we are well advised to refrain from any predictions with regards to the future of the country. Given the prevailing dynamics, however, one can hardly be optimistic. The international community has lost all the credibility it once had with the local politicians and the European Union has so far proven unable to assume the firm role that it probably should have. During the elaboration of the study, I was repeatedly cautioned that one could not talk seriously to the Bosnians by which both the people and the political elites were usually meant. I was told that the people and their representatives would only understand the language of brute force and were genuinely immune to the concept of win-win-situations. Often times I have been pointed to the mandate of Paddy Ashdown as the ultimate blueprint of how one should behave with the Bosnian politicians. Often, these statements came with practical advice on how to proceed from here. The European Union should stop sending money to Bosnia; the International Monetary Fund should stop all loans; and the OHR should impose the necessary legislation to

---

ploring Pathways in Contemporary Bosnia-Hercegovina. Special Volume of Transitions 51, no. 1,2 (2011): 99–114; Daniel Bochsler, "Let the People Decide? Learning from Swiss Direct Democracy in a Comparative Perspective," Francis Cheneval and Sylvie Ramel, ed. *From Peace to Shared Political Identities. Exploring Pathways in Contemporary Bosnia-Hercegovina. Special Volume of Transitions* 51, no. 1,2 (2011): 115–119.

move the country forward. The advice givers were convinced that only such hard action would make the local political elite live up to their responsibilities.

While I have much sympathy for a stronger course of action from international actors towards the Bosnian political elite, I strongly dislike the underlying premise of such statements. If taken seriously, these statements ultimately mean that the Bosnians are not ready for democracy and that the Bosnian state as such is not sustainable without outside intervention. I have yet to find out on what grounds such statements are made, something none of the advice givers have been able to tell me in greater detail. Furthermore, I suspect that the people making such statements are not really aware of the latter's further impact. But despite such fundamental flaws, it would be a mistake not to listen to such claims. After all, what those statements also express is a deep trust in the capacity of the internationals to handle the Bosnian situation and get the country out of the dead-end in which the local political elites have manoeuvred it. Especially the European Union, which has lost much credibility within the political elite, still enjoys some reputation within the public. And both the public and the political leaders seem convinced that the United States could do something if it really wanted.

The international community as a whole has thus the responsibility to help the state. This is not only true for moral and historical reasons that emerge out of the inaction in the 1990s but for practical concerns. They are the only ones that can help set the local political system on track once again. What is needed is a clear strategy in this regard as well as political will and determination. Conversely, abandoning ship under the present circumstances in Bosnia and, for example, closing the OHR without any subsequent arrangement or a clear EU perspective must be interpreted as the ultimate capitulation of international intervention in this country. What consequences this would have for the people, is presently unclear. I doubt, however, that they would be benign.

Epilogue

12 A Short Postscript on other Cases: Macedonia[1] and Kosovo

In the conclusion, I discussed the possibility of applying the analytical framework of an 'imposed consociation' to other cases. In the following, I would like to tentatively and shortly attempt this with respect to the cases that, following a most similar systems design, seem most comparable to the Bosnian situation: Macedonia[2] after the Ohrid Agreement of 2001 and Kosovo after the imposition of constitutional framework of 2001. In methodological terms, the comparability of these cases has been established through many comparative studies so that I need not restate the respective reasoning.[3] Furthermore, as it is not feasible to follow the methodological approach of the study in this short and summary section, I shall limit myself to analysing secondary literature with regards to the questions of interest in the present study. After a brief introduction to the historical context, I shall follow the same analytical framework employed for the Bosnian case in chapter 10.

12.1 The historical context

The Albanian-Macedonian conflict is a fairly recent dichotomy in Macedonian history. Until the 1980s, Yugoslav Macedonia had a rather positive relationship to the central government in Belgrade. The federal state supported the Macedonian party and republican leadership in their nationalising policies, which sought to strengthen a particularly Macedonian cultural identity.[4] The apparent success of such policies became obvious only in the 1980s as a result of rising ethnic tensions in neighbouring Kosovo. These events increased Albanian activity in revolutionary groups within Macedonia. More importantly, they led to a change in the

---

1   The findings in this postscript referring to Macedonia have previously been presented in the form of a paper at the UMD Global Conference in Skopje. Cf. Adis Merdzanovic, "Imposing Compromise. Consociational Arrangements in Macedonia and Bosnia-Herzegovina" (presented at the 4th Global Conference of the United Macedonian Diaspora, Skopje, 2013).

2   Throughout the text, I shall use Macedonia instead of the official name 'Former Yugoslav Republic of Macedonia' (FYROM).

3   See for example Thorsten Gromes, *Ohne Staat und Nation ist keine Demokratie zu machen: Bosnien und Herzegowina, Kosovo und Makedonien nach den Bürgerkriegen* (Baden-Baden: Nomos, 2012); Bieber and Keil, "Power-Sharing Revisited"; Bieber, "The Balkans."

4   Justin L. C. Eldridge, "Playing at Peace: Western Politics, Diplomacy and the Stabilization of Macedonia," *European Security* 11, no. 3 (2002): 50.

ethnic composition of the Macedonian population. Between the Yugoslav census of 1953 and the admittedly controversial Macedonian census of 1994, the Albanian share of the total population rose from 12.5 to 23 per cent; in other words, almost doubling within forty years.[5] The reason for this shift lies in a high birth rate of Albanians, but also in the influx of many Kosovar Albanian refugees. Until the mid-1990s, around 130,000 Kosovar Albanians came to Macedonia and many of them assumed prominent positions within the revolutionary groups.[6] In this respect, the ethnic conflict between Macedonians and Albanians was not a genuinely Macedonian product but the consequence of spill-over effects.[7]

But the conflict also had internal causes. The local Albanians boycotted the 1991 independence referendum and, in spring 1992, even organized an illegal plebiscite over the issue of autonomy with the goal to show the world that Macedonia was not ready for international recognition because the rights (i.e. autonomy) and demands (recognition of Kosovo) of the Albanians were neither respected nor met.[8] Even though the reality did not necessarily reflect the alleged discrimination, there were some genuine reasons for friction between the Albanian population and the Macedonian state: the complex question of the Albanian University, the general situation in the minority education system, and the underground activities of the Albanian separatists.[9] Room for improvement was espe-

---

[5]   Nada Boškovska, "Im Zentrum des Balkans und am Rande des europäischen Interesses: Makedoniens schwierige Lage in den 1990er Jahren," in *Tranformation und historisches Erbe in den Staaten des europäischen Ostens*, Carsten Goehrke and Seraina Gilly, ed. (Bern: Peter Lang, 2000), 463. In 2002, a census was conducted as part of the Ohrid Agreement. It showed that ethnic Macedonians comprised 64.18% and Albanians 25.17% of the population. See Saso Ordanoski and Aleksandar Matovski, "Between Ohrid and Dayton: The Future of Macedonia's Framework Agreement," *Südosteuropa Mitteilungen* 4 (2007): 57.

[6]   Boškovska, "Im Zentrum des Balkans und am Rande des europäischen Interesses," 460.

[7]   This 'foreign connotation' is why the Albanian side remained split during the 2001 conflict. The 'older' Albanian elites had a deeper connection to the Macedonian state than the newly arrived and substantially radicalized political agitators. In fact, one reason why the war could be contained was exactly the passivity of the older Albanian population that did not buy into the concept of a 'larger Albania'. See Stefan Troebst, "Vom ethnopolitischen Schlachtfeld zum interethnischen Stabilitätspol: Gewalt und Gewaltfreiheit in der Region Makedonien im 'langen' 20. Jahrhundert," in *Das makedonische Jahrhundert: Von den Anfängen der nationalrevolutionären Bewegung zum Abkommen von Ohrid 1893-2001*, by Stefan Troebst (München: Oldenbourg Verlag, 2007), 36.

[8]   Boškovska, "Im Zentrum des Balkans und am Rande des europäischen Interesses," 464.

[9]   Stefan Troebst, "Von der 'Makedonischen Frage' zur 'Albanischen Frage': Der Balkan am Ende des 20. Jahrhunderts," in *Das makedonische Jahrhundert: Von den Anfängen der nationalrevolutionären Bewegung zum Abkommen von Ohrid 1893-2001*, by Stefan Troebst (München: Oldenbourg Verlag, 2007), 369.

cially present with regards to the integration of the Albanians into the state administration; a failure to do so left them economically and socially disadvantaged. It also constituted some form of discrimination that the 1991 constitution mandated Macedonian, in Cyrillic, as the only national language and specifically recognized only the Macedonian Orthodox Church by name.[10] The central character of the state thus seemed distinctly Macedonian. Consequently, Albanians complained of having to live under the 'tyranny of the Macedonian majority', for their constitutional status was downgraded compared to the 1974 Yugoslav constitution that had granted them (together with Turks) constitutional equality with Macedonians.[11] For precisely this reason, no specific minority-related concessions by the Macedonian authorities could have changed the general outline of the inner Macedonian conflict. The Albanians wanted to become a constituent people within the state of Macedonia, their language recognized as official, and to be represented in all state institutions according to their share in the population, which they saw as around forty per cent.[12] In the 1990s, the Macedonian authorities paid little attention to this kind of political and identity-related inclusion of the sizable Albanian minority. They regarded the Albanians as merely another national minority subject to the general rule of an inherently Macedonian state, and effectively neglected their constitutive character.[13]

Due to the largely inexistent historicity of the underlying division, a split in Albanian leadership, and the engagement of the internationals, the intensity of the 2001 conflict was rather low. Battles between the Albanian National Liberation Army (NLA) and the Macedonian authorities lasted some eight months and resulted in 200 dead, 650 wounded, and around 140,000 internally displaced people.[14] Even though there is no direct correlation between casualties and the characterization of the situation as 'war', Stefan Troebst's description of the 2001 events in Macedonia as '*drôle de guerre*'[15] is certainly accurate; at no point did the fighting actually amount to full-fledged war.

In Kosovo, we find a distinctively different situation that is highly shaped by historical connotations. The cultural and religious importance of *Kosovo Polje* with-

---

[10]   Eldridge, "Playing at Peace," 55.

[11]   Armend Reka, "The Ohrid Agreement: The Travails of Inter-Ethnic Relations in Macedonia," *Human Rights Review* 9, no. 1 (1 March 2008): 56.

[12]   Boškovska, "Im Zentrum des Balkans und am Rande des europäischen Interesses," 463.

[13]   Troebst, "Vom ethnopolitischen Schlachtfeld zum interethnischen Stabilitätspol," 36.

[14]   Pavlos I. Koktsidis, *Strategic Rebellion. Ethnic Conflict in FYR Macedonia and the Balkans* (Bern: Peter Lang, 2012), 187.

[15]   Stefan Troebst, "Gross-Kosovo," in *Das makedonische Jahrhundert: Von den Anfängen der nationalrevolutionären Bewegung zum Abkommen von Ohrid 1893-2001*, by Stefan Troebst (München: Oldenbourg Verlag, 2007), 393–405.

in Serb national mythology and ecclesiastical history has been sufficiently ex-plained in the first part of the present study. I shall therefore not repeat it here, even though it forms an important part of understanding the historical connotation of the Kosovo war. Suffice it to say that the Serb nation has a deeply rooted con-nection to the area of modern Kosovo so that nationalist sentiments can be easily mobilised within large parts of the population when this specific strip of land is concerned. While Macedonia's statehood was recognised through the status of a Yugoslav republic after 1945, Kosovo merely received the status of an autono-mous region in 1948; and it was only in 1974 that it became an autonomous prov-ince thus receiving direct representation in the federal executive.[16] The general accommodation tendency in terms of national demands in post-1960 Yugoslavia directly threatened the traditional Serb dominance within Kosovo's party and fed-eral structures. While the respective census data is subject to much debate, it seems widely acknowledged that the Serb population in Kosovo, which was around 25 per cent between 1945 and 1961, started to decline thereafter. In the early 1970s, the Serbs made up roughly 18 per cent of the local population, com-pared to about 70 per cent Albanians; it is estimated that during the sixties and seventies the Serb population fell at the same rate of about five per cent per dec-ade.[17] The reasons for this decline are of lesser importance in the present context and probably the result of higher birth rates among Albanians as well as a con-stant emigration by the Serbs with both causes being linked to the poor economic development of the province.[18] Those demographic changes soon transformed in-to political influence. As Bieber and Keil note, 'in the 1970s and 1980s, power in Kosovo shifted increasingly from the Serb minority to the Albanian majority.'[19] While we still lack reliable census data with regards to the present situation, it is estimated that there are roughly 130,000 Serbs in contemporary Kosovo; this would correspond to six or seven per cent of the total population.[20]

Since the 1980s at the latest, therefore, there was an imbalance between de-mographics and political representation. The resulting political conflict was made worse by the fact that Kosovo did not enjoy the status of a republic but formally remained under Serbian sovereignty. Accordingly, Serbia had a great interest in keeping the Serb forces in power in the province and thus kept supporting their respective struggles. The entire conflict, therefore, was 'less within Kosovo, but

---

[16]   Bieber and Keil, "Power-Sharing Revisited," 341.

[17]   The respective numbers are taken from Momčilo Pavlović, "Demographic Changes in Kosovo - 1974–1981," *TransConflict*, 5 April 2013, http://www.transconflict.com/2013/04/demographic-changes-in-kosovo-1974-1981-054/.

[18]   For a deeper discussion of these arguments, see Ibid.

[19]   Bieber and Keil, "Power-Sharing Revisited," 342.

[20]   European Stability Initiative, *The Lausanne Principle. Multiethnicity, Territory and the Future of Kosovo's Serbs* (Berlin/Pristin: European Stability initiative, 7 June 2004), http://www.esiweb.org/pdf/esi_document_id_53.pdf.

rather between Serbia and Kosovo'.[21] After Milošević realised the potential of revived nationalist ideology in this respect, the catastrophe took its course. While the Albanians fought for their rights as a national group in the forms of sovereignty and autonomy for Kosovo, the Serbs opposed any such plans and denied the legitimacy of any respective institutions. Soon enough, the fight took a violent form between the Kosovo Liberation Army (KLA) and the Yugoslav Army that showed little mercy to the local population. In fact, the Kosovo war of 1999 was the direct result of Milošević's attempt to produce a *fait accompli* and solve the issue once and for all by military means. It is only due to the international community and its humanitarian intervention that a larger tragedy within the Kosovar population could be averted.

12.2 The Assumptions of an 'Imposed Consociation' in Macedonia and Kosovo

An 'imposed consociation' assumes intra-group competition and the presence of a consociational system. Both conditions are fulfilled in the Macedonian case. Given the relatively low intensity of the war and its comparatively small historicity, the post-Ohrid Macedonian constitution was adapted to reflect the principles of a liberal consociation. The state kept its 'unitary character'[22] and the Albanians, together with other peoples, were recognised as part of the citizenry of Macedonia.[23] Their position was furthermore advanced through changes in the local self-government law, which stipulates that 'if an ethnic community numbers more than 20% in the total population within the municipality, its language and alphabet automatically become official.'[24] This provision is of particular interest, for the groups are not pre-determined; the 20 per cent rule could potentially apply to any group, provided it has a significant size. Macedonia furthermore does not know the instrument of reserved seats for ethnic communities, but 'employs a system of proportional representation with electoral districts designed to ensure minority representation in the state legislature'.[25] Territorial autonomy is inexistent as far as the constitutional structure is concerned. In parliament, the so-called Badinter principle constitutes a consociational veto right: for laws directly affecting culture, the use of language, education, personal documentation, and the use of symbols, a double majority, i.e. in parliament and within non-majority com-

---

[21] Bieber and Keil, "Power-Sharing Revisited," 357.

[22] Article 1.2 of the Ohrid Framework Agreement (OFA).

[23] Annex A, OFA, Preamble to the Constitution.

[24] Reka, "The Ohrid Agreement," 59.

[25] Bieber and Keil, "Power-Sharing Revisited," 347.

munity representations, is needed.[26] Lastly, Macedonia's grand coalition governments have been based on informal rather than formal arrangements. Since 1992 there has been a general willingness towards informal power sharing between Macedonians and Albanians in the executive branch. In recent years, this willingness even transformed into pre-election coalition governments with parties from smaller minorities.[27] In its totality, the Ohrid Agreement is therefore an extremely flexible document. Its provisions 'are particularly agile for solving interethnic problems because they do not confine the actors through too many details and strictly defined procedures of how to implement the items elaborated in the Agreement.'[28]

As Ordanoski and Matovski explain with respect to party competition, we find indications for ethnic outbidding in post-Ohrid Macedonia: Since 'two parties in each ethnic community have comparable chances of winning the majority of votes from their related ethnic groups' and the tradition demands including one party of each community in the government, the 'political struggle centres on the interests of the respective ethnic constituents, so habitually, the major ethnic opposition parties would take a more radical stance to advance these interests vis-à-vis the other groups'.[29] This dynamic within the Macedonian electoral corpus—between the VMRO-DPMNE and the SDSM—and the Albanian electoral corpus—between the DUI and the DPA*[30]—is not an uncommon result of consociational systems. However, as long as these dynamics work properly, ethnic outbidding in the election phase is compensated by a generally coalescent behaviour in government according to consociational theory.[31]

When analysing the post-war situation in Kosovo, we are in a worse position than with Macedonia or Bosnia. For while the Kosovo case is usually perceived as a consociational polity, we lack a unique document like the DPA or the OFA in which the respective provisions are recorded. The Kumanovo Agreement[32] and UN Security Council Resolution 1244 meant the end of the war and the estab-

---

26   Reka, "The Ohrid Agreement," 59. See also article 69.2 of the Macedonian constitution, as amended by Annex A of the OFA.

27   Bieber and Keil, "Power-Sharing Revisited," 351–2.

28   Ordanoski and Matovski, "Between Ohrid and Dayton," 49.

29   Ibid., 54.

30   VMRO-DPMNE: Internal Macedonian Revolutionary Organization-Democratic Party for Macedonian National Unity; SDSM: Social Democrats; DPA*: Democratic Party of Albanians (the asterisk is used in order to avoid confusion with the Dayton Peace Agreement); DUI: Democratic Union for Integration.

31   Daalder, "The Consociational Democracy Theme."

32   The Military Technical Agreement between the International Security force ('KFOR') and the Governments of the Federal Republic of Yugoslavia and the Republic of Serbia, available online: http://www.nato.int/kosovo/docu/a990609a.htm. Accessed 29 December 2013.

lishment of a full-fledged protectorate over the territory (see next section regarding the competencies of the UNMIK mission). In 2001, the Special Representative of the Secretary-General, Hans Haekkerup, imposed a constitutional framework for the provisional self-government of Kosovo.[33] This framework established constitutional institutions, such as the assembly, the presidency, the government, and the courts under the limits of international supervision. Ethnic, national, or linguistic communities were given the right to use their language and alphabets in contact with the state administration, receive education and information in their national language, enjoy equal opportunities with respect to employment in public service, display their respective community symbols, enjoy free access to and representation within public media, etc. In order to fill the 120 seats of the assembly, a system of proportional representation was introduced; however, it included 20 reserved seats for non-Albanian communities (10 for Serbs and 10 for other minorities). Similarly, the framework stipulated that at least two ministers in government had to come from communities other than the community having a majority in the assembly, with one of them necessarily being a Serb. The framework thus had a strongly consociational character, which was 'largely emulated by the Kosovo Constitution adopted in June 2008'.[34] However, like in the Macedonian case, the framework did not foresee the consociational principle of territorial autonomy. Instead, 'Macedonia and Kosovo redrew municipal borders to create new municipalities where the non-dominant community would be most numerous'.[35]

While Kosovo does *de jure* possess the consociational makeup upon which an 'imposed consociation' relies, the same cannot be said for intra-group competition. In fact, the mere concept of party politics is inaccurate when we are confronted with the Kosovar case. In Bosnia as well as in Macedonia, the notion of non-cohesive groups was a precondition of intra-group competition for governmental seats or representation in parliament. It was thus based on a general acceptance of the political system and a readiness to enter into competition within the respective political framework. In Kosovo, we do not find such a dynamic. The Serb side always rejected participation within the consociational state structures since it deemed the Kosovar state illegitimate. Serb participation in the elections has happened, but never to such a degree that we could assume the respective results to be accurate. Consequently, the respective mechanisms could not be developed and the consociational system remained merely formal and non-functional.

---

33   See the Constitutional Framework for Provisional Self-Government in Kosovo, UNMIK regulation 2001/9, available online: http://www.assembly-kosova.org/com mon/docs/FrameworkPocket_ENG_Dec2002.pdf, accessed 29 December 2013.

34   Bieber and Keil, "Power-Sharing Revisited," 344.

35   Ibid., 356.

12.3 The International Regulating Body

The model of the 'imposed consociation' centres on the role international actors
played in establishing the consociation as well as their continued interference
with the system through International Regulatory Bodies with intervention prerogatives. As far as Macedonia is concerned, the first assumption is clearly fulfilled. In fact, one reason why the Macedonian conflict never really amounted to a
war lies in the international environment. With the end of the Kosovo conflict and
the establishment of an international protectorate in 1999, the international community was omnipresent in the region. Moreover, it had learnt from previous mistakes and was now determined not to let Macedonia's conflict get out of hand.
NATO, the United States, and the European Union pressured both parties in the
conflict not to apply unnecessary force and to seek a negotiated solution. This is
why, despite violent outbursts by Macedonian extremists and the Albanian guerrillas, the conflict could largely be contained.[36] In late July 2001, six months after
the beginning of the fighting, 'NATO brokered security arrangements between
the government security forces, [while] the EU and US encouraged the political
dialogue and confidence-building measures that proved to be necessary to end the
fighting.'[37] Of course, those diplomatic efforts were supported by a general reluctance to use excessive force for political purposes on both sides of the conflict.
Ultimately, this meant that the radicalisation tactics of the extremist elements
never gained much traction.[38] As with the Dayton Agreement, the international
negotiators tried to seclude the group representatives, which is why NATO and
EU officials shifted the negotiations from Skopje to Ohrid in order to 'isolate the
negotiators and protect them from negative media exposure and popular reactions.'[39]

The Ohrid Agreement foresaw a specific role for the international community within the implementation efforts. Article 8.3 of the OFA invites the international community to convene a donor's conference and to provide financial support for 'measures to be undertaken for the purposes of implementing this
Framework Agreement'.[40] The role of the internationals is further specified in
Annex C of the agreement dedicated to implementation and confidence-building

---

[36]   Troebst, "Vom ethnopolitischen Schlachtfeld zum interethnischen Stabilitätspol," 36.

[37]   Eldridge, "Playing at Peace," 65.

[38]   Troebst, "Vom ethnopolitischen Schlachtfeld zum interethnischen Stabilitätspol," 37.
       This "lack of enthusiasm for interethnic confrontation" was not only a constraint to
       the use of ethnic populism in 1990s politics, but also helps one understand the gen-
       eral stability of the Ohrid arrangement. See Ordanoski and Matovski, "Between
       Ohrid and Dayton," 53.

[39]   Koktsidis, *Strategic Rebellion*, 184.

[40]   Similarly, Article 3.3 of Annex C states that the European Commission and the
       World Bank should convene a meeting of international donors, while Article 4.1 of
       the same annex asks for support to strengthen the 'financial basis of municipalities'.

measures. Here, the international community is invited to 'facilitate, monitor and assist in the implementation' of the agreement while the parties 'request such efforts to be coordinated by the EU in cooperation with the Stabilization and Association Council'.[41] Apart from assisting in the area of refugee return, the international community—in the form of the OSCE, the European Union, and the United States—were also charged with assisting to achieve a representative composition of the police forces and in training those police forces *inter alia* with regard to professional conduct and human rights. Furthermore, international assistance was sought in the areas of jurisprudence, higher education and the media sector. On a military level, the international community's engagement in Macedonia is underlined by NATO actions undertaken as part of the operation 'Essential Harvest,' whose goal it was to collect weapons of the NLA and to supervise its demobilisation.[42] In general, these provisions contain a clear-cut differentiation between the internationals and the locals. While it is clear that the main task of the parties signing the agreement is to implement it, the international community is asked to *assist* in this process. However, it is not mere assistance the agreement foresees, but a substantial support in terms of *modernising* the country's infrastructure and administration. By their nature, such provisions presuppose the existence of a functioning, albeit not ideal political system and a generally accepted statehood. We thus do not have the condition of some sort of IRB with certain intervention prerogatives in the Macedonian case.

External actors were crucial in the establishment of the Kosovo consociation. After international intervention forced Serbia to abandon all forms of control in post-war Kosovo, the United Nations established a full-fledged protectorate over the territory. Security Council Resolution 1244 tasked the military security presence, i.e. KFOR, *inter alia* with maintaining the ceasefire, demilitarising KLA forces, ensuring a secure environment for refugee return, establishing public safety, ensuring the freedom of movement, as well as supervising the security situation until the 'international civil presence' could take over. In the form of the United Nations Mission in Kosovo (UNMIK), the latter was tasked 'to provide an interim administration for Kosovo under which the people of Kosovo can enjoy substantial autonomy within the Federal Republic of Yugoslavia, and which will provide transitional administration while establishing and overseeing the development of provisional democratic self-governing institutions to ensure conditions for a peaceful and normal life for all inhabitants of Kosovo' (paragraph 10). According to paragraph 11 of the resolution, its main responsibilities included *inter*

---

[41]   The articles cited in this paragraph all refer to Annex C of the OFA. Concretely, I refer to Articles 1.1, 3, 5.2, 5.3, 5.4, and 6.

[42]   Ulf Brunnbauer, "The Implementation of the Ohrid Agreement: Ethnic Macedonian Resentments," *Journal on Ethnopolitics and Minority Issues in Europe*, no. 1 (2002): 6.

alia the establishment of substantial autonomy and self-government in Kosovo, performing basic civilian administrative functions where and as long as required, organising and overseeing the development of provisional institutions for democratic and autonomous self-government (including elections), gradually transferring the responsibility for those institutions to the locals, and, in a final stage, overseeing the transfer of authority from Kosovo's provisional institutions to institutions established under a political settlement. The resolution thus tasked the UNMIK with setting up the state and running it whilst it encouraged both conflict parties to pursue further negotiations aimed at finding a permanent political solution for the makeup of the state.

Such a permanent solution proved impossible to find. After many rounds of negotiations between representatives of Serbia and Kosovo had failed, Kosovo unilaterally proclaimed its independence in February 2008. Since a number of states, including some larger nations, accepted the sovereignty of Kosovo, the Kosovar-Serb debate was elevated to the international level. Serbia, determined not to let the province secede, started an international counter campaign that also included the request of an advisory opinion by the International Court of Justice on the legality of Kosovo's independence proclamation. In 2010, the court ruled that the proclamation was in accordance with international law.[43] From that moment on, it seemed clear that a solution to the Kosovar situation would have to be found between Serbia and Kosovo and not through any distinct action of the international community within the state of Kosovo. Since the proclamation of independence, UNMIK has drastically reduced its activity in Kosovo. In practice, it has been replaced by several other international agencies: the European Commission Liaison Office, the EU Special Representative that heads the International Civilian Office, and the EULEX, which advises Kosovo on judicial reform. As Florian Bieber has pointed out, this international confusion of different institutions with different roles has some real-life consequences:

> For example, international missions in Kosovo are divided between the 'status neutral' and those supportive of Kosovo's independence; this, along with the multitude of actors, often makes communication difficult and blurs lines of responsibility. The European Union's various roles accentuate its different priorities; in trying to appeal to everybody - from EU members which don't recognise Kosovo, to the Serbian government, Serbs in the enclaves and the Kosovo government - it risks living in contradiction.[44]

---

[43] The advisory opinion is accessible here: http://www.icj-cij.org/docket/files/141/15987.pdf. Accessed 29 December 2013.

[44] Florian Bieber, "Kosovo: One Year on," *openDemocracy*, 17 February 2009, http://www.opendemocracy.net/article/kosovo-one-year-on. Accessed 29 December 2013.

With the proclamation of independence, the policy of the international community on the ground thus changed dramatically. Ultimately, this step also decreased its importance with respect to the existing political system.

12.4 The incentive structure in post-conflict Macedonia and Kosovo

In Macedonia, we can find a twofold development with respect to the functionality of the political system. On the one hand, it took the international community a lot of arm-twisting in order to get the system going. As Ulf Brunnbauer has shown for the first year, '[t]he whole process of implementing the Framework Agreement proved that external monitoring, support and occasionally [sic] intervention is crucial for the realization of the planned reforms because, without international mediation, the political parties in the Republic of Macedonia hardly find compromises on those vital issues.'[45] Brunnbauer's statement is based on the controversies surrounding NATO's declaration of successful completion of operation 'Essential Harvest' after 3,800 weapons had been collected (the government claimed that the NLA possessed up to 85,000 weapons), as well as controversies about delays in passing the law on local self-government. As he convincingly shows, Macedonian opposition was crucially responsible for those delays. But interestingly enough, 'opposition rose mainly to those provisions which dealt with the identity of the state and had a more symbolic character. The far-reaching changes concerning the official use of other languages, or the introduction of "double majorities" in parliament did not, by contrast, provoke much public debate.'[46] Opposition to the OFA had thus an ethno-nationalist character and 'was mostly aired by nationalist intellectuals, the Macedonian media and political hardliners who all should not be taken as representatives of the whole ethnic Macedonian population'.[47] Such an analysis is supported by the fact that the first post-Ohrid elections in 2002 were won by the Social Democrats who, 'despite the strong negative image of this party in the Macedonian electorate'[48] subsequently entered into a governing coalition with the DUI, the winner of the Albanian ballot and the political wing of the former Albanian guerrillas. Even though the consociational system seemingly worked, a significant challenge occurred in 2006. The VMRO, which has a distinctly nationalist orientation, won the elections and, acting against tradition, chose to enter into a coalition not with the winner of the Albanian ballot, the DUI, but with the runner-up, the DPA*. The DUI claimed that while not illegal, such an action was clearly directed against the spirit of the OFA.

---

[45]   Brunnbauer, "The Implementation of the Ohrid Agreement," 7.

[46]   Ibid.

[47]   Ibid., 17.

[48]   Ordanoski and Matovski, "Between Ohrid and Dayton," 55.

Unimpressed by such accusations, the VRMO 'decided to resist rather than accommodate DUI'; as a consequence, 'the Badinter majority in parliament became DUI's main instrument in its dealings with the executive.'[49] The DUI thus used its veto potential to protest the general setup of the government. Macedonia was thus on its way to embark on the same incentive structure that the model of an 'imposed consociation' predicts.

Due to the reaction of the international community, however, it did not. Therein lies the second tendency of post-conflict Macedonia. Lacking a structural intervention prerogative, the 'crisis' was resolved by US and EU pressure; those led to direct VMRO-DUI negotiations and an agreement to reinforce the legal provisions for the use of the Badinter majority.[50] The international community thus acted *indirectly* and managed to resolve the crisis without actual imposition. Since the OFA did not foresee a civilian component to the agreement's implementation, the international community had no other choice than to act indirectly. The parties themselves had to find a solution within the settings provided by the political system. It is precisely for this reason that the role of the EU Special Representative (EUSR) and the OSCE 'have been limited in the post-conflict period' and the EUSR 'and key foreign embassies have only been informally key mediators in conflicts of the implementation of the Ohrid Agreement.'[51]

As further developments showed, systemic pressure towards extremist positions were not eradicated with the VMRO-DUI agreement. However, this agreement opened up the possibility of cooperation between those two rather antagonistic parties. External events helped foster this cooperation (something also in line with consociational theory). At the 2008 NATO summit in Bucharest, Greek objections towards Macedonia's name prevented the latter from becoming a member of the military alliance, a goal both local ethnic groups supported. As a reaction, Macedonia's political elites chose to hold early elections, during which Prime Minister Gruevski of VMRO campaigned 'on a platform of ethnic pride based in part on an idiosyncratic view of Macedonians' glorious ancient past that he had developed after coming to office in 2006 and advanced with an aggressive media campaign.'[52] The VMRO won the elections in a landslide and formed a coalition government with the DUI. Greek politics thus not only united Macedonian and Albanian political elites but also allowed for a revival of purest Macedonian nationalism that has continued to dominate the political sphere ever since. Gruevski's policies have thereby a dual character: they are designed towards

---

49   Ibid., 56.
50   Ibid.
51   Bieber, "The Balkans," 315.
52   International Crisis Group, *Macedonia: Ten Years after the Conflict*, Europe Report (Skopje/Istanbul/Brussels, 2011), 1, http://www.crisisgroup.org/en/regions/europe/ balkans/macedonia/212-macedonia-ten-years-after-the-conflict.aspx.

achieving EU and NATO membership, but also possess a strong nationalist connotation as exemplified by the efforts to promote Macedonia's ancient heritage in the form of the Skopje 2014 project.[53] While this project raised concerns on the international level and put into question the commitment to a multi-ethnic Macedonia, VMRO's coalition partner DUI supported it, albeit not with much enthusiasm and probably within the context of some political bargain. Nevertheless, when the VMRO-DUI coalition received a second mandate in the early elections of 2011, the DUI insisted on a more effective role in government, feeling that its engagement previously had been cosmetic. A common platform was adopted and focused on five priorities: economic development, Euro-Atlantic integration, corruption and organized crime, further implementation of Ohrid and investments in education.[54] DUI's role in the coalition was strengthened, for it assumed responsibility for Macedonia's Euro-Atlantic agenda, for the Ministries of European affairs and defence were now to be held by an Albanian.

Admittedly, such commitments may seem cosmetic even today and, as the International Crisis Group argues, there are certain indications that Macedonia's civic character has not yet been sufficiently reflected by the political structures and implemented policies.[55] In fact, actions directed against the freedom of the media and the rule of law put into question the democratic character of the Macedonian government.[56] Ethnic tensions remain high, not least as a result of the nationalising policy of the present government. But it would be inaccurate to assume the general inadequateness of the political system as such, since the increased influence of the DUI in the government is a genuine product of a largely functioning political system. In other words, it is a success of consociationalism—at least for the moment.

The situation in Kosovo is much more complex than the one in Macedonia; and we are far from understanding the respective structures as clearly. As I have already explained, the Kosovar political system had never really started working, which is why the consequences of an 'imposed consociation' could hardly be observed. The general problem in analysing the Kosovar case with the present framework is the numerical minority of the Serbs in the state as well as their factual rejection of participating in any Kosovar political system. When a group opposes the consociational system that is designed to accommodate its interests, the model is deprived of its primary purpose. Furthermore, some of the minority

---

[53]   Ibid., 2–3.

[54]   Ibid., 6.

[55]   International Crisis Group, *Macedonia*.

[56]   Emily Thompson, „Big Censorship Fears in Little Macedonia," *Radio Free Europe Radio Liberty,* 21 October 2014, http://www.rferl.org/content/big-fears-of-censor ship-in-little-macedonia/26562554.html, accessed 21 October 2014.

rights provisions do not apply to core legislation, which puts into question the effectiveness of the consociational setup. Pointing to this aspect and the general situation, Bieber and Keil detect a 'problematic situation of power-sharing arrangements in Kosovo' and thus exclude the case from comparative analysis.[57] Since a serious analysis of the respective mechanisms would require much more space and research than the scope of this short postscript provides, I am inclined to follow their suggestion. In addition to the undetermined character of the system due to the Serb rejection of the new state, I also believe that such course of action is permissible since Kosovo's future will probably be decided on the international level. According to the website 'Kosovo Thanks You',[58] 105 out of 193 UN Member states recognised the independent state of Kosovo by the end of 2013. Even though such a number may seem impressive for a state that is in existence for some six years, the real battle for Kosovo's recognition lies in the relations between Kosovo and Serbia.

In this respect, the 15 point agreement brokered by the European Union in April 2013 is surely of extreme importance.[59] While Serbia still refuses to recognise Kosovo as a sovereign state, the agreement nevertheless includes provisions that secure full sovereignty of the Kosovar state over the Serb dominated municipalities. However, those municipalities are given the right to form an association or community so that the powers awarded to municipalities following the European Charter on Local Self Government and respective Kosovo law can be exercised collectively. While the agreement foresees special provisions in order to ensure Serb representation in the judiciary as well as the establishment of a special Police Regional Commander for the four northern Serb majority municipalities, these municipalities should be fully integrated within the respective legal and security systems of the central state. As the example of the municipal elections shows rather clearly, the agreement is far from being fully implemented and its consequences remain to be seen. As such, the situation in Kosovo still remains largely unpredictable.

12.5 Conclusion

The goal of this short postscript was not to present a full analysis of post-conflict developments in Macedonia and Kosovo, but simply to test out the limits of the 'imposed consociation' as an analytical framework. As even such a superficial analysis has shown, the model cannot be directly applied to explain these two cases. In the Macedonian situation, a strong international presence in the form of

---

[57]   Bieber and Keil, "Power-Sharing Revisited," 344 fn. 20.

[58]   Cf. http://www.kosovothanksyou.com/. Accessed 29 December 2013.

[59]   The full text of the Agreement can be found here: http://www.europeanvoice.com/page/3609.aspx?&blogitemid=1723. Accessed 29 December 2013.

an IRB is absent, whereas in the case of Kosovo the consociational system as such is boycotted by one of the major groups. Under those conditions, we cannot expect the incentive structures or anything similar to what we have observed in the Bosnian case to develop. Nevertheless, I strongly believe that the 'imposed consociation' framework is not useless for such cases, as it directs our attention to the deviations and, in the form of clear assumptions, offers a functional approach to their analysis. It helps us structure our analysis by pointing to certain otherwise neglected factors. Naturally, a much more detailed and methodologically more sophisticated approach would be needed to either strengthen or discredit the model as such.

13 Annex

13.1 Topic guide for interviews with local political leaders

<u>OBJECTIVE:</u> To explore why and under what circumstances political leaders/elite in Bosnia and Herzegovina cooperate or do not cooperate and to evaluate the influence external actors (in this case the international community/OHR) have in promoting cooperation between these leaders.

1. <u>INTRODUCTION</u>
   - Introduce self and basic sketch of study, get permission to audio record

2. <u>GENERAL SITUATION IN BOSNIA</u>
   - <u>Political challenges in Bosnia</u>
     - What are the major political challenges in Bosnia today?
     - How is his party handling these, what are the strategies/ideas/concepts?
       - If not mentioned, probe for:
         - importance of EU accession process
         - importance of constitutional reform
   - <u>General life together of the three groups</u>
     - In his view, how is it functioning?
     - What are the challenges?

3. <u>DECISION MAKING PROCESS</u>

   - <u>Elements accounted for before making decisions</u>
     - What are the basic principles guiding personal decision making?
     - How does he reach his position?
     - What factors/elements influence decision making?
       - If not mentioned, probe for:
         - group allegiance/interests
         - positions of the other group leaders
         - economic implications
         - foreign policy implications
         - security concerns

- <u>Negotiation / Cooperation</u>
  - Once a decision has been made, how does he go about implementing it?
  - What factors guide his decision in choosing a strategy for implementation?

    If not mentioned, probe for:

    inclusion of other group leaders (cooperation)
    importance of state structure
  - Why and when does he choose to include the other group leaders? When not?

4. IMPORTANCE OF FOREIGN ACTORS / THE OHR

- <u>General</u>
  - How does he feel about…. (also: why)

    presence of international community/OHR in Bosnia in general
    politics of the international community in general
    politics of the international community in relation to his group
  - How would he characterise the *influence* of the OHR in terms of quality in general (what are benefits and disadvantages)? For what reason? Examples?
- <u>Influence in decision making</u>
  - What is the importance of the OHR/international community in his decision making?
  - How is this influence manifest/shown?
  - Examples

    probe for: Bonn powers
  - Are there changes in this influence depending on political fields?
  - What is the effect of international pressure to cooperate with other group leaders?

5. BOSNIA'S FUTURE

- <u>Future of the OHR</u>
  - Does he think the OHR/the international community should remain in Bosnia?

    Why, why not? For how long? In what form?

- <u>Vision</u>
  - What is his vision for Bosnia's future?
  - What state structure is preferred and why?

13.2 List of Interview Partners

	Name	Function	Date of interview	Place of interview
Locals	Haris Silajdžić	Founder and long-time president of SBiH (Bosniak), prime minister of BiH 1993-1996, co-prime minister 1997-2000, member of BH state Presidency 2006-2010	15 May 2012	Sarajevo (BiH)
	Božo Ljubić	Former President of HDZ 1990 (Croat), currently member of BH Parliament, at the time of interview vice-chairman of Parliamentarian Assembly	20 June 2012	Sarajevo (BiH)
	Mladen Ivanić	President of PDP (Serb) and Serb member in the BiH Presidency; former member of BH Parliament, House of Peoples; former BH foreign minister and RS prime minister	7 July 2012	Banja Luka (BiH)
	Mladen Bosić	President of SDS (Serb) and at the time of the interview member of BiH Parliament, House of Representatives; former BH ambassador to Slovenia and deputy foreign minister of BiH	16 May 2012	Sarajevo (BiH)
	Dragan Čović	President of HDZ BiH (Croat) and Croat member in the BiH presidency; former member of BH Parliament, House of Peoples; Croat member of BiH Presidency 2002-2005 (removed from office by Paddy Ashdown), minister in Federation government 1998-2001	19 June 2012	Mostar (BiH)
	Nebojša Radmanović	Member of BH state Presidency from Republika Srpska between 2006 and 2014 (Serb), vice-president of SNSD (president of the board) at the time of the interview.	7 November 2012	Sarajevo (BiH)

Internationals	Željko Komšić	Member of BH state Presidency between 2006 and 2014 (Croat); long-time SDP (multi-national) vice-president, currently President of DF (liberal); former BiH ambassador to Serbia	9 November 2012	Sarajevo (BiH)
	Carlos Westendorp	High Representative 1997-1999, currently Secretary General of Club de Madrid, before that foreign minister and Spanish ambassador to the UN	11 September 2012	Madrid (S)
	Wolfgang Petritsch	High Representative 1999-2002, currently Austrian ambassador to the OECD, before EU special envoy for Kosovo (1998-9), EU chief negotiator at Rambouillet (1999), and Austrian ambassador in Belgrade (1997-9)	4 December 2012	Paris (F)
	Paddy Ashdown	High Representative 2002-2006, currently member of the House of Lords, before long-time member in the British House of Commons and president of the Liberal Democrats	23 October 2012	London (UK)
	Christian Schwarz-Schilling	High Representative 2006-2007, international mediator for the Federation of BiH 1995-2004	23 August 2012	Büdingen (D)
	Miroslav Lajčák	High Representative 2007-2009, currently foreign minister of Slovakia	17 December 2012	Bratislava (SK)

13.3 List of OHR Decisions

	1997	1998	1999-1	1999-2	2000	2001	2002-1	2002-2	2003	2004	2005	2006-1	2006-2	2007-1	2007-2	2008	2009-1	2009-2	2010	2011	2012	2013
	CW	CW	CW	WP	WP	WP	WP	PA	PA	PA	PA	PA	CSS	CSS	ML	ML	ML	VI	VI	VI	VI	VI
(1)	1	6	5	2	7	3	15	13	14	12	18	1	0	3	2	0	0	9	1	2	0	0
(2)	0	8	1	1	29	5	1	14	11	6	3	1	9	3	0	3	0	0	0	2	0	0
(3)	0	0	3	0	4	7	9	35	31	30	30	2	14	6	5	1	2	3	0	0	0	0
(4)	0	4	5	0	1	2	13	17	4	19	1	0	2	3	0	0	0	5	1	0	0	0
(5)	0	6	8	24	28	14	13	8	7	6	34	7	15	2	1	2	0	9	6	1	3	1
(6)	0	2	1	2	5	3	4	1	0	0	0	0	0	0	0	0	0	0	0	0	0	0
(7)	0	3	19	19	12	20	7	3	11	0	4	0	6	4	7	3	0	1	0	1	0	0
(8)	0	0	0	0	0	0	0	0	18	85	1	0	0	0	1	3	1	1	2	4	1	0
N 1	1	29	42	48	86	54	62	91	96	158	91	11	46	21	16	12	3	28	10	10	4	1
(9)	0	0	0	1	0	0	1	0	0	0	30	7	13	2	0	3	2	9	8	5	4	1
(10)	0	0	0	0	0	0	0	0	0	0	1	0	2	0	0	0	0	0	0	0	0	0
N 2	0	0	0	1	0	0	1	0	0	0	31	7	15	2	0	3	2	9	8	5	4	1
(11)	1	29	42	47	86	54	61	91	96	158	60	4	31	19	16	9	1	19	2	5	0	0

Legend: (1) decisions relating to state symbols and state level matters and constitutional issues, (2) decisions in the field of economics, (3) decisions in the field of judicial reform, (4) decisions relating to the Federation, Mostar, and Herzegovina-Neretva Canton, (5) removals and suspensions from office, (6) media restructuring decisions, (7) decisions in the field of property law, the return of displaced persons and refugees and reconciliation, (8) decisions relating to individuals indicted for war crimes in the former Yugoslavia; (N1): total number of decisions (9) lifts of bans and revocations, (10) decisions limiting the scope of Bonn power usage, (N2) total number of repeals, (11) corrected N total: N total minus N repeals, (CW) Carlos Westendorp, (WP) Wolfgang Petritsch, (PA) Paddy Ashdown, (CSS) Christian Schwarz-Schilling, (ML) Miroslav Lajčák, (VI) Valentin Inzko.
Source: OHR Website: http://www.ohr.int/decisions/archive.asp (last accessed 26 December 2013).

14 Bibliography

Aitken, Rob. "Cementing Divisions?" *Policy Studies* 28, no. 3 (2007): 247–67.

Alic, Anes. "Influential Bosnian Croat Trio Arested." *Transitions Online*, January 26, 2004. http://www.tol.org/client/article/11490-influential-bosnian-croat-trio-arrested.html.

———. "The Bosnian War, My Way." *ISA Intel*, April 24, 2012. http://www.isaintel.com/2012/04/24/the-bosnian-war-my-way/.

Anderson, Benedict. *Imagined Communities*. London and New York: Verso, 2006.

Apter, David E. *The Political Kingdom in Uganda: A Study in Bureaucratic Nationalism*. Princeton, N.J.: Princeton University Press, 1961.

Ashdown, Paddy. *A Fortunate Life*. London: Aurum, 2009.

———. *Inaugural Speech by Paddy Ashdown, the New High Representative for Bosnia & Herzegovina*. Sarajevo: Office of the High Representative, May 27, 2002. http://www.ohr.int/ohr-dept/presso/presssp/default.asp?content_id=8417.

———. Personal Interview in London (UK), October 23, 2012.

———. *Speech by the High Representative for Bosnia and Herzegovina Paddy Ashdown to the BiH House of Representatives*. Sarajevo: Office of the High Representative, December 17, 2002. http://www.ohr.int/ohr-dept/presso/presssp/default.asp?content_id=28736.

———. "Statement by the High Representative, Lord Paddy Ashdown to the Venice Commission." Appendix 1 of CDL-PV (2004) 003, Venice, October 8, 2004.

———. *Swords and Ploughshares: Building Peace to the 21st Century*. London: Weidenfeld & Nicolson, 2007.

Baer, Josette. *Revolution, Modus Vivendi or Sovereignty?: The Political Thought of the Slovak National Movement from 1861 to 1914*. Stuttgart: Ibidem, 2010.

———. *Slavic Thinkers or the Creation of Polities: Intellectual History and Political Thought in Central Europe and the Balkans in the 19th Century*. Washington, DC: New Academia Publishing, 2007.

Banac, Ivo. *The National Question in Yugoslavia. Origins, History, Politics*. Ithaca and London: Cornell University Press, 1988.

Bardos, Gordon N. "Balkan Ethnoconfessional Nationalism: Analysis and Management." *Südosteuropa* 59, no. 2 (2011): 192–213.

Barry, Brian. "Review Article: Political Accommodation and Consociational Democracy." *British Journal of Political Science* 5, no. 04 (1975): 477–505.

———. "The Consociational Model and Its Dangers." *European Journal of Political Research* 3, no. 4 (1975): 393–412.

Beetham, David. *Max Weber and the Theory of Modern Politics*. Cambridge; New York, NY, USA: Polity Press ; B. Blackwell, 1985.

Bekkers, Victor, and Arthur Edwards. "Legitimacy and Democracy: A Conceptual Framework for Assessing Governance Practices." In *Governance and the Democratic Deficit Assessing the Democratic Legitimacy of Governance Practices*, edited by Victor Bekkers, Geske Dijkstra, Arthur Edwards, and Menno Fenger, 35–60. Aldershot, England; Burlington, VT: Ashgate Pub., 2007.

Bellamy, Alex J. *The Formation of Croatian National Identity: A Centuries-Old Dream?*. Manchester: Manchester University Press, 2004.

Belloni, Roberto. *State Building and International Intervention in Bosnia*. London and New York: Routledge, 2007.

Bieber, Florian. "Kosovo: One Year on." *openDemocracy*, February 17, 2009. http://www.opendemocracy.net/article/kosovo-one-year-on.

———. *Post-War Bosnia. Ethnicity, Inequality and Public Sector Governance*. Hampshire and New York: Palgrave Macmillen, 2006.

———. "Power Sharing after Yugoslavia: Functionality and Dysfunctionality of Power-Sharing Institutions in Post-War Bosnia, Macedonia, Kosovo." In *From Power Sharing to Democracy. Post-Conflict Institutions in Ethnically Divided Societies*, edited by Sid Noel, 85–103. Montreal/Kingston: McGill-Queen's University Press, 2005.

———. "The Balkans: The Promotion of Power Sharing by Outsiders." In *Power Sharing in Deeply Divided Places*, edited by Joanne McEvoy and Brendan O'Leary, 312–26. Philadelphia: University of Pennsylvania Press, 2013.

Bieber, Florian, and Soeren Keil. "Power-Sharing Revisited: Lessons Learned in the Balkans?" *Review of Central and East European Law* 34, no. 4 (2009): 337–60.

Bildt, Carl. *Peace Journey: The Struggle for Peace in Bosnia*. Weidenfeld & Nicolson, 1999.

Bilefsky, Dan. "War's Lingering Scars Slow Bosnia's Economic Growth." *The New York Times*, February 8, 2009. http://www.nytimes.com/2009/02/08/world/europe/08bosnia.html.

Bochsler, Daniel. "Let the People Decide? Learning from Swiss Direct Democracy in a Comparative Perspective." Edited by Francis Cheneval and Sylvie Ramel. *From Peace to Shared Political Identities. Exploring Pathways in Contemporary Bosnia-Hercegovina. Special Volume of Transitions* 51, no. 1,2 (2011): 115–19.

Bogaards, Matthijs. "Democracy and Power Sharing in Multinational States: Thematic Introduction." *International Journal on Multicultural Societies* 8, no. 2 (2006): 119–26.

———. "The Favourable Factors for Consociational Democracy: A Review." *European Journal of Political Research* 33, no. 4 (June 1, 1998): 475–96.

———. "The Uneasy Relationship between Empirical and Normative Types in Consociational Theory." *Journal of Theoretical Politics* 12, no. 4 (2000): 395–423.

Bogaards, Matthijs, and Markus M.L. Crepaz. "Consociational Interpretations of the European Union." *European Union Politics* 3 (2002): 357–81.

Bose, Sumantra. *Bosnia after Dayton: Nationalist Partition and International Intervention*. London: C. Hurst, 2002.

Bosić, Mladen. Personal interview in Sarajevo (BiH), May 15, 2012.

Boškovska, Nada. "Im Zentrum des Balkans und am Rande des europäischen Interesses: Makedoniens schwierige Lage in den 1990er Jahren." In *Transformation und historisches Erbe in den Staaten des europäischen Ostens*, edited by Carsten Goehrke and Seraina Gilly, 441–74. Bern: Peter Lang, 2000.

Breuilly, John. "Reflections on Nationalism." *Philosophy of the Social Science / Philosophie Des Sciences Sociales* 15, no. 1 (1985): 65–75.

Brubaker, Rogers. *Nationalism Reframed. Nationhood and the National Question in Europe*. Cambridge: Cambridge University Press, 1997.

Brunnbauer, Ulf. "The Implementation of the Ohrid Agreement: Ethnic Macedonian Resentments." *Journal on Ethnopolitics and Minority Issues in Europe*, no. 1 (2002): 1–24.

Calic, Marie-Janine. *Geschichte Jugoslawiens im 20. Jahrhundert*. München: Beck, 2010.

———. *Krieg und Frieden in Bosnien-Hercegovina*. Erweiterte Neuausgabe. Frankfurt: Suhrkamp Verlag, 1996.

Caspersen, Nina. "Contingent Nationalist Dominance: Intra-Serb Challenges to the Serb Democratic Party." *Nationalities Papers: The Journal of Nationalism and Ethnicity* 34, no. 1 (2006): 51–69.

Chandler, David. *Bosnia: Faking Democracy after Dayton*. London; Sterling, Va.: Pluto Press, 2000.

Cohen, Roger. "Enough of the Daytonians." *The New York Times*, July 18, 2013, sec. Opinion / Global Opinion. http://www.nytimes.com/2013/07/19/opinion/global/roger-cohen-enough-of-the-daytonians.html.

———. "How Bosnia Heals." *The New York Times*, July 15, 2013, sec. Opinion / Global Opinion. http://www.nytimes.com/2013/07/16/opinion/global/roger-cohen-how-bosnia-heals.html.

Čović, Dragan. Personal interview in Mostar (BiH), June 19, 2012.

Daalder, Hans. "The Consociational Democracy Theme." *World Politics* 26, no. 4 (1974): 604–21.

Dahl, Robert A. *Democracy and Its Critics.* New Haven: Yale University Press, 1989.

Dahl, Robert A. *Polyarchy: Participation and Opposition.* New Haven: Yale University Press, 1971.

Deutsche Welle. "Nordkosovo wiederholt die Kommunalwahl." *DW.DE*, November 17, 2013. http://www.dw.de/nordkosovo-wiederholt-die-kommunalwahl/a-17229796.

Easton, David. *A Systems Analysis of Political Life.* New York: Wiley, 1965.

Eldridge, Justin L. C. "Playing at Peace: Western Politics, Diplomacy and the Stabilization of Macedonia." *European Security* 11, no. 3 (2002): 46–90.

Engelen, Ewald, and Monika Sie Dhian Ho, eds. *De Staat Van de Democratie: Democratie Voorbij de Staat.* Amsterdam: Amsterdam University Press, 2004.

European Commission for Democracy through Law (Venice Commission). *Opinion on the Constitutional Situation in Bosnia and Herzegovina and the Powers of the High Representative.* Venice: CDL-AD (2005) 004, March 11, 2005.

European Stability Initiative. *The Lausanne Principle. Multiethnicity, Territory and the Future of Kosovo's Serbs.* Berlin/Pristin: European Stability initiative, June 7, 2004. http://www.esiweb.org/pdf/esi_document_id_53.pdf.

Filandra, Šaćir, and Enes Karić. *Bošnjačka ideja.* Zagreb: Narodni zavod Globus, 2002.

Fine, John. *The Bosnian Church: Its Place in State and Society from the Thirteenth to the Fifteenth Century: From the Twelth to the Fourteenth Century.* London: Saqi Books, 2007.

Friedman, Francine. *The Bosnian Muslims. Denial of A Nation.* Colorado: Westview Press, 1996.

Frontal.ba. "Istraživanje stavova građana BiH." *Frontal.ba*, August 28, 2013. http://www.frontal.ba/novost/64739.

Fukuyama, Francis. "Nation-Building and the Failure of Institutional Memory." In *Nation-Building. Beyond Afghanistan and Iraq*, edited by Francis Fukuyama, 1–16. Baltimore: The Johns Hopkins University Press, 2006.

Funk, Julianne. "'Invisible' Believers for Peace: Religion and Peacebuilding in Postwar Bosnia-Herzegovina." Doctoral Dissertation, KU Leuven, 2012.

Fuster, Thomas. "Bosniens Serben krebsen zurück: Verzicht auf das umstrittene Volksreferendum nach einem Überraschungsbesuch der EU-Aussenbeauftragten Ashton." *Neue Zürcher Zeitung*, May 14, 2011, sec. International. http://www.nzz.ch/aktuell/international/bosniens-serben-krebsen-zurueck-1.10571555.

Gallup Balkan Monitor. *The 2010 Gallup Balkan Monitor. Focus on Bosnia-Herzegovina.*, 2010. http://www.balkan-monitor.eu/files/Gallup_Balkan_Monitor-Focus_On_Bosnia_and_Herzegovina.pdf.

Gellner, Ernest. *Nations and Nationalism*. Ithaca: Cornell Univ Pr, 2009.

Gromes, Thorsten. "Democratisation of Post-War Societies: A Mission Impossible?" *European Journal of Political Science and Theory* 5 (2009): 418–41.

———. *Ohne Staat und Nation ist keine Demokratie zu machen: Bosnien und Herzegowina, Kosovo und Makedonien nach den Bürgerkriegen*. Baden-Baden: Nomos, 2012.

Hadžikadunić, Emir. *Od Dejtona Do Brisela (From Dayton to Brussels)*. Sarajevo: ACIPS, 2005.

Hartzell, Caroline A., Matthew Hoddie, and Donald Rothchild. "Stabilising the Peace after Civil War: An Investigation of Some Key Variables." *International Organization* 55, no. 1 (2001): 183–208.

Hastings, Adrian. *The Construction of Nationhood. Ethnicity, Religion and Nationalism*. Cambridge: Cambridge University Press, 1997.

Hawton, Nick. "Ashdown Strives to Atone for the West's Sins over Bosnia." *The Times*. December 26, 2002. http://www.ohr.int/ohr-dept/presso/pressa/default.asp?content_id=28812.

Hoare, Marko Attila. *History of Bosnia: From the Middle Ages to the Present Day*. London: Saqi Books, 2007.

———. *How Bosnia Armed*. London: Saqi Books, 2004.

Hobe, Stephan, and Otto Kimminich. *Einführung in das Völkerrecht*. 8. Auflage. Tübingen and Basel: A. Fracke Verlag, 2004.

Hobsbawm, Eric J. *Nations and Nationalism since 1780: Programme, Myth, Reality*. 2nd ed. Cambridge: Cambridge University Press, 1990.

Hodžić, Edin, and Nenad Stojanović. *New/Old Constitutional Engineering. Challenges and Implications of the European Court of Human Rights Decision in the Case of Sejdić and Finci v. BiH*. Sarajevo: Analitika, 2011.

Holbrooke, Richard. *To End a War*. New York: Random House USA, 1999.

Horowitz, Donald L. "Constitution-Making: A Process Filled With Constraint." *Review of Constitutional Studies* 12, no. 1 (2006): 1–17.

————. *Ethnic Groups in Conflict*. 2nd Revised edition. Berkeley, Los Angeles, London: University of California Press, 2000.

Hösch, Edgar. *Geschichte der Balkanländer: Von der Frühzeit bis zur Gegenwart*. 5., aktualisierte und erweiterte Auflage. München: Beck, 2008.

Hroch, Miroslav. *Das Europa der Nationen. Die moderne Nationsbildung im europäischen Vergleich*. 1st ed. Göttingen: Vandenhoeck & Ruprecht, 2005.

Hutchinson, John, and Anthony D. Smith. *Ethnicity*. Oxford and New York: Oxford University Press, U.S.A., 2009.

————. *Nationalism*. Oxford and New York: Oxford University Press, U.S.A., 2001.

Huyse, Lucien. *Passiviteit, Pacificatie en Verzuiling in de Belgische Politiek: een sociologische studie*. Antwerp: Standaard Wetenschappelijke Uitgeverij, 1970.

Ibrahimagić, Omer. *Bosanski identitet i suverenitet*. Sarajevo: Univerzitet u Sarajevu, Institut za istraživanje zločina protiv čovječnosti i međunarodnog prava, 2012.

Imamović, Mustafa. *Historija Bošnjaka*. Sarajevo: Preporod, Bošnjačka Zajednica Kulture, 1996.

International Crisis Group. *Bosnia's Alliance for (Smallish) Change*. Balkans Report. Sarajevo/Brussels: International Crisis Group, August 2, 2002.

————. *Bosnia: State Institutions under Attack*. Europe Briefing. Sarajevo/Istanbul/Brussels: International Crisis Group, May 6, 2011.

————. *Dayton: Two Years On. A Review of Progress in Implementing the Dayton Peace Accords in Bosnia*. Bosnia Report. Brussels: International Crisis Group, November 19, 1997.

————. *Macedonia: Ten Years after the Conflict*. Europe Report. Skopje/Istanbul/Brussels, 2011. http://www.crisisgroup.org/en/regions/europe/balkans/macedonia/212-macedonia-ten-years-after-the-conflict.aspx.

Inzko, Valentin. *Address by High Representative and EU Special Representative Valentin Inzko to the BiH Parliamentary Assembly*. Sarajevo: Office of the High Representative, December 5, 2009. http://www.ohr.int/ohr-dept/pres so/presssp/default.asp?content_id=43453.

Ivanić, Mladen. Personal Interview in Banka Luka (BiH), July 7, 2012.

Jelavich, Barbara. *History of the Balkans: Volume 1*. Cambridge: Cambridge University Press, 1999.

————. *History of the Balkans: Volume 2*. Cambridge: Cambridge University Press, 1999.

Jovic, Dejan. *Yugoslavia: A State That Withered Away*. West Lafayette, Indiana: Purdue Univerity Press, 2008.

Judah, Tim. *The Serbs: History, Myth and the Destruction of Yugoslavia*. New Haven: Yale University Press, 2009.

Juncos, Ana E. "Europeanization by Decree? The Case of Police Reform in Bosnia." *Journal of Common Market Studies* 49, no. 2 (2011): 367–89.

Karger, Adolf. "Das Leopardenfell. Zur regionalen Verteilung der Ethnien in Bosnien-Herzegovina." *Osteurope* 42 (1992): 1102–11.

Kasapović, Mirjana. "Bosnia and Herzegovina: Consociational or Liberal Democracy?" *Politička Misao* XLII, no. 2 (2005): 3–30.

Keil, Soeren. *Multinational Federalism in Bosnia and Herzegovina*. Farnham: Ashgate, 2013.

Kerr, Michael. *Imposing Power-Sharing: Conflict and Coexistence in Northern Ireland and Lebanon*. Dublin/Portland OR: Irish Academic Press, 2005.

Knaus, Gerhard, and Felix Martin. "Travails of the European Raj." *Journal of Democracy* 14, no. 3 (2003): 60–74.

Koktsidis, Pavlos I. *Strategic Rebellion. Ethnic Conflict in FYR Macedonia and the Balkans*. Bern: Peter Lang, 2012.

Kolind, Torsten. *Post-War Identification. Everyday Muslim Counterdiscourse in Bosnia Herzegovina*. London: Verso, 2008.

Komšić, Željko. Personal Interview in Sarajevo (BiH), November 9, 2012.

Kriesi, Hanspeter. *Vergleichende Politikwissenschaft 1: Grundlagen. Eine Einführung*. Baden-Baden: Nomos, 2007.

Lajčák, Miroslav. Personal Interview in Bratislava (SK), December 17, 2012.

Lehmbruch, Gerhard. "Consociational Democracy in the International System." *European Journal of Political Research* 3, no. 4 (1975): 377–91.

———. *Proporzdemokratie: Politisches System Und Politische Kultur in Der Schweiz Und in Österreich*. Tübingen: Moor, 1967.

Lemarchand, René. "Consociationalism and Power Sharing in Africa: Rwanda, Burundi, and the Democratic Republic of the Congo." *African Affairs* 106, no. 422 (2007): 1–20.

Lewis, Arthur. *Politics in West Africa*. London: Allan and Unwin, 1965.

Lijić, Lejla. "Brčko distrikt." In *Država, Politika i Društvo u Bosni i Hercegovini. Analiza postdejtonskog političkog sistema*, 417–36. Sarajevo: University Press Magistrat Izdanja, 2011.

Lijphart, Arend. "Consociational Democracy." *World Politics* 21, no. 2 (1969): 207–25.

———. "Consociation and Federation: Conceptual and Empirical Links." *Canadian Journal of Political Science / Revue Canadienne de Sciences Politique* 12, no. 3 (1979): 499–515.

———. "Constitutional Design for Divided Societies." *Journal of Democracy* 15, no. 2 (2004): 96–109.

————. *Democracy in Plural Societies: A Comparative Exploration*. 4th ed. New Haven: Yale University Press, 1980.

————. "Democratization and Constitutional Choices in Czecho-Slovakia, Hungary, and Poland 1989-91." *Journal of Theoretical Politics* 4 (1992): 207–113.

————. "Power Sharing, Ethnic Agnosticism, and Political Pragmatism." *Transformation* 21, no. 1993 (1993): 94–99.

————. *Power-Sharing in South Africa*. Berkeley: University of California Press, 1985.

————. *The Politics of Accommodation: Pluralism and Democracy in the Netherlands*. Second Revised Edition. Berkeley, Los Angeles, London: University of California Press, 1975.

————. "The Puzzle of Indian Democracy: A Consociational Interpretation." *The American Political Science Review* 90, no. 2 (1996): 258–68.

————. "The Wave of Power-Sharing Democracy." In *The Architecture of Democracy. Constitutional Design, Conflict Management, and Democracy*, 37–54. New York: Oxford University Press, 2002.

————. *Thinking about Democracy: Power Sharing and Majority Rule in Theory and Practice*. Routledge Chapman & Hall, 2008.

————. "Typologies of Democratic Systems." *Comparative Political Studies* 1, no. 3 (1968): 3–44.

Linz, Juan J., and Alfred Stepan. *Problems of Democratic Transition and Consolidation: Southern Europe, South America, and Post-Communist Europe*. Baltimore: Johns Hopkins Univ Pr, 1996.

Ljubić, Božo. "Croat Question—Key to the Stability of Bosnia and Herzegovina." Pittsburgh, USA, June 4, 2011.

————. Personal Interview in Sarajevo (BiH), June 20, 2012.

Malcolm, Noel. *Bosnia: A Short History*. New Updated. New York: New York Univ Pr, 1996.

Marković, Goran. "Ustavne promjene u Bosni i Hercegovini." In *Država, Politika i Društvo u Bosni i Hercegovini. Analiza postdejtonskog političkog sistema*, 71–104. Sarajevo: University Press Magistrat Izdanja, 2011.

Martens, Michael. "Schwarz-Schillings nicht ganz freiwilliger Abschied." *FAZ.NET*, January 25, 2007. http://www.faz.net/aktuell/politik/ausland/bosnien-hercegovina-schwarz-schillings-nicht-ganz-freiwilliger-abschied-1409649.html.

Matuz, Josef. *Das Osmanische Reich: Grundlinien seiner Geschichte. 6. Auflage*. Darmstadt: Primus-Verlag, 2010.

May, Jonathan. "How Bosnia Changed Paddy." *East European Politics and Societies and Cultures* 27, no. 4 (2013): 593–618.

McCrudden, Christopher, and Brendan O'Leary. "Courts and Consociations, or How Human Rights Courts May De-Stabilize Power-Sharing Settlements." *European Journal of International Law* 24, no. 2 (2013): 477–501.

McGarry, John, and Brendan O'Leary. "Iraq's Constitution of 2005: Liberal Consociation as Political Prescription." *International Journal of Constitutional Law* 5, no. 4 (2007): 670–98.

McGarry, John, and Brendan O'Leary. "Power Shared after the Death of Thousands." In *Consocitional Theory. McGarry and O'Leary and the Northern Ireland Conflict*, edited by Rupert Taylor, 15–84. London and New York: Routledge, 2009.

Merdzanovic, Adis. "Imposing Compromise. Consociational Arrangements in Macedonia and Bosnia-Herzegovina." Skopje, 2013.

———. "The Consequences of Ratko Mladić's Ideology for Today's Bosnia." *New Eastern Europe*, 2012. http://www.neweasterneurope.eu/node/332.

Miller, Nicholas J. "The Nonconformists: Dobrica Ćosić and Mića Popović Envision Serbia." *Slavic Review* 58, no. 3 (1999): 515–36.

Mujanovic, Jasmin. "It's Spring at Last in Bosnia and Herzegovina," February 11, 2014. http://www.aljazeera.com/indepth/opinion/2014/02/it-spring-at-last-bosnia-herzegov-2014296537898443.html.

Mujkić, Asim. "Beyond Consociation: The Case of Brčko Arbitration." Edited by Francis Cheneval and Sylvie Ramel. *Special Issue of Transitions: From Peace to Shared Political Identities. Exploring Pathways in Contemporary Bosnia-Herzegovina* 51, no. 1–2 (2011): 81–97.

———. *Mi, Građani Etnopolisa*. Sarajevo: Šahinpašić, 2007.

Nezavisne novine. "Mladen Bosić: BiH se pretvara u partokratiju." *Nezavisne novine*, March 5, 2012. http://www.nezavisne.com/novosti/intervju/Mladen-Bosic-BiH-se-pretvara-u-partokratiju-131072.html.

Nordlinger, Eric A. *Conflict Regulation in Divided Societies*. Cambridge: Center for International Affairs, Harvard University, 1972.

Office of the High Representative. "Comment by the High Representative on Re-Cantonisation in BiH," April 24, 1998. http://www.ohr.int/ohr-dept/presso/pressr/default.asp?content_id=4603.

———. "Decision Enacting the Law on Changes and Amendments to the Law on the Council of Ministers of Bosnia and Herzegovina," October 19, 2007. http://www.ohr.int/decisions/statemattersdec/default.asp?content_id=40687.

———. "Decision Enacting the Law on the Center for the Srebrenica-Potocari Memorial and Cemetery for the Victims of the 1995 Genocide," June 25, 2007. http://www.ohr.int/decisions/plipdec/default.asp?content_id=40028.

———. "Decision Further Limiting the Scope of the Ban from Public Office in the Removal Decisions Issued by the High Representative," April 4, 2006. http://www.ohr.int/decisions/removalssdec/default.asp?content_id=36919.

———. "Decision Imposing the Law on Citizenship of BiH," December 16, 1997. http://www.ohr.int/decisions/statemattersdec/default.asp?content_id=343.

———. "Decision Imposing the Law on the Flag of BiH," February 3, 1998. http://www.ohr.int/decisions/statemattersdec/default.asp?content_id=344.

———. "Decision Lifting the Ban from Office within Political Parties in the Removal Decisions Issued by the High Representative," June 7, 2006. http://www.ohr.int/decisions/removalssdec/default.asp?content_id=37615.

———. "Decision Removing Ante Jelavic from His Position as the Croat Member of the BiH Presidency," March 7, 2001. http://www.ohr.int/decisions/removalssdec/default.asp?content_id=328.

———. "Decision Removing Mr. Nikola Poplasen from the Office of President of Republika Srpska," March 5, 1999. http://www.ohr.int/decisions/removalssdec/default.asp?content_id=267.

———. "Decision Suspending All Disbursement of Budgetary Itemisations for Party Funding to the HDZ BiH, the SDA, the HDZ 1990—HZ and the SBiH from the Budget of the Bosnia and Herzegovina, the Budget of the Federation of Bosnia and Herzegovina and the Budget of the Herzegovina-Neretva Canton and Reducing Party Funding to the HDZ BiH, the SDA, the HDZ 1990—HZ and the SBiH from the Budget of the Herzegovina-Neretva Canton," May 29, 2007. http://www.ohr.int/decisions/mo-hncantdec/default.asp?content_id=39853.

———. "Order Seizing Travel Documents of Persons Who Obstruct or Threaten to Obstruct the Peace Implementation Process," July 10, 2007. http://www.ohr.int/decisions/war-crimes-decs/default.asp?content_id=41138.

O'Leary, Brendan. "Debating Consociational Politics: Normative and Explanatory Arguments." In *From Power Sharing to Democracy. Post-Conflict Institutions in Ethnically Divided Societies*, edited by Sid Noel, 3–43. Montreal/Kingston: McGill-Queen's University Press, 2005.

———. "Foreword: The Realism of Power-Sharing." In *Imposing Power-Sharing. Conflict and Coexistence in Northern Ireland and Lebanon*, by Michael Kerr, i—d. Dublin/Portland OR: Irish Academic Press, 2005.

———. "Power Sharing in Deeply Divided Places: An Advocate's Introduction." In *Power Sharing in Deeply Divided Places*, edited by Joanne McEvoy and Brendan O'Leary, 1–64. Philadelphia: University of Pennsylvania Press, 2013.

O'Neill, Shane. "Recognition, Equality, Difference." In *Consociational Theory. McGarry and O'Leary and the Northern Ireland Conflict*, edited by Rupert Taylor, 87–98. London and New York: Routledge, 2009.

Ordanoski, Saso, and Aleksandar Matovski. "Between Ohrid and Dayton: The Future of Macedonia's Framework Agreement." *Südosteuropa Mitteilungen* 4 (2007): 46–59.

Oslobođenje. "Dodik: Serbs Have Two Countries—Serbia and Republika Srpska." *Oslobođenje*, May 15, 2013. http://www.oslobodjenje.ba/daily-news/dodik-serbs-have-two-countries--serbia-and-republika-srpska.

Papagianni, Katia. *Power Sharing, Transitional Governments and the Role of Mediation.* Oslo: Centre for Humanitarian Dialogue, 2008. http://www.hdcentre.org/uploads/tx_news/60Powersharingfinal.pdf.

Papić, Žarko. "The General Situation in B-H and International Support Policies." In *International Support Policies to South-East European Countries: Lessons (not) Learned in Bosnia and Herzegovina*, 17–37. Sarajevo: Müller, 2001.

Pappalardo, Adriano. "The Conditions for Consociational Democracy: A Logical and Empirical Critique." *European Journal of Political Research* 9, no. 4 (1981): 365–90.

Pavlović, Momčilo. "Demographic Changes in Kosovo - 1974–1981." *TransConflict*, April 5, 2013. http://www.transconflict.com/2013/04/demographic-changes-in-kosovo-1974-1981-054/.

Pavlowitch, Stevan K. *Serbia: The History Behind the Name*. London: C Hurst & Co Publishers, 2002.

Peace Implementation Council. *Communique by the PIC Steering Board*. Vienna: Office of the High Representative, March 15, 2006. http://www.ohr.int/pic/default.asp?content_id=36760.

———. *Communiqué of the Steering Board of the Peace Implementation Council*. Sarajevo: Office of the High Representative, November 20, 2008. http://www.ohr.int/pic/default.asp?content_id=42667.

———. *Communiqué: Political Declaration from Ministerial Meeting of the Steering Board of the Peace Implementation Council (Sintra Conference)*. Sintra: Office of the High Representative, May 30, 1997. http://www.ohr.int/pic/default.asp?content_id=5180.

———. *Declaration by the Steering Board of the Peace Implementation Council*. Sarajevo: Office of the High Representative, June 19, 2007. http://www.ohr.int/pic/default.asp?content_id=39997.

———. *Declaration by the Steering Board of the Peace Implementation Council*. Sarajevo: Office of the High Representative, February 27, 2008. http://www.ohr.int/pic/default.asp?content_id=41352.

———. *Declaration of the Political Directors of the Peace Implementation Council Steering Board*. Sarajevo: Office of the High Representative, September 24, 2002. http://www.ohr.int/pic/default.asp?content_id=27982.

————. *Joint Statement: Meeting of the Steering Board with the Presidency and the COM Chairs*. Sarajevo: Office of the High Representative, November 6, 1997. http://www.ohr.int/pic/default.asp?content_id=5181.

————. *PIC Bonn Conclusions*. Bonn, December 10, 1997. http://www.ohr.int/pic/default.asp?content_id=5182.

Pearson, Sevan. "Bošnjaci instead of Muslimani: A Symbolic Change in Wartime Bosnia-Herzegovina in 1993." Edited by Francis Cheneval and Sylvie Ramel. *Special Issue of Transitions: From Peace to Shared Political Identities. Exploring Pathways in Contemporary Bosnia-Herzegovina* 51, no. 1–2 (2011): 201–20.

Peter, Fabienne. "Political Legitimacy." *The Stanford Encyclopedia of Philosophy (Summer 2010 Edition)*, January 22, 2012. http://plato.stanford.edu/archives/sum2010/entries/legitimacy/.

Petritsch, Wolfgang. *Bosnien und Herzegowina fünf Jahre nach Dayton - Hat der Friede eine Chance?*. Second Edition. Klagenfurt: Wieser Verlag, 2001.

————. Personal Interview in Paris (F), December 4, 2012.

————. "The Future of Bosnia Lies with Its People." *Wall Street Journal Europe*, September 17, 1999. http://www.ohr.int/ohr-dept/presso/pressa/default.asp?content_id=3188.

Petritsch, Wolfgang, and Christophe Solioz, eds. *Ownership Process in Bosnia and Herzegovina : Contributions on the International Dimensions of Democratization in the Balkans*. Vol. Band 159. Baden-Baden: Nomos, 2003.

"Political System." *Encyclopedia Britannica*. Accessed December 25, 2013. http://www.britannica.com/EBchecked/topic/467746/political-system.

Powell, G. Bingham Jr. *Social Fragmentation and Political Hostility: An Austrian Case Study*. Stanford: Stanford University Press, 1970.

Radmanović, Nebojša. Personal Interview in Sarajevo (BiH), November 7, 2012.

Ramet, Sabrina Petra. *Balkan Babel: The Disintegration Of Yugoslavia From The Death Of Tito To The Fall Of Milosevic*. 4th ed. London: Westview Press, 2002.

Rawls, John. *Justice as Fairness: A Restatement*. Cambridge: Harvard University Press, 2001.

Reka, Armend. "The Ohrid Agreement: The Travails of Inter-Ethnic Relations in Macedonia." *Human Rights Review* 9, no. 1 (March 1, 2008): 55–69. doi:10.1007/s12142-007-0029-z.

Renan, Ernest. "Qu'es-ce qu'une nation?," 1882. http://archives.vigile.net/04-01/renan.pdf.

Ritchie, Jane, and Jane Lewis. *Qualitative Research Practice: A Guide for Social Science Students and Researchers*. London: Sage, 2003.

Sahadžić, Maja. "Izbori i izborni sistem Bosne i Hercegovine." In *Država, Politika i Društvo u Bosni i Hercegovini. Analiza postdejtonskog političkog sistema*, 397–415. Sarajevo: University Press Magistrat Izdanja, 2011.

———. "Priroda političkog sistema u Bosni i Hercegovini." In *Država, Politika i Društvo u Bosni i Hercegovini. Analiza postdejtonskog političkog sistema*, 15–37. Sarajevo: University Press Magistrat Izdanja, 2011.

Saračević, Nermina. "Parlamentarna Skupština Bosne I Hercegovine." In *Država, Politika I Društvo U Bosni I Hercegovini. Analiza Postdejtonskog Političkog Sistema*, 223–52. Sarajevo: University Press Magistrat Izdanja, 2011.

Sarajlić, Eldar. "The Convenient Consociation." Edited by Francis Cheneval and Sylvie Ramel. *From Peace to Shared Political Identities. Exploring Pathways in Contemporary Bosnia-Hercegovina. Special Volume of Transitions* 51, no. 1–2 (2011): 61–80.

Scharpf, Fritz. *Governing in Europe: Effective and Democratic*. Oxford: Oxford University Press, 1998.

Schneckener, Ulrich. "Making Power-Sharing Work: Lessons from Successes and Failures in Ethnic Conflict Regulation." *Journal of Peace Research* 39, no. 2 (March 1, 2002): 203–28.

Schumpeter, Joseph. *Capitalism, Socialism and Democracy*. New York: Harper and Row, 1956.

Schwarz-Schilling, Christian. "Europa und Deutschland müssen sich ihrer Verantwortung stellen." In *Bosnien im Fokus. Die zweite politische Herausforderung des Christian Schwarz-Schilling*, edited by Erich Rathfelder and Carl Bethke, 260–98. Berlin/Tübingen: Verlag Hans Schiler, 2010.

———. Personal Interview in Büdingen (D), August 23, 2012.

———. *Speech by the High Representative, Christian Schwarz-Schilling, to the BiH Parliament*. Sarajevo: Office of the High Representative, 05 2006. http://www.ohr.int/ohr-dept/presso/presssp/default.asp?content_id=37224.

Silajdžić, Haris. Personal Interview in Sarajevo (BiH), May 15, 2012.

Smith, Anthony D. *Ethnic Origins of Nations*. London: Blackwell, 1986.

———. *National Identity*. Nevada: University of Nevada Press, 1991.

———. *Nationalism*. Cambridge: Polity Press, 2001.

Solioz, Christophe. *Turning Points in Post-War Bosnia: Ownership Process and European Integration*. Baden-Baden: Nomos, 2007.

Solioz, Christophe, and Wolfgang Petritsch. "The Interview: The Fate of Bosnia and Herzegovina: An Exclusive Interview of Christophe Solioz with Wolfgang Petritsch." *Journal of Southern Europe and the Balkans Online* 5, no. 3 (2003): 355–73.

Srna. "Dom naroda danas glasa o smjeni ministara i zamjenika iz SDA." *Klix.ba*, October 22, 2012. http://www.klix.ba/vijesti/bih/dom-naroda-danas-glasa-o-smjeni-ministara-i-zamjenika-iz-sda/121021085.

Steiner, Jürg. *Gewaltlose Politik und kulturelle Vielfalt: Hypothesen entwickelt am Beispiel der Schweiz.* Bern/Stuttgart: Haupt, 1970.

———. "In Search of the Consociational 'Spirit of Accommodation.'" In *Consociational Theory. McGarry and O'Leary and the Northern Ireland Conflict,* edited by Rupert Taylor, 196–205. London and New York: Routledge, 2009.

Štiks, Igor. "Being Citizen the Bosnian Way. Transformations of Citizenship and Political Identities in Bosnia-Herzegovina." Edited by Francis Cheneval and Sylvie Ramel. *Special Issue of Transitions: From Peace to Shared Political Identities. Exploring Pathways in Contemporary Bosnia-Herzegovina* 51, no. 1–2 (2011): 245–67.

Stojanović, Nenad. *Dialogue sur les quotas. Penser la représentation dans une démocratie multiculturelle.* Paris: Presses de Sciences Po, 2013.

———. "Limits of Consociationalism and Possible Alternatives: Centripetal Effects of Direct Democracy in a Multiethnic Society." Edited by Francis Cheneval and Sylvie Ramel. *From Peace to Shared Political Identities. Exploring Pathways in Contemporary Bosnia-Hercegovina. Special Volume of Transitions* 51, no. 1,2 (2011): 99–114.

———. "The Dilemma of Ethnic Quotas in Power Sharing Theory: The Case of Bosnia and Herzegovina." In *The Western Balkans: A European Challenge,* edited by Milan Bufon, Anton Gosar, Safet Nurkovic, and Andre-Louis Sanguin, 331–47. Koper: Publishing House Annales, 2006.

Šuško, Dževada. "Reaktionen der bosnischen Öffentlichkeit auf Christian Schwarz-Schilling als Hoher Repräsentant." In *Bosnien im Fokus. Die zweite politische Herausforderung des Christian Schwarz-Schilling,* edited by Erich Rathfelder and Carl Bethke, 299–309. Berlin/Tübingen: Verlag Hans Schiler, 2010.

Taylor, Rupert, ed. *Consociational Theory: McGarry and O-Leary and the Northern Ireland Conflict: McGarry and O'Leary and the Northern Ireland Conflict.* 1st ed. London and New York: Routledge, 2009.

———. "Introduction." In *Consociational Theory. McGarry and O'Leary and the Northern Ireland Conflict,* edited by Rupert Taylor, 1–11. London and New York: Routledge, 2009.

Thompson, Paul. *The Voice of the Past. Oral History.* Third Edition. New York: Oxford University Press, 2000.

Thompson, Emily. „Big Censorship Fears in Little Macedonia," *Radio Free Europe Radio Liberty,* 21 October 2014, http://www.rferl.org/content/big-fears-of-censorship-in-little-macedonia/26562554.html.

Troebst, Stefan. "Gross-Kosovo." In *Das makedonische Jahrhundert: Von den Anfängen der nationalrevolutionären Bewegung zum Abkommen von Ohrid 1893-2001*, by Stefan Troebst, 393–405. München: Oldenbourg Verlag, 2007.

———. "Vom ethnopolitischen Schlachtfeld zum interethnischen Stabilitätspol: Gewalt und Gewaltfreiheit in der Region Makedonien im 'langen' 20. Jahrhundert." In *Das makedonische Jahrhundert: Von den Anfängen der nationalrevolutionären Bewegung zum Abkommen von Ohrid 1893-2001*, by Stefan Troebst, 21–42. München: Oldenbourg Verlag, 2007.

———. "Von der 'Makedonischen Frage' zur 'Albanischen Frage': Der Balkan am Ende des 20. Jahrhunderts." In *Das makedonische Jahrhundert: Von den Anfängen der nationalrevolutionären Bewegung zum Abkommen von Ohrid 1893-2001*, by Stefan Troebst, 363–72. München: Oldenbourg Verlag, 2007.

Westendorp, Carlos. "Lessons From Bosnia." *Wall Street Journal Europe*, July 29, 1999. http://www.ohr.int/ohr-dept/presso/pressa/default.asp?content_id=3186.

———. Personal Interview in Madrid (S), September 11, 2012.

World Bank Group. *Bosnia and Herzegovina Partnership Country Program Snapshot*. Sarajevo: World Bank Country Office Bosnia and Herzegovina, April 2013. http://www.worldbank.org/content/dam/Worldbank/document/eca/BH-Snapshot.pdf.

"Writing the Past." *The Economist*, January 5, 2013. http://www.economist.com/news/books-and-arts/21569007-teaching-children-about-history-nationalism-and-right-and-wrong-writing-past.

ibidem-Verlag / *ibidem* Press
Melchiorstr. 15
70439 Stuttgart
Germany

ibidem@ibidem.eu
www.ibidem-verlag.com
www.ibidem.eu